54.50
I

Repression and Fear

THE SERIES IN CLINICAL AND COMMUNITY PSYCHOLOGY

CONSULTING EDITORS
Charles D. Spielberger and Irwin G. Sarason

Auerbach and Stolberg Crisis Intervention with Children and Families
Burchfield Stress: Psychological and Physiological Interactions
Burstein and Loucks Rorschach's Test: Scoring and Interpretation
Cohen and Ross Handbook of Clinical Psychobiology and Pathology, volume 1
Cohen and Ross Handbook of Clinical Psychobiology and Pathology, volume 2
Diamant Male and Female Homosexuality: Psychological Approaches
Froehlich, Smith, Draguns, and Hentschel Psychological Processes in Cognition and
  Personality
Hackfort and Spielberger Anxiety in Sports: An International Prospective
Hobfoll Stress, Social Support, and Women
Janisse Pupillometry: The Psychology of the Pupillary Response
Krohne and Laux Achievement, Stress, and Anxiety
London Personality: A New Look at Metatheories
London The Modes and Morals of Psychotherapy, Second Edition
Manschreck and Kleinman Renewal in Psychiatry: A Critical Rational Perspective
Morris Extraversion and Introversion: An Interactional Perspective
Muñoz Depression Prevention: Research Directions
Olweus Aggression in the Schools: Bullies and Whipping Boys
Reitan and Davison Clinical Neuropsychology: Current Status and Applications
Rickel, Gerrard, and Iscoe Social and Psychological Problems
  of Women: Prevention and Crisis Intervention
Smoll and Smith Psychological Perspectives in Youth Sports
Spielberger and Diaz-Guerrero Cross-Cultural Anxiety, volume 1
Spielberger and Diaz-Guerrero Cross-Cultural Anxiety, volume 2
Spielberger and Diaz-Guerrero Cross-Cultural Anxiety, volume 3
Spielberger and Sarason Stress and Anxiety, volume 1
Sarason and Spielberger Stress and Anxiety, volume 2
Sarason and Spielberger Stress and Anxiety, volume 3
Spielberger and Sarason Stress and Anxiety, volume 4
Spielberger and Sarason Stress and Anxiety, volume 5
Sarason and Spielberger Stress and Anxiety, volume 6
Sarason and Spielberger Stress and Anxiety, volume 7
Spielberger, Sarason, and Milgram Stress and Anxiety, volume 8
Spielberger, Sarason, and Defares Stress and Anxiety, volume 9
Spielberger and Sarason Stress and Anxiety, volume 10: A Sourcebook of Theory and
  Research
Spielberger, Sarason, and Defares Stress and Anxiety, volume 11
Spielberger, Sarason, and Strelau Stress and Anxiety, volume 12
Strelau, Farley, and Gale The Biological Bases of Personality and Behavior, volume 1:
  Theories, Measurement Techniques, and Development
Strelau, Farley, and Gale The Biological Bases of Personality and Behavior, volume 2:
  Psychophysiology, Performance, and Applications
Ulmer On the Development of a Token Economy Mental Hospital Treatment Program
Williams and Westermeyer Refugee Mental Health in Resettlement Countries

IN PREPARATION

Spielberger and Diaz-Guerrero Cross-Cultural Anxiety, volume 4
Spielberger and Vagg The Assessment and Treatment of Test Anxiety
Suedfeld Psychology and Torture

Repression and Fear

A New Approach to Resolve the Crisis in Psychopathology

Yacov Rofé
Bar-Ilan University
Ramat-Gan, Israel

○ HEMISPHERE PUBLISHING CORPORATION
A member of the Taylor & Francis Group

New York   Washington   Philadelphia   London

REPRESSION AND FEAR: A New Approach to Resolve the Crisis in Psychopathology

1 2 3 4 5 6 7 8 9 0   B C B C   8 9 8 7 6 5 4 3 2 1 0 9

This book was set in Times Roman by Hemisphere Publishing Corporation. The editors were Evelyn Walters Pettit, Mark A. Meschter, and Todd W. Baldwin; and the typesetter was WorldComp, Inc. Cover design by Sharon Martin DePass.
BookCrafters, Inc. was the printer and binder.

Library of Congress Cataloging-in-Publication Data

Rofé, Yacov.
    Repression and fear: a new approach to resolve the crisis in psychopathology / Yacov Rofé.
        p. cm.—(The Series in clinical and community psychology)
    Bibliography: p.
    Includes index.

    1. Psychology, Pathological.   2. Repression (Psychology)   3. Fear.
    I. Title.   II. Series.
    [DNLM: 1. Behaviorism.   2. Fear.   3. Neurotic Disorders.
    4. Psychoanalytic Theory.   5. Psychotherapy-methods.   6. Psychotic
    Disorders. 7. Repression. Wm 193.5.R4 R719r]
    RC437.5.R64 1989
    616.89'001—dc20
    DNLM/DLC
    for Library of Congress   89-11012
    ISBN 0-89116-056-6   CIP
    ISSN 0146-0846

Dedicated with love
to my mother, Mrs. Shoshana Rofé;
to my in-laws, Mr. & Mrs. Avraham and Zehava Erlich;

and to the memory of my father, Nisan Rofé.

Contents

PART VI
TOWARD A UNIFIED THEORY IN PSYCHOTHERAPY

Preface

Today psychopathology is dominated by three major theoretical approaches—psychoanalysis, behaviorism, and the medical model—among which there is profound disagreement. In fact, from a scientific point of view, psychopathology seems to have reached a standstill. The advocates of each of these camps continue to "manufacture" the same type of evidence to which we have become accustomed throughout the years, and there remains little hope that decisive proof will be found to resolve the endless dispute that exists between them. This book extensively and critically reviews the relevant literature and suggests a new theory for the explanation of neurosis, psychosis, and fear that is capable of integrating within its framework the seemingly conflicting data accumulated over the years.

The proposed theory—psychobizarreness—contends that a sharp distinction should be made between bizarre behavioral symptoms (e.g., agoraphobia, paranoid delusional systems), which are considered the essence of abnormality, and the more common behavioral deviations (e.g., smoking, fear of dogs). Bizarre behaviors are conceptualized as coping strategies, consciously and actively chosen by the individual to deal with unbearable stress. Thus, the theory denies that these behaviors are imposed by unconscious mechanisms, conditioning, or biological processes.

Although psychobizarreness theory strongly opposes psychoanalysis, the concept of repression is its cornerstone. However, repression is conceptualized in an entirely different way and, unlike the Freudian formulation, is consistent with both clinical and experimental findings. Repression is conceived as a conscious rather than an unconscious process, having no connection with childhood events. Further, a distinction is made between normal and abnormal repression. Normal repression consists of distractive maneuvers that do not require an adoption of bizarre behaviors. It operates in a flexible and selective manner. Under unavoidable stress attention is almost completely diverted from the situation. Under avoidable stress, repression enables one to overlook superfluous anxiety-provoking elements so that attention is exclusively focused on the task at hand. For example, during wartime a soldier will be more efficient if he can focus entirely on the necessities of battle and avoid thinking about other irrelevant stress stimuli (e.g., family problems that may result from his injury or death). A growing body of research indicates that flexible and selective reality distortion buffers the potential damage of stressful events and enhances the individual's coping ability. In contrast, abnormal repression is an unhealthy mechanism because distraction is achieved by bizarre symptoms and because it totally disconnects the patient from the source of stress. Thus, a search for more appropriate coping devices becomes very difficult.

Although psychobizarreness theory denies the existence of an unconscious entity, it recognizes the vital importance of accounting for the patients' inability to provide a plausible explanation for their bizarre behavior—a phenomenon that led Freud to suggest his theory of the unconscious. Psychobizarreness attributes this state of obliviousness to sophisticated self-deception mechanisms activated by consciousness itself.

The book is also concerned with the explanation of fears. Many investigators believe that behaviorism is adequate to account for the development of fears. However, this does not seem to be the case for either clinical phobias or simple fears. For example, in the vast majority of cases no significant frightening events precede the development of agoraphobia, and often conditioned fear does not occur even when people are exposed to extremely frightening situations. Moreover, the hope that Seligman's preparedness theory would resolve some of these difficulties proved to be unfounded since it gained very meager empirical support. This book proposes (1) a revised version of the Pavlovian paradigm—the cognitive–automatic conditioning theory—for the explanation of simple fear and (2) the psychobizarreness theory to account for clinical phobias.

It is widely accepted that psychosis develops as a result of adverse genetic predisposition or neurochemical changes. However, in recent years this theory has run into serious difficulties. For example, while earlier studies reported a concordance rate of almost 90% of schizophrenia among identical twins, more recent evidence shows that only about 40% would develop the "illness" if their twin had already developed it, while 60% would not become schizophrenic despite their faulty genetic constitution.

The diathesis-stress model cannot account for this problem simply because it lacks sufficient supportive data. For example, according to this conception a highly stressful situation of any type should cause an automatic increase in the rate of psychosis. However, a thorough review of studies of people during wartime, including both men who were in combat and civilians who survived the concentration camps, failed to support this claim. Although psychobizarreness theory also attributes the causes of psychosis to stress, and in fact views it as almost the sole factor, it proposes a totally different conceptualization of this variable. For example, based on the assumption that psychosis is a personal choice one makes when better coping options are unavailable, it is argued that this choice is made only when one experiences stress the causes of which one attributes to oneself. That is, the self is viewed as the prime cause of the stress. Genetic predispositions do not directly cause the symptoms, but expose the patient to an unbearably high level of personal stress, which "triggers" display of "crazy" behavior.

The book is divided into six parts. Part I reviews the relevant studies on repression and, by referring to various areas of related research, attempts to point out the scientific inadequacies of the psychoanalytic doctrine of repression. Part II deals with a theory of normal repression. Part III discusses the foundations of psychobizarreness theory and its value in explaining neurotic symptoms. In order to demonstrate the usefulness of the new conceptualization of repression, a review of studies on hysteria is presented. An attempt is made to show that this Freudian "stronghold" of repression can be better explained by the psychobizarreness theory than by psychoanalytic or behavioral approaches. Part IV exposes the weakness of traditional and contemporary theories of fear. To a certain degree this part is a continuation of efforts made in the discussion of hysteria, which attempts to show the advantages of psychobizarreness theory over other models. Like hysteria in psychoanalysis, fear is the stronghold of learning theories, inasmuch as the vast majority of the studies on behavioral deviations are related to this phenomenon. Thus, one of the major objectives of this part is to show that learning theories are inadequate for explaining psychopathological deviations by demonstrating that they cannot account for the production of even simple fears. Psychobizarreness theory is offered as a plausible explanation for the development of clinical fears, while the cognitive–automatic conditioning theory is presented to handle nonclinical behavior in this domain. Part V puts forth psychobizarreness theory as an explanation for the development of bizarre symptoms in psychoses.

The theoretical confusion in psychopathology is no less than in psychotherapy. A unified therapeutic theory, which synthesizes findings from different research schools, is suggested in the last chapter of the book (Part VI). This chapter also provides a multidimensional therapeutic strategy for treatment of neurosis, a guideline principle for treatment of psychosis, and a new cognitive approach for treatment of depression. The advantage of this approach over that of Beck's cognitive therapy is emphasized.

At this opportunity I would like to express my deepest gratitude to Professor Charles D. Spielberger, of the University of South Florida, Tampa, for his invaluable assistance in promoting the publication of this book. The inclusion of this book in the Series in Clinical and Community Psychology, edited by Professor Spielberger and Professor Irwin G. Sarason, of the University of Washington, Seattle, is a great honor for me, and I wish to thank them both. Special thanks is given to Professor Cyril M. Franks and Professor Paul M. Lehrer, both of Rutgers University, Piscataway, New Jersey, who read the manuscript and endorsed its publication. In addition, Professor Lehrer was kind enough to write the foreword to my book and to support my theoretical ideas. I would also like to thank my colleagues and friends at Bar-Ilan University—Professors Isaac Lewin, Leonard Weller, and Daniel Algom—as well as Richard Ertl at Washington University, St. Louis, for their encouragement and thoughtful comments. Especially, I want to thank Professor Lewin, who carefully read the manuscript. I was happy to discuss with him my new ideas and gain further insight into my theory. I thank as well Professor Noach Milgram of Tel-Aviv University, from whom I learned much about the publication process. Thanks are also given to Ms. Kathleen A. Roach, Mr. Ron E. Wilder, and Mr. Todd Baldwin, Hemisphere's editors, for being so efficient in handling the publication of this book. In addition, I thank Mrs. Elizabeth Segal for her incomparable secretarial skills and, Miss Brenda for her great editorial assistance. Finally, I thank my dear wife, Sara, for her patience, emotional support, and wise advice, and my three children Yoav, Esti, and Yochai for the patience, joy, and enthusiasm they provided me during my long period of work.

Yacov Rofé

Foreword

Paul M. Lehrer
University of Medicine and Dentistry of New Jersey
R. W. Johnson Medical School
and
Rutgers—The State University of New Jersey

The field of abnormal psychology is now in transition. Rofé describes three of the major theoretical approaches that purport to explain abnormal behavior: the psychoanalytic, the behavioral, and the biological. By the mid-1980s, none of these can be said to be new. Rofé argues that the time has come for a new synthesis.

In some sense it is not yet clear that the limit of these older approaches has yet been reached. New psychodynamic explanations of borderline and other difficult personality disorders (e.g., Kernberg, 1984) have recently emerged, and the field of short-term dynamic psychotherapy has given new insights into working with people in a more time-limited manner. Although primarily a clinical field, the psychoanalytic tradition has spawned considerable recent empirical research on various aspects of theory and therapy (Masling, 1986). The behavioral tradition also has recently attacked the problem of personality disorders (Linehan, 1987), and has spawned new approaches to the study of anxiety (e.g., Barlow, 1988), obsessive–compulsive disorders (Foa, Grayson, & Steketee, 1988), and treatment noncompliance (Marlatt & Gordon, 1985). It has largely abandoned the 1960s emphasis on reciprocal inhibition of anxiety, and has more recently emphasized cognitive contributions to psychopathology and therapeutic use of extinction procedures. Biological approaches, meanwhile, have been discovering brain mechanisms for the whole gamut of emotional disorders, while producing ever more effective medical treatments, with lower and more acceptable levels of side effects.

Despite the current productivity in each of these traditions independently, there is increasing realization that none has *the* complete explanation or treatment for psychopathology. While researchers from all traditions have always given at least lip service to the notion that biological and psychological factors interact in the etiology and treatment of emotional problems, only recently have attempts at genuine theoretical integration (e.g., Schwartz, 1981) and at active collaboration between behavioral and biological researchers (cf. the review of recent work on anxiety disorders by Pecknold, 1987) been made. That such collaboration is necessary has become increasingly clear because of valid criticisms of comparative studies done by one group from the point of view of the other. For example, behavioral–medical comparative studies of anxiety disorders done by biological researchers have been criticized for offering behavioral treatments that are overly mechanistic and inflexible (e.g., by not offering training to criterion levels, by failing to treat cognitive components by using inexperienced therapists, etc.), whereas such studies done by behaviorists have been criticized for offering inflexible medical treatments that do not take into account differential sensitivities to various drugs, or do not allow the full variety or proper dosages of medications to be used. A similar rapprochement is now occurring between psychoanalytic and behavioral clinicians (e.g., Wachtel, 1977;

Arkowitz & Messer, 1984), and here too dialogue and collaboration are occurring. The biological and psychodynamic combination flourishes in almost all American psychiatry departments.

Such dialogue comprises more than simple translation from one tradition to another. These have not proven very satisfying. For example, Dollard and Miller's (1950) early translation of psychoanalytic into behavioral terminologies has been accused of setting the field of behavior therapy behind by not encouraging the development of radically new approaches to treatment. More recent behavioral–psychoanalytic collaborations have also been criticized for ignoring philosophical differences between orientations that may be mutually contradictory (Messer & Winokur, 1980). In this book Rofé similarly criticizes "translations" of biological and psychological approaches into each other's terms, with little benefit shown in the development of new clinical or research approaches.

The various approaches differ in more than the philosophical and scientific dimensions. Historical and sociological forces play a role as well. The psychoanalytic tradition emanated from the clinical situation, and asks the kinds of ideographic questions about the full complexity of individual cases that the health care practitioner needs in order to treat the "whole person." Psychoanalytic theory has thus addressed such issues as: What patterns of conflicting motivations contribute to patterns of abnormal (and normal) behavior and thought? How do people express these motivations? Can the behavior of the patient toward the therapist be used to understand the complexity of his or her behavior toward significant others? What therapeutic techniques can best clarify these relationships (e.g., the therapist acting as a "blank wall," refraining from giving advice, interpreting slips of the tongue or dreams, etc.)? What is the structure of personality? How does it develop? Many of these questions do not lend themselves well to empirical research, but lead to heuristic theories of assessing personality and devising treatment strategies. As Messer and Winokur (1980) point out, the goal of psychoanalytic treatment is often not even symptom alleviation. This approach sees the human condition as inevitably plagued by conflicting forces of motivation, which can be understood and managed, but never eliminated. Psychoanalysis also was formed at a time when health care professionals were generalists and life-long companions who took care of their patients emotionally and physically, but who were unable to reverse many of the severe disease processes that currently can be cured. Traditions of treatment were handed down from teacher to student. Although scientific advances occurred, their pace was relatively slow by today's standards. Also, health care was a luxury of the relatively wealthy, who could afford treatment by a physician who cared about their long-term welfare and who was willing, for a fee, to devote considerable professional time to understanding, caring for, and helping the individual patient.

In contrast, the behavioral tradition originated in the psychology laboratory, from psychologists who had two overlapping motives for advancing a new comprehensive theory: (1) to bring psychological knowledge from the laboratory to the clinic and to explore the power of laboratory models of behavior to explain and to treat emotional disorders, and (2) not inconsequentially, to establish themselves as independent health care practitioners with a unique set of scientifically based tools. It is interesting in this latter regard that the behavioral approach never achieved the status of other approaches among nonpsychologist mental health professionals. To some extent the laboratory origins have defined the strengths and weaknesses of the behavioral approach. It offers a systematic approach to short-term management of specific problems, and even though the pace of clinical practice often far exceeds the pace of scientific research on the theory and outcome of behavioral technique, "behavior therapy" is at least *researchable*. Also, its short-term nature is compatible with the modern pattern of medical specialization and subspecialization and with universal health care, paid by cost-conscious third-party payers. A major weakness of this laboratory-based tradition is in its approach to the etiology and structure of psychopathology. It is at best simplistic to assume that the same processes are involved in the natural development of complex human problems as in laboratory analogues, with the latter sometimes even involving lower animals. Even with the incorporation of cognitive social psychology within the behavioral framework, behavioral theories often fall short of explaining or even describing the richness of human experience.

The biological approach to psychopathology now appears to be the dominant one in many academic departments of psychiatry. Like the behavioral approach, it addresses the modern need for brevity, clearness of results, and inexpensiveness. It also is quintessentially attuned to the modern practice of medical subspecialization, and its currency is affected by professional concerns and biologically oriented practitioners. As attested by recent falling enrollments in psychiatric residency programs, the psychiatric specialty is in trouble. Psychotherapeutic services are now widely offered by psychologists and social workers at considerably lower cost, and even some somatic treatments are now offered by other specialties, particularly neurology and family practice. Biological psychiatry is, however, the only professional approach that carries the biological model to its limit, with some of its more radical proponents offering *only* biological approaches to diagnosis and treatment. Whatever the shortcomings of this way of treating emotional illness, it is, as Rofé points out, woefully inadequate in offering a complete explanation of psychopathology.

So where does the field go from here? In this book Rofé boldly offers a new approach that is much more than just a translation or even an integration of psychodynamic, behavioral, and biological models. Drawing heavily on information-processing cognitive models, it presents a new theory that purports to incorporate all that its predecessors have explained, and to fill some of the gaps that these other methods have left. Whether it succeeds depends on whether it captures the imagination of researchers and practitioners in the field. I, for one, think it is worthy of their notice and consideration. It is a genuinely new, internally consistent, and comprehensive general theory of psychopathology. It is an undertaking whose time has arrived.

REFERENCES

Arkowitz, H., & Messer, S. B. (1984). *Psychoanalytic therapy and behavior therapy. Is integration possible?* New York: Plenum.

Barlow, D. (1988). *Anxiety and its disorders.* New York: Guilford.

Dollard, J., & Miller, N. E. (1950). *Personality and psychotherapy.* New York: McGraw-Hill.

Foa, E., Grayson, J. B., & Steketee, G. S. (1988). Success and failure in the treatment of obsessive compulsives. *Journal of Consulting and Clinical Psychology, 51,* 287–297.

Linehan, M. (1987). Dialectical behavior therapy for borderline personality disorder: Theory and method. *Bulletin of the Menninger Clinic, 51,* 261–276.

Kernberg, O. (1984). *Severe personality disorders: Psychotherapeutic strategies.* New Haven, CT: Yale University Press.

Marlatt, G. A., & Gordon, J. R. (1985). *Relapse prevention.* New York: Guilford.

Masling, J. (Ed.) (1986). *Empirical studies in psychoanalytic theory* (Vols. 1 and 2). Hillsdale, NJ: Lawrence Erlbaum.

Messer, S. B. (1986). Eclecticism in psychotherapy: Underlying assumptions, problems, and trade-offs. In J. C. Norcross (Ed.), *Handbook of eclectic psychotherapy* (pp. 379–397). New York: Brunner/Mazel.

Messer, S. B., & Winokur, M. (1980). Some limits to the integration of psychoanalytic and behavior therapy. *American Psychologist, 35*, 818–827.

Pecknold, J. C. (1987). Behavioral and combined therapy in panic states. *Progress in Neuropsychopharmacology and Biological Psychiatry, 11*, 97–104.

Schwartz, G. E. (1981). A systems analysis for psychobiology and behavior therapy: Implications in behavioral medicine. *Psychotherapy and Psychosomatics, 36*, 159–184.

Wachtel, P. (1977). *Psychoanalysis and behavior therapy.* New York: Plenum.

Repression and Fear

Introduction

Inadequacy of Current Theories in Psychopathology

At the beginning of this century, two major theories were proposed for understanding normal and pathological behavior of human beings: Freud's psychoanalytic doctrine and Watson's behaviorism. Since then, clinicians and researchers of psychopathology have been divided into two diametrically opposed camps. The two approaches, which at the time of their formulation were revolutionary, not only radically changed scientific thinking and treatment strategies in psychopathology but also greatly influenced wide areas of Western culture such as sociology, philosophy, and literature. The many theorists and investigators who followed these two schools of thought contributed to the expansion of the two respective empires. But, despite more than 50 years of extensive research and theoretical work, the basic beliefs and assumptions of the two movements have remained essentially unchanged.

The optimism and enthusiasm that characterized the scientific community for many years following the formulation stage of these theoretical approaches are now being replaced by growing dissatisfaction and pessimism. Most reviewers are convinced that currently accepted personality theories leave much to be desired and that the word *crisis* is not an unreasonable description of the state of the art (Pervin, 1985). In psychopathology, the situation seems to be even more severe. In fact, as we attempt to show in this book, the central assumptions of both of the abovementioned theoretical models are not supported by cumulative research findings on the pathological behavior of human beings. Thus, psychoanalysis and behaviorism seem little more than two systems of beliefs in psychopathology, each with its own advocates.

This state of affairs seems to be much more characteristic of Freudian theory. Psychoanalysis is accused (Gross, 1979) of having

> an anti-science attitude which resists investigation of its methods and results. Its theory is challenged as being imaginative Victorian speculation posing as science. Its cure has been described as an overly complex disguise for simple suggestion. Its orthodoxy is seen as a form of cultism blocking open inquiry into the mind. (p. 196)

Like Freud himself (see Erdelyi & Goldberg, 1979), the proponents of this approach are so confident of their clinical observations that they feel no need to plan empirical research for examining the validity of their constructs. When evidence inconsistent with their position emerges, it is either totally ignored, as for example the bulk of studies on repression–sensitization (e.g., Bell & Byrne, 1978), or defended via a number strategies developed to cope with the threat. The main defensive devices consist of (1) attacking available research tools, claiming that only their clinical observations can testify to the validity of their theoretical constructs (Bowers, 1984; Erdelyi & Goldberg, 1979); (2) accusing investigators of a hostile attitude toward psychoanalysis (see Erwin, 1980); (3) defending

1

their position by what is termed *ex post facto formulation* (Kazdin, 1978, p. 20); and (4) attempting to fit inconsistent data into their theoretical framework (Wachtel, 1977). These defensive maneuvers are to a certain extent legitimate as long as they do not serve as substitutes for controlled research. The unrigorous approach taken in psychoanalysis was recognized, for example, by Silverman (1976), one of the strongest advocates of this theory. In cases where scientific studies were conducted (Silverman, 1976, 1978, 1983), the findings have often gone unreplicated (Condon & Allen, 1980; Hapsel & Harris, 1982; Heilbrun, 1980, 1982; Oliver & Burkham, 1982; Porterfield & Golding, 1985). It is quite clear that if a theory in any other area of science, such as chemistry or physics, had not succeeded in producing convincing evidence to demonstrate its basic assumptions, especially so many years after it was originally proposed, it would certainly have lost its scientific respectability. However, psychoanalytic doctrine continues to enjoy scientific status, mainly because no better theory has come along to replace it, but also because the interpretive case study evidence of its practitioners conveys the impression of solid scientific data.

The behaviorists are, in general, more scientific in their approach, and they have certainly made an important contribution to understanding many psychological processes, for example, motor skills, habits, memory, and forgetting. However, the same scientific rigor has not generally been applied to psychopathology, and the behaviorists' theoretical concepts do not seem adequate for explaining behavioral deviations in clinical populations (Breger & McGaugh, 1965; Emmelkamp, 1982). This can be attributed to the fact that research efforts in behavior are often concentrated on the wrong target. Even though their therapeutic techniques are more successful than other methods (Rachman & Wilson, 1980), they are still limited (Barlow & Wolfe, 1981; Chambless, 1985a; Hafner, 1976, 1983; Hand & Lamontagne, 1976), and do not necessarily validate their theoretical assertions (e.g., Emmelkamp, 1982; Kirsch, Tennen, Wickless, Saccone, & Cody, 1983; H. B. Lewis, 1981).

Thus, the major problem facing behaviorists is that they have still not succeeded in demonstrating that their animal model is applicable in explaining human pathological behaviors.

> *When we look at the way conditioning principles are applied in the explanation of more complex phenomena, we see that only a rather flimsy analogy bridges the gap between such laboratory defined terms as stimulus, response, and reinforcement and their referents in the case of complex behavior. (Breger & McGaugh, 1965, p. 343)*

Similarly, Brewer (1974) indicated, on the basis of a massive reanalysis of the conditioning literature, that "behavioristic psychology could not explain even simple behavior" (p. 1) in adult humans. Along the same lines, Maltzman (1977) noted that "it now seems apparent that classical conditioning in normal adults, as ordinarily studied in the laboratory, is a consequence largely of thinking rather than vice versa" (p. 112). Even their explanation of the development of fear, which for years was thought of as a flawless paradigm of classical conditioning, today faces serious challenges (Emmelkamp, 1982; Jacobs & Nadel, 1985; Rachman, 1977, 1978, 1985a; Saigh, 1984a, 1984c). After more than 50 years of research on the subject, such a severe lack of experimental evidence on the inducement of pathological responses with human subjects exists that behaviorists often return to Watson's case study of little Albert in order to show the generality of their findings regarding the development of behavioral disturbances in humans (e.g., Rimm & Somervill, 1977; Wolpe & Rachman, 1960). However, even the validity of this case can be questioned; its limited scientific worth has been demonstrated by Harris (1979). The weaknesses of the behaviorist model are much more prominent when it comes to unusual behaviors. This is demonstrated, for example, by Rachman (1978; see also Rachman & Seligman, 1976), one of the leading investigators in the behaviorist camp. He describes several cases of neurotic patients with very bizarre symptoms, the development of which could not be explained in terms of learning theories. We describe briefly one of these cases to illustrate the basic problems the behaviorists face.

Rachman (1978) reports a case of a phobic woman who experienced an extremely high level of fear when exposed to chocolate or any stimulus that was even remotely associated with it. The phobia developed some time after the death of her mother, but no specific frightening events could be found to justify the onset of this bizarre response. In addition, intensive behavioral treatment did not succeed in diminishing her fears. In the absence of an adequate theory, Rachman (1978), whose strong position against psychoanalysis is well known (e.g., Wolpe & Rachman, 1960), noted that even though "psychoanalytic theory cannot succeed as a comprehensive account of human fears, it may help us ultimately to understand some of the more unusual fears" (p. 222).

The serious difficulties that the conditioning theory is encountering today with respect to all kinds of fear will be elaborated on in later chapters. In this context, however, it may be worth noting that while, with regard to normal fears, the conditioning model has at least some face validity inasmuch as frightening events often precede the onset of acquired fear, this is by no means the case in bizarre fear. A growing body of data shows that these responses often develop in spite of the absence of any significant frightening event to justify them in terms of learning theory (Emmelkamp, 1982; Jacobs & Nadel, 1985; Mathews, Gelder, & Johnston, 1981; Rachman, 1978, 1984a; Rachman & Seligman, 1976). Even when such an event occurs prior to the onset of the agoraphobic symptoms, the intensity of the "acquired" fear response is so out of proportion and usually so resistant to extinction that one must be very naive to attribute the disturbance to that event. As is shown throughout this book, bizarre symptoms, such as those of the chocolate phobia or of agoraphobia, are not at all trivial. These types of symptoms pose the real problems for psychotherapy, not fears of spiders, snakes, exams, cigarette smoking, and the like, on which the behavior-oriented investigators have expended most of their time and energy. To a great extent, it was this bizarre sort of behavior that led Freud to develop his psychoanalytic theory (Maddi, 1980; Peters, 1958; Shevrin & Dickman, 1980). Essentially, an admission that the traditional learning principles are inadequate to explain the production of bizarre symptoms is tantamount to an admission of failure of the behavioral models in explaining psychopathological disorders, namely, neuroses and psychoses.

Cases such as that of the woman with the chocolate phobia not only expose the basic weaknesses of learning theories, but may also compel adherents of the behaviorist approach to reconsider their position with regard to fundamental questions that they have refused, on principle, to regard as necessary for understanding human pathological behaviors. Two of the most fundamental issues involve questions as to the existence of the unconscious and of defense mechanisms. Since the woman with the chocolate phobia could not explain the reasons for her bizarre responses and her inability to suppress them, one may be easily tempted to believe that these behaviors must be controlled by unconscious autonomous processes. Indeed, this is the type of evidence that supporters of psychoanalysis use even today to attempt to convince the scientific community that it is necessary to assume the existence of an autonomous unconsciousness. This investigative strategy (to be elaborated later, pp. 54–55) is used, for example, by Bowers and Meichenbaum (1984) when they refer to a bizarre case of shoplifting in the introduction to their book *The Unconscious Reconsidered*. Examples of such seemingly unexplained bizarre responses may incline one to move closer to the traditional positions of psychoanalytic doctrine and accept the idea that the origins of these behaviors lie in traumatic childhood experiences, which are kept in the patient's unconscious store and cause him or her to be highly vulnerable to certain types of stressful events (see Wachtel, 1977; R. W. White & Watt, 1981). A variation of this fundamental idea is adopted, for example, by Jacobs and Nadel (1985), whose basic orientation is behaviorist. Faced with the inadequacy of behaviorist principles for explaining clinical phobias, Jacobs and Nadel make an implausible synthesis of conditioning principles and psychoanalytic ideas. (This will be discussed in more detail further on.) Essentially, Jacobs and Nadel argue that conditioning events in infancy predispose an individual to the onset of clinical bizarre phobias. They attribute to the events and circumstances of infancy an almost demonic power to wreak havoc later in an adult's life if certain suitable conditions prevail.

Even though one can hardly deny the obvious facts that psychiatric patients are completely unaware of the causes of their bizarre symptoms and that researchers should make this the focus of their interest, it is very difficult to accept the basic psychoanalytic assumptions, or a synthesis of these ideas with behavioristic principles, because they have no convincing empirical basis. What the assumption of the autonomous unconscious implies, in fact, is that inside our heads is an ongoing, independent psychological process similar to a "little man" who can pull the strings and propel us to behave quite bizarrely, sometimes for a prolonged period and without our awareness. It is difficult to accept this notion, particularly in view of the fact that proponents of psychoanalysis do not seem to have a convincing body of evidence to defend it.

In fact, from a scientific point of view, psychoanalytic doctrine does not seem to be very different from the demonology theory of ancient times. Like psychoanalysis, this theory claimed that a devil (or an early traumatic event) could dwell within the mind (or unconsciousness) without the individual's knowledge, making him or her vulnerable to certain types of illness. The only chance to escape the outbreak of these diseases was to avoid making the devil angry (or not exposing oneself to stressful situations similar to those stored in the unconsciousness; see, e.g., R. W. White & Watt, 1981, pp. 198–199). However, since the devil was completely autonomous and one had no knowledge of his existence, the onset of serious illness (or bizarre symptoms) was almost inevitable. In order to save the subject from this fate (or cure him after the onset of the illness), the devil (or traumatic event) had to be detected and eliminated from the mind (or brought under the control of the individual's consciousness). However, this process could be very painful and might be accompanied by strong resistance (Erdelyi & Goldberg, 1979; Perry & Laurence, 1984, p. 24). Thus, exorcism (or hypermnesia, i.e., lifting of amnesias; see Erdelyi & Goldberg, 1979) could not be accomplished without the assistance of a priest (or psychoanalyst). During the entire operation of this "omnipotent person," the patient remained unaware (Perry & Laurence, 1984, p. 24) and only the former could tell whether or not the operation had succeeded (Erwin, 1980).

The demonology theory did not gain scientific respect because no one could demonstrate the existence of devils. Psychoanalytic theory, on the other hand, is difficult to refute, mainly because its proponents can always find an early traumatic event in a subject's "unconsciousness," which, according to psychoanalytic belief and interpretation, is responsible for the mental illness. It may be worthwhile to note that, therapeutically, there is no reason to expect demonology to be less efficient than psychoanalysis.

This is because, as will be shown, the rate of successful treatment by psychoanalysis is no higher than no treatment at all (Erwin, 1980; Gross, 1979; Rachman & Wilson, 1980). It appears, then, that the major psychological theories have not succeeded in enlisting much scientific support for the validity of their basic theoretical positions.

The third theoretical approach in psychopathology is the medical model, which suggests that psychiatric symptoms result from adverse physiological changes. With regard to the explanation of bizarre neurotic symptoms, such as hysterical, agoraphobia, and obsessive–compulsive reactions, psychoanalytic and behaviorist approaches have succeeded in defending their theoretical territory. The failure of the medical model theorists to find significant empirical support for genetic–biological explanations for these disorders (Emmelkamp, 1982; Gottesman, 1962; R. S. Levy & Jankovic, 1983; Mathews et al., 1981) prevented adoption of this approach to treatment of neuroses. However, the story is quite different where psychoses are concerned. Early reports of the strong dominance of genetic factors in these behavioral disturbances (Kallmann, 1953, 1958) discouraged most investigators from accepting the idea that psychological variables play a critical role in this process. This view was strengthened by the severity of the bizarre responses, the patients' inability to explain their behavior or control it, and the poor therapeutic value of the psychological tools. The popularity of the medical or biological models increased, particularly with the growing decline in the scientific status of psychoanalysis (Reich, 1982). The psychiatric literature is now flooded with articles and books conveying the message that bizarre psychotic symptoms are nothing more than expressions of illness induced by adverse neurochemical changes (Davison & Neale, 1982; McKinney & Moran, 1981; Nagler & Mirsky, 1985; Spring & Coons, 1982).

However, the theoretical confusion surrounding psychosis is no less than that surrounding neurosis (Spring & Coons, 1982; Zigler & Glick, 1984; Zubin & Spring, 1977). Increasing numbers of investigators have begun to raise questions about the wisdom of accepting the medically oriented point of view. This includes, for example, Skrabanek (1984), who called the data presented by the medical model theorists pseudo-scientific evidence, and Rose (1984), who said that describing mental processes in biological terms is merely a translation of the problem from one language to another rather than an explanation. Furthermore, proponents of the biological–medical theory very rarely present experimental findings. In most cases, they use correlational data, in which the cause–effect relationship is difficult to determine. Moreover, even when both experimental and correlational data are presented, the findings often suffer from inconsistencies and contradictions (G. C. Davison & Neale, 1982; Siegel, Niswander, Sachs, & Stavros, 1959; Skrabanek, 1984). When more refined research tools were employed, the effect of genetic components was found to be much weaker than had been believed by the early investigators (Coleman, Butcher, & Carson, 1984; Faraone & Tsuang, 1985; Marshall & Pettitt, 1985; Rose, 1984). For example, the concordance rate for schizophrenia among monozygotic twins is now accepted as being between 40% and 50% rather than 86.2%, as the earlier studies by Kallmann (1953, 1958) had reported. In many cases, no "psychotic illness" develops despite the presence of genetic predisposition (Coleman et al., 1984), and in other cases psychotic reaction in the form of acute schizophrenia (R. W. White & Watt, 1981) or paranoia (Coleman et al., 1984; Zigler & Glick, 1984) develops even in the absence of genetic factors. In addition, no genetic evidence has been documented for the most essential characteristic of schizophrenia, namely, thought disorder (Berenbaum, Oltmanns, & Gottesman, 1985).

In view of these increasing difficulties, theorists with a medical orientation have attempted to modify their position by suggesting an interactive model of genetic–biological factors and stress (Spring & Coons, 1982). However, their theoretical formulation still affords primacy to biological factors. In many psychotic cases, no genetic predisposition could be detected. In many other cases, a prior stressful event could not be identified or, if it was, the event was too minor to justify the onset of the schizophrenic individual's extremely bizarre behavior (Rabkin, 1980). Other evidence shows that the incidence of psychotic symptoms in wartime (B. P. Dohrenwend & B. S. Dohrenwend, 1969; Hemphill, 1941; Hopkins, 1943; Kolb, 1977; A. Lewis, 1942) and in concentration camps (Eitinger & Strom, 1981; Helweg-Larsen et al., 1952; Nathan, Eitinger, & Winnik, 1964; Nirembirski, 1946; Shuval, 1957/1958) is unusually low, despite the intensive stress these situations cause. These findings are inconsistent with the simple interaction theory, since one would expect such stressful situations to cause significant increases in the rate of psychosis.

Furthermore, since genetic predisposition is not a necessary condition for the development of psychotic symptoms, medically oriented theories should be able to tell us why we should apply different sets of principles to account for the onset of bizarre neurotic and psychotic symptoms. If these principles can be generalized to neurosis as well, it is necessary to explain why this point of view is so rarely supported empirically, not even by correlational data. Nor is the principle of stress alone sufficient to explain the onset of neurotic disorders, since one may then ask why the same type of stress causes such diverse symptoms in different subjects and sometimes no symptoms at all (Emmelkamp, 1982). We are not minimizing the importance of stress or its interaction with genetic–biological factors. On the contrary, these ideas are strongly emphasized in our theoretical approach as well. However, we claim that current models are premature, failing to capture the full complexity of the problem, and that a more advanced theoretical approach to stress is needed. We believe, moreover, that any interaction model should give priority to psychological factors rather than to neurochemical changes.

In conclusion, the very selective number of studies cited so far may not be sufficient to show the impoverished scientific condition of current theories in psychopathology. We have no doubt that when the cumulative research findings are considered in a more thorough and detailed manner, even the most skeptical reader will come to the inevitable conclusion that a new theoretical approach in psychopathology is in order. However, despite our harsh criticism, it seems that such an approach should be based on the framework of thinking of both psychoanalysis and behaviorism. We will attempt to demonstrate that by making several fundamental changes in these theories and by adding a number of basic principles, a more valid theory can be suggested to explain behavioral deviations. Before specifying these proposals, we will discuss the basic shortcoming common to traditional theories (which seems to be largely responsible for their meager scientific success in psychopathology) and indicate the cardinal problems that need theoretical clarification.

BASIC SHORTCOMING OF TRADITIONAL THEORIES

In a general sense, despite basic and sharp differences, all three theories share the same fundamental deficiency in their basic conceptualization of the human being. They all give more or less the same answer to philosophical questions like "What is the nature of the human?" and "Are humans free to choose their behavior?" All three approaches have a deep, general disrespect for human consciousness. They treat their patients in a very mechanistic and deterministic way, as though they were devoid of consciousness. In fact, the possibility that consciousness may have an important role in determining pathological responses is not even considered. The exhibition of bizarre neurotic or psychotic symptoms is attributed to the autonomous activity of the unconscious (Bowers & Meichenbaum, 1984; Nemiah, 1984; Sackeim, Nordlie, & Gur, 1979), to automatic learning mechanisms over which the subject has no control (Schwartz, 1978), or to some adverse neurochemical changes (Emmelkamp, 1982; Jacobs & Nadel, 1985; Spring & Coons, 1982). The general attitude of psychoanalysis toward consciousness is best described by Freud's declaration that the mind is like an iceberg, nine tenths of which is submerged (C. S. Hall & Lindzey, 1967, p. 30). This is Freud's statement regarding the normal, functioning individual; it should hold true to an even greater extent for psychiatric patients.

The position of behaviorist theory is even more mechanistic than that of psychoanalysis. In this model, the causes of behavior are attributed almost entirely to environmental events. "The idea that people are autonomous and possess within them the power and the reasons for making decisions has no place in behavior theory" (Schwartz, 1978, p. 6). The theorists in this camp, particularly Skinner (Ewen, 1980; Schwartz, 1978), truly believe that the rat's "mind" can supply us with satisfactory answers to the basic questions of how bizarre behaviors develop in psychiatric patients. These behaviorists refuse to recognize that in many respects, their animal model cannot be generalized to the human being for the simple reason that humans are endowed with superior cognitive abilities. Mackintosh (1983), for example, noted that the human brain is a machine of an altogether more sophisticated nature than investigators of animal learning had previously believed. When investigators begin to realize the "full complexity of the way in which we see the world, think, reason, and learn to talk; then it is no longer possible to take seriously the pretensions of the reflexologists" (p. 2). Currently, the study of learning processes is dominated by "cognitive psychologists grappling with problems altogether more complex than anything envisioned by Watson" (p. 2).

Our criticism of this mechanistic conceptualization of the human being applies not only to the traditional learning theories, but also to current models such as that of Seligman's (1971) preparedness theory, Rachman's (1984a) safety-signal theory, and Jacobs and Nadel's (1985) model of stress-induced recovery of fears and phobia, all of which make an intensive theoretical effort to overcome the problems the behaviorists have come up against in recent years. In the chapters that follow we show that these new attempts are equally inadequate in explaining the bizarre behavioral deviations of humans. This is basically because these new attempts display the same (or even more extreme) adherence to the mechanistic conception of the human being as that of the original behaviorists.

In this respect, the position of the medical or biological models is even worse than the other two. For example, Reich (1982) states that these models are even more deterministic than the environmental theories. In psychoanalysis, and to a large extent in behaviorism as well, there is some optimism about the capacity of the human to change or to be cured. However, this is not so in the case of the medical models, which usually make no reference to the human's psychological capacities.

Perhaps one of the most extreme expressions of this general deterministic and mechanistic attitude is their research attempts to extrapolate information from the study of the rat's brain and nervous system and apply it to understanding of the causes of bizarre psychotic symptoms, such as the paranoid's persuasion belief (e.g., see McKinney & Moran, 1981). Skrabanek (1984) notes that it is

startling when one reads about attempts to use animal models of schizophrenia. It is an understate-
ment to write that "the fact that schizophrenia is a thought disorder complicates the creation of
animal models." . . . A paranoid rat? A hallucinating guinea pig? A thought insertion in the ass?
(p. 226)

As is elaborated throughout this book, the long affair of psychopathology with the Watsonian animal model has borne very little fruit, and we suspect that its "biological successors" are likely to terminate their own association with the model, with nothing more to show for it. Bizarre psychiatric symptoms such as hysteria, agoraphobia, obsessive–compulsive behavior, or psychotic symptoms do not characterize any non-human creature in the animal kingdom, certainly not the rat. Like language, these behaviors are unique to the human being, and we are convinced that unless this basic fact is taken into consideration, very little progress in psychopathology will be made. In this respect, our position is consistent with that of Breger and McGaugh (1965), namely, that the phenomenon of neurosis can be facilitated more by using "analogies from the area of psycho-linguistics and language learning rather than, as has typically been done, from studies of classical and operant conditioning" (p. 343).

SEVERAL CARDINAL PROBLEMS IN
PSYCHOPATHOLOGY

We would like to be so bold as to suggest that nearly all the central theoretical questions in the field of psychopathology remain unanswered. First, there is the problem of whether the difference between abnormal and normal behavior is essentially a matter of degree, as psychoanalysis and behaviorism teach, or there are sharp, qualitative differences between these two types of behavior, as is claimed in the present work. Should the same theoretical concepts be applied to the understanding of both normal fears (such as fear of dogs) and clinical phobias (e.g., the bizarre chocolate fear), as is claimed by psychoanalytic clinicians (Moss, 1960) and behaviorists? Or are different sets of principles needed, as some investigators (Jacobs & Nadel, 1985) have recently suggested? Do bizarre paranoid persecution beliefs and the realistically suspicious behavior of a normal person belong in the same category, as is claimed, for example, by Zigler and Glick (1984)? Or are these two types of responses entirely different and controlled by different psychological processes?

One of the central causes for the difficulties of "mechanistic" theories is that they have never demonstrated that the assumption of continuity between normal and abnormal behavior is scientifically more profound than the idea of discontinuity. We argue that bizarreness is the central characteristic of abnormality and that normal individuals very rarely display this type of behavior. Moreover, even when bizarre behavior is shown by nonclinical subjects, for example, the bizarre shoplifting case reported by Bowers and Meichenbaum (1984), it lasts for a very short period, and it stems entirely from different causes, as recent research evidence indicates (Reason, 1984a, 1984b; Reason & Lucas, 1984).

It will be demonstrated in this book that the prolonged behavioral bizarreness of abnormal subjects is a coping strategy adopted in order to deal with unbearable stress. It will be seen, for example, that failure to take this point into consideration is, to a large extent, responsible for the fact that the question "What is schizophrenia?" continues to be asked today, despite tremendous research effort that has been invested (Carpenter, 1984; Rifkin, 1984; Strauss & Carpenter, 1983).

Another fundamental issue that requires theoretical attention is the concept of unconsciousness. As stated previously, Freud formulated his theory of the unconscious because he realized that subjects with bizarre responses could neither control their behavior nor provide rational explanations for it. Watson and Skinner's campaign against introspection succeeded in convincing many investigators that the question of unawareness either is redundant or has no scientific legitimacy in psychology. However, this line of thinking has run into trouble because of behaviorism's failure to provide valid explanations for psychopathological behavior. The vast majority of behavioristic studies on psychopathology have been devoted to an examination of fear; yet, as has been indicated, it has become clear in recent years that conditioning principles are inadequate to explain the development of bizarre fear or agoraphobia, not to mention more complicated behavioral disorders such as schizophrenia. Thus, we are left either to accept the Freudian theory of unconsciousness and attribute the onset and persistence of bizarre symptoms to a "mysterious black box" or to provide a more plausible answer to Freud's original dilemma, namely, why are patients so unaware of the causes of their bizarre symptoms?

Another central issue concerns the causes of bizarre symptoms. The rejection of traditional mechanistic theories raises the question of how these symptoms develop. Despite our criticism of the genetic–stress model, we maintain that the level of psychological stress to which the individual is subjected at a given time is the key factor in understanding this process. An increasing number of investigators have become aware of the importance of this concept, even with regard to schizophrenia (e.g., see review by Lukoff, Snyder, Ventura, & Neuchterlein, 1984). In reviewing significant research and clinical data, we attempt to show the central importance of stressful life events in determining the development of neurotic and psychotic symptoms. Moreover, we claim that childhood experiences and genetic predispositions play an important role in this process, mainly because they can cause severe deficits in subjects' ability to cope with daily life requirements or stressful demands. As already noted, the attempts that stem from a simplistic, mechanistic conception of stress are not satisfactory in this respect, and a new, more elaborate theoretical approach seems to be called for.

Another important question concerns the choice of symptoms. What causes an individual to exhibit one particular bizarre behavior from the entire range of pathological symptoms? The psychoanalytic idea that these are determined by adverse experiences during the early psychosexual stages has very little empirical support (Emmelkamp, 1982), and this has remained one of the most puzzling questions in psychopathology. This issue cannot be swept under the rug any longer, and no theory of psychopathology can be complete without providing a plausible solution to this chronic problem.

An additional question that demands attention is the development of normal fear. Why is it that in fear-inducing situations in real life (e.g., war), long-lasting fear does not develop in the vast majority of people, despite the presence of favorable conditions? This question was originally raised by Rachman (1978, 1985a) and Saigh (1984a, 1984b) as one of the major difficulties confronting conditioning theory. Seligman's (1971) preparedness theory is one of the frequent attempts to provide a solution to these problems of learning theories. However, as will be pointed out later, the cumulative research findings (Delprato, 1980; Zafiropoulou & McPherson, 1986) raise serious doubts about the validity of this theory as well.

Several other questions that may be of less theoretical importance than those already mentioned also remain without satisfactory answers. It is still unclear why, for example, nearly all types of phobias (Gray, 1971; Marks, 1969, 1978), hysteria (Folks, Ford, &

Regan, 1984; Jones, 1980; Kroll, Chamberlain, & Halpern, 1979), and depression (Krauthammer & Klerman, 1979; Weissman & Klerman, 1977) are more prevalent among females than males. Why are phobias and hysteria (Chambless, 1985b; Folks et al., 1984; Jones, 1980) as well as schizophrenia (Cockerham, 1978; Davison & Neale, 1982) much less frequent in higher socioeconomic groups, while this is not necessarily the case for other disorders such as psychotic depression (Cockerham, 1978)? There is, as yet, no satisfactory explanation of why suicide and mortality rates are highest among schizophrenic patients (Aisenberg, Weizer, & Munitz, 1985; Day & Semard, 1978; Lester, 1983). Why is the rate of onset of schizophrenia highest in the early years of adulthood (Bleuler, 1964; Gottesman & Shields, 1982)? Why should a kibbutz be a more pathogenic social environment for the development of schizophrenia than a city (Mirsky, Silberman, Latz, & Nagler, 1985), even though the quality of social life appears to be better in the kibbutz? This is a very small sample of the problems that need clarification. Our purpose, then, is to present a theoretical framework in the hope of shedding light on these fundamental questions.

OUR GENERAL THEORETICAL APPROACH

Consciousness and Repression

In the present work, we argue that one of the key factors in resolving several major difficulties in psychopathology is the total abandonment of the mechanistic view that neurotic or psychotic bizarre behaviors are imposed on the individual by unconscious processes, neurochemical changes, or conditioning mechanisms. Instead, we suggest that these behaviors are consciously selected by the individual due to a lack of better strategies for coping with unbearable stressful situations. This view requires a reorienta-tion of the traditional, deterministic philosophical position regarding the basic nature of the human being and a reinstatement of the concept of consciousness, which was expelled from psychopathology by the combined forces of psychoanalysis, behaviorism, and biological–medical models. Even though some human behavior consists of strong habits, many human responses are voluntary and determined by cognitive analysis of the individual's present circumstances. One of the intrinsic and unique characteristics of the human being is the ability to consciously invent or adopt bizarre responses as part of a strategy to cope with unbearable stress. And only a human can then mislead himself or herself by sophisticated methods into thinking that he or she is not responsible for this bizarre behavior. Thus, the traditional mechanistic views regarding the nature of humans seem to have brought psychopathology to a dead end. It is our position that no breakthrough can be achieved in this field unless it is recognized that human beings are first and foremost conscious creatures and that cognitive factors play a vital role in determining many of their behaviors, particularly those of a bizarre nature.

Although consciousness is one of the central aspects of this book, it is not the primary focus. Rather, the primary concept is repression. We will attempt to show that all bizarre symptoms are essentially a response to current stressful experiences and that repression is the key concept in the understanding of psychological phenomena. Freud (1914/ 1959) considered repression the "foundation-stone on which the whole structure of psychoanalysis rests" (p. 297). Indeed, this concept has attracted the attention of researchers more than any other notion in psychoanalysis, and "hundreds of psychologi-cal investigations have been interpreted as either propping up or tearing down this cornerstone" (Gur & Sackeim, 1979, p. 167). Some investigators like Erikson (see

Ewen, 1980, p. 224) and Murphy (1975) consider the notion of unconsciousness to be one of the most important discoveries of the modern age. However, leaving aside the lack of scientific evidence for this claim, we side with Freud in promoting repression, rather than unconsciousness, as the most important contribution of psychoanalysis. Thus, in spite of our strong opposition to psychoanalysis, including the psychoanalytic doctrine of repression, we agree with Freud's basic thesis that repression is the essence upon which any theory of psychopathology should be built. We, therefore, propose to modify the psychoanalytic concept of repression and use it as the foundation of a new theoretical model.

In psychoanalytic doctrine, repression and unconsciousness are strongly related. In the present work, these two concepts are separated. In our theory, repression is viewed as a conscious and deliberate effort to withdraw attention from a threatening stimulus. This conceptualization is in accordance with more recent experimental work on repression (D'Zurilla, 1965; Holmes, 1972, 1974; Holmes & Schallow, 1969; Stam, Radtke-Bodorik, & Spanos, 1980), conflicting with early, less controlled experiments by Zeller (1950a, 1950b, 1951) and others (see Holmes's critical review, 1974). Thus, unlike Freud, who used subjective, clinical observations and showed no interest in laboratory investigation of repression (Mackinnon & Dukes, 1964), we rely on laboratory research findings as our major source of evidence for clarification of the repression concept and construction of our "psychoanalytic" theory.

Moreover, in order to render the concept of repression appropriate for its new use, it must be freed from its strong links with two additional concepts in psychoanalysis—maladjustment and childhood memories. In psychoanalytic theory, repression and/or detachment from reality is considered an unhealthy psychological process under almost all conditions (Fenichel, 1946; Nemiah, 1984; Perry & Laurence, 1984; Singer, 1970; Taylor, 1983). This point of view is based on observations of abnormal patients who exhibit pathological repression. In contrast, a growing body of new evidence (e.g., Lazarus, 1979, 1983; McCrae & Costa, 1983; Rofé, Hoffman, & Lewin, 1985; Rofé & Lewin, 1979; Taylor, 1983) indicates that detachment from reality, deluding oneself or presenting oneself in a positive way, may enhance, rather than retard, reality adjustment. Thus, we maintain that Freud and his followers may have been wrong in their assumption that clinical findings on repression or other psychological processes can be automatically generalized to nonclinical subjects. Maddi (1980), in criticizing this methodological approach with respect to the notion of defense mechanisms, noted,

Psychoanalysts have been known to make conclusions on the basis of striking observations of as few as one or two patients. However exciting these conclusions may be, they may not apply to people in general, even though it is typical to assume that they do. (p. 207)

The cumulative research and clinical evidence suggests that abnormal and normal subjects employ radically different means for achieving withdrawal of attention from anxiety-provoking stimuli. Repression is thus conceptualized not as a defense mechanism, but rather as a coping strategy that is employed by normal, neurotic, and psychotic people. Hence, while Freud restricted repression to normal and neurotic subjects, we expand it to include psychotic patients as well. However, unlike the healthy use of repression, abnormal individuals use pathological measures for achieving repression. Furthermore, we claim that the phenomenon of unconsciousness is mainly characteristic of abnormal people and that this is, to a large extent, an integral part of the maladjusted use of repression, as this was originally argued by Janet (see Perry & Laurence, 1984).

As will be demonstrated, abnormal subjects use very sophisticated methods to deceive themselves as to their lack of direct conscious involvement in producing their bizarre symptoms. Thus, we accept the phenomenon of unconsciousness or unawareness as a product of the conscious, but deny its existence as an autonomous entity.

Regarding the linkage of repression to childhood events, Freud promoted the idea that traumatic childhood memories, for which adult subjects could not recall any details, may be kept in the unconscious store and that psychoanalytic means may help expose them in their full freshness. This notion is vividly described by Wachtel (1977), a contemporary psychoanalytic theorist, as follows:

> *Freud's description of the persisting influence of the past is reminiscent of the tales of wooly mammoths found frozen in the Arctic ice, so perfectly preserved after thousands of years that their meat could be eaten by anyone with a taste for such regressive fare. (p. 28)*

Not only did Freud not even consider the possibility that the patient's complete inability to recall traumatic material from childhood may simply reflect its loss from the system, but he believed, as other psychoanalysts do still, that the preservation of these "memories" becomes possible as a result of this lack of conscious access to them (see Wachtel, 1977).

However, this psychoanalytic assumption is of questionable scientific status. Not only does psychoanalytic doctrine lack a convincing body of evidence to support this hypothesis (other than the type Freud supplied), but also the cumulative research findings, presented throughout this book, tend to refute it. These data indicate that patients' reports about their past are unreliable and may be nothing more than pure confabulations (Erdelyi & Goldberg, 1979; E. F. Loftus & G. R. Loftus, 1980; Neisser, 1982, 1984). Accordingly, in the present work it is argued that in many cases these stories are part and parcel of the patient's sophisticated methods of self-deception.

We do not deny, of course, the important influence of early childhood in shaping one's personality. Rather, we claim that patients' symptoms have no direct or indirect relationship to early events in their lives. As stated, we maintain that childhood events and/or genetic predisposition may prepare the individual to experience a high level of stress due to severe deficits in certain important qualities or behaviors. However, a subject's pathological responses are determined by cognitive evaluation of his or her present life, and in no case are these automatically aroused by particular events stored in the patient's memory system. In this respect, our theoretical approach is similar to that of the behavioral paradigm as well as the ideas of Lewin (see C. S. Hall & Lindzey, 1967).

In view of the sharp differences between the psychoanalytic usage of repression and the sense indicated here, another term (e.g., *denial* or *distraction*) may be more exact. Nevertheless, we prefer the traditional concept, primarily because many studies have examined it without any specific connection to other psychoanalytic ideas or data. And, as stated before, we are interested in formulating our proposal in accordance with this empirical base. It may be worthwhile to note that our view of repression as a conscious and deliberate effort to distract attention from stressful stimuli not only is consistent with research findings, but also can be seen as congruent with Freud's original meaning of the concept, at least according to Erdelyi and Goldberg's (1979) interpretation of that work.

A Theoretical Proposal

Our proposal includes three theories, or sets of principles, one for the explanation of neurotic and psychotic symptoms, a second for understanding the coping mechanism of repression as it is used by a normal person, and a third to explain normal human fears. This line is taken in order to avoid the shortcomings of traditional theorists, who believed that one set of theoretical concepts is sufficient for understanding the complicated abnormal and normal behavior of human beings and, according to the behaviorists, of other animals as well. Each of the three theoretical proposals can be considered part of a single theoretical model, and all belong to the same psychological spectrum, namely, response to stress. Nevertheless, since each of them deals with a different area of research, we refer to each component, or set of principles, as a theory. In addition, generalization from one area to another either is quite limited (as is the case regarding normal and abnormal individuals, who, in our view, employ qualitatively different types of repression as coping strategies) or is impossible (as seems to be the case with regard to normal vs. bizarre fear).

Our first proposal, a theory of psychopathology, constitutes the major portion of the book as well as its most important contribution. Like psychoanalysis, the theory is based heavily on the concept of repression, although its meaning has been highly transformed. In a certain sense, it endeavors to preserve the essence of psychoanalysis without its traditional contents. In order to emphasize this similarity, we designate our approach *psychobizarreness theory*. Another reason for choosing this name is that, in our view, *bizarreness* is the most appropriate term for distinguishing between the behavioral deviations of abnormal and normal people. In this approach, agoraphobia and the chocolate phobia are considered pathological, mainly because they are very unusual and they drastically affect the individual's global functioning. In contrast, fear of dogs or insects is regarded as normal, except in those very rare cases (e.g., see Jacobs & Nadel, 1985) when their burden on the individual's general adjustment capacity becomes very heavy. Thus, psychobizarreness theory attempts to explain the production and persistence of bizarre behaviors, but not the development of normal behavioral deviation. The exact criteria for differentiating between bizarre and nonbizarre behavioral dysfunction will be delineated later. According to the proposed theory, all bizarreness responses are responses to stress, and this applies not only to neurotic but to psychotic reactions as well. In fact, the most impressive evidence for this theory has been gathered from clinical data and research on psychotic behaviors.

The objective of the second theory, which we call the *theory of normal repression*, is to show that the type of repression used by normal human beings is a healthy and efficient coping strategy. Research findings that demonstrate the beneficial effects of repression, including the body of studies on the repression–sensitization (R–S) scale, will be carefully reviewed. These studies have been rejected or totally ignored by repression theorists (Holmes, 1974; Wachtel, 1977). One of the reasons for their rejection is the strong correlation of the R–S scale and self-report anxiety scales (e.g., Taylor Anxiety Scale), social desirability, and various measurements of maladjustment; this correlation indicates that repressors are generally healthier individuals than nonrepressors (Bell & Byrne, 1978; Epstein & Shontz, 1971; Rofé & Lewin, 1979). It will be shown that these studies are quite relevant; rather than rejecting or ignoring them, it may be more appropriate to revise the psychoanalytic conception of repression. Thus the proposed theory of normal repression emphasizes the beneficial effects of repression for normal people. Within this theoretical framework, it should be possible to resolve the apparent inconsistencies between repression and the abovementioned data from the R–S studies, which caused theoretical concern among investigators in this field (Bell & Byrne, 1978; Epstein & Shontz, 1971).

The third theory in our proposal is a conditioning model for the explanation of normal fears of humans and animals. Both Rachman's (1978) and Jacobs and Nodel's (1985) efforts to expose the weaknesses of the traditional learning theories will be examined and elaborated on. It will be shown that these theories cannot explain the acquisition of either normal or bizarre fears. Against this background, it will be proposed that with substantial modification, particularly by taking into account cognitive processes, the old learning model of conditioning may again be useful in explaining the production of normal fears. We will attempt to show that even with respect to animals, the Tolmanian cognitive explanation of learning makes more sense in understanding the acquisition of fear than Hull's mechanistic point of view (see Bower & Hilgard, 1981; Mackintosh, 1983). As far as normal fear is concerned, humans seem to have a basic similarity to animals, and comparative study may, to some limited extent, enhance understanding of normal fear. However, this is not likely to be the case with regard to bizarre phobias, which in our opinion are unique to human beings. A revised theory of conditioning has been designated the *cognitive–automatic conditioning theory of normal fears*, indicating an integration of cognitive factors into the conditioning process. Unlike Tolman's cognitive theory, our theory also includes several other variables, such as personality and social factors, which, according to various research data, seem to play an important role in facilitating or retarding humans' acquisition of normal fear.

The three proposed theories clearly differ from one another. Yet, they share one common element: All three emphasize the central role of consciousness or cognitive processes in determining human as well as animal behavior. Our theoretical work, of course, has important implications for therapy, and chapter 18 is devoted to this subject. The confusion surrounding psychotherapy is probably no less than the lack of clear answers in theoretical aspects of psychopathology. We do not yet know why the rate of therapeutic success of psychoanalysis is not higher than the absence of treatment (Erwin, 1980; Rachman & Wilson, 1980), why behavioral (Hafner, 1976, 1983) or biological intervention (Hogarty, Goldberg, & the Collaborative Study Group, Baltimore, 1973; D. A. Lewis & Hugi, 1981) indicates a low rate of success and a substantial rate of relapse, and why nonprofessional psychological intervention, such as treatment by a witch doctor, may succeed in curing an individual, even one suffering from a serious physical illness (as reported in a case study published in the *AMA Journal* in 1981 by Kirkpatrick; see also N. R. Hall & Goldstein, 1986). We hope to show that psychobizarreness theory can provide insight into these problems as well.

CONCLUSIONS

The main objective of this book is to show the necessity for a new theoretical approach in psychopathology, by demonstrating the inadequacy of traditional theories. In particular, the book challenges three deeply entrenched beliefs in the field of psychopathology. The first, which has become an integral part of Western culture, concerns the existence of an autonomous unconscious entity or unconscious processes and the idea that a serious therapeutic approach must revive traumatic childhood memories buried in the unconscious. The second belief is the idea that all fears, including clinical phobias, are most amenable to explanation by behaviorist concepts. And the third is that bizarre psychotic symptoms are the result of adverse neurochemical changes.

These three assumptions are the main pillars of psychopathology, and any attempt to question them can be expected to meet with strong opposition beyond objective considerations. For example, Armstrong (1982a), based on his review of empirical research about the acceptability of manuscripts in scientific journals (see Armstrong, 1982b; Mahoney, 1985), noted that in order to increase the likelihood and speed of publication, authors should "(1) not pick an important problem, (2) not challenge existing beliefs, (3) not obtain surprising results, (4) not use simple methods, (5) not provide full disclosure, and (6) not write clearly" (p. 197). Armstrong's formula applies to journals, and we would probably encounter great difficulties if we had to use that channel of scientific communication for our purpose. An attempt to challenge the beliefs just mentioned requires an extensive review of an enormous body of research, which is beyond the scope of a journal article.

Rejection of traditional theories in psychopathology and acceptance of a new one cannot be achieved unless one can convincingly demonstrate the superiority of the new theory in explaining the findings that have accumulated over the years (e.g., see Kuhn, 1962). Thus, we hope to show that the idea that patients represent a mechanical entity controlled by unconscious, conditioning, or neurochemical processes is much less adequate in explaining human pathological behavior than our claim that these are deliberately adopted by human consciousness as a coping mechanism against unbearable stress.

In a certain sense, this theoretical approach is close to the behaviorist position, which emphasizes the individual's current situation rather than his or her historical background. However, our theory is in general much closer to that of psychoanalysis, since the concept of repression and the phenomenon of the unconscious constitute its most important base.

Despite our strong criticism of psychoanalysis, without doubt no one has contributed to the understanding of pathological processes more than has Freud. He concluded that the concepts of repression and unconsciousness are the essence of all psychopathological disorders. However, the undeveloped scientific state of psychology in his time could not allow him to formulate his theory more validly. Freud's ideas were proposed at a time when the entire field of psychology was just beginning to awaken from a long period of hibernation, and human behavioral deviations were beginning to be considered a valid subject for scientific observation. It is too much to expect that Freud's formula could provide a theoretical framework to explain the scientific material that has gathered over the years. This task can be fulfilled more efficiently by psychobizarreness theory, since its "psychoanalytic concepts" have been formulated in accordance with these data. Hariman (1982), attempting to demonstrate that hypnosis is nothing more than a state of superalertness, stated that the new studies on hypnosis

actually pose insuperable difficulties to [Freud's] conception of the unconscious in general and "repression" in particular. Notwithstanding, the essential criticality of Freud's methodology renders possible the possibility that he might have agreed to this point had he lived long enough. (p. 85)

In line with this, it is likely that Freud would agree that psychobizarreness theory is a natural scientific development of psychoanalysis and therefore its most legitimate successor.

I

INADEQUACY OF THE PSYCHOANALYTIC DOCTRINE OF REPRESSION

Freud based his psychoanalytic theory of repression entirely on data collected from his work with abnormal people. The theory was then automatically generalized to normal individuals. Despite the subjectivity of the observations, neither he nor his followers ever expressed any doubt as to the validity of the theory of repression, at least with regard to normal subjects. Freud (1914/1959) so vigorously believed in his theory that he declared,

> If anyone should seek to regard the theory of repression and of resistance as assumptions instead of as results following from psychoanalysis, I should oppose him most emphatically . . . the doctrine of repression is the outcome of psycho-analytic work, a theoretical inference legitimately drawn from innumerable observations. (p. 298)

Freud did not feel any necessity to examine the validity of his theory by objective means. For example, in a response to an early experimental study on repression by Rosenzweig and Mason (1934), who sent him a copy of their article, he stated, "I have examined your experimental studies for the verification of the psychoanalytic assertions with interest. I cannot put much value on these confirmations because the wealth of reliable observations on which these assertions rest make them independent of experimental verification" (cf. MacKinnon & Dukes, 1964, p. 703).

In this part of the book, we want to take the course opposite to that of Freud. Instead of relying on subjective clinical case studies and generalizing the conclusions drawn from these cases to the entire population, we will attempt to see what repression is, according to empirical research with a nonclinical population, and to discover to what extent the data support psychoanalytic doctrine in general. Later, in the second part of this book, we will examine how these findings can advance a new formulation of psychopathology theory.

The first chapter attempts to clarify the concept of repression according to the cumulative research findings without any exception or prior theoretical obligation. Thus, we take a different position from that of the previous investigators, whose attempts to examine this notion failed to relate to all research areas on repression, mainly because of their prior theoretical predispositions. For example, Holmes (1974), in his endeavors to demonstrate the lack of experimental support for Freud's theory of repression, overlooked the studies on repression–sensitization (R–S) and perceptual defense. Holmes (1974) justified the omission of the repression–sensitization studies by noting that "there is no way of distinguishing between individuals who have symptoms but do not report them (repressors) and individuals who do not have symptoms and therefore cannot report them (nonrepressors)" (p. 649). Thus, even though these studies may shed some light on the theory of repression, he preferred to disregard them only because they did not fit the traditional linkage of repression with maladjustment. Holmes also overlooked the extensive studies on perceptual defense, indicating that their methodological shortcomings had been exposed by other investigators. However, there appears to be no justification for the criticisms to which these studies were subjected, as will be shown shortly. Thus, these studies should also be taken into consideration in the attempt to clarify the concept of repression.

A similar selective attitude to empirical investigation of repression was taken by Erdelyi and Goldberg (1979). They, like Holmes, completely ignored the studies on repression–sensitization. At the same time, in their critique of Holmes's (1972, 1974) work, they accused him of "complete neglect of the wealth of clinical evidence for repression, which is the empirical foundation of repression concept to begin with" (p. 359). Moreover, they tended to devalue Holmes's experimental findings, indicating that the existence of repression should not be judged by the success of experimental psychologists in producing the phenomenon in the laboratory. Erdelyi and Goldberg (1979) justified their position by arguing "since when, and by what philosophy of science, is a phenomenon's existence predicated on the laboratory science's ability to create it?" (p. 359). However, a philosophical approach of this type may "immunize" psychoanalysis from experimental testing. This line of thought implies that if experimental examination fails to confirm psychoanalytic theory, we must continue to believe in the interpretive case studies of Freud and his followers. However, contrary to Erdelyi and Goldberg's position, we believe that after this long and disappointing journey with psychoanalysis, it is time to change horses. We ought to first disconnect ourselves from psychoanalytic theory and its interpretive case study material, and take a look at what repression is according to experimental observations per se. Then, and only then, should we try to see whether this can be applied to enhancing our understanding of clinical cases. In fact it seems that Holmes's controlled experiments advanced our understanding of the nature of repression more than have hundreds of clinical case studies. If Holmes had not invalidated Zeller's (1950a, 1950b) explanation of repression, psychoanalysts could continue to argue that their theory is consistent not only with clinical observations but with experimental data as well.

We now describe briefly the content of this part of the book. Generally speaking, our prime purpose is to evaluate the scientific status of the psychoanalytic theory of repression according to empirical data, excluding clinical observations. The first chapter reviews the experimental findings on repression, including three main areas: repression proper, perceptual defense, and repression–sensitization. The latter will be examined more thoroughly in order to show its legitimacy for inclusion in any attempt to build a new theory of repression.

Chapter 2 aims to strengthen the notion implied by R–S studies that psychoanalysis has no convincing body of research to justify the linkage between repression and maladjustment. The chapter attempts to show that the psychoanalytic strategy of encouraging the expression of anger in order to prevent psychosomatic illnesses, such as hypertension, is not supported by scientific research.

Chapter 3 reexamines the idea that childhood memories or memory in general is permanent. It particularly attempts to show that psychoanalysts have no scientific support for their central claim that childhood experiences, of whose existence subjects have not even the slightest idea, still exist in the adult's cognitive system.

Chapter 4 reconsiders the evidence regarding the existence of the autonomous unconscious mind. It reviews the different conceptions of the unconscious in the scientific literature, and shows that there is no support for the psychoanalytic theory.

In Chapter 5 we strengthen the criticism against the psychoanalytic model by showing that, therapeutically, this theory has no greater rate of success than does absence of any treatment. The chapter also shows that behavioral approaches are much more successful and that psychoanalysis has difficulty in coping with this challenge. Concluding remarks regarding the data reviewed in this part are given at the end of this chapter.

1

Repression in the Light of Empirical Findings

REPRESSION PROPER

Freud distinguished between two types of repression, which he termed *repression proper* and *primal repression* (see MacKinnon & Dukes, 1964). Repression proper refers to a subject's failure to remember anxiety-provoking experiences of which he or she was once aware and which can be retrieved to consciousness by removal of the threat. Primal repression involves "a denial of entry into consciousness to the mental (ideational) presentation of the instinct" (Freud, 1915/1925, p. 86). This section concerns studies on repression proper. Studies relevant to primal repression will be discussed in the section on perceptual defense.

Repression proper is the most dominant type in the psychodynamic doctrine of repression, and its confirmation or disproval is of crucial importance for the basic validity of the entire psychodynamic approach. The experimental evidence on repression proper is extensively reviewed by Holmes (1974). The earlier experimental studies by Zeller (1950a, 1950b, 1951) and some other investigators were considered confirmation of the psychoanalytic notion of repression. Typically in these studies, subjects first learned a set of nonsense syllables and then the experimental, but not the control, subjects were given a failure experience, which was supposed to arouse in them a high degree of "ego threat." These studies consistently found that subjects in the experimental group exhibited poorer recall of the syllables at first, but when the threat was removed their recall improved and became equal to the level of the control group. These findings were interpreted as providing strong support for the psychodynamic idea of repression.

This interpretation of the early experiments was challenged by D'Zurilla (1965), Holmes and Schallow (1969), and Holmes (1972). D'Zurilla successfully repeated the basic findings of the earlier experiments, but data from a postexperimental interview led him to conclude that distraction hypothesis might better interpret the findings than the psychodynamic concept of repression. When subjects were asked what they had been thinking about during the poststress retention interval, they were found contrary to the psychodynamic conceptualization, to have been worrying and thinking about the threatening event rather than avoiding it. Of these subjects, 62% reported thinking about things related to the threat, as compared to 24% in the control group. Thus the poorer recall of the experimental group was attributed to disruption caused by "irrelevant cognitive responses" elicited by the threatening event rather than by transference of the threatening material to an unconscious store.

The interference or distraction hypothesis was further strengthened by findings of Holmes and Schallow (1969). They demonstrated that subjects whose attention during the retention period was occupied by irrelevant tasks displayed decline of recall similar to the ego-threat subjects, and both groups were significantly poorer in recall than were the control subjects. After the debriefing, however, the performance of the two experimental groups improved and became equal to the level of the control group. Moreover, analyses of the specific words forgotten by the distraction and ego-threat groups rule out the possibility that the improved recall in the ego-threat group was the result of a specific association between content of the forgotten words and the threat. Additional experimentation by Holmes (1972) soon provided more impressive support for the distraction hypothesis. Subjects learned a list of words and then took a Rorschach test in which the words were used as stimuli. Subjects were then given either ego-threat (i.e., they were told that their choice indicated maladjustment), ego-enhancing (i.e., they were told that they were creative and high in leadership ability), or neutral feedback. Following this, they were tested for recall, debriefed, and retested for recall. Results showed that the ego-threat and ego-enhancing groups performed alike and showed poorer recall on the postfeedback test than did the control group. After the debriefing, however, while the control group did not show a change in recall performance, the other two groups did show an improvement. It was these findings, in essence, that led Holmes (1974) to claim that there is no experimental evidence for the psychoanalytic notion of repression.

Further study that strengthens Holmes's conclusion is reported by Stam, Radtke-Bodorik, and Spanos (1980). These authors repeated the experiment of Clemes (1964), which had been used by several investigators (Cooper, 1972; W. Epstein & Shontz, 1971; Touhey, 1977) to support psychoanalytic theory. Clemes found that when subjects were given posthypnotic amnesia suggestion to the effect that they would remember only 10 out of 18 previously learned words, they were more likely to forget the words with negative affect. However, Stam et al. (1980) did not succeed in replicating these findings, and they concluded that the psychoanalytic concept of repression cannot account for these data.

In contrast, in accord with Holmes's (1974) distraction hypothesis, Stam et al. (1980) used the inattention idea to explain their findings as well as the general phenomenon of posthypnotic amnesia. Thus, they indicated that

> according to the inattention hypothesis, amnesia occurs to the extent that subjects withdraw their attention from the task of recalling target material during the suggestion period. Following the cue to cancel amnesia, subjects once again focus attention on the recall task and therefore recover the amnesic material. (p. 557)

Holmes (1974) used these findings for rejecting altogether the psychodynamic theory of repression. As an alternative, Holmes (1972) considered the possibility of interpreting his findings in terms of the traditional concept. However, he rejected this. His main objection is that "the unconscious plays a crucial role in the process traditionally associated with the process of repression, while it plays no role whatsoever in the interference process" (pp. 169–170). This point was not taken into consideration by Wachtel (1977), who attempted to interpret Holmes's results in line with psychoanalytic approaches. In the psychoanalytic doctrine not only is the operation of repression unconscious but the repressed materials are stored in an autonomous unconscious storage, where they remain intact for an indefinite period. These notions are very strongly emphasized by Wachtel himself (1977, 1984) and are completely inconsistent with Holmes's conceptualization. Repression proper constitutes the most important aspect of psychoanalytic doctrine with regard to both the manner in which psychiatric symptoms are developed and the way in which they are removed. Therefore, the findings of D'Zurilla (1965), Holmes (1972, 1974), Holmes and Schallow (1969), and Stam et al. (1980) raise serious questions as to the validity of the traditional psychoanalytic approaches.

PERCEPTUAL DEFENSE

Another area of research, which according to various investigators (Maddi, 1980; MacKinnon & Dukes, 1964) has direct relevance to repression, particularly to primal repression, is the bulk of experiments on perceptual defense. In these studies, anxiety-provoking stimuli (usually taboo words having either sexual or aggressive connotations) were presented tachistoscopically to each individual. (Tachistoscopic procedure involves presenting a stimulus below the subject's absolute thresholds and then gradually increasing the exposure duration.) Immediately after each exposure, the subject was to guess what the stimulus was. The abovementioned studies consistently found that some individuals displayed perceptual avoidance namely, they failed to recognize the anxiety-arousing stimuli when they were presented somewhat below their absolute threshold, while others exhibited "perceptual sensitization" or "vigilance," that is much quicker perception as compared with their response to emotionally neutral stimuli.

This series of experiments was initiated by Bruner and Postman (1947). Subjects were first administered a word-association test in which their time reaction to various kinds of words was measured. Then the words were presented for tachistoscopic perception. Bruner and Postman found that for some subjects, words associated with longer reaction time (which according to the authors' assumption is an indication of emotional disturbance) required longer tachistoscopic exposures for recognition than did words associated with shorter reaction times. In contrast, other subjects displayed the opposite pattern of reaction—the words associated with longer reaction times were more quickly identified than were the words associated with shorter reaction times. In addition, several other experiments (N. F. Dixon, 1958; McGinnies, 1949) found that not only did the slower observers fail to recognize the supposedly anxiety-provoking stimuli, but they also displayed more intense galvanic skin response (GSR) (a measure of emotional arousal) before they "consciously" identified the stimuli than they did when exposed to neutral stimuli. These results were interpreted as evidence of "autonomic discrimination without awareness." Somehow, enough information is transmitted to the autonomic nervous system to yield differential GSR responding to the two classes of stimuli, but the information is insufficient to produce awareness.

However, this theoretical position was not unanimously accepted by all investigators, and the interpretation of the perceptual defense findings produced one of the most bitter controversies in the history of psychology (N. F. Dixon, 1981). Critics have argued, for example, that the taboo words may have been perceived as quickly as, or even more quickly than, the neutral words, but that the subjects may have been too embarrassed to utter them. It has also been claimed that the subjects correctly identified the words, but did not act on their guesses because it seemed to them unlikely that anyone would have shown them words of this kind. Another criticism raised is that taboo words are less familiar or less frequently used than neutral ones. This argument may account for the threshold differences, but it would not explain the subjects' psychogalvanic discrimination before their awareness of the taboo words (Dember, 1960).

We do not intend to thoroughly review here the perceptual defense studies and discuss their possible limitations. This task has been very well done by a number of investigators (N. F. Dixon, 1981; Erdelyi, 1974; Eriksen & Pierce, 1968; Maddi, 1980).

Our prime interest is to examine whether these studies may enhance our understanding of repression. As was indicated previously, Holmes (1974), convinced that these studies had serious shortcomings, chose not to discuss their implications for the theory of repression. However, Erdelyi (1974) in an intensive critical review concluded that perceptual defense is a valid phenomenon even after all the criticisms have been taken into account. Similarly, N. F. Dixon (1981), after reviewing the studies in this area, concluded that the findings put "the validity of the perceptual defense effect, as a manifestation of sensory regulation, beyond any reasonable doubt" (p. 146).

Erdelyi (1974) and N. F. Dixon (1971, 1981) made the most intensive theoretical effort to explain the phenomenon of perceptual defense. The central problem, which according to some investigators (e.g., see Haber & Hershenson, 1973) caused the decline of interest in this area, is what Erdelyi (1974) termed the *logical paradox:* "How can the perceiver selectively defend himself against a particular stimulus unless he first perceives the stimulus" (p. 3). It does seem, however, that Erdelyi's (1974) theory on perceptual defense provides a satisfactory answer to this problem. According to this theory, perceptual defense-vigilance effect is a special instance of selectivity in the perceptual system. It is argued that the processes of selectivity are complex phenomena that are not restricted to certain regions of the perceptual activity but rather may take place along all stages of the cognitive continuum, from input to output. These processes are regulated by control commands at the long-term memory storage that examine and analyze the stimulus input at the iconic storage and/or at the latter stages of perception. The examination of the input material at the iconic stage does not by itself produce storage in the long-term memory. Further operations such as encoding the selected information into short-term storage, rehearsal, etc., are needed until the material has been transferred to the long-term memory. However, the control commands may, on the basis of analysis of information held in an earlier buffer (e.g., iconic storage), terminate further processing through commands to transfer systems (e.g., stop further encoding of the information currently in iconic storage). Erdelyi proposed that the conscious identification or phenomenal awareness of the input stimulus takes place in or near the region of the short-term memory, beyond the encoding system but prior to long-term memory. Accordingly, *perceptual defense* denotes a failure of emotional input to reach this region.

Erdelyi suggested, on the basis of many studies, several mechanisms by which traumatic input is prevented from reaching the short-term memory region. These mechanisms include looking strategies, namely, fixating away from the emotional stimulus and closing the eyelids, contracting the diameter of the pupils, and accommodation of the lenses. Defensive processes may also operate at later stages of perception through selective rehearsal and/or reporting strategies, including one of the earliest explanations of perceptual defense, namely, avoidance of reporting the troublesome material. Thus, Erdelyi overcame the logical problem mentioned above by arguing essentially that the rejected material was available to the perceiver for "a fraction of a second" before it was permanently lost with the rapid decay of the information from the iconic memory. Though not clearly expressed, Erdelyi's article implies that the selective defensive processes are conscious and voluntary and that subjects in the perceptual defense studies may have been conscious of the rejected material for a fleeting moment before it vanished from their memory system.

N. F. Dixon's (1971, 1981) suggestion for explaining perceptual defense phenomena is a neurophysiological model. It is argued that defense effects are mediated by an interaction between sensory processes, activities in the cortical projection areas and the reticular formation system. The awareness of visual stimuli depends on the coincidence in the visual cortex of impulses arriving from a specific stimulus and those coming from upward discharge of the reticular activity system. Raised or lowered perceptual thresholds for emotional stimuli stem from cortical control of the reticular system. When stimuli are presented below the awareness threshold, their meaning is recognized by the cortex, and the cortex may affect the reticular system toward either enhancement or inhibition of cortical activation. Thus, for awareness to occur, a specific sensory area in the cortex must be activated, together with arousal by the reticular formation system. N. F. Dixon (1971, 1981) mentioned only a few studies that confirm his theory, and it seems that more studies are needed for more careful evaluation of his proposals. It may be worthwhile to note, however, that Dixon's theoretical position is not incompatible with Erdelyi's approach. In fact, Dixon's emphasis on the involvement of the reticular formation mechanism indicates that he too attributes a vital role to the attentional processes in producing the perceptual defence phenomenon, inasmuch as attention is, to a large extent, controlled by this neurophysiological mechanism.

One of the important contributions of both Erdelyi's (1974) and Dixon's (1981) theories was that they renewed acceptance of the phenomenon of perceptual defense. Nisbett and Wilson (1977) noted, in reference to Erdelyi's article, that the theory provides a satisfactory answer to the problem of logical paradox, for it shows that "we cannot perceive without perceiving, but we can perceive without remembering" (p. 230). They further indicated that

> the basic question of whether people can respond to a stimulus in the absence of the ability to verbally report on its existence would today be answered in the affirmative by many more investigators than would have been the case a decade ago. (p. 239)

Positive acceptance of the phenomenon of perceptual defense is expressed also by Shevrin and Dickman (1980) and by Bowers (1984).

Thus, the perceptual defense literature seems to be quite relevant and important for clarification of the concept of repression. There is, however, no convincing evidence that necessitates accepting the notion that these findings support the psychoanalytic doctrine of repression, in which the unconscious element is strongly emphasized. Consistent with Holmes's (1972, 1974) conceptualization of repression, it may be argued that the looking strategies, by which, according to Erdelyi (1974), the perception of threatening material is prevented, are attentional distractive mechanisms controlled by conscious rather than unconscious mechanisms. However, the subject appears to be unconscious because the looking responses are performed very rapidly before the stimulus input has a chance to pass much further beyond the region of iconic memory. Thus, due to rapid decay processes in this region of memory, the subject cannot remember either the threatening input or his own coping responses. This interpretation is in fact what is suggested by Erdelyi's (1974) theoretical analysis of perceptual defense. A different interpretation of these findings—that they are controlled by the unconscious system—would raise the question of logical paradox mentioned above, namely, how can the perceiver selectively defend himself against a particular stimulus input unless he is first aware of the stimulus? It may be worthwhile to indicate that this conception of perceptual defense is also consistent with Erdelyi and Goldberg's (1979) point of view, according to which repression is a conscious and deliberate process by which undesirable material is rejected from the conscious region.

DIMENSIONS OF REPRESSION–SENSITIZATION

Overview

The repression–sensitization (R–S) scale generated an unusual number of studies since its development by Byrne (1961), and these are summarized in several review articles (Bell & Byrne, 1978; Byrne, 1964; Chabot, 1973; W. Epstein & Shontz, 1971). As mentioned, due to the strong relationships of the scale with self-report measurements of anxiety, social desirability, and indices of maladjustment, investigators usually are uncertain as to its true meaning (Bell & Byrne, 1978; W. Epstein & Shontz, 1971; Holmes, 1974). In the present section, we want to reconsider the studies that have examined the validity of the scale and show that there is no reason for their being rejected in developing a theory of repression. Then the research that examined the relationship between the R–S scale and the abovementioned variables will be reviewed. The inconsistency of these findings with psychoanalytic theory will be emphasized. However, at this stage no attempt will be made to settle the apparent inconsistencies between repression, anxiety, social desirability, and maladjustment. This will be postponed until the second part of the book.

Validity of the R–S Scale

The earliest attempt to examine the validity of the R–S scale was performed by Tempone (1964a, 1964b). In one study, clinical psychologists were requested to fill out a copy of the scale as they thought a repressor would do. In addition, psychiatric residents rated their patients on the degree of repression–sensitization observed in each. Results showed 90% agreement between the clinical judgments and Byrne's revised version of the R–S scale. Further, a significant correlation ($r = .43$) was found between the psychiatric ratings and the clinical judgments. Thus, this study demonstrated some correspondence between repression measured by the R–S scale and the clinical use of the concept.

In his second study, Tempone (1964b), using experimental manipulation similar to that employed in perceptual defense studies, showed that repressors displayed higher thresholds for threatening words than did sensitizers. However, no significant differences were found between the two groups in thresholds for neutral or positive words. Similar findings were reported by Hutt and Anderson (1967), using nonsense syllables paired with threatening words, and by Schill and Althoff (1968) in an auditory task. In the same way, S. Epstein and Fenz (1967) found that repressors showed greater elevation in thresholds for taboo words and lesser increase in GSR magnitude when exposed to these words than did sensitizers. In the second stage of the experiment, in which subjects were asked to produce associations to the stimulus words, repressors displayed greater GSR arousal in response to the taboo words than did sensitizers. The authors concluded that repressors are well defended against perceiving threatening materials, but are more vulnerable once they perceive the threat. It is interesting to note that the expected perceptual threshold differences were obtained even when subjects were only led to believe that the stimuli were threatening (see M. D. White & Wilkins, 1973).

Consistent with these studies, Haley (1974) found that repressors had a greater tendency to avoid looking at the aversive content of a stressful film than sensitizers, but neither differed significantly from the intermediates. The tendency of repressors to avoid looking at stressful pictures was also demonstrated by S. F. Brown (1970). It may be worthwhile to note that similar findings were obtained by Luborsky, Blinder, and Schimek (1965), when projective measurements were used to classify subjects as repressors, and by Eberhage, Polek, and Hynan (1985), when the Manifest Anxiety Scale (MAS) was used for the same purpose.

Some inconsistent findings were reported by Van Egeren (1968), who discovered no significant differences between repressors and sensitizers in the recognition of affective and neutral words. It is worthwhile to note, however, that before the subjects' perception was examined, they were allowed 10 minutes to learn the words. It is likely that this research procedure obscured the threatening aspect of the words by way of adaptation. Additionally, the Ulman's rather than the Byrne R–S scale was used for classification of subjects into repressors or sensitizers.

Further evidence that reinforces the validity of R–S scale was provided by Markowitz (1969). Extreme repressors and sensitizers were instructed to learn a list of nonsense syllables, where each syllable appeared in the center of a card. At the corner of each card was printed either a negative, a neutral, or a positive word. Half the subjects were told that the learning task was a measure of intelligence, and the other half were told that the experimenter was interested in finding out the average performance of college students. The results showed that repressors displayed less incidental learning, that is they showed less recall of the peripheral words under the ego-threat than under the non-ego-threat condition. In contrast, sensitizers displayed greater learning of these words under the threatening condition than nonthreatening condition. The differences between the two personality types could not be attributed to differences in intellectual or learning ability. In reference to this study, Donelson (1973) indicated that "repressors, who tend to look around little anyway, respond to threat with a narrowed attention. Sensitizers tend to look around more and respond to threat with increased vigilance and broader attention" (p. 372).

In terms of adjustment, the repressors' mode of response to threat, as was demonstrated in this study, seems to be quite efficient. This coping response increases the probability that attention will be focused only on the relevant stimuli when the ego is threatened. However, at the same time, a cognitive orientation to avoid threatening stimuli may sometimes result in poorer cognitive performance, even when the stimulus appears to be nonthreatening. Bergquist, Lewinsohn, Sue, and Flippo (1968) reported that repressors displayed poorer short-term memory than sensitizers for both threatening and nonthreatening words. The authors indicated that these findings raise some doubt about the validity of the scale, as they expected to find an interaction between R–S and the type of words presented. However, it seems that the reduced recall of the nonthreatening words by repressors was due to the experimental procedure by which subjects were exposed to the words. Each of the 54 recall trials involved successive presentation of two words, one threatening and one nonthreatening. It is quite possible that after a few trials repressors realized that each display involves an aversive stimulus, and since they could not know in advance exactly when the threatening stimuli were due to appear, they chose to withdraw their attention from both types of words.

The tendency of repressors to show avoidance cognitive orientation to threatening stimuli was demonstrated by several other investigators as well. Gossett (1964) found that repressors exhibited a greater tendency to forget syllables that had previously become associated with failure than did sensitizers. Similarly, Eriksen and Davids (1955) found that subjects with a greater tendency to forget traumatic experiences or anxiety-arousing topics scored lowest on the Manifest Anxiety Scale (MAS). As will be shown soon, R–S is highly correlated with self-report scales of anxiety, particularly the MAS. Therefore, these two scales seem to have the same psychological meaning (Golin, Herron, Lakota, & Reineck, 1967; P. F. Sullivan & Roberts, 1969).

Consistent with these findings, Hare (1966) found that repressors tend to avoid thinking about the threatening stimuli. Similarly, Gleason (1969) reported that repressors displayed greater decrease in their level of anxiety if the experimenter's confederate avoided talking with them about the threatening topics as compared to situations where he ruminated about them at length. In the same way, Carroll (1972) showed that repressors elaborated less freely about their experiences when confronted with threatening stimuli than did sensitizers. In addition, it was reported that repressors tend to avoid verbalizing associations to threatening material. While sensitizers show the opposite pattern of behavior (Haney, 1974; D. L. Shapiro & Rosenwald, 1975).

In psychoanalysis and in perceptual defense studies, sexual and aggressive stimuli were linked with defensive operations or threat. Thus, if the R–S scale is valid, one would expect repressors and sensitizers to show avoidance and approach behavior, respectively, in response to such stimuli. Indeed, evidence from several studies confirms this expectation with both sexual (Burns & Tyler, 1976; Byrne & Lamberth, 1971; Byrne & Sheffield, 1965; Galbraith & Lieberman, 1972; Haney, 1974; Schill, 1969; Wolff, 1966) and aggressive stimuli (Altrocchi & Perlitsh, 1963; Altrocchi, Shrauger, & McLeod, 1964; McDonald, 1965, 1967; Palmer & Altrocchi, 1967; Parsons, Fulgenzi, & Edelberg, 1969; Scarpetti, 1974). Some inconsistent evidence was reported by Good and Levine (1970), who found no significant differences between repressors and sensitizers in the pupil dilation response to sexual and aversive stimuli. However, the authors noted that the experimental design of repeated measures that they employed "resulted in a fairly insensitive procedure for assessing the role of R–S dimension in pupillary reactivity" (p. 634). Furthermore, they indicated that the categorization of the emotional and neutral stimuli in their study is not to be recommended.

Overall, these findings seem to indicate fairly consistent evidence showing that repressors display avoidance of threatening or aversive stimuli and sensitizers approach these stimuli. These findings give strong legitimacy to the relevance of these studies to the concept of repression. Therefore, any new theory of repression must integrate these data within its framework. With respect to the nature of defense or coping mechanisms of repressors, it seems that the idea of conscious distraction, which was used for explaining the studies on repression proper, posthypnotic amnesia, and perceptual defense, may be applied to this area of research as well. It may be worthwhile to note that this conceptualization of repressors was also suggested by Donelson (1973).

Thus, the notion of attentional interference or distraction seems to be the common denominator of the abovementioned four areas of research (i.e., repression proper, posthypnotic amnesia, perceptual defense, and R–S) that empirically examined the concept of repression. Therefore, as far as experimental studies with nonclinical populations are concerned, the mechanism of attentional distraction appears to be the most suitable meaning of repression. It should be noted, however, that no evidence exists that would necessitate the assumption that this mechanism is controlled by unconscious processes. Rather, the findings suggest the opposite, or at least this seems to be the most plausible and parsimonious explanation of these observations.

Repression–Sensitization, Anxiety, and Social Desirability

Strong relationships between R–S and self-reports and anxiety (e.g., Golin, et al., 1967; Joy, 1963), and measures of social desirability (e.g., Feder, 1967; Joy, 1963; Silber & Grebstein, 1964) were reported by various investigators. The coefficient correlations with MAS ranged from .87 (Abbott, 1972; Golin et al., 1967) to .91 (Joy,

1963; P. F. Sullivan & Roberts, 1969). The correlation between the two scales remained remarkably high (.76) even after omission of the 29 common items (P. F. Sullivan & Roberts, 1969) or after removing items that have a high rating of social desirability (Highland, 1980). It is worthwhile to note that despite these correlations, investigators of MAS or social desirability scales often fail to relate to studies on R–S and do not even mention the high correlations with R–S. This attitude was reflected for example by Millham and Jacobson (1978) in their intensive review on social desirability research.

Freudian or psychodynamic-oriented investigators would be willing to accept the R–S scale as a measure of repression if repressors would score low on self-reported scales but high on other measurements of anxiety such as physiological indices. However, while repressors consistently described themselves as less anxious (e.g., Early & Kleinknecht, 1978; Rofé & Lewin, 1982b, 1986; J. Weinstein, Averill, Opton, & Lazarus, 1968), this is not the case when other measurements of anxiety are applied. Some investigators found that repressors showed more signs of anxiety than sensitizers on physiological measurements (Y. N. Goldstein, 1977; Hare, 1966; Scarpetti, 1973) and on a word-association test (Lomont, 1965). However, others obtained the opposite results with respect to physiological arousal, namely, repressors were less anxious than sensitizers (P. O. Davidson & Watkins, 1971; Early & Kleinknecht, 1978; Snortum & Wilding, 1971). Consistent with the later findings, Dykman, Reese, Galbrecht, and Thomasson (1959) found that high scorers on the MAS showed greater autonomic arousal than did the low scorers (i.e., repressors) while thinking about "emotional" questions. This inconsistent pattern of results with regard to physiological as opposed to self-report measurements of anxiety is reflected also in the work of J. Weinstein et al. (1968). In reanalyzing six previous experiments, they found no significant differences between repressors and sensitizers with respect to physiological indices. In some experiments, repressors tended to show more autonomic arousal than did sensitizers, while in others this pattern was reversed. Repressors, however, consistently claimed to be less anxious than did sensitizers. Similarly, Rofé and Lewin (1982b) found no significant differences between the two groups in their blood pressure level during pregnancy and immediately before delivery, but repressors described themselves as being less anxious than did sensitizers. Insignificant relationships between R–S and physiological measurements of anxiety were reported also by Baldwin (1972), by Barton and Buckhout (1969), and by Simal and Herr (1970). In the same way, several studies (Hodges & Spielberger, 1966; Katkin, 1965; Lewinsohn, 1956) failed to find significant relationship between MAS and autonomic response to stress.

Thus two main conclusions may be drawn from the studies reviewed in this section:

1. A strong positive relationship between R–S and self-report scales of anxiety was found in a normal setting. Moreover, in stressful situations repressors consistently described themselves as experiencing a low level of anxiety in contrast to sensitizers, who described themselves as highly anxious.

2. Despite the high correlation between R–S and measures of social desirability there is no confirmation of the psychoanalytically derived hypothesis that the repressors' experience of less anxiety exists only on a conscious level while unconsciously they are more anxious. When measurements of anxiety other than self-report scales were employed, some studies found that repressors displayed a higher level of anxiety, some found the opposite, and others reported no significant relationship between R–S and anxiety. The evidence in the next section, which shows that repressors are better

adjusted individuals, reinforces the view that repressors genuinely and not spuriously, as would be claimed by psychoanalytic doctrine, have a lower level of anxiety.

It appears then, that repressors experience less anxiety, at least cognitively, because they have the ability to distract themselves from anxiety-arousing stimuli. In contrast, sensitizers behave like clinically anxious subjects (MacLeod, Mathews, & Tata, 1986; Mathews & MacLeod, 1985), who also display attentional bias to stress-related stimuli. Thus, whether or not one experiences anxiety in stressful situations depends to a large extent on one's attentional vigilance to such stimuli. We will elaborate on this issue later in the book.

Repression–Sensitization and Maladjustment

Inspired by Freudian theory, Byrne (1964) raised the hypothesis that "if each end of the repression-sensitization continuum represents an extreme of the respective defense modes, scores on the R–S scale would be expected to have a curvilinear relationship with various indices of psychological adjustment" (p. 190). Theoretically, psychoanalytic proponents could also argue that while a repressive coping mechanism is an unhealthy process, a sensitive coping style should enhance the likelihood of adjustment.

> *Sensitization denotes awareness and acceptance of impulses, accessibility to consciousness of the full reality of inner mental life. A sensitizer should therefore be a picture of psychological well-being, aware of the forces that activate his own behavior and free to experience all things. (W. Epstein & Shontz, 1971, p. 389)*

Yet, contrary to both of these psychoanalytic expectations, the vast majority of the studies found that repressors are better adjusted individuals than are sensitizers (e.g., see Byrne, 1964; Byrne, Golightly, & Sheffield, 1965; Byrne, Steinberg, & Schwartz, 1968; Feder, 1967, 1968; Foulds & Warehime, 1971; Joy, 1963; Rofé & Lewin, 1979; Schill, Adams, & Bekker, 1982; Tempone & Lamb, 1967; Thelen, 1969; Turner, Giles, & Marafiote, 1983). These studies show that repressors describe themselves on various self-report scales, such as CPI, MMPI, POI (a measure of self-actualization), self-concept scales, etc., as better adjusted individuals than do sensitizers. In the same way, these studies also show that repressors report less frequency and/or severity of emotional and physical difficulties.

Some investigators raised the question of whether self-report scales disclose the true psychological condition of repressors. However, the abovementioned studies reported that repressors displayed the same pattern of psychological health when other types of measurements were employed as well. Thus, repressors, as compared with sensitizers, seek psychiatric and medical help less frequently and are found less often among psychiatric population (e.g., Feder, 1967; Foulds & Warehime, 1971; Thelen, 1969; Turner et al., 1983). It appears then that repressors are less likely to be afflicted with psychiatric disorders than are sensitizers. In a study titled "Who Adjust Better: Repressors or Sensitizers?" Rofé and Lewin (1979) attempted to give a more valid answer regarding the relationship between R–S and maladjustment by using external criteria for evaluating adjustment, with high school students as subjects. They found that repressors were chosen more frequently as friends by their peers and were rated more positively by their teachers on several personality characteristics as compared with sensitizers. In a further study of this type, Rofé (1985) found that not only

REPRESSION IN THE LIGHT OF EMPIRICAL FINDINGS   31

repressors but their spouses as well, irrespective of their own personality type, described their marriage as more happy than did sensitizers or their spouses. Thus, socially at least, repressors have more attractive personalities than do sensitizers. These findings were attributed to the repressors' ability to create a better psychological atmosphere for themselves as well as for others by tuning their attention to the positive aspects of their environment and avoiding the negative ones.

Indeed, evidence by Merbaum and Kazaoka (1967) show that repressors as opposed to sensitizers have the ability to focus their attention on the positive rather than negative aspects of their personal life. In line with these findings, Haley (1974) reported that repressors but not sensitizers avoided looking at the aversive content of a stressful film. In discussing these results, Haley (1974) noted that ". . . the connotation that 'repressors' ' responses are maladaptive should be avoided. In view of the non-functional aversive nature of the film, it would seem that facility to switch off the input is indeed adaptive" (p. 93). Similarly, Clark and Neuringer (1971), in referring to their findings that repressors exceeded sensitizers in verbal aptitude, noted that "fewer self-doubts and less attention to upsetting situations might actually permit greater facility for controlled or directed thinking as opposed to undirected associated thinking" (p. 187).

The tendency of repressors to focus their attention on the positive aspects of life, as these studies imply, and their inclination to avoid talking about aversive materials (e.g., Carroll, 1972; Gleason, 1969) may be one of the prime reasons for their social attractiveness as friends (Rofé & Lewin, 1979) and their success in marriage (Rofé, 1985). This is consistent with Rofé's (1984) utility theory and some other studies (Rofé, Hoffman, & Lewin, 1985; Rofé & Lewin, 1986; Rofé, Lewin, & Hoffman, 1987) that show that people do not like to be with miserable individuals or to talk about depressing topics, as well as with data (Hammen & Peters, 1978) demonstrating that depressed individuals are more strongly rejected than are nondepressed individuals. The general tendency of repressors to behave less aggressively (see p. 28), and their tendency to appease others even when they are painfully attacked by them (Scarpetti, 1974) may be an additional important reason for their success in interpersonal relationships.

The ability of repressors to endure more pain (Merbaum & Badia, 1967) and to be less sensitive to the pain of others (Von Baeyer, 1982) may also help them cope with stressful situations. Von Baeyer (1982) noted in this respect that "temporal disavowal of reality . . . can help one to deal with the situation without becoming disabled by anxiety" (pp. 319–320).

However, even though there is fairly consistent evidence that repressors are better adjusted individuals than are sensitizers, some data indicate that they are more vulnerable to physical illness. Thus, M. S. Schwartz, Krupp, and Byrne (1971), using medical patients at the Mayo Clinic as subjects, found that while sensitizers tended to develop disorders with psychological components, repressors tended to have purely organic diagnoses. Similarly, Lazarus (1979) reported that the most common reaction among a group of women with a breast lump was denial mixed with rationalization. He noted that

> they wouldn't accept the possibility that the lump might mean cancer, and came up with all sorts of reasons for their being right. Unfortunately, their denial led to delay in going to a doctor, which added to the danger of metastasis if the lump was malignant. (pp. 47–48)

Evidence that cancer patients are prone to use avoidance defenses, especially denial and repression, rather than approach coping strategies were reported also by C. D.

Bahnson and M. B. Bahnson (1966). Thus, the above findings show quite consistently that psychologically repressors are better adjusted individuals than are sensitizers. At the same time, some evidence suggests that repressors are more likely to develop organic disease due to their avoidance coping mechanism.

CONCLUSIONS

In conclusion, the studies reviewed in the last section of this chapter show that R–S findings are highly relevant to the general concept of repression and that there is no justification for the tendency of Holmes (1974) and others to overlook the importance of these findings for a comprehensive theory of repression. The most important message of these studies for a theory of repression is that the traditional strong linkage between repression and maladjustment should be reconsidered. At least among the nonpsychiatric population, repression seems to be a healthy coping mechanism. We believe that the theory of repression that will be presented later will not only clarify the relation of repression to normal and pathological behaviors but will also shed some light on the reasons for the strong relationships among R–S, MAS, and social desirability scales. However, at the present stage the "difficulties inherited in the theory of repression itself make it impossible to draw a clear conclusion about whether the R–S scale measures what it is supposed to measure" (W. Epstein & Shontz, 1971, p. 389).

2

Repression, Hostility, and Hypertension

OVERVIEW

Besides the studies on R–S, the only body of research that empirically examined the relationship of repression to maladjustment among the nonpsychiatric population is the one dealing with repression versus expression of hostility or anger. Psychoanalytic theorists often warn against the maladaptive consequences of repressed hostility and emphasize the importance of expression of anger in their attempt to alleviate psychiatric symptoms (Berkowitz, 1962, 1970; Geen & Quanty, 1977). Holt (1970), criticizing Berkowitz's negative attitude to psychoanalytic catharsis theory, indicated that in an individual who repeatedly developed a variety of psychosomatic symptoms,

> problems of one sort or another with inhibited rage, or anxious expectations of being aggressed against, have been implicated by psychoanalysts in the etiology of rheumatoid arthritis, hives, ance vulgaris, psoriasis, peptic ulcer, epilepsy, migraine, Raynaud's disease, and essential hypertension. (p. 9)

The research efforts to examine the validity of this psychoanalytic notion were concentrated almost exclusively in the area of blood pressure or essential hypertension. This research can be divided into two groups: field studies and experimental studies. We now examine the main findings of these studies.

FIELD STUDIES

Franz Alexander (1932, 1939, 1950), the most notable psychoanalytic theorist on the subject of psychosomatic illnesses, concluded on the basis of his own clinical observations and some psychiatric data that essential hypertension is developed mainly because the prehypertensive individual represses feelings of hostility instead of expressing them. He noted that "quite frequently these patients were extremely compliant and agreeable and would go out of their way to please their associates" (Alexander, 1950, p. 147). This theoretical conception continued to dominate the view of many investigators in recent years as well. Thus R. W. White and Watt (1981) stated in their book on abnormal personality that hypertensive individuals can never openly express anger or even become aware of these feelings:

> we can scarcely assume that hostility is dead in these people; we must therefore suppose that it is aroused but somehow spends itself internally. . . . Perhaps the anger is bottled up with no outlet except a chronic raising of the blood pressure or some other physiological effect. (p. 130)

However, when the empirical findings are carefully examined, support for this psychoanalytic hypothesis is found to be quite meager. Although the earliest studies tended to support this theory (Cochrane, 1971), recent ones raise serious doubts regarding the validity of these findings (e.g., see reviews by Diamond, 1982; Harrell, 1980). Inconsistent with psychoanalytic theory, several investigators found no relationship between repressed hostility and blood pressure level (Cochrane, 1973; Goldberg, Comstock, & Graves, 1980; Rofé & Lewin, 1982b; Steptoe, Melville, & Ross, 1982; Weatley et al., 1975), and some found that hypertensives displayed a higher level of hostility than normotensives (Baer, Collins, Bourianoff, & Ketchel, 1979; Mann, 1977, 1984; Whitehead, Blackwell, De Silva, & Robinson, 1977). Baer et al. noted that their results are not consistent with "the notion of suppression in the form of denial" (p. 328), an opinion held by many clinicians and personality investigators. Similarly, Mann (1977) concluded that his findings "run contrary to the accepted theory of repressed hostility" (p. 659). In the same way, Mann (1984) stated that his "findings do not provide support for the view that repression of hostility is associated with hypertension. . . . If anything, the hypertensive subjects displayed more self-criticism and reported more expression of hostility than normotensive subjects" (p. 31).

In line with these findings, other studies reported that expression of hostility and the personality dimension of Type A, which correlates significantly with expression of anger (T. W. Smith, 1984), are both significantly related with coronary heart disease (Chesney, Black, Chadwick, & Rosenman, 1981; Matthews, Glass, Rosenman, & Bortner, 1977; Williams et al., 1980).

Several studies conducted by Harburg and his co-workers appear to be inconsistent with these findings (Gentry et al., 1983; Gentry, Chesney, Hall, & Harburg, 1981; Harburg et al., 1973). These investigators found that suppression of anger was related to a higher level of blood pressure than was expression of anger. However, the meaning of suppression of anger in these studies is completely different from the psychoanalytic notion of repressed hostility as is reflected in the abovementioned quotations by Alexander (1950) and R. W. White and Watt (1981). In the studies of Harburg and his associates, *suppression* refers to conscious and active inhibition of anger in anger-provoking situations. Those who reported that they use suppression did not state that they succeeded in eliminating feelings of anger from their consciousness. Rather, they only stated that if some high authority figure such as their boss got angry and blew up at them for no good reason they would hold in their anger. Evidence consistent with these data were also reported by Schneider, Egan, Johnson, Drobny, and Julins (1986). Comparing borderline hypertensives whose blood pressure also remained high outside the clinic with subjects whose blood pressure returned to normal at home, the authors found that the former were higher on both anger-expression scales (conscious experiencing of anger) and anger-in scales (conscious suppression of anger). Similar findings were reported by Ploeg, Buuren, and Brummelen (1985).

Thus, three main conclusions can be drawn from the field studies on hostility and hypertension reviewed so far:

1. Experiencing anger or hostility seems to be one of the prominent characteristics of hypertensive subjects (see also Diamond, 1982).

2. There is no convincing evidence to support the psychoanalytic hypothesis that hypertensive patients are "extremely compliant and agreeable" (Alexander, 1950, p. 147) and "can never openly express aggression nor even become aware of hostile feelings" (R. W. White & Watt, 1981, p. 130).

3. Both expression of anger and conscious efforts to inhibit or suppress anger were significantly related to hypertension. This may indicate that frequent arousal of anger, irrespective of whether it is expressed or held in, is one of the important causes of

hypertension. This possibility is consistent with evidence showing that anger produced the greatest increase in cardiovascular activity, greater even than did fear (G. E. Schwartz, Weinberger, & Singer, 1981).

Psychoanalysis attributes great importance to repression (including repression of hostility) that takes place during childhood (Fenichel, 1946). However, with regard to hypertension, not only is there no evidence that the phenomenon of hypertension is related to repressed hostility in childhood, but some data suggest that even those who use suppression had long been in the habit of expressing their anger. Alexander (1950) indicated that anamnestic reports of hypertensive patients usually show a typical history of aggressive personality. Then, within a short period of time, often during puberty, they radically change their behavior and act as if they were intimidated and meek.

Sometimes such patients report that the change from belligerency to meekness took place as a result of conscious effort; that they had to control themselves in order not to lose their popularity or because they had suffered defeats as a result of the expression of their aggressive impulses. (p. 50)

Thus, judging from this report, psychoanalysts cannot attribute the development of hypertension to repression originated in childhood, as they have often done with other psychiatric symptoms. Moreover, it is possible that if these prehypertensive subjects had learned in early childhood to inhibit (or repress) rather than express anger, they would be less likely to develop angry personality types and, hence hypertension. However, when this attempt is made after a prolonged period of repetition of the hostile behavior and without developing an alternative coping mechanism to deal with frustration-provoking situations (such as distraction), it has little chance of success. Furthermore, these subjects may have a somewhat greater chance to develop hypertension than those who continue to express their anger, as the abovementioned studies of Harburg and his co-workers indicate (except that of Harburg, Blakelock, & Roeper, 1979, which found the opposite). Since they feel anger or stress with no ability to discharge or overcome it in any other way, they may remain physiologically aroused for a longer period and are thereby more prone to develop hypertension.

Some further evidence shows that a modified form of suppression of anger may be quite efficient in avoiding hypertension. Thus, Harburg et al. (1979) found that subjects who used a "reflective" coping style displayed a lower blood pressure level than did those who employed expression or suppression coping mechanisms. The reflective group also suppressed their anger, but at the same time they analyzed the problem that had made them angry and tried to clarify their reasons for being attacked. Similar findings were reported by Ewart, Taylor, Kraemer, and Agras (1984). These authors were interested in examining whether teaching hypertensive patients more effective coping skills in handling conflicts, particularly with their spouses, could make long-term blood pressure control easier to achieve. One of the important elements of this training was the inhibition of aggressive responses. This involved "speaking a code word" (e.g., *time out*), taking a deep breath, exhaling slowly while focusing on a calming thought or image, and agreeing to continue discussing the problems later if necessary. This method seems to involve a strong component of distraction. Ewart et al. (1984) found that subjects who had mastered these coping skills engaged in fewer hostile exchanges during marital discussions than did the untrained control group. Trained subjects also achieved a significantly greater reduction in systolic blood pressure than did the control group. Thus, suppression of anger is not always bad behavior, as is suggested in psychoanalysis.

It appears then that the cumulative research findings, at least from field studies, tend to refute the psychoanalytic explanation of hypertension. These data do not suggest that expression of anger is an efficient means of reducing the likelihood of hypertension. At most, the findings indicate that suppression by itself may not be an adequate coping response. However, even this may apply primarily to subjects who have a prolonged history of aggressive behavior and attempt to make an extremely abrupt shift in their habitual mode of reaction.

EXPERIMENTAL STUDIES

A fairly large body of experimental evidence shows that expression of anger that has been experimentally aroused leads to a rapid decrease in the level of blood pressure and general physiological arousal (Baker & Schaie, 1969; Gamaro & Rabin, 1969; Hokanson, 1961; Hokanson & Burgess, 1962b; Hokanson & Shelter, 1961; Ranschburg, 1983; Schill, 1972; Van Egeren, Abelson, & Thornton, 1978). These findings were used by various authors (e.g., Duke & Nowicki, 1979; R. W. White & Watt, 1981) to strengthen the popular psychoanalytic notion that "if people have to 'sit on' their anger for long periods of time, their blood pressure may rise and stay high even after the cause of their frustration has been removed" (Duke & Nowicki, 1979, p. 283). However, more careful examination of these data suggests that these studies, like the correlational ones, cannot be considered to support the psychoanalytic repression hypothesis.

First, the short-term decrease in blood pressure level immediately after expression of anger does not occur under all circumstances. This is limited only to situations where such behavior is not likely to make the attacker experience anxiety (see Geen & Quanty's review, 1977). For example, when anger is directed against a high-stature frustrator either no reduction in blood pressure level takes place, or it may even increase slightly (Hokanson & Burgess, 1962a; Hokanson & Shelter, 1961). In addition, the individual's learning history in reacting to frustrating experiences plays an important role in determining whether or not a reduction in blood pressure or general autonomic arousal will occur. Subjects who characteristically react to threat passively or who were experimentally rewarded for reacting in a friendly manner to provocation displayed quicker decreases in their physiological arousal if they responded nonaggressively to an experimental provocation than if they reacted in a hostile manner (Hokanson, Willers, & Koropsak, 1968; Scarpetti, 1974; Sosa, 1968; L. J. Stone & Hokanson, 1969).

Second, it may be argued (Berkowitz, 1962, pp. 197–198; 1970, p. 6) that in line with learning theories the immediate "tension reduction" and some other reinforcements that one may gain by an aggressive act may in the long run increase the tendency to react to frustrating situations with anger. This pattern of behavior may in the long run lead to further increase in the subject's blood pressure level. Findings consistent with this hypothesis were found by Geen, Stonner, & Shope (1975) and by Kahn (1966). These investigators reported that expression of anger was followed by both a reduction in blood pressure and an increase in the level of aggressiveness. These findings and many other data (Berkowitz & Geen, 1967; Berkowitz, Green, & Macaulay, 1962; DeCharms & Wilkins, 1963; Downey, 1973; Ebbesen, Duncan, & Konecni, 1975; Goldman, Keck, & O'Leary, 1969; Loew, 1967; E. A. Nelson, 1969; Wheeler & Caggiula, 1966) indicating that expression of anger increases rather than decreases the likelihood of aggressive reaction on subsequent occasions are in sharp contrast to the psychoanalytic notions of catharsis and repression of hostility (Geen & Quanty, 1977; Holt, 1970).

Third, expression of anger invites retaliation and negativism as noted by Alexander (1950): "the relatives of such patients often remark that although the treatment may have improved the patient's physical status, it has made him a more difficult person to live with" (p. 153). Most likely the relatives of Alexander's patients restrained their retaliatory responses because the patient had the status of an "ill person" and had gained the support of the therapist. In normal circumstances, an aggressive attitude may impair the subject's relationship with his close social network. As was indicated, Alexander (1950) stated that this type of stress, produced by a maladjustive type of reaction, was among the main motivators of prehypertensive subjects to change their previously habitual, angry behavior. In view of the position of stress as one of the most important psychological factors in rising blood pressure level (Cochrane, 1971; Kasl & Cobb, 1970; McGinn, Harburg, Julius, & McLeod, 1964; Rofé & Goldberg, 1983) and at the same time the great importance of social support in coping with both physiological and psychological stresses (Berkman & Syme, 1979; Cobb, 1976; Eaton, 1978; Gottlieb, 1981; Larocco, House, & French, 1980; Linn & McGranahan, 1980), it appears that the encouragement of expression of anger as a conventional mode of reaction may in the long run have devastating effects on both the physiological and the psychological condition of a hypertensive patient. More fruitful results may be had through relaxation training (Pinkerton, Hughes, & Wenrich, 1982) accompanied by therapy directed to teaching the individual to be less sensitive to frustrating events (particularly by way of distraction, denial, and postponement of any inclination to react angrily) and to behave in a peaceful and friendly manner toward others.

Holt (1970), in describing the maladaptive consequences of not expressing anger, indicated that "it can cause the person to withdraw, to make fewer attempts to communicate, so that empathy is not reestablished and the air is never cleared. Love dies in such a chilly climate" (p. 9). In the absence of controlled studies on this issue, a recent study by Rofé (1985) may be relevant. Criticizing the idea that suppressed hostility is undesirable in marital relationships (see Barry, 1970, pp. 47–48), Rofé found that repressors are more likely than sensitizers to love each other, and have satisfactory marital relationships. Rofé indicated that social interactions with close persons inevitably involve many minor conflicts and that the ability to overlook such conflicts and contain feelings of hostility is essential for a happy marriage. Such a pattern of avoidance and overlooking can create a positive atmosphere, while expression of anger is likely to increase tension and distance between spouses. A study by Scarpetti (1974) indicates that repressors do inhibit feelings of anger and respond to attack in a friendly and peaceful manner, and yet these responses were most effective in reducing their physiological arousal. Thus, Holt's psychoanalytic argument that love may die if one avoids expressing anger is not based on solid data.

CONCLUSIONS

Although the findings in both field and experimental studies do not support the psychoanalytic doctrine of repression, it is still possible that in some cases expression of anger can help to reduce a subject's blood pressure. This is because stress, as noted previously, is one of the most important factors in determining the level of blood pressure, and sometimes aggressive behavior may be essential for removal of the stress. However, even in these cases the beneficial effect of such a mode of reaction does not stem from expression of anger per se, as the psychoanalytic notion of energy implies, but rather from the removal of the stress-inducing factors. In most cases, a coping mechanism of such type may lead to harmful rather than beneficial results, as has been indicated in this chapter. It appears that the best reaction strategy for reducing the probability of developing high blood pressure is to adopt a coping response likely to inhibit intense and frequent arousal of the autonomic nervous system.

Finally, it may be that we should avoid exaggerating the importance of psychological factors in the development of hypertension. Steptoe (1981), indicating that a significant proportion of hypertensives are not under medical care, stated that "the elevated hostility or neuroticism levels reported among diagnosed hypertensives may not be typical of the group as a whole, but characterize only those who have contact with medical services" (p. 141). Genetic factors or food habits, which seem to be highly important (e.g., Obrist, 1981), may better explain individual differences in blood pressure than do psychological factors (see also Rofé & Lewin, 1982b).

3

Permanence of Childhood Memories

OVERVIEW

The essence of psychoanalysis is not repression per se, as might be understood from Freud's statement regarding repression as being the cornerstone of his theory, but rather repression of childhood traumatic experiences. According to the psychoanalytic doctrine, adult personality, with its normal and abnormal functioning, is deeply rooted in events that happened during early childhood. Furthermore, relieving patients' difficulties or symptoms "in any lasting and extensive way would seem to require an uncovering of the residue of the past. To attempt to intervene at the level of current functioning and current influences would appear futile" (Wachtel, 1977, p. 22). Repression of traumatic memories is considered to be the most significant cause of almost any psychiatric symptom. Therefore, the lifting of repression, thereby reevaluating these repressed memories, is the essential prerequisite for a true and enduring therapeutic outcome (E. F. Loftus & G. R. Loftus, 1980, p. 413; Messer, 1986; Wachtel, 1977, pp. 18–23, 26–29). Freud as well as current psychoanalytic theorists such as Wachtel (1977) believe that these "repressed memories . . . remained fresh, retaining in an unmodified way their original significance and intensity. The unconscious memories were viewed as 'timeless,' in contrast to memories of unrepressed events, which gradually lost their preoccupying significance" (p. 28). Apparently, due to the influential position of psychoanalysis, this theory gained predominance among many psychologists. Thus, theorists in the psychology of memory (Shiffrin & Atkinson, 1969; Tulving, 1974) believe that although material may become inaccessible, once it is registered in the long-term memory, it is never lost from the cognitive system. The extensive influence of this belief among psychologists is reflected in the finding in an informal survey by E. F. Loftus and G. R. Loftus (1980) that 84% of respondents believed that everything we learn becomes permanently stored in our memory bank though much of the information may not be retrievable.

The psychoanalytic position is of course much more radical than the belief of some memory theorists. The theory claims not only that memories are permanent, but also that some of the events a subject does not remember at all may have tremendous devastating effects on his or her current behavior. However, the psychoanalysts have neither reliable empirical evidence to prove the second part of their claim (as the previously reviewed evidence indicates) nor a satisfactory scientific basis for the first part of this hypothesis. This is due to the fact that "recent research into the nature of human memory has been increasingly critical of the 'videotape' concept of memory" (M. C. Smith, 1983, p. 388). Our main purpose in this chapter is to show that the claim that past experiences that we can no longer remember nevertheless exist in the cognitive system and are able to be retrieved into the consciousness is not more scientific than the notion that they are, in most cases, entirely lost from memory storage.

PERMANENCY THEORY RECONSIDERED

An alternative approach to the permanency hypothesis of memories is the old theory of disuse, which prior to the 1930s was the primary explanation for forgetting (see Hintzman, 1978). The theory claims that memory traces, if not used or exercised, tend to fade away. For almost five decades this theoretical position was largely ignored and the research efforts were primarily concentrated on the interference theory, originally proposed by McGeoch (1932) as the sole or main cause of forgetting. The newly revived interest in the decay theory raises serious doubt regarding McGeoch's position that passage of time does not affect the strength of memories.

Gleitman (1971), for example, claimed that

> the assumption that memory traces are permanent is no more plausible than the assertion that they. . .gradually disintegrate. Under the circumstances we might do worse than to entertain decay theory seriously as a genuine alternative. . . . Indeed, some investigators concerned with biological basis of memory seem to have moved toward a decay hypothesis. (pp. 36–37)

Gleitman further indicated that the belief that memory traces are permanent is rooted more deeply in conviction than in factual evidence. The same view is held by Hintzman (1978), who stated that "the interference theorists have not proved that time-dependent decay does not occur" (p. 354). Hintzman thought that an adequate theory of forgetting must include both the interference factor and the time-dependent decay factor.

Unfortunately, due to the neglect of this theory by researchers over the last 50 years, not enough evidence exists to validate the importance of this factor as a determinant of forgetting. Nevertheless, the few data available tend to support the decay theory. Thus, Gleitman (1971) mentions a number of studies on goldfish showing that retention deteriorated with increasing interval between learning and memory test and with increasing temperature during the interval. However, keeping the goldfish in conditions that slowed down their metabolic processes decreased the rate of forgetting. In the same way, Hintzman (1978) indicated that studies on long-term retention have always found some forgetting in situations in which no proactive or retroactive interference was deliberately introduced. Forgetting could be attributed to interference from nonexperimental sources, however, there is no solid basis to support this hypothesis. As an example, Hintzman stated that the time-dependent decay may be applied to explain why a List 1 learned just prior to a List 2 caused more proactive interference than one learned 3 days earlier (Underwood & Freund, 1968).

One of the prime arguments that was frequently used to disprove the passive-decay theory and that was among the main reasons for the decline of interest in it was the demonstration by Jenkins and Dallenbach (1924) and by Van Ormer (1932) that more rapid forgetting occurs during wakefulness than during sleep. These results were reinforced by subsequent studies (Lovatt & Warr, 1968; Ekstrand, 1967). However, Wickelgren (1977) indicated that there is now considerable research evidence that is inconsistent with the interference explanation of the sleep effect.

First, Yaroush, Sullivan, and Ekstrand (1971) demonstrated that forgetting is substantially slower over the first half of a night's sleep than over the second half. If the wakefulness that precedes sleep is the reason for the small amount of forgetting that occurs during sleep, as the interference theorists believe, than this ought to produce more forgetting during the first half of a night's sleep. An even greater discrepancy with the interference theory is the occurrence of forgetting over the second half of a night's sleep at approximately the same rate as during a comparable wakefulness period.

The second half of the sleep period has a greater frequency of dreaming than the first half, so the differences in the forgetting rate between the two periods might be attributed to interference from dreams. However, evidence from a study by Ekstrand, Sullivan, Parker, and West (1971) shows that this is unlikely. They found that after an interval of 7 hours of sleep, there was no difference in retention of two paired associative lists between subjects who had been deprived of dreams and those who had not. Empson and Clarke (1970) obtained different results, but their findings were equally inconsistent with the interference theory. These authors found that dream-deprived subjects displayed poorer retention than subjects who had not been deprived of dreams. On the basis of these findings, Wickelgren (1977) concluded that it is necessary to reinterpret the sleep effect as a result of slower rate of temporal decay or faster rate of consolidation during the first half of a night's sleep.

Second, Hockey, Davies, and Gray (1972) found that recall after a 5-hour retention interval at night was superior to recall after a 5-hour retention interval during the day, irrespective of whether subjects were awake or asleep during the interval period. Once again, these findings imply that the slower rate of forgetting during sleep may result from reduction of decay rate or increase in consolidation rate during the night.

Third, research data (cf. Ekstrand, 1972) indicate that if, after completing a learning assignment, a subject sleeps 8 hours and then stays awake 16 hours, retention is much better than if he stays awake 16 hours and then sleeps 8 hours. These findings, reported by three different studies (cf. Ekstrand, 1972) disagree with the interference explanation of the sleep effect, since a delay between the original and similar interference learning should not affect the magnitude of interference.

In addition to these findings on sleep effect, Wickelgren (1977) used four types of evidence to show that temporal decay is an important source of forgetting in long-term memory. One type refers to the fact, derived from the normal course of forgetting and retrograde amnesia studies, that the rate of forgetting continually decreases with increasing trace age. Since no evidence exists to indicate that interference decreases with the increasing memory trace age, the only viable explanation for this phenomenon is the temporal decay concept. Wickelgren assumed that, due to the consolidation process that continues throughout the lifetime of the memory trace, the effect of temporal decay decreases with the increasing trace age.

The second type of evidence refers to the complete failure of the research efforts (cf. Keppel, 1968, 1972) to demonstrate that forgetting material learned in the laboratory, from one day to the next, was primarily caused by prior or subsequent learning outside the laboratory. Wickelgren noted that the degree of similarity between the two types of learning, and therefore also the magnitude of interference, is so small that it is unlikely to explain the forgetting over the retention intervals of a day to a week that have been used to study this question.

The third piece of evidence used by Wickelgren to defend that passive-decay theory is the findings mentioned previously that conditions that slow down the metabolic activity, such as decreasing of temperature, cause a decrease in the forgetting rate as well.

The fourth argument is that in fitting retention functions, the magnitude of the time decay parameter does not vary much for different types of material under different conditions.

All these findings clearly argue against the idea suggested by some memory investigators (Shiffrin & Atkinson, 1969; Tulving, 1974) that once information is registered in the long-term memory it is never lost. Moreover, permanent loss of information may be due not only to disuse. As some findings (Hintzman, 1978, p. 354) suggest, new learning may sometimes cause permanent loss of the previously learned material. Data consistent with this hypothesis were also provided by B. F. Loftus and G. R. Loftus (1980).

Proponents of the permanence of memory traces and the Freudian concept of repression (Wachtel, 1977) typically defend their position by arguing that currently available retrieval techniques, namely, electrical stimulation of the brain (Penfield, 1969; Penfield & Perot, 1963: Penfield & Roberts, 1959), hypnosis (Cheek & LeCron, 1968), and psychoanalytic procedures (cf. Erdelyi & Goldberg, 1979) can uncover previously forgotten information. However, E. F. Loftus and G. R. Loftus (1980), in evaluating the evidence in each case, raise considerable questions about their validity. With regard to brain stimulation, E. F. Loftus and G. R. Loftus indicated that memory recovery occurred in only 3.5% of the patients examined by Penfield. Moreover, when they eliminated patients who claimed hearing only music or voices from their past and those whose responses were too vague to classify, fewer than 3% of the patients reported lifelike experiential responses.

Furthermore, "detailed examination of even these patient protocols leaves one with the distinct feeling that they are reconstructions or inferences rather than actual memories" (E. F. Loftus & G. R. Loftus, 1980, p. 414). Similar interpretation of brain-stimulation reports was offered by Neisser (1967), who concluded that Penfield's work tells us nothing new about memory. A brain-stimulation study by Mahl, Rothenberg, Delgado, and Hamlin (1964) is consistent with this reinterpretation of Penfield's findings.

Similar doubts were raised with regard to the traditional interpretation of hypnosis. E. F. Loftus and G. R. Loftus (1980) indicated that instances where hypnosis succeeds in reviving temporarily inaccessible memory do not necessarily mean that hypnosis has awesome, mysterious power. Hypnosis may simply encourage people to relax more, cooperate more, or concentrate more than they otherwise would. Subjects under hypnotic trance are motivated to behave in a way that pleases the hypnotist. People in such a state often produce a wealth of recollections, but much of this information may be fabricated. Knowing even a few details of an event may provide enough basis to create a highly detailed "memory" of the entire event.

No convincing body of evidence exists to show that recall during hypnosis is more accurate or complete than in the waking condition (Barber, 1965; Geiselman, Fisher, MacKinnon, & Holland, 1985; Neisser, 1967; M. C. Smith, 1983; Yuille & McEwan 1985). Moreover, some studies (Putnam, 1979; Sheehan & Tilden, 1983, 1984; M. C. Smith, 1983) show not only that hypnosis does not reduce retrieval difficulties, but also that distortion of memory may be even greater in the hypnotic state. Sheehan and Tilden (1984) noted that their "results are generally quite contrary to the notion that memory capacity is enhanced in hypnosis. Distortion, and not overall increased accuracy, characterized the memory of hypnotic subjects for material that was highly meaningful" (p. 55). In line with this, Erdelyi and Goldberg (1979) noted that evidence by Bernstein (1956) grants subjects under hypnosis the power to retrieve "inaccessible memories not only from childhood but from previous reincarnations" (p. 369). In the same way, Erdelyi and Goldberg (1979) indicated that some experiments (Kline, 1958; Rubenstein & Newman, 1954) have shown

that subjects imaginatively responding to hypnotic suggestions will confidently recall events not only from the past but from the future as well. . . . When a physician employs hypnosis with a patient it is wise always to be aware who may be hypnotizing whom. (p. 370)

In the same line, Hintzman (1978) stated, after reviewing some of the evidence concerning age regression, that "the most reasonable conclusion regarding the permanent memory hypothesis, at the present time, is that it is probably incorrect" (p. 804). Neisser (1982) indicated that

> when hypnotized subjects are "age-regressed," for example, their vivid descriptions of long-past events are often taken at face value by well-trained scientists. This is a mistake: Careful studies of hypnotic age regression demonstrate that it produces much confabulation and little or not hypermnesia. (p. 44)

Similarly, M. C. Smith (1983), arriving at the same conclusion, noted that in an age-regression study, "the experimenters were shocked to find that some of the individuals so vividly described had not even been members of the subjects' class" (p. 390). M. C. Smith noted that while such findings are of little concern in therapy, the situation is quite different where accuracy of the recalled material is important: "Imagine if Freud had acted on his patients' recollections and urged the authorities to imprison the fathers for incest" (p. 390).

A third line of evidence that may seem to support the notion of permanency of memory is the phenomenon of spontaneous and prompted recoveries. This phenomenon refers to spontaneous reappearance of items that seemed to have been forgotten or prompting the recall of such items by providing particular cues (Crowder, 1976; Tulving & Thomson, 1971, 1973). A related phenomenon is that of initially unreported elements of a stimulus emerging in daydreams, or free associations. In criticizing this argument, E. F. Loftus and G. R. Loftus (1980) indicate that these phenomena do not prove that all memories are potentially recoverable. Moreover, with regard to the effect of fantasy activities on memory, Erdelyi (1970) pointed out that rather than intensifying the memory itself, fantasy induces people to adopt a lax criterion for reporting so that low-confidence memory items, which otherwise might not be reported, are recalled.

The fourth argument put forth for defending the permanency notion concerns the psychoanalytic claim that supposedly repressed traumatic material can be retrieved using various techniques. However, this claim should be reconsidered because "even some of those who believe in the concept of repression have argued that it is possible that subjects purportedly recovering lost memories are in fact generating not memories of true events but fanciful guesses, fantasies, or plain confabulations" (E. F. Loftus & G. R. Loftus, 1980, p. 415). Erdelyi and Goldberg (1979) indicated that this problem was underestimated by clinicians and noted that even

> Freud himself fell prey to this methodological trap when, being too credulous of his early patients' apparent hypermnesias of childhood seductions, he rushed into his "infantile seduction theory" of hysteria only to be obliged to recant it in short order. (p. 369)

Further evidence against the permanency theory of memory is E. F. Loftus and G. R. Loftus's (1980) experimental findings that under certain circumstances stored information may be replaced by perceptual information and that in this process the original information may vanish completely from the memory system. The authors concluded that "the implication of the notion of non-permanent memory is that it should give pause to all who rely on obtaining a 'truthful' version of an event from someone who experienced that event in the past" (p. 419). This position is consistent with Neisser's (1984) view that "the widely held belief in permanent storage of specific experiences has essentially no basis in fact" (p. 33).

PROLONGED RETENTION

Although all these findings place the permanency theory in serious doubt, some evidence that memories may be highly resistant to forgetting may appear inconsistent with them. One argument often raised against the notion of decay or disuse is that motor skills such as swimming, driving, etc., are very well retained even when they have not been practiced for years (e.g., see Hilgard, R. C. Atkinson, & R. L. Atkinson, 1975; Kendler, 1968). This common experience has been strongly supported by many empirical studies showing no decrement in ability to perform motor skills even after a long period of no practice (e.g., see Adams, 1964; E. A. Bilodeau & I. M. Bilodeau, 1961; Fleishman & Parker, 1962).

Even though this phenomenon seems to be a characteristic of motor skills, new evidence shows that it may occur in other types of learning as well (H. P. Bahrick, 1979, 1983, 1984c; H. P. Bahrick, P. O. Bahrick, & Wittlinger, 1975; H. P. Bahrick & Karis, 1982). H. P. Bahrick (1984c) tested the retention of a foreign language (Spanish) learned in school over a period of 50 years during which there was very little rehearsal. It was found that although subjects evidenced marked decline in the first 3– 6 years of the retention interval, it remained unchanged, subsequently, for periods up to 30 years before showing a further pronounced decline. Moreover, a larger portion of the originally acquired knowledge remained accessible for a period of 50 years without being used at all. A similar effect was demonstrated with regard to retention of names and faces of high school classmates and to retention of the map of a city (H. P. Bahrick, 1979, 1983; H. P. Bahrick et al., 1975).

The permanency of both motor skills and other types of learning was attributed to degree of learning and acquisition of a plan or scheme (H. P. Bahrick, 1984a, 1984b, 1984c; Cofer, 1984; Deese & Hulse, 1967; Travers, 1972). Deese and Hulse (1967) noted that what is learned in motor skills is not a series of movements or sensorimotor coordinations, but rather some schematic plan or program for performing things in a certain way. Similarly, Neisser (1984) said that instead of acquiring a set of isolated responses the Spanish students in Bahrick's study discovered a structured system of relationships. Their knowledge of vocabulary, their ability to recognize idioms and to state rules of grammar, and especially their ability to understand Spanish texts depended on their mastery of that system. Bahrick (1984a), however, unlike Neisser believes that the degree of learning does affect the memory trace and thereby constitutes a major factor in determining the longevity of retention. Bahrick claims that his data offer definite evidence that the level of Spanish-language training determined the proportion of knowledge that survived for 25 years or longer. Thus, Bahrick does not agree with Neisser's suggestion that remembering is essentially similar to problem solving or reconstruction processes. He views it, rather, as a process primarily involving a repro- duction of exact past experiences. Bahrick argues that while the organizational factors have an important influence on memory, we cannot disregard the work of associational psychologists like Thorndike and Skinner, who showed that memory largely depends on the strengthening of individual responses.

With respect to the issue of the permanence of memory, one can by no means conclude from these findings that all or most memory traces are permanent and/or that these findings invalidate the law of disuse. The data only suggest that memory traces may be immune to decay or interference if the learned items are practiced until they reach some critical level, especially if the items are structurally organized. Furthermore, despite the factors of overlearning and structured organization, even Bahrick's subjects forgot much of their learning during the first 6 years, and the rate of forgetting was further accelerated after 25 years. Similarly, also with regard to motor skills, particularly complex skills such as piano playing, some decrease in retention does occur in the absence of practice. At any rate, none of these findings can be used to defend the psychoanalytic claim regarding availability of unconscious memories, that is, that even if a subject cannot remember an event by the usual means, it nevertheless exists in the memory system and can be retrieved if special techniques are applied.

The claim that the amount of rehearsal is crucial for prolonged retention may seem inconsistent with a number of studies (R. Brown & Kulik, 1977; Sheingold & Tenney, 1982; Winograd & Killinger, 1983; Yarmey & Bull, 1978), which examined the recall of salient childhood events, such as the assassination of President John F. Kennedy, the resignation of President Richard M. Nixon, and the birth of a younger sister or brother. Based on the subjects' reports, these authors found that a significant amount of the subjects' personal experiences associated with the salient childhood event could be recalled even many years after their occurrence. While R. Brown and Kulik (1977) attributed this phenomenon to rehearsal, others (Sheingold & Tenney, 1982; Winograd & Killinger, 1983) did not find a significant correlation between reported rehearsal and recall scores. These latter reports may seem inconsistent with the rehearsal hypothesis. Nevertheless, Winograd and Killinger (1983) indicated that the question of the mediating role of rehearsal remains open for at least two reasons: first, subjects were asked only about overt but not covert rehearsal; second, "whether covert or overt, rehearsals themselves may not be accessible to recall, particularly when they occur at an early age" (p. 418).

A more serious argument against the phenomenon of salient childhood memory concerns the validity of the reported memories. Neisser (1982), who raised this criticism with regard to the study of R. Brown and Kulik (1977), noted that various studies show "over and over again that vivid recollection and accurate testimony may be wrong" (p. 44). Neisser also cited two examples, one from his own personal experience and another from a study (Linton, 1975) about experiences associated with the assassination of President Kennedy, which show that such memories may be complete fabrications. According to Neisser (1982, 1984), memories of remote experiences are fabrications or new constructions resulting from internalized schema that are applied when an attempt is made to remember these experiences. Being aware of the possibility of fabrications or errors in our memory, Linton asserted that "the researcher must know (or perhaps control) the details of events being remembered" (p. 387). Indeed when such a method was employed (Robbins, 1963), recall proved to be very poor and inaccurate.

CONCLUSIONS

The studies reviewed in this chapter show that widespread belief among many psychologists (see E. F. Loftus & G. R. Loftus, 1980) that information is never lost once it has been registered in the memory system is not defendable. The cumulative research evidence places this hypothesis in serious doubt. This applies particularly to the psychoanalytic theorists, since the permanency belief is most deeply rooted among them. Psychoanalysis claims that humans are endowed with a "magic box," or unconsciousness, in which information from childhood can be stored or frozen in its original form with no time limitation and can be retrieved in its full vitality without damage (see Wachtel, 1977, pp. 28–29). In order to prove this thesis it is not enough to show that some memories are resistant to forgetting. Solid data must be brought to prove that experiences, particularly remote childhood experiences that subjects cannot remember by themselves and that become available by employing psychodynamic techniques, are true events rather than fabrications. Moreover (Erdelyi & Goldberg, 1979), "even if the recovered memories can be shown to be veridical (i.e., to constitute 'hits' rather than 'false alarms'), there remains the residual methodological issue of whether the subject is actually recalling (i.e., remembering) more or merely reporting more" (p. 370). A subject may be aware of certain experiences and yet avoid discussing them with his or her therapist until a more comfortable relationship has been established.

Furthermore, even if psychoanalytic investigators were to succeed in proving that the lost memories are true events, they would still have to prove their claim (Fenichel, 1946; Singer, 1970; Wachtel, 1977) that these memories are the cause of neurotic symptoms. However, despite more than 50 years of intensive work, psychoanalysis still does not have a convincing body of evidence for its assumptions concerning the "buried" memories and their effects on behavior, which are the essence of the theory. The interpretive case study approach cannot by any means be a substitute or the main scientific source for defending these central assumptions. The poor scientific quality of this approach will be shown later by discussing some of the psychoanalytic cases. At this stage, we say with much confidence that belief in the unconscious storage of the forgotten events, particularly those of the childhood stage, has no more scientific validity than the assertion that the events were completely lost from the memory system through disuse or decay.

4

Unconsciousness Reconsidered

OVERVIEW

The main objective of this chapter is to show that, as in other areas, proponents of psychoanalysis have no convincing body of research to support their psychodynamic concept of the unconscious. In the psychological literature the general term *unconscious* is very ambiguous. While in the psychodynamic theory, unconscious is strongly linked with the concept of defense mechanisms (Maddi, 1980; Wachtel, 1984), in general psychology, the term refers to a condition of lack of awareness, with no connection to the idea of defense. The research findings of this concept of unconscious cannot of course be used for defending the psychodynamic notion. In view of this, the chapter is divided into two sections, each dealing with one of these two concepts of unconscious.

NON-FREUDIAN CONCEPTIONS OF THE UNCONSCIOUS

Apart from psychodynamic notion, the concept of unconscious has at least three additional uses: (1) lack of awareness of mental or physiological activities that are always performed without one's awareness, (2) lack of awareness in performance of motor skills, and (3) lack of awareness of the cognitive determinants of behavior.

Permanent Lack of Awareness

Many of our internal activities, for example, the firing of the nervous system, are never consciously perceived (Kihlstrom, 1984; P. White, 1980). Similarly, many of our mental processes such as those by which a subject retrieves memories or solves problems never gain access to one's consciousness (Nisbett & Wilson, 1977). Freud used the notion of the unconscious primarily to refer to experiences that were conscious at the time they occurred, but that subsequently ceased to be available to awareness. Occasionally he used the term with respect to mental activities that had never been and could never be conscious. He apparently used unconscious in this connection because he was influenced by Jung's theory of collective or racial unconscious, but he felt uneasy using it this way (see Maddi, 1980). Use of the term unconscious to denote events that can never gain access to awareness seems to have little practical value in psychotherapy (see also Maddi, 1980); therefore, it is suggested the term not be used in this sense.

Automatism of Motor Skills

The term unconscious is sometimes used to refer to automatic performance of motor skills. However, this concept seems not to be needed; the automatism phenomenon can be very well explained by the term *minimal attention* (Lewin, 1982; Morris, 1981; Reason,

1983, 1984a, 1984b). Unconscious carries the connotation of divided consciousness (Gur & Sackeim, 1979; Sackeim & Gur, 1978; Sackeim, Nordlie, & Gur, 1979), and this meaning does not advance the understanding of motor skills. It is simpler to argue instead that the more a motor skill is practiced the less attention is required for its performance. Lewin (1982), for example, delineates three stages in the process of learning skills: the cognitive, the associative, and the autonomous. The required attention or awareness if quite high in the cognitive stage, but gradually declines in the associate stage, and become very minimal at the autonomous stage. Lewin noted that beginning drivers asked to describe what they have done during the previous 15 minutes, are likely to remember mostly the details of their behavior. Slightly more advanced drivers may describe their behavior in more general terms. However, experienced drivers may fail to remember their driving activities and may even admit that they were not aware of having passed through traffic lights on green.

Similarly, Morris (1981) differentiated two types of mental activities, intentional and nonintentional. Intentional behaviors are assumed to be controlled by "Boss System," that is, a top cognitive system responsible for planning one's behaviors. Nonintentional responses are controlled by "Employee Systems," that is, lower cognitive processes that function to fulfill the general programs, plans, and intentions of the Boss system. "A new skill, for example, may at first demand Boss control, but as it is perfected Boss is freed to control other activities" (Morris, 1981, p. 196).

To some extent Morris's distinction is consistent with the abovementioned idea that during practice of motor skills, including verbal learning, a program or schema is developed in the subject's cognitive system (Deese & Hulse, 1967; Neisser, 1984). Thus, it seems that once such a program is developed, very minimal attention is needed for executing the responses. Reason's (1983, 1984a, 1984b) analyses show that even when a specific skill is highly practiced, minimal attention is always required for adequate performance of the task. If, during the automatic performance of the task, attention is "captured" either by internal preoccupation or as a result of an external distraction, the subject may fail to carry out the task. Reason argued that such absentmindedness was apparently the cause for many disasters associated with motor skills. Thus, *reduced attention* seems to be a much more appropriate term for describing the automatism phenomenon in motor skills than is unconscious, which is characterized by ambiguous and multiple meanings.

Conscious Access to Cognitive Processes

A third meaning of unconscious involves the controversial question of whether people do or do not have conscious access to their cognitive processes or to the reasons for the behaviors. Nisbett and Wilson's (1977) answer to this question is negative. The most important aspect of their theory is their claim that people are unaware of the cognitive determinants of their behavior. Nisbett and Wilson argued that subject's reports about the causes of their responses are based on a priori, implicit causal theories, or on judgment about the extent to which a particular stimulus is a plausible cause of a given response, rather than on direct access to their mental processes. Thus, an accurate report of behavioral determinants may be given only by chance when the subject's beliefs coincide with the real causes.

In order to support their position, Nisbett and Wilson used findings from various areas such as cognitive dissonance, attribution studies, and subliminal perception. However, being aware of the limitations of retrospective data, Nisbett and Wilson performed several experiments to test their model. In one of these experiments, for example, subjects memorized a list of word pairs intended to generate associative processes that would elicit target words in a word association task performed afterwards. Immediately after this task, subjects were asked to indicate what, in their opinion, affected their responses to the word association test. Results showed that despite the ability of the subjects to recall nearly all the word pairs, they were unaware that their responses were influenced by the memorization task.

In a further experiment, subjects were asked to evaluate articles of clothing, which were arranged in a row. Nisbett and Wilson found that the position at which the article was located markedly affected the subjects' preference. However, when asked about the reasons for their choices, none of the subjects was aware of the effect of position.

As one would expect, Nisbett and Wilson's argument raised strong criticism by many investigators (Ericsson & Simon, 1980; Shotter, 1981; E. R. Smith & Miller, 1978; P. White, 1980), who tend to reject Nisbett and Wilson's hypothesis on both theoretical and methodological grounds. Some of the objections raised are as follows:

1. The hypothesis was formulated in a form that could not be falsified. This meant that not only incorrect responses but also occasional correct reports would be consistent with the hypothesis. However, there is no clear and testable indication as to what conditions would cause correct reports to be considered as disproving the hypothesis.

2. The time interval between the cognitive processes and the report increases the likelihood of forgetting. This is consistent with experimental studies on sensory perception, showing that much of stimulus input may be apprehended but not stored for longer than a second or so, or at least not in a manner that can be reported. Thus, the incorrect reports may reflect the failure of the memory rather than indicate lack of awareness. For example, a driver may remember very little of the trip upon reaching a destination, but this does not mean that he or she was unaware of important stimuli (e.g., stop signs, curves, etc.,) along the way.

3. Verbal reports have shortcomings as an index of awareness. They are subject to influences such as social desirability and demand characteristics, so that incorrect reports need not indicate lack of conscious access to mental process.

4. Nisbett and Wilson used a criterion that was too stringent for detecting awareness, that is, subjects were expected to be aware of something that was systematically and effectively hidden from them by the experimental design.

5. *Cause* may have a different meaning to the experimenter and the subject. E. R. Smith and Miller (1978), who raised this criticism, refer as an example to Nisbett and Wilson's position experiment mentioned above. As was indicated, subjects denied that position of the articles affected their choices. However, Smith and Miller argued that the position per se was not necessarily the real cause of the subjects' choice. Rather, it might be a wrong impression caused by the way the subjects examined the clothing. If all the articles presented to the subject were of the same quality, and the subject examined them by going from left to right, one would expect that successive comparisons of the quality of the articles would lead to marked preference for the right-most article because it was the one examined last, not because it occupied the right-hand position in space. In this case the subject might correctly report on his or her procedure for choosing, but might fail to mention the position effect since this was not the real cause for the choice. However, since this is not consistent with the experimenter's hypothesis, the subject would be classified by Nisbett and Wilson as having no access to his or her cognitive processes.

6. Furthermore, contrary to Nisbett and Wilson's theoretical position, experimental findings by the abovementioned investigators show that people do have access to causal processes. Moreover, when conducted properly, introspective reports may yield important insights into the nature of cognitive processes underlying task performance.

7. Several of the studies that Nisbett and his associates conducted to support their hypothesis used inappropriate statistical tests. A reanalysis of one of their experiments revealed that contrary to the original interpretation, subjects were correctly aware of their cognitive processes.

Some more recent experimental findings by Kellogg (1982; see also Kellogg, 1980) and Hill (1984) may appear consistent with Nisbett and Wilson's position. Kellogg's study consisted of two main experimental conditions: a dual- and a single-task condition. In the dual-task condition, subjects performed difficult mental multiplication designed to maximally occupy their attentional capacity, while pictures of faces were presented as secondary stimuli. One group of subjects was instructed to ignore the faces, namely, to look at the faces but to regard them as distractions. They were asked to avoid consciously thinking about the faces and concentrate fully on the primary task of multiplication. A second group was asked to split their attention, namely, to concentrate on the multiplication task, but to pay attention to the faces if possible. In the single-task condition, subjects were not required to multiply while examining the faces. Instead, they were asked to attend consciously to the faces presented to them in isolation. A delayed-surprise-recognition test of the faces was then given. After viewing the faces, subjects were asked to rate on a 5-point scale how much they consciously thought about the faces. Results showed that although the attend conditions produced superior recognition performance, the ignore condition resulted in a small but significant amount of learning as well. The introspection data revealed that in the single-task condition, the more subjects claimed to have attended to the faces the greater was the amount of learning they demonstrated. In contrast, the introspective ratings of subjects in the dual-task conditions bore no relation to their recognition scores. Kellogg (1980) concluded that "conscious attention is useful but not necessary for long-term storage" (p. 379).

Hill (1984) hypothesized that people can accurately report the casual effects of stimuli on their performance, provided that memory and attentional capacities are not overly taxed. To examine this hypothesis, a learning task was devised in which one variable was highly influential in that it greatly facilitated learning, while another was irrelevant or noncausal but perceptually salient. Results showed that subjects' reports were more accurate when these two factors were presented separately than when they were combined in the learning task. These findings were interpreted in line with Nisbett and Wilson's position.

However, it appears that neither of these studies can give definite support to Nisbett and Wilson's view. Thus, it may be claimed that the dual-learning condition in Kellogg's experiment did not allow accurate introspection because the minimum attention required for learning to occur prevented sufficient rehearsal. Hence, poor retention and thereby "lack of awareness" were caused. This might be particularly true due to the fact that "introspection ratings were collected several minutes following presentation of the last face. With such a long delay before introspection, information concerning conscious processes might have been forgotten" (Kellogg, 1982, p. 142). With regard to this possibility, Kellogg (1982) noted that "although this criticism is plausible, it is unclear why introspection succeeded for subjects in the single-task conditions and yet failed for those in the dual-task conditions. The delay for both conditions was equivalent" (pp. 142–143). However, Kellogg might not have rejected this alternative explanation if he had considered the possibility that the rehearsal time, and therefore strength of learning, was less in the dual-task conditions. The fact that memory scores under the dual-task conditions were lower than under the single-task conditions seems to be consistent with the latter hypothesis.

Similarly, consistent with Holmes's (1974; see pp. 21–22 in this book) distraction hypothesis, it may be argued that the combined condition in the Hill's experiment prevented an accurate report because the salient but irrelevant factor distracted the individual's attention from the real factor. The subject's attention was so intensively occupied by the irrelevant variable that it prevented adequate rehearsal of the relevant one, and as a result he or she appeared to be unaware. It is also possible that rehearsal was sufficient, but that the salient factor distracted the individual's attention from the real factor only at the reporting stage.

Nisbett and Wilson's (1977) position was defended also by Bowers (1984), who used two main arguments for this response. First, they claimed that "causality is simply not subject to direct observation" and that "what is true for observation is no less true for introspection" (p. 249). However, inference processes might indirectly enable the individual to understand the causes of his or her behavior. If the inference processes are inappropriate, then the determinants of one's behavior remain unconscious. To support this claim, Bowers referred to a conditioning experiment which he had conducted several years earlier (Bowers, 1975). In that experiment, subjects were presented with series of paired postcards, each pair comprising one landscape and one portrait. Subjects were asked to state which of the two cards in each pair they preferred. After the initial baseline was determined, subjects were verbally reinforced for the nonpreferred type of painting. Bowers (1984) reported that one subject who had initially preferred portraits increased her preference for landscapes as a function of reinforcement. However, a short postconditioning interview revealed that she was unaware of this change. Bowers claimed that her lack of information of naïvete about the function of reinforcement in the learning process precluded her understanding and hence her awareness of the determinant of her behavior. Bowers's (1984) second argument is that psychological research would be "totally redundant" if a subject would have direct access to cognitive determinations of his behavior: "So the need for psychological research testifies to the insufficiencies of introspection to deliver a fully informed understanding about the variables controlling thought and action" (p. 250).

It seems, however, that neither of Bowers's two arguments can defend Nisbett and Wilson's position. Before discussing these arguments, it may be worthwhile to note that Bowers almost completely overlooked all the serious criticisms raised against Nisbett and Wilson's hypothesis. With respect to Bowers's first arguments, it seems that his generalization from observation to introspection may not necessarily be valid. This is exactly the issue over which the investigators diverge. Empirical data are needed for settling this dispute. The conditioning evidence Bowers used to defend his position seems to be insufficient. Essentially, there is not much difference between Bowers's conditioning experiment and the bulk of the research on verbal conditioning (see review by Rofé, 1973) that was precipitated by Greenspoon's (1951, 1955) pioneering work. As is well known, Greenspoon's claim that reinforcement had an automatic effect without the subject's awareness generated very bitter controversy among the investigators in this field. Moreover, when more sensitive postexperimental interview procedures were employed for assessing awareness, no confirmation was found for Greenspoon's hypothesis (Denike, 1964; Dulany, 1961, 1962; Spielberger, 1962; Spielberger, Bernstein, & Ratliff, 1966; Spielberger & Denike, 1966; see also Brewer, 1974). Thus, it may be that Bowers's female subject only appeared to be unaware. Bowers's short questionnaire for assessing awareness may not have been sensitive enough. It is also possible that she did not feel comfortable admitting that she had been complying with the experimenter's wishes.

Bowers's second argument, that the value of psychological research for understanding causal influences on human behavior stems primarily from lack of direct access to cognitive processes, is also questionable. First, while it may be true that sometimes introspection is insufficient to supply information about variables controlling our behavior, this may be due to reasons other than lack of direct access to cognitive processes. Some of these are as follows:

1. In some cases one of the components involved in the cause–effect relationship may fail to gain a mental representation. Thus, introspection would be inadequate, for example, in detecting the causal relationship between hormonal changes and behavior or between anger and elevation of blood pressure. Cognitive access to these relationships is impossible because neither hormonal changes nor variations in blood pressure are mentally represented in the consciousness.

2. Due to processes of decay, the causes of the subject's response may no longer be available in his or her cognitive system at the time of introspection. This may apply, for example, to the perceptual defense studies discussed earlier (Erdelyi, 1974) and to more remote experiences of one's childhood period.

3. As was pointed out with regard to Hill's (1984) experiment, sometimes a salient nonrelevant factor may gain such dominance over the individual mind that it completely distracts the subject's attention from the real causes of his or her behavior, which had been available a moment previously. Another example is a case where a subject becomes involved in a serious motor accident. The individual's consciousness may be so powerfully controlled by the immediate and terrible consequences of the accident that he or she may fail to rehearse, and hence to remember, how the accident took place (Erdelyi, 1974).

4. Sometimes one utilizes self-deception mechanisms for hiding the threatening determinants of behavior from oneself. This issue constitutes one of the central theses of our psychobizarreness theory, and therefore we prefer to defer the clarification of this possibility until we present the theory later in this book.

Thus, psychological research may be valuable in discovering the entire range of causes of human behavior and in clarifying why introspection is sometimes inadequate for this purpose.

Second, even when introspection can provide valid explanation for behavior, psychological research is not necessarily redundant if it uses introspection as a tool for detecting the causes of behavior. Such research may help in disproving some popular beliefs in psychology about the real determinants of human behavior. For example, Bowers and Meichenbaum (1984) presented a bizarre case of shoplifting. Because the motives of the subject appear to be unexplainable, they are attributed to the unconscious. However, research by Reason and Lucas (1984), who utilized introspective data for inquiry about this phenomenon, show that shoplifting is not necessarily determined by unconscious motives (we will elaborate on this shortly).

Thus, there seems to be no sufficient support for Nisbett and Wilson's (1977) hypothesis that people have no direct access to their cognitive processes. Even if the data were consistent with this theory, it would not be adequate for the psychoanalytic concept of unconscious. Nisbett and Wilson's hypothesis of unawareness makes no reference to threat or defense. In contrast, these concepts are an integral part of the Freudian theory. However, although Nisbett and Wilson's hypothesis is not directly concerned with psychoanalytic concepts, it was important to mention this area of research. A confirmation of this hypothesis would reinforce the traditional, mechanistic conception of the human being. According to this conception, which characterizes both psychoanalysis and behaviorism, human behavior is essentially determined by automatic factors. However, now that Nisbett and Wilson's idea runs into difficulties, we can continue to maintain the view that human beings are, by and large, conscious creatures, who in most cases are aware of the factors determining their behavior and in many cases freely choose their responses. As will be demonstrated later, this assertion is one of the important assumptions of our theory of psychopathology. Let us now examine the evidence supporting the psychoanalytic notion of unconsciousness.

PSYCHOANALYTIC CONCEPTION OF THE UNCONSCIOUS

The psychoanalytic concept of the unconscious is characterized by four fundamental features. The first and most important aspect of the theory is that the consciousness is divided rather than unitary. This means that at least psychologically (Gur & Sackeim, 1979; Sackeim & Gur, 1978; Wachtel, 1984), and some maintain that even physiologically (Galin, 1974; Galin, Diamond, & Braff, 1977), conscious and unconscious are two entirely separate entities. Second, the unconscious is characterized by the unusual ability to preserve emotional experiences in their full vitality and for an indefinite length of time. For example, Fischer and Pipp (1984) referred to Freud's unconscious theory as follows:

> memories stored in the unconscious are like photographs or tape recordings—accurate copies of what was originally perceived. . . . When the person tries to bring forth the memories, they are subject to distortion by impulses within the unconscious. But in their original, recorded state, they are perfect, "immaculate" copies. (p. 90)

The same view is expressed by Wachtel (1977), one of the prominent figures in the field of psychoanalysis (see p. 12). Third, the unconscious is characterized by active processes that are strongly linked with the defense mechanism of repression (Gur & Sackeim, 1979; Maddi, 1980; Sackheim & Gur, 1978; Shevrin & Dickman, 1980). Fourth, almost all behavioral deviations are attributed to the unconscious processes over which the subject has no control (Bowers & Meichenbaum, 1984; Maddi, 1980; Nemiah, 1984; Shevrin & Dickman, 1980; Silverman, 1976).

It is claimed here that proponents of psychoanalysis have no reliable or defensible evidence to support any one of the four main aspects of their theory of the unconscious. Let us examine the types of evidence often used to defend the theory.

Bizarre Behaviors

Various investigators noted that the unconscious concept was developed by Freud to account for behaviors that patients could neither explain nor control (Maddi, 1980; Peters, 1958; Shevrin & Dickman, 1980). Maddi (1980), referring to Peters's work, indicated that Freud would never have suggested the concept of unconsciousness if he had been convinced by explanations provided by patients for their peculiar behaviors:

> Peters generalizes from this to say that it is only when the explanation persons give for their behavior does not convince us that we should look to the possibility of unconscious motivation. This is what Freud would have done, and what we should do too. (p. 425)

As previously stated, the same type of unexplained abnormal behaviors led Rachman (1978) to assert that psychoanalysis may help us ultimately understand some of the more unusual fears. He raised this possibility, not out of belief in the truth of the theory, but rather due to lack of an alternative explanation.

A similar type of evidence was used by Bowers and Meichenbaum (1984), in the introduction to their book *The Unconscious Reconsidered*, to justify the assumption of existence of the unconscious. After more than 60 years since the theory of unconscious was proposed, they seem to have no more convincing data to justify this conceptualization than the story about a case of shoplifting by a powerful Quebec politician. The man was caught shoplifting a $120 sportcoat and consequently had to resign his cabinet seat in disgrace. He was greatly puzzled by his action and "called the theft 'probably an attempted political suicide. . . . I didn't need that coat. I could have paid for it many times over' " (pp. 1–2).

It is doubtful whether such evidence can be accepted as scientific data to prove existence of autonomous unconscious processes. First, in the absence of adequate scientific data, the argument that such bizarre behaviors as those described in this shoplifting case are controlled by unconscious forces makes no more sense than a demonology argument that they are induced by an invisible devil. What psychoanalytic explanation in fact assumes is what Maddi (1980) termed *person within person*:

> If there is an active process whereby conflicts are held out of awareness, then there must be some part of the person that can perceive reality, and decide what the rest of the person shall and shall not be permitted to know about. (p. 206)

In the area of perceptual defense this argument was termed the *Homunculus Bugaboo* (Erdelyi, 1974, p. 4) and was formulated by Spence (1967) in the following way:

> Do you have to presuppose . . . that a little man is inside, pulling the strings, or, as Bruner and Postman suggested, that the superego, peering through a Judas eye, is scanning incoming precepts in order to decide which shall be permitted into consciousness. (p. 184)

Thus, as long as unequivocal evidence is provided for existence of the autonomous unconsciousness entity, there seems to be no scientific justification for continuing to hold this system of belief.

Second, as far as episodic bizarre behaviors among normal people, for example, shoplifting, slips of the tongue or other examples of oddities are concerned (Reason, 1984a, 1984b), rational explanation based on scientific observations is now available. In this respect, Reason's "absentmindedness" theory (Reason, 1983, 1984a, 1984b; Reason & Lucas, 1984; Reason & Mycielska, 1982) can very well replace the Freudian theory of unconscious. Generally speaking, Reason's theory demonstrates that odd behaviors of the type just mentioned are the results of "attentional capture, either by some internal preoccupation or as the result of any external distraction" (Reason, 1984b, p. 181).

Since absentmindedness is not the focus of our attention, a detailed account of Reason's interesting work will not be given. However, in order to refute Bowers and

Meichenbaum's (1984) explanation of the shoplifting case, we will review Reason and Lucas's (1984) two-part study on shoplifting. In the first part, 150 men and women were asked how often they had experienced each of 24 varieties of mental lapses while shopping. If they had not actually suffered a particular lapse, they were asked to judge the likelihood of its happening to them. In the second part, 166 letters written by 67 individuals who felt they had been wrongly accused of shoplifting were analyzed.

Results of the first part showed that lapses carrying the risk of being accused of shoplifting were reported as occurring far less frequently, and were judged as less likely to happen, than either "embarrassing" or "nuisance" lapses. The findings in the second part showed that 63% of the subjects mentioned being distracted or preoccupied when the incident occurred. Distractors tended to be of two kinds: some novel or engaging feature of the immediate surroundings that demanded their attention or something in the store environment that triggered distressing ruminations. Half the subjects were involved in negative life events, such as a divorce or the discovery of a spouse's infidelity. The authors indicated that many, if not most, of the shoplifting cases occurred while the shopper's limited attention was heavily engaged by something other than the immediate task. About a quarter of the sample were receiving medical treatment when the incident occurred, and many of them were taking psychotropic drugs. Thus, these subjects' attentional deficits were likely to have been further intensified by medication. An additional contributing factor in a number of cases was the employment of some unwise practice such as using shopping bags to keep items separate or transferring bulky items to a carrier beneath a stroller.

The following two shoplifting cases, mentioned in Reason and Lucas (1984), may more vividly describe the notion of absentmindedness and the superfluity of the Freudian concept of unconscious in explaining episodic, bizarre behavioral responses. In one case, a 31-year-old man went into a shop to buy a pair of glasses and some small toiletries. He had just broken up with his girlfriend, for whom he had recently left his wife and family. He chose the sunglasses and automatically slipped them into his shirt pocket. He then paid for the other items, but forgot to declare the sunglasses. In another case, a 56-year-old woman, suffering a severe migraine attack, went into a store to buy a flannel bag. On leaving, she was stopped by the store detective, who accused her of not having paid for some items in her handbag valued at less than one dollar. She claimed that she had taken her glasses out of the bag in order to read some price tags and then absentmindedly put the small items into the handbag along with her glasses. It is clear, then, that Reason's theory of absentmindedness or attentional deficit (Reason, 1983, 1984a, 1984b; Reason & Lucas, 1984; Reason & Mycielska, 1982) for the explanation of episodic bizarre behaviors among normal individuals, such as shoplifting, is more plausible and empirically based than Bowers and Meichenbaum's (1984) Freudian explanation. However, there is still not a more plausible explanation than the psychoanalytic theory to account for bizarre behaviors (e.g., chocolate phobia; see Rachman, 1978) among neurotic and psychotic patients. These bizarre symptoms differ completely from oddities among normal people because they are not episodic, but rather continuous responses that their subjects claim to be powerless to prevent. These patients appear to be completely unaware of the reasons for their bizarre behaviors. As has been noted, it was essentially these unexplained behaviors that led Freud to develop his theory of the unconscious. Thus, anyone who rejects this theory must provide an alternative answer to the problem that bothered Freud. It is hoped that the psychobizarreness theory, to be presented later in this book, will provide a satisfactory solution to this problem.

Wachtel's Evidence for the Theory of the Unconscious

Wachtel (1977, 1984) used two main sets of empirical findings to defend the Freudian concept of the unconscious. One set of data cited in his book *Psychoanalysis and Behavioral Therapy* (Wachtel, 1977) concerns Penfield's work showing that brain stimulation could revive forgotten childhood experiences. These findings were used to support the psychodynamic notion that the human mind consists of a "store" where childhood experiences may be preserved in their original form for an undefined period of time (Fischer & Pipp, 1984, p. 88; Wachtel, 1977, pp. 28–29). However, as was previously indicated, Penfield's findings were misinterpreted and can therefore not be used to validate the psychoanalytic theory.

The second set of data is concerned with Silverman's (1976, 1978, 1983; Silverman, Ross, Adler, & Lustig, 1978) research on "one of the central aspects of psychoanalytic theory: the relationship between psychopathology and unconscious wishes" (Silverman, 1976, p. 621). Silverman and others (Bryant-Tuckett & Silverman, 1984; Dauber, 1984) explored this relationship by means of a "subliminal psychodynamic activation" method. Wachtel (1984), in a preface to Bowers and Meichenbaum's book *The Unconscious Reconsidered,* indicated that "Silverman's consistent findings pose a serious challenge to those who dismiss psychoanalytic notions . . . any effort to assess the evidence for unconscious processes and their nature is incomplete without coming to terms with this remarkable body of work" (p. xi). However, these findings cannot be considered a challenge because several investigators have failed in their attempts to replicate the findings of Silverman and his associates (Condon & Allen, 1980; Hapsel & Harris, 1982; Oliver & Burkham, 1982; Porterfield & Golding, 1985). Both Heilbrun (1980) and Porterfield and Golding (1985) noted that with the exception of several doctoral dissertations conducted in collaboration with Silverman, the evidence for "subliminal psychodynamic activation" comes entirely from studies conducted by Silverman.

Shevrin and Dickman's Evidence on Perception

In an attempt to find empirical support for Freudian unconsciousness theory, Shevrin and Dickman (1980) used findings from research on selective attention, subliminal perception, and visual perception. According to them, these findings imply that much of our perception takes place outside consciousness. However, much of the research they reviewed has no relationship to the psychoanalytic concept of unconscious that is strongly linked to the defense mechanism of repression (e.g., Hariman, 1982; Wachtel, 1977). For example, one of the areas of research to which Shevrin and Dickman refer concerns the phenomenon of retinal image stabilization. When an image is stabilized on the retina it gradually fades from the conscious level. This type of data is not at all relevant to the psychodynamic theory. Indeed, Shevrin and Dickman (1980) themselves indicated, in reference to some of their data, that "a considerable gap" exists between the type of evidence reviewed by them and the psychoanalytic notion of unconscious:

> For instance, none of these theoreticians discusses the possibility that precepts can be stored in long-term memory and can exert an active influence on simultaneous conscious processes, even though they may never enter into awareness or may not do so until long after they were originally perceived. (p. 426)

This same argument was more strongly emphasized by Kihlstrom (1984), who stated that Shevrin and Dickman *have attempted to reconcile the conception of the unconscious offered by contemporary cognitive psychology with that held by Freudian psychoanalysis. . . . The attempt ultimately fails, however, because the nature of these unconscious contents, and the principles of their operation, are so radically divergent from the proposals of psychoanalysis. (p. 156)*

Gur and Sackeim's Research on Self-Deception

In an attempt to find empirical support for psychoanalytic repression and the unconsciousness theory, Gur and Sackeim (1979; see also Sackeim & Gur, 1978) did an experimental study on self-deception. Sackeim and Gur (1978) indicated that the psychodynamic concept of repression "requires that consciousness be shown to be nonunitary and nontransparent and, in particular, that cognitions that are not subject to awareness be stored in an unconscious" (p. 142). However, at the same time they also noted that "it is difficult to imagine how one might go about demonstrating the existence of an unconscious and what sorts of evidence would be relevant to such a conclusion" (p. 142). Indicating that repression is a special case of self-deception, they suggested that as a first step, this latter concept be investigated: "If self-deception does not exist, it is unlikely that repression exists" (p. 142).

Sackeim and Gur (1978) listed four conditions they considered necessary and sufficient for proving the existence of self-deception: The individual must (1) hold simultaneously, (2) two contradictory beliefs, (3) where one of them is nonaware, and (4) this nonawareness is motivated. To test their theory, two experiments were conducted. In one, subjects were asked to listen to voices from a tape and to indicate whether they thought each voice was their own or that of someone else. The results were that hearing one's own voice, as compared with hearing others' voices, significantly increased the subject's galvanic skin response (GSR) level and that there were no significant differences in GSR level between subjects who correctly identified and those who misidentified their own voices. Data from postexperimental questionnaires revealed that the latter subjects were not aware that they had misidentified their own voices. Thus, the experimenters succeeded in demonstrating three of the four criteria necessary for proving the existence of self-deception, namely, that subjects simultaneously held two contrary beliefs without being aware. The motivational basis of the misidentifications of the voices was inferred from questionnaire data that were supposed to measure aversiveness of self-confrontation and the tendency to engage in self-deception. However, in order to examine the motivational factor more validly, subjects in the second experiment were given either success or failure experience before being exposed to the voice stimuli. Consistent with their hypothesis, Gur and Sackeim found that the failure group more frequently misidentified themselves, whereas the success group more frequently misidentified others.

Gur and Sackeim (1979; see also Sackeim & Gur, 1978) interpreted these findings to mean that consciousness is nontransparent. Although this is not clearly shown, they appear to consider these findings as supporting the Freudian concept of unconscious. Their psychoanalytic orientation is also demonstrated in their theoretical position on hysteria (see Sackeim, Nordlie, & Gur, 1979), which will be considered later. However, the results reported here may be explained without assuming the existence of unconscious processes. Basically, Gur and Sackeim's experiment seems to be quite similar in nature to perceptual defense studies (e.g., Bowers, 1984), where presentation of an aversive stimulus also aroused an elevation in GSR and subjects failed to identify the stimulus. Thus, consistent with Erdelyi's (1974) theoretical explanation of perceptual defense, it may be argued that subjects who misidentified their own voice may have, prior to their report, correctly identified the voice for a fraction of a second.

However, inasmuch as the voice (i.e., aversive stimulus) heard from a tape was not identical to the subject's usual perception of his or her own voice (i.e., contained dissimilar elements) and since the exposure time was very short, subjects could easily cope with the stress by directing their attention to the dissimilar aspects. They could thereby easily convince themselves that this was not their own voice. Thus, there is no necessity to argue that subjects simultaneously held two contradictory beliefs. Instead, it may be claimed that at the first stage of perception they recognized their voice (and this aroused their GSR), but at the second stage they convinced themselves, by deliberately directing their attention to the dissimilar elements, that the voice was not their own. The rapid decay of processes in the iconic memory (e.g., see Erdelyi, 1974), on the one hand, and the priority given to the dissimilar aspects in the second stage of perception, on the other hand, should have discouraged a conscious identification of their voices as well as any experience of uneasiness at the reporting stage. This interpretation is consistent with the widely accepted notion that "perception represents not a locus, but a vast region, of processing space" (Erdelyi, 1974, p. 14); it also agrees with the abovementioned arguments against Nisbett and Wilson's (1977) theoretical position. As was indicated, one of these criticisms was that the time interval between the cognitive processes and report increases the likelihood of forgetting. Thus, a postinterview questionnaire does not seem a reliable measurement of a subject's awareness at the initial stage of perception.

It is difficult to determine whether Gur and Sackeim's interpretations or ours are more valid. However, if indeed part of a subject's attention or consciousness at the initial stage were occupied by considerations of coping strategy, one would expect that reaction time, as well as level of uncertainty, would be greater among subjects in whom negative rather than positive emotions were aroused when they heard their own voice. Indeed, Gur and Sackeim (1979) reported in their second experiment that subjects in the failure condition were slower and less certain on the trials of self-identification than were subjects in the success condition. However, it should be noted that even if Gur and Sackeim's interpretation were valid, this would not be sufficient to verify psychoanalytic concepts of repression or unconsciousness, as the authors themselves admit.

One important point that deserves some consideration concerns the tendency of Sackeim and Gur (1978) and some other researchers (Galin, 1974; Galin, Diamond, & Braff, 1977) to associate the right hemisphere with the Freudian concept of unconscious. This idea, however, is rejected by Kihlstrom (1984) and by Corballis (1980). In this respect, Kihlstrom noted that

> the right hemisphere is fully conscious in its own way, except that its disconnection from the left hemisphere precludes verbal expression. All other requirements for consciousness—attention, perception, memory, judgment, categorization, and action planning—are shown by the right hemisphere. (p. 160)

Hypnosis

Traditionally, psychoanalytic investigations (e.g., Kihlstrom, 1979, 1984; Sackeim et al., 1979) interpreted hypnosis as supporting the notion of the unconscious. However, as was indicated in the previous chapter, many investigators (E. F. Loftus & G. R.

Loftus, 1980; Sheehan & Tilden, 1984) raised serious doubts regarding the belief of psychoanalytic theorists that hypnosis could reliably reflect the content of unconscious memories. Moreover, in recent years hypnosis has been conceived in terms of attention alertness rather than the unconscious (Hariman, 1980, 1982; Sheehan & McConkey, 1982; Stam, Radtke-Bodorik & Spanos, 1980). For example, Hariman (1982) argued that hypnosis is a conscious and deliberate process obtained by a subject's willingness and ability to concentrate exclusively and intensively on the hypnotic suggestion. Hypnotic amnesia or dissociation is not the product of the unconscious, as psychoanalytic proponents have traditionally assumed, but rather a result of the subject's exclusive attention to other matters. Hariman (1982) asserted that Freud regarded hypnotic amnesia as the very paradigm of unconsciousness. However, the new studies on hypnosis make this theoretical approach unlikely. Hariman further stated that it is quite possible that Freud would have agreed with this new conceptualization of hypnosis had he lived long enough.

CONCLUSIONS

We have not, of course, reviewed all the evidence used by psychodynamic proponents to defend the Freudian concept of unconsciousness. However, the data reported here are the main empirical findings in this area. To our knowledge, no other important, objective, and convincing body of research exists. However, even if we have failed to refer to some other relevant research data, we doubt whether this omission would affect the conclusion that psychoanalysis theorists have not been able to present a convincing body of research for proving any of the major aspects of their concept of the unconscious. No evidence exists that consciousness is divided or nonunitary, or that the mind contains a "mysterious box," where childhood experiences are preserved intact. On the contrary, the evidence tends to disprove this idea. Neither does any support exist for their claim that normal bizarre behaviors are controlled by the unconscious autonomous processes.

Moreover, apart from lack of empirical support, this psychoanalytic concept provides us with no more theoretical benefit except the illusion that we have a profound explanation for the human being's behavioral deviations. But even here, many fundamental questions remain unanswered. For example, apart from the general claim that these responses are unconsciously determined, psychoanalytic theory does not clarify how a specific symptom is unconsciously selected. R. W. White (1964) formulated this problem as follows:

> a dynamic theory leaves one question untouched: it does not explain the choice of neurosis, the appearance of one symptom syndrome rather than another. How does it come about that the patient develops just this kind of neurotic symptoms rather than some other kind? (p. 276)

Psychoanalysis provides very general ideas in its attempt to answer this question, but the empirical support for these ideas is very poor. For example, psychoanalysis asserted that the development of obsessive–compulsive neurosis is related to the anal personality type. However, after careful examination of the research data, Emmelkamp (1982) came to the definite conclusion that "there is no evidence whatever to support the psychoanalytic theory that relates anal eroticism to the obsessive-personality and to the development of obsessional neurosis" (p. 188). Thus, no scientific reason seems to exist to justify the continuation of this belief system. We need, of course, to explain the phenomenon of unawareness, which is characteristic of people displaying prolonged bizarre behaviors, but as will be demonstrated later, we do not need the concept of autonomous unconscious for this purpose. Psychopathology has not benefitted much from its long "affair" with this "troublesome" concept, and it appears that only by completely abandoning this mechanistic conception and accepting instead the notion that the human being is essentially a conscious creature can the road to understanding human psychopathology be paved.

5

Effectiveness of Psychoanalysis and Behavior Therapy

EYSENCK'S ARGUMENT: A REEVALUATION

The theoretical foundation of psychoanalytic therapy is heavily based on the Freudian concept of repression. This is consistent with Freud's assertion that repression is the cornerstone of psychoanalysis. The therapy is designed "to help the patients dig under the layer of repression" (E. F. Loftus & G. R. Loftus, 1980, p. 413) so that the locked-in emotional experiences will be released and integrated with the rest of the personality (Wachtel, 1977, p. 38). Thus, while positive empirical findings regarding the efficiency of psychoanalytic therapy would not be enough to validate the theoretical foundations of psychoanalysis, lack of such evidence may constitute a serious threat to psychoanalytic theory, particularly with respect to the notion of repression. This is especially true when it is combined with the findings reviewed thus far.

The failure of psychoanalysis to prove its therapeutic value is associated with the psychological term *Eysenck argument,* which is used by several investigators (Erwin, 1980; Rachman & Wilson, 1980). On the basis of massive research data, Eysenck (1952, 1966) concluded that the research findings fail to prove that psychoanalytic therapy facilitates the recovery of neurotic patients. According to Eysenck (1952), the empirical evidence shows that "roughly two-thirds of a group of neurotic patients will recover or improve to a marked extent within about 2 years of the onset of their illness, whether they are treated by means of psychotherapy or not" (p. 322). As could be expected, this assertion incited the rage of proponents of psychoanalysis, and instead of providing positive data for defending their thesis, they invested their energy in criticizing Eysenck's conclusion. However, after carefully considering all the criticisms and reevaluating the cumulative evidence, old and new, both Rachman and Wilson (1980; see also Rachman, 1971) and Erwin (1980) came to the definite conclusion that Eysenck's argument is still valid. Thus, Rachman and Wilson (1980) stated that "there is no acceptable evidence to support the view that psychoanalysis is an efficient treatment" (p. 76). Moreover, Erwin (1980) asserted that this argument applied not only to orthodox theory, but to other psychoanalytically oriented therapy as well.

All these findings, together with other data by Gross (1979) showing the poor therapeutic value and antiscientific position of psychoanalysis, raise serious doubt regarding the entire theory. Indirectly, these findings should shake the psychoanalytic cornerstone of repression.

EFFECTIVENESS OF BEHAVIOR THERAPY

In contrast to psychoanalysis, many empirical findings (e.g., see Rachman & Wilson's 1980 book on the efficiency of psychological therapy) show that behavioral techniques may be quite efficient in treating psychiatric symptoms. Discussion of these

61

findings is relevant to a theory of repression for two main reasons. First, they intensify the doubts regarding the validity of psychoanalysis. Second, they may convey the impression that learning principles are sufficient for both the explanation and cure of psychiatric disorders, so that there is no need for a new theory. Thus, the purpose of this section is, on the one hand, to present the difficulties produced by this evidence for psychoanalysis and, on the other hand, to indicate why these findings are insufficient to defend the theoretical position of behavioral therapy.

According to psychodynamic theories (Fenichel, 1946; Gordon & Zax, 1981; Silverman, 1976; Singer, 1970; Wachtel, 1977), symptoms or behavioral deviations are the result of repression of traumatic experiences and/or conflicts between an instinctual drive pressing for discharge and the ego's efforts to restrain these impulses. If only symptoms are removed and the underlying unconscious or repressed causes are neglected, the subject may be left without defenses and, consequently, flooded with intense anxiety. As a result, the subject may develop new symptoms even more severe than the original ones. Behaviorists like Rimm and Masters (1979) often compare the psychoanalytic model of maladjustment to a closed hydraulic system. If pressure is raised due to some interruption in the normal functioning of the system,

this may cause a surface rupture, with fluid rushing out. However, since fluids are not compressible, dealing with the rupture (analogous to treating symptoms) only increases the likelihood that a rupture will occur elsewhere. If this analogy is appropriate to human psychology functioning, symptom substitution is a very plausible notion. (p. 7)

Thus findings, which show that symptoms-oriented techniques may be quite efficient (Rachman & Wilson, 1980; Rimm & Masters, 1979), raise theoretical difficulties for psychodynamic approaches and, hence, for the psychoanalytic doctrine of repression. Rimm and Masters (1979), for example, noted that both case studies and controlled experiments are overwhelmingly inconsistent with the notion of symptom substitutions.

As usual, however, psychoanalytically oriented investigators (Gordon & Zax, 1981; H. B. Lewis, 1981; Wachtel, 1977; Weitzman, 1967) defend their theoretical position by intensive intellectual effort to integrate the behaviorist findings within their theoretical framework. For example, Weitzman (1967) indicated that Wolpe's desensitization procedure may just as well be interpreted in terms of psychodynamic approaches. He stated that according to his own observations, the scenes presented by the therapist in desensitization undergo a series of transformations and elaborations by the patient's internal psychological processes. On the basis of this, he asserted that "with this information at hand, it is not surprising, to a dynamically oriented therapist, to find that a wealth of dynamically rich and exciting material results from desensitizations obtained with Wolpe's method" (Weitzman, 1967, p. 305). Essentially, the same theoretical position was adopted by Wachtel (1977) and H. B. Lewis (1981).

However, while psychoanalytic proponents may be right in their claim that therapeutic success of the behavioral techniques cannot be considered to validate the behavioral theories (see H. B. Lewis, 1981, p. 86), their proposal for overcoming the theoretical difficulties caused by these findings cannot be taken seriously. As long as psychoanalytic investigators cannot supply acceptable scientific data to prove the validity of their central concepts, their theoretical arguments for resolving the inconsistencies between their approach and behavioral findings do not have much scientific value.

Despite the empirical evidence regarding the efficiency of behavioral techniques, the position of behavioral theorists is no better than that of psychoanalysts. First, the cumulative research evidence (e.g., see Emmelkamp, 1982; Rachman, 1978), which will be specified later in this book, indicates very strongly that Breger and McGaugh (1965) were quite right in their claim that simple principles of classical conditioning and reinforcement cannot "provide useful explanation for clinical phenomenon." This argument is most valid with regard to clinical problems or bizarre behaviors seen in the clinical setting, such as agoraphobia, but it is also applicable to the acquisition of simple fears. Behavioral investigators have no convincing empirical evidence to demonstrate that their "animal model" can explain the production of neurotic symptoms. As previously indicated, in the vast majority of cases no frightening experiences precede the development of agoraphobic symptoms (e.g., Emmelkamp, 1982; Jacobs & Nadel, 1985; Mathews, Gelder, & Johnston, 1981; Rachman, 1978). Moreover, most people do not develop even simple fears or other anxiety symptoms even when conditions are optimal for the occurrence of classical conditioning (Rachman, 1978). Behavioral investigators have plenty of evidence to demonstrate development of fears among animals but they suffer from an extreme shortage of empirical findings showing that learning principles can sufficiently explain the production of fears or other psychiatric symptoms in humans. Thus, inasmuch as learning principles do not seem to be useful for explaining the production of psychiatric symptoms, it is doubtful whether these principles may explain the behavioral improvement obtained by behavioral therapy techniques. Emmelkamp (1982) noted, in this respect, that "behavior therapists claim that their clinical practices are based on experimental evidence. This seems to give behavior therapy a scientific reputation in the field of psychotherapy" (p. 8). However, Swan and MacDonald's (1978) national survey in the United States shows a considerable difference between behavior therapy as practiced in research and behavior therapy as applied clinically. This evidence casts doubt on the scientific basis of this mode of therapy.

Second, the cumulative research findings show that Rimm and Masters's (1979) strong conviction that behavioral treatment does not lead to symptom substitution is not valid. For example, Kazdin (1979), one of the prominent proponents of the behavioral approaches, indicated that "as behavior therapy developed, it was clear in many instances, that behavioral treatment might well lead to a return of problem behaviors or to manifestations of problems that were not evident initially" (p. 633). Similarly, in his recent review article on symptom substitution, Kazdin (1982) noted that "proponents of behavior modification have acknowledged several circumstances where new problems might emerge after treatment" (p. 350). In the same way, Gordon and Zax (1981) indicated that "the behavioral literature on symptom substitution falls far short of proving empirically that it is, at best, a nonexistent and, at worst, a negligible phenomenon" (p. 44). It is very doubtful whether the intellectual efforts of a number of investigators (Bandura, 1969; Blanchard & Hersen, 1976; Cahoon, 1968) to explain the phenomenon of symptom substitution in terms of learning principles can provide an adequate answer for the theoretical difficulties of the behaviorist camp. In this respect, the assertion made with regard to psychoanalysis appears to be applicable here as well. As long as these investigators are not able to prove the validity of their central concepts, namely, that conditioning and reinforcement principles are indeed among the central causes for development of neurotic symptoms, their theoretical efforts to explain the phenomenon of symptom substitution cannot be considered more than an interesting intellectual exercise. For example, Blanchard and Hersen (1976) suggested accepting the behavioristic principles with regard to phobias and the dynamic point of view with respect to hysteria. However, as stated, the research findings on fear, particularly clinical phobia, are inconsistent with the behaviorist's position, so that this proposal is not acceptable for settling the dispute between the behavioral and dynamic approaches.

The third criticism often raised against behavioral therapy techniques is that the majority of the studies on which the behaviorists rest their claim that symptom substitution is a negligible phenomenon are conceptually and/or methodologically flawed. For example, Gordon and Zax (1981) indicated that successful elimination of symptoms, such as thumb sucking, cigarette smoking, or fear of spiders, is not relevant to the psychodynamic notion of symptom substitution, since these symptoms are not necessarily caused by internal conflicts (see also H. B. Lewis, 1981). Similarly, Emmelkamp (1982), referring to the fact that the vast majority of studies on fears were conducted on animals or people with normal fears, indicated that due to some marked differences between "clinical and analog populations, the clinical value of such studies has been questioned" (p. 9). Emmelkamp (1982) asserted, "I doubt seriously whether the hundreds of analog studies concerning anxiety and phobias have been of much value for developing and evaluating treatments for clinical patients" (p. 10). In his more recent article, Emmelkamp and his colleagues (Emmelkamp, Mersch, & Vissia, 1985) suggested that with respect to some phobias, results of analog studies may be generalized to the clinical population, but this is not justified with regard to agoraphobia. Consistent with these criticisms, it may be worthwhile to note that the efficiency of behavioral techniques in treating clinical fears is quite limited (Barlow & Wolfe, 1981; Hafner, 1976, 1983; Hand & Lamontagne, 1976), and sometimes no therapeutic effect is gained, despite intensive application of these methods (Rachman & Seligman, 1976).

It appears, then, that the main contribution of the behavioral therapy research is that it helps to further undermine the scientific status of psychoanalysis. However, as was stated previously, this does not mean that behavioral theoretical suggestions can provide a better solution for the psychopathological problems. In fact, it appears that while some of the behavioral suggestions may be incorporated in a new theoretical model in psychopathology, the fundamental assumptions of such a model should remain within the framework of the psychodynamic approach. However, we suggest abandoning the basic concepts of psychoanalysis, namely, unconscious and repressed memories, and their implications with regard to processes by which psychiatric symptoms develop or are removed. An attempt will be made to show that all psychiatric symptoms seen in the clinical setting, both neurotic and psychotic, are coping strategies used by the subject to deal with current stressful situations. As such, it is suggested that the behavioral therapy techniques are sometimes efficient, not because they recondition the subject, but mainly because they provide the subject with tools for coping more successfully with life stress, thus removing the need for maladjusted coping mechanisms. It is further implied that the concepts "reconditioning," "relearning," or "extinction," which behavior therapists have traditionally used to explain their findings, are valid only with regard to simple symptoms such as thumb sucking, cigarette smoking, and fear of dogs.

CONCLUSIONS

As has been demonstrated throughout the book thus far, not even one of the central concepts of psychoanalytic theory is supported by a convincing body of research. The experimental evidence regarding the most fundamental notion in psychoanalysis, namely, repression proper, runs contrary to the accepted and dominant view among psychoanalytic investigators. Similarly, with regard to the concept of primal repression, the evidence in perceptual defense does not necessarily indicate that subjects were not aware at the time of perception. They may have been aware for a fraction of a second and then been unable to remember the stimuli because of the decay of the cognitive process.

Freudian theory is also inconsistent with the bulk of studies on repression–sensitization, the research on essential hypertension, and studies dealing with catharsis of hostility. The findings provide no justification for the inclination of some investigators to regard the studies on repression–sensitization as illegitimate with regard to the theory of repression. The results of these studies raise a serious threat to Freudian theory inasmuch as they show that repressors are more adaptable individuals than other type of subjects. Another yet-unsolved problem is the strong linkage between R–S scale and measurements of social desirability or self-report scales of anxiety.

With respect to hypertension, there is no evidence that it develops as a result of repression of hostility. Here again, the results tend to refute the psychoanalytic conception. A similar conclusion has been reached with respect to the catharsis theory of aggression: Expression of hostility does not lead to its reduction, but rather to its enhancement.

The proponents of psychoanalysis have also failed to provide empirical evidence for their theory of memory. First, the cumulative research evidence shows that the acceptance of the permanency theory of memory and the rejection of the decay theory were premature. Second, there are no convincing data to show that humans are endowed with a "magic box," namely, the unconscious, where forgotten emotionally charged materials of early childhood are kept intact for an indefinite period of time. Likewise, there is no convincing evidence that these experiences can be retrieved to the consciousness by psychoanalytic techniques. Finally, there are no empirical data to support the view that these "unconscious memories" are the origin of psychiatric symptoms. And psychoanalysis has no evidence to support any of the other aspects of its concept of unconscious. Perhaps one of the most bitter failures of psychoanalysis is its inability to show that its therapeutic suggestions are more efficient than the absence of treatment.

Overall, the supporters of psychoanalysis have failed to provide a convincing body of evidence for any of the central concepts of the theory. This lack of support was also recognized by Silverman (1976), one of the most prominent advocates of psychoanalytic theory. He noted that evidence from the psychoanalytic couch is insufficient to demonstrate the validity of the theory "particularly because this material rarely meets reasonable criteria for the admissibility of clinical data as supporting theoretical propositions. . . . Thus, such data must be supplemented and complemented by data from more formal research procedures" (p. 622). In a series of studies, Silverman and his colleagues claimed that they obtained some empirical support for psychoanalytic theory. However, as is usually the case in psychoanalysis, several attempts to replicate his findings met with failure (e.g., see Condon & Allen, 1980; Hapsel & Harris, 1982; Heilbrun, 1980, 1982; Oliver & Burkham, 1982; Porterfield & Golding, 1985). A new theory may be given a limited period of time to enlist support for its concepts. However, if after almost a century of concentrated research effort, psychoanalysis is still striving for scientific recognition, it is doubtful that it can be regarded as little more than a system of convictions.

II

THEORY OF NORMAL REPRESSION

Why are many psychologists and psychiatrists still reluctant to give up psychoanalysis despite chronic lack of supportive scientific evidence? Why have behaviorists, whose therapeutic techniques are far more successful than psychoanalytic intervention, and who appear to be more scientific, failed in their long campaign to challenge the psychodynamic models?

While this may perhaps be attributed partly to people's conservative tendency, which to some extent characterizes also the scientific community (Mahoney, 1985), the major reason seems to be lack of a more attractive theoretical model. As will be elaborated later, the behaviorists' suggestions are far from satisfactory in dealing with the core problems of psychopathology. What psychopathology urgently needs is a theory that can adequately explain how neurotic and psychotic bizarre symptoms develop, and why patients are so incompetent in providing plausible reasons for abrupt changes in their behavior. The behaviorist animal model seems to be too simplistic in providing an adequate explanation in this area.

As stated, we agree with Freud's idea that repression is the key to understanding abnormal behavior and to a certain extent normal behavior as well. However, unless this concept is radically changed to make it more consistent with the cumulative research data, it will remain controversial and will hardly advance our understanding of human behavior. Not only should repression be disconnected from the autonomous unconscious, but this latter concept, which has brought to psychopathology nothing but trouble, should be totally abrogated from psychology.

It is also important to abandon the Freudian energy model that conceptualizes the differences between normals and abnormals with respect to repression solely in quantitative terms. It is highly essential to realize that these two types of populations use different types of repression, normal and pathological, respectively.

In this book, repression, as well as the state of unconscious that is so typical of normal subjects, is conceived solely in terms of attention. The perception of the world, our feelings and our conscious experiences, are by and large determined by what we have in our focus of attention. Repression is conceptualized as a deliberate effort to push away threatening cognitions from the attentional domain. The difference between normal and abnormal subjects is that while the former use normal means to achieve distraction, the latter employ pathological maneuvers for the same purpose. These distractive pathological tools prevent threatening cognitions from resuming control in the attentional zone. Thus, a state of unconscious regarding those cognitions is created by refocusing on the highly demanding attentional stimuli, i.e., bizarre symptoms. In addition, sophisticated self-deceptive mechanisms are employed in order to prevent the subject from becoming aware that he or she has enacted the symptoms. The threatening cognitions, including the subject's knowledge that he or she has adopted the bizarre symptoms, remain in the long-term memory, but are blocked by the attention given to the symptoms. However, it is possible that with time the decay process may eliminate both the threatening cognitions and the knowledge that the subject has utilized bizarre symptoms. The concept of unconsciousness that is presently used is different from that of Freud in that it does not refer to an autonomous unconscious entity, but rather the simple lack of attention.

This part presents the theory of normal repression. Although its main purpose is to propose a new conceptualization of repression, it also attempts to resolve the apparent inconsistencies in this area of research, particularly in studies on repression–sensitization. The theory of pathological repression will be discussed in the later parts of this book.

6

Beneficial Effects of Repression

DEFINITION OF REPRESSION

Erdelyi and Goldberg (1979), in discussing the definition of the concept of repression, noted that "the meaning of repression has been a subject of great and continuing confusion, both within as well as outside of Psychoanalysis" (p. 360). Holmes (1974), in his critique on the psychoanalytic notion of repression noted that "in considering an alternative theory of repression it is important for it to be broad enough to encompass all the experimental findings as well as what appear to be instances of repression observed in the clinical setting" (p. 650).

It appears that the most promising way to resolve the confusion discussed by Erdelyi and Goldberg and to satisfy Holmes's requirement is to define *repression* on the basis of objective laboratory observations and then generalize it to the clinical area. The studies that seem relevant for this purpose are those dealing with repression proper, perceptual defense, and posthypnotic amnesia, as well as those concerning the typical response of repressors and sensitizers to threatening stimuli. As shown in Chapter 1, the most prominent feature in all these studies is a distraction of attention. Thus, based on these findings, repression may be defined solely in attentional terms as follows: Repression is a coping mechanism by which threatening inputs are consciously, actively, and intentionally prevented, by means of normal or pathological distraction, from gaining access to the domain of attention or, in the case of penetration, these inputs are deliberately removed.

Attention, in our theoretical approach, refers to that part of the consciousness by which an awareness of a stimulus occurs. The consciousness itself encompasses a larger part of the cognitive system, so that in addition to the attentional system it includes the higher mental activities, namely, thinking, judgment, and verbal processes. The term *threatening stimuli* refers to any stimulus input, originating from either the internal (e.g., deviant sexual demands) or the external environment, that is likely to cause undesirable emotional arousal.

We now discuss in more detail the three main aspects emphasized in our definition of repression (i.e., active distraction, awareness, and coping mechanism) to see in what respects it differs from the psychoanalytic doctrine of repression.

Active Distraction

In contrast to psychoanalysis, in which the element of forgetting is strongly emphasized (Wachtel, 1977), the new definition indicates that repression is nothing more than active withdrawal of attention from a threatening stimulus. Of course, forgetting also takes place according to the new conceptualization, as was indicated in our discussion of perceptual defense experiments and the studies on repression proper. However, this process occurs indirectly, due to the withdrawal of attention and not due to activation

69

of a mysterious, unconscious autonomous system. Active distraction differs from passive distraction in the sense that prevention or elimination of the disturbing stimulus from attention is not caused by outside events or intervention, such as accidental occupation of one's attention by unexpected stimuli, but rather by deliberate activities initiated by the person himself or herself. Among these self-induced responses, we include not only highly conscious activities but also habitual avoidance activities, namely, patterns of avoiding responses that have become fairly automatic, as a result of repetition, so that their operation requires minimal attentional effort. This latter possibility is consistent with Bower's (1984) position on repression when he indicated that "it is possible, for instance, that the act of avoiding an idea, though quite conscious at the outset, can with repetition become a habitual and eventually an automatized act that is no longer subject to conscious awareness" (p. 243). This idea may apply, for example, to repressors since, as has been shown, avoidance of threat is one of the strongest parts of their personality structure.

Active distraction may include four main types of distractive maneuvers:

1. *Physical Escape*   The individual removes himself or herself from the environment in which the threatening events occur or are expected to occur. Bowers (1984) cites this type of response as an instance of repression and he illustrated it as follows:

> Consider, for example, that a movie can generate an impending sense that "something awful" is going to happen, even if it does not telegraph precisely what that "something" is going to be. One could, at that point, walk out of the theater. (p. 243)

2. *Obstructing the Sensory System*   This mechanism includes manipulation of the senses so that the subject's relationship with the threatening stimuli is disconnected or disrupted. These operations include various looking strategies, discussed by Erdelyi (1974) in his theoretical work on perceptual defense (see p. 24 in this book), and diversion of hearing to irrelevant stimuli in response to auditory threatening messages.

3. *Interference Activities*   The individual's attention is occupied by distractive activities, such as work, reading, socializing, or irrelevant internal thoughts.

4. *Suppression*   The individual concentrates his or her effort on avoiding paying attention to threatening material that has been stored in the long-term memory. He or she may even actively intervene to prevent their retrieval by methods such as rapid shift of attention and active rehearsal of competitive materials or the avoidance of situations and thoughts that might recall the "banned material." These operations should, in the long run, decrease the attentional power of these stimuli and increase the likelihood of their being entirely lost from the system. This claim is consistent with the notions of passive nonrehearsal and selected rehearsal as well as the general concept of directed forgetting, which are discussed by various investigators (Bjork, 1972; Erdelyi, 1974; Erdelyi & Goldberg, 1979; Geiselman, Bjork, & Fishman, 1983; Kihlstrom, 1983).

Our definition of repression is consistent with Holmes's (1974) interpretation of repression proper, Erdelyi's (1974) theoretical analysis of perceptual defense, and the studies on repression–sensitization. This conceptualization of repression is also consistent with S. M. Miller's (1979, 1980, 1981) theoretical work emphasizing the importance of distraction as a major coping mechanism and with Murphy's (1970, 1975) concept of self-deception. Murphy's evidence shows that when exposed to stress-arousing stimuli, subjects tend to deceive themselves by avoiding looking at these stimuli and/or by directing their attention to the more pleasant aspects of the perceptual field.

Is this aspect of repression consistent with the psychoanalytic doctrine of repression? To a limited extent it appears to be so. Erdelyi and Goldberg (1979), in their discussion on the concept of repression, noted that according to Freud himself, "the essence of repression lies simply in the function of rejecting and keeping something out of consciousness" (p. 360). The authors stated that this basic definition does not stipulate the methods of rejection from consciousness—whether by inhibition, attentional withdrawal, or single or combined set of techniques. Erdelyi and Goldberg (1979) further indicated that

> "the response of interference" or "disturbed attention" arguments per se cannot be viewed as criticisms of repression but only—at best—as theoretical conceptualizations of repression (or at worst, terminological wrangles). Without any doubt, Freud's own concept of repression is an interference one (though he did not, of course, use behavioristic terminology); moreover, Freud specifically viewed the withdrawal of attention ("attention cathexis") as one means by which repression is effected. (p. 378)

However, even if Erdelyi and Goldberg (1979) are right in their interpretation of Freud's original theory, their conceptualization by no means represents the dominant viewpoint of psychoanalytic theorists, such as Fenichel (1946) and Wachtel (1977). According to the psychoanalytic doctrine, repression is not simply the rejection of threatening material from attention. The most important aspect of the concept involves automatic transference of the material to unconscious store, where in most cases it is no longer available or retrievable at the individual's wish. Moreover, this repressed material continues to preserve its vitality and to affect, sometimes very bizarrely, the individual's current behavior (e.g., see Bowers & Meichenbaum, 1984; Fenichel, 1946; Fischer & Pipp, 1984; D. S. Holmes, 1974; Jacobsen & Steele, 1979; Singer, 1970; Wachtel, 1977). Furthermore, to the best of our knowledge, Erdelyi and Goldberg's interpretation of Freud's view is inaccurate. In Freudian theory, this concept is strongly related to the notion of hypermnesia, or lifting of repression, and this constitutes the essence of the entire psychodynamic approach. With respect to this element, our new conceptualization of repression differs radically. First, the existence of an autonomous unconscious store is completely denied. Second, our notion of distraction or withdrawal of attention implies that this coping strategy reduces the chance that the threatening material will remain in the subject's memory system. Moreover, contrary to psychodynamic conceptualization, our new formulation of repression implies (as is elaborated at length in this chapter) that rejection of the threatening material from the attentional system is, in many cases, beneficial, in that it enhances individual adjustment (see Taylor, 1983).

Awareness Versus Unawareness

The second important aspect of the new definition of repression is its emphasis on awareness or conscious operation of repression itself. This notion is consistent with Holmes's (1972, 1974) conception of repression (see p. 22) and to some extent with Erdelyi's (1974; see also Erdelyi & Goldberg, 1979) theoretical approach to perceptual defense.

This aspect of repression may also appear to be consistent with Freud's definition of repression. Erdelyi and Goldberg (1979) claimed that the unconscious nature of repression never played a crucial role in Freudian theory; the authors stated that Freud never made a consistent suggestion that the mechanisms of defense are operated unconsciously. In fact "repression was often portrayed as a conscious or sometimes conscious process. . . . it nevertheless remains the case that the contexts in which the terms occur make it very clear that at least at times, repression is a conscious, deliberate act" (pp. 364–365). Erdelyi and Goldberg (1979) further indicated that Freud did not make a clear distinction between repression and suppression (i.e., between unconscious and conscious rejection of threatening material from consciousness) but used the two terms interchangeably. Moreover, according to Erdelyi and Goldberg's (1979) point of view, "a particular repression that is unconscious may have originally started out as a conscious process" (p. 366).

Again, it should be indicated that although Erdelyi and Goldberg's position is quite interesting, and consistent with my theoretical view, they seem to be wrong in their interpretation of Freud's real intention. MacKinnon and Dukes (1964) noted that Freud first used the terms *repression* and *suppression* to refer to a single mechanism and defense; however,

in the course of time the term "suppression" disappeared almost entirely from Freud's writing, and increasingly his use of the term "repression" implied that the process was not a conscious, voluntary one but rather one which went on without any conscious awareness of it. (p. 681)

Moreover, Laplanche and Pontalis (1968) indicated that as a result of the incorrect English translation of the two terms, some investigators were misled into thinking that Freud did not differentiate between repression and suppression.

Even if Erdelyi and Goldberg's interpretation of Freud's real intentions is valid, it should not affect our attitude toward psychoanalysis as a doctrine. Our controversy is not with Freud himself but rather with his impact on psychotherapy. According to the psychoanalytic doctrine of repression (Donelson, 1973), "material of the dynamic unconscious is subject to repression, which operates automatically and without conscious intent. It is not a passive forgetting, but an active, dynamic process of holding down certain mental events and keeping them from becoming conscious" (p. 37).

The psychoanalytic concept of repression. . . is closely linked to the Freudian idea of an unconscious mind. . . . Suppression occurs when one voluntarily and consciously withholds a response or turns attention away from it deliberately. Unconscious repression, in contrast, may function as an automatic guardian against anxiety. (Mischel, 1971, p. 357)

Similarly, Alexander (1932) viewed repression as "a kind of unconscious censorship which reacts automatically to unacceptable tendencies. . . . It is comparable with a conditional reflex rather than with a deliberate judgment" (p. 113). In discussing Freud's theory, Ewen (1980) said that "we are not cognizant of using repression because it originates from the unconscious part of the ego, which expends psychic energy in order to prevent a dangerous object-choice from taking place" (p. 24). The same position was adopted by Stafford-Clark (1966), who in his book *What Freud Really Said* indicated that Freud viewed repression as "the dynamic, compulsive, but completely unconscious forgetting of unbearable, threatening or disturbing experiences" (p. 26). Fenichel (1946) said that repression

consists of an unconsciously purposeful forgetting or not becoming aware of internal impulses or external events. . . . However, although the repressed is not felt consciously it remains effective. . . .

In repression proper, based on continual counter-cathexis, the repressed remains effective from the unconscious. (p. 148)

Thus, the operation of repression itself is, in psychoanalytic doctrine, strongly linked with unconscious, nonvoluntary, and automatic processes. Moreover, some psychoanalytically oriented investigators (e.g., see Gur & Sackeim, 1979; Sackeim & Gur, 1978; Sackeim, Nordlie, & Gur, 1979) imply that the concept of repression requires the assumption that consciousness is a nonunitary entity. In this regard, our emphasis on the conscious and deliberate aspect of repression is completely inconsistent with psychoanalytic doctrine.

Coping Mechanisms Versus Defense Mechanisms

In the new definition of repression we abandon the term *defense mechanisms* and adopt instead the concept of *coping mechanisms* for the following reasons:

1. The notion of defense mechanisms is too strongly related to psychoanalytic doctrine, which is not supported by enough scientific evidence.

2. In psychoanalysis the prime source of stress is found within the individual: the term defense mechanism conveys the notion that the "ego" defends itself from the powerful "id." According to Maddi (1980), the concept of defense in all theories that use this notion "is a technique for avoiding the anxiety that would be aroused by recognition that there existed in you some thought or action that would lead to punishment, guilt or feelings of unworthiness" (p. 203). This concept of stress in psychodynamic theories is one of the main sources of controversy between them and behavioral approaches, which, unlike them, attribute the source of stress to outside agencies. Thus, by replacing the term *defense* with *coping,* we emphasize that repression may be activated not only by internal sources of stress (i.e., conflicts, unacceptable needs), as the psychoanalytic theories assert, but also by external stresses. For example, as will be clarified, pathological distraction or repression coping strategies may be adopted in response to current life stress conditions, such as war or social ostracism (e.g., see pp. 107–110 in this book), which are not necessarily related to internal conflicts. The idea that the coping mechanisms of distraction may be activated by external sources of stress is also suggested in S. M. Miller's (1979, 1980, 1981) monitoring/blunting theory.

3. In psychoanalytic theory, defense has a negative connotation. Even if the defensive set has some beneficial effects, the source of stress is not eliminated but remains within the individual. He or she is, however, protected from all or some of its potential emotional damage. For example, Maddi (1980) noted that

the defense is instituted virtually at the same time as the arousal of anxiety, and therefore not much anxiety is actually experienced, if the defense is effective. Once instituted, the defense tends to persist, because the underlying conflict also persists. (p. 203)

In psychoanalysis, all defenses except sublimation are pathogenic (Singer, 1970, pp. 167–168). In contrast, the term *coping* is much more neutral and may be either positive or negative. As will be demonstrated shortly, normal use of repression, according to the new theoretical approach, helps to reduce or even eliminate altogether the threatening aspects of a stressful situation from the individual's cognitive system, and this enhances his or her ability to adjust. However, repression becomes pathological when abnormal means are used for achieving distraction from a threat. If there is validity to our argument that repression can be beneficial, sometimes even to the point of totally eliminating stress, then it seems that the term coping is much more appropriate than the concept of defense.

We now elaborate on the beneficial value of repression from the psychoanalytic perspective as well as from our standpoint, since this constitutes the central idea of the proposed theory of normal repression.

ADJUSTMENT VALUE OF REPRESSION

Psychoanalytic Position

As noted, psychoanalysts view repression, except for sublimation, as a negative process since the subject runs away from a problem instead of solving it. In Freudian theory,

> repression weakens the capacity to deal with reality. Furthermore, repression usually cannot be undone when it is no longer needed. . . . Childhood repressions therefore persist into adolescence and adulthood, where they prevent true self-knowledge, help bring about self-defeating behavior, and may even lead to the development of troublesome neurotic symptoms. (Ewen, 1980, p. 25)

In the psychological literature, it is sometimes argued (R. L. Atkinson, R. C. Atkinson, & Hilgard, 1983) that repression may help the individual to adjust, but this position does not agree with the psychoanalytic model. Psychoanalysis sees the human psyche as an energy system in which any process that raises the individual's energy level, without an outlet for expression or energy discharge, is nonbeneficial and even harmful. The behavioral theorists (Kazdin, 1978; Rimm & Masters, 1979) compared this concept to a closed hydraulic system. If normal expression of the psychic energy is shut off, energy may be discharged in a maladjusted way. Although repression in individuals who function normally may not lead to immediate production of psychophysiological symptoms, it impoverishes the personality. Fenichel (1946), who is acknowledged as the major exponent of Freudian psychoanalytic thinking, noted that every individual uses a certain degree of defensive forces. However, as long as the instinctual energies are not strong enough to break through,

> the person may suffer from a certain impoverishment of his personality but otherwise remain relatively well. But any disturbance of this equilibrium brings the danger of a breaking through of the repressed impulses and the necessity to develop new and effective means of defense—in other words, the danger of a neurosis. (p. 121)

Thus, in psychoanalysis all defenses are pathogenic except those related to sublimation (e.g., see Fenichel, 1946; Nemiah, 1984; Perry & Laurence, 1984; Singer, 1970). However, sublimation is possible only after the removal of repression (see Fenichel, 1946; Singer, 1970):

> substitution process can take place only when the originally repressed impulse is no longer repugnant to the patient. The impulse itself need not necessarily become acceptable as a basis for action but must become acceptable as part of oneself. Therefore the recovery of memories of past impulses which were repressed assumed crucial therapeutic importance. (Singer, 1970, p. 167)

Singer noted that although Freud refined his system and thinking considerably, this remained his position to the very end. Thus, as an energetic model, psychoanalysis cannot accept conceptually the notion of good repression.

Freud was strongly influenced by Darwin's theory (H. B. Lewis, 1981), and it appears that Freud's extremely negative conceptualization of repression is related to Darwinism. In Darwin's theory, an organism must, for adaptive reasons, be in close touch with reality. It must see the world exactly as it is. Any detachment from reality is undesirable and may be harmful. This notion was adopted by Freud and psychoanalytically oriented clinicians (Taylor, 1983, pp. 1167–1168). Thus, according to psychoanalytic thinking, any mechanism or characteristic that causes even slight deviation from reality, such as repression, self-deception, or social desirability (see pp. 80–81), is undesirable because it may hinder the individual's adjustment (a similar point of view is expressed by Murphy, 1970, 1975). However, as will soon be demonstrated, the empirical evidence indicates that Freud was wrong. Darwin's concept seems to be correct for animals, and it may apply also to abnormal people who display gross deviation from reality, but not to normally functioning subjects. Indeed, psychoanalytically oriented investigators based their claim almost entirely on data from their clinical work.

Perspective of the Proposed Theory

Theoretical Assumptions

The general assumption of the proposed theory is that repression is one of the most important variables in determining the individual's ability to adjust. Inevitably, life is characterized by pain and bitterness, which in the vast majority of cases are physically inescapable. To be able to function normally, individuals need a mechanism by which they can cognitively disconnect themselves from stress situations. In cases where a total disconnection from the threatening situation might be harmful, according to the individual assessment of the reality, a selective and flexible mechanism of repression is needed to prevent the emotion-loaded components of the stressful situation from gaining access to one's attentional domain.

Elsewhere I argued, in a theoretical work on stress and affiliation (Rofé, 1984), that stress may be divided into two main categories, the avoidable and the unavoidable. In an avoidable stress situation (e.g., war), something practical can be done (e.g., fighting) to reduce or eliminate the stress. In an unavoidable stress situation (e.g., incurable disease), no practical action can be taken to remove the sources of the stress. In principle, it may be physically possible to escape from avoidable stress (e.g., desert from the military to avoid the war), but in practice this option is not exercised in most cases because of the high price of punishment it may involve or because the alternative situation is just as stressful. In this respect, we are totally different from animals. Our advanced cognitive development may prevent disconnection from the stress components even if we are physically distant from them.

Certainly, in the case of unavoidable stress the best coping response seems to be use of various techniques of repression for preventing any access to cues that directly or indirectly remind us of the stress. Repressive coping mechanisms may, to a limited extent, also enhance our ability to cope with avoidable stress but only on condition that they are used in a selective manner. *Selectivity* means that subjects remain faithful to the important aspects of reality, while at the same time ignoring or deliberately denying access to the focus of their attention of redundant, emotionally arousing cues that may only hinder efficient interaction with reality. Complete faithfulness to reality may sometimes be harmful even in respect to avoidable stress. For example, a soldier at war would function more efficiently if he focused intensively on the job to be done, so that his attention would not be accessible to anxiety-arousing cues and thoughts such as possibility of death or injury, the strength of the enemy, etc. For this reason, the presence of a fearful soldier, who may be more in touch with reality than a brave one, may be harmful because he may disrupt the distractive efforts of the others. It appears, then, that anxiety and frustration are not determined by what exists in the outside world but rather by what exists in the subject's attentional domain. Indeed, recent evidence (MacLeod, Mathews, & Tata, 1986; Mathews & MacLeod, 1985, 1986) shows that clinically anxious subjects display attentional bias to threat-related stimuli. Feelings of anxiety, frustration, and probably pain as well (McCaul & Malott, 1984) can be avoided or reduced if the attentional channels are intensively occupied by nonrelevant stimuli. Moreover, it is further hypothesized that habitual response to positive aspects of reality, ignoring the negative, nonchangeable ones, is likely to increase the individual's adaptive capacity.

This theoretical framework is consistent with the theoretical positions of S. M. Miller's (1979, 1980, 1981) "blunting" or distraction hypothesis, Rofé's (1984) utility theory, Bandura's (1971b) cognitive theory of fear, and Taylor's (1983) theory of cognitive adaptation. According to S. M. Miller's theory,

> *arousal remains high in uncontrollable aversive situations to the extent that an individual is alert for and sensitized to the negative aspects of the events. Arousal is reduced when an individual can cognitively avoid and psychologically blunt objective sources of danger. (see S. M. Miller & Mangan, 1983, p. 231)*

However, unlike our theoretical position, S. M. Miller's (1981) blunting or distraction hypothesis is restricted to the uncontrollable-stress situation only. In controllable stress, "monitoring" or alertness for threat-relevant information was suggested as the coping modality. In my opinion, a selective and flexible repressive mechanism, namely, a combination of monitoring and blunting strategy is much more efficient in dealing with avoidable or controllable stress than is monitoring alone.

Rofé's (1984) theory emphasizes the utility considerations in responding to stress situations. It suggests that in unavoidable stress situations, subjects tend to avoid others like themselves and refrain from talking about the threatening events because these "may increase the mutual panic and awareness of the threat, keep the individual within the undesirable psychological state, and cause embarrassment" (p. 240). In avoidable stress situations, the individual tends to prefer the company of a helpful rather than a fearful person. In addition, a subject tends to talk about topics relevant to the stress in an attempt to gather information for coping with it better. However, there is no indication as to whether pure monitoring or a combination of monitoring and repressing is a better coping mechanism.

Bandura's (1971b) cognitive theory states that conditioned emotional responses are typically mediated by thought-producing arousal rather than directly evoked by external events. It is the conscious evaluation of the various stimuli that is important rather than its occurrence per se. People can frighten themselves by fear-provoking thoughts, and prevent arousal by calm thoughts. This means that self-distractive measurements can prevent arousal of fears in fear-provoking situations, such as war. Similarly, Taylor

(1983), in his cognitive theory of adjustment, indicated that humans are endowed with an impressive ability to withstand severe personal tragedy successfully: "The majority of people facing such blows achieve a quality of life or level of happiness equivalent to or even exceeding their prior level of satisfaction" (p. 1161). Taylor (1983) noted that "in the past, mental health researchers and clinicians have assumed that positive mental functioning depends upon being in touch with reality" (p. 1167). However, according to Taylor's theory, successful adjustment to frustrating life events "rests fundamentally upon the ability to form and maintain a set of illusions" (p. 1161). Similarly, Lazarus (1979, 1983), in his new look at denial, pointed out that denial is no longer rejected as a primitive, ultimately unsuccessful defense. Clinicians and health psychologists are now recognizing its value in protecting people against crises.

Generally speaking, our theoretical approach is also consistent with the view of T. A. Ribot, who wrote in 1882 that

> *without the total obliteration of an immense number of states of consciousness, and the momentary repression of more, recollection would be impossible. Forgetfulness, except in certain cases is not a disease of memory, but a condition of its health and life. (p. 61)*

Our concept of distraction is at variance with H. S. Sullivan's (1953/1968) notion of selective inattention. Although he recognized that distraction may have some beneficial value, he regarded it primarily as disadvantageous: "Selective inattention is, more than any other of the inappropriate and inadequate performances of life, the classic means by which we do not profit from experience which falls within the areas of our particular handicap" (H. S. Sullivan, 1953/1968, p. 319). Sullivan, like Freud, based his theoretical concepts on work with deviant subjects, who use faulty distractive tools, as will be elaborated on later. Normal people do not employ bizarre symptoms for distractive activities, preferring normal and flexible means that are in accord with adjustment demands. They do not dwell on unavoidable stressful situations, and when the stress is avoidable, they are likely to use selective inattention. Moreover, their distractive maneuver consists partly of attentional bias to pleasant aspects of reality.

Research Evidence

We now review the available research data that seem to be relevant to this theoretical position. These findings are organized under four categories: (1) studies dealing with medical patients; (2) studies relating to war or dangerous situations; (3) studies dealing with R–S, anxiety, and social desirability; and (4) studies that have examined the beneficial effect of distraction in reducing the risk of depression. The first two groups of studies more or less correspond with the first two hypotheses in the following list, respectively, the third and fourth groups correspond with the third hypothesis, which formally represents our theoretical approach.

1. Repression is the most efficient coping strategy in responding to unavoidable stress situations.
2. A combination of repression and monitoring is a more efficient coping mechanism in responding to avoidable stress than is repression or monitoring alone.
3. Paying attention to the positive aspects of self and others combined with a tendency to exaggerate these aspects and to some degree ignore or play down the negative aspects increases the probability of better adjustment as compared to an accurate perception of self or others.

Studies in Medical Settings. Consistent with the first hypothesis, various studies show that medical patients prefer to avoid rather than seek information relevant to their condition. Before specifying these studies, let us first refer to a statement made by S. M. Miller and Mangan (1983), who investigated this issue:

> One key situational property that has consistently been found to affect stress is whether the individual has maximal information (predictability) or minimal information (unpredictability) about the event and its effects. . . . Laboratory evidence shows that most (but not all) people prefer to have information about the timing and nature of an aversive event. . . . However, in less artificial studies that mirror real life (e.g., providing external distractors in the unpredictability condition), the preference reverses: The majority of individuals then prefer to distract themselves from threat-relevant information. (p. 223)

Also, in this respect, according to Rofé (1984) laboratory stress may not represent stress in real life. Laboratory stress encourages approach behavior because, unlike real-life situations, the stress is kept to a minimum and the subject has the option to escape at a small price if it becomes intolerable.

Several investigators reported findings showing that when stress was unavoidable, medical patients preferred to avoid rather than seek relevant information. For example, Cohen and Lazarus (1973) found that patients who avoided information prior to surgery spent fewer days in the hospital and had fewer postsurgical complications than did those who sought information. Similarly, Langer, Janis, and Wolfer (1975) reported that information increased arousal and delayed recovery. Along the same lines, S. M. Miller and Mangan (1983) found that patients at risk for cancer who were to undergo an aversive diagnostic procedure expressed less anxiety, pain, and depression when given minimal information. Moreover, information increased self-reported distress not only on the day of the examination but also on several following days. Further results showed that subjects with "blunter" personality types (i.e., those who tended to avoid threatening information) showed less psychological arousal in the low-information condition, while those with "monitor" personality types (i.e., information seekers) displayed less arousal in the high-information condition.

Consistent with these findings, Rofé and his associates found that cancer patients (Rofé, Hoffman, & Lewin, 1985; Rofé, Lewin, & Hoffman, 1987) as well as pregnant women immediately before delivery (Rofé & Lewin, 1986; Rofé, Lewin, & Padeh, 1977) avoided both talking about topics related to their stressful condition and being with people like themselves. These findings are consistent with Rosenheim and Reicher's (1986) finding that cancer patients and their spouses displayed very low interest in joining support groups. In line with these findings, data from other research areas show that a person emotionally shocked by a traumatic death prefers to be left alone and/or avoid talking about the anxiety-provoking subject of death (Latané & Wheeler, 1966; Sheatsley & Feldman, 1964; Vernon, 1970, p. 167).

Other relevant data were reported by Taylor (1983) and by Katz, Weiner, Gallagher, and Hellman (1970). These researchers showed that denial or illusion are among the most prominent and efficient coping techniques used by cancer patients for overcoming their feelings of distress. Taylor (1983) provided much additional data to support his cognitive theory of adaptation, which emphasizes the beneficial effects of the illusion or denial coping mechanisms (see also Lazarus, 1979, 1983).

Thus, the overall findings clearly show that people confronted with unavoidable stress, such as an incurable disease, tend to adopt the coping strategies of repression, denial, or illusion and that these coping styles enhance the subject's adjustment ability.

These findings are, of course, inconsistent with the psychoanalytic conception of repression and are in line with our theoretical position.

Studies in War or Other Dangerous Conditions. The distraction hypothesis received additional support from research on responses of civilian populations in wartime. Rachman's (1978) review of the studies on psychological reactions during World War II showed, surprisingly, that the vast majority of people had usually evidenced indifferent or calm reactions and rapid adaptation to bombing attacks. This type of reaction characterized adults and children, including people who were repeatedly exposed to great danger and intense stimulation. Similar findings were reported by Saigh (1984a, 1984b) with regard to subjects who were exposed to traumatic conditions during the Israeli invasion of Beirut.

Rachman pointed out that this unexpected calm response is inconsistent with the conditioning theory of fear. In animals, conditioning takes place under almost all conditions of fear. However, this is not the case with human beings. As will be elaborated on later, one of the prime reasons for this state of affair seems to be that humans have the ability to distract their attention from the fear stimuli and, thereby prevent emotional arousal.

Some evidence consistent with this hypothesis is found in the results of these wartime studies. Janis (1951), one of the prominent investigators of the psychological reactions during World War II, stated that "people who face danger tend to feel less fearful if they are able to engage in some form of useful overt activity" (p. 120). A similar conclusion was reached by A. Lewis (1942), who surveyed neurotic children during the war. In an attempt to explain why fighter pilots in World War II reported less fear than did other members of the air crews, Rachman (1978) suggested that "concentration of attention upon a distracting task in a situation of stress reduces anxiety" (p. 82). He further noted that some other investigators of the psychology of aviation had reached a similar conclusion. For example, Flanagan (1948) observed that even activities that were not very efficient in reducing danger but merely kept one busy tended to decrease anxiety. Elsewhere, Rachman (1978) explained that inactivity may raise the individual's anxiety level because "it forces one to experience the full impact of the fearful stimuli. Distraction, by diminishing that impact, may help even if it has no influence on the probability of the event itself occurring" (p. 262).

Further evidence that distraction plays a vital role in coping with dangerous situations is reported in the autobiographical accounts of two dedicated scientists: Admiral Richard Byrd, who spend six solitary months in the Antarctic, and Dr. Alain Bombard, who sailed alone across the Atlantic on a lift raft for 65 days. The two explorers reacted to their loneliness, isolation, and dangerous life conditions in almost identical ways. "Both men used the same mechanisms to fight off depression: controlling their thoughts, dwelling only on pleasant past associations and experiences and refusing to allow themselves to think about the anxiety producing aspects of their situations" (P. Solomon, Leiderman, Mendelson, & Wexler, 1957, p. 363).

Other evidence of the effectiveness of repression in coping with dangerous situations was reported by Rofé and Lewin (1980, 1982a). These authors found that Israeli children raised in a border town that was frequently a target of terrorist activities displayed more repressive behaviors than did children who grew up in a town away from the border. The former group had a lower score on Byrne's R–S scale and reported fewer fearful dreams and unpleasant daydreams than did the latter. The authors (Rofé & Lewin, 1982a) concluded that constant living in a war environment from early childhood might lead to the development of a personality type that uses repression and denial mechanisms to make life more tolerable; young subjects

> *having no means at their disposal to remove the threat either directly by defeating the enemy, or indirectly by leaving the place, would make an effort to avoid thinking about the potential danger in order to reduce their tension and thereby make life more tolerable. (p. 67)*

Overall, these findings reinforce the idea that repression enhances rather than disrupts the individual's adjustment capacity. The data suggest that when the situation is dangerous but something may be done to reduce or eliminate the stress, the individual's coping resources may be utilized more efficiently if attention is occupied by the job that needs to be done and the redundant, anxiety-provoking aspects are overlooked. In the absence of such distractive capacity, attention may become overwhelmed by the fear-arousing stimuli and, thereby, the individual's behavioral output is likely to be less mature. These studies also indicate that one who is exposed to an unavoidable stressful environment from early childhood may develop a repressive type of personality that "immunizes" him or her from the noxious conditions of such a surrounding.

Repression–Sensitization, Anxiety, and Social Desirability. The bulk of studies on repression–sensitization, which show that repressors are better adjusted individuals than are intermediates or sensitizers, provide additional support to our theoretical position. As has been demonstrated, repressors consistently show avoidance responses to anxiety-arousing conditions on both perceptual and behavioral levels. These data confirm the legitimacy of the R–S studies to be included in a theory of repression. Nevertheless, two major sets of findings, which caused some investigators to doubt whether the R–S scale in fact measures repression, need some theoretical clarification.

One set concerns the fact that at least on the cognitive level, repressors tend to be less anxious than are sensitizers. From a Freudian perspective, one would expect that either repressors would be more anxious or that both ends of the R–S continuum would be highly anxious. However, in view of the increasing findings that demonstrate the efficiency of distraction or denial, one can hardly be surprised that cognitively, repressors experience low anxiety. Naturally, people who distract their attention from anxiety-provoking stimuli should experience less anxiety than those who direct their attention to them. We have become accustomed to thinking differently only because the psycho-analytic theoretical position is so deeply rooted.

The second set of findings are those showing a high correlation between the R–S scale and measures of social desirability. It has been argued that repressors only appear to be better adjusted because they are motivated to impress others. Adherence to the Freudian model has encouraged the idea that a tendency to exaggerate one's positive characteristics and deny or minimize the negative ones is a reflection of maladjustment (Millham & Jacobson's review, 1978; Millham & Kellogg, 1980). This line of thought led several investigators to claim that studies showing repressors to be better adjusted than sensitizers might be invalid.

Millham and Kellogg (1980) are among the two strongest advocates of this theoretical position. In their empirical work on social desirability, they demonstrated that this personality dimension is characterized by two components of deception: self-deception and other deception. *Self-deception* refers to the repressive type of behavior where individuals believe, independent of a motivation to impress others, that they possess certain positive characteristics that they do not actually have. This tendency was reflected in some earlier findings such as those provided by S. E. Berger (1971), who reported that high scorers on the Marlowe–Crowne social desirability scale would cheat to avoid apparent failure even when they believed that no one but themselves would have access to the data. *Other deception* refers to individuals who are motivated by a desire to avoid negative evaluation and who deliberately distort the truth in order to impress others. Millham and Kellogg indicated that reality distortion is more prominent in deception of the self than in deception of others since only in the latter is behavior modifiable with a changing environment.

These two types of deception are independent of each other although both are related to a need for social approval, as measured by Marlowe–Crowne's scale. However, self-deception was more powerfully related to social desirability scores than was deception of others. Results further showed that after subjects were presented with a descriptive adjective list, highly self-deceptive persons recalled more positive than negative evaluative traits, while highly other-deceptive subjects recalled more negative than positive evaluative traits. In addition, highly self-deceptive persons recalled fewer socially undesirable traits than did low-scoring self-deceptive persons. The highly other-deceptive subjects recalled more socially undesirable traits than did low-scoring other-deceptive persons.

These findings were consistent with Millham and Kellogg's (1980) assumption that self-deceptive persons would tend to deny, fail to attend, or otherwise avoid negatively evaluative stimuli. In contrast, other-deceptive persons would tend to be more alert to negative information in the environment that they could use in adjusting their behavior to the requirements of others.

In discussing the implications that their findings might have on psychopathology, Millham and Kellogg claimed that although social desirability responding was traditionally seen as negative because of its tendency to reduce the validity of pathological measures, in itself it was not regarded as reflecting an independent dimension of pathology. However, according to Millham and Kellogg (1980),

> to the extent that highly unrealistic and distorted conceptions of self can be viewed as psychopathological or maladaptive, then social desirability responding as self-deception may be viewed as a dimension of pathology itself, independent of any other pathology dimension being evaluated. (p. 465)

Thus, Millham and Kellogg's view of social desirability as a reflection of maladjustment is even more extreme than the traditional conception. Moreover, inasmuch as there is a high correlation between the R–S scale and measures of social desirability, this theoretical approach further implies that repressors are maladjusted individuals. However, neither Millham and Kellogg nor previous investigators provide any empirical evidence to support their psychoanalytic claim that social desirability responding is associated with pathology. Furthermore, a hypothesis opposing the traditional view makes more sense both theoretically and empirically. On the theoretical level, one may argue that being alert to the demands of others is an integral part of social competence and highly important for maintaining satisfactory social relationships. Similarly, presenting oneself positively and focusing one's attention on one's positive qualities is likely to increase self-confidence and to elicit positive response from others. Dwelling on one's negative aspects may intensify the negative self-image and reduce happiness. Additionally, self-awareness might not be beneficial in producing change because the negative aspect may be inherently unchangeable, or it may require a great effort that the subject may not be ready to make.

These claims are consistent with Bandura's (1977a) self-efficiency theory, which argues that expectations of personal mastery affect both initiation and persistence of coping behavior. They are also in line with Rofé's (1984) utility theory, which implies that subjects tend to avoid the company of unhappy persons or those whose attention is focused on the negative aspects of reality. Consistent with this claim, Hammen and Peters (1978) reported that depressed subjects were more likely to be rejected than were nondepressed individuals, especially by members of the opposite sex. Subjects who interacted with a depressed person were themselves significantly more depressed afterward, apparently because the experience focused attention on emotionally negative stimuli. This agrees with other data showing that depressed individuals focus their conversations on inherently depressive topics (see Coyne, 1976).

Indeed, the cumulative research findings clearly negate the traditional conceptualization and support the view that high social desirability characteristics tend to reinforce adjustment. McCrae and Costa (1983), in reference to the as-yet-unsettled dispute concerning the exact meaning of the social desirability scale (see, e.g., Linehan & Nielsen, 1983; Nevid, 1983), noted: "Many psychologists still regard correlations with social desirability (SD) scales as evidence of the invalidity of measures, despite 20 years of research showing that this interpretation is usually unjustified" (p. 882). In an attempt to resolve this dispute, McCrae and Costa compared self-report data of 215 subjects with the external criterion of spouse ratings on a range of personality traits in the areas of neuroticism, extraversion, and openness to experience. Subjects also completed the Marlowe–Crowne social desirability scale and the Eysenck Personality Inventory (EPI) Lie scale. The authors found considerable agreement between self-report and external ratings. In most cases, correction of self-reports by taking into account social desirability scores from either the Marlowe–Crowne questionnaire or Eysenck's scale lowered the validity coefficients instead of raising them. The largest decrease was of traits in the area of neuroticism, particularly when the Marlowe–Crowne was used. Both social desirability scales were substantively related to neuroticism, and to a lesser degree to extraversion and closedness. A comparison of correlations of social desirability scores with self-rating and external ratings showed a highly similar pattern of results. McCrae and Cresta (1983) concluded that "individuals in this study who obtained high scores on the Marlowe–Crowne and EPI Lie scales were in fact better adjusted, friendlier and more open than those who scored low" (p. 886).

Additional findings supporting this interpretation were reported by Rofé (1985), who compared the marital happiness of repressors and sensitizers. Rofé reported that not only repressors themselves but their spouses as well (external criterion), irrespective of personality type, described their marriages as happier than did sensitizers or their spouses. In discussing these results, Rofé (1985) stated that

> many marital conflicts are minor in importance, or may be perceived so when the individual has distance from them, and some conflicts are insoluble. Individuals who have no ability to deny or ignore conflicts or delay their responses, may create an antagonistic atmosphere which detracts from marital happiness. (p. 78)

Further findings consistent with this hypothesis were reported by Kundu and Chandidas (1981) and by Rofé and Lewin (1979). The former found that secondary school students with high sociometric status scored significantly higher on the Marlowe–

Crowne social desirability scale than did those with low sociometric status. Rofé and Lewin, using the same type of population, reported that as compared with sensitizers, repressors obtained higher sociometric ranks and were evaluated more positively by their teachers. Some other relevant findings are those showing that feelings of hopelessness are more widespread among subject with low than with high social desirability scores (Linehan & Nielsen, 1981, 1983; Nevid, 1983).

Thus, the cumulative research findings that subjects scoring high on social desirability tend to function better than do those scoring low argue against the traditional conceptualization of this personality dimension. High social desirability seems to be an essential part of a healthy use of repression. Therefore, it appears that the theoretical difficulties that were posed in the past by the correlation between social desirability and R–S stemmed from a misconception of the notion of repression.

Depression and Detachment from Reality. Many studies (see pp. 237–240) show that depression and apathy are strongly associated with stress, particularly unavoidable stress, among both animals and humans (e.g., H. F. Harlow & M. K. Harlow, 1965; Kaufman & Rosenblum, 1967a, 1967b; Seligman, 1974). However, while animals seem to be unable to detach themselves from reality when the stress is inescapable, thereby avoiding the onset of depression, humans are able to do so. This ability to detach oneself from the bitterness of reality seems to be quite important in determining whether or not a person will develop depression (Taylor, 1983). For example, Lewinsohn, Mischel, Chaplin, and Barton (1980) reported that, surprisingly, the self-perception of depressed patients were more realistic than were those of control subjects. Depressed patients saw themselves as they were seen by others, whereas control subjects perceived themselves in a more positive light. This realistic outlook of depressed patients tended to decrease in the course of treatment. The overall findings in this research area show that depressed people tend to perceive reality more accurately and to be less likely to succumb to an "illusion of control" than nondepressed people (Abramson & Alloy, 1981; Alloy & Abramson, 1979, 1982; Alloy, Abramson, & Viscusi, 1981; DeMonbreun & Craighead, 1977; Golin, Terrell, & Johnson, 1977; Golin, Terrell, Weitz, & Drost, 1979; Martin, Abramson, & Alloy, 1984).

These findings are consistent with results of several studies showing that people perceive reality as being much brighter than it really is. Thus, they remember themselves as having been more successful and more often correct than they have actually been, attribute good results to themselves much more than bad ones, believe that the present is better than the past and that the future will be even better, and expect to succeed and improve in the future. Depressed people are less susceptible than nondepressed subjects to a number of cognitive biases that would allow them to perceive themselves and their interaction with the environment with a rosy glow (Abramson & Alloy, 1981; Lewinsohn, Mischel, Chaplain, & Barton, 1980; Nelson & Craighead, 1977; Rozensky, Rehm, Pry, & Roth, 1977; Taylor, 1983). The inability of depressive people to delude themselves and deny the unpleasant aspects of reality may explain the fact that as compared with control subjects, they display greater recall of negative than of positive or nondepressive information about themselves (Bradley & Mathews, 1983; Derry & Kuiper, 1981).

The importance of the ability to detach oneself from reality in response to a stressful situation may be demonstrated more vividly by examining two modes of responding to the horrible conditions that existed in the Nazi concentration camps. One mode, described by Bettelheim (1960), was that of prisoners whose attention was almost completely dominated by the bitter fact of reality. They believed that they would never leave the camp alive. Bettelheim noted that

> *these prisoners were in a literal sense, walking corpses. . . . They were people who were deprived of effect, self-esteem, and every form of stimulation, so totally exhausted, physically and emotionally, that they had given the environment total power over them. (pp. 151–152)*

Thus, these people were completely aware of the horrible conditions of their reality, but they paid a very high price for this awareness. Evidence both from the concentration camps and from Americans who were prisoners of war in Korea showed that death was more probable when apathy and depression, which are inevitable in such a mode of reaction were predominant (Frankl, 1968; Strassman, Thaler, & Schein, 1956). A completely different type of response is demonstrated in Frankl's (1968) book *Man's Search for Meaning*. When one carefully examines Frankl's cognitive responses to the horrible experiences he had to undergo, one can hardly avoid the impression that mentally, Frankl was not at the concentration camps. Throughout his book are many expressions indicating that Frankl succeeded in distracting himself from the bitterness of reality by directing his attention to those extremely few and rare elements of reality that could inspire him with hope and good feelings. Moreover, when the reality was extremely stressful and such elements were not available, he used his imagination to invent encouraging cognitions.

Upon arrival at the camp, instead of thinking about his tragic plight, as one would normally do, Frankl (1968) found a positive aspect of the environment to focus his attention on: "Just the sight of the red cheeks and round faces of those prisoners was a great encouragement" (p. 8). Similarly, on his journey from Auschwitz to a Bavarian camp, which might have been his journey to death, he nevertheless "beheld the mountains of Salzburg with their summits glowing in the sunset . . ." (pp. 38–39). Elsewhere, he relates: "I practically trained a friend of mine who worked next to me on the building site to develop a sense of humor. I suggested to him that we would promise each other to invent at least one amusing story daily" (p. 42).

A special means of overcoming his miserable life conditions was the hallucinating of his wife's encouraging image. In describing one of the difficult times while he was enduring the Nazi cruelty, he noted that

> *my mind clung to my wife's image, imagining it with an uncanny acuteness. I heard her answering me, saw her smile, her frank and encouraging look. Real or not, her look was then more luminous than the sun which was beginning to rise. (p. 36)*

It should be noted that Frankl knew that his wife's conditions might not have been better than his own, yet he did not imagine how miserable she must be but concentrated only on the glory of her image.

Recently, a young Israeli man, lost on a journey in the jungles of South America and near death, also used similar encouraging hallucinations as a coping device. In describing one of his very desperate moments (Ghinsberg, 1985), he wrote that

> *I know that this was purely imaginative, but she was lying beside me weeping and yelling. I did not know who she was, a girl friend, or my wife. . . . I knew only that we were lovers. She was crying in desperation. . . . Get up, Yosi, I encouraged myself, you must be an example for her. Encourage her. I removed myself from the mud and gently helped her get up. (p. 242)*

We are aware of the possible criticism that these two descriptions are retrospective data and that their scientific value is, therefore, questionable. However, these excerpts shed some light on the coping value of self-deception and appear to be consistent with the cumulative research evidence presented previously. Thus, generally speaking, both the empirical findings and the autobiographical reports reviewed here strongly support the view that illusion and self-deception are not necessarily bad. On the contrary, when used in a selective and controlled manner, they are likely to enhance the subject's coping ability and hence serve as an important barrier against depression.

CONCLUSIONS

In this chapter, we demonstrated that the most legitimate definition of repression concordant with the laboratory data is one that emphasizes a conscious and deliberate distraction. It was also suggested that the term coping mechanism is more appropriate in describing a subject's response to any stressful conditions, either internal or external, than the traditional psychoanalytic concept of defense mechanism. At the same time, due to reasons specified earlier (p. 12), we do not suggest abandoning the term repression in favor of distraction. However, not all distractive activities are regarded as repression in our new definition. Rather, in a manner similar to the strong linkage between the psychoanalytic concept of defense and the idea of dynamism, only active or self-induced distractions are included in the new conceptualization. An additional reason for preserving the term repression is its strong connection, in the psychoanalytic doctrine, with the idea of unconscious. As previously stated, although we deny the existence of the autonomous entity of unconscious, we accept that under extremely stressful conditions, the conscious may use very sophisticated maneuvers for producing a state of unconscious. Like repression in psychoanalysis, active distraction plays a crucial role in this process. All these issues will be dealt with in part III.

One of the most important messages of this chapter is that as far as normal people are concerned, there seems to be no scientific support for the psychoanalytic conception that repression is an unhealthy psychological process. In fact, contrary to this approach and in line with the present theoretical model, the findings strongly indicate that repression is a very important mechanism in coping with both avoidable and unavoidable stress situations, and it reduces the likelihood of psychological damage such as depression. Moreover, there is no confirmation for the widely accepted belief that a positive relationship should exist between social desirability and maladjustment. Repression is strongly correlated with social desirability, and these two personality dimensions positively relate to measures of adjustment. Thus, the tendency to exaggerate positive characteristics of self and/or others and to play down negative aspects helps preserve a positive self-image and increases the chances of being liked by others.

Is it appropriate to generalize the conclusions in this chapter to the area of psychopathology? Can one, for example, claim that detachment from reality or repression is beneficial for abnormal people as well? Certainly not. We have no intention of repeating Freud's mistake and generalizing the observations from one population to another. Normal and abnormal people are two different and distinct populations, and at least with regard to repression there seems to be a very sharp difference between them. It is argued that normal and abnormal individuals have the same goal of distracting their attention from a stressful situation, but the means by which this is achieved are radically different. The pathological nature of repression is the focus of our attention in the next part of the book.

III

PSYCHOBIZARRENESS THEORY AND ITS APPLICATION TO NEUROSES

7

Pathological Repression

DEFINITION OF BIZARRENESS

As was indicated in the introduction to this book, the traditional psychopathological theories make no clear distinction between normal and abnormal behavioral dysfunctions. The differences between the two types of behaviors are conceptualized in quantitative rather than qualitative terms. As previously stated, this line of thought is characteristic of all psychopathology theories and continues to be upheld among today's theorists (e.g., see Zigler & Glick, 1984). The same set of rules is applied for explaining all behavioral deviations. In principle, the dreadful fear of going outside the home, namely, agoraphobia, is conceptualized by all approaches, including psychoanalysis (Moss, 1960), in the same way as fear of dogs.

Theoretically, however, these two types of symptoms cannot be included in the same category. Until now, this argument was not seriously made because of the investigators' conviction that the theoretical positions of the traditional theories were based on solid scientific ground. However, in light of cumulative data that raise serious doubt regarding the basic assumptions of the dominant theoretical approaches in psychotherapy, it may be beneficial to abandon this unproved assumption.

It may be worthwhile to adopt instead the view that the behavioral deviations displayed by psychiatric patients necessitate entirely different theoretical conceptions than those shown by nonclinical populations. This seems to be a prerequisite for any new attempt at genuine understanding of human psychopathology. It is suggested that the essence of abnormality is the bizarreness feature of behavior and cognitions. Neurotic or psychotic disorders differ from other types of behavioral disturbances (e.g., fear of animals, stuttering, thumb sucking, etc.) by the element of bizarreness. Unlike normal deviations, the bizarre behavioral symptoms should be regarded as coping devices adopted by an individual in a conscious and deliberate manner in response to an unbearable stress situation. Thus, it is claimed that the subject, lacking normal means of controlling stressful situations and reluctant or even unable to endure the resulting anguish, has little choice but to resort to bizarre symptoms. These selected reactions help the individual to cope both because of their high attentional demands, which make attention inavailable to the stress-related cognitions, and their dramatic effect on the social environment, which helps to reduce environmental demands. Before elaborating on this point of view, we will delineate four main criteria for distinguishing between a bizarre and an ordinary behavioral deviation: (1) rarity and strangeness of the symptom, (2) its effect on the individual's total adjustment, (3) mode of its onset, and (4) its impression on the social environment.

Rarity and Strangeness

Unlike normal behavioral deviations, which are quite common and usual, bizarre clinical symptoms are very rare, unusual, and strange. For example, while normal fears, such as fear of animals or darkness are quite frequent, bizarre or clinical phobias, such as agoraphobia or the chocolate phobia described earlier, are very unusual and rare (Agras, Sylvester, & Oliveau, 1969; Brandon, 1960; Ingram, 1961; Marks, 1969, 1973; Mathews, Gelder, & Johnston, 1981; Rachman & Seligman, 1976). Another example of rarity and strangeness is that of obsessive–compulsive symptoms (Brooker, 1982; Rachman & Hodgson, 1980). Rachman and Hodgson noted that a compulsive cleaner often exhibits a "bizarre mixture" of excessive cleanliness and dirtiness. The lavatory might be kept brightly clean and strongly disinfected while parts of the kitchen may be caked with month-old food remains. Patients of this type may wash their hands 200 times a day but leave their legs and feet unwashed for months and wear the same dirty underwear for weeks.

> *In one extreme case the patient had been trying to complete the cleaning of the motor of his second automobile for almost three years. . . . This immobilized car was kept in the well-protected garage, while the more valuable vehicle that was in daily use was left unsheltered in the street outside. (Rachman & Hodgson, 1980, p. 65)*

Effects on Total Activity or Adjustment

The criterion of rarity is not, however, sufficient for classifying behavior as abnormal. As was shown previously in the case of shoplifting (pp. 54–55), normal people may sometimes display very rare and strange behavior as well. In such a case however, the bizarre behavior is episodic. The necessary condition for considering behavior as abnormal is that it must have an unusual effect on the subject's total behavior. The neurotic or psychotic symptoms disturb the subject's daily functions to a great degree, and the individual pays unusual attention to them. This is demonstrated, for example, in cases of agoraphobia and of hysteric blindness or deafness (Coleman, Butcher, & Carson, 1980) as well as in the case of chocolate phobia mentioned earlier. Another interesting example of the extreme effect of a bizarre symptom on a subject's attention and total activity is the case of a young woman who had an obsessive fear that her heart might stop beating unless she concentrated on counting the beats (see Dollard & Miller, 1950). A further example concerns a patient who felt compelled to repeatedly rearrange objects on top of a bookcase to keep them from falling down on someone's head. However, by continuously rearranging the objects, she greatly increased the danger of their actually falling and hurting someone (Fenichel, 1946, p. 271). In reference to this case, Emmelkamp (1982) indicated that although there is little empirical support for the psychoanalytic point of view, one cannot help but be impressed by some of the clinical observations made by psychoanalysis, especially by Freud and by Fenichel. The most prominent element of all the cases cited here is the tremendous burden that these symptoms, unlike normal ones, place on a subject's attention and their devastating effects on his or her daily activities for a relatively prolonged period.

Mode of Onset

In most cases, the onset of an abnormal symptom is bizarre in that it is sudden and dramatic. There is a radical change in behavior for which the subject can give no plausible explanation. There is also no evidence for a significant environmental change that could justify the onset of the peculiar responses. For example, the onset of agoraphobia is usually associated with the occurrence of spontaneous and sudden panic attacks whose cause the patient is unaware of (Garssen, van Veenedaal, & Bloemink,

1983; Ley, 1985; Mathews et al. 1981). No traumatic or frightening event of the type required by the classical conditioning model occurs to explain the response (e.g., Buglass, Clarke, Henderson, Kreitman, & Presley, 1977; Jacobs & Nadel, 1985). Rachman (1978) notes that the process by which agoraphobia is developed remains a puzzle; we do not know yet "why the fear arose on the day that it did, at the time that it did. And why do they acquire it when on hundreds or thousands of previous exposures to the same set of stimuli, they remained unaffected?" (p. 196).

Even if a frightening event precedes the phobia, the intensity of the reaction and the extent of generalization are totally out of proportion (Jacobs & Nadel, 1985). Similarly, in the absence of any organic causes (Brady, 1966) or in response to motor accidents in which they are only slightly injured (R. W. White & Watt, 1981), patients may suddenly develop very unusual symptoms such as blindness. In some cases, such as the chocolate phobia described by Rachman (1978), the bizarre symptom may be developed gradually over an extended period of time. Nevertheless, the criterion "mode of onset" may still be applicable to these symptoms if the subjects can provide no plausible explanation for their queer behavior, and no evidence exists of significant change in the subject's environment that would justify the response.

Impression on the Social Environment

The first three criteria might be sufficient for distinguishing between normal and abnormal behavioral deviations. Nevertheless, another criterion is useful, namely, the evaluation of behavioral dysfunction by an ordinary normal individual. Although this criterion may be less reliable than the first three, it is mentioned in particular because traditional theories disassociate themselves from common sense experience. It appears that only in psychological literature may one encounter considerable confusion as to what is the essence of abnormality and under what exact conditions behavioral deviations should be considered abnormal (Coleman, Butcher, & Carson, 1984).

Among ordinary, naïve individuals who have no sophisticated psychological background, the confusion seems to be much less. An ordinary person would classify the patient with chocolate phobia as a clinical case with little hesitation. Similarly, if a woman with a successful business career suddenly became terrified of insects and bugs, so that she

> regularly inspect[ed] her desk and office for the presence of insects . . . afraid to sleep at night because she found a small bug on her bed covers 3 weeks ago . . . her fears have begun to interfere with her marriage, her career, and her maternal life (Jacobs & Nadel, 1985, p. 512)

most people would consider this response as queer. In contrast, they would not regard behavioral deviations such as a regular fear of insects as bizarre but rather as ordinary behavioral dysfunctions. The naïve individual might not be successful in making distinctions among various psychiatric deviations, apart from indicating the level of bizarreness. However, this state of affairs exists among practiced clinicians as well. For example, as will be shown later, diagnostic confusion with regard to classification of schizophrenia, affective disorders, and paranoia is not unusual. It will be demonstrated that this unfortunate condition stems, to a large extent, from a lack of realization of the essence of abnormality, namely, bizarreness. It may be worthwhile noting that to some extent our last criterion of bizarreness is consistent with Bandura's (1971a) claim that "the designation of behavior as pathological thus involves social judgement" (p. 3).

Thus, a pathological behavioral symptom may be defined as a bizarre behavioral response if it seems strange and rare; its mode of onset is sudden and dramatic with no plausible circumstances to justify it; the subject genuinely appears unaware of its causes; it poses an unusual burden on the individual's attention and adjustment resources; and it is highly peculiar to the social environment.

It seems, then, that the four criteria of bizarre symptoms discussed here cover the entire range of abnormal symptoms, namely, hysteria, clinical phobia, obsessive–compulsive disorders, anxiety neuroses, affective disorders, and schizophrenic reactions. It is these types of responses that the psychobizarreness theory aims at explaining.

THE NATURE AND ROLE OF REPRESSION
IN NEUROSES

Freud's Options for Explaining Bizarre Symptoms

As was stated, Freud developed the concepts of repression and unconsciousness essentially because his patients could not provide a plausible explanation for their bizarre symptoms. Thus, Freud observed two important behavioral phenomena in his patients' behavior, namely, bizarreness and unawareness. This observation could have led him to one of these three conclusions:

1. The state of unconsciousness preceded the symptoms and was among the prime causes of their formation.

2. Unconsciousness and the bizarre symptoms occurred simultaneously, brought about by an independent factor, such as conditioning events or neurochemical changes, over which the subject had no control.

3. The bizarre symptoms preceded the phenomenon of unawareness, and they were in fact among the prime causes of the formation of a state of unawareness.

Freud chose the first alternative and used clinical case studies to justify his position (Fenichel, 1946; H. B. Lewis, 1981; Singer, 1970; Wachtel, 1977; R. W. White, 1964). In our opinion, this choice was the fatal theoretical mistake made by Freud and his followers. In fact, given Freud's deterministic, mechanistic view of the human being, he could not have made a better choice. Moreover, within the context of this alternative, Freud had no better option than to attribute the root of his patients' bizarre responses to repressed traumatic events that had taken place sometime during early childhood and were stored in the unconscious. He could have attributed the causes of the symptoms to the individuals' recent stressful life events. However, he did not even consider the possibility that the symptoms might have been caused by external factors. This was due both to his own strong deterministic convictions and to the lack of scientific progress in the field of psychopathology at that time, particularly in the area of stress.

This suggestion would also raise many difficult questions, such as why patients did not articulate troublesome events if they had taken place only recently, and why the same type of stress may cause different pathological reactions in different individuals (these questions will be dealt with in chapter 8). Moreover, it may be argued that Freud's clinical setting was a "manufacturer" of misleading information that prevented him from realizing that he had made the wrong theoretical choice. The demand characteristics of the clinical setting generated pressure on the patient to comply with the therapist's expectations, namely, to make up stories of stressful childhood events. At the same time, the patients themselves had their own reasons to collaborate with Freud. If indeed our assumption that they consciously adopted the response is valid, then the patients would have had a strong need for self-deceptive information in order to remove tension associated with this knowledge. They would have had a great need for appropriate material to develop a system of belief that they were not responsible for their bizarre actions. The Freudian clinical setting seems to have been an ideal condition for this purpose since, apart from some secondary gains and expectations of real help, a respected therapist led them to the conclusion that they were being "betrayed" by some interior psychological mechanisms over which they had no direct control. This analysis may perhaps explain why patients spent so much of their energy, time, and money in such therapy despite its low therapeutic benefits (see p. 61).

Behaviorist and Medical Model Approaches

The abovementioned second hypothesis, namely, that both unawareness and bizarre symptoms are simultaneously caused by a third factor, represents more or less the points of view of the behaviorist's and the medical models. Behaviorists have always claimed that deviant responses develop through conditioning events, and at least the earlier learning investigators contended that conditioning takes place in an automatic manner and in absence of the subject's awareness (e.g., see P. W. Dixon & Oakes, 1965; Greenspoon, 1955; T. D. Kennedy, 1970, 1971). Similarly, medical models attribute the development of psychiatric symptoms to a mechanistic factor (i.e., neurochemical changes) of which the subject has no direct awareness. In later chapters it will be demonstrated that these hypotheses have no more scientific support than does psychoanalysis.

Since neither the Freudian approach nor the other mechanistic points of view succeeded in proving their theses, we suggest abandoning these theories and exploring instead the abovementioned third hypothesis.

Approach of Psychobizarreness Theory: Repression as a Product of the Consciousness

The basic assumption of the psychobizarreness theory is that both repression and the phenomenon of unconsciousness follow the onset of bizarre symptoms. It is argued that bizarre symptoms are consciously and deliberately chosen by the patient, and that repression is not the cause but rather the by-product of the symptoms. We assume that all feelings of distress, particularly anxiety and depression, result from the presence of negative and intolerable cognitions in the focus of attention. An individual with no means of reducing a highly stressful situation and unable to either bear the stress or disregard it is likely to take drastic measures to eliminate the emotion-arousing cognitions from his or her attentional domain. Thus, it can be assumed that one of the prime functions of bizarre symptoms is to free the subject's attention from the dominating negative cognitions, thereby avoiding or reducing the feelings of anxiety or depression. The bizarre symptoms cause feelings of distress as well, but they are less costly than the feelings the patient would have without them. As will be discussed later, in psychoses withdrawal of attention constitutes the most important and almost the only function of the bizarre symptoms. By contrast, in neuroses this is only one of their prime functions. Their more important goal, which will be elaborated in chapter 8, is to achieve control over the real sources of the stress by pathological means, as the individual has no better coping devices at his or her disposal. Once bizarre symptoms are adopted, self-deceptive mechanisms are activated and the subject succeeds in deceiving himself or herself concerning his or her conscious role in producing the symptoms.

Distractive Value of a Stimulus

Two important concepts of the psychobizarreness theory are the distractive value of a stimulus and willpower. The first concept refers to the fact that stimuli are not equally powerful in attracting an individual's attention. The distractive value of a stimulus is its power to eliminate from one's attention other stimuli or cognitions that currently occupy it and to prevent them from resuming their control. The stronger the power of the stimulus to attract the individual's attention and the greater its ability to prevent rival stimuli from renewing their control on one's attention, the stronger its distraction value. The characteristics that determine the distraction value of a stimulus are its degree of strangeness, newness, danger, and complexity; its importance to the individual's needs and his or her general life conditions and goals; and the behavioral demands that the stimulus or activity impose on the individual.

An example of the distractive value of a stimulus may be seen in the act of driving on a highway: The automatic act of driving needs very little attention, and it cannot significantly prevent the driver from thinking about various matters or carrying out activities such as talking or listening to a radio. A medium level of distraction would be reached upon approaching a dangerous intersection. Attention becomes so intensively occupied that very little room is left for other cognitions. A high level of distraction would occur if the driver became involved in an accident. Such an event might have a distractive value so powerful that it could totally eliminate cognitions that previously occupied the driver's attention, and it might also prevent their regaining control for some time. It is known that in highly distractive conditions, people sometimes feel no pain despite severe injury. For example, a family is injured in an accident, an individual member of the family may not feel pain if he or she is actively involved in attempting to save the others. The individual's attentional channels may become so intensely occupied by the rescue activities and the severe conditions of the family that the sensations of pain have no chance of gaining access to them. It should be noted that this last suggestion is a new hypothesis, although many investigators have emphasized the importance of distraction in reducing feelings of pain (see McCaul & Malott's review, 1984). Another example of high distractive value is the hearing of very unusual good or bad news—a person who has just been informed that he or she has won a tremendous amount of money or a sexually deprived person who is exposed to a very attractive nude person of the opposite sex. Stimuli have differing distraction value for each individual; let us examine this notion of distraction with respect to bizarre behaviors.

Distractive Value of Bizarre Symptoms

A subject may achieve distraction in a self-directed manner as was done, for example, by Frankl (1968) (p. 84). However, the stress-producing stimuli may so powerfully control the subject's cognition that his or her internal resources would not be sufficient to eliminate them from consciousness. Concentrated cognitive effort or willpower may be enlisted in order to actively prevent anxiety- or depression-provoking inputs of the external or internal environment (negative thoughts, memories, or information) from gaining access to one's consciousness. However, this solution is very costly in terms of energy required, and it cannot therefore be an adequate, long-lasting solution for a chronic high level of stress that is beyond the subject's normal coping ability. The internal cognitive effort (i.e., willpower) to set up a barrier to the undesirable input can be reinforced by occupying oneself with attention-demanding tasks (work, reading, etc.). However, these options are not always available, and even if they are, their distraction value may not be high enough for coping with a very high level of stress. Apart from committing suicide or continuing to suffer, the best solution for alleviating the burden of emotional distress is to adopt bizarre behaviors or cognitions. These symptoms have a very high distractive value since their load on a subject's attentional capacity is very high. The higher the level of bizarreness, the higher its distractive value. For example, the chocolate phobia demanded an unusual level of attention form the woman who developed it (Rachman & Seligman, 1976). She constantly thought about it and spent a lot of energy avoiding stimuli that might remind her of the feared object. Her fear of chocolate kept her in the same state of distraction in which she would have been had she thought a bomb were planted on every corner. It is claimed that among other beneficial outcomes she derived from her symptoms, these cognitions, and related fearful responses they elicited, occupied her attentional channels so intensively that they helped her to avoid more terrible and unbearable cognitions that for her were extremely intolerable. The bizarre symptoms freed her from more costly emotional consequences (see pp. 185–186 for a more detailed discussion of the case).

This conceptualization of abnormal symptoms is consistent with the position of some family theories. Some of these investigators claim that the "sick" family members, especially children, serve to deflect attention from underlying conflicts in the family relationships. For example, by developing anorexia symptoms, the "sick" member provides an alternative focus of attention, thereby reducing tension among family members (Minuchin, 1974; Minuchin et al., 1975).

However, the bizarre symptoms would not have much distractive value if the subject remained aware of his active role in their development. They might cause feelings of great discomfort and even anxiety. Thus, it is essential that the subject use some mechanism for misleading himself or developing a belief that he was not consciously responsible for the process of symptom formation. It is argued, therefore, that the adoption of bizarre symptoms is simultaneously accompanied by several factors or mechanisms that result in the state of unconsciousness. The neurotic mechanisms that seem to be responsible for covering up the forbidden solution that the individual has chosen will be clarified soon, and those used by psychotic subjects will be elaborated upon later. Let us first discuss the subject's emotional and cognitive condition when making this decision.

Psychological State at the Stage of Adoption

The idea that bizarre symptoms are consciously and intentionally adopted may bring to mind the picture of a malingerer consciously faking the symptoms of a disease. One might imagine that the subject is in a relatively calm emotional condition and in a normal state of cognitive awareness during the stage at which the decision to adopt the bizarre symptom is made. However, some research and clinical evidence suggests the opposite. The subject seems to be in a high level of emotional arousal, in strong conflict as to whether to adopt the "crazy" behavior, and in a reduced state of awareness. For example, data from various sources (e.g., see Garssen et al., 1983; Ley, 1985), show that the onset of agoraphobic symptoms is associated with the occurrence of spontaneous panic attacks. This mode of reaction is illustrated in the autobiographical report of an agoraphobic, to be discussed in chapter 8, as well as in another case study of a subject who developed hysterical blindness (R. W. White & Watt, 1981, pp. 214–216). Consistent with these data, Coleman et al. (1984) outlined three stages in the adoption of hysterical symptoms. In the first stage, the subject wants to escape from an unpleasant stressful situation. In the second stage, a fleeting wish to be sick in order to avoid the situation is experienced. Then, under additional or continued stress the individual eventually adopts a physical ailment.

We believe that the psychological process in developing bizarre neurotic symptoms is in some way similar to the psychological state of a person shortly before committing suicide. Research data show the severity of neurotic symptomatology and the serious-ness of suicidal behavior to be significantly related to stress level (see Harder, Strauss, Kokes, Ritzler, & Gift, 1980; Paykel, 1976, 1978). It also appears that in both situations the subject is in a high state of emotional arousal and conflict before making the crucial decision. With respect to suicide, Coleman et al. (1984) noted that "the irreversible choice is made when they are alone and in a state of severe psychological stress, unable to see their problems objectively or to evaluate alternative courses of action" (p. 326). Like the would-be suicide victim, the neurotic subject must pay a high price, although not as high as paid by the potential suicide, for the decision to adopt bizarre symptoms. The price is paid in terms of expected social embarrassment and limitation of freedom or adjustment ability. For example, agoraphobic symptoms, the peculiar phobias like fear of chocolate or vegetables (Rachman & Seligman, 1976), or hysterical blindness are very embarrassing socially and disruptive to overall ongoing adjustment. Thus, deciding whether or not to adopt neurotic symptoms must be quite a difficult task emotionally and cognitively. This is consistent with research findings (Donelson, 1973; Janis, 1982; Janis & Mann, 1977) demonstrating that a person who has to make an important decision experiences marked emotional arousal. However, it is very likely that once the decision is made or immediately after the adoption stage, the subject's level of emotional arousal is significantly reduced. The subject feels much better since he or she is no longer in a state of cognitive unclarity. In addition, the symptom successfully distracts the subject's attention from the problems that are the real cause of anxiety and, as will be discussed later, gives the subject substantial control over the source of stress.

At the stage of adoption, it appears that the whole process of decision making takes place at a very low level of awareness. Awareness seems to be low because the decision is made when attention is heavily occupied by the stress-related cognitions. It seems obvious that stress causes a significant reduction in the subject's attentional capacity. For example, Reason and Lucas (1984), in their attempt to apply the absentmindedness theory to the shoplifting phenomenon, showed that many of the subjects accused of shoplifting were involved in stressful life events that heavily occupied their attentional resources. Moreover, as research and clinical evidence suggests (Anisman & LaPierre, 1982; Coleman et al., 1984; Janis, 1982), stress may cause biological deterioration either directly or indirectly by causing sleeplessness or loss of appetite. As a result, the subject's level of awareness and ability to make rational judgments are further reduced.

Furthermore, such mental and biological conditions increase the likelihood that the subject will respond in a manner inappropriate and possibly destructive to his or her own physical or social environment. There is then a significant increase in the probability of destructive events, such as motor accidents (e.g., see case study on hysterical blindness in R. W. White, 1964, pp. 243–245) or other disasters, as a result of absentmindedness (Reason, 1983, 1984a, 1984b; Reason & Lucas, 1984; Reason & Mycielska, 1982) as well as physical illness (the strong relationship between stress and illness is well established in the research literature). It is possible that the occurrence of these stress-producing events is due not only to absentmindedness or impaired judgment, but that the subject himself plays an active part in their creation either by adopting a careless attitude, by intensifying minor stressful events that happening accidentally, or even by deliberately exposing himself or herself to situations in which the potential for such events is high. As will be demonstrated, these events are used by the subject for purposes of self-deception and choice of symptoms. At any rate, with respect to awareness, these stressful events, irrespective of whether they were caused by absent-mindedness, carelessness, or purposely, place an additional burden on the subject's already heavily loaded attentional capacity. Thus, all these factors are likely to reduce the individual's awareness at the stage that the bizarre symptom is adopted to an extremely low level.

There seem to be two modes by which bizarre symptoms are adopted: dramatic and gradual onset. In the dramatic mode, the symptom emerges in its full intensity all at once, without any warning signals. In the second mode, the symptom develops gradually over an extended period. For example, the bizarre chocolate phobia reached its full intensity over a number of years (Rachman & Seligman, 1976). We believe that each step in this gradual intensification of the symptom is taken when the subject's stress level increases or when the bizarreness level of the symptom is no longer sufficient to cope with the stressful demands. It is also possible that the reinforcement or controllability benefit that the subject derives from the symptom plays an important role in this process. Presumably the level of awareness is lower in the gradual than in the dramatic mode, and this may be one of the reasons for the tendency of some subjects to prefer the former mode.

A State of Unconsciousness

As was stated, the distractive value and, to some extent, the controllability value (this will be discussed later in this chapter) of the bizarre symptoms are not of much benefit if lack of awareness regarding the subject's own deliberate involvement is not achieved. The subject must "bury" the secret of his or her involvement deep in memory or the symptoms would lose their value for coping with stress. Two sets of factors seem to be involved in producing this state of unconsciousness or unawareness:

1. Memory-inhibiting factors, which deal with the subject's immediate situation and serve as a barrier to the immediate knowledge of his or her involvement.
2. Self-deceptive mechanisms, which are aimed at producing a prolonged or permanent state of unawareness of self-involvement.

Memory-Inhibiting Factors

As has been stated, the decision to adopt bizarre symptoms apparently takes place at a low level of awareness. This would mean that rehearsal of the anxiety-provoking information, in the process of transference from short- to long-term memory, must already be quite weak and limited. This is expected to be the case particularly with respect to the gradual mode of symptom adoption. In addition, there seem to be three main factors that inhibit retrieval of this information from the long-term memory to consciousness.

The first factor concerns the emotional and cognitive changes that apparently take place immediately after the symptoms are adopted. It is assumed that the symptom causes a rapid and substantial reduction of the subject's emotional distress and cognitive unclarity. Moreover, sometimes as is the case with fugue, where the patient escapes a stressful environment (see case study on pp. 122–124), the adopted symptom causes significant changes in the subject's physical and social environment as well. Thus, consistent with the cue-dependent theory of forgetting (Hulse, Egeth, & Deese, 1980), it is claimed that these stimulus changes inhibit memory of the anxiety-evoking cognition. Indeed, consistent with this line of thought, Bower (1981) demonstrated that a change in the subject's emotional state may drastically reduce recall. Subjects displayed significantly less recall of a list of words learned under one emotional state (happy or sad mood) if tested under a different mood condition.

The second factor concerns the feelings of well-being and reduced tension the subject feels, as compared with the state of intensive arousal, helplessness, and despair felt shortly before the onset of the symptoms. These positive feelings are likely to provide the subject with some moral justification for the decision to fake the symptom and encourage a strong intentional resistance to relating to stimuli that might directly or indirectly remind the subject of how the symptom was originated. The subject would actively avoid thinking, talking, or exposing himself or herself to these stimuli, as repressors regularly do with regard to anxiety-arousing stimuli (see pp. 26–28). This theoretical position is also consistent with the notion of directed forgetting (Bjork, 1972; Erdelyi, 1974; Erdelyi & Goldberg, 1979; Geiselman, Bjork, & Fishman, 1983; Kihlstrom, 1983). As has been indicated, in Freudian theory this inhibiting factor would be designated as suppression or repression, according to Erdelyi and Goldberg's (1979) interpretation of Freud's theory. In our theory, this factor is regarded as one of the normal distractive devices.

Another important factor that helps to deepen the state of unconsciousness is self-induced hypnosis. The strong relationship between hypnosis and psychopathology was recognized by many investigators (Kihlstrom, 1979, 1984). In Freudian theory, hypnosis was viewed as an unconscious phenomenon achieved by activation of the unconscious mind. However, the new conceptualization of hypnosis recently suggested by Hariman in his "concentration theory of hypnosis" (Hariman, 1980, 1982; see also Leuba, 1960) negates this traditional point of view. According to this theory, the hypnotic state is attained through subjects' willingness and ability to concentrate exclusively and intensely on the hypnotist's suggestions. If conflicting ideas enter their consciousness, they may activate their willpower to shift their attention away from the ideas so that the hypnotist's suggestions remain the sole cognition in the subject's consciousness. Hypnotic capacity is latent in every individual, and research evidence shows that subjects are as capable of hypnotizing themselves as of being hypnotized by others. Hariman (1982), as well as other investigators (Spanos, 1981; Stam, Radtke-Bodorik, & Spanos, 1980), conceptualized hypnotic amnesia as an active cognitive process in which the subject deliberately fails to attend to the material to be remembered. Hariman's explanation of hypnosis in attentional terms is consistent with much of the relatively recent empirical evidence (see review by Sheehan & McConkey, 1982). These findings, as indicated by Hariman (1982), pose insuperable difficulties to Freud's conception of the unconscious in general and repression in particular. Thus, in recent years hypnosis has come to be conceived as a state of "superattention" rather than as reduced attention or a phenomenon controlled by the unconscious. In line with this conceptualization, it may be argued that bizarre behaviors provide an excellent stimulus for self-hypnosis because of their high potential to focus and occupy one's attention. In other words, a person who believes, for example, that a piece of chocolate is a very dangerous object or that he or she has become blind, then the chocolate or the blindness should be for the person a stimulus with very high potential for attentional arousal. The active concentration on this bizarre cognition along with the attentional demand it requires and the responses it elicits would be so strong that it would enable the patient to exclude any disruptive thought from consciousness. Thus, the "crazy behavior" not only enables the patient to distract himself or herself from the unbearable stress, but it also helps the patient forget his or her own responsibility for behaving in such a bizarre manner.

Self-Deceptive Mechanisms

As stated previously, the bizarre symptoms cannot reach their maximum distractive and/or controllability efficiency if the subject retains knowledge of his or her active involvement in faking the symptoms. The memory-inhibiting factors seem to be quite efficient in securing the goal of unawareness in the period immediately after the adoption stage. However, although they may remain in effect as long as the symptom persists, they are not sufficient for achieving prolonged persistence of unawareness. Humans are rational creatures, and as such, they themselves, or others, may pose threatening questions. If questions remain unanswered as to why the individual's behavior is so different from in the past or why his or her behavior is so different from that of other people, the person may be reminded of the deception. Thus, the neurotic patient must develop a misleading belief in order to depress self-threatening thoughts and cope adequately with anxiety-provoking questions. It is suggested that this objective is attained by the operation of self-deceptive mechanisms. This term refers to the use of the cognitive system for perceiving and interpreting reality in a distorted way, thereby strengthening the barriers to the subject's attentional domain in a more permanent manner. The manipulation of the self-deceptive mechanism is aimed at keeping the individual's most secret information away from the attentional zone, thereby maximizing the ability of the bizarre symptoms to distract and control the stress-relating stimuli.

A deliberate distortion of reality for the purpose of developing a self-deceptive belief is not beyond a subject's ability. It is well established that an individual's emotional condition, his or her motives, beliefs, and values may radically affect the way he or she perceives or interprets reality. Input from the outside world is integrated and coordinated in such a way that information will have the meaning the individual desires. He or she attends to the useful aspects of reality, but ignores or modifies the others (Bruner, 1973; Buckhout, 1974; R. J. Davidson, 1980; D. G. Miller & E. F. Loftus, 1976; Neisser, 1967, 1976).

The self-deceptive beliefs seem to be of two kinds. Subjects may either recognize that something is wrong with their behavior but attribute its causes to some internal or external agency beyond their control or else deny that their behavior is dysfunctional by inventing a fictitious reason that seemingly explains the peculiar responses. We term these two self-deceptive mechanisms *projection* and *intellectualization,* respectively.

Before elaborating somewhat on these two mechanism, we would like to delineate the main differences between them and the Freudian concepts on this matter. Although in psychoanalysis repression is considered as a primary defense and the remaining defenses as secondary ones (Erdelyi & Goldberg, 1979; Fischer & Pipp, 1984; Maddi, 1980), all have the same goal: to cope with interior stresses by keeping them away from the conscious domain. If repression fails to execute its defensive function, the secondary defenses come to its aid. For example, by employing projection or intellectualization, either unacceptable impulses or thoughts that have succeeded in breaking through the conscious zone are attributed to external sources (projection) or their personal threat is neutralized by various cognitive means (intellectualization). These may include cutting off or isolating their affective charge (Coleman et al., 1984, p. 65), inventing a socially acceptable fictitious reason to explain them (Maddi, 1980, p. 299), or taking the emotional conflicts into the sphere of intellect and, thereby, divesting them of affective and personal meaning (R. W. White & Watt, 1981, pp. 174–175).

In contrast, in the psychobizarreness theory the mechanisms of projection and intellectualization are not aimed at coping with unbearable stress. This function is assigned to the bizarre symptoms, which are expected to distract the individual's attention and gain some control over the sources of stress. The self-deception mechanisms are aimed at creating appropriate conditions so that the bizarre symptoms would be able to do their job. Moreover, while in psychoanalysis the secondary defenses are not necessarily present in all types of neuroses (e.g., hysteria) and come into effect mainly when repression is insufficient as a defensive maneuver, this is not the case in psychobizarreness theory. Projection or intellectualization must unexceptionally accompany all bizarre symptoms. Some form of false belief must be developed in order for consciousness to be misled.

In an attempt to achieve this goal, the cognitive system is activated in a malformed way. In both projection and intellectualization, attention may be directed to those parts of reality that are congruent with the false belief, while the incongruent elements are ignored. The meaning of the perceptual events may be modified to agree with the belief or the subject may engage in an active search for self-deceptive information. For example, hysterical patients with bizarre complaints of pain or fear of heart attack may direct their attention to body sensations, overly amplify the significance of minor pains that normally would pass unnoticed, and thereby, find "evidence" to strengthen the false complaint. Moreover, as will be elaborated in chapter 8, subjects often choose symptoms that have some basis in reality, thereby facilitating the formation of the self-deceptive belief. Thus, a subject experiencing an unbearable degree of life stress, such as intense marital conflict, may take advantage of an accident in which he or she unexpectedly or unintentionally becomes involved and develop bizarre symptoms, such as blindness. The patient may then use a slight injury from the accident and attribute his or her symptoms to it. (This is a summary of an actual case study; for more information see R. W. White, 1964, pp. 243–245. An additional case study of the same nature is described later in this book, pp. 187–192; see also p. 114). In a similar manner, a person accidentally involved in an emotionally arousing situation may deliberately intensify the unpleasant emotion to the point of terror, attributing the source of his or her bizarre response to the situation. This idea is consistent with the arousal-attribution model mentioned by Emmelkamp (1982). To illustrate this point, Emmelkamp used a hypothetical example of a woman in a state of marital distress who experiences emotional arousal while shopping in a supermarket. The woman may be tempted to take advantage of this emotional arousal by intensifying it and attributing it to the crowded supermarket. "Blaming crowding may provide a more acceptable explanation for experienced arousal than facing her marital unhappiness and the possibility of a divorce" (Emmelkamp, 1982, p. 36). Emmelkamp expressed the view that such misattribution may account for the development of agoraphobia in a number of cases. Another way of using projection might be to actively search out evidence to reinforce the self-deceptive belief. As will be demonstrated in our discussion of psychosis, this self-deceptive strategy is carried to the extreme by paranoid subjects. However, this mode of reaction may characterize neurotic patients as well. For example, hypochondriac patients may simultaneously consult a number of physicians to seek self-deceptive information (e.g., see Davison & Neale, 1982). In a similar fashion, patients with some psychoanalytic knowledge may, ironically, take advantage of this and attribute the causes of their bizarre behavior to "unconscious" traumatic childhood events. A case study illustrating this is described in chapter 8. Moreover, these patients may prefer psychoanalytically oriented therapists because such therapists can supply a wealth of "evidence" to support their tendency to attribute their behavior to factors over which they have no direct control. The need to gain supportive evidence for the self-deception may be so strong that in combination with anticipation of secondary gains such as sympathy, comfort, or acceptance, it motivates a patient to spend a great deal of time, energy, and money on such therapy, despite the prospect of little therapeutic gain (Erwin, 1980; Gross, 1979; Rachman & Wilson, 1980). This may be more characteristic of subjects with a high level of intelligence or education since, as will be discussed in chapter 8, they may have more difficulty with distorting reality. A prestigious, dynamically oriented therapist may facilitate the process of self-deception by providing a "scientific basis" for deception. In a similar manner, now that behaviorist theories have become generally known, a person with agoraphobic symptoms may use his knowledge of psychology to attribute his fears to conditioning mechanisms (see studies mentioned on pp. 146–148).

Another projective device likely to be used, especially by less sophisticated subjects, is simply to attribute the symptom to an unknown source. Subjects may lead themselves to believe that it is unlikely that they could intentionally adopt such self-destructive bizarre symptoms. They may come to the conclusion that they must be "mentally ill" or "crazy," which means that the cause of their behavior should be attributed to sources other than themselves (a case study describing such a possibility is reported by Coleman et al., 1980, p. 216).

Usually, intellectualization is used by patients with obsessive–compulsive symptoms. For example, a 14-year-old Israeli patient I treated developed an unusual praying ritual in combination with a few other compulsive behaviors. The patient came from a nonobservant family, and before this ritual began, he had never performed religious activities, including prayer. The patient denied that his behaviors were deviant or irrational by insisting that he was doing this in order to protect his parents and two brothers from danger. He argued that many people had recently been killed and wounded by terrorist activities and motor accidents and that the prayers would help protect his family. A similar case study demonstrating the use of intellectualization, described by Coleman (1964, p. 225), is that of a 13-year-old boy who engaged in compulsive ritualistic washing due to guilt over masturbation:

> When asked to explain his concern regarding cleanliness, he stated that he realized that he washed more than other boys, but that in his case there were real reasons. He believed that his skin was of such a texture that it retained dirt and germs, and he therefore was forced to wash and scrub himself. (Coleman, 1964, p. 225)

As stated in psychoanalytic doctrine, intellectualization refers to a group of defensive processes (R. W. White & Watt, 1981, p. 174). One of its dominant versions is a situation where the conscious is continuously and heavily engaged by philosophical thoughts. Although these thoughts are formulated in quite general terms, they are closely related to the subject's stressful problems. We believe that the main function of these defensive processes is to strengthen the distractive function of the bizarre symptoms. The distractive value of these symptoms may not be high enough to seal off all attentional leaks so that the stressful thoughts may succeed in gaining limited access to the attentional domain. In such a case, a sophisticated individual may shift these thoughts to general cosmopolitan, religious, scientific, or political problems that relate to his personal anxiety-provoking problems only very remotely. Thus, using Murphy's (1970) descriptive terminology for self-deception it may be said that these patients continuously insert "noise in their cognitive system." Attention is continuously occupied by distractive philosophical thoughts rather than by the patient's real problem. It should be noted, however, that usually these subjects also use intellectualization in the previously described way. They attribute their symptoms to some fictitious reason that "necessitates" these responses.

In accord with psychoanalysis, which also attributes defense operations to normally functioning individuals, it seems that self-deceptive maneuvers are not at all unique to subjects with bizarre symptoms. This is demonstrated, for example, in the classic book *When Prophecy Fails* by Festinger, Riecken, and Schachter (1956), where false belief was developed to account for the failure of their prophecy. With normal people, however, the self-deceptive operations do not involve prolonged, gross, and rigorous distortion of reality. They are part of the normal subject's general coping strategy for adjusting to demands of reality rather than devices for defending the use of bizarre symptoms. The subject temporarily perceives reality from a more convenient angle until the stress ceases or is overcome, as was done, for example, by Frankl (see p. 84). A normally functioning individual never adopts a prolonged state of unawareness as a coping strategy. A subject who appears unaware may have forgotten the original factors that formulated the deviant behavior. This point will be elaborated later, when we discuss the frequent observation that subjects may be unaware of the original circumstances that formulated their normal fearful responses. As will be demonstrated, psychoanalytically oriented investigators also attribute this type of fear to repressed traumatic events (e.g., see Moss, 1960).

CONCLUSIONS

In conclusion, there are sharp differences between the psychoanalytic and the psychobizarreness conception of the phenomenon of unconsciousness. In psychoanalytic doctrine, consciousness and unconsciousness are regarded as two different psychological entities operating by different rules and even, according to some investigators, associated with two distinct areas in the brain (see p. 58). In psychobizarreness theory, unconsciousness is conceived merely as a psychological state of unawareness produced by sophisticated conscious maneuvers. These operations consist of attentional level reduced primarily by adoption of symptoms with highly distractive value, memory-inhibiting factors, normal forgetting processes, and self-deceptive devices by which self-misleading beliefs are developed.

Moreover, in contrast to the mechanistic-automatic conceptualizations of both psychoanalysts and behaviorists, who play down the role of the conscious in determining bizarre symptoms, psychobizarreness theory views the conscious as the agent responsible for creation and maintenance of bizarre behavior. Thus, the conscious not only initiates the adoption of the symptom, but it never ceases its active involvement in determining the subject's behavior. It continues to play some minimal role in determining the continued occurrence of the pathological behavior even after the adoption stage and the development of the state of unawareness. The attentional domain is never completely sealed off, no matter how extreme the distractive value of the symptom. In other words, the emission of the pathological responses never become entirely automatic. The impaired consciousness continues to assess reality and the subject's needs and to manipulate his or her pathological responses accordingly. For example, patients exhibiting hysterical epilepsy rarely, if ever, injure themselves and have attacks only in the presence of others (see Coleman et al., 1984). Similarly, hysterically blind individuals avoid walking in front of cars, tripping over furniture, and so on (e.g., see Brady, 1966; Janet, 1929), although they appear to be genuinely unaware of the causes of their symptoms. Similarly, inasmuch as an undifferentiated, automatic agoraphobic response might place an impossible burden on the subject's capacity to continue functioning in daily life (since it would mean indefinite self-imprisonment), the consciousness invents excuses for deceiving oneself and/or others, thereby giving the person greater control of the degree and timing of the fear response. Clinical and research data (see Rachman, 1984a, 1984b; and p. 184 in this book) show that agoraphobics can control their fear when accompanied by a talisman or a spouse or when having access to safety (e.g., sitting near the door in a restaurant). Furthermore, research findings demonstrate that at least some schizophrenic patients can manipulate at will the emission of pathological responses according to their coping needs (B. M. Braginsky & D. D. Braginsky, 1971; B. M. Braginsky, D. D. Braginsky, & Ring, 1969; B. M. Braginsky, Grosse, & Ring, 1966; Fontana & Klein, 1968; Fontana, Klein, Lewis, & Levine, 1968; F. S. Kelly, Farina, & Mosher, 1971; Price, 1972; see also Ryan & Neale, 1973, who found inconsistent results). May and Simpson (1980a, p. 1197) noted that schizophrenic patients are to some extent aware of their illness, and that they are never entirely and continuously psychotic.

Finally, we believe that awareness and unawareness should not be conceived in terms of all or nothing, as psychoanalysis seems to imply, but rather as a continuum. In addition, we have some doubt whether a clear boundary exists between a neurotic subject and a malingerer. As stated, the neurotic symptoms have two main functions, distraction and controllability. It is likely that some subjects may exhibit bizarre behavior in response to a level of stress that, although quite high, is still not high enough to motivate them to perform the necessary activities for attaining "unawareness." However, to the extent that the symptoms are successful in controlling the sources of stress, the reinforcement gained may lead malingerers, in the long run, to develop a belief that their bizarre symptoms (e.g., blindness) are real. This position is consistent with the point of view both of Grosz and Zimmerman (1965) and of Brady (1966). Grosz and Zimmerman (1965) indicated that there is "no way of proving either hysteria or malingering" and that both conditions may "co-exist in the same patient at the same time" (p. 257). Similarly, Brady strengthened this point of view, stating that "it is more accurate to say that hysteria and malingering are on a continuum, there being some elements of both apparent in almost all cases" (p. 321). Brady indicated further that patient status along the hysteria–malingering continuum is not fixed but may change by variables such as exposure to other psychiatric patients, therapeutic maneuvers, changes in secondary gains, etc. Both Grosz and Zimmerman (1965) and Brady (1966) use the same case study of hysterical blindness to demonstrate their point of view.

8

Choice of Neurotic Symptoms

OVERVIEW

Perhaps one of the most fundamental and difficult problems unresolved in psychopathology is the choice of symptoms. The mechanistic conceptualization of human beings has led investigators to believe that choice of symptoms is automatically determined. However, no evidence as yet supports this claim. In psychoanalytic theory, the selection of symptoms is controlled by unconscious processes and is strongly related to the concept of fixation, which it is assumed, takes place during psychosexual development (e.g., see Emmelkamp, 1982; Fenichel, 1946; D. Shapiro, 1965; R. W. White, 1964). However, the validity of the psychosexual stages, particularly with respect to choice of symptoms, has never received consistent support (e.g., see Emmelkamp, 1982). Moreover, neither psychoanalysis nor other models have been able to explain why two of the three major neurotic bizarre symptoms, namely, hysteria and clinical phobia, are much more prevalent among females and members of low socioeconomic classes than among males and members of high socioeconomic classes. Psychoanalysis can bring no convincing evidence to show that these subjects experience stronger psychosexual fixations. Similarly, obsessive–compulsive disorders are equally common among the two sexes (H. B. Lewis, 1981), but "there is no evidence whatever to support the psychoanalytic theory that relates anal eroticism to the obsessive personality and to the development of the obsessive neurosis" (Emmelkamp, 1982, p. 188; see also Pollak, 1979). Furthermore, the evidence reviewed in this chapter shows that the attempts of many investigators to relate the choice of symptoms to personality or constitutional factors has gained very little support.

Thus, a new theoretical approach seems to be needed to explain this phenomenon. Our basic assumption is that the direct causes of pathological responses are the subject's current stress experiences. This suggestion may hardly sound novel, and naturally a question may be raised as to why different individuals have different responsiveness to stress. How do stress and different forms of pathology interact? In order to find satisfactory answers to these questions, it is proposed that we abandon the mechanistic conception of this process. It does not seem likely that such an abrupt and dramatic change in the subject's behavior, which sometimes involves very complicated and organized activities, as in fugue reaction (see pp. 122–124) is controlled by automatic mechanisms. At any rate, in view of the lack of scientific progress, we suggest, like Adler (1933/1964), who conceptualized neurosis as "a creative act, and not a reversion to infantile and atavistic forms" (p. 131), that the selection of symptoms be regarded as a decision-making process in which the conscious plays a dominant role, as in any other action of choice. This does not mean that the choice is made with a high level of awareness or that patients are free to choose any symptom they desire. On the contrary, the subject's cognitive clarity at the stage of decision-making is very low, and as the level of stress increases, so does the bizarreness of the chosen symptom intensify, as in the case of psychosis (see chapter 14).

It appears, then, that a subject overwhelmed by a stressful situation is likely to choose bizarre symptoms that greatly enhance his or her coping maneuvers. However, the selection action is not randomly based, but is guided by three major principles: controllability, saliency-availability, and cost–benefit considerations. The first principle indicates that the choice of a symptom is largely determined by the specific demands of the stressful situation. The second principle states that among the symptoms that can fulfill the distractability and controllability demands, those that, for various reasons, gain more saliency in the individual's attention, are more likely to be adopted. The principle of cost–benefit denotes that a symptom would not be adopted if it were likely to increase rather than decrease the individual's overall tension. Cost considerations may even lead the conscious to prefer suicide rather than bizarre symptoms. Though the subject's main decision is controlled by these principles, sometimes a specific symptom is chosen also because of its symbolic meaning, as in the chocolate phobia (see pp. 185–186).

Before elaborating these three principles, we would like to make two important comments: (1) Although we recognize that constitutional and developmental variables may increase the individual's sensitivity and accessibility to stress, and hence the probability for developing psychiatric symptoms, we deny that these variables have any automatic, etiological effect on the selection process. Moreover, it is not our concern in this book to clarify how maladjustive personality tendencies are developed. No doubt this could facilitate the broadest understanding of human psychopathology, but it is not directly concerned with the selection of bizarre symptoms. What is more important in our case is whether or not the subject experiences stress at the adoption stage, rather than the historical reasons for developing a sensitive personality type. Thus, unlike the dynamic theories, and some other new behaviorist approaches (Jacobs & Nadel, 1985), which attempt to understand the development of pathological symptoms in terms of historical causes or to explain the course of personality development and psychopathology by the same principles, our approach makes a clear distinction between these two areas of research. (2) According to our theoretical standpoint, people who display a great tendency to adopt bizarre symptoms are not necessarily characterized by an immature personality, in contrast to those who lack such symptoms. First, those lacking symptoms may simply be lucky and not encounter situations that prompt such responses. Second, the price involved in adopting bizarre symptoms may deter some from selecting them. These people would remain in stress and continue their coping efforts. While such attempts would increase their chances of eliminating the stress, they may also increase the likelihood of biological damage, such as hypertension, which to a large extent is caused by stress (see findings and studies reviewed by Rofé & Goldberg, 1983), or even the option of suicide. We hope to clarify these issues in this and following chapters (see also chapter 17).

PRINCIPLE OF CONTROLLABILITY

The distractive value of bizarre neurotic symptoms is important, but by itself is generally not sufficient to motivate a subject to adopt them. A necessary condition for the adoption of a bizarre neurotic symptom seems to be the expectation that it will increase the likelihood of stress control, not in an illusory but in a very real sense. This control is obtained by reduction or elimination of the sources of stress, by removal of the patient from the stressful situation, or by the subject's becoming more alert to the threatening aspects of the stress so that the probability of damage is significantly reduced.

The notion of controllability is strongly related to Rofé's (1984) conception of avoidable versus unavoidable stress, which was specified earlier (see p. 75). As was stated, avoidable stress refers to any stress condition in which some specific actions can be taken to reduce the stress or eliminate its sources. This includes situations from which subjects can remove themselves or over which they are able to gain some control. In contrast, unavoidable stress refers to situations in which nothing can be done to reduce or eliminate the stress. It renders the individual completely helpless and prompts resort to an illusionary control, namely, psychosis. These stresses include situations in which damage has already taken place (e.g., irreversible loss or failure) as well as situations in which damage is currently taking place, but the subject is completely helpless to stop the process. This category also includes situations, such as the Nazi concentration camps, in which a person is dominated by a very powerful force.

It is claimed that apart from a few exceptional cases, to be discussed later, bizarre neurotic symptoms always develop in situations where stress is actually avoidable, but the subject's normal coping resources are inadequate to alleviate it. The subject must either live with it, commit suicide, or be willing to use pathological devices. Examples illustrating such willingness in relation to the stresses of war, ostracism, marital conflict, and unbearable internal demands are presented throughout this chapter and chapter 9. Avoidable stress would become unavoidable for a specific individual who did not have the capacity to remove or reduce it significantly and, at the same time, was unwilling to adopt bizarre symptoms. In such cases, emotional distress in the form of anxiety and depression is likely to develop. We now examine the concept of controllability in more detail by referring to the three major neuroses—hysteria, clinical phobia, and obsessive–compulsive disorder.

Controllability Value of Hysteria

Clinical and research evidence suggests that hysterical symptoms tend to be associated with external rather than internal stress, and one of their prime objectives is gaining control over the source of the stress. This is consistent with the viewpoint of Rimm and Somervill (1977), who stated that in most cases the so-called secondary gain is the primary drive of the disorder:

> Thus, the airmen with visual problems are attempting to avoid an external task that they find frightening. The wife who systematically develops an "incapacitating" headache whenever her spouse makes sexual advances is similarly avoiding an external event—intercourse with her husband—that she finds distasteful. (pp. 81–82)

Similarly, Ironside and Batchelor (1945) reported that conversion reactions among airmen during World War II were closely related to the nature of their duties. For example, the pilots developed visual symptoms such as blurring or night blindness that made flying impossible. Similar findings were reported by Halpern (1944) and Wagner (1946). In the same way, Mucha and Reinhardt (1970) concluded, after considering the social environment of their patients, that their physical symptoms were the only socially acceptable ones they could have chosen for escaping the unbearable external military demands.

Consistent with these findings, Lehmkuhl (1983) described a case study of a 13-year-old girl who developed a complete paralysis of one leg in an "unconscious" attempt to avoid a marriage arranged by her parents. In another case, Grosz and Zimmerman (1970) reported the case of a 15-year-old girl who developed blindness for reading printed letters. Both her parents were so engrossed in their personal goals and careers that they not only neglected to pay attention to her, but also required her to take care of her siblings. By adopting the bizarre symptom, the girl succeeded in greatly reducing her stress since the mother was compelled to spend all her free time reading homework assignments to her (for more details regarding the unconscious aspect of the case, see pp. 128–130). In another case (Malmo, 1970), a 19-year-old girl developed hysterical deafness as a result of family tension. The symptoms enabled the patient to screen out the nagging voice of her mother, with whom her relations were particularly strained.

Although most of the evidence suggests that hysterical symptoms are associated with external stresses, some data show that these symptoms are sometimes adopted in order to gain control over unacceptable and threatening impulses. For example, Abse (1959) described a case study of a man who developed total paralysis of his legs after his wife left him for another man. The husband had a strong wish to pursue his wife and kill her and her lover, and the paralysis was apparently aimed at avoiding the execution of this internal demand. In a similar case study (Coleman, Butcher, & Carson, 1984, pp. 216–217), a female subject, who had physically attacked her father, subsequently developed a marked tremor and partial paralysis of the right arm and hand. She had clutched at and torn open the father's shirt with her right hand. Coleman et al. suggest that the paralysis represented a sort of symbolic punishment of the "guilty party," while preventing a recurrence of the forbidden aggressive behavior.

We have the impression that the latter two case studies do not represent the type of stress usually associated with hysteria. As will be discussed in this chapter, the evidence suggests that unacceptable impulses tend to be associated more with bizarre phobias, particularly obsessive–compulsive disorders. More studies are needed to clarify this issue. At any rate, the data presented so far very clearly demonstrate the controllability value of hysterical symptoms.

Controllability Value of Bizarre Phobias

As in the case of hysterical symptoms, the principle of controllability seems to be one of the important factors in determining the choice of bizarre phobias. It seems that like hysteria, these symptoms are mostly associated with external rather than internal stresses. However, bizarre phobias are also associated with unacceptable impulses, apparently to a greater extent than hysteria. Thus, it appears that one of the prime objectives of bizarre phobias (in addition to distraction) is to distance the individual from external stresses and in some cases to remove him or her from situations likely to arouse or intensify a threatening internal demand. We will examine in detail one case study that demonstrates both the controllability and distractive values of phobias, on the one hand, and the inadequate explanation of the case by psychoanalysis, on the other.

Leonard's Case Study

Description. The case is an autobiographical account by William Ellery Leonard (1927; see R. W. White & Watt, 1981), a poet and university lecturer who developed a crippling phobia that kept him from going even a short distance from home. By renting a room across the street from the university, he was able to resume his work as a teacher, but trips away from home, even short walks, were quickly curtailed by a rising panic. The symptoms first appeared sometime after Leonard's wife had committed suicide. The woman was the daughter of a highly respected family, and the community, which had come to regard Leonard as demanding and self-centered, almost unanimously blamed him for her death. The first panic attack occurred when Leonard, feeling very lonely and desperate, was standing alone on a bluff overlooking a quiet lake, along the other shore of which a freight train was moving. Later, Leonard attributed his bizarre fears mainly to two frightening episodes that he claimed had occurred during his childhood and were stored in his unconscious. One was a frightening incident with a train when he was 2 years old. He had almost been run down by a thundering locomotive while standing near the track on a station platform. The other was being chased out of the schoolyard at the age of 9 by a group of jeering children after having disgraced himself by making a puddle under his desk. Leonard claimed that he remembered these incidents while under autohypnosis, which he had done to increase recall of earlier frightening events.

Psychoanalytic Interpretation. R. W. White and Watt (1981) used these memories, without raising any doubts regarding their validity, as an example demonstrating the claim of psychoanalysis that repressed childhood fears may make an individual vulnerable to current stress. They noted that

> *not uncommonly a phobia assumes extreme proportions at some point in adult life after having been quiescent since early childhood. This requires the assumption that something has happened recently to increase the strength of the anxiety response so that it reaches a newly disruptive level.* (p. 198)

However, there seem to be serious questions regarding the validity of this type of traditional psychoanalytic explanation. First, it is highly probable that the two episodes, which were "remembered" under "autohypnosis" were pure products of Leonard's poetic imagination (Erdelyi & Goldberg, 1979; E. F. Loftus & G. R. Loftus, 1980; Neisser, 1967, 1984; see also pp. 42–43 in this book). Moreover, even if these two episodes actually occurred, it is still doubtful whether they had any effect on Leonard's panic attacks. At least with regard to the train episode it seems highly unlikely, because Leonard had traveled by train many times since that occasion. Therefore, the fear must have been extinguished. Furthermore, even if the fear had not completely vanished from his cognitive system and a recent stressful event had revived his fear, as suggested in Jacobs and Nadel's (1985) recent theory (see pp. 153–154 in this book), Leonard should have displayed a train phobia, not agoraphobic symptoms. Similar considerations can be applied to the second episode. Since Leonard did not subsequently avoid people, the extinction process should have either eliminated the fear altogether or reduced it to a nonsignificant level.

An Alternative Explanation. Another explanation, which seems to be more plausible than the psychoanalytic one, is that Leonard invented his agoraphobic symptoms to cope with an unbearable level of stress. The objective of these symptoms was to alleviate the unbearable feelings of anxiety, guilt, and depression generated, in all likelihood, by his wife's suicide and to cope with the unbearable external stress of his rejection by the entire community. Many people would feel extremely miserable if they were in Leonard's position, and some would perhaps commit suicide. However, Leonard chose instead a less drastic "suicidal act." It can be argued that while on the bluff, Leonard consciously intensified the feelings of anxiety and fear that he actually experienced due to his extremely stressful life situation. Apparently, these feelings of distress reached a peak when Leonard was standing alone in a very secluded place (see also the discussion of the availability principle in this chapter). The intensification of these fears to a bizarre level not only provided him a powerful distractive stimulus to ward off the depressive and/or anxiety-provoking cognitions that gained vigorous control over his attentional domain, but also effectively solved his rejection by the community. It enabled him to distance himself from the source of stress by avoiding encounters with his enemies and to some extent punish them by in effect saying, "Look what you have done to me by blaming me for my wife's death." At the same time, Leonard reduced the potential damage of the symptoms to his career by restricting the fear to certain areas, excluding places associated with his work at the university (see the discussion on the principle of cost–benefit). A more viable solution for Leonard might have been to leave the distressing area. However, this option was apparently not possible for him because of some attracting forces, such as his work. Moreover, it is doubtful whether the environmental change in itself would have helped remove the stress-arousing cognitions that apparently controlled his consciousness quite power-fully.

Leonard's autobiography was published in 1927, by that time he was possibly familiar with Freudian psychoanalytic concepts. Thus, it may be hypothesized that Leonard used this knowledge for fooling himself into believing that his fears were formed not by his conscious, but by repressed childhood memories that he probably truly believed were stored in his unconscious.

Additional Evidence

We elaborate more on the issue of bizarre fear when discussing the psychology of fear in the next part of the book. Here, however, we present more data demonstrating the controllability value of phobic responses. Coleman et al.'s (1984) position, which emphasized the important role of stress in developing phobias, is somewhat consistent with our theoretical paradigm. For example, Coleman (1964) described the case of a young man who developed claustrophobia after realizing that his business venture was doomed to failure. Thus, the phobia kept the patient from facing the unbearable stress of failure. Another example by Coleman, Butcher, and Carson (1980) is the hypothetical case of an insecure person who works in an office on the 40th floor of a building and who fears being discharged for inefficiency. One possible coping strategy the subject may adopt in order to avoid confrontation with this threat of self-devaluation and embarrassment is development of an elevator phobia. Although elevator phobia is quite common, this specific case should be regarded as a "bizarre" response if no significant frightening event preceded its onset. Even if such an event did take place, it still should be viewed with a great suspicion as to whether the subject were in fact taking advantage of the situation. One must remember that, apparently, riding in elevators had been one of the patient's habitual practices and that conditioned fear rarely develops even in extremely frightening situations (Rachman, 1978; see also p. 144 in this book).

Clinical evidence indicates that phobia is associated not only with external but also with internal stressful demands. The symptoms in this case are aimed at distancing patients from environmental stimuli likely to arouse or intensify the threatening thoughts or demands. For example, R. W. White and Watt (1981) described a boy of 17 who had severe conflicts over masturbation and developed a morbid dread of encountering another boy who also masturbated. In a similar fashion, a husband may develop a phobia about lakes and swimming pools because on previous occasions he had persistent thoughts of drowning his wife (Coleman et al., 1980).

This evidence seems sufficient to demonstrate the controllability value of the bizarre phobia in response to external and/or internal stresses. The theories and research findings regarding fear and phobia are thoroughly discussed later in this book. As will be shown, it is necessary to distinguish between normal and bizarre phobias. The psychobizarreness theory provides an explanation of bizarre phobias that seems more plausible than that of any other theory, while conditioning principles are most appropriate for the explanation of normal fears.

Our explanation of phobia may provide the solution to one of Freud's theoretical dilemmas. According to Freud, phobia is the result of repression, which itself is activated by the existence of anxiety. Thus, repression, which is aimed at coping with feelings of anxiety, causes, in these cases, arousal of these feelings.

> *How can anxiety be the effect or product of repression when it can also be seen—in the case of Little Hans for one thing—to be the cause of repression coming into play? Freud did not pretend that he had the solution to this puzzle. On the contrary, he expressed his puzzlement by invoking the Latin phrase "non liquet." (H. B. Lewis, 1981, pp. 63–64)*

This issue poses no problem for the psychobizarreness theory. Like psychoanalysis, this theory views repression as motivated by anxiety or stress. However, according to psychobizarreness theory, repression of unbearable stress may be achieved only by producing some bizarre behavior that has the ability to occupy the subject's attention. Phobia should be considered one type of bizarre response subjects can use to cope with unbearably stressful situations. Internally, subjects do a great deal: they adopt a fictitious problem that enables them to distract their attention from a problem that is even more anxiety provoking and to gain some direct control over the sources of their problem. Of course, the bizarre actions also place a burden on their adjustment capacity, but the total emotional cost is still lower than it was before. The selection of a bizarre symptom other than phobia (e.g., hysterical blindness) may be emotionally less costly because the anxiety experienced would be lower, but the limitation it might place on the subject's adjustment resources might be higher. Thus, despite the high level of emotional arousal a bizarre phobia produces, this symptom is sometimes more economical than other types of bizarre symptoms in terms of total adjustment.

Controllability Value of Obsessive–Compulsive Symptoms

Obsessive–compulsive disorders are usually associated with internal stress-producing impulses, namely, hostility and unacceptable sexual feelings (H. B. Lewis, 1981; D. G. Miller's findings and literature review, 1983; R. W. White & Watt, 1981). However, the cumulative research evidence shows that hostility and anger play a more central and dominant role in the development of this neurosis. The strong link between these two variables was demonstrated not only by indirect measurements of hostility, but also when self-report scales were employed (D. G. Miller, 1983).

Obsessive–compulsive behavior seems to be the best neurotic coping strategy in dealing with threatening internal feelings. The stress in these cases stems from two sources: fear of losing control and guilt feelings.

Fear of Losing Control

Subjects might be afraid that internal demands will compel them to unexpectedly perform acts severely damaging to themselves and/or others. The damage to oneself might include punishment, social embarrassment, and serious impairment of one's social relationships. It may be noted, for example, that consistent with this claim Salzman (1968) emphasized the desire of the obsessive–compulsive patient to gain absolute control, along with the feelings that any loss of control would constitute an intolerable public display of inadequacy and imperfection. These patients' fear of losing control is demonstrated in Button and Reivich's (1972) study of women who had obsessive thoughts of killing their children: "The obsessional-thoughts were typically experienced not so much as an impulse to harm the child but as an apprehension that such an impulse might occur and be uncontrollably acted upon" (p. 238).

The obsessive–compulsive symptoms consist of two modes of coping mechanisms, both of which attempt to increase the subjects' control over their threatening impulses. One mode involves bizarre compulsive rituals such as checking behaviors (Emmelkamp, 1982). This mode of reaction aims to distract subjects' attention from cognitions likely to arouse the anxiety-provoking impulses, and at the same time to increase their supervision of their own behavior so that they will not act unexpectedly. The second mode of reaction is the use of obsessive thoughts. The cognitive aspect of the threatening impulse, excluding its emotional component, is amplified to a bizarre or absurd level. This amplification is probably obtained in a self-deceptive manner. The actual threatening thought may spontaneously, through free associative thinking, lead to sporadic bizarre thoughts. While such thoughts generally pass unnoticed, subjects with an intense fear of losing control may use these cognitions (or even create them deliberately) and direct their attention to them. Thus, if for some reason they have intense feelings of hate toward somebody they love, they may use this method to occupy their attention to a great degree with bizarre aggressive thoughts that are only remotely connected with the actual aggressive intention. This amplification of bizarre aggressive thoughts should distract subjects' attention from the actual aggressive intention and at the same time increase their alertness to the potential danger of acting unexpectedly. Due to the absence of an appropriate emotional component, the bizarre aggressive thoughts are less likely to lead to actual aggressive behavior than are the original relatively moderate intentions. Moreover, by sharing the bizarre thoughts with others, subjects can increase their feelings of being supervised, which may give them the feelings that others will watch them and prevent their acting in a "crazy" manner. Furthermore, inasmuch as the bizarre obsessive thoughts are not accompanied by parallel intensification of the emotional aspect of the impulse, which may be deliberately suppressed, subjects may deceive themselves into thinking that they are not responsible for their occurrence.

A case study illustrating this coping style, reported by Coleman et al. (1980), is that of a man who developed obsessive thoughts of hitting his 3-year-old son over the head with a hammer. The patient was completely unable to explain his "horrible thoughts." He indicated that he loved his son very much and thought that he must be going insane to have such thoughts. It was later discovered that the patient's wife had suffered great pain in childbirth and since then had refused to have sexual relations with him. Additionally, she directed all of her attention to her son, and their previously happy marriage was now disrupted by quarreling and bickering. Coleman et al. (1980) noted that the patient vigorously and sincerely denied the therapist's explanation that he harbored hostile feelings toward his son. "Because his fantasies were lacking in affect, they did not seem to him to represent his real feelings at all" (Coleman et al., 1980, p. 216).

Guilt Feelings

The arousal of unacceptable impulses, particularly when they involve forbidden behaviors such as masturbation, may arouse unbearable feelings of guilt. In the case of hostility, this may be especially true when the feelings of hate are directed toward a loved person, such as a spouse or child (Button & Reivich, 1972; Coleman et al., 1984; R. W. White & Watt, 1981). A typical compulsive behavior often adopted to cope with these stressful feelings is compulsive hand washing. This pattern of behavior is more prevalent among women than men (Emmelkamp, 1982) apparently because hostility is socially less acceptable in females, and they are therefore more prone than males to experience guilt feelings. (An interesting case study of this pattern of behavior in connection with guilt feelings is reported by Coleman et al., 1984, pp. 204–205.) Hand washing is not, of course, restricted to hostility. It may also be aroused by guilt feelings associated with sexual behavior, as illustrated in a case study by Coleman (1964, p. 225) involving a 13-year-old boy who engaged in compulsive ritual activities because of guilt feelings with regard to masturbation.

One of the most efficient types of bizarre behaviors for coping with both types of stress of the obsessive–compulsive disorders (aggression and sex) is to adopt an opposite pattern of behavior. This coping style is termed *reaction formation* by psychoanalysis. An example of such behavior is described by Masserman (1946, p. 43). This mechanism not only enables the subject to reduce the probability of carrying out the dangerous actions and experiencing feelings of guilt, but it has another important advantage as well. Self-deception in these cases is easier to achieve than in other types of bizarre behavior such as hand washing or checking rituals.

Finally, one may argue that obsessive–compulsive reactions do not provide the individual with real control over internal stress since the stress is not actually eliminated. However, internal stress is the result of the subject's internal subjective environment, and research evidence shows that obsessive–compulsive symptoms in fact reduce the subject's level of anxiety (see reviews by Emmelkamp, 1982). Thus, while the symptoms may not eliminate the unacceptable stressful internal impulses, they provide the subject with some control or supervision that helps reduce his or her level of anxiety. Moreover, with respect to feelings of guilt, the obsessive–compulsive coping mechanism may, like religious praying rituals, lead to complete elimination of the stress.

PRINCIPLE OF SALIENCY–AVAILABILITY

As was noted, distraction and controllability demands can be fulfilled by more than one bizarre neurotic symptom. What then determines the adoption of one specific bizarre symptom rather than another? One of the important factors appears to be the saliency of the symptom in the individual's cognitive system. This principle indicates that a symptom is selected because it has gained more prominence in the subject's cognitive system due to the individual's learning history, which resulted in greater familiarity with the symptom, and/or because the adopted symptom is more powerfully suggested by the immediate environment than other symptoms. The symptom or the pathological coping device may have been present in the subject's cognitive system for quite a long time, but was not expressed externally due to lack of suitable conducive conditions. Thus, in line with Tolman's latency principle (e.g., see Bower & Hilgard, 1981), it may be argued that throughout life, particularly during childhood, the subject internalizes pathological coping devices by observing them in the close social environment or through other informational channels. These latent coping mechanisms are used when a subject's normal coping strategies are no longer adequate, according to his or her cognitive appraisal, to deal with experience of stress. However, a symptom may also be selected because some changes in the subject's immediate environment increased their salience in the subject's cognitive system. Let us now examine the evidence supporting these suggestions.

Many findings are consistent with the saliency–availability principle, particularly with regard to hysterical symptoms. Thus, Ullman and Krasner (1975) indicated that patients with hysterical symptoms either have observed relatives who suffered from organic difficulties or have themselves had such difficulties. Arconac and Guze (1963) reported that somatization disorders were found in about 20% of first-degree relatives of hysterical subjects. This is also demonstrated in a case study by Brady and Lind (1961). Similarly, Mucha and Reinhardt (1970), in examining conversion reactions among naval aviation students, found that in 70% of the cases the patient's parents had suffered from illness in the same organ system the patient used in the conversion reaction, and the majority of patients had had multiple physical symptoms of actual illness prior to their hysterical reactions. Similarly, research findings (E. A. Weinstein, Eck, & Lyerly, 1969) show that hysterical symptoms are commonly located in the organ system that was the site of a previous injury or disability. Apparently this type of response is adopted not only because of familiarity with the symptom, but also because it may make deception of self and others easier. The subject may believe and claim that he never completely recovered from his or her illness. Another study supporting the saliency–availability principle was reported by Volkmar, Poll, and M. Lewis (1984). In examining hysterical symptoms among children, the authors found that in comparison with a control group consisting of children with adjustment difficulties, significantly more subjects had been hospitalized in the year prior to the psychiatric referral. Moreover, a model of illness similar to that of the child was more often observed in the family members of conversion cases. A case study demonstrating the tendency of the hysterical patient to utilize previous somatic illnesses for solving present psychological difficulties is described by Davison and Neale (1982, p. 182).

The choice of hysterical symptoms may sometimes be based on the subject's present life conditions. The unique stimulus characteristics of the present situation may make these particular symptoms more salient than other ones in his or her cognitive system. The subject who presently suffers from a temporary illness or injury may intensify or prolong the available symptoms in order to escape unbearable psychological stress (e.g., see R. W. White & Watt, 1981). A case study demonstrating this type of response, described by R. W. White and Watt (1981, pp. 214–216), involves a man made very uneasy by his wife's having become pregnant and given birth to a child. On his way to the hospital to visit them, he sustained minor injuries in a motor accident. He took advantage of his injury and developed hysterical blindness; his first remark to the psychiatrist was that he could not tie his wife down to a blind man and would now divorce her. A similar case study is discussed elsewhere in this book (pp. 187–192).

Finally, hysterical symptoms may gain priority in a subject's cognitive system due to the specific nature of the stress and/or because, according to the subject's appraisal, those particular symptoms have the highest controllability value in that particular stressful situation. These observations are consistent with evidence, mentioned previously, that conversion reactions among World War II airmen were closely associated with the nature of their duties as well as with findings that somatic symptoms have often been the only socially acceptable symptoms subjects could choose for escaping stressful demands of a military situation (see Mucha & Reinhardt, 1970).

The principle of saliency–availability may play a more dominant role in developing conversion symptoms because symptoms of illness are more prevalent than other kinds of symptoms, such as phobia. Yet, this principle plays an important part in development of other symptoms as well. As in the case of hysteria, there seems to be a close relationship between a subject's fearful behavior and parental responses (see studies reviewed by Emmelkamp, 1982, on vicarious learning). In a national survey in the United Kingdom (Thorpe & Burns, 1983, p. 21), 43% of the agoraphobic subjects described their mothers as being over anxious. Thus, in a manner similar to that of hysterical patients, subjects may take advantage of fearful responses they have observed in others and display them when their normal coping devices collapse. A subject who already has a fearful personality will be likely to exhibit fear reactions to stress, and thus the salience of this response in the cognitive system is likely to increase. Thus, subjects whose normal coping mechanisms have collapsed may be tempted to utilize their fear reaction as a pathological coping strategy. The fear reactions are intensified to a bizarre level because this type of response is more available to them than another type of symptom. Another factor likely to motivate subjects to adopt this type of strategy is that self-deception in this case would be much simpler. Inasmuch as they have already become automatically aroused to a high level, due to their fearful personality type, an intensification of this reaction to a bizarre level would be less noticeable, particularly if it occurred in a gradual manner, than would adoption of a bizarre symptom that had no basis in the subject's present response repertoire. Thus, the correlation between prior tendency to fearfulness or dependency with agoraphobia (Emmelkamp, 1982) does not necessarily reflect an etiological relationship, which is how these observations are generally interpreted. Rather, it may reflect utilization of these symptoms for coping needs as suggested by the saliency–availability principle.

Ideas of particular bizarre fears may also be transmitted by information or instruction just as is the case with regard to normal fear (Rachman, 1977). A case study demonstrating this possibility, reported by Emmelkamp (1982), concerns a patient whose mother suffered from a heart condition, which did not upset the daughter very much. However, when the mother was advised by her physician to stay at home in order to prevent a heart attack, the daughter subsequently developed severe agoraphobic symptoms. She was afraid that she might die from a heart attack if she ventured out of her home.

Another factor likely to motivate subjects to adopt bizarre phobia is exposure to fear-arousing circumstances during the stress stage. Such conditions may supply subjects with ideas for bizarre fears, as well as with excuses for self-deception based on their own particular belief systems, such as psychoanalysis or conditioning theory.

This idea may be illustrated in the case of Leonard, detailed earlier. As stated, Leonard was already in a high state of arousal due to his severely stressful situation. However, the onset of his panic attack occurred when he was subjected to secluded frightening conditions that greatly increased the salience of fear responses in his cognitive system. In describing his psychological frame of mind immediately prior to the outbreak of his symptoms, Leonard repeatedly emphasized his "weird isolation" while looking out over the "silent and vacant water," and noted that he had felt "diffused premonitions of horror." At this stage he saw a freight train and heard it blowing its whistle, which aggravated his fear to a state of panic. There may have been two reasons for the train's effect: (1) a sudden and unexpected strong noise such as a train's whistle in a silent and isolated surrounding, especially when one is intensively absorbed in one's own internal world, is likely to cause spontaneous arousal in many people; (2) most likely, Leonard had been contemplating suicide.

The train episode made these thoughts salient in his cognition, though they were still not strong enough to actually be carried out. Indeed, Leonard vividly imagined that the train was "about to rush over" him. The image was so strong that he could not get it out of his mind:

> I say to myself (and aloud), it is half a mile across the lake—it can't touch you . . . I rush back and forth on the bluffs. . . . My God, won't that train go; my God, won't . . . "Won't that train go away!" I smash a wooden box to pieces . . . against my knee to occupy myself against panic. (R. W. White & Watt, 1981, pp. 162–163)

It seems then, that Leonard deliberately intensified the spontaneous arousal he was feeling until it resulted in a state of agoraphobia. Moreover, since the shift in his feelings was, to a large extent, spontaneous and his active involvement in producing the symptoms was minimal, he could use his psychoanalytic knowledge to deceive himself that he was not in any way responsible for his bizarre agoraphobic behavior.

It should be indicated that Leonard's report is retrospective. He claimed that he forgot the experience almost immediately and that he remembered only that he had had some sort of attack on the bluff. He recovered the full memory more than 10 years later during states of relaxation. Although we cannot accept Leonard's psychoanalytic interpretation of his panic attack and agoraphobic symptoms due to reasons specified earlier, it is quite possible that Leonard's report regarding the circumstances in which the first attack occurred has a kernel of truth. Apparently, the loneliness intensified Leonard's level of anxiety and feelings of depression. He could no longer continue to bear this stressful situation and was desperately looking for a coping mechanism. He chose agoraphobic symptoms both because they satisfied his coping demands and because the circumstances in which he was found made fear responses most salient in his focus of attention. These coping responses also required the fewest efforts at self-deception. It seems, then, that the principles of controllability and availability provide an explanation for Leonard's bizarre fear no less plausible than that suggested by psychoanalytic theory.

The saliency–availability principle may apply to obsessive–compulsive disorders as well. Research data (Emmelkamp, 1982) show that the vast majority of obsessive–compulsive patients (71–72%) had a moderate to marked degree of premorbid obsessive–compulsive personality traits, compared to 53% of nonobsessive control patients. As claimed by Emmelkamp, these findings suggest the existence of a strong relationship between premorbid personality traits and development of obsessive–compulsive symptoms. However, in our opinion, these findings may be interpreted by the saliency–availability principle. Subjects are likely to intensify their premorbid personality traits in order to cope with a stress when they are consistent with controllability demands. Moreover, when a symptom is an intensification of an existing strong habit, self-deception may be easier. In evaluating our explanation of this relationship, one should bear in mind Emmelkamp's (1982) statement that "there is not evidence whatever to support the psychoanalytic theory that relates anal eroticism to the obsessive personality and to the development of obsessional neuroses" (p. 188).

Premorbid obsessive personality traits are not a necessary condition for the development of obsessive disorders. In a substantial number of cases, these symptoms develop in the absence of any such personality traits. However, other findings show that typically these patients are raised by very strict and controlling parents and are characterized by high moral standards (Emmelkamp, 1982; R. W. White & Watt, 1981). Thus, it appears that these patients are quite vulnerable to internal stresses associated with hostility and/ or unacceptable sexual impulses. Individuals subjected to this type of stress are likely to develop obsessive–compulsive symptoms because they are the most suitable for their controllability demands. Other types of bizarre neurotic symptoms (hysterical blindness) are less likely to increase the individual's supervision of his or her responses. Additionally, other symptoms appear to be more costly in terms of total adjustment (see the following discussion on the principle of cost–benefit). Thus, apparently, the saliency–availability principle enters into play only if the more readily available symptom fulfills the requirements of controllability and cost–benefit.

The principle of saliency–availability may also explain why compulsive washing behavior is more common among females than males (Emmelkamp, 1982). These responses are adopted both because symbolically they are suitable for controllability of guilt feelings, and also because they tend to characterize females more.

As was stated, the saliency–availability principle is consistent with Tolman's principle of latent learning. It appears that this principle is also, to some extent, consistent with Boles's theory of defense reactions (see Hulse, Egeth, & Deese, 1980). Boles theorized that organisms possess innate, characteristic methods of responding to danger. Danger signals evoke these innate reactions, which remove the animal from danger. However, if these reactions fail to work, other response strategies close to the natural coping devices emerge. In a similar manner it may be argued that when faced with stress, humans use their dominant normal coping skills to remove the stress. However, if these methods prove to be inadequate, the likelihood of using pathological measures increases. Those that gain salience in a subject's cognitive system are more likely to be employed provided that they are consistent with controllability demands and that the subject has no less costly symptoms at his or her cognitive disposal.

PRINCIPLE OF COST–BENEFIT

The third principle that appears to guide subjects' choice of bizarre neurotic symptoms involves cost–benefit considerations. This principle states that in the process of adopting a symptom the subject evaluates not only its benefits in terms of distraction and controllability, but also the price that must be paid to adopt it. The subject takes into account the degree of cognitive involvement that will be required in order to achieve self-deception, the total burden on his or her general adjustment, social embarrassment, etc. Some subjects will never adopt bizarre symptoms at any level of stress, either because their value system and/or their advanced cognitive development does not allow them to cheat themselves and/or because the expected devastating effect on social status or general adjustment would be too high. These subjects may continue to bear their suffering and, as a result, increase their chance of eventually finding an appropriate solution to their problem. On the other hand, this may also increase their chance of developing a somatic illness such as heart attack, ulcer, and hypertension or of committing suicide.

The cost–benefit principle seems to be one of the most important factors dominating human behavior. Such considerations characterize our daily behavior. We are aware that a person may be quite helpless in inhibiting some responses (e.g., cigarette smoking) despite the expectation of high cost. However, this seems to be the case only with respect to those behaviors that have a long reinforcement or conditioning history. Moreover, we are concerned here with the adoption of bizarre operant behavior, the onset of which is in most cases sudden and dramatic, rather than with inhibition of the strong nonpathological responses that were the focus of the animal learning theories. In our opinion, one of the important variables determining the adoption of these behaviors, and possibly many nonpathological responses as well, is cost–benefit considerations. This idea is accepted to some extent by the learning theorists as well. However, the behaviorists' anticognitive philosophical approach to the human caused the proponents of the behaviorist camp to conceive the effects of reinforcement–punishment in terms of a Thorndikian–Skinnerian mechanistic approach, rather than in a Tolmanian conceptualization, which regards these effects as informational input that guides the organism in its relationship with the environment (Mackintosh, 1983).

The importance of cost–benefit considerations in determining human behavior in the area of stress and affiliation was recently emphasized in Rofé's (1984) "utility theory" and in several other studies that have examined these ideas (Rofé, Hoffman, & Lewin, 1985; Rofé & Lewin, 1986; Rofé, Lewin, & Hoffman, 1987). Affiliation preferences at times of stress seem to be determined by an analysis of the expected cost–benefit of being with others. In our opinion, unless this principle is generalized to psychotherapy as well, some long-standing problems in the area of psychiatry—such as the greater prevalence of neurotic symptoms (and, as will be demonstrated in the last part of this book, psychotic symptoms as well) among the low than the high social classes and among women than among men—will remain unsolved. Let us demonstrate this with regard to the three major categories of neuroses.

Hysterical symptoms seem to have very high value in terms of controllability and distraction. In Western society at least, these symptoms tend to be the most acceptable excuse for escaping intolerable external demands (Mucha & Reinhardt, 1970; R. W. White & Watt, 1981). Similarly, of all bizarre neurotic symptoms, hysteria seems to have the highest distractive value. This is because unlike the other type of neurotic disorders, these symptoms are always available for attentional focus, that is, their expression is not limited to a certain place or time. Thus, in the case of neurotic symptoms other than hysteria, the anxiety-provoking cognitions can more easily resume their attentional control. This positive coping value of hysteria symptoms is consistent with Freud's clinical observations that repression reaches its maximum efficiency in hysteria.

However, the use of hysterical reactions may be too costly, particularly for men and for high-social-class subjects, who tend to avoid adopting these symptoms (Folks, Ford, & Regan, 1984; Jones, 1980; Kroll, Chamberlain, & Halpern, 1979). Men are expected to work and to be physically strong. Thus, somatoform disorders may intensify rather than decrease their general adjustment capacity because they may seriously disrupt their ability to work, cause social embarrassment, and threaten their social status. In contrast, the expected damage is considerably lower for females.

Similar considerations may explain why hysterical symptoms are less common among high socioeconomic classes or more sophisticated individuals (Folks et al., 1984;

CHOICE OF NEUROTIC SYMPTOMS   119

Jones, 1980; Rangaswamy & Kamakshi, 1983; Stephansson, Messina, & Meyerowitz, 1976; Ullmann & Krasner, 1975). These symptoms appear to be less beneficial for these people because their sophistication stands in the way of their developing self-deceptive beliefs and hence of achieving distraction.

Nevertheless, despite these disadvantages in using somatoform symptoms, both men and members of the high socioeconomic classes do develop such symptoms when the stress becomes highly intolerable and no other options are available (Jones, 1980; Mucha & Reinhardt, 1970; Ziegler, Imboden, & Meyer, 1960). However, as noted by R. W. White and Watt (1981), "the dramatic old-fashioned symptoms like glove anesthesia are no longer available to educated people, especially those trained as physicians, nurses, or medical secretaries. More often among relatively sophisticated people the physical symptoms take the form of pain" (p. 217).

Other data consistent with cost–benefit considerations show that hysteric hemianesthesias and hemiparalyses are more frequently located on the left than on the right side (Galin, Diamond, & Braff, 1977). These findings were interpreted by Galin et al. as a sign that hysterical symptoms are controlled by unconscious mechanisms, which they believe are located in the right hemisphere. However, as was noted previously, the attempt to link this hemisphere with the Freudian notion of unconscious was rejected by Corballis (1980), who indicated that except for verbal disability, the right hemisphere is endowed with all the other requirements for consciousness, such as attention, perception, memory, judgment, etc. Moreover, with respect to the abovementioned findings on hysteria, Kihlstrom (1984) noted that "a more parsimonious explanation, one considered and rejected by Galin et al. (1977), is that the symptoms are lateralized where they will do the least harm" (p. 160).

Cost–benefit considerations similar to those used for explaining sexual differences in hysteria may be applied to account for the higher frequency of bizarre fears, particularly agoraphobia, among females (Davison & Neale, 1982; Marks, 1969; Rachman, 1978; Thorpe & Burns, 1983). The social pressure to act fearlessly is greater for boys than for girls (Emmelkamp, 1982; Marks, 1973). Females feel less embarrassed to display fearful behavior than do males (Emmelkamp, 1982; Gerard & Rabbie, 1961; Lynch, Watts, Galloway, & Tryphonopoulos, 1973). Thus, these considerations, together with the ability of agoraphobia or other types of bizarre fears to seriously disrupt the work ability of males, may explain why these psychiatric disorders are so rare among men. We are quite aware of the existence of some other explanations for these sexual differences (Emmelkamp, 1982, p. 38). For example, it has been suggested that "females are more willing to report phobias than males. . . . After similar traumatic experiences, males are expected to continue working and are therefore automatically exposed to the phobic situations. Such exposure can result in the extinction of anxiety" (Emmelkamp, 1982, p. 38). A more recent attempt to account for the sexual differences in the incidence of agoraphobia was made by Rachman (1984a, 1984b) in his safety-signal theory. However, as will be comprehensively demonstrated later in our discussion of the psychology of fear, none of the available models can explain the production of bizarre fears. For example, the abovementioned explanation of these sexual differences is based on the conditioning paradigm. However, the cumulative research findings raise serious questions regarding the validity of this conceptualization, inasmuch as agoraphobia and other bizarre fears are usually manifested in the absence of any frightening events that could lead to conditioning.

The cost–benefit principle may also help us understand why obsessive–compulsive symptoms are far more prevalent among males than are hysterical or phobic symptoms

(H. B. Lewis, 1981; Slade, 1974). The obsessive–compulsive symptoms seem to be the most efficient and least costly behavioral deviation in dealing with the unacceptable hostile impulses that appear to be more frequent among men. While these symptoms seem to be highly efficient in satisfying the controllability demands in dealing with such types of stress, their expected damage to the patient's work ability is quite minimal compared with hysteria or agoraphobia. While in many cases of hysteria, such as blindness, deafness, and paralysis, the symptoms severely limit the subject's total adjustment, this does not exist in obsessive–compulsive disorders. In hysteria, subjects also have less flexibility in the way they display the symptoms because the symptoms must be in accord with medical knowledge. However, subjects with obsessive–compulsive disorders can arbitrarily avoid displaying the symptoms when they feel uncomfortable without being accused of inconsistency. They have greater flexibility in finding excuses for not displaying the symptoms than do hysterical patients. The burden in obsessive–compulsive disorders is also lighter than that of bizarre phobia disorders. The former do not cause intensive emotional arousal and do not restrict the subject's movements in the environment. The restriction of movement often includes quite a wide area of the environment due to the ease of stimulus generalization that appears to characterize phobia more than any other bizarre symptom. Another advantage of obsessive–compulsive symptoms is that they do not disable the person in the sense of causing dependency on others, as hysteria or bizarre phobia often do.

CRITICAL DISCUSSION

The purpose of this section is to clarify two issues that relate to ideas raised in this chapter. The first issue concerns the three principles discussed here, namely, controllability, saliency–availability, and cost–benefit. One may disagree with these principles, arguing that the choice of neurotic symptoms is determined mainly by biological and personality variables. The second issue relates to the claim that neurotic symptoms are associated with avoidable rather than unavoidable stress. It may be argued that these symptoms are also aroused in response to unavoidable stress. Let us discuss each of these two issues separately.

Effects of Biological and Personality Variables

We have three main arguments against the idea that a specific type of neurotic symptom is determined by biological–genetic or personality factors:

1. As far as genetic or biological tendencies are concerned, the research findings show either no significant relationship between these factors and neurotic symptoms or at the most a very weak one. This claim is true with respect to hysteria (Gottesman, 1962; studies reviewed by R. S. Levy & Jankovic, 1983; Slater, 1961), phobia (Emmelkamp, 1982; Mathews, Goldberg, & Johnston, 1981), as well as obsessive–compulsive disorders (Emmelkamp, 1982).

2. Consistent with the abovementioned studies, the research generally reports a weak relationship between a specific premorbid personality type and the development of hysteria (Chodoff, 1974; Jones, 1980; studies reviewed by Sackeim, Nordlie, & Gur, 1979; R. W. White & Watt, 1981) or phobia (Aitken, Lister, & Main, 1981; Buglass, Clarke, Henderson, Kreitman, & Presley, 1977; Emmelkamp, 1982; Mathews et al., 1981). The correlation data are more impressive with regard to obsessive–

compulsive symptoms (Emmelkamp, 1982). However, as was indicated earlier, in a significant number of cases the obsessive–compulsive symptoms may also develop in the absence of a premorbid obsessive personality type.

3. Even when a significant relationship is found between certain personality characteristics and specific neurotic symptoms, this does not necessarily point to an etiological relationship, as is sometimes implied in the literature (Jones, 1980; D. Shapiro, 1965). First, these relationships might be spurious rather than genuine. For example, the greater prevalence of hysteria is among females and subjects who are less educated or of a low socioeconomic level does not necessarily mean that femininity or a naïve personality type causes the adoption of hysterical symptoms. These subjects may prefer these symptoms as coping mechanisms because for them the price is low. Thus, it may be that the correlation between these symptoms and certain personality characteristics would be diminished if the cost–benefit involved in adopting these symptoms were held constant. Second, as was suggested with respect to obsessive–compulsive reactions, the correlation between certain premorbid personality types and a specific type of neurotic symptom may be high because these personality tendencies gained high salience in the subject's cognitive system. Thus, such correlation data might be interpreted as implying an etiological relationship while, in fact, the subject is utilizing his acquired weaknesses for coping purposes.

Despite these arguments, it seems that personality variables as well as biological constitution play an important role in the development of neurosis. On the one hand, we do not believe, as do the traditional theorists, that the type of neurosis one develops is determined in a direct and automatic manner by these or other factors. However, at the same time, it seems that certain acquired personality traits or a constitutional impairment or weakness may increase vulnerability to stress and hence to neurosis. These factors may lead to sensitivity or overreaction to stress or to the lack of coping skills and thereby may increase the risk of the individual's developing bizarre neurotic symptoms. The clarification of these risk factors is not among the central aims of this book (although the subject will be considered in somewhat more detail with respect to psychosis); however, it is of great importance to the comprehensive understanding of psychopathological phenomena and deserves careful theoretical attention and intensive research effort.

Effects of Unavoidable Stress

We have suggested that the development of bizarre neurotic symptoms tends in most cases to be associated with avoidable stress. However, in a few cases unavoidable stress is an important etiological factor in the development of neuroses. These cases are classified here into two main categories termed *readiness for explosion* and *inevitable danger*.

Readiness for Explosion

Sometimes, an avoidable stress may not in itself be sufficient to cause the adoption of neurotic symptoms because it has not yet reached a certain level and/or because of some inhibiting situational or personality factors. However, the avoidable stress causes the individual to be in a state of readiness for explosion or on the edge of breakdown. Any significant new stress that would not in itself be enough to cause the adoption of pathological coping devices may upset the subject's delicate state of equilibrium and mobilize him or her to take such measures.

This possibility is demonstrated in a case study (Masserman, 1946) of a 42-year-old woman who developed a fugue reaction to a prolonged unhappy marriage. The woman had entered into a loveless marriage to a man chosen by her parents, after recovering from a severe depression over an incident of unrequited love during her academic studies. The way of life of her husband, a clergyman engaged in missionary work, was completely different from what she had wanted for herself. Despite her deep frustration and unhappiness, she continued to bear the situation for several years. Finally, when the patient was 37, the culmination of her disappointments came with the illness and death of her youngest and favorite child. The next day, she disappeared from home without any explanation or trace, and her whereabouts for the next 4 years were unknown to her family. Eventually, she was located in the college town of her youth, over 1,000 miles away. During all these years she called herself by a different name and completely lost all conscious knowledge relating to her true identity. Her new identity was that of a college girlfriend with whom she had shared a room during her academic studies, and whom she had adored. Under the new identity, she began to earn a living playing and teaching piano. She was so rapidly successful that within 2 years she became the assistant director of a music conservatory. During the 4 years of her escape reaction, the patient lived as though she were another person until she was eventually identified by an acquaintance who had known both her and the woman she was impersonating.

Thus, it may be argued that due to her prolonged period of stress the patient was in a state of preparedness to develop bizarre neurotic symptoms. With the death of her favorite child, the stress was intensified beyond her stress threshold and thus triggered the onset of the neurotic symptoms. It does not seem plausible that the death of the child played a primary etiological role in the development of the symptoms. Such an event should at the most have caused depression or even suicide, but not fugue. Yet, the high distractive value of the symptoms probably also served to alleviate or prevent feelings of depression over the death. It is possible that the woman's level of stress was sufficiently high even before the child's death, but she avoided displaying the symptoms because she was strongly attached to her youngest child, who, due to his youth, needed her support.

Why didn't the patient choose a normal course of action, namely, divorce, or another pathological response? Many factors may have discouraged her from divorce—procedural difficulties involved in such a move, her fanatic religious parents, or guilt feelings in view of her intensive religious education. Additionally, the decision to adopt the pathological option was taken when the patient was subject to an unusual level of stress that pressed for an immediate solution. She particularly needed a course of action that could provide strong distractive value and that would immediately alleviate her unbearable feelings of depression. In such a psychological state, when the thinking processes and logical consideration of all available options are impaired (e.g., see Neuringer, 1976), the likelihood of adopting bizarre symptoms or committing suicide (Coleman et al., 1984, p. 326) is greatly intensified.

The question of why the patient chose fugue rather than another mode of bizarre reaction is difficult to answer. However, it seems that three main factors were involved in increasing the salience of the pathological escape reaction in her cognitive system. The first factor involves the characteristics of the stress situation itself, which strongly suggested the idea of escape. The second variable was the college town of the subject's youth, where she spent the happiest period of her life, due largely to the girlfriend whom she adored and to whom she was deeply attached. The third factor was the hypocritical religious behavior of her parents. On one hand, they were fanatically religious, but on the other hand they did not live according to the morality which they preached. Thus, in a way the patient adopted as a coping strategy the two-facedness of her parents, which had been latent in her cognitive system since childhood.

This case study may also serve to demonstrate some of the ideas mentioned in the previous chapter with regard to the creation of a state of unawareness. Three factors seem to have been involved in producing this psychological state:

1. The drastic environmental and emotional changes that the escape response caused discouraged the patient from spontaneously recalling that she had consciously and deliberately initiated the escape and the adoption of the new identity.

2. In all likelihood, the patient made a conscious effort to avoid thinking about her past (suppression) and avoided exposing herself to stimuli that might remind her of it. Masserman (1946) noted, for example, that the patient "chose friends who would not be curious about her past . . . and thereby eventually established a new social identity which soon removed the need for introspection and ruminations" (p. 46). Adopting a new name was, of course, one of the conscious maneuvers she utilized in order to forget her past.

3. Compared with her former environment—a small village that prohibited movies, recreation, secular music, etc.—the new town was like a new world where she could fulfill her dreams and aspirations. Additionally, the new place was the college town of her youth, which was emotionally loaded with many happy memories related to the adored girlfriend. Thus, the town had great distractive value for her. Her consciousness was so powerfully occupied by activities and memories associated with the new place that she hardly had free time to think about her miserable past life. One of the areas that occupied her attention very intensively was playing the piano. As was stated, her success in this area was rapid and quite unusual. Most probably, this was obtained by a great deal of effort and attentional investment.

The evidence appears to suggest that the patient had developed a strong belief in her new identity. When she was eventually found, she "sincerely and vigorously denied this identification" and insisted that she had never seen her parents, husband, and child. However, we have some doubt as to her sincerity. On the one hand, it is very likely that during the 4 years of her escape she had succeeded in building a strong barrier against thoughts related to her past. This was achieved by the three factors mentioned above, by the strong aversion that such thoughts aroused, and by reinforcements she received for behavior in accordance with her new identity. On the other hand, we doubt whether the barrier was absolute and particularly whether she was really sincere in her new encounter with her family. With respect to this, it may be worthwhile to point out that her immediate response to the new confrontation was one of perturbation and anxiety. Only afterward did she deny any connection with her family. Thus, as was stated earlier we have some doubt as to whether in this case, or in any other psychiatric state involving bizarre responses, there exists a state of an absolute lack of awareness, and whether there is a clear boundary between the behaviors of a neurotic subject and a malingerer (Brady, 1966; Grosz & Zimmerman, 1965; and pp. 103, 131 in this book). Masserman (1946) noted that even in her new identity the patient neither married again nor permitted herself any form of direct sexual expression. He explained that these behaviors were avoided "since deep in her unconscious such unfaithfulness or bigamy would have been untenable" (p. 34). However, in our opinion these avoidance reactions may be considered another indication of the existence of a minimum level of conscious control.

Masserman (1946) uses this case study as an illustration of the psychoanalytic concept of repression, which he defined as "the automatic and unconsciously defensive process of banishing dangerous desires, affects or ideas . . . from awareness to the unconscious" (p. 296). However, the patient's bizarre responses, from the emergence stage and throughout the 4 years, were so well organized that it does not seem plausible to ascribe them to automatic unconscious processes. Can one really believe that the escape to a town so far from her village, the choice of her new identity, her ability to "forget" the very powerful memories of her past life, and the creation of the new identity could be achieved by automatic processes without intensive involvement of the consciousness?

Another case that can illustrate the idea of "readiness for explosion" is that of the chocolate phobia case, which is discussed in more detail later in this book (pp. 185–186). Here, as in the previous case study, the bizarre symptom emerged after the death of a beloved person, the patient's mother. Thus, one could argue that bizarre symptoms were adopted to cope with the unavoidable stress of death. However, a careful examination of the case reveals that the woman was in a state of chronic stress before her mother died. She was extremely dependent on her mother, sexually inadequate, and most probably, like the former patient, dissatisfied with her marriage. It seems that she could not sever her marriage due to her dependent personality. However, the ongoing stress placed her in a constant state of preparedness to take some action in order to cope with this avoidable stress. Her mother's death probably freed her from some restraining forces and intensified the acuteness of this problem. It is highly doubtful whether she would have adopted her bizarre fears if she had not hoped to effect some desired change in her marital relationship, most probably in the form of increased attention from her husband. Thus, we believe that the death in itself would not have been sufficient to cause the bizarre neurotic symptoms.

However, in addition to the controllability demands, the symptoms had another important goal. After the loss of the central supporting figure in her life, to whom she was unusually attached, the woman became progressively depressed. It appears, then, that her unusual bizarre symptoms were chosen for their high distractive value in order to free the consciousness from intense occupation by stimuli related to the loss and other distressing factors and to thereby prevent further intensification of the depression.

In reference to this case, we do not altogether exclude the possibility that in some cases the distraction value may have been almost the sole function of bizarre neurotic symptoms. In other words, it is possible that in a small minority of cases, unavoidable stress will motivate a subject to adopt neurotic symptoms, primarily in an attempt to prevent the development of severe depression. However, we believe that the symptoms in these cases would tend to be unusually bizarre, as they were in the case of the chocolate phobia.

Inevitable Danger

Sometimes, bizarre neurotic symptoms emerge in response to anticipation of an inevitable impending event such as the expected death of a loved one or the expectation of inevitable failure. However, we do not classify these stresses as "unavoidable" since the events have not yet occurred but merely exist in the individual's cognitive system. The bizarre symptoms not only provide an efficient tool for distraction, but they also supply the subject with some direct control over the stress. The symptom may either cause the stress to be eliminated from the subject's cognitive system or reduce its damaging effect by modifying its meaning. An example demonstrating the first possibility is a case study (R. W. White & Watt, 1981, pp. 205–208) of an 11-year-old boy who was unusually attached to his grandfather. The boy was quite apprehensive about his grandfather's expected death, and as a result he developed unusual ritualistic behaviors. Inasmuch as the event had not yet occurred, it may be argued that the rituals caused not only distraction, but also the "actual" elimination of the stress. In a way, this interpretation is consistent with some experimental findings showing the importance of illusory control in coping with stress-provoking depression or anxiety (see studies mentioned on pp. 83–84). For example, Geer, Davison, and Gatchel (1970) found that subjects who were led to believe that they could control the amount of stress to which they were subjected in the course of an experiment displayed less anxiety arousal than did members of the control group. Geer and his colleagues concluded that

> *man creates his own gods to fill in gaps in his knowledge about a sometimes terrifying environment . . . creating at least an illusion of control which is presumably comforting. Perhaps the next best thing to being master of one's fate is being deluded into thinking that he is. (pp. 737–738)*

Two examples mentioned earlier illustrate the modification of the meaning of the stress to a less damaging one. One is the case of the young man who developed claustrophobia after realizing that his business was doomed to failure, and the other is the case of the man who developed elevator phobia in response to his expected inevitable discharge from work (see p. 110). In both these cases, the development of the bizarre symptoms enabled the subjects to change the meaning of their stress; they were able to attribute the stress to factors other than the self and thereby prevent feelings of self-devaluation and self-blame. Being afraid of an elevator is less damaging to the ego than the acknowledgment that one is inadequate at one's job.

9

Hysteria: A Theoretical Discussion

In the psychoanalytic doctrine of repression, hysteria has special theoretical importance since, according to this theory, repression reaches its ultimate level of efficiency in this neurotic reaction. Thus, a more detailed theoretical discussion of this disorder may be expected to shed some additional light on the theory of repression. This discussion may more clearly expose the weaknesses of psychoanalysis and further strengthen the position of the psychobizarreness theory.

In psychoanalysis, the causes of hysteria are primarily attributed to repressed childhood conflicts. Repression of anxiety-provoking childhood events plays an important role in all neuroses, but is particularly emphasized in the etiology of hysteria (Chodoff, 1974; Erdelyi & Goldberg, 1979; Fenichel, 1946; H. B. Lewis, 1981; Sackeim, Nordlier, & Gur, 1979; Wachtel, 1977). Fenichel (1946) formulated this point of view as follows:

> In conversion, symptomatic changes of physical functions occur, which unconsciously and in a distorted form, give expression to instinctual impulses that previously had been repressed. . . . the specific type of distortion being determined by the historical events that created the repression. (p. 216)

As has been stated, psychoanalysis attributes tremendous importance to repression of traumatic events in the exploration of all neuroses. The retrieval of these experiences is of great importance in producing therapeutic changes (Erdelyi & Goldberg, 1979; Fenichel, 1946; H. B. Lewis, 1981; Wachtel, 1977). However, as was indicated previously, psychoanalysis has no reliable evidence to verify its repression theory. On the contrary, the experimental evidence argues against its validity. As we have already shown and will continue to demonstrate later (pp. 138–142, 187–189), psychoanalytic investigators have never proved that the information they gathered in their case studies regarding forgotten childhood events reflects actual events. Moreover, even if they could supply such evidence, they would still have to prove that these events play a direct role in the etiology of hysteria or other neuroses. They would also need to explain why psychoanalytic therapeutic methods that make an intensive effort to revive the memories buried in the unconsciousness are generally ineffective (Erwin, 1980; Gross, 1979; Rachman & Wilson, 1980) while other techniques that do not involve recall of childhood events are beneficial in curing neurotic symptoms such as hysteria (Blanchard & Hersen, 1976; Liebson, 1969; Parry-Jones, Santer-Westrate, & Crawley, 1970).

One problem that especially concerns hysteria is the psychoanalytic claim of unconsciousness conversion of psychological energy into a somatic ailment. The antagonism toward this concept is reflected in statements such as the one Rimm and Somervill (1977) made expressing their antagonism toward this idea by stating that "it is unfortunate that the label conversion is still used" (p. 79). They noted that the concept has neither descriptive nor theoretical value. "Precisely how a psychological conflict, or the energy associated with such a conflict, can somehow be transferred into an apparent physical ailment has never been clarified" (p. 79). Similarly, Ziegler and Imboden (1962) noted that investigators "found no scientific evidence in support of the 'transmutation of energy' (or of 'libido') theory of the mechanism of conversion, and consider that the term 'conversion reaction' should be used only in a metaphorical sense, not a literal sense" (p. 285). However, Gedo (1979) dismissed altogether the concept of psychic energy when he declared that ". . . I have become persuaded that neither a literal nor a metaphorical interpretation of the concept of psychic energy is epistemologically tenable" (p. 165). A similar conclusion is arrived at by Mendelson (1982).

In this respect, we propose that if the concept *conversion of energy* has any theoretical value, then its formulation in terms of the psychobizarreness theory may make it more plausible. Hysterical patients, instead of investing their attentional energy in their stressful psychological problems are in fact converting this energy by actively directing the attention to bizarre physical symptoms that have for them both unusual distractive (in Freudian terms "defensive") and controllability value.

Another chronic problematic issue in the psychoanalytic theory of neurosis is the concept of the unconscious. We have discussed the issue in detail elsewhere, and as was stated, the scientific evidence in support of this psychoanalytic concept is meager. However, one research study on hysteria may appear to be consistent with the psychoanalytic model. Sackeim et al. (1979) claimed, in accordance with the psychoanalytic theory, that hysterical blindness is determined by automatic unconscious defense operations. To support their claim, they presented four previously reported case studies of hysterical blindness (see Brady & Lind, 1961; Grosz & Zimmerman, 1965, 1970; E. Miller, 1968; Theodor & Mandelcorn, 1973; Zimmerman & Grosz, 1966). In three of these cases, the patients' performance on a visual test was below chance level, namely, different than what would be expected from a truly blind person. For example, in one study (Grosz & Zimmerman, 1965; Zimmerman & Grosz, 1966), three triangles were projected onto a screen that contained three windows. In each trial, two of the figures were inverted and the third was upright. If the subject selected the switch below the upright triangle, he was informed that his response was correct. If, however, he chose either of the other two switches, he was informed that his response was incorrect. The triangles were randomly projected so that the upright triangle appeared equally often in each of the three windows. The subject's correct responses in the absence of the visual stimuli (first stage) were then compared with correct responses obtained when the stimuli were projected onto the windows (second stage). The results showed that the patient's performance in the second stage was significantly below the chance level determined at the first stage. To examine whether the patient's correct responses could be experimentally manipulated, the experimenter's collaborator told the subject that the doctors knew or thought that he could see because he had made fewer correct responses than a blind person would. He was also told the number of correct responses required for chance-level performance. As one would expect, in a subsequent visual test the subject's correct responses increased to a chance level. Similar results were obtained in the other two case studies, where similar experimental procedures were employed. In the fourth case study (Grosz & Zimmerman, 1970), the patient, a 15-year-old girl, demonstrated almost perfect vision, despite her claim to be blind. Sackeim et al. (1979) utilized these data, particularly the latter case study, to build a psychoanalytically oriented model of hysterical blindness, according to which visual experiences of the hysterically blind subjects are mediated by autonomous, unconscious processes.

To further strengthen their position that unconscious processes exist, Sackeim et al.

referred to an additional case study, previously reported by Weiskrantz, Warrington, Sanders, & Marshall (1974), of a subject who had suffered from a lesion in a certain area of his visual cortex that caused lack of visual experience in the left visual field. As in the abovementioned fourth case, although this patient denied any sense of "seeing" on the damaged visual field, he succeeded in correctly guessing the visual stimuli presented to him in this field.

In our opinion, this evidence is by no means sufficient to support Sackeim et al.'s psychoanalytic model of hysteria or the existence of autonomous, unconscious processes. Alternative explanations are possible for all five of these case studies. First, the below-chance-level performance of the first three cases may be explained by our previously discussed assumption that the attentional barrier against threatening inputs is never complete. A minimal level of awareness remains in effect under all conditions no matter how much attention is occupied by the bizarre symptom. Some knowledge of the stressful demands that had induced the individual to adopt and maintain the symptoms, and thoughts that he himself had faked the bizarre responses for coping purposes would penetrate, from time to time, the attentional domain. However, subjects usually succeed in warding off these threatening inputs through various attentional manipulation devices, such as rapid shift of attention and utilization of the belief system developed by self-deception mechanisms. Thus, when the individual's coping mechanism is threatened, as in the abovementioned case study by Grosz and Zimmerman (1965), a subject would consciously and deliberately manipulate her behavior to cope with the threat.

Second, in our opinion, Sackeim et al. misinterpreted the evidence of the fourth case study. The authors maintained that the 15-year-old girl identified visual stimuli at a high level of accuracy even though she claimed to be blind. Sackeim et al. rejected the idea of malingering (i.e., conscious denial) as an interpretation of these data by arguing that "a consciously malingering patient would be unlikely to maintain claims of blindness while giving correct identification of visual stimuli" (p. 479). However, upon close examination of the case one many realize that the statement that the girl claimed total blindness is highly questionable. It is true that she occasionally demonstrated some blurred vision, but her complaints of blindness were primarily limited to printed letters. This is clearly indicated in the text of the case on several occasions. For example, Grosz and Zimmerman (1970) noted that "her behavior showed no signs of any visual deficits except when asked to read small or large print" (p. 118). Similarly, sometime after the experimental visual test when "her condition was still essentially unchanged . . . she scored 100% loss of vision for reading in both eyes" (p. 121). Thus, the girl was hysterically blind only to reading, and it may be argued that her perfect performance in the visual test was due to the presentation to her of geometrical shapes (triangles) rather than letters. It appears, then, that the apparent discrepancy between the patient's visual performance and her verbal report was due to the experimental procedure employed. The functional selectivity in hysterical symptoms is well known (Coleman, Butcher, & Carson, 1984; Rimm & Sommervill, 1977). It can be argued that the patient developed blindness for reading because this was consistent with her controllability demands. The girl was subjected to a chronic lack of attention by her ambitious parents, who "appeared to be very busy pursuing their own activities and seemed always to be in a rush to go somewhere or to work on some project" (p. 117). The girl's level of stress was especially high because as the eldest of four children she had to take care of her siblings. The hysterical blindness for reading freed her from this responsibility and compelled her mother to spend practically all her free time helping the patient with her homework assignments. In addition to its high controllability value this symptom probably had high distractive value as well, because a continuous manifestation of such behavioral deviation requires a great deal of attentional investment. As in this case study, evidence presented by various investigators (Blanchard & Hersen, 1976; Rangaswamy & Kamakshi, 1983; Volkmar, Poll, & M. Lewis, 1984) clearly demonstrates the strong link between hysterical symptoms and stressful life events in children or adolescents.

Sackeim et al.'s reference to the brain-damage case is also open to an alternative explanation. First, this case study has not even a remote relationship to Sackeim et al.'s notion of unconscious, in which the element of defense is highly emphasized. Second, it may be argued that the cortical area was not completely damaged and that some dull visual information was transmitted to the conscious attentional area. This information may not have been strong enough to produce normal sight but, because the stimulus was presented to the intact visual field shortly before exposure to the damaged field and because it was sufficiently large, it provided him enough information to correctly guess the stimulus. For example, in one of the visual tasks the letters "X" and "O" were first presented in the intact area of the patient's visual field and then they were projected on the "blind field." The subject correctly guessed the letters but claimed that he had no sense of seeing. However, when questioned more he said that he "perhaps had a 'feeling' that the stimulus was either . . . 'smooth' (the O) or 'jagged' (the X)" (Weiskrantz et al., 1974, p. 721). Moreover, the patient was able to correctly guess or "unconsciously see the stimuli" only if they were large enough.

Thus, at the most, Sackeim et al.'s autonomous unconscious model of hysteria is based on questionable if not inaccurate data. The authors attempted to get additional confirmation of their model by induction of hypnotic blindness to normal subjects. However, research of this type is too far from the target of their theory—real cases of hysteria—and, therefore, it cannot provide any scientific validation of their theory. Moreover, even if one would be willing to accept their interpretation of the abovementioned cases, it is hard to see how and in what sense psychopathology would benefit from this vigorous effort (Gur & Sackeim, 1979; pp. 57–58 in this book) to prove existence of autonomous, unconscious processes. How, for example, would this help one cope with the problem of choice of symptoms?

The dissatisfaction with the psychoanalytic explanation of hysteria led to several additional attempts to explain the phenomenon (e.g., see Chodoff, 1974; Rimm & Somervill, 1977; Szasz, 1975; Ullmann & Krasner, 1975). These models, which are behavioristic in their basic approach, emphasize the controllability value of hysteria. Essentially the behaviorists do not make much of a distinction between the hysteric and the malingerer (Parry-Jones et al., 1970; Rimm & Somervill, 1977; Ullmann & Krasner, 1975). For example, Rimm and Somervill (1977) noted that

> regardless of his level of awareness, the patient has learned to cope with the environment in a manner that is burdensome to himself and to others. In this light, it does not make a great deal of difference whether we use the label of hysteric or malingerer. (p. 82)

This theoretical model may seem to be similar to our explanation of the disorder, but in fact the two theories are fundamentally different.

First, although our theory, like the behaviorist's approach, emphasizes the controllability value of hysterical symptoms, we attribute, as does psychoanalysis, great importance to the distractive or repressive value of these symptoms. Neurotic bizarre symptoms are adopted not only with the aim of reducing the stress-causing stimuli or of deriving some benefit from the social environment, but also in order to divert one's attention from the unbearable stressful situation. Although the controllability value of the symptoms plays a vital role, in most cases the distractive value is just as important. As a result, most neurotic subjects succeed in achieving a high level of unawareness. Thus, as in other areas of psychotherapy, the behaviorists completely neglect to relate to unconscious aspects of neuroses such as hysteria.

We have mentioned the possibility that in some cases there might be no clear distinction between a neurotic patient and a malingerer. Sometimes the controllability, rather than the distractive value, becomes dominant because the level of stress is insufficient to motivate the subject to perform the activities necessary for attaining a high state of unconsciousness. Thus, in this regard our position is closer to that of the behaviorists, who make no clear distinction between the hysteric and the malingerer. However, we do not suggest automatically classifying all malingerers as hysterics, as the behaviorists imply. The classification of a malingerer as a hysteric should be the exception rather than the rule. Only if convincing evidence is presented that the individual is subjected to a high level of stress may he or she be given the status of a hysteric neurotic. We are aware that in some cases it would be difficult to distinguish between a subject who adopted the symptoms in response to unbearable stress (true hysteric) and one who created the symptoms only in order to gain some benefit (true malingerer), such as monetary rewards following an accident (Coleman et al., 1984). However, it may be that a discrimination between these two types of behavioral responses would be easier if—apart from employing the somewhat simple traditional discriminative method, according to which malingerers tend to conceal their "symptoms" and display them only to a few authority figures while the hysteric subjects demonstrate readiness to share their problems with everybody (Coleman et al., 1984)— the clinician would carefully examine the individual's level of stress prior to the development of the symptoms.

The second fundamental difference between behaviorism and the psychobizarreness theory is that the former employs different sets of concepts for explanation of hysteria and of bizarre fears. On the one hand, hysteria is explained in terms of reinforcement (e.g., see Blanchard & Hersen, 1976), which is somewhat similar to our notion of controllability. On the other hand, bizarre phobia is explained on the basis of the classical conditioning paradigm. The possibility that certain phobias, namely pathological ones, might be operant behaviors in the same manner as hysteria and that the same principles should therefore apply in their explanation is not considered by the behaviorists. Principally, apart from their blind adherence to the mechanistic animal model, the behaviorists seem to have no plausible argument as to why their suggestion that hysteric symptoms are displayed for reinforcement purposes should not also apply to bizarre fears, particularly in view of the total collapse of their classical conditioning theory for bizarre phobias (see chapter 10). In this regard, psychobizarreness theory is similar to psychoanalysis (H. B. Lewis, 1981) because both apply the same set of principles for explanation of hysteria, bizarre phobias, and in fact all types of pathological symptoms.

One possible argument the behaviorists might raise against our theoretical model is that therapeutically it makes little difference whether behavioral deviations, such as hysteria, are regarded as coping strategies or as operant tools for obtaining reinforcement. However, while our main concern here is not the beneficial effects of therapeutic strategies, it may be worthwhile to note that research data show that the behaviorists' methods are not as successful as they claim. With regard to hysteria, these data show that symptom substitution and/or return is not an unlikely phenomenon when their methods are applied (Blanchard & Hersen, 1976; Zimmerman & Grosz, 1966). Moreover, in accord with our theoretical claim, evidence presented by Blanchard and Hersen (1976) demonstrated that the therapeutic effectiveness of behavioral-extinction procedures in treating hysterical symptoms may be greatly enhanced if the patient is taught more useful skills "to cope with both the usual and more unusual stresses encountered in life" (p. 127).

To some extent, our explanation of hysteria synthesizes ideas from both behaviorism and psychoanalysis. As does psychoanalysis, the psychobizarreness theory emphasizes the distractibility (or repressive) function of hysteria and the idea that hysteria and bizarre phobias share the same etiological basis. We have also shown that the psychobizarreness theory is similar to behaviorism in respect to the controllability aspect of hysteria. Another similarity is that both behaviorism and psychobizarreness theory emphasize the role of subject's current life conditions in motivating him or her to adopt the bizarre responses, rather than dealing with his past. Indeed, a growing body of research demonstrates the vital importance of the individual's current life events in the etiology of hysteria (Blanchard & Hersen, 1976; Brady, 1966; Coleman et al., 1984; Jones, 1980; Rangaswamy & Kamakshi, 1983; Volkmar et al., 1984). However, in this context, it may be worthwhile to indicate that the experiencing of stress is determined not only by situational factors, but by personality factors as well (Appley & Trumbull, 1967; Janis, 1983; Keane, 1985; Monat & Lazarus, 1977). This principle is demonstrated in the case of hysteria, inasmuch as research data (Horowitz, 1977; Jones, 1980; Marks, 1973; D. Shapiro, 1965) strongly suggest that prehysterical patients tend to overestimate and overreact to stressful situations. However, apart from a general deficit in the personality makeup, hysterical patients do not appear likely to have a specific personality profile. Cleghorn (1967), for example, noted in this respect that "the available evidence indicates that conversion reactions occur in a wide variety of personality disorders, and that there is no good reason for identifying them solely with the hysterical personality, although the association is frequent enough to be intriguing" (p. 553). Yet, one of the prominent characteristics of hysterical patients is that like schizophrenic subjects, they exhibit a lack of habituation to repeated auditory stimuli (Horvath, Friedman, & Meares, 1980; Lader & Sartorius, 1968). It is possible that the difficulty in habituation stems from their inability to exclude stressful stimuli from their focus of attention by concentrating on a competitive nonstressful stimulus. In other words they need more drastic measures to achieve distraction when they encounter stressful events.

In conclusion, it appears that of all theoretical models the psychobizarreness theory provides the most plausible explanation of the development of hysteria.

CONCLUSIONS TO PART III

In this part, we laid down the foundations of the psychobizarreness theory. This theory includes the concepts of pathological repression, memory-inhibiting factors, and self-deception mechanisms, as well as the principles of controllability, saliency–availability, and cost–benefit. Another important suggestion is the replacement of the concept of defense mechanism with the more general and neutral concept of coping mechanism.

Throughout this book, particularly in the first part, we have demonstrated the scientific inadequacy of the psychoanalytic theory. Not only is there no direct scientifically acceptable evidence to support its central assumptions, particularly the concept of repression and unconsciousness, but the cumulative research findings are inconsistent with the theory. Moreover, many important issues, particularly the long-standing problem of choice of symptom, remain unanswered. Yet, despite this poor scientific basis, psychoanalytic concepts continue to dominate the field of psychopathology and personality theories, and unfortunately, to guide the work of most clinicians as well. While this state of affairs may be partly due to insufficient awareness of the lack of scientific validation of psychoanalysis, its main cause seems to be the lack of an alternative theory to explain psychopathological phenomena more adequately. As will be demonstrated in the next part of this book, the mechanistic learning concepts cannot substitute for the psychoanalytic ideas. As the problems behaviorists encounter today in the area of psychopathology are not less severe than those of psychoanalysis, that the scientific halo of the behavioristic concepts has become somewhat tarnished. Thus, in order to bring about a radical change in this area, namely, the abandonment of these theoretical empires, it is necessary to offer an alternative theory that can provide a more comprehensive explanation to the psychopathological disorders and that is consistent with the cumulative research findings. As was pointed out by Kuhn (1962),

> *Once it has achieved the status of a paradigm . . . a scientific theory is declared invalid only if an alternative candidate is available to take its place. . . . The decision to reject one paradigm is always simultaneous with the decision to accept another. (see Holmes, 1974, p. 650)*

In the same way, Conant (1948, cited in Holmes, 1974, p. 650) indicated that "a theory is not overthrown by data but by a better theory." Similarly, Holmes (1974) in his important critique on the psychoanalytic repression theory noted that "in considering an alternative theory it is important for it to be broad enough to encompass all of the experimental findings as well as what appear to be instances of repression observed in the clinical settings" (p. 650).

It appears, then, that psychobizarreness theory provides satisfactory answers to the problematic issues that psychopathology encounters today and synthesizes the basic ideas of rival theories. It also encompasses in its framework seemingly inconsistent research and clinical evidence in the field.

IV

PSYCHOLOGY OF FEAR AND PHOBIAS: TRADITIONAL MODELS VERSUS THE COGNITIVE– AUTOMATIC CONDITIONING THEORY OF FEAR

As with neuroses, the cumulative research and clinical evidence to be presented in this part raises serious doubts as to the validity of the traditional theories in explaining the acquisition of fears of all kinds. The objective of this part is to present an alternative theory to explain the development of normal fears. Consistent with our conceptualization, we argue that it is necessary to distinguish between bizarre and normal fears. The former symptoms are explained in terms of psychobizarreness theory, while for explanation of the latter, we suggested revising the traditional conditioning paradigm. The most important aspect of the revised theory is its emphasis on involvement of the conscious in the conditioning process. However, the new model was termed *cognitive– automatic conditioning theory of fear* to emphasize that both cognitive and automatic processes are involved in the development of normal fears.

In chapter 10, we attempt to show the weaknesses of all the dominant theories of acquisition of fear and, thereby, to demonstrate the need for a new theoretical model of the development of fears among human subjects. No attempt is made to thoroughly review the research data in this area, and the interested reader is advised to refer to several reviews on this topic (Emmelkamp, 1982; Gray, 1971; Marks, 1969, 1978; Rachman, 1978). Chapters 11 and 12 present the new theoretical model of conditioning, and in chapter 13, we discuss some theoretical problems that stem from our two proposed theories of fear and analyze two case studies mentioned in the literature in order to demonstrate more vividly the usefulness of these theories.

10

Inadequacy of Traditional Theories

PSYCHOANALYTIC MODEL

Theory

As is the case with hysteria, in psychoanalysis the concept of repression is very central to the explanation of phobias or fears. This is well implied by Freud's suggestion that phobia be called *anxiety hysteria* (H. B. Lewis, 1981, p. 63). In psychoanalysis, phobia is conceptualized as a defense against anxiety produced by conflicts or by the id's impulses, which in most cases had been repressed since early childhood. The phobia symptoms represent displacement of anxiety to fear of an object or situation that has some symbolic relationship to threatening internal demands that could not be discharged by normal means (e.g., see Fenichel, 1946). Perhaps the best example to demonstrate this conceptualization is Freud's famous case history of little Hans (see H. B. Lewis's summary and analysis of the case, 1981). Freudian-oriented investigators regard even fear reactions to spiders, snakes, and dogs in psychoanalytic terms (Abraham, 1927; H. B. Lewis, 1981; Moss, 1960; Newman & Stoller, 1969; Sperling, 1971). In an article for the American Psychoanalytic Association, Sperling (1971) noted that "most investigators seem to agree that the spider is a representative of the dangerous (orally devouring and anally castrating) mother, and that the main problem of these patients seems to center around their sexual identification and bi-sexuality" (p. 493). Similarly, H. B. Lewis (1981) noted, with regard to the relatively high prevalence of fear of snakes, spiders, and heights, that these fears might be "metaphors" of "forbidden emotional states" (p. 84).

Consistent with this theoretical approach, other psychodynamic investigators suggested that phobias may develop not only due to repression of anxiety-arousing impulses, but also because of repression of traumatic experiences. Accordingly, using the case studies method, several psychodynamic investigators (Marks, 1969, pp. 86–89) demonstrated that recall of the original trauma was sufficient to cause gradual disappearance of the fear reaction. More recently, Arieti (1979) suggested that a phobia may develop because of the repression of an emotional shock experience in the area of interpersonal relationships. In order to support his model, Arieti, like other psychoanalytic investigators, presented a case study of a phobic subject. However, it appears that none of the psychoanalytic models has enough data to defend its position and, therefore, they all should be rejected.

Criticisms

Argument 1: Poor Scientific Quality of Case Studies

Psychoanalysis relies almost completely on material from case studies to prove its position. We agree that use of this research method cannot be completely excluded in psychopathology. However, one must regard this source of evidence with suspicion and great caution. This is particularly so when an entire theory is based solely on this type of evidence, and when the data collection is not made by an independent observer. The poor scientific quality of psychoanalytic case studies may be demonstrated quite strongly by referring to Freud's case study of little Hans. Even today this case continues to be regarded as one of the main sources of the psychoanalytic theory of phobia (H. B. Lewis, 1981). In an excellent reanalysis of the case, Wolpe and Rachman (1960; see also Rachman, 1978) show that the gathering of information did not fulfill even very minimal requirements of scientific work. They indicated, for example, that Freud saw little Hans only once and that the material upon which Freud built his theory was supplied primarily by little Hans's father, who kept Freud informed by regular written reports. Moreover, the father's account of Hans's behavior was in several instances suspect. For example, he twice presented his own interpretation of Hans's behavior as observed facts. Many of the views and feelings purported to be Hans's were actually those of the father. Essentially, only material related to psychoanalysis was collected, while other factors were ignored. Furthermore, the boy himself was encouraged directly or indirectly to provide material relevant to psychoanalysis. Wolpe and Rachman (1960) concluded that the "facts of the case need to be treated with considerable caution" (p. 141).

As an alternative explanation of the case, Wolpe and Rachman suggest the classical conditioning paradigm. Hans experienced several unpleasant incidents with horses. The last one occurred just prior to the onset of the phobia. He was witness to an incident in which a horse and wagon were overturned. These experiences led Wolpe and Rachman (1960) to suggest that

> just as the little boy Albert (in Watson's classic demonstration) reacted with anxiety not only to the original conditioned stimulus—the white rat, but to other similar stimuli such as furry objects, cotton wool and so on; Hans reacted anxiously to horses, horse-drawn bases, vans . . ." (p. 146)

However, the behaviorists have problems with their own case of little Albert, which behavioristic clinicians (e.g., Rimm & Somervill, 1977) often use for defending their simplistic theoretical model due to lack of sufficient experimental evidence from human subjects in the area of fear and phobia. As will be elaborated soon, Harris (1979) showed, in a critical review of the case of little Albert, that it does not have much scientific value.

Argument 2: Poor Reliability of Childhood Memories

Apart from the poor scientific quality of the psychoanalytic theorists' general methodological approach, which may lead to distortion in the collection of information, there is a question regarding the validity of the data (i.e., recollection of childhood memories) upon which their theory of fear is based. Even if the investigators collect the information in a very reliable way, it is still quite uncertain whether the events reported by the patients actually occurred. Moreover, even if they had, it is very doubtful whether these "lost memories" are responsible for the subjects' fears or whether recovery of these memories is what caused the disappearance of the fears reported in psychoanalytic case studies. Let us demonstrate this claim more vividly by examining three case studies reported by Moss (1960) and Bagby (1922).

Moss's Case Study. This case concerns a 45-year-old woman who had suffered from a fear of dogs for many years. The patient wanted to rid herself of this fear because she wished to give her daughter a puppy as a birthday present. Her decision to turn to a psychoanalyst was made soon after she saw the movie *The Three Faces of Eve*. The patient was treated by the method of hypnosis. After four hypnotic sessions, the childhood pathogenic experience which supposedly had occurred at the age of 4 was, according to the report, uncovered and revivified. Then, after four additional therapeutic sessions, the fear gradually disappeared. Moss (1960) introduced the case as a "brief successful treatment of a phobia reaction in which the patient's repressive defenses were penetrated, leading to a simple, convincing demonstration of the childhood learning of the phobic response and its subsequent ramifications" (p. 266). However, the case is subject to three major faults.

First, careful examination of the case raises serious doubt regarding the actual occurrence of the repressed "childhood traumatic episode." This is because the patient's mother "continued to deny that the event had ever happened" (p. 269), and the patient herself expressed considerable doubt as to its occurrence. This is reflected by the fact that in a meeting 1 year later she opened the discussion by asking, "Suppose the event I recalled wasn't true; could the mind make up something like that?" (p. 269). Moss chose to ignore this possibility completely. Moreover, faithful to psychoanalytic doctrine, the question was interpreted as a reflection of "evidence of some residual resistance against a complete emotional acceptance of her childhood trauma" (p. 269). If such a question would be directed to a memory expert such as Neisser (1982), he would answer it very definitely in the affirmative, and it would support this claim from his own personal experience (see also p. 45). It is worthwhile noting that Moss's comment that the traumatic episode "recalled" by the patient's hypnosis was quite similar to the death incident in *The Three Faces of Eve*, which had prompted the patient to seek therapy. It is very likely that this experience affected the patient's "recollections" during hypnosis.

Indeed, empirical evidence by a number of investigators shows that a subject's experiences prior to hypnosis do influence his or her responses in the hypnotic trance (Klinger, 1970; Orne, 1959; Sheehan & Bowman, 1973). Moreover, there is much data showing that a subject's behavior in both hypnotic and nonhypnotic states may be affected by the demand characteristics of the situation (see review by Ullmann & Krasner, 1975). Thus, it may be argued that the therapist's expectations, which were conveyed to the patient very clearly, caused her to invent the story during the hypnotic session. For example, at the end of the third session "she was given the post-hypnotic instruction that the meaning of her life-long fear of dogs would begin to manifest itself between sessions" (p. 264). It may be argued that it took her four hypnotic sessions until these memories were "communicated" to her from her "unconscious" because throughout this period she had some moral reservation about inventing a story and had to overcome her resistance before she was able to comply with the therapist's implicit demands.

Second, as a faithful psychoanalyst, Moss approaches the case with an implicit assumption that the patient's fear must have been developed through some traumatic experience in her early life and that this event must have been retained in her memory's system despite her display of complete forgetfulness. However, fear of animals may also be acquired through observational learning and/or cultural training (see p. 164). Moreover, even if the fear were developed as the result of a traumatic event, a subject may fail to remember the original event, not necessarily because the experience was transferred to a "mysterious black store," but because of the normal course of forgetting, which may cause the event to vanish completely from one's memory system.

Third, the successful treatment outcome can by no means be considered even a partial verification of Moss's psychoanalytic claim that it was attained by the recall of the original traumatic event. Hundreds of behavioral studies (e.g., see Rachman & Wilson, 1980) show that fear may be eliminated without any reference to the original conditions under which it developed. Moreover, when Moss's method of treatment is carefully examined, one may notice that it is much more plausible to attribute the beneficial effect of the therapy to the patient's strong motivation to overcome her fears (which is very obvious throughout the paper) and to an informal desensitization process, of which the therapist was not aware. Let us examine some of this evidence.

The first two sessions were devoted to training the patient in achieving a hypnotic state. It may be argued that as in the conventional desensitization procedure, the subject was first trained to relax. Indeed, the relaxation benefit was so outstanding that it spread to the patient's behavior outside the therapy room. Thus, Moss (1960) noted, with respect to the first two sessions, that "one immediate benefit of these sessions was that for the first time she and her husband had been able to talk freely about . . . a painful period in their lives" (p. 266). The actual extinction or desensitization process began at the fourth session, during which the patient, in the relaxed state of hypnosis, talked about the supposedly repressed material, namely, fear of dogs. In the interval between the fourth and fifth sessions, the patient patted a dog and had a dream in which she was attacked by a large dog but managed to calm it. It may be argued that both the relaxation training and a personal conviction that she had reached the "root" of her fears during the fourth session, motivated her to initiate these approach responses. Further evidence that gradual self-initiated exposure had taken place was reported with respect to the 1-month interval between the seventh and last sessions. While on a skiing vacation with her daughter, she patted several dogs she encountered. This was done with the encouragement of her daughter, who yelled, "Oh, look, Mommy used to be afraid of dogs and isn't any more." Most likely this in vivo desensitization was practiced on other occasions as well. Thus, the informal desensitization procedure, the subject's strong motivation to recover, and the placebo or cognitive effects (Bootzin, 1975; Kirsch, Tennen, Wickless, Saccone, & Cody, 1983; Rachman & Wilson, 1980) appear to be the true factors that resulted in the extinction of the dog phobia, rather than recall of the "pathogenic experience." In this respect, Kirsch et al.'s (1983) findings that "a highly credible expectancy modification procedure" is just as effective as systematic desensitization in reducing fear of snakes may shed important light on Moss's therapeutic procedure. In the study by Kirsch et al., subjects were told that clinical research had shown certain childhood events to be related to fear of snakes, and they were encouraged to relive their fantasies with free association regarding them. In actual fact, these events were common to most children (e.g., the first day of school) and had no relation to snake phobia. Kirsch et al. reported that this psychoanalytic placebo procedure resulted in significant improvement of the same degree attained by systematic desensitization. Thus, there seems to be no need for the unproved and complicated theoretical assumptions of psychoanalysis to explain the extinction of animal phobias.

Bagby's Case Studies. Bagby (1922) described two cases of phobia. The first is that of a young woman who suffered from a severe phobia of running water. The phobia was very intense and disturbed her in many ways for about 13 years. The patient succeeded in overcoming her fear after she met her aunt, whom she had not seen for 13 years. Upon meeting her, her aunt said, "I have never told." According to Bagby, these magic words were sufficient to retrieve a traumatic episode that had occurred when the patient was 7 years old and with her aunt. As a result of this recall experience, the very intense, long-lasting fear gradually subsided.

The second case, which is similar, is that of a man who suffered from a fear of being grasped from behind. The phobia had begun in early childhood and continued to disturb the patient severely until the age of 55. Then, he returned to his hometown, where he met an old man who had been a shopkeeper during the patient's childhood. The man reminded him of the traumatic episode; he said that when the patient had been a child, he used to pass the store and take a handful of peanuts from the stand in front. One day, the shopkeeper had jumped out and grabbed him from behind, which had terrified the boy. He had suffered from the phobia after that. According to Bagby, this patient's fear also gradually subsided after the traumatic episode was recalled.

Bagby used these two cases to support Freud's theory of repression. However, when reading these cases, one can hardly avoid feeling a lack of confidence in the reliability of the data. Bagby does not indicate the source of his information. It is very unlikely, however, that he himself witnessed the recall episodes. It is very doubtful that he even met the two patients, and it is not unlikely that Bagby got the information from a second or more remote source. If this were indeed the case, then the scientific value of this evidence is no greater than that of gossip. It may be worthwhile to indicate that Harris (1979) demonstrated, in regard to Watson's case of little Albert, that gross distortion of information is likely to occur when the material is reproduced by a second or third source.

The cases reported by Bagby contain two additional puzzling aspects. According to psychoanalytic theory (Perry & Laurence, 1984, p. 24), a subject should be strongly resistant to exposure to, or recall of, the original fearful condition (see case studies by Kendler, 1968, pp. 459–460; and by R. W. White, 1964, pp. 61–68). How, then, could Bagby's second patient have voluntarily gone to visit the place where the repressed traumatic event had occurred, and why did the first patient instantly recall the episode at the first hint? How can psychoanalysis explain these inconsistencies?

Another puzzling question concerns the tendency of prolonged fear responses to be very resistant to extinction (Jacobs & Nadel, 1985). In Bagby's report, however, one gets the impression that the fears almost magically disappeared upon retrieval of the lost memories. For example, in his reference to the common features of the two cases, Bagby (1922) noted that "the symptoms disappear when recall is effected. No sublimation, transference, or treatment by suggestion was required" (p. 18).

Thus, psychoanalytic investigators have no convincing evidence to defend their proposition that the persistence and/or elimination of fears are related to repression of childhood memories. They do not have enough evidence to prove the validity of the reported "memories" and their connection to the persistence or disappearance of the fears. As was stated, these "memories" may be no more than total fabrication (Erdelyi & Goldberg, 1979; E. F. Loftus & G. R. Loftus, 1980; Neisser, 1982).

Further evidence, which weakens the psychoanalytic claim that repressed childhood traumatic events form the basis of adult fears or phobias, is the lack of significant relationship between separation anxiety in childhood and agoraphobia or panic disorders (Thyer, Nesse, Cameron, & Curtis, 1985; Thyer, Nesse, Curtis, & Cameron, 1986). Thyer et al. (1986) noted that

> numerous published case histories and uncontrolled descriptive studies initially did suggest that childhood separation anxiety was a precursor to the development of agoraphobia in adults, but subsequent control-group studies comparing agoraphobic vs. other psychiatric patients have failed to find the predicted selective history of childhood separation trauma with respect to the agoraphobic patients. (p. 209)

Argument 3: Sexual Anxiety

Rachman (1978) noted that Freud specifically asserted that phobias never occur if the person has a normal sexual adjustment (see also Bagby, 1922). However, he stated that this claim remained unproven and almost certainly incorrect. Rachman (1978) asserted that in the course of 20 years of psychotherapeutic work, he and his colleagues "have assessed and treated a substantial number of phobic patients and although many of them do report multiple problems, including sexual difficulties, a large number have satisfactory sexual lives" (p. 220).

Argument 4: Vulnerability to Phobia

The psychoanalytic approach asserts that repression of frightening childhood events may make one vulnerable to the development of phobia later in life, even if the subject displays a complete forgetfulness of the event and no signs of fear during the prolonged interval. A stressful new event, which would normally pass with no marked effect, may awaken the "sleeping devils" and cause the spontaneous eruption and persistence of a very intense and peculiar fear. This idea was expressed by R. W. White and Watt (1981) in their discussion on the agoraphobic case study of Leonard that was mentioned previously. In addition, this psychoanalytic idea is deeply embedded in Jacobs and Nadel's (1985) theory of fear, which will be discussed later in this chapter.

However, apart from case studies, which can be interpreted differently, there is no convincing empirical evidence to support these thoughts. Moreover, this claim is inconsistent with the bulk of studies reviewed earlier that show the beneficial effects of repression or denial of reality. These studies suggest that successful forgetting of traumatic events (i.e., the subject shows no sign of fear or other disturbances when subsequently dealing with stimuli related to the forgotten event) may have a beneficial effect on the subject's total mental functioning.

Argument 5: Effectiveness of Behavioral Techniques

We have already discussed this point in our critique of psychoanalysis in general. However, this criticism is particularly relevant here because behavioral techniques can be efficient in treating fears (Goisman, 1983; Mathews, Gelder, & Johnston, 1981; Rimm & Masters, 1979; Telch, Agras, Taylor, Roth, & Gallen, 1985), including sexual phobias, without any reference to repressed memories of childhood or any other period of one's life. This is in contrast to the conspicuous therapeutic inferiority of psychoanalysis (Erwin, 1980; Rachman & Wilson, 1980). It is true that behavioral treatment of bizarre fears may cause symptom substitution or a relapse of the fear (see pp. 178, 262–263). However, in many cases the treatment is quite successful and this does not happen (Mathews et al., 1981). Moreover, even when the treatment is not totally successful, it is not necessarily due to lack of reference to childhood memories. As will be shown later in this book, other alternative explanations are possible.

Argument 6: Sex Differences

Neither psychoanalysis nor behavioral approaches provide a satisfactory answer as to why fears of all types are much more prevalent among women than among men (Davison & Neale, 1982; Gray, 1971; Marks, 1969; Mathews et al., 1981; Rachman, 1984a). Gray (1971) noted in this respect, that *the Freudians have seen sexual significance in this fact, regarding snakes as symbolic of the penis. No doubt they would find support for this interpretation in the fact that women report significantly more fear of snakes than do men. (They also claim to be more frightened of worms, rats, mice, and spiders). However, the fear of snakes is also found among our primate cousins, so we must seek a less extravagant explanation for this intriguing difference between the sexes in Man (unless we are to conclude that the chimpanzee—who is, admittedly, a very clever animal—is capable of symbolic sexual fears). (p. 15)*

Thus, the disproportion of fears between the two sexes constitutes a major problem for theoreticians (Rachman, 1984a), and psychoanalysis seems to have no satisfactory answer to it.

In conclusion, apart from these arguments, the psychoanalytic theory of fear is subject to all the criticism that were raised against psychoanalysis in general. The major criticism is the lack of evidence for the existence of an autonomous unconscious and the preservation of forgotten events. All these arguments, together with the findings reviewed previously, raise serious doubts as to the validity of the psychoanalytic explanation of fears and phobias.

BEHAVIORAL MODELS: CONDITIONING THEORY

Theory

Parallel to the decrease in the number of investigators and clinicians who remain faithful to the psychoanalytic doctrine of fears and phobias, more and more investigators and therapists turned to the rival camp, namely, the behavioral models. However, in recent years cumulative research data show that the theoretical gap left by psychodynamic approaches cannot be filled by learning theories.

The dominant behavioral theory for explanation of the etiology of fears and phobias is the Pavlovian conditioning paradigm. Historically, it was largely Watson and Rayner's (1920) pioneering work with little Albert that promoted the idea that the classical conditioning model might be useful in explaining human fears. Behavioral theoreticians, such as Wolpe and Rachman (1960) and Eysenck (1960), used this case for defending their behavioral explanation of fear.

However, data reviewed by Harris (1979) shows that there was much exaggeration and inaccurate reporting by Watson himself and by later investigators who referred to this case in their writings: "Critical reading of Watson and Rayner's . . . report reveals little evidence either that Albert developed a rat phobia or even that animals consistently evoked his fear" (p. 154). Harris (1979) further noted that "a more serious problem with clinicians' citing of the Albert study is the failure of Watson's contemporaries to replicate his work" (p. 155). Harris concluded that the conditioned-avoidance model of phobias does not seem to be in accord with more recent experimental and clinical data. Harris also criticized Seligman's (1971) preparedness theory of human phobias (to be discussed later in this chapter) as being based on an erroneous interpretation of Watson and Rayner's experimental work.

The learning theorists' conception of the conditioning model as the prime mechanism by which fear is developed was proved to be insufficient in explaining the phenomenon of resistance to extinction of fear responses (Hulse, Egeth, & Deese, 1980). This problem led behavioral investigators to adopt Mowrer's (1947, 1960) two-factor theory of fear. Mowrer claimed that at the first stage, an organism acquires fear responses by classical conditioning. Anxiety reduction attained by the escape or avoidance response serves to maintain the fear reactions. This theoretical model proved to be unsatisfactory, however, and was seriously criticized by many investigators, some of whom suggested alternative or modified explanations (de Silva & Rachman, 1984; Emmelkamp, 1982; Herrnstein, 1969; Hulse et al., 1980; Rachman, 1976, 1984a, 1984b). However, our main concern here is not this specific model but rather the difficulties of the conditioning theory itself, which serves as the basic theoretical model for all behavioral theorists in explaining the development of human fear responses. In the following section, we present arguments against the conditioning theory of fear. The first six were originally raised by Rachman (1976, 1977, 1978). Additional data that strengthened Rachman's claims, together with three more arguments raised by Jacobs and Nadel (1985), are also reviewed.

Criticisms

Argument 1: Failure to Acquire Fear

Contrary to conditioning theory, findings from research done during and shortly after World War II show that both children and adults failed to acquire conditioned fears even after repeated exposure to traumatic events or extremely frightening situations (see Rachman, 1977, 1978). Evidence of this was recently reported by Saigh (1984a, 1984b) as well. Subjects exposed to the traumatic war conditions in Beirut did not develop conditioned fear. On the contrary, the subjects' level of anxiety decreased markedly after exposure to the traumatic conditions. Saigh concluded that his results are incompatible with conditioning theory, and he suggested instead a cognitive model of fear acquisition. Interestingly, findings similar to those reported by Saigh were found on the other side of the Lebanon border (see Rofé & Lewin, 1980, 1982a). Emmelkamp (1982) reported additional findings that support the conclusions of Saigh or Rachman concerning the inadequacy of the conditioning paradigm to explain the development of fear symptoms among humans.

Saigh's conclusion was criticized, however, by Heimberg (1985) and by Keane (1985), who noted that results of studies on Vietnam War veterans appear to be consistent with the conditioning model. Saigh (1985) responded by pointing out that the cumulative research data from his own studies and other sources, such as those reported by Rachman (1978), were sufficient "to question the validity of the conditioning formulation." A similar approach is taken by Rachman (1985a), who noted that although positive findings from some sources indicate that there is some merit in the conditioning theory, "the 20-year-old (plus) theory is hard to defend as a satisfactory, sufficient and comprehensive theory of fear acquisition" (p. 427).

Argument 2: Conditioning Human Fears

Research evidence shows that attempts to condition human beings, infants or adults, have not been very successful. For example, a meticulous experimental attempt by Bregman (1934) to condition fear in 15 normal infants was a failure. This is consistent with evidence that people fail to develop conditioned fear in air raids. Other findings consistent with these observations show that patients treated with electrical aversive therapy do not develop fear under treatment. Most of these patients reported indifference to the conditioned stimuli employed in electrical aversion therapy. Similar findings were obtained in two experimental studies by Hallam and Rachman (1976), which were intended to provide an analogue to electrical aversion therapy.

Argument 3: Equipotential Premise

One of the assumptions of conditioning theory is that all stimuli have an equal chance of being associated with fear. According to Rachman (1977, 1978), this assumption does not seem valid because various evidence appears to support Seligman's (1971) preparedness theory, which says that fears, which on the evolutionary ladder had greater survival significance to organisms than did other stimuli, are more easily acquired. One of these findings is Valentine's (1930) report that he succeeded in conditioning his young daughter to fear a caterpillar but not a pair of opera glasses. However, many other findings (Delprato, 1980), which will be discussed shortly, place the validity of Seligman's preparedness theory in serious doubt. Thus, Rachman's evidence may not be enough to disprove the equipotential premise. Rachman's next argument, however, provides additional evidence against it.

Argument 4: Distribution of Fears

The distribution of fears, whether in the general population or in psychiatric samples, does not coincide with predictions from the equipotential premise. For example, fear of snakes is too common to be explained on the basis of the probable frequency of frightening experiences with snakes. An epidemiological study by Agras, Sylvester, and Oliveau (1969) revealed that the fear of snakes is far more prevalent than the fear of dentists or of infection, despite the much greater frequency of exposure to the latter. Rachman stated that according to conditioning theory, we should expect equal distribution of fear toward many objects and situations in our environment. Yet, some fears are far too common and others are far too rare. For example, fear of the dark is commonly seen among children while pajama phobia is not. Thus, if Seligman's preparedness theory is indeed invalid, as seems to be the case (see pp. 148–151), then conditioning theory is left with no answer to the question of why certain fears are more easily acquired than are others.

Argument 5: Vicarious Transmission of Fear

Observational learning exhibited by both humans (Bandura, 1969, 1977a) and animals (Cook, Mineka, Wolkenstein, & Laitsch, 1985; Mineka, Davidson, Cook, & Keir, 1984) raises difficulty for conditioning theory since such learning shows that fear may be acquired even if one has never seen the direct object of the fear-arousing stimulus.

Argument 6: Patients' Reports of Fear Onset

In the clinical setting, it is often difficult to determine the origin of a patient's phobia. Patients often fail to recall any traumatic experiences that might have initiated their phobias. Marks (1969) indicated that "there are many phobias . . . where there was no apparent trauma to initiate the phobia. In these cases learning theory provides no adequate explanation of the onset" (p. 92). Goorney and O'Connor (1971) demonstrated this in their study of excessive fears among aircrews during peace time. In only a quarter of the cases could the fears be attributed to specific precipitants such as accidents or frightening incidents. In the remainder, either no discernible cause could be found, or the precipitants were not of a traumatic or conditioning type. In agoraphobia or other types of bizarre fears, the inability of patients to recall a traumatic event that could have been responsible for their phobia becomes much more acute (Emmelkamp, 1982; Jacobs & Nadel, 1985; Mathews et al., 1981; Rachman, 1984a; Rachman & Seligman,

1976). Emmelkamp (1982) noted that "most studies investigating the development of clinical phobias could not support a classical conditioning interpretation to account for the acquisition of fears" (p. 18).

Argument 7: Clinical Phobias Are Independent of Environmental Context

In contrast to the Pavlovian model, once a clinical phobia has developed, its manifestation is often not bound to a specific environmental context:

> Anxiety or phobic reactions may strike at work, in an automobile, or even in the safety of one's own home. This runs counter to most known forms of learning. For example, Pavlovian fear conditioning appears to be largely context specific. A change in the context in which a conditional fear stimulus is presented can dramatically decrease both the intensity of the conditioned emotional response and the behavioral manifestation of that response. (Jacobs & Nadel, 1985, p. 514)

Argument 8: Broad Generalization

Unlike laboratory fears, generalization of clinical phobias is often unusually broad. Fear may generalize "so broadly that in some cases . . . the individual may not be able to tell us what is frightening" (Jacobs & Nadel, 1985, p. 514).

Argument 9: Resistance to Extinction

Pathological fears may be unusually resistant to extinction. Such responses "often fail to show extinction after many years of exposure to the feared stimulus, even in the absence of any aversive consequences. . . . This is at odds with the typical fear extinction pattern found in the laboratory" (Jacobs & Nadel, 1985, p. 514; for an example, see Rachman & Seligman, 1976).

Discussion

These arguments provide sufficient reason to question the validity of conditioning theory as an explanation of human fears. The theory seems totally incapable of explaining the development of clinical or bizarre phobias, and in its present form it cannot even satisfactorily explain the development of normal fears. This conclusion is consistent with Rachman's (1978) assertion that "at its best the conditioning theory can provide a partial explanation for the genesis of some fears" (p. 192).

However, despite these criticisms, Ost and Hugdahl (1981, 1983, 1985; Ost, 1985) insist that conditioning theory is the best explanation of clinical and normal fears. This position is based on data collected by having subjects answer short questionnaires on the origin of their phobias. The questions were formulated to be answered in a yes–no manner. Using this method, they found that most of their subjects attributed their phobias to conditioning experiences. To some extent, Ost and Hugdahl's position is supported by data from two studies by other investigators (McNally & Steketee, 1985; Rimm, Janda, Lancaster, Nahl, & Dittmar, 1977), who also used the questionnaire method. The latter investigators, however, examined only animal or specific phobias but not agoraphobia. In our opinion, moreover, these data cannot be used to defend conditioning theory for these reasons:

1. Questionnaire data cannot validate conditioning theory. The original behavioral theorists expressed strong opposition to the introspective method. First, subjects may not remember the origin of their phobias, particularly those that began in childhood.

For example, in McNally and Steketee's (1985) study, 91% of the subjects reported that their animal fears began before the age of 10, and 77% of all subjects could not recall the onset of their phobia. Second, even when subjects claim to remember the causes of their fears, their memories may be inaccurate. Subjects may distort the memories either unintentionally or in an attempt to rationalize their responses. This was acknowledged by McNally and Steketee (1985), who stated that

> even in those instances when patients did cite a specific event, it may not necessarily have been the actual cause of the phobia. It is possible that individuals postulate plausible triggering events when at a loss to explain the cause of their irrational fears. Therefore, more precisely, the present study concerns the causal attributions . . . made by patients to account for their phobia. (p. 434)

This assertion may be particularly applicable to the studies of Ost and Hugdahl since "rationalization responding" appears to be easier when the questions are posed in a way that can be answered by yes or no.

2. Ost and Hugdahl did not refute any of the arguments against the conditioning theory specified earlier. In fact, they seem to have overlooked them. Thus, if their claim that fears, particularly "clinical phobias . . . are acquired via direct conditioning experiences in a large majority of the cases" (Ost & Hugdahl, 1985, p. 33) were valid, the question still remains as to why fear frequency does not develop despite the existence of optimal conditions.

3. One of the most peculiar findings of Ost's studies concerns agoraphobia. According to these studies, between 81% (Ost & Hugdahl, 1983) and 88.8% (Ost, 1985) of the subjects attributed their agoraphobia to direct conditioning experiences. Ost and Hugdahl (1983) believed the subjects' reports and claimed that "conditioning theory holds fairly well when it comes to explaining the acquisition of agoraphobia" (p. 629). They do not mention any reservation as to whether the questionnaire data actually reflect the truth. Do Ost and Hugdahl really believe that an adult would be terrified to leave home due to some environmental fear? Why, then, is this type of syndrome so rare among children "when people of all ages are exposed to the rigours of going into open spaces and streets?" (Marks, 1969, p. 75). From the perspective of learning theories, the adult's learning history should have "immunized" him or her to a bizarre fear such as that of going to safe places like supermarkets. How, then, can a person become conditioned to fear supermarkets while traumatic events such as wars fail to produce conditioned fears (e.g., Rachman, 1978; Saigh, 1984a, 1984b)? It should be noted that Ost and Hugdahl (1983) came to their conclusion despite their acknowledgment that it "is quite the contrary to that of Mathews et al. . . . ." (p. 623), who reported that agoraphobics cannot as a rule recall any traumatic events that might have caused the development of their fears. Faced with this difficulty, Ost and Hugdahl (1983) stated that they

> agree that it is only a minority of the cases for which the UCS to the first anxiety attack can be identified. However, after the first occurrence the anxiety attack reappears in the situations that will be avoided and this certainly serves as a repeated fearful event. (p. 629)

Thus, what the authors seem to imply is that conditioning takes place due to the emotional arousal in the first or subsequent attacks. However, it is difficult to accept this position. A necessary condition for the acquisition of fear, according to conditioning theory, is the existence of UCS. Since conditioning theorists cannot provide data for the existence of such events, the theory remains without scientific support. Moreover, an acceptance of conditioning theory for the explanation of agoraphobia raises some additional difficulties. For example, the spontaneous and sudden recovery from agoraphobia that sometimes occurs (Wolpe, 1982, pp. 286–287) seems to be unexplainable in terms of conditioning theory, particularly in view of the high resistance of normal fears to extinction (see studies mentioned by Hulse et al., 1980; Jacobs & Nadel, 1985; R. L. Solomon & Wynne, 1954). Equally unexplainable is that an intensive application of behavioral technique, which might be effective against a normal fear, may produce no change at all in the intensity of a bizarre phobia (e.g., Rachman & Seligman, 1976). Another surprising phenomenon is that brief exposure or minimal therapeutic intervention may sometimes be effective in reducing agoraphobic symptoms (de Silva & Rachman, 1984; Emmelkamp, 1974) but not normal fears (W. L. Marshall, 1985). Such conflicting findings are unexplainable in terms of conditioning theory.

Ost and Hugdahl's (1985) strong advocacy of conditioning theory may be due to the high percentage of their agoraphobic subjects who attributed their symptoms to conditioning. However, as was explained in psychobizarreness theory, such responses may reflect the need of subjects who have bizarre symptoms to mislead themselves or rationalize their odd responses. In the past, when psychoanalysis enjoyed wide support and subjects were more familiar with it than other theories, agoraphobic patients like Leonard (see pp. 108–110) tended to attribute their fears to their unconscious motivations. However, with the increase in the acceptance and popularity of behaviorist ideas, agoraphobic subjects became inclined to rationalize their fears in a new way. It is also possible that one of the main reasons that a high percentage of Ost and Hugdahl's agoraphobic subjects attributed their phobia to traumatic experiences was the way in which the questions were posed.

4. Ost and Hugdahl (1985) as well as McNally and Steketee (1985) stated that their findings "are in contrast to most studies on analog Ss . . . where the indirect ways of acquisition account for a majority of the cases" (Ost & Hugdahl, 1985, p. 32–33). In an attempt to reconcile these conflicting results, the authors of both studies suggested that clinical phobias or intense fears are acquired by conditioning, while milder fears result from observational and/or instructional/informational learning. However, this compromise cannot be accepted because no convincing data seem to exist to support this claim. Moreover, in its present form, it cannot adequately explain the development of normal fears. A new theory of conditioning must answer all the criticisms raised before. It appears, then, that only by substantial revision of the old model can conditioning theory be made adequate for the explanation of normal human fears. However, we must abandon the notion that this or any other theory that can explain normal fear would also be suitable for explaining the development of bizarre fears.

SELIGMAN'S PREPAREDNESS THEORY

Theory

The arguments of equipotentiality and the distribution of fears that were specified in the preceding sections led Seligman (1971; see also Seligman & Hager, 1972) to suggest the preparedness theory of fears. Essentially, the theory claims that biologically evolutionary processes have programmed various types of organisms to become more easily conditioned to stimuli that have potential survival value. According to Seligman (1971), "phobias are highly prepared to be learned by humans, and, like other highly prepared relationships, they are selective and resistant to extinction, learned even with degraded input, and probably are noncognitive" (p. 312). A fear would be considered extremely prepared if it were aroused from the very first presentation of the conditioned stimulus, and only moderately so if the response were evoked after few conditioning trials. However, if the "response emerges only after many pairings, the organism is unprepared. If acquisition occurs after very many pairings or does not occur at all, the organism is said to be contraprepared" (p. 313).

It appears from Seligman's theory that the acquisition of prepared phobia is completely automatic. This is reflected in the following statement by Seligman (1971):

> Unprepared contingencies are learned and extinguished cognitively, i.e., by such mechanisms as expectations, intentions, beliefs or attention, while prepared associations are learned more primitively or noncognitively. Prepared associations may be the blind associations that Pavlov and Thorndike had thought they were studying. (pp. 315–316)

Criticisms

Argument 1: Lack of Evidence for Inherited Mental Images

Preparedness theory is similar to Jung's notion of archetypes (see Ewen, 1980) in that both theories imply that some types of inherited mental images or other forms of representation of stimuli with a high danger potential are "printed" in the organism's nervous system. Without the existence of such images, both theories would have difficulty explaining how the quick identification or conditioning of these stimuli is made. However, there is no evidence to support this implicit assumption of Jung's and Seligman's theories.

Argument 2: Conditioning Experiments with Infants

One source of evidence often used (Rachman, 1977; Seligman, 1970, 1971) to support preparedness theory is conditioning experiments with infants conducted by several earlier investigators. The results of these studies imply that infants are more easily conditioned to animals than to inanimate objects. This type of evidence was seriously criticized by Harris (1979) and Delprato (1980). As was indicated previously, Harris contended that "much of Seligman's . . . discussion of human phobias is based on an erroneous interpretation of Watson and Rayner's . . . work" (p. 156). Delprato arrived at a similar conclusion with regard to the other conditioning experiments with infants, such as that of Bregman (1934) and Valentine (1930).

Argument 3: Taste-Aversion Studies

Another area of research on which the preparedness theory was based is the taste-aversion conditioning studies by Garcia and his colleagues (Garcia, Ervin, & Koelling, 1966; Garcia & Koelling, 1966). The principal finding of these experiments was that rats were easily conditioned to avoid drinking saccharine-flavored water if it were followed by illness. Taste-aversion effect was obtained even if there was a long delay between the taste and the subsequent illness. However, conditioning aversion effect could not easily be obtained if the taste were followed by electric shocks. Shocks were effective in producing avoidance behavior toward the water when it followed an audiovisual stimulus (click–flashing light) but not a taste. These findings, which were repeated by many experiments (Delprato, 1980; Hulse et al., 1980), were interpreted as supporting the evolution-preparedness theory (Seligman & Hager, 1972).

However, this interpretation was rejected by several investigators (Delprato, 1980;

Jacobs & Nadel, 1985). The main arguments are that the proponents of the preparedness theory did not notice the similarity or belongingness aspects of taste–illness and failed to take into account the developmental history of the learner. Regarding the similarity hypothesis, it has been argued that stimuli that belong to the same modalities or location are easier for animals to associate than stimuli that belong to two different modalities or are dissimilar to each other. With respect to the rat's learning history, it has been argued that from birth, rats learn to associate gustatory stimuli with the internal state rather than with stimulation at the body surface. Thus, the rat's learning history, rather than evolutionary history, has prepared it to associate taste–illness more easily than taste–shock. Direct evidence for this hypothesis was provided by L. G. Sullivan (1979, cited in Jacobs & Nadel, 1985). Rats were raised in a controlled environment in which visual cues were made predictive of ingestive consequences while taste cues were made irrelevant. Sullivan found that these rearing conditions resulted in the conditioning of rats to the visual rather than to taste stimuli. Thus, when we consider the similarity or belongingness hypothesis and Sullivan's findings along with some other experimental data (see Delprato, 1980; Jacobs & Nadel, 1985) inconsistent with those of Garcia and his colleagues, the necessity for the concept of preparedness greatly diminishes.

Argument 4: Inadequacy of Ohman's Studies

The main source of evidence in support of preparedness theory came from several experiments conducted by Ohman and his colleagues (for review, see Delprato, 1980; Emmelkamp, 1982). Subjects in these experiments were classically conditioned to two types of pictures. One type consisted of fear-relevant or potentially phobic stimuli (pictures of snakes and spiders), and the other type consisted of fear-irrelevant or neutral stimuli (pictures of mushrooms, flowers, houses, faces, etc.). Electrical shocks or loud noises were used as the UCS. The results of these studies showed that electrodermal responses conditioned to fear-relevant stimuli were more resistant to extinction than were responses conditioned to neutral stimuli. However, these findings are not enough to validate preparedness theory for the following reasons.

First, as indicated by Emmelkamp (1982), the evidence supporting the theory was provided by one research group only—Ohman and his colleagues. The results of three studies conducted by other investigators (McNally, 1986; another two mentioned by Emmelkamp, 1982) are inconsistent with the preparedness theory.

Second, the central idea of preparedness theory is that "prepared" stimuli are more easily learned than are unprepared stimuli. However, except for a single experiment (Hugdahl, Fredrikson, & Ohman, 1977), Ohman and his associates failed to confirm the acquisition effect. The same result was recently reported by McNally (1986). Similarly, McNally and Reiss (1982) found no significant difference in learning not to fear certain conditioned stimuli when the safety signal (i.e., the discriminative stimulus) was a picture of a snake or a picture of a flower.

Third, Delprato (1980) argued that Ohman and his colleagues did not take into consideration the developmental history of the subjects. The fear-irrelevant stimuli used, such as houses and flowers, are associated with neutral and positive experiences, while the fear-relevant stimuli, such as snakes, are associated with negative experiences. Thus "any of several factors in the subject's experiential histories (e.g., parental modeling, folklore) rather than natural selection could account for the result of the Ohman experiments" (Delprato, 1980, p. 89). Delprato (1980) noted also that the picture of the mushroom used in Ohman's studies is not neutral in terms of survival value since many species of mushrooms are poisonous: "It is reasonable to suspect that mushrooms have posed a greater threat to the survival of the human species than have spiders and snakes combined" (p. 89). Thus, these criticisms greatly minimize the value of Ohman's findings in support of the preparedness concept.

Argument 5: Inappropriate Application to Clinical Setting

Emmelkamp (1982), referring to some prominent differences between Ohman's experiments and the clinical phobia (e.g., the use of normal nonphobic subjects, minimal level of aversiveness), asserted that "it is certainly a very bold claim to generalize these findings to human phobias" (p. 29). Indeed, Rachman and Seligman (1976) described two cases of bizarre phobias—a chocolate and a plant phobia—that were clearly unprepared and yet were both highly resistant to extinction. In another study, de Silva, Rachman, and Seligman (1977) rated the evolutionary significance or the preparedness of phobic and obsessive–compulsive disorders. The rating data indicated that the large majority of these symptoms were judged as significant from an evolutionary point of view. However, the degree of preparedness did not predict the outcome of therapy, the suddenness of the onset of the disorder, the severity of the impairment, the intensiveness of the treatment received, or the age of onset. The authors concluded that the lack of relationship of preparedness to the therapeutic outcome "seriously weakens the clinical usefulness of the concept of preparedness" (pp. 74–75). Recently, Zafiropoulou and McPherson (1986) repeated this study and obtained the same pattern of results.

Argument 6: Unexplainable Sex Differences

In the animal kingdom, males are more susceptible to fear and stress than are females (Gray, 1971). This trend seems to exist also among human beings. For example, duodenal ulcer is 10 times more common among men than women (Gray, 1971). Thus, from the perspective of the preparedness theory, which emphasizes the importance of the genetic component, as opposed to the effects of training in the development of fear, one would expect a higher level of fear among men than women. In fact, however, fears of all types are more prevalent among women (e.g., Gray, 1971; Marks, 1969). In conclusion, taking all these arguments into account, it seems that the preparedness concept has hardly advanced our understanding of human or animal fears.

COGNITIVE–BEHAVIORAL APPROACHES

Theory

Another theoretical approach in the explanation of the genesis of fears is that of the cognitive–behavioral theories, mainly the controllability theory and Ellis's (1962) irrational-thinking theory (see also Davison & Neale, 1982; Emmelkamp, 1982; S. M. Miller, 1981; Rachman, 1978, 1984c).

The controllability notion indicates that fear is aroused whenever we feel unable to control the probable outcome of a threatening situation. This concept is prominent also in Seligman's (1974) theory of learned helplessness. Seligman suggested that anxiety is the initial response to a stressful situation. However, it is replaced by depression if the person comes to believe that the stressful event is uncontrollable. The notion of controllability is strongly related to the concept of the predictability of stress. The predictability theories (S. M. Miller, 1981; Rachman, 1978) share the view that predictable aversive events are less stressful than unpredictable aversive stimuli. However, although both controllability and predictability, as well as Ellis's theory, are of considerable significance, they are not sufficient, nor are they the dominant factors, in the acquisition of fears and phobias.

Criticisms

Argument 1: Absence of Fear Despite Lack of Controllability

The widespread phenomenon of habituation in conditions of war (Rachman, 1978, 1984c; Rofé & Lewin, 1980, 1982a; Saigh, 1984a, 1984b), where subjects did not develop fearful responses despite the uncontrollability and unpredictability of the stressful events, should cause one to doubt whether these notions alone can provide an adequate examination of the development of fear. Rachman (1978) noted that these theories "would have predicted that people subjected to dangers and uncertainty of air raids will develop intense fears, and the failure of this prediction leaves a vacuum" (p. 45).

Argument 2: Presence of Fear Despite Controllability

Rachman (1978) noted that an individual may perceive a situation as controllable and nevertheless experience fear: "He knows that he can control the harmless snake as it lies in its box in the laboratory. No uncontrollable aversive event is expected. But he nevertheless experiences palpitations and sweating, and refrains from approaching the box" (p. 260). Rachman indicated, further, that 17% of the combat veterans who responded to a survey during World War II continued to express intense fear during combat despite their growing sense of self-confidence in their military abilities.

Argument 3: Value of Distraction

The traditional theories of predictability (S. M. Miller, 1981) claim that in a potentially aversive situation, a person needs more information about the aversive event even if the stress is unavoidable. These theories derive their main support from laboratory studies (see S. M. Miller & Mangan, 1983). However, the cumulative research data show that in a real-life stress situation, the general tendency is to avoid getting information about the aversive event when the stress is unavoidable. Subjects in these conditions prefer to distract themselves rather than have information about the stressful events (S. M. Miller, 1981; S. M. Miller & Mangan, 1983; Rofé, 1984; Rofé, Hoffman, & Lewin, 1985; Rofé & Lewin, 1986; Rofé, Lewin, & Hoffman, 1987; Taylor, 1983). Moreover, this seems to be the case with infants as well as with adults. Mussen et al. (1984) noted, for example, that an infant confronting a stranger is more likely to experience a high level of anxiety if there is no possibility, such as an opportunity to play with a toy, of diverting his or her attention.

Argument 4: Inability to Explain Clinical Phobia

Controllability in its present form cannot explain why individuals may suddenly become incapable of coping with very simple and harmless situations over which they had very good control for many years prior to the outbreak of the phobia. The controllability theory does not seem to adequately explain how and why subjects develop what appear to be nonsensical beliefs that they have no control over these harmless situations.

Cognitive–behavioral theories (e.g., see Latimer & Sweet, 1984), such as Ellis's

(1962) rational emotive therapy or Beck's (1976) cognitive theory, attributed emotional disorders, such as phobia and depression, to irrational beliefs or distorted ways of thinking. Indeed, several studies (Emmelkamp, 1982) show that such beliefs are related to phobias. However, Emmelkamp (1982) noted that "while the results of these studies might indicate that such irrational beliefs are causally linked to anxiety evocation, it is equally plausible that increased emotional arousal in certain situations may sensitize individuals to certain irrational expectancies" (p. 26). Furthermore, according to Emmelkamp these studies may not be applicable to clinical phobia, because none of the studies investigated the thoughts of phobic patients. A similar criticism was made by Beidel and Turner (1986) in an excellent critical review of the theoretical bases of cognitive–behavioral theories. Referring to studies showing differences in cognitive content between behavioral-disorder subjects and normal individuals, the authors noted that "evidence of this type requires inferring causality as a result of preestablished group differences, however, and does not rule out the possibility that these cognitions merely accompany or result from the psychological state . . ." (p. 183). The authors added that in order to test a causality hypothesis stating that deviant cognitions precede pathology, a cognitive assessment of individuals who exhibit no form of psychopathology is required. The hypothesis would gain confirmation if those reporting negative or deviant cognitions would demonstrate signs of psychopathology at a later stage. However, when such methods were applied, no confirmation was found for the cognitive–behavior theories.

Thus, although clinical data do indicate the presence of maladaptive thoughts among subjects with emotional disorders such as phobias, no existing theory seems capable of explaining how and why these beliefs are generated.

JACOBS AND NADEL'S CONDITIONING THEORY

Theory

In an attempt to overcome the difficulties of conditioning theory in explaining clinical phobias, Jacobs and Nadel (1985) proposed a new theoretical framework for conditioning. Their basic assumption is that clinical phobias develop as a result of Pavlovian conditioning. However, in view of the frequent inability of phobic subjects to report when and where the feared stimulus was paired with a noxious event, they suggest that the acquisition of human phobias resembles the kind of learning that takes place during the "amnesic" period of infancy. They claim that, neurophysiologically, learning that occurs in infancy is different from adult learning. Two main neuroanatomical systems are postulated to be involved in the conditioning process. The first is the class "taxon systems," which are responsible for the acquisition of skills (stimulus–stimulus) and S–R (stimulus–response). The second involves the hippocampus, in which the information regarding the time–space context of experiences is stored. The phenomenon of infantile amnesia occurs because learning in infancy, unlike that of later periods, is controlled solely by the taxon systems in the absence of the influential effects of the hippocampus, which begins to function sometime after 18–36 months postpartum. Conditioned fears that are controlled solely by taxon systems are not tied to any given environmental context, and they manifest themselves very broadly. They are also highly resistant to extinction, as is the case with clinical phobias.

Conditioned fears that were established in infancy and subsequently forgotten constitute the basis for the development of powerful phobias at a later period. These experiences prepare the taxon system for the acquisition of strong conditioned fears later in life.

Exposure to stressful conditions suppresses the functioning of the hippocampus, and as a result, learning strongly resistant to extinction, resembling that of infancy, can occur:

> *Early experiences have prepared those parts of the taxon learning systems representing conditional and unconditional stimuli, and those pathways mediating any associative connections between them. Given this early preparation, subsequent environmental contingencies may be highly degraded, and yet robust, long-lasting (re)learning can still occur. (Jacobs & Nadel, 1985, p. 518)*

The authors further stated that once acquired, the conditioned fears might never be eliminated using traditional extinction or counterconditioning procedures. Instead, they outlined several of their own ideas for facilitating extinction.

Criticisms

Argument 1: Lack of Evidence Demonstrating the Validity of the Theory for Clinical Phobia

As was stated, Jacobs and Nadel assume that Pavlovian conditioning is the mechanism by which clinical phobia is produced. However, they provide no evidence that conditioning could have been responsible for the onset of clinical phobia. To the best of our knowledge, no such evidence exists, and, therefore, no scientific justification for Jacobs and Nadel's assumption seems to exist. The phobic patient's apparent lack of memory may simply reflect the fact that the onset of the phobia was not caused by conditioning events, but rather that the events were forgotten, as Jacobs and Nadel assume. Thus, no scientific basis seems to exist for the superficial similarity between infantile amnesia and clinical phobia.

Argument 2: Clinical Phenomena Are Not Explained by Their Mechanistic View of Stress

Jacobs and Nadel attribute the sudden eruption of clinical phobia and its broad generalization to automatic effects of stress. Stress suppresses the functioning of the hippocampus, and as a result, the subject becomes automatically controlled by neuroanatomical systems that may compel him or her to display bizarre fears and behave in an infantile manner. Consciousness is not discussed at all as a mediating factor. This mechanistic point of view raises several difficulties.

First, if this approach were indeed valid, why is clinical phobia very prevalent among women and very rare among men and children? Stress should disrupt the hippocampus functioning of men and children in the same way as it supposedly does that of women, unless one can prove that there is a difference in the hippocampus sensitivity of these groups. One could argue that men and children are exposed less frequently to stress. However, even if this were the case, one still would have to find the same proportion of phobias among subjects of these three groups who were exposed to the same level of stress. However, as yet no evidence of this type exists, and we suspect that it will not be found. Bizarre fears seem to be extremely rare among children, and yet, we know that many children are exposed to high levels of stress. It also remains to be proven that women are exposed to much higher levels of stress than are men.

Second, if stress has an automatic effect, one would expect the traumatic situation of war or concentration camps to cause a substantial increase of clinical phobias such as agoraphobia. However, to the best of our knowledge, a review of studies in these two areas (see pp. 144, 205) does not indicate that this is the case.

Third, a mechanistic view of stress cannot explain the wide range of psychiatric effects of stress. Not only is stress related to phobia, but also it may cause other disorders such as hysteria, depression, and psychosomatic disorders, as research evidence reviewed in this book shows. What, then, are the particular characteristics of stress that cause the development of clinical phobia, or the suppression of the hippocampus and the activation of the taxon systems, rather than other psychiatric symptoms? Jacobs and Nadel do not answer this question. Another problem is the choice of the phobic stimulus. Different objects or situations may become associated with eruption of intensive panic reaction. Sometimes the choice of the feared object is unusually bizarre such as the chocolate or the vegetable phobia. Can this be related to the effects of stress or to some conditioned fear in infancy? We think that a mechanistic view of stress cannot cope with these problems.

Argument 3: Lack of Evidence for the Tyranny of Infancy

Jacobs and Nadel's theory is a synthesis of two approaches in psychopathology. One is what they termed *the tyranny of childhood,* and the other is the learning theories. According to their model, infantile experiences may have an unusual effect on the tendency to develop psychological fear. In this respect, Jacobs and Nadel's theory appears to be even more extreme than psychoanalysis. Not only is the subject unaware of the frightening infantile events, but he or she can never become aware of them; according to Jacobs and Nadel's belief, it is very difficult or almost impossible to free the individual from the poisoning effects of these events. In its basic approach, this model is reminiscent of ancient demonology, since both approaches indicate that a demonic power that has lain dormant for many years may, under certain circumstances, suddenly awaken and make one's life unusually miserable. Once freed, the genie is difficult to return to the bottle. However, Jacobs and Nadel provide no clinical evidence such as a case study to demonstrate their claim. In view of this fact and inasmuch as psychoanalysis has not succeeded in proving its thesis regarding the tyrannical effects of childhood, there seems to be no reason for accepting Jacobs and Nadel's more extreme position of the tyranny of infancy.

Argument 4: Lack of Distinction Between Different Types of Clinical Phobias

Although Jacobs and Nadel realize the need for making a distinction between clinical and nonclinical fears, they seem to list all fears observed in the clinical setting under the same category. This approach does not seem to be justified, however, since clinical phobias may stem from completely diverse causes. Let us illustrate this claim by referring to two hypothetical examples of phobias that Jacobs and Nadel describe at the beginning of their article. One example concerns a woman who, after the birth of her child, began to experience a severe fear of insects, which greatly disrupted her daily life:

> She has begun to feel uncomfortable in her office and in her home. She regularly inspects her desk and office for the presence of insects. She is afraid to sleep. . . . Her housekeeper of 11 years was dismissed. . . . Her fears have begun to interfere with her marriage, her career and her material life. (Jacobs & Nadel, 1985, pp. 512–513)

While this phobia seems bizarre because of its sudden and dramatic appearance, its rarity, and particularly its unusual effects on the subject's total adjustment, this does not appear to be the case with regard to Jacobs and Nadel's second example. The latter concerns a man whose fear of heights was successfully treated, but resurfaced several years later when he was involved in an air accident in which he lost his wife and his only son, and in which he himself was injured. The patient had trouble sleeping, concentrating, and interacting in his office, but as time passed these intense reactions diminished. His fear of heights remained unchanged, and this disturbed him a great deal because his office was in a windowed high-rise building. Unlike the former patient, he was fully aware of the causes of his fear, attributing it to the traumatic circumstances.

In their paper, Jacobs and Nadel make no theoretical distinction between the two cases. In our opinion, however, totally different sets of theoretical concepts should be applied to explain them. While it is very difficult to explain the first cause in conditioning terms, it is very easy to do so with the second one. This case bears much similarity to laboratory fears and, as will be shown later, fears of this type can be satisfactorily explained by a revised conditioning theory.

In conclusion, these arguments seem to be sufficient for rejecting Jacobs and Nadel's theory, even though more objections could be raised. Essentially, this theory remains within the same deterministic and mechanistic theoretical framework of the traditional theories, either psychoanalysis or behavioral approaches. Human pathological behavior is seen to be dominated by strong interior and/or exterior powers, and the possibility that these behaviors were consciously invented as strategies for coping with unbearable stress is not considered.

CONCLUSIONS

As demonstrated, none of the existing theories is able to adequately explain the acquisition of fears. What, then, are the mechanisms that determine the development of fear? As a prerequisite to any further attempt at resolving this question, it seems necessary to distinguish between bizarre and normal fears, as suggested by psychobizarreness theory. The external similarity of responses in these two types of fears led to the misleading assumption that all fears stem from the same source. However, in recent years theorists in the field have become increasingly aware of the need to distinguish between clinical and normal fears (Emmelkamp, 1982; Hallam, 1978; Jacobs & Nadel, 1985; Rachman, 1978).

As was indicated in psychobizarreness theory, bizarre phobias appear to be much more similar to bizarre neurotic symptoms, such as hysteria, than to normal fears. This was recognized by Freud (Fenichel, 1946; H. B. Lewis, 1981) when he suggested the term anxiety hysteria for phobias. Indeed, the cumulative research evidence shows that as in the case of hysteria (e.g., Blanchard & Hersen, 1976; Brady, 1966; Rangaswamy & Kamakshi, 1983: Volkmar, Poll, & M. Lewis, 1984) the onset of bizarre fears is strongly associated with stressful life events or conflicts (Last, Barlow, & O'Brien, 1984; Marks & Herst, 1970; Mathews et al., 1981; Mendel & Klein, 1969; Rachman & Seligman, 1976; L. Solyom, Beck, C. Solyom, & Hugel, 1974). Similarly, bizarre fears, like hysterical symptoms (see p. 118), are more prevalent in females (e.g., Rachman, 1978; Emmelkamp, 1982) and in lower socioeconomic levels (e.g., see studies mentioned by Chambless, 1985b). In addition, as was argued in the case of other types of bizarre symptoms, no special type of traumatic incident or particular personality structure appears to be associated with bizarre fears. For example, although the onset of agoraphobia is significantly related to stressful life events and personality weaknesses, agoraphobia does not develop in response to a particular type of stress, nor is it associated with unique personality traits (see reviews and research findings by Emmelkamp, 1982; Fisher & Wilson, 1985; Mathews et al., 1981; Thyer et al., 1985, 1986). For example, Last et al. (1984) found that while interpersonal conflict was the most frequently cited stressor, other stressful life events (e.g., birth, miscarriage, death, or illness of a significant other) were reported as precipitants of agoraphobia as well.

Another interesting finding demonstrating the similarity of bizarre fears to other bizarre neurotic symptoms is that unlike specific phobias, agoraphobia, social phobia, and anxiety state (Lader & Mathews, 1968), as well as hysteria (Horvath, Friedman, & Meares, 1980; Lader & Sartorius, 1968) are associated with a lack of or a slow rate of habituation to disturbing stimuli. These findings seem to indicate that people likely to develop bizarre responses to stress are deficient in their ability to distract their attention from stress and need more radical measures to achieve this goal when the stress becomes intolerable.

Thus, as was stated previously, bizarre fears should be viewed as a coping strategy intended, like other bizarre neurotic symptoms, for the double purpose of distracting one's attention and gaining some control over the sources of stress.

While psychobizarreness theory seems to be most suitable for explaining bizarre fears, the conditioning model appears to be the most efficient theoretical framework for explaining normal fears. However, as has been shown, conditioning theory in its present form is inadequate and in need of substantial revision. It seems to us that a new conditioning theory must take into account the organism's cognitive processes, as does the psychobizarreness theory. Automatic or mechanistic terms are not sufficient for understanding even normal fears. Therefore, we have termed our theory the *Cognitive–Automatic Conditioning Theory of Fear*.

Before presenting this theory, we must clarify precisely what we mean by the term *normal fear*. Generally speaking, the term refers to fearful responses that cannot be categorized as bizarre on the basis of the four criteria of neurotic bizarre symptoms specified previously. Considering these criteria and some additional data reviewed so far, normal fears seem to be characterized by the following four critical aspects:

1. These fears are quite common and are not regarded by others as bizarre.

2. They tend to be aroused by a very restricted range of stimuli.

3. In most cases, they have a very marginal effect on a subject's total adjustment or daily activity. In a few cases, however, the activity affected by the fear is of great importance in the subject's daily routine, and it is difficult for him or her to give it up or find a substitute activity. For example, two persons may develop acrophobia after being involved in an air accident. The first person, whose daily routine does not include tall buildings or any other heights, is hardly affected, but the second person, employed in a high-rise office building, is.

4. Usually, these fears exist in a subject's behavioral repertoire for many years, often from early childhood (e.g., see McNally & Steketee, 1985), or they appear after the experience or observation of some traumatic incident. When the fear exists from childhood, in most cases subjects would not remember the circumstances under which it originated (e.g., see McNally & Skeketee, 1985). However, if the onset of fear was recent, the subject will usually remember the traumatic events that preceded the onset, as in the example of acrophobia just described.

Finally, in our opinion there are no qualitative differences between normal fears and laboratory-produced fears, and the latter should be integrated into the framework of any new theory of normal fear.

11

Cognitive–Automatic Conditioning Theory of Fear

INTRODUCTION

Despite the many criticisms of classical conditioning theory, it seems that this paradigm should constitute the basis of any new theoretical effort to explain the development of normal fears. The findings from six areas of research indicated by Rachman (1978) can be used to defend this claim:

1. The research on induction of fears in animals constitutes "the strongest and most systematic evidence" (p. 176) for the conditioning paradigm.
2. A minority of people developed significant lasting fears during World War II. "The forms of these fears and the conditions under which they arose are consistent with conditioning theory" (p. 177).
3. In a number of cases of young children, fear was successfully induced by classical conditioning procedures (see also Delprato, 1980).
4. Research on dental phobias seem to indicate that they were caused by traumatic dental experiences.
5. Incidental observations arising from the use of aversion therapy, a technique explicitly based on the classical conditioning model, provide some support for the theory.
6. A number of experiments on the effects of traumatic stimulation are consistent with this model. Most subjects who were given injections of scaline, which produces a temporary suspension of breathing, developed intense fear of stimuli encountered in or connected with the experimental situation. The intensity of their fears tended to increase, even in the absence of further aversive trials.

This all provides strong support for the role of conditioning in producing fears. However, while conditioning, according to the classical model, consistently causes fear among animals, this is not true among humans, as has been shown. In addition, the traditional theory is confronted with many other problems such as the unequal distribution of fears or differences between males and females. It appears that in order to resolve these problems it is essential to change the traditional behaviorist conceptualization that viewed conditioning entirely as an automatic process (Mackintosh, 1983). We suggest conceiving of conditioning as a two-stage process. The first stage involves a cognitive assessment of the entire situation the results of which will determine whether or not an automatic bonding will develop between the conditioned stimulus and arousal of fear. The second stage is the actual bonding process, an idea that will be elaborated in the next section.

AUTOMATIC VERSUS COGNITIVE
CONCEPTUALIZATIONS OF CONDITIONING

As was previously noted the strongest support for the conditioning theory comes from the laboratory studies that show animals always developing fear when a CS is paired with a traumatic event (UCS). These findings may be explained in two alternative ways. One interpretation is that the entire learning process is controlled by automatic mechanisms. The alternative explanation is that the CS is first cognitively assessed as dangerous or as a sign of forthcoming danger and that this is a necessary but not sufficient condition for an automatic S–R bonding between the CS and fear. This latter interpretation is consistent with Talman's learning theory, which viewed conditioning, not as the acquisition of new reflexes, but rather as the acquisition of new knowledge about the world (e.g., Bower & Hilgard, 1981; Brewer, 1974; Mackintosh, 1983).

Even though these two theoretical approaches are equally plausible, the automatic conceptualization came to dominate psychological thinking. Moreover, when the equipotential premise, which is one of the most important assumptions of this conceptualization, proved to be inadequate (Rachman, 1978, and p. 145 in this book), even with regard to animals (Gray, 1971, pp. 11–14), the notion of "automatic biological preparedness" was invented by Seligman (1971) to fill the theoretical gap. In an attempt to support the automatization notion, Seligman refers, for example, to the fact that human phobias are not readily modified by information: "Showing or telling that cats are not going to hurt him is rarely effective" (Seligman & Hager, 1972, p. 495). However, as was demonstrated, the preparedness concept does not seem to rest on a sound scientific basis, so that the problems faced by the theory of conditioning still apply. In addition, much new evidence exists to show that cognitive intervention can be effective in reducing fear (Bandura, 1977b; Kirsch, Tennen, Wickless, Saccone, & Cody, 1983; Lick, 1975; Lick & Bootzin, 1975; Marcia, Rubin, & Efran, 1969; Meichenbaum, 1971, 1975).

Thus, in view of these difficulties it may be helpful to try the second alternative in an attempt to understand the conditioning process. Such an approach would be consistent with Bandura's (1971b, 1977b) conditioning theory of self-arousal. Bandura (1977b) indicated that "in behavior theory . . . classical conditioning, is commonly viewed as a process wherein conditioned stimuli are directly and automatically connected to responses evoked by unconditioned stimuli. . . . Closer examination revealed that it is in fact cognitively mediated" (p. 87). To reinforce this claim, Bandura (1971b, 1977b) reviewed two sets of empirical evidence showing that

1. People fail to be conditioned if they are unaware that the CS signifies an aversive stimulus. For example, when subjects were informed that a certain word in a series would be followed by a shock they quickly developed anticipatory heart rate response, whereas those who were led to believe that the shock was not related to their verbalization were not conditioned.

2. When subjects were told that the CS would no longer be followed by painful events, the conditioned autonomic responses were promptly eliminated, whereas subjects who were not told lost their fear only gradually.

Essentially the same conclusion was reached by Brewer (1974) with respect to conditioning theory, both classical and operant paradigms. Reviewing massive research data on conditioning with humans, similar to those reviewed by Bandura, Brewer concluded that

> all the results of the traditional conditioning literature are due to the operation of higher mental processes, as assumed in cognitive theory, and that there is not and never has been any convincing evidence for unconscious, automatic mechanisms in the conditioning of adult human beings. (p. 27)

On the basis of these research findings, Bandura (1977b) proposed conceptualizing conditioning of fear in terms of self-arousal theory, according to which conditioned reactions are evoked through fear-producing thoughts: "For individuals who are aware that certain events forebode distress, such events activate fear-arousing thoughts, which in turn produce emotional responses" (p. 69). Conditioning is a matter of belief that the past contingencies remain in effect, and the more severe the effects one expects, the stronger the emotional arousal will be. However, even though in principle Bandura's theory is consistent with our general approach, it is not sufficient to explain the effects of conditioning or development of fear for the following reasons:

1. One of the prominent characteristics of phobic responses is their automatic arousal and resistance to extinction (Hulse, Egeth, & Deese, 1980; Jacobs & Nadel, 1985). Typically, the subject is aware that the feared stimulus is not harmful and yet is unable to control the arousal of fear. People who have an intense fear of snakes will continue to experience fear and display avoidance behavior even in the presence of a toy snake (Rachman, 1984b, p. 638). The limited effect of cognition on arousal of fear was recognized by Bandura, who stated that these responses are not always susceptible to cognitive control. In an attempt to solve this problem, Bandura proposed two alternative solutions. The first, originally suggested by Bridger and Mandel (1964), assumes that the conditioning process involves two components: self-arousal, which is readily modifiable by altering one's thoughts, and automatic response, directly evoked by external events. However, neither Bridger and Mandel (1964) nor Bandura explained precisely what they meant by these ideas. Inasmuch as conditioning is conceived as an automatic process, they did not explain exactly what is the role of the cognitive component. As a second alternative, Bandura suggested that when people undergo painful experiences, the external stimuli become such powerful elicitors of fear-arousing thoughts that they are not easily subject to voluntary control. For example, acrophobics become fearful when they are looking down from the rooftop of a tall building because they are unable to turn off thoughts about the horrendous things that could happen to them despite the obvious safety of the situation. However, it is doubtful whether this idea can explain the automatic arousal of phobic reactions. Recently, for example, S. L. Williams and Watson (1985) found that perception of danger was a very weak predictor of acrophobic behavior. Moreover, when subjects were carefully questioned regarding their perception of danger as they struggled to cope with the height task in vivo, a number of subjects denied that they had any belief that they might fall or that any other harm would come to them (S. L. Williams, Turner, & Peer, 1985).

2. Another problem associated with Bandura's cognitive theory of conditioning is that it does not specify the conditions that determine whether or not conditioning is likely to occur. For example, this theory cannot adequately explain why fear rarely develops during wars, despite the existence of appropriate conditions for production of fear-arousing thoughts, and why unusually intense fears such as agoraphobia sometimes develops despite the total lack of suitable circumstances such as dangerous events.

3. Bandura's self-arousal theory does not seem able to explain the prevalence of different types of fear among females and young children (Rachman, 1978, p. 117).

4. The theory cannot explain why animals acquire conditioned fear much more readily than do humans. It is doubtful whether laboratory animals studies can be integrated within this theory.

Bandura's self-arousal theory appears too simplistic to serve as an alternative to the traditional conception of the conditioning process although it makes a significant contribution in this direction. Of particular importance is the idea that conditioning may be composed of two factors, cognitive and automatic. Elaboration of this idea is an important element of our proposed theory.

DISTINCTION BETWEEN PROCESS AND PRODUCT

It seems that one of the main flaws of traditional conditioning theory is the lack of differentiation between the process through which conditioning is generated and its final product. Similar to the process of motor-skill acquisition, in which cognitive factors are centered in the initial stages and become reduced in the later stage (Deese & Hulse, 1967; Lewin, 1982), the conditioning process is composed of two main stages. The first stage is essentially a cognitive screening, which determines whether or not conditioning will take place, while the second stage involves a process during which the relationship between the CS and arousal of fear becomes similar to a reflex. In the cognitive-screening stage, a cognitive evaluation of the CS is made to determine whether or not the stimulus is dangerous. Among animals, this evaluation process is very simple, and a noxious event will nearly always be sufficient to produce the bonding in the second stage. Among humans, due to their greater cognitive complexity, several other variables (which will shortly be specified) may be involved. While in motor-skill acquisition the cognitive stage is quite long, in conditioning it appears to be very brief. This may be one of the main reasons that most of the traditional conditioning theorists failed to realize the importance of this stage. Since their observations were concentrated on the final product of conditioning, they concluded that conditioning is essentially an automatic process. In our opinion, this is a mistaken conclusion, comparable to the observation by an investigator of the final product of a motor-skill-acquisition process.

In this section, a general outline of our conditioning theory has been presented. This theory is based on four main assumptions, which are discussed in the next section. The first three assumptions are concerned with the cognitive screening stage of conditioning, and the fourth deals with the formation of permanent bonding between the CS and the arousal of the autonomic system.

FOUR MAIN ASSUMPTIONS OF THE PROPOSED THEORY

Assumption 1: Two Minimum Requirements for the Occurrence of Conditioning—Appraisal of Danger and Emotional Arousal

It appears that two basic requirements must be filled in order for the conditioned fear to develop. The CS must be appraised as dangerous, or as a signal of a dangerous event, and the organism must experience an increase of emotional arousal with presentation of the CS.

A stimulus seems likely to be perceived as dangerous if it can cause harm or if its presence increases the probability of harm. Whether or not a stimulus will be perceived as such depends to a large extent on the harmful input from the stimulus. The stronger the noxious element in the informational input regarding the external stimulus, the stronger the likelihood it will be perceived as dangerous. The question is also affected, however, by the perceiver's characteristics (Heimberg, 1985; Keane, 1985). These characteristics may intervene in order to neutralize or intensify the dangerous input signals. Generally speaking, low cognitive development and strong feelings of helplessness increase the likelihood that a threatening situation will be perceived as dangerous. Therefore, it should be expected that animals, infants, and children up to a certain age will be more likely to develop conditioned fear in the context of a threatening situation (e.g., pain as in laboratory animals experiments) than will older persons. More mature individuals, being cognitively more advanced and less helpless, base their judgment of the extent of danger in a situation on more comprehensive information than the presence or absence of a noxious stimulus. For example, adult subjects are usually less likely to develop fear of a dentist than are small children because the adults are less likely to appraise the situation as dangerous. Moreover, even if an adult concludes that a situation might be dangerous, emotional arousal would not necessarily follow. Subjects with a higher level of cognitive development seem to have better ability to control arousal. At the same time however, adults may more readily develop conditioned fear in a situation, such as war, in which the appraisal or perception of danger requires a higher level of cognitive development. A minimum or more advanced cognitive development is needed in order to appraise danger in certain situations. Fear of strangers does not develop among either chimpanzee or human infants before the age of 4–6 months (Gray, 1971) because they do not yet have schema for judging strangeness (Mussen, Conger, Kagan, & Huston, 1984).

Our second requirement regarding the necessity of emotional arousal immediately after the organism's exposure to the CS is consistent with the view of Emmelkamp's (1982), who asserted that "a minimum requirement of the classical conditioning paradigm is that not only should a traumatic experience be identified, but also that the subject should have experienced pain or anxiety in the situation that subsequently led to his phobia" (p. 20). Essentially, the same point of view was recently expressed by Keane (1985). Thus, if a situation is perceived as dangerous but, for various reasons that will be specified later, no arousal occurs, conditioned fear will not be produced. Moreover, even if the situation is perceived as dangerous and the subject is in a general state of arousal, such as in a war situation, no conditioning would be expected to occur unless the subject experienced an increase in emotional arousal immediately after perception of the danger.

Assumption 2: Irrelevance of the Mode of Fear Arousal

Our second assumption concerns the techniques by which conditioning may be produced. In the classical conditioning paradigm, the UCS is an essential factor of conditioning. However, inasmuch as the two critical variables in producing conditioned fear are danger input signals and the experience of fear and since these can also be obtained by other techniques, we suggest viewing the UCS as one of several methods by which conditioning may occur. In other words, the specific technique by which arousal takes place is not an essential part of the conditioning paradigm.

Among lower animals, which served as the subjects in the vast majority of laboratory studies on fear, the use of a UCS is the only technique for arousing fear. However, among subjects with more advanced cognitive ability, namely, primates, the experience of danger and fear, thereby conditioning, can be produced by other techniques as well. Thus, several investigators (Cook, Mineka, Wolkenstein, & Laitsch, 1985; Mineka, M. Davidson, Cook, & Keir, 1984) demonstrated that laboratory-born rhesus monkeys, who had previously not displayed a fear of snakes, developed intense fearful reactions to snakes after observing such responses by wild-born monkeys. Similarly, R. E. Miller, Murphy, and Mirsky (1959) showed that monkeys whose conditioned fear responses to CS (another monkey) were extinguished, redisplayed these responses when they were exposed to a frightening monkey. Moreover, the fear responses were elicited when the conditioned animals viewed photographs of frightening monkeys as well. The applicability of the observation method for producing conditioned fear in humans has been demonstrated in many experiments (Bandura, 1971a; Bandura & Rosenthal, 1966; S. M. Berger, 1962). This has also been evident in real-life situations such as circumstances of war (Kipper, 1977; Rachman, 1978). Thus, the difference between Pavlovian and observational conditioning seems to be one of technique rather than substance.

A further procedure by which conditioned fear may be produced is the instruction-informational method (Rachman, 1977, 1978). In this technique, various social agencies, including television and books, are used to convey the belief that a certain stimulus is dangerous, and thereby fear is aroused. The way the danger is presented and the credibility of the social agency seem to be quite important in determining the arousal intensity and hence the strength of conditioning. Fearful messages conveyed by a mother concerning particular stimuli may cause a child to feel intense fear no less than will the noxious stimulus itself. A subject with more advanced cognitive development may be more immune to noxious information and thereby also to the development of conditioned fear.

The claim that the instruction-informational method is an important procedure for producing conditioned fear is consistent with Bandura's (1973, 1977b) self-arousal theory previously presented. Some research evidence consistent with this prediction can be found in Murray and Foote's (1979) research. Using questionnaire data, the authors found that a variety of observational and instructional learning experiences communicating negative information about snakes were related to fear of snakes. Emmelkamp (1982) noted that the instruction-informational method has a great advantage over Pavlovian and vicarious conditioning paradigms in "that it provides a basis for explaining the development of fear in individuals who neither experienced a traumatic event nor observed this occurring to others" (p. 24). However, Emmelkamp asserted that "it seems to make more sense to hold that information processes play a dominant role in the acquisition of normal fears" (p. 25).

Thus, if we accept the view that conditioned fear may be produced by a variety of techniques and that there are no substantial differences between them in terms of the underlying learning processes, we may be helped to deal with many of the issues that cause difficulty for the traditional theory of conditioning. This view is consistent with Mackintosh's (1983) point of view that classical conditioning is an acquisition of knowledge about relationships between events in the subject's environment.

Assumption 3: Facilitating and Suppressing Factors in Conditioning

The third assumption claims that the strength of emotional arousal is determined not only by the noxious stimulation, but also by social and personality variables. Thus, it is argued that the overall factors that facilitate and/or suppress arousal must be taken into consideration in order to determine the strength of conditioning.

Research evidence from various sources (Bandura & Rosenthal, 1966; Emmelkamp, 1982; Sartory & Eysenck, 1976; R. L. Solomon & Wynne, 1954) indicates that the stronger the emotional arousal, the stronger the strength of the conditioning. It appears that due to their higher cognitive abilities and to a large extent due to their social training, humans, unlike animals, can control the extent of their emotional arousal. Several variables may enhance or suppress the emotional arousal and hence the strength of conditioning. It appears that unless these factors are taken into account, the reason the same frightening circumstances lead to acquisition of fears of varying strength may be difficult to explain. It is assumed that the strength of the conditioned fear is a function of the net arousal, which is determined by overall facilitating and suppressing factors. Conditioning would not take place if the suppressing factors succeeded in depressing the net arousal below some minimum level.

Factors Facilitating Conditioning

Absence of Others. Rachman (1978) reviewed numerous examples from World War II showing that conditioned fear was more likely to develop if the individual were alone at the time of the emotional arousal. Rachman noted that with few exceptions, people appear to be more susceptible to fear when they are alone, and he explained this susceptibility in terms of controllability and social demands for courageous behavior. This tendency to react more fearfully in the absence of others is consistent with many findings on stress and affiliation (Cottrell & Epley, 1977; Rofé, 1984), indicating that arousal in a dangerous stressful situation remains higher when the subject is alone than with others.

Lack of Controllability. Various investigators (Emmelkamp, 1982; S. M. Miller, 1981; Rachman, 1978, 1984a, 1984b) showed that when confronted with stress, people tend to become fearful if they believe that they are incapable of coping with it. This notion is consistent with Bandura's (1977a, 1982) self-efficacy theory, which suggests that perception of self as lacking efficacy to cope with potentially aversive events makes one fearful, while perception of self as possessing coping efficacy diminishes fear arousal. Thus, lack of control should act to enhance conditioning in a situation perceived as dangerous.

Dependency. Several authors (Emmelkamp, 1982) have suggested that dependency may be related to the development of phobias. Dependency is strongly related to the notion of controllability, dependent people may feel more helpless when confronted with stressful situations and may, therefore, more readily develop conditioned fear. Dependency is more prevalent among females (Crandall & Rabson, 1960; Emmerich, 1966; McCandless, Bilous, & Bennett, 1961; Rachman, 1984a), and this seems to be one of the reasons for the higher prevalence of fears among them (Gray, 1971; Marks, 1969).

Sensitization. This variable refers to a situation in which one has difficulty removing his or her attention from the anxiety-arousing aspects of the stressful condition because of either the strong nature of the stress itself or the subject's poor distractibility. Conditioning is enhanced because attention remains focused on the anxiety-arousing stimulus and is diverted before the onset of relaxation responses. If the subject would continue to attend to the conditioning stimulus long enough, relaxation responses would eventually occur and the conditioning strength would decrease as a result. However, attention is diverted when the arousal becomes no longer tolerable. It makes little difference whether the period of attention is short or long. The most important variable is whether or not the CS were associated with arousal. Yet, the longer the period of arousal, the greater the intensification of conditioning. This may take place in an actual confrontation with the feared stimulus, upon contemplating or imagining the situation, or through exposure to the stimulus in other ways (e.g., seeing a picture of it or reading a story about it). The more frequently attention is focused on the fear-arousing elements of the feared event, the stronger the conditioned response will be, provided that attention is removed before the onset of calm responses.

The sensitization hypothesis is consistent with Bandura's (1971b, 1977b) conditioning theory that thoughts produce arousal, S. M. Miller's (1981) monitoring/blunting theory, which indicates that some people tend to be more anxious because of their greater tendency to tune their attention to the dangerous cues, as well as with the bulk of studies on repression–sensitization (see pp. 28–30) which show that sensitizers tend to be more anxious individuals. Findings from two other areas of research, which are consistent with this theoretical approach, are the studies on covert sensitization (Rimm & Masters, 1979) showing that aversive conditioning may take place when the subject deliberately imagines the CS in conjunction with some aversive event and evidence on the phenomenon of incubation, which shows that fear may be intensified over a period of time (Rachman, 1978).

Sensitization may seem to be inconsistent with the notion of implosive therapy because this approach indicates that fear tends to diminish when a subject deliberately imagines and very intensively experiences the anxiety-arousing event. However, the effectiveness of this therapy method is controversial, and some research shows that this approach may even intensify a subject's emotional distress (e.g., see Rachman & Wilson, 1980; Rimm & Lefebvre, 1981). In addition, research evidence from in vivo exposure (e.g., Gauthier & W. L. Marshall, 1977; W. L. Marshall, 1985) suggests that implosive therapy may be efficient only if a subject is exposed to the feared stimulus for a prolonged period, that is, attention is not removed before the onset of relaxation responses. Brief exposure may produce little or no beneficial change (W. L. Marshall, 1985) or, as most studies in this area show, may even cause the fear to intensify (B. V. Miller & Levis, 1971; Rohrbaugh & Riccio, 1970; Rohrbaugh, Riccio, & Arthur, 1972; Sartory & Eysenck, 1976; Silvestri, Rohrbaugh, & Riccio, 1970; N. M. Stone & Borkovec, 1975).

It appears that among human subjects, sensitization in imagination is more likely to occur than is sensitization in vivo, at least with some fears. McNally and Steketee (1985), in attempting to explain the persistence of their subjects' severe animal phobias, which typically began in childhood, indicated that subjects "consistently avoided their animal phobia and fled following surprise encounters" (p. 434). However, while this may be one reason for the intense animal fear, it is very likely that "cognitive fleeing" rather than "in vivo fleeing" played the dominant role in the production of severe animal fear. The reason for this assertion is that an actual encounter with animals may be rare, particularly because the phobic subject may make an appropriate arrangement to avoid the feared stimulus. In contrast, cognitive confrontation, such as reading about subjects that bring it to mind or seeing a picture of it, may be quite common and difficult to avoid. Emotional arousal in these conditions, which is accompanied by quick cognitive escape, is likely to enhance conditioning and prevent extinction.

Genetic Predisposition. Data from studies on both animals and humans (Emmelkamp, 1982; Gray, 1971; Sartory & Eysenck, 1976) suggest that to some extent normal fears, but not the clinical ones, are related to genetic factors. Thus, the genetically predisposed organisms react more fearfully to distress situations (e.g., see Gray, 1971), and they are thereby more likely to acquire conditioned fears. Research evidence consistent with this prediction was reported by Sartory and Eysenck (1976). Using different strains of rats as subjects, they found that differences in the acquisition and extinction of fear responses are controlled by genetic factors. The findings suggested that the higher the basal level of fear, the stronger the acquired fear response and the more time required for its extinction.

Strength of Subjects' Belief Regarding the Extent of Danger. Subjects' belief regarding the extent of harm that the CS might cause would have important effect on arousal and hence conditioning. This is consistent with MacCorquodale and Meel's formulation of Tolman's expectancy theory (Bower & Hilgard, 1981) as well as with Mackintosh's (1983) position. In lower organisms, the strength of this belief is determined by the frequency and intensity of arousal that confrontation with the CS may cause. Among human subjects, however, the strength of this belief may be determined by a more comprehensive evaluation of the situation. For example, in the instruction–informational method the credibility of the source of information may be an important variable in determining the subject's strength of belief. Similarly, calm or fearful messages by others during an actual exposure to a threatening stimulus may have an effect on the appraisal of the situation and on the emotional arousal. Other variables that may affect the strength of one's belief regarding the expected harm are the subject's cognitive level, past learning experiences, and personality variables, as well as the reactions of others to the situation. With regard to cognitive level, some research evidence shows that subjects with less intellectual ability or lower educational level tend to display greater emotional arousal (Rachman, 1978, Rofé, Lewin, & Hoffman, 1987) and to develop more psychiatric symptoms (Z. Solomon, Noy, & Bar-On, 1986) when exposed to stressful conditions. As suggested by Rachman (1978), these subjects tend to acquire fear more readily than do those with better cognitive development. The relationship between level of intelligence and emotional arousal in reaction to stress may be one of the reasons for the general decline of fears with the increase in age (Agras, Chapin, & Oliveau, 1972).

Factors Suppressing Conditioning

As was stated, in human subjects several factors might intervene to depress emotional arousal and hence to retard or prevent conditioning.

Embarrassment. Social expectation of courageous behavior tends to suppress overt expression of fear and perhaps prevents its arousal as well. Embarrassment to respond fearfully, which seems to be more frequent among males than females (Gerard & Rabbie, 1961; Lynch, Watts, Galloway, & Tryphonopoulos, 1973), may be one of the important factors that retard the development of conditioned fears. In times of war, not only men but women as well are expected to suppress feelings of fear, and this may be one of the reasons for the lower prevalence of fears during war among both sexes (Rachman, 1978; Saigh, 1984a, 1984b).

Habituation. This variable refers to reduction of sensitivity or emotional arousal in response to a frightening stimulus as a result of prolonged exposure to that stimulus (W. L. Marshall, 1985; Rachman, 1978). Habituation may explain not only the reduction or elimination of conditioned fears (W. L. Marshall, 1985; Rachman, 1978), but also the prevention of the conditioning process itself. Prolonged exposure to stressful stimuli tends to depress emotional arousal (W. L. Marshall, 1985), leading to an indifferent and apathetic attitude (Bettelheim, 1943; Strassman,

Thaler, & Schein, 1956), and possibly causing reappraisal of the situation as being less dangerous. All these should decrease the strength of conditioning or prevent it altogether. These data may also explain why most people have not developed long-lasting fears while in wars (Rachman, 1978; Saigh, 1984a, 1984b), concentration camps (see studies mentioned on p. 205), or prisoners of war camps (Strassman et al., 1956), despite intensely stressful conditions.

Social Support. An increasing number of studies on social support and stress (Eaton, 1978; Gore, 1978; Gottlieb, 1981; Haggerty, 1980; Larocco, House, & French, 1980; Linn & McGranahan, 1980) show that social support increases the individual's ability to cope and buffers the potential damage of stressful events on mental or physical health. Accordingly, it appears that social support suppresses arousal of fear and the perception of a situation as dangerous. It can, therefore, be expected that even when conditions optimal for occurrence of conditioning exist, social support could prevent or reduce to a great degree the occurrence of conditioning. It is very possible that this is one of the major reasons that conditioned fear during war is quite rare (Rachman, 1978; Saigh, 1984a, 1984b).

Controllability. As was indicated previously, fear is less likely to be aroused in people who believe that they are sufficiently competent to cope with the stress. Accordingly, it is expected that controllability would reduce the likelihood of conditioning in a dangerous situation, such as war (Rachman, 1978). Consistent with this prediction, laboratory experiments with rats demonstrated that less fear is conditioned to a neutral stimulus paired with controllable events (escapable) as opposed to uncontrollable (inescapable) shock (Mineka, Cook, & Miller, 1984). These findings indicate that the conclusions derived from experiments using the traditional Pavlovian paradigm may not be applicable to conditioning taking place in everyday life. This is because, unlike experimental condition, in a real-life situation, a subject may have some

> control over the US and/or some feedback that the US has terminated and will not happen again for a while. . . . Such factors play an important role in how much fear is conditioned. . . and/or how quickly such fear, once acquired, will extinguish once the situation has changed slightly. (p. 322)

Distraction. The efficiency of distraction in coping with stress has been discussed at length. Distraction decreases the likelihood of conditioning, because "when people direct their attention to extraneous features or irrelevant events, they may neither experience nor recognize the predictive stimulus" (Bandura, 1977b, pp. 71–72).

Generalization. Generalization from previous learning may either enhance or sup-press emotional arousal and thereby the likelihood of conditioning. Indeed, a recent study by Mineka and Cook (1986) found that an immunization procedure, in which monkeys were given extensive preexposure to a model displaying nonfearful behavior with snakes, effectively prevented later acquisition of fear.

In conclusion, the first three assumptions are summarized in Fig. 11.1.

Assumption 4: Automatic Nature of Conditioning and Resistance of Extinction

Conditioning trials result in a physiological bonding between the CS and the autonomic nervous system as well as in a belief that the CS may be dangerous and/or that the emotional arousal it causes is beyond the subject's control. This fourth

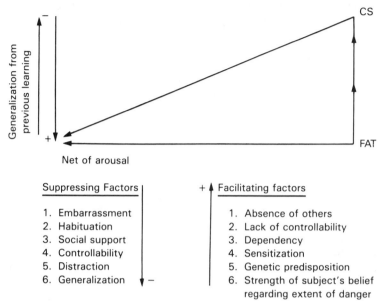

Suppressing Factors | + ↑ Facilitating factors

Suppressing Factors	Facilitating factors
1. Embarrassment	1. Absence of others
2. Habituation	2. Lack of controllability
3. Social support	3. Dependency
4. Controllability	4. Sensitization
5. Distraction	5. Genetic predisposition
6. Generalization ↓ −	6. Strength of subject's belief regarding extent of danger

Figure 11.1 The new conditioning paradigm of fear. CS, a stimulus that is appraised as being an integral part of a dangerous event; FAT, fear-arousal techniques: UCS, observation, instruction, self-analysis.

assumption concerns the lack of voluntary control over conditioned fear and its resistance to extinction (Campbell, Sanderson, & Laverty, 1964; Hulse et al., 1980; Jacobs & Nadel, 1985; R. L. Solomon & Wynne, 1954). We assume that both these phenomena are caused by two main factors. The major variable is some type of direct physiological bonding between perception of the CS and arousal of the sympathetic nervous system that seem to take place during the conditioning trials. The second factor consists of two beliefs. The first, developed at the beginning of the conditioning, is a conviction that the CS is dangerous. The second, which makes its appearance at a more advanced stage, is the belief that emotional arousal is inevitable and difficult to cope with.

Physiological Bonding

It appears that once an organism perceives a stimulus as dangerous and reacts to it emotionally, a permanent S–R bonding is set up in the subject's nervous system: A presentation of the CS would automatically activate the sympathetic arousal system even if cognitively the stimulus were appraised as nonharmful. The stronger the emotional arousal and/or the greater the number of conditioning trials, the stronger the S–R bonding between the CS and the sympathetic nervous system.

This theoretical position is consistent with that of R. L. Solomon and Wynne (1954) and Jacobs and Nadel (1985). In their review of conditioned fear, the former authors indicated that a conditioned stimulus paired with a very intense pain–fear reaction is likely to cause "a permanent increase in the probability of occurrence of an anxiety reaction in the presence of that conditioned stimulus pattern. . . . A neurophysiological correlate might be the permanent reorganization of central nervous system networks"

(p. 361). Similarly, according to Jacobs and Nadel's theory, conditioning tends to generate a permanent physiological change in a neuroanatomical system which they termed *taxon system*. Once conditioning is generated, particularly in a high-stress situation, it is highly resistant to extinction. Thus, even though we criticized Jacobs and Nadel's theory with regard to pathological fear (see pp. 153–156), their suggestions seem to be of value with respect to normal fears.

R. L. Solomon and Wynne (1954) tend to associate the permanent physiological change with intensive emotional arousal only. In our opinion, however, the physiological linkage between the CS and fear is generated at all levels of emotional arousal, but when arousal is low or moderate, the automatic relationship is less noticeable. In this case, the conditioned response is more amenable to cognitive control and able to be more easily extinguished.

Before concluding this section, we will discuss the theoretical implications of some evidence presented by Mackintosh (1983) against the strict S–R theory. Although Mackintosh made no special reference to fear, these data appear to be relevant to our general theoretical position. Mackintosh reviewed two sets of research data in order to demonstrate that conditioning is essentially a cognitive process. One set of findings shows that conditioning can be produced even if the occurrence of the unconditioned response is prevented during the course of conditioning. For example, in one of these experiments the drug atropine was used to block salivation during the presentation of CS with acid, and yet when tested later the subject exhibited a normal salivary response to the CS. The second set of data shows that manipulation of either the UCS or the CS, after conditioning has been established, may affect the subject's reaction to the CS. For example, if an aversion to food is produced after Pavlovian association between this food and the CS has been established, then the subject is unlikely to salivate or show other signs of attention to the CS. These findings are considered inconsistent with the S–R theory because, according to this formulation, changing the status of the UCS should not affect the CS–CR bonding. On the basis of these results, Mackintosh concluded that conditioning is an acquisition of knowledge about the events in an animal's environment.

However, this departure from the S–R conditioning model seems to be much too extreme, certainly with regard to fear. As was pointed out with respect to Bandura's theory, knowing that the feared stimulus is no longer harmful does not eliminate the fear. Autonomic responses are automatically aroused when the CS is presented. Thus, consistent with Konorski's (1967) theory, some kind of S–R bonding between the CS and internal responses of fear must be assumed. Konorski suggested that one aspect of conditioning involves automatic bonding between the CS and diffuse expressions of a general emotional state (see also Mackintosh, 1983). However, in line with Mackintosh's cognitive theoretical position, it seems that the escape or operant coping maneuvers (as opposed to respondent emotional reactions), by which the subject removes himself from the fear-arousing stimuli, are not controlled by the S–R relationships. In animals, these responses may be determined essentially by the subject's innate defensive maneuvers (see Bolles, 1972, 1975, 1978). In humans, however, these coping devices are adopted according to a cognitive analysis of the stressful situation. An individual whose natural coping resources, such as running away, fighting, or refusing to be reexposed to the feared stimulus, are inadequate may employ a sophisticated pathological strategy. For example, an Air Force serviceman who acquired an intensive fear reaction to flying due to a traumatic combat accident may be uncomfortable admitting feelings of fear, even to himself.

This may also be an inefficient coping strategy, since he might not be freed from his duties on such grounds. A more sophisticated response would be development of symptoms of a physical illness that would make him incapable of fulfilling his duty and would lead others as well as himself to believe that they are genuine responses. A case study demonstrating this possibility will be discussed in chapter 13.

Cognitive Expectation

The second factor that acts to strengthen the automatic arousal of fear and reduce its amenability to extinction consists of two cognitive variables. One is the strength of the belief that the CS is dangerous, and the second is the subject's belief in his or her ability to cope with the feared stimulus, particularly the emotions he or she expects it to arouse.

As implied by our previous assumptions, as long as the organism believes that the CS is dangerous, any new encounter with it that is accompanied by emotional arousal will strengthen the conditioning. The stronger the subject's belief, the greater the likelihood of quick emotional arousal. Thus, the elimination of this belief seems to be a condition necessary to any effort to extinguish the fear.

The effects of expected danger usually appear to be much more prominent in the early stages of conditioning. In many cases involving humans, particularly adults, the belief that the CS is dangerous gradually weakens owing to reasoning and increased experience, and it may eventually disappear altogether. Research evidence shows that among subjects with prolonged phobias, fear of a harmful outcome either is rarely mentioned (e.g., see S. L. Williams, & Watson, 1985) or is not the major reason mentioned by subjects (e.g., McNally & Steketee, 1985). However, it seems that as the S–R physiological bonding becomes more firmly established, intensification in a second cognitive variable occurs. The spontaneous arousal of fear upon reconfrontation with the CS, and the subject's inability to overcome this arousal, may lead him or her to the conclusion that he or she is incapable of coping with the fear: repeated failures act to deepen this belief. This hypothesis is consistent with Bandura's (1977a, 1978, 1982) self-efficacy theory as well as with what Mathews, Gelder, & Johnston (1981) termed *fear of fear*. Thus, although cognitive intervention aimed at eliminating this belief would not in itself be sufficient, it may facilitate the extinction process.

Several recent investigators examined whether the belief of self-efficacy is dependent on or independent of expected harmful outcomes. Kirsch et al. (1983) reported a high correlation between self-efficacy and expected anxiety, and they arrived at the conclusion that these two concepts are a single construct. In contrast, S. L. Williams and Watson (1985) argued that self-efficacy is independent of expected harmful outcomes. Using acrophobic subjects, they found that self-efficacy predicted approach responses toward the phobic stimulus with perceived danger and anxiety arousal held constant, whereas the latter two variables did not significantly predict approach behavior with self-efficacy held constant. Similar results were reported by Lee (1984) in examining the relationships between self-efficacy and anticipated anxiety, on a behavior of approach toward snakes.

However, we have several reservations regarding these latter results. First, the high correlation between self-efficacy and expected fear indicates that at least as far as arousal of fear is concerned (as opposed to avoidance–approach responses), these two concepts are not independent of each other. Second, S. L. Williams and

Watson's subjects had suffered from their height phobia for an average of 27 years. Thus, at best, the independence of the approach responses and expected harmful outcomes might apply only to a very advanced stage of conditioning. Third, these findings may not be valid with regard to all types of subjects. It is possible, for example, that in children, perception of danger continues to play a vital role in determining avoidance behavior for a long time after the first conditioning trials. Fourth, the concept of self-efficacy in the area of fear, as was measured in these studies, appears to be very ambiguous. Generally speaking, self-efficacy seems to have two distinct meanings. One meaning, which seems appropriate mainly in the case of motor skills, indicates a conviction in one's ability to successfully perform the required operant behaviors. The second meaning, which seems to apply mainly to fear, concerns the belief in one's ability to cope with the expected emotional and/or dangerous outcomes that an approach to the feared stimulus may affect. Thus, it is not clear what the acrophobic subjects of S. L. Williams and Watson understood when they were asked to state their "confidence in their ability to ascend and stand at the railing of each balcony looking down." It is very likely that the subjects' responses reflected the second meaning, that is, their ability to cope particularly with the expected emotional arousal that the approach behaviors toward the feared stimulus might cause. Two subjects may have the same level of anxiety toward the CS, but one may believe she has the competence to cope with the expected arousal feelings of fear and embarrassment, while the other may not have such a belief. Thus, while the actual or expected arousal may be insufficient to predict differences in approach behavior when self-efficacy is held constant, the latter variable may adequately differentiate between the two in this respect. If this is indeed the case, then S. L. Williams and Watson's conclusion that avoidance–approach behavior is independent of the expected emotional or dangerous outcomes would be inaccurate.

In conclusion, we suggest, as the fourth assumption of our theory, that automatic arousal of fear is determined mainly by S–R bonding between the CS and arousal of the autonomic nervous system. This is also the prime factor in retarding the extinction process, but cognitive variables play an important role as well. At the very early stages of conditioning, the belief that the CS may be dangerous is the only cognitive factor in enhancing the conditioned fear or in retarding the extinction process. However, at a more advanced stage a decrement in this belief and a parallel increase in a belief in the inability to cope with the fear is likely to occur. The stronger this belief, the slower the extinction process.

The factors involved in producing the automatic nature of conditioning and retarding extinction are summarized in Fig. 11.2.

Extinction Procedures

The idea that physiological rather than cognitive components constitute the major factor in the inhibition of extinction of conditioned fear is consistent with research evidence (Bandura, 1977b; Ladouceur, 1983; R. L. Solomon & Wynne, 1954) that cognitive intervention is not sufficient for extinction, though it may facilitate the process. R. L. Solomon and Wynne (1954) noted, for example, that

> forced reality testing should result in "reorganization of the cognitive field" such that the organism no longer "perceives the situation as dangerous." . . . However . . . while the anxiety will be reduced in intensity, it will never be completely removed, and the avoidance response may therefore reappear even after long periods of reality testing. (p. 363)

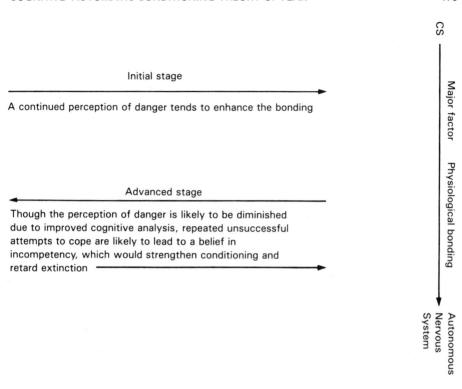

Figure 11.2 Factors involved in enhancing conditioning and retarding extinction processes.

Additional research evidence showing the facilitation effect of cognitive intervention has been reported by several other investigators (e.g., Denney, Sullivan, & Thiry, 1977; W. L. Marshall, 1985). However, the most efficient intervention seems to be prolonging exposure to the feared stimulus, at least up to the point where anxiety has subsided, and better yet for some period of time after this point (Gauthier & W. L. Marshall, 1977; Jacobs & Nadel, 1985; W. L. Marshall, 1985). Such intervention seems to be efficient because it makes possible new emotional experience, or counter-conditioning, which can neutralize or inhibit the previous physiological S–R bonding. This idea is consistent with notions suggested by R. L. Solomon and Wynne (1954) and Jacobs and Nadel (1985).

The view that cognitive intervention is insufficient for producing extinction of conditioned fear may seem inconsistent with Kirsch et al.'s (1983) findings that a highly credible expectancy-modification procedure was as efficient as application of systematic desensitization in reducing fear of snakes. However, let us point out that the subject's fear was only reduced, but not eliminated. This agrees with the idea that cognitive intervention may be only partly effective or may serve as a facilitating factor. Second, Kirsch et al. did not examine the maintenance of the therapeutic gains beyond the experimental setting. Research data by W. L. Marshall (1985) indicate that therapeutic gain of phobic subjects, evidenced in the experimental setting, may be lost or the phobia may become even worse after a one-month follow-up. However, relapse was less likely to occur when subjects were given prolonged exposure, particularly when this was combined with some cognitive intervention.

CHILDHOOD MEMORIES AND THE ISSUE OF "AWARENESS"

As indicated earlier, psychoanalysis generalizes its therapeutic methods to the treatment of normal fears (see pp. 138–142). We believe that our theoretical framework can explain any therapeutic benefits claimed by the proponents of psychoanalysis in the treatment of normal fear. Contrary to psychoanalysis, we argue that the psychoanalytic technique of retrieving memories has only an indirect effect on the extinction process. A subject led by a prestigious therapist to believe that retrieval of emotionally loaded memories releases him from the "poisoning effect" of the unconsciousness (e.g., catharsis) is likely to change his belief regarding his coping ability, and to motivate him to expose himself in vivo and/or via the imagination to the noxious stimulus until relaxation responses set in. The placebo effect of retrieving childhood "memories" in diminishing normal fear was demonstrated in our reanalysis of Moss's (1960) case study (pp. 138–140) and empirically confirmed by Kirsch et al. (1983; see p. 140 in this book).

With regard to the issue of awareness, subjects in many cases do appear to be "unaware" of the original causes of their fears, particularly when these fears have their roots in early childhood. However, it seems that this unawareness should be attributed to the normal course of forgetting rather than to repression. It may be the result of decay processes (see pp. 41–43; and some evidence presented by Jacobs & Nadel, 1985) and/or the consequences of interfering effects. Interference is very likely to produce unawareness inasmuch as the fear responses are evoked in many circumstances where similarity to some dominant aspects of the original conditioning situation exists. Sometimes, subjects claim that they remember the original events; however, some of these events may be invented to rationalize the unexplained fear. Some research findings by McNally and Steketee (1985) are relevant to this discussion. These authors found that 77% of their animal phobic subjects could not recall (in psychoanalytic terms, "repressed") the onset of their phobia, reporting that they had had the fear as long as they could remember. The rest attributed their fears to frightening encounters with animals. However, McNally and Steketee (1985) noted that

> in those instances when patients did cite a specific event, it may not necessarily have been the actual cause of the phobia. It is possible that individuals postulate plausible triggering events when at a loss to explain the cause of their irrational fears. (p. 434)

COGNITIVE READINESS AS A SUBSTITUTE FOR PREPAREDNESS

As was stated, the preparedness theory was formulated in order to explain the failure of the equipotentiality premise, namely, that stimuli have an equal chance to be conditioned (see p. 145). In view of the problematic nature of the preparedness concept, which we have demonstrated previously, it is suggested that some stimuli have higher conditioning value because they are characterized by certain qualities that enable one to more easily perceive them as dangerous. The cognitive effort needed for their being appraised as dangerous is less than in other types of stimuli. As cognitive creatures, animals and humans as well have a cognitive readiness to perceive danger more easily in the presence of certain qualities of stimuli than in their absence. These qualities are strangeness, movement, and lack of controllability.

Strangeness refers to a high level of discrepancy between the organism's cognitive representation of its prior experiences (schema) and perception of a new event. Mussen, Conger, Kagan, and Huston (1984) indicated that for human infants, a usually low or moderate level of discrepancy elicits attention, excitement, and even a smile. However, a high level of discrepancy elicits signs of distress and fear. For example, an infant may cry if its mother is wearing an unfamiliar hat that makes her look different. Fear of strangeness is, of course, not limited to humans (Mussen et al., 1984), but characterizes animals infants as well (Collard, 1967; H. F. Harlow & Zimmermann, 1959). It appears that strangeness tends to arouse fear because the organism cannot be certain that the stimuli are harmless.

Movement in itself should not cause fear, but the perception of danger is intensified when the strange object moves. An organism appears to know from its own movements and other experiences that moving objects have a power to inflict harm. Thus, dogs show greater fear of strange moving objects than of similar stationary objects (Melzack, 1952). Similar observations were reported with regard to chimpanzees (R. M. Yerkes & A. W. Yerkes, 1936). The authors noted that an object, to be really frightening, had to be characterized by properties of "visual movement, intensity, abruptness, suddenness or rapidity of change in stimulus" (R. M. Yerkes & A. W. Yerkes, 1936, p. 64). Some further research findings supporting the notion that movement may play an important role in eliciting fear are reviewed by Delprato (1980).

Arousal of fear is also associated with the extent to which an unfamiliar object is amenable to control or increases the lack of the subject's control in his or her immediate situation. Some relatively new evidence (Gunnar, 1980; Gunnar-von Gnechten, 1978) shows that human infants display fearful reactions if the unfamiliar object seems uncontrollable to them. However, fear responses cease when control over the object is obtained. Other evidence shows that for both human and animal infants, the presence of attachment figures and familiar surroundings reduces fearful behavior (Bowlby, 1973; Campos, Emde, Gaensbauer, & Henderson, 1975; H. F. Harlow & Zimmermann, 1959). Further evidence demonstrates that control of aversive events reduces arousal responses in both adult humans and animals (Averill, 1973; Bandura, 1982). In addition, Rachman (1978) showed that one of the most important elements likely to arouse fear during wartime was lack of control. A sense of controllability and personal competence were associated with a low level or lack of fear.

It appears, then, that these three qualities of stimuli together with the principles of the new conditioning theory are sufficient to explain the examples of fear that the proponents of the preparedness theory employed to validate their theoretical claims (Rachman, 1978; Rachman & Seligman, 1976; Seligman, 1971). Thus, it may be argued that both humans and chimpanzees display fear of snakes (Gray, 1971) partly because snakes are highly discrepant of their cognitive schema in respect to shape and movement. Other important factors in the development of fear of snakes are observational learning (Cook et al., 1985; Mineka, Cook, & Miller, 1984) and cultural influences (e.g., Murray & Foote, 1979). The former investigators found that laboratory-born monkeys, which were not previously afraid of snakes, developed an intense fear after they observed such responses in wild-born monkeys. Cook et al. (1985) indicated that "several studies . . . have suggested that a majority of wild-reared monkeys exhibiting snake fear probably acquired that fear observationally, rather than through direct traumatic conditioning" (pp. 606–607). This appears also to be true of humans, as Murray and Foote's (1979) data show. The authors concluded that Seligman and Hager's preparedness concept cannot account for the acquisition of fear of snakes. Other information that can strengthen this conclusion is that among members of an Indian community in Canada, certain dangerous animals do not arouse fear, but some harmless creatures, notably frogs and toads, do (Rachman, 1977).

Thus, strangeness and cultural training may explain why fear of snakes develops at an early age and is common among humans and animals. If one wishes to believe that an organism has some physiological mechanism, such as a small "picture" inside its head, that sensitizes it to fear of snakes, as is implied in the theories of Seligman as well as Jung, then one should argue that this is also the case with regard to the fear responses of the infant who sees its mother wearing a strange hat.

This theoretical approach may also explain why Valentine (1930) succeeded in conditioning his infant to fear of a caterpillar, but not to fear of opera glasses. As mentioned earlier, this is one of the examples used for defending the preparedness concept (Rachman, 1977, 1978). Another example often used is the fear of darkness. However, this response may be attributed to the reduction of controllability caused by darkness.

The principles mentioned here may also be used to explain some of the "innate" or prepared, fears among birds. For example, Tinbergen (1951) reported that ducks and geese exhibit more fear when exposed to a model of a hawk moving about their heads than when exposed to models of harmless birds. The hawk's short neck was thought to be an innate releasing mechanism of fear reactions. However, Gray (1971) noted that the interpretation of Tinbergen's observations remains very much in doubt. Firstly, Tinbergen's birds were more familiar with geese than with hawks as they had been reared in a natural environment. "Now novelty is itself an important stimulus for fear, so Tinbergen's hawk shape might have been more frightening simply because it was more novel. And, secondly, other investigators, working under more controlled conditions, have failed to repeat Tinbergen's findings" (p. 13). The first of these criticisms may be strengthened by Schneirla's (1965) hypothesis that a necessary factor for the hawk–goose effect is a sudden, massive increase in retinal stimulation produced by the hawk and the goose. With respect to this hypothesis, Delprato (1980) indicated that although the results of one research study (M. Green, R. Green, & Carr, 1966) did not support Schneirla's hypothesis, Schneirla (1965) and Hinde (1970) cited a variety of research findings in line with it. Gray's second criticism is also supported by several research studies reviewed by Delprato (1980).

Rachman (1977, 1978) used the preparedness theory for explaining the low incidence of conditioned fear during the "trauma and stress of bombing" of World War II. Rachman (1978) indicated that this theory may explain "the curious composition of a species that readily displays fear of spiders and snakes, but possesses a psychological resilience that enables it to endure the dangers and destruction of bombing attacks, repeated by day and by night" (p. 46). It appears that this phenomenon may be partly explained by the principle of strangeness and also social training, which prepares the individual to show courageous reaction to war-related stimuli, but not to stimuli such as snakes or spiders. Thus, like the unconscious concept in psychoanalysis, the preparedness notion of the behavioristic approach, which in the Jungian theory was termed the *collective unconscious*, appears to be superfluous.

12

Inadequacy of Learning Concepts for Explaining Bizarre Fear

THE NEW CONDITIONING PARADIGM

Even though we have rejected classical conditioning theory, it is still possible to argue that the new conditioning theory may be applied to bizarre fears, since the two minimum requirements of conditioning are nevertheless fulfilled. One could also claim that the fact that behavioral techniques are sometimes effective in treating bizarre fears such as agoraphobia (Hafner, 1983; Mathews, Gelder, & Johnston, 1981) may indicate that the phobia was developed through conditioning. However, this possibility should be rejected for the following reasons.

First, the argument that the two minimum requirements are fulfilled is inaccurate. In fact, only one of them is satisfied—the display of fear. There is not indication, however, that what is supposed to be the CS is genuinely perceived as dangerous. In normal fears, the CS signifies danger at least in the early stages of conditioning. The appraisal of danger is based either on direct experience, on information that the subject gets from observing others behaving fearfully toward the CS, or on information from a highly credible third source (e.g., parents). The subject genuinely believes that the CS may be harmful, and his or her previous knowledge either is consistent with this belief, or is too limited to disprove it. In contrast, the cognition of danger is missing in the case of bizarre fear. In bizarre phobias, the feared stimulus is never viewed as being able to cause real damage. It does not sound plausible to argue that a stimulus, such as a supermarket or chocolate, to which an adult subject is safely exposed hundreds or thousands of times, will suddenly be perceived as likely to cause real harm without any significant alteration in the environment that would justify such a change of attitude. Even when a traumatic or frightening event does occur concomitant with the onset of the panic, as is sometimes the case (Rachman, 1984a), it is highly doubtful whether the peculiar fear responses are the result of the perception of danger. There is no indication that people exposed to terrorist activities, such as bombings of supermarkets and buses, develop any bizarre fears such as agoraphobia. They may develop normal, but not bizarre fears. People know from their own previous experiences that these familiar places are not dangerous in and of themselves. They learn to adjust to their fears and may continue to visit these places feeling safe as long as they are certain that proper safety precautions have been taken. Thus, it appears that conditioning theory is not suitable for explaining the onset of bizarre fear even when it is associated with a recent traumatic event. As was stated, the psychobizarreness theory offers a more plausible explanation in these cases. The event is used by the subject for self-deception when the need arises to adopt bizarre behaviors for coping with unbearable stress (see pp. 114–115, 192).

One may continue arguing that conditioning in bizarre fears develops after the onset of the first panic attacks. The subject may then perceive the feared stimulus as dangerous. However, this notion must also be rejected. An agoraphobic patient may develop a conviction that the phobic stimulus is emotionally dangerous for him or her and that it may cause a heart attack from excessive stress (Rachman, 1984b). However, we do not believe that the patient perceives at any stage that the phobic stimulus itself can directly cause damage, that is, that the stimulus itself is objectively dangerous. As a rational being who has normal reality testing, the agoraphobic subject is well aware that he or she becomes fearful not because of some concrete danger in the outside world, but rather because of some other reason that he or she cannot adequately explain (e.g., see the case of Leonard, pp. 110–111). Some evidence supporting this claim was reported by Rappoport and S. L. Williams (1981; cited in S. L. Williams & Watson, 1985) in their analysis of in vivo thought patterns among agoraphobics. Subjects reported their thoughts while exposed to their phobic stimuli. Although they frequently referred to their coping ability, they only rarely were concerned about harmful outcomes.

Second, behavioral techniques are only partially successful in treating bizarre phobias. In some cases no positive results are attained despite intensive application of these techniques (Rachman & Seligman, 1976). Empirical evidence shows that the improvement rate of agoraphobia is approximately 49% (Barlow & Wolfe, 1981). Hafner (1983, see also Hafner, 1976), for example, reported that 44% of agoraphobic men and 12% of agoraphobic women either refused treatment or dropped out prematurely. Moreover, symptom substitution, relapse, or interpersonal complications are likely to occur after symptomatic treatment (Bland & Hallam, 1981; Hand & Lamontagne, 1976; Hudson, 1974; Milton & Hafner, 1979). The evidence shows that agoraphobics who were dissatisfied with their marriages either showed no change in their level of neurotic symptomatology (with some patients actually showing an increase) or, over the course of time, lost most of the improvement they had achieved through therapy. Some couples even experienced acute marital crises following the removal of the client's phobic symptoms. There is, however, some conflicting evidence indicating that marital adjustment of agoraphobics is independent of treatment outcome and that an improvement in phobic symptomatology may lead to an overall increase in marital satisfaction (see Himadi, Cerny, Barlow, & Cohen, 1986).

Third, there is no general agreement about the mechanism by which behavioral techniques reduce agoraphobic escape responses (Mathews et al., 1981; Michelson, Mavissakalian, & Marchione, 1985). Evidence shows that behavioral techniques remain effective despite striking variation in the method of application (Rachman, 1984a). For example, Emmelkamp (1974) demonstrated that with agoraphobic subjects, minimal therapeutic intervention was as effective as prolonged exposure. Similarly, de Silva and Rachman (1984) reported experimental findings showing that, contrary to the "Mowrerian Prediction," agoraphobics who were required to escape the fear-inducing situation when their anxiety reached a high level improved to the same extent as those who stayed in the target situation until their self-rated anxiety dropped by half.

These findings are in sharp contradiction to research findings (see W. L. Marshall's review, 1985) showing that for animals or nonclinical analogue subjects brief exposure either is not beneficial or may even aggravate the subject's level of anxiety; the findings constitute a further challenge to those who insist on explaining agoraphobia in conditioning terms. Marshall endeavored to resolve these inconsistencies by attributing the findings of the Emmelkamp (1974) and de Silva and Rachman (1984) studies to methodological problems (e.g., improper statistical analysis, size of sample). However, this does not seem to be an adequate solution to the problem since Rachman, Craske, Tallman, and Solyom (1986) found the same results when they repeated de Silva and Rachman's work. Brief exposure resulted in significant and equivalent improvements on all measures of agoraphobia, as did prolonged exposure. Moreover, these changes were still evident 3 months later. Thus, agoraphobic subjects seem to follow different rules than do fearful animals or analogue subjects. In view of many other differences between normal and bizarre fears, it appears preferable to resolve these conflicting findings by acknowledging that these two types of fears cannot be categorized together. Brief exposure cannot reduce normal fear because, as stated earlier, a necessary requirement for this is new emotional experience or counterconditioning for neutralizing the previously acquired S–R bonding. This rule does not apply to agoraphobia since such bonding had never taken place. As will be elaborated in the next section, agoraphobics may sometimes continue to display their symptoms despite their having become accustomed to the original stress or its even having been altogether eliminated. Brief exposure may be efficient in these cases because it can, for example, provide a self-deceptive excuse for the agoraphobic to rationalize his or her "cureness."

Another challenge to the conventional explanation of extinction effects by behavioral techniques is that sometimes the agoraphobic symptoms spontaneously disappear. For example, Wolpe (1982) reported a case history of a married agoraphobic woman who fell in love with another man and left her husband to live with him for a month in another city. During this time her agoraphobic symptoms completely disappeared. She was "able to go about on her own any distance without the least discomfort" (p. 287). However, when she returned to her husband, her agoraphobia reappeared in full force. When it became clear that the patient's marriage could not be improved, the therapeutic efforts were directed at enabling her to separate from her husband. Wolpe trained her in self-assertion and desensitized her to other areas of unadaptive anxiety. She then separated temporarily from her husband. During the first week, the agoraphobia gradually faded away, and she was completely free of it in the second week. She then returned to her home to make the legal arrangements for a permanent separation. "Her return did not produce any recurrence. . . . Three years later she was still free from the handicap of agoraphobia" (p. 287). We do not see how incidents such as these can be accounted for by the conventional model of extinction.

REASONS FOR THE EFFECTIVENESS OF BEHAVIORAL TECHNIQUES IN THE TREATMENT OF BIZARRE FEARS

As was previously stated, in many cases behavioral intervention does succeed in reducing and sometimes in eliminating bizarre fears. Choosing to reject the traditional behavioral explanation of the underlying causes of these fears raises the question of why these techniques are in fact sometimes effective.

It appears that the therapeutic effectiveness of behavioral techniques stems from two main factors. First, the techniques improve the subjects' coping ability and, second, they help to invalidate the subjects' beliefs regarding their inability to cope with their particular fears.

With regard to the first factor, research and clinical evidence reviewed earlier in this book (see pp. 108–110 and 156–157) has indicated, in line with psychobizarreness theory, that the onset of bizarre fears is associated with unbearable stress. It appears that in many cases, the coping skills the subject acquired in symptomatic behavior therapy are also used in dealing with the trouble that was the initial cause of the adoption of the bizarre fears. For example, if Leonard, in the case study described previously, had been treated behaviorally with symptomatic treatment for his agoraphobia, he could have used the skills acquired (relaxation, desensitization, assertive training) to deal with the true underlying causes of the disorder, namely, his guilt feelings following his wife's suicide and with the anxiety and rejection resulting from the community boycott. Sometimes a behavioral therapist intentionally teaches coping skills to help relieve the stress that caused the subject to adopt the bizarre symptom. This was done, for example, by Wolpe (1982) in the case study mentioned in the previous section. Thus, spontaneous recovery from bizarre phobias may occur either when a subject acquires efficient coping strategies or when life circumstances cause the disappearance of the stress. Consistent with this explanation, recent behavior investigators use the term *coping skills* to describe the effectiveness of behaviorist techniques with regard to bizarre neurotic symptoms such as agoraphobia (Michelson et al., 1985; Rachman, 1984a, 1984b) or hysteria (Blanchard & Hersen, 1976).

As we said previously with regard to normal fear, the effectiveness of the behavior-extinction procedures stems partly from their help in changing the subject's belief in his or her ability to cope with the expected harmful outcomes, particularly with the inevitable emotional arousal, by means of forced reality testing (e.g., see R. L. Solomon & Wynne, 1954). This therapeutic effect of behavioral techniques also seems to be effective with respect to bizarre fears. Agoraphobia is a disorder that often persists for many years (Mathews et al., 1981). Consequently, agoraphobics are likely to develop a strong belief that they are genuinely unable to control their fear even if they have become habituated to the original stress that led them to invent the bizarre responses. Thus, behavior therapy may help patients to revise their belief in their inability to cope with the fear. This hypothesis seems to be consistent with Mathews et al.'s (1981) argument that behavioral techniques do not cause extinction of fear of certain classes of stimuli but rather "extinction of fear of the fear itself" (p. 92). In line with this suggestion, some research data show that a behavioral approach in treating agoraphobia becomes more effective when the cognitive manipulation is more explicit (Ascher, Schotte, & Grayson, 1986; Michelson et al., 1985; Michelson, Mavissakalian, Marchione, Dancu, & Greenwald, 1986).

We do not have sufficient evidence to support our claim that the maintenance of agoraphobic symptoms may be largely the result of self-deception and/or belief of "fear of fear." However, as we have stated (pp. 131 and 156–157), according to both psychoanalysis and the psychobizarreness theory, agoraphobia and hysteria have similar etiological factors. Thus, research evidence on hysteria may be applicable to agoraphobia. Experimental evidence by R. S. Levy and Jankovic (1983) demonstrates that the manifestation of hysterical symptoms is determined purely by the subject's belief. By manipulating the belief of a female patient, Levy and Jankovic succeeded in controlling the manifestation of her hysterical symptoms. It is our opinion that the idea that hysteria is a matter of belief is true of bizarre fears as well.

It appears then that the persistence of bizarre fears is determined by two main factors: (1) unbearable stress, which caused the eruption of the fear, and (2) the strength of patients' belief that they are unable to cope with the fear. The more chronic the symptoms, the stronger this belief would be.

For some patients, particularly those who have suffered their bizarre fears for a relatively long period, behavioral intervention may have another beneficial effect. These patients may have become habituated to the stress that originally caused the appearance of the symptoms, and it may even be that the subjects continue to display the symptoms after the stress has been removed. Cognitively, the patient may feel a certain uneasiness in abandoning the defunct coping tools. Implicit social pressures may also exist to prevent the behavior change as removal of the symptoms may challenge the family or spouse to adapt to the patient's new role (Hafner, 1984; Hand & Lamontagne, 1976). For example, Hand and Lamontagne described the case of a man who had suffered from agoraphobia for 26 years. He had "to fight with his wife for 'permission' to try the flooding treatment. She felt that the whole family, including two very disturbed children, had adapted to his phobia" (p. 408). Hafner (1984) reported that "large improvements in patient's phobias and general symptoms were negatively associated with her husband's subsequent increased well-being" (p. 224). Thus, the behaviorist approach may relieve the individual's cognitive uneasiness (or dissonance) by providing an excuse for self-deception and may also help family members accustom themselves to the patient's new role, by involving them in the therapy. This conclusion is supported by research that has shown that involvement of the patient's spouse in the course of treatment may be an essential ingredient for its success (see Himadi, Boice, & Barlow, 1986). Similarly, Symonds (see Merskey, 1979) has treated cases of hysterical fugue by telling his patients, "I know from experience that your pretended loss of memory is the result of some intolerable emotional situation" (pp. 264–265). He then says to the patient that if told the whole story he will respect the patient's confidence, even to the point of telling the patient's doctor and relatives that he has been cured by hypnotism. According to Symonds, his patients never failed to admit that they had been faking their symptoms.

Behavioral symptom-oriented therapy may be less efficient or entirely ineffective in cases where the agoraphobic symptoms have only recently manifested themselves. In such cases, a dynamically oriented therapy may be more promising. The notion of a dynamic approach that we recommend is different from the traditional psychodynamic concept. Rather than reinstating "lost childhood memories from the unconscious," we suggest that such therapy should lead to insights regarding the pathological coping mechanisms that the patient has adopted and should encourage the patient to use more appropriate coping devices. Such a therapeutic strategy may incorporate some of the symptomatic behavioral tools such as relaxation. As we stated previously, Blanchard and Hersen (1976) have shown that with regard to hysteria, reinforcement of a subject's coping skills is crucially important for maintenance of therapeutic gain, and it may also be crucial for bizarre fears. The therapeutic suggestions presented here should be regarded as preliminary (see also chapter 18). More intensive theoretical work, which is beyond the scope of this book, is required to develop an efficient therapeutic strategy for countering bizarre fear and other neurotic disorders.

We have seen, then, that there is no need for the conditioning paradigm to explain the formation, the maintenance, or the removal of bizarre fears.

CLARIFICATION OF SOME ISSUES RELATED TO BIZARRE PHOBIAS

The objective of this section is to clarify three issues associated with bizarre phobias: (1) the psychological function of bizarre fears; (2) the rarity of these fears among children; (3) Rachman's safety-signal theory of agoraphobia.

Psychological Function of Bizarre Fears

The psychobizarreness theory stated that bizarre neurotic symptoms have two main psychological functions: distracting the patient's mind from the stressful stimuli and reducing the sources of the stress by removing the patient from the stressful environment and/or by effecting some desirable change to it.

With regard to the first function, it appears that one important purpose of bizarre symptoms is to avoid the escalation of depression, one of the most prominent characteristics of the preagoraphobic individual (Breier, Charney, & Heninger, 1984; Mathews et al., 1981; G. L. Thorpe & Burns, 1983), by redirecting attention to less depressive distracting thoughts. The likelihood that the removal of phobic symptoms will aggravate agoraphobics' depression provides supportive evidence for our hypothesis. Just such evidence is to be found in Hand and Lamontagne (1976), who described several cases in which removal of the agoraphobic symptoms by behaviorist procedures resulted in a significant increase in depression.

However, agoraphobics do not form a homogeneous group (e.g., Hafner & Ross, 1984), and therefore, the notion that agoraphobia serves as a barrier against intense feelings of depression may not apply to all subjects with bizarre fears. This distracting function of bizarre fear may play a more dominant role in cases where the phobia develops in conjunction with illness or with the death of a significant person (Rachman, 1984a). Our approach is consistent with Zigler and Glick's (1984) theory that bizarre paranoid reactions are strategies for coping with depression. Zigler and Glick's theory will be discussed in more detail later in relation to psychotic depression and paranoia.

As for the second function, bizarre fears, like other neurotic symptoms, give individuals some control over the sources of their stress by removing them from the stressful environment (see the case of Leonard, pp. 108–110). Bizarre fears are often associated with interpersonal conflicts, particularly marital ones (Last, Barlow, & O'Brien, 1984; Mathews et al., 1981; Rachman, 1984a). It appears that in these cases, the objectives of the symptoms is to effect desired changes in interpersonal relationships, particularly between spouses (e.g., see Rachman, 1984a), such as increasing attentional services and decreasing family demands. The need for attention seems to play an important role in the development of agoraphobic symptoms, since dependency is one of the common personality traits among agoraphobic subjects (Emmelkamp, 1982; Rachman, 1984a).

Evidence reviewed by Rachman (1984a) shows that fear of illness is frequently found among agoraphobics, although they are no less healthy than the rest of the population. Buglass, Clarke, Henderson, Kreitman, and Presley (1977) found that more than 50% of the agoraphobic subjects had feared fatal illness. It is quite likely that these symptoms are part of the agoraphobic's distraction tactics and/or help with their efforts to satisfy their strong need for dependency and attention.

Rarity of Bizarre Fears Among Children

Bizarre phobia in general and agoraphobia in particular (Marks, 1969) are very rare among children. Children are more likely to use hysterical symptoms in response to stress (Volkmar, Poll, & M. Lewis, 1984). Bizarre symptoms are used less by children for coping with stress for the following three reasons: (1) they are less familiar with bizarre fear and its coping value than with the symptoms of hysterical illness; (2) they lack both the breadth of experience required to feign bizarre fear and the high level of sophistication needed for the deception involved; and (3) the restriction placed on the agoraphobic's freedom of movement and the excessive emotional arousal that they undergo is too high a price for children to pay (as opposed to women, among whom staying at home is more acceptable and emotional arousal is more prevalent).

Rachman's Safety-Signal Theory of Agoraphobia

In light of the difficulty involved in explaining the development of agoraphobia in accordance with conditioning theory, Rachman (1984a, 1984b) suggested an alternative understanding of the disorder. Since the onset of agoraphobia is sometimes associated with loss or bereavement, he proposed that it is induced by events that significantly reduce the individual's sense of safety. Rachman further theorized that this pathological syndrome is more likely to occur in people who tend to be anxious and who have a dependent personality. This idea is used to explain some of the characteristics of the disorder, such as the higher rate of occurrence in women, especially those in their mid-20s, who (for reasons that Rachman elaborates) have a high level of dependence and/or anxiety.

In our opinion, however, this theoretical model cannot sufficiently explain agoraphobia for the following reasons, some of which Rachman himself pointed out:

1. Agoraphobics do not conceive of their problems as stemming from a lack of safety. Relatively few patients give spontaneous accounts that are consistent with the safety-signal theory (Rachman, 1984a).

2. The theory "makes no particular contribution to understanding the reasons for the association between agoraphobia and anxiety, or for the common association between agoraphobia and depression" (Rachman, 1984a, pp. 68–69).

3. Like the traditional approach of learning theories, the safety-signal theory neglects the most puzzling aspect of bizarre fears, namely, the lack of awareness of the agoraphobic patients of the causes of the sudden and dramatic changes in their lives.

4. Although the bizarre aspect of the agoraphobic syndrome was earlier recognized by Rachman (1978), it is not incorporated in the safety-signal theory. It makes little sense to argue that a sudden, intense, and lasting fear of certain familiar places, such as supermarkets, can automatically be aroused in a rational adult, as a result of a general feeling of insecurity. The inability of this theoretical approach to account for the bizarre aspects of phobias becomes even more blatant when we consider the more extreme bizarre fears, such as the chocolate and vegetable phobias that Rachman himself had difficulty explaining (Rachman & Seligman, 1976). How and why do neutral stimuli such as supermarkets, chocolate, or vegetables become objects of very intense and enduring fears? Can automatic mechanisms explain the selection of these as stimuli that engender fear? Surely one must recognize that the rat's mind, from which the notion of safety signal was originally derived (see Gray, 1971; Rachman, 1984b), cannot supply the basic answers for sophisticated human pathological processes. Though rats may display normal fear, they cannot display bizarre phobias for the simple reason that their minds are too restricted to enable them to invent responses (see also Mackintosh, 1983, p. 2).

5. Rachman also failed to explain why a feeling of insecurity should cause only agoraphobia and not other bizarre neurotic symptoms. As was stated earlier, the onset of neurotic symptoms, such as hysteria (pp. 107–108 and 156) is also associated with stress (see also Emmelkamp, 1982). What, then, are the automatic mechanisms that

determine the emergence of agoraphobia in preference to other peculiar responses, under such stressful or unsafe conditions?

6. The safety-signal theory claims that loss of a relative or friend may seriously undermine one's sense of safety and may automatically cause agoraphobia, particularly among people who are generally anxious and who have a dependent personality. Were this indeed the case, we should expect that the stress of war or concentration camps should give rise to a high degree of agoraphobia among soldiers, civilians, and camp survivors. However, the evidence simply does not confirm this expectation (e.g., see Rachman, 1978, on war, and the studies on concentration camp survivors mentioned on p. 205).

One set of data that Rachman (1984a, 1984b) used to support the safety-signal theory is that provided by G. L. Thorpe and Burns (1983) showing that agoraphobics feel comfortable when they have access to safety. The specific comfortable situations when they are away from home include having a way open for a quick return, being accompanied by their spouse, and sitting near a door in a restaurant. However, these findings can also be explained in terms of psychobizarreness theory. It can be argued that a strict adherence to agoraphobic symptoms is unusually difficult. From time to time, subjects need to take a break from their self-imposed confinement. However, arbitrary breaks are not possible since the agoraphobe would then seem inconsistent both to himself or herself and to the social surroundings. Self-deceptive excuses, such as those listed previously, are therefore needed for alleviating the burden of the agoraphobic symptoms. This explanation may also be applied to account for the frequently observed phenomenon that agoraphobics become attached to or dependent on a talisman, without which they are reluctant to venture outside (see Rachman, 1984a, 1984b).

CONCLUSIONS

In conclusion, it seems that none of the existing theories, including the safety-signal theory, is adequate. The two theories we have suggested, namely the theories of cognitive–automatic conditioning and psychobizarreness, provide the most plausible explanations for the onset of normal and bizarre fears, respectively.

Before concluding this part of the book, we would like to reanalyze two clinical case studies reported in the literature, in order to demonstrate the superiority of our two theories.

13

Reanalysis of Two Case Studies of Fears: The Chocolate and Aviation Phobias

CASE 1: CHOCOLATE PHOBIA

The case of chocolate phobia (Rachman & Seligman, 1976) has been mentioned on several occasions in this book, but it has not yet been fully described. Before more thoroughly analyzing the case, we first recount it in greater detail.

The patient, Mrs. V, was admitted to the hospital with a chronic neurotic disorder, whose main features were compulsive rituals centered on a powerful fear of chocolate. When confronted with any object or place slightly resembling or reminiscent of chocolate, she displayed an extreme fear reaction. As the fear became exacerbated over the years, she had to stop working and became increasingly confined to home. The phobia had begun several months after the death of her mother, to whom she had been abnormally attached. Prior to this, she had enjoyed eating chocolate, but her pleasure seemed to have waned gradually during the period following her bereavement. After her mother's death, Mrs. V became depressed for a prolonged period, and she also became aware of a strong aversion to and fear of cemeteries and funeral parlors.

Rachman and Seligman mentioned no specific frightening experience that could justify the patient's unusual fear of chocolate. Although the information available is scarce, it appears that the case is still amenable to explanation in terms of psychobizarreness theory. First, when reading a description of the case, one cannot avoid forming the impression that the phobia had an unusually high level of distractive value for the patient, since it almost entirely occupied her attention. Her reactions resembled those of one who has been informed that wherever he goes, a bomb may be planted, ready to explode. Second, the death of her mother constituted a very intense emotional shock that caused prolonged depression. It seems clear that the patient was desperately in need of a coping mechanism to arrest further intensification of depressing feelings. A stimulus with an extremely strong distractive value was therefore required to eliminate the powerfully depressing thoughts that had succeeded in dominating her consciousness. The chocolate phobia could fulfill this function quite well. Although the phobia seriously limited the patient's general adjustment, it was much less distressing for her than the prospect of enduring her dominating depressive thoughts. Third, the patient was hypochondriacal, sexually inadequate, and abnormally dependent. One can imagine that in the face of these personality traits, her relationship with her husband was already stressed and that her mother's death no doubt increased Mrs. V's dependence on him. Moreover, it is quite possible that because of her impoverished personality she had cultivated only poor social relationships, which could otherwise have enabled her to relieve her depression (see p. 242). Thus, it may be argued that apart from the distraction function, the chocolate phobia was aimed at maneuvering her husband into playing a mother's role, that is providing support and satisfying her unusual need for dependency.

It appears that the patient struck quite a good bargain: she replaced very dominating depressive thoughts (stemming from the loss of her life support), which might have led to suicide, with an artificial phobia, which helped her secure support and attention from her husband and other people. This interpretation is also consistent with the theoretical approach of Fontana, Klein, E. Lewis, and Levine (1968) that a person may be motivated to present himself or herself to others as crazy, sick, and incompetent to attain certain desirable goals. When viewed

in this way, people are not likely to make demands on him or are not likely to persist in their demands. . . . Passivity and gratification of dependency needs are legitimized, since society accepts the position that the sick cannot care for themselves and must be cared for. (p. 111)

Why did the patient choose the chocolate phobia and not another type of symptom as a coping mechanism? We believe that the choice of symptoms is not at all arbitrary but is, in fact, quite limited. As indicated in psychobizarreness theory, some symptoms are less costly and lend themselves more easily to self-deception than others. In this case, the patient could have chosen less costly symptoms, that is, symptoms with much lower distractive value, but they might not have been strong enough to overthrow the powerful depressive thoughts and/or to secure social support. Moreover, the evidence indicates that immediately or a short time after her mother's death, chocolate spontaneously aroused in her a very moderate level of uneasiness or fear. By gradual intensification of this symptom, she could easily deceive herself into thinking that the phobia was imposed on her by an uncontrolled source. Apparently, the original mild fear of chocolate was caused by the following two responses: (1) As the patient had previously enjoyed eating chocolate, it is very possible that the chocolate reminded her of her mother's death since it symbolized a loss of the sweetness of her life. Rachman and Seligman did indeed indicate that "there seemed to be a close connection for her between chocolate and the death of significant people in her life" (p. 337). (2) The patient was obliged to see the coffin containing the body of her mother. She reported that she believed the coffin was dark brown in color and that it may have contributed to the association she had established between chocolate and death. In addition, she saw a bar of chocolate in the room containing the coffin. Thus, these stimulus characteristics of chocolate were enough to arouse in the subject a moderate level of discomfort, and in accordance with our principle of saliency–availability, these "normal symptoms" were intensified to an absurd level in order to meet the patient's psychological needs.

The explanation of the case in terms of psychobizarreness theory seems more plausible than an interpretation based on either the conditioning model or psychoanalytic theory. An adequate explanation in terms of conditioning is unattainable due both to a lack of prominent fear-evoking events that could justify the unusual lack of fear and to the extreme resistance of the phobia to extinction despite very intensive application of behavioral therapy techniques.

Psychoanalytic clinicians would of course connect the onset of the chocolate symptom to some traumatic childhood episode—most probably a sexual one. However, in addition to much research that seriously questions the validity of this approach, no plain evidence exists in the case study itself to support such an interpretation. Nevertheless, we do not rule out the possibility that the patient's childhood experiences, which shaped her extremely dependent personality and were at the root of her strong attachment to her mother, "prepared" her to develop a pathological reaction to a relatively moderate level of stress.

CASE 2: AVIATION PHOBIA

The following case, reported by Grinker and Spiegel (1945; see R. W. White, 1964), can illustrate the inadequacy of both the psychoanalytic approach and the traditional conditioning paradigm in explaining intense acquired fears. It will be demonstrated that concepts from both the cognitive–automatic theory of conditioning and the psychobizarreness theory may sometimes be necessary for understanding the development of psychiatric symptoms. Let us first describe the main details of the case.

Description

The case concerns a young man called Pearson Brack, who was a bombardier in the U.S. Army Air Corps during World War II. On his ninth mission, his plane was suddenly jolted. It rolled over and began to fall. During the fall, Brack received a heavy blow on his chest and at once began to cough up blood. Eventually, the pilot regained control, and in spite of his injury Brack dropped his bombs on the target and the mission was successfully completed. After 4 weeks of hospitalization, he returned to duty. However, on his next two missions he fainted when the plane reached an altitude of 10,000 feet.

In several psychiatric interviews, Brack vigorously denied that he had felt anxious during the flights, and he consistently attributed his fainting to an organic defect. Medical examination, however, ruled out this possibility. The patient did not show any signs of fear even when he was given a Pentothal interview. He remembered the ninth mission in great detail, but he remained completely calm and unemotional. Still unconvinced, the psychiatrist tried another approach. He accompanied Brack on a practice flight to observe his reactions while in the air. On the way to the airfield and during the early stages of the flight, Brack was exceedingly talkative and jocular, showing no signs of fear. However, as soon as the aircraft reached an altitude of 10,000 feet, he began to tremble. His face became pale, and his breathing became rapid. Nevertheless, he denied that he was experiencing fear, saying that he felt sleepy and closing his eyes. The patient was ordered to breathe slowly and deeply, and fainting was thereby avoided.

Brack was then sent on another mission. He performed his tasks efficiently but returned completely exhausted. He was again sent to the hospital, where he was informed that he would be suspended from flying for 6 months. When he returned home to the United States, he enjoyed his leave with his wife and child, but as time passed, he became increasingly nervous and depressed. Brack was readmitted to the hospital, where he met with the same psychiatrist who had treated him previously. He admitted at once that the doctor had been right about his nervousness, although he himself had not recognized it at the time. During a subsequent Pentothal interview, Brack again described his ninth mission, but this time he reported having felt fear. However, it was only after several additional interviews (one of which included the use of Pentothal) that he was able to admit having felt extreme fear while not under the influence of the drug. After a short course of conventional psychodynamic therapy, during which the therapist claimed that Brack had gained insight into the causes of his symptoms, the depression and nervousness gradually disappeared. However, on the basis of the patient's childhood experiences, the therapist concluded that Brack did not have enough strength to cope with combat flying, and he was, therefore, assigned to ground duty.

Inadequacy of the Psychoanalytic Interpretation

The case was originally interpreted in terms of the psychoanalytic concept of repression. It was claimed that Brack's central problem was an inability to admit weakness and that he could not bear the idea of experiencing fear in response to a traumatic event. Consequently "his denial was not simply a conscious concealment from others; the anxiety was actually repressed out of his own awareness" (R. W. White, 1964, p. 66). It was argued that the patient was motivated to repress experiences of fear because they would constitute a threat to his ego ideal. However, when the physical symptoms of fear (trembling, palpitations, rapid breathing, etc.) became evident and panic threatened to invade his consciousness, Brack's only remaining mechanism was fainting. Fainting enabled him to defend his ego ideal since it prevented him from recognizing his terror. R. W. White (1964) stated that this response "was a completely involuntary protective device" (p. 66).

As usual in psychoanalysis, the patient's dysfunctional responses were attributed to his childhood experiences. The anamnestic interview revealed that Brack's father was an alcoholic who had used drink to escape his difficulties. White stated that Brack internalized this negative image and during adolescence exhibited a personality style similar to his father's. One day, his grandfather had taken him aside for a serious talk in which he warned Brack that he might grow up to be just like his father. This shocked Brack into making an abrupt change in his way of life. White claimed that Brack rejected his father's example and internalized a new ego ideal in the image of his grandfather. Furthermore, the threat of being like his father strongly motivated Brack to repress weaknesses and experiences of fear.

The change in Brack's symptoms after his return to the United States was attributed to the weakening of the repressive forces. On the one hand, Brack felt some relief at his removal from the dangerous zone, but at the same time, he remained somewhat apprehensive since eventually he had to return to combat. It has been argued (R. W. White, 1964) that this psychological state "relaxed the whole system of defense just enough to let anxiety creep into his dreams and into waking behavior in the form of nervousness. This necessarily brought about depression . . . " (p. 68). Further, this loosening of the defense mechanism enabled the psychiatrist "to assist his insight and give him the encouragement necessary to restore his confidence and self-respect" (p. 68).

This psychoanalytic interpretation poses several problems that render its acceptance difficult. Our first objection concerns one of the fundamental assumptions of psychoanalysis, namely, that a denial of negative personality traits or weaknesses is necessarily a sign of maladjustment or even of pathological disturbance (Millham & Kellogg, 1980; see also pp. 74–75 in this book). This stems from the general philosophical approach that denial of reality is necessarily harmful (e.g., see Taylor, 1983). However, as shown by extensive research reviewed previously, this assumption is not consistent with the facts. An increasing amount of research demonstrates that mental functioning depends on illusion and denial (Lazarus, 1983; Taylor, 1983) and that presenting oneself in a positive light is associated with improved mental functioning (see pp. 81–83). Furthermore, in line with these findings, the behavioral responses of Pearson Brack portray a picture quite the opposite of the psychoanalytic description of him. Brack's unusual strength of personality was to some extent recognized by R. W. White (1964) himself who stated

we must admit that Brack had strength. . . . Not everyone could have dropped bombs accurately on a target a few minutes after staring straight into the face of death and while spitting blood from a painful injury. Not everyone could have forced himself to enter a plane for another mission. (p. 65)

It is sometimes amazing how psychoanalytic procedures can lead a therapist to a conclusion so inconsistent with the obvious facts.

Our second objection is that in the absence of convincing evidence arguing for the existence of an autonomous unconscious entity, the idea that the fainting symptoms were automatic responses entirely controlled by involuntary unconscious mechanisms is purely psychoanalytic speculation. Scientifically, there is no difference between this idea and an assertion that the fainting was controlled by an invisible devil.

No plausible case can be made for the claim that Brack's resistance to admitting fear stemmed from an unconscious repressed anxiety of being like his father. Moreover, if this were indeed the psychological factor underlying Brack's psychiatric symptoms, then his being sent home either should have had no effect on the defense mechanism he used or should have intensified the mechanism rather than "relaxed" it, as was presumed by White. Being at home while the country was in the throes of a war and while other young men were at the front should have caused an intensification of Brack's feelings that he was acting like his father. While according to the psychoanalytic conceptualization this should have led to an intensification of Brack's psychiatric symptoms, at the same time it should have reinforced his resistance to remembering the "repressed" traumatic episode. In fact, contrary to this psychoanalytic prediction, the opposite happened. Why?

It has been shown that treatment of combat stress is more effective when administered in close proximity to the combat zone than when soldiers are airlifted and treated behind the lines (e.g., Z. Solomon & Benbenishty, 1986). In view of these findings, it seems reasonable to assume that Brack's military dysfunction could have been desensitized at the front had behavioral approaches such as desensitization been applied. Thus, it appears that the notion of resistance to admitting weakness should be regarded not so much as reflecting defense mechanisms employed by Brack, but rather as a defense strategy used by the psychiatrist himself to rationalize the failure of his psychoanalytic therapeutic procedure.

Our third objection is that the authors have no evidence validating Brack's "story" regarding his childhood experience. Furthermore, even if this story has some truth, there is no solid evidence that the patient's symptoms were directly affected by these experiences. Moreover, from the point of view of both psychoanalytic and learning theories, it is highly unlikely that one conversation with his grandfather during adolescence, when his personality had already been shaped, could have produced so substantial a change in Brack's personality.

In our opinion, these objections cast serious doubt on the psychoanalytic interpretation of the case.

Inadequacy of the Classical Conditioning Model

As will be illustrated shortly, it is quite apparent that the traumatic event did lead to conditioned fear and that this played an important role in the determining of Brack's psychiatric symptoms. However, we claim that the patient's responses cannot be explained by the traditional conceptualization of conditioning. Mackintosh (1983), in his critique of conditioning theory, reviewed findings that called into question the mechanistic behaviorist conception that classical conditioning produces stimulus–response (S–R) bonding between the conditioned stimulus (CS) and the overt unconditioned response (UCR) (see p. 172). Brack's behavioral symptoms seem to be a case in point, inasmuch as they contain no indication of overt UCR apart from emotional arousal. The fainting response did not occur immediately after the traumatic incident (unconditioned stimulus [UCS]), nor during the interval between this event and the completion of the traumatic mission, but only on the subsequent flights. In the same way, Brack's verbal expressions during his reexposure to the CS during the practice flight did not contain any element that could be considered similar to the UCR. Instead of an expression of fear, there was a denial of fear. Moreover, one would expect that the traumatic event would cause resistance to exposure to situations that might arouse discomfort, as is usually the case with phobic subjects. However, Brack's insistence on returning to flying and his willingness to expose himself to situations that bore a close relationship to the original CS evidences a reaction opposite to what would be expected by S–R formulation. Thus, his behavioral symptoms during the flights after the traumatic events and his overall behavioral reaction did not coincide at all with the traditional S–R conceptualization of conditioning.

Moreover, even if Brack's responses could be explained in terms of classical conditional theory, it would nevertheless be difficult to accept this explanation, since much of the research reviewed earlier (see pp. 144–146; and Mackintosh, 1983) raises serious doubt regarding the general validity of the theory. One of the main findings that has direct relevance to this case is that conditioned fear is very rare during times of war (see p. 144). The fact is that the vast majority of people do not develop conditioned fear despite their being exposed to optimal conditions for the occurrence of such responses in terms of the S–R theory of conditioning. Thus, an automatic conceptualization of conditioning necessitates justifying why only a minority of people, like Brack, develop conditioned fear. All these considerations should discourage one from using the Pavlovian model to explain the case of Brack. The one theory that appears capable of adequately integrating the seemingly conflicting research findings in the area of conditioning, as well as cases like that of Brack, is the cognitive–automatic theory of conditioning.

Alternative Interpretation

Brack presumably experienced a high level of stress prior to the occurrence of the traumatic event. Most normal married men with children would be concerned and scared in wartime, even if fear were not evident in their overt behavior. Evidence from the Lebanon War (Z. Solomon, Noy, & Bar-On, 1986) indicating that older soldiers (26 years of age and above) who have wives and children are more likely to develop combat stress reaction than younger, single soldiers supports the assumption that Brack would have been under stress. Nevertheless, Brack succeeded in overcoming his fears and fulfilled his duty efficiently. The traumatic incident, however, so dramatically increased Brack's stress level that his normal coping resources were no longer adequate. This increase in stress was due to the following three reasons:

1. Brack's belief that he might be killed was strengthened. R. W. White (1964) stated that from Brack's remarks during the first Pentothal interview, "one could infer a deep conviction that he would die on a mission" (p. 63). The belief that he might die was probably present before the traumatic incident, since occupations involving dangerous tasks intensify the awareness of possible death. Being so close to death on this mission, however, raised this awareness or belief to such an extent that it greatly diminished Brack's efficiency as a soldier.

2. Consistent with our cognitive–automatic theory of conditioning, it seems that the

traumatic event did cause automatic bonding between flying at a certain altitude (CS) and the arousal of the sympathetic nervous system (UCR).

3. It is very likely that conditioned fear was weak at the time of the incident and intensified only later. In other words, in line with our principle of sensitization and Bandura's (1977b) conditioning theory of self-arousal, it is possible that during the 4 weeks of hospitalization shortly after the ninth mission Brack frightened himself by hallucinating about the original traumatic episode and/or other dangerous episodes. Thereby the conditioned fear gradually intensified. Z. Solomon and Benbenishty's (1986; see also Kolb, 1977, pp. 535–543) findings, that delaying psychiatric intervention in treating combat stress reduces the effectiveness of treatment as compared with immediate intervention, would seem to reflect our assumption that during Brack's protracted stay in the hospital, his condition worsened.

It is possible then that Brack's report during the first Pentothal interview, regarding his emotional arousal during the traumatic flight, was quite accurate and that much of the conditioning strength developed afterward. Brack had exceptional ability to control his emotional arousal. This is borne out by his ability, despite his injury, to release the bombs on the target, and by his successful completion of another mission after the practice flight, despite his fears. Thus, Brack either did not experience much fear during the traumatic incident, or his ability to control arousal and concentrate on the job to be done prevented most of the emotional-arousal signals from reaching his focus of attention. If this were indeed the case, then the automatic bonding between the CS and arousal, on the traumatic mission, ought to have been weak. Thus, had he been treated immediately for his fear symptoms, Brack would possibly not have developed a strong conditioned fear. However, for him this was not possible because his physical injury necessitated hospitalization.

A possibility does still exist that Brack reacted very emotionally during the traumatic incident but due to embarrassment did not reveal this to the psychiatrist at the first Pentothal interview. Men do tend to depress feelings of fear because of embarrassment (Gerard & Rabbie, 1961; Lynch, Watts, Galloway, & Tryphonopoulos, 1973).

Why did Brack not admit that he feared flying? It may be argued that apart from embarrassment, Brack avoided this type of response because of a moderately strong approach–avoidance conflict: he did and did not want to continue carrying out his dangerous military task. The approach tendency may have been affected by the following factors: (1) Brack may have had a strong ego ideal, perhaps shaped in part by the grandfather, as the therapist assumed. The strong ego ideal would have been one of the principal reasons for his strong devotion to duty and his unwillingness to admit fear. It should be noted, however, that this is by no means exceptional. Men are educated to be brave, and a refusal to admit weakness is an integral, positive part of the self-image of many men, encouraged by various social agencies (not only by grandfathers). (2) Another factor that may have strengthened the approach tendency in Brack is the degree of attachment to his comrades, whose respect he might have feared losing if he had admitted weakness. The strength of the bond between soldiers during a war inhibits the expression of fear (e.g., Rachman, 1978). (3) A third factor that could have played some role in strengthening Brack's approach tendency is his identification with the goals of the war. Brack may have been quite in agreement with these goals, and he may not have wanted to admit to himself that he lacked the strength to make a significant contribution in defeating the enemy.

Thus, it appears that all these factors motivated Brack's resistance to admitting fear and his overt verbal desire to resume his previous duties. However, on the other hand, his normal coping mechanisms were no longer strong enough to bear the intensified level of stress. In such a predicament, fainting was just about the most efficient coping strategy possible. In other words, consistent with our principle of saliency–availability, by using the fact that he had received a heavy blow on his chest, Brack could easily deceive himself into thinking that his inability to fly at the high altitude necessary for bombing missions stemmed from his injury rather than from fear. The selection of the fainting response, combined with the belief that his inability to carry out his military duty stemmed only from his physical injury, were personally less costly than admitting a psychological incapability would have been.

After Brack's return home, the approach tendency apparently intensified (this is consistent with N. E. Miller's, 1944, 1951, theory that in an approach–avoidance conflict, avoidance drops off more rapidly with distance from the conflicting goal than does the approach motive). He was "troubled by self-reproach because he had not been able to complete his tour of duty overseas" (R. W. White, 1964, p. 64) and probably was socially embarrassed at being home during wartime. These factors may explain Brack's change in mood during his vacation in the United States. Emotionally, Brack was at this point ready to cooperate and play the role demanded of him by his psychoanalytic therapist. Therefore, in the psychiatric interviews that followed his return home, he was willing to admit fear. Although less likely, it is also possible that as a result of moral scruples Brack was ready to abandon his self-deceptive mechanism and tell the psychiatrist exactly how he felt during the traumatic event in the hope that this would facilitate his return to duty.

It should be noted, though, that the psychoanalytic therapy had only very limited success. In view of the therapist's finding that Brack was incapable of resuming his previous military assignment, it is doubtful whether his original fear symptoms were eliminated at all. Moreover, the therapist's eventual solution of sending Brack to work in ground duty could have been effective without his having expended time and effort in therapy.

We have seen, then, that conditioning alone sometimes cannot provide a sufficient explanation when symptoms other than fear appear after exposure to fear-evoking circumstances. At the same time, there is no need to attribute these symptoms to pathogenic childhood memories preserved in an "unconscious black box." The phenomena may be more simply explained by analyzing the subject's current stressful condition and by involving the consciousness in the symptom-production operation.

CONCLUSIONS

We have shown that none of the current available theories can provide a comprehensive explanation of either normal or bizarre fear. The fundamental problem in all these approaches, is their insistence on viewing the human as basically an automatic, rather than a cognitive creature. It was not apparent to their formulators that humans, and to some extent animals too, are wise creatures who can cognitively analyze the current stimulus conditions and determine their behavior accordingly. It seems that one of the main reasons for the mistaken assumption of the S–R theorists, at least with regard to conditioned fear, is that they analyzed the final product of conditioning and failed to realize that conditioning, like motor skills, is composed of two basic processes: the assessment-screening stage and the consolidation or automatization process. The conceptualization of conditioning as both a cognitive and an automatic process seems to represent more faithfully the phenomenon of conditioning of fear. Using these terms, it has been argued that the classical Pavlovian paradigm is not an essential part of the conditioning process but merely one of the techniques by which conditioning can be produced. Thus, one of the advantages of the new conditioning theory is its ability to integrate the various learning models of fear into one theoretical framework.

Another distinct flaw in the traditional theories of fear is the belief that the simple model of animal behavior can explain the complex behavior of the human. According to the proposed theory, variables unique to humans, apart from consciousness, such as presence or absence of other people, a sense of controllability, embarrassment, and social support, may have a crucial effect on the conditioning process.

Another advantage of the new model is that preparedness theory, which has gained wide recognition in the psychology of fear over the last 18 years, is made redundant. It was shown that the various examples used by proponents of this theory to validate the concept of preparedness may be more simply explained by the new conditioning theory together with a few simple additional principles.

None of the conditioning models, including the new paradigm, can adequately explain the development and persistence of bizarre phobias. These types of fear are unique to humans, and most probably they are consciously invented or adopted as part of a pathological coping style in response to an unbearable level of stress. Thus, psychobizarreness theory seems to be the most efficient model for explaining clinical fears. Moreover, it was indicated that while the behavioral techniques may have limited success in treating these fears, a dynamic approach aimed at producing insight into the pathological nature of the patient's coping style, together with encouragement to adopt a more adaptive coping strategy, may be beneficial. Indeed, it may be the only useful therapy for many patients who cannot benefit from behavioral approaches.

V

APPLICATION OF PSYCHOBIZARRENESS THEORY TO PSYCHOSIS

14

Psychobizarreness and the Inadequacy of Traditional Models

INTRODUCTION

Fundamental Theoretical Issue in Psychosis

Our main objective in the part of this book is to demonstrate the applicability of psychobizarreness theory to psychosis. We emphasize that we are not primarily concerned with the depression or anxiety these patients experience. Depression and anxiety are not the sole property of humans, and they are displayed by infant animals as well, inasmuch as they seem to be spontaneous reactions to stress (see chapter 17). However, bizarre responses are unique to human beings, and our main intention is to clarify whether bizarre psychotic behavior is mechanistically determined either by the unconscious, by conditioning, or by neurochemical mechanisms, or whether it is consciously chosen by the individual as a coping strategy, as the psychobizarreness theory asserts.

We do not mean to imply by our use of the word *chosen* that psychotics are completely free to choose their behavior and that they could behave normally if they so desired. No one can deny the crucial importance of genetic or biological components, childhood experiences, or other environmental factors in shaping the individual's behavior and overall ability to adjust. However, the question is whether these variables compel the bizarre psychotic symptoms through some automatic mechanisms or whether they merely expose individuals to an extremely high level of stress, which although greatly limiting their choice of behavior, still leaves them with several options. They may choose to bear the suffering and remain deeply depressed, to commit suicide, or to adopt certain convenient pathological coping devices. The decision to adopt the bizarre symptoms is not usually made while the individual is in a full state of awareness. On the contrary, all our previously mentioned considerations with regard to neurosis (see pp. 95–97) are applicable to psychosis as well. Moreover, awareness in these subjects is likely to be far lower than in neurotic patients. The excessive stress to which they are subjected produces adverse psychological and neurochemical changes that greatly reduce the individual's alertness and power of judgment. This is consistent with data indicating that high arousal is likely to decrease the efficiency of various mental processes (Nuechterlein & Dawson, 1984, p. 167). So the claim that "crazy behavior" is freely chosen should not be understood to mean that the decision to act in this manner is made while the subject is entirely lucid.

Thus, the fundamental question is whether we should continue to conceptualize psychosis in behavioral, psychoanalytic, or biological deterministic terms, or whether we should see it as a consciously selected strategy for coping with unbearable stress? Do humans lose the freedom to choose their mode of behavior during the prepsychotic stage, or do they remain relatively free even when acting "crazy"?

Unfortunately, despite tremendous effort invested over the last century, the fundamental theoretical questions regarding psychosis have remained unanswered. No theory yet exists that can provide a satisfactory explanation of the causes of psychosis and integrate the many research findings to a unified theoretical framework. As Zigler and Glick (1984) point out,

> *the confusion which currently surrounds the field of psychopathology may be due largely to the lack of clear knowledge about the causes of the disorders of central concern. . . . Perhaps it should not be too surprising, then, that even after a century of work there are still no widely accepted cause– effect formulations for the two major psychoses, schizophrenia and affective disorder. With regard to these disorders, the field is currently split between those who champion biogenic versus psychogenic etiological determinants. Still others do not view these two classes of determinants as mutually exclusive and have adopted an interactive position in which a biological proclivity toward the disorder is seen as triggered by experiential factors. (pp. 44–45)*

A similar view is expressed by Zubin and Spring (1977); in discussing the merits of various models of schizophrenia, they noted that "after tremendous strides in the last decade in both description and etiology, the study of schizophrenia has come to a stand still. . . . A new, fresh view of the entire subject seems to be necessary if we are to move ahead" (p. 103). Indeed, this is the main objective of this part of the book. However, before seeing whether psychobizarreness theory is adequate in providing a more comprehensive explanation of psychotic reactions, it may be worthwhile to discuss briefly the basic weaknesses of the existing major theories in this field.

INADEQUACY OF PSYCHOANALYSIS, BEHAVIORISM, AND THE MEDICAL MODELS

Psychoanalysis

We have already shown the inadequacy of psychoanalytic and behavioral approaches in the field of neurosis. With psychotic behavior, as with neurosis, no research data exist to support the psychoanalytic concept (Fenichel, 1946; Ginsberg, 1979) that bizarre psychotic behaviors are automatically determined by unconscious forces created in early childhood. Aware of the low scientific status of psychoanalysis, Silverman (1976, 1978, 1983), one of the strongest advocates of this theory, conducted several experiments with schizophrenic patients and succeeded in providing empirical validation for psychoanalytic theory. However, the enthusiasm these findings generated in the psychoanalytic camp (Wachtel, 1984) was short-lived, as all subsequent attempts to replicate these findings met with failure (Condon & Allen, 1980; Hapsel & Harris, 1982; Heilbrun, 1980, 1982; Oliver & Burkham, 1982; Porterfield & Golding, 1985). In light of this chronic lack of empirical support, it seems that we would be justified in suggesting that this theory be considered invalid until fresh evidence is produced.

Behaviorism

In the understanding of bizarre psychotic symptoms, behavioral concepts (Davison & Neale, 1982; Rimm & Somervill, 1977; Spring & Coons, 1982; Ullmann & Krasner, 1975) are of no greater value than are psychoanalytic concepts. With regard to neurosis, and particularly the bizarre phobias, behaviorists can defend their position with seemingly relevant scientific evidence, which has at least some superficial validity. However, with psychosis, where bizarre behavior reaches its ultimate, they have hardly any supportive evidence and do not themselves attribute much credibility to their own concepts. For example, Rimm and Somervill (1977), who generally have a favorable attitude toward the behavioristic learning models of neurosis, declare that "in essence, a purely operant account of the etiology of schizophrenia is at best an oversimplication" (p. 137). Similarly, Zubin and Spring (1977) noted that

> *beyond studying reinforcements that elicit and maintain schizophrenic behavior, this model has generally not dealt with basic causes of schizophrenic behavior. Thus it has not explained why events and reinforcements that catapult one individual into an episode of schizophrenia leave another individual unaffected. (p. 108)*

Similarly, no supportive evidence was found for Mednick's (1958) conditioning model of schizophrenia (see studies reviewed and findings presented by Kugelmass, Marcus, & Schmueli, 1985). It may be true that behavioral techniques, particularly token economy, can modify certain aspects of psychotic behavior. However, as was claimed with regard to neurosis (see p. 62) and as seems to be the case with psychoses as well (Rimm & Somervill, 1977, p. 138), this does not prove that the bizarre psychotic behaviors were acquired through operant or classical conditioning. Moreover, the therapeutic success of the behavioral techniques with psychosis is highly limited, much more so than with neurosis.

Medical Models

Attractiveness of the Medical Models

In recent years, with the declining faith in the ability of psychoanalysis and other environmental approaches to explain human psychopathology, medical models (Reich, 1982; Skrabanek, 1984; Steinglass, 1987) have been held in higher esteem, particularly for their insights into psychosis. An indication of this turnabout is the increasing number of biologically oriented books and articles published in the major psychiatric journals. The basic assumption of the various medical models (Davison & Neale, 1982; McKinney & Moran, 1981; Nagler & Mirsky, 1985; Reich, 1982; Rimm & Somervill, 1977; Skrabanek, 1984; Spring & Coons, 1982) is that bizarre psychotic symptoms are directly imposed by neurochemical changes, brought about by the imperfect genetic constitution of the individual, or by his or her imperfect constitution in conjunction with environmental stress. Thus, these models regard psychosis as being essentially a physical illness. They completely disregard the possibility that the consciousness is directly involved in assuming bizarre behavior. Reich (1982) claimed that the medical models are even more deterministic than the environmental theories, such as psychoanalysis, since with the latter, there is at least some optimism about the capacity of the individual to change or be cured. However, the "pseudoscientific evidence" (Skrabanek, 1984) that the proponents of the medical theory display is far from convincing and falls far short of proving their mechanistic point of view. The medical model, however, has been attractive to scientists for two basic reasons:

The first reason (applicable to all mechanistic theories) is the fundamental and implicit assumption that such damaging, bizarre behavior cannot be deliberately and consciously self-inflicted. This assumption is all the more attractive in view of the inability of patients to give credible reasons for their psychoses.

Second, the inadequacy of psychoanalysis and behaviorism, on the one hand, and the encouraging early results of genetic research, on the other, led to the belief that neurochemical change must be the mediating mechanism causing psychotic illness.

Arguments against the Medical Model

1. The position of the biologically oriented theories has been undermined by the cumulative findings of recent researchers (Coleman, Butcher, & Carson, 1984; Gottesman & Shields, 1976, 1982; Kessler, 1980; J. R. Marshall, 1984; J. R. Marshall & Pettitt, 1985; Rose, 1984) that the poor research methods of previous investigators have greatly exaggerated the significance of the genetic factor in psychotic disorders. For example, while previous evidence conveyed the impression that the concordance rate for schizophrenia among monozygotic twins is about 86%, the new data show that it is at most about 50% (Coleman et al., 1984; Faraone & Tsuang, 1985; Lukoff, Snyder, Ventura, & Nuechterlein, 1984). Moreover, researchers such as J. R. Marshall and Pettitt (1985) claim that the concordance rate is even lower than this and that the imperfect methods employed even today in biologically oriented research falsely diminish the role of the environment and bolster the role of genetic factors.

2. Despite this criticism, genetic factors undoubtedly play a vital role in the development of psychosis. However, the medical interpretation of the genetic findings is not the only plausible one. Psychobizarreness theory states that the genetic constitution may make the individual vulnerable to stress, but it is the strain of the stress (whether it be a product of the environment or of a genetic disorder) that causes the consciousness to select bizarre symptoms as a coping mechanism, not the neurochemical changes that cause psychosis. Imagine a case where a genetic flaw seriously impairs a subject's use of both legs, causing him or her to live in a world in which normal adjustment with such a handicap is virtually unattainable. Suppose also, that such cases are extremely rare and that society is therefore unaware of the handicap and ignorant of the person's special needs. If a subject in such circumstances developed bizarre symptoms, would it be possible to argue that these symptoms were necessarily caused by neurochemical changes? Surely, bearing in mind the harshness of this person's life, it is more than reasonable to suggest that he or she voluntarily adopted the bizarre symptoms. Thus, it may be argued that an adverse genetic constitution directly exposes the individual to an unbearably stressful condition or that it reinforces stressful life experiences, and only indirectly causes the adoption of bizarre symptoms.

3. The proponents of the medical theory would encounter great difficulty in explaining why environmental factors alone are sometimes sufficient to bring about the so-called illness. Research findings (Coleman et al., 1984; R. W. White & Watt, 1981; Zigler & Glick, 1984) indicate that psychotic disorders, such as acute schizophrenia or paranoia, may develop in the absence of any genetic predisposition. If the illness is the automatic result of adverse neurochemical changes, as the medical theory claims, then the advocates of this theory must show that stress in itself is sufficient to induce the profound biological changes required to trigger the bizarre psychotic symptoms.

4. The medical theory investigators attempted to defend their position by arguing that in some cases genetics alone might not be sufficient to induce the illness and that stressful events are also necessary to stimulate the neurochemical changes that eventually "trigger" the psychosis (Spring & Coons, 1982). If genetic factors or the interaction of genetic predisposition with stress can automatically cause bizarre behavior, then why do relatively negligible events sometimes precipitate psychosis (Rabkin, 1980) while the extremely stressful conditions of war and concentration camps do not?

Psychoanalysis would argue that stresses of the latter type lack psychodynamic meaning. But if this is true, how do they nevertheless frequently cause neurosis or other psychiatric symptoms?

Although much research supports the hypothesis that genetic factors interact with stress to produce psychosis (Lukoff et al., 1984), these findings do not prove that bizarre psychotic symptoms are caused by neurochemical changes. A genetic impairment may predispose an individual to experience stress at a much higher level. For example, constitutional damage in the attentional system can prevent the acquisition of certain social skills and essential coping mechanisms, and this would in turn increase the individual's vulnerability to stress. The occurrence of a relatively moderate stressful life event may elevate the tension to such an unbearable level that the consciousness is "obliged" to adopt the pathological coping strategy, having no better answers at its disposal.

5. The proponents of the medical model may use the limited efficiency of drug treatment in psychoses (Hogarty, Goldberg, & the Collaborative Study Group, Baltimore, 1973; D. A. Lewis & Hugi, 1981) as proof of the validity of their theoretical model regarding the etiology of the disorder. However, as was indicated with respect to the behavioristic model, therapeutic efficiency cannot be used to prove a theoretical position regarding causes. Rose (1984) argued, for example, that if a certain drug reduces a symptom, this does not mean that

> the biochemical system on which the drug acts is the "cause" of that symptom, or even its brain correlate. If aspirin reduces toothache, it does not follow that investigating the biochemical mode of action of aspirin will cast light on some "prostaglandin hypothesis" for toothache. (p. 355)

Moreover, the medical model should also explain why there may sometimes be significant therapeutic results in the absence of any medical intervention (Spring & Coons, 1982). Rose (1984) indicated, for example, that the evidence consistently shows that in about 30% of all cases, the success of treatment with antidepressant drugs can be attributed to a placebo effect. As Rose says "I may have missed it in the literature, but I am not aware of any biological psychiatrist endeavoring to answer the question: How does the placebo exert its effect?" (p. 358).

6. In order to establish the validity of the genetic-biological point of view, it is necessary, as with physical illness, to demonstrate that the bizarre symptoms can be induced in a healthy individual or at least that they can be artificially intensified or diminished among patients. Correlational data alone are by no means satisfactory. However, there does not seem to be any reliable evidence of this sort. We refer to one set of studies to illustrate our claim.

After a series of studies, Heath (1960; see also Heath & Krupp, 1967; Heath, Martens, Leach, Cohen, & Angel, 1957) reported the successful identification of a certain substance in the blood serum of schizophrenic patients, which he called *taraxein*. The author claimed that this substance is produced genetically and that its presence in the blood causes the schizophrenic symptoms. Heath further argued that schizophreniclike symptoms were produced when the substance was administered to nonschizophrenic subjects. Findings of such a type demonstrate quite well how successful the medical model may be. Unfortunately, however, another group of investigators (Siegel, Niswander, Sachs, & Stavros, 1959) have failed in their efforts to replicate Heath's findings.

It should be noted that this failure of replication is not exceptional but typical of the psychobiological studies of psychosis. In the vast majority of cases, these studies are not of an experimental type as were Heath's, but rather of a correlational nature, and even then, replication of the findings is unsuccessful. For example, Skrabanek (1984) indicated that

> *if someone suggests that schizophrenia is due to hyperactivity of prostaglandins, you may be sure that you will find someone else who claims the opposite. Or, for example, if five articles show that naloxone ameliorates schizophrenic symptoms and another five report no effect, does it mean that the reports mutually neutralize themselves? Not at all. It will be pointed out that the naloxone dose, the type of schizophrenic symptoms, and the selection of patients were not comparable. (p. 225)*

Similarly, Davison and Neale (1982) stated:

> *The history of research on whether biochemicals figure in schizophrenia has been one of discovery followed by failures to replicate. Many methodological problems plague this research, and many confounds, unrelated to whether or not a subject is schizophrenic, can produce biochemical differences. . . . Furthermore, studies on biochemicals can indicate only that a particular substance and its physiological processes are associated with schizophrenia. Dopamine activity might become excessive after rather than before the onset of the disorder. (p. 433)*

A similar view was expressed by Rose (1984, p. 354).

7. Findings concerning neurosis pose additional difficulties to the medical models. Both psychosis and neurosis are characterized by bizarre behavior, and they differ psychologically only in the degree of bizarreness. The similarity between the two necessitates one common theoretical explanation. In the past, medical models dealt largely with psychosis. This could be justified by a belief that a genetic disorder was a precondition for psychosis, but not for neurosis. However, the evidence presented previously, that psychosis can develop in the absence of any genetic predisposition, invalidates this belief. Thus, the medical theories no longer have any "excuse" for the exclusion of neurotic behavior from their model. However, research has demonstrated that the role of genetic or biological factors in the onset of neurosis is either very small or nonexistent (Emmelkamp, 1982; Gottesman, 1962; R. S. Levy & Jankovic, 1983; Mathews, Goldberg, & Johnston, 1981). Thus, a new theory is needed that can synthesize within its framework both neurosis and psychosis, and that does not require the presence of an adverse genetic predisposition for the development of these disorders.

Thus, the biologically oriented theories must explain: (1) How can environmental effects, and which ones, produce neurochemical changes sufficiently intense to cause such dramatic and bizarre behavior in cases where a genetic predisposition is absent? (2) Will genetic predisposition alone be sufficient to induce the adverse biochemical changes? Under what conditions would this be true? (3) Why, among monozygotic twins of whom one is schizophrenic, do more than 50% of the others (who would be presumed to have a genetic predisposition to psychosis) not develop the illness? In other words, which environmental conditions cause "biological immunization," that is, inhibit the production of the adverse neurochemical changes, and which stimulate them among those who do develop the illness? (4) Why does schizophrenia tend to occur in early adulthood (Bleuler, 1964; Gottesman & Shields, 1982; Richter, 1976)? (5) Why is nonparanoid schizophrenia strongly associated with people of lower IQ and paranoid reaction with people of higher IQ (Zigler & Glick, 1984)? How can all these facts be integrated within the biological mechanistic theoretical framework? At this stage at least, the biologically oriented theorists do not seem to have satisfactory answers to any of these questions.

The increasing dissatisfaction with the medical theory is expressed, for example, by Skrabanek (1984), who indicated that this

> *may be a wrong model. Schizophrenia may not have a cause in a medical or biological sense. If abnormal behavior had a biochemical cause, then normal behavior would also have a biochemical cause. It seems epistemologically, methodologically, and conceptually unsound to reduce behavior to biochemistry. (p. 224)*

It appears, then, that despite vast research efforts, all the traditional mechanistic theories have failed to prove their central theses, and it is high time to "change horses." We believe that abandoning the mechanistic conception of the human is a precondition of any genuine breakthrough in this field. For example, as indicated by Skrabanek (1984), the biologists must abandon their recent fruitless and absurd efforts to understand the underlying causes of bizarre psychotic symptoms, such as paranoid reactions, by observing the effect of various drug treatments on rats. Bizarre psychotic behavior is unique to humans and is adopted by the consciousness in an attempt to cope with unbearable stress. This is the basic premise of our proposed theory, and throughout this part of the book we will show this to be the most plausible approach to psychosis.

Before demonstrating the merits of our theory with regard to schizophrenia and affective disorders, we present two basic principles that we see as common to all psychoses.

BASIC PRINCIPLES OF THE PSYCHOBIZARRENESS THEORY OF PSYCHOSIS

Principle 1: Psychosis Is Most Likely to Be Caused by Stress That Is Truly Unavoidable or Perceived to Be So

Some fundamental differences distinguish neurosis from psychosis. As stated in the previous chapters, bizarre neurotic symptoms are adopted mainly in response to avoidable stress situations and for two major purposes—distraction and controllability. Unavoidable stress in itself very rarely sparks the adoption of bizarre neurotic symptoms. Its main effect is to facilitate the adoption of these responses when the experienced avoidable stress is not in itself sufficiently high to motivate the subject to adopt a bizarre form of behavior.

Bizarre neurotic symptoms lose much of their appeal in situations of unavoidable stress, since the subject can do nothing, even through bizarre behavior, to control the sources of the stress. However, as the unavoidable stress intensifies, the individual's attention will be so powerfully dominated by stress-related stimuli that a distracting coping strategy will be desperately sought. A need for control, even if it is only illusory, may also be strongly desired. Research data (Geer, Davison, & Gatchel, 1970; Taylor, 1983) suggest that illusory control is desirable even under normal stressful life conditions, as it can alleviate the damaging effect of stress.

However, since bizarre neurotic symptoms have limited distractive value, neurotic behavior will not meet the distractive requirement of the subject. Nor will it fulfill the need for a feeling of control. In contrast, bizarre psychotic symptoms can well meet the subject's psychological needs. Psychotic behavior has both a high distractive value, due to its extreme bizarreness, and a high degree of illusory control inasmuch as the subject is disconnected from reality.

In neurosis, bizarreness is mainly limited to one's belief system and to overt responses while the cognitive processes essentially remain intact. In psychosis, however, the bizarre symptoms expand their "territorial activities" to the cognitive system as well, so that normal attention and thinking processes are seriously impaired. The area in which the stress-related cognitions, such as compulsive worrying and self-devaluation, are produced, becomes the favorite target for the bizarre symptoms. Whereas in neurosis, distraction is obtained by heavily but harmlessly occupying the attentional channels to prevent access to stressful inputs, in psychosis, the cognitive processes themselves are intentionally damaged. Activating the cognitive system in a pathological manner (e.g., by the production of nonsense words or thoughts, rapid shifts of attention, deliberate absorption of oneself in hallucinatory images, etc.) prevents the processing of unbearable thoughts.

What is common to all psychoses is that attention, perception, and thought processes become severely damaged. This is consistent with the fact that thought disorder characterizes all psychotic reactions, schizophrenic and nonschizophrenic alike (Andreasen, 1979a, 1979b; Andreasen & Powers, 1974; Harrow & Quinlan, 1977; Marengo & Harrow, 1985; Sengel, Lovallo, Pishkin, Leber, & Shaffer, 1984). It will be shown that psychotics are exposed to such an unusually high level of stress that except for the all-too-common path of suicide (Aisenberg, Weizer, & Munitz, 1985; Day & Semard, 1978; Fernando & Storm, 1984; Gottesman & Shields, 1982; Lester, 1983), the deliberate disturbance in the normal functioning of consciousness caused by psychotic behavior is the only option left to many patients.

Principle 2: Psychosis Normally Requires the Unavoidable Stress to Be Personal Rather Than Universal

Clinical and research findings suggest that psychotic symptoms tend to be associated with personal unavoidable stress. Universal unavoidable stress is less likely to arouse psychosis.

Personal unavoidable stress refers mainly to two types of situations—stress due to incompetence (trait stress) and stress due to occasional error (state stress):

1. *Trait Stress*   Some stresses result, not so much from a particular event, but rather from a genuine incompetence leading to constant failure in coping with the normal everyday demands of life, which constitute no special problem for the vast majority of people. This type of stress can sometimes be better dealt with by increasing the individual's coping skills. Nevertheless, the stress would still be considered unavoidable because it is very diffuse, encompassing so wide a range of the subject's everyday life that he or she may feel totally incapable of overcoming it, not even by adopting neurotic symptoms.

2. *State Stress*   These irreversible stressful situations, such as loss or failure caused by personal inefficiency or assessed as having been caused by personal inefficiency, are due to an exceptional error, not to a genuine pervading incompetence. (An example might be the loss of one's family in an accident that was due to one's own carelessness.)

Universal unavoidable stress refers to such things as natural disasters, incurable diseases, and absolute confinement (e.g., concentration camp internment).

The first type of personal unavoidable stress matches Mechanic's (1967) conception of stress as the perception of one's inability to meet life demands. The subject is defeated not so much by the stressful event itself as by the constant stress caused through a lack of coping skills. He or she develops such a severely handicapped personality that adjustment to life essentially becomes impossible. In the second type, it is the severity of the stressful life events that brings about the psychosis, though the contribution of personality traits (e.g., competitiveness and ambitiousness) and of a genetic predisposition are not to be ignored. As will be shown, schizophrenic and paranoid reactions tend to be associated with the first type of stress, whereas affective disorders are associated with the second.

In both types of personal stress, the subject is completely helpless in removing the stress, and the self becomes the highly disrespected focus of the subject's own intense resentment. Attention is heavily dominated by stressful cognitions, particularly by negative self-reference.

However, the focus of our attention in this section is not personal but rather universal unavoidable stress. The self plays a minor or insignificant role in producing these types of stress. Based on evidence from research on the concentration camp experience, universal unavoidable stress appears to be less likely to spark adoption of bizarre neurotic or psychotic symptoms than does personal stress. To the best of our knowledge, researchers who have examined the psychiatric functioning of camp survivors after their release report no evidence suggesting that the frequency of psychotic or even neurotic symptoms of a bizarre nature is higher among them than among the rest of the population (Eitinger & Strom, 1981; Helweg-Larsen et al., 1952; Leon, Butcher, Kleinman, Goldberg, & Almagor, 1981; Nathan, Eitinger, & Winnik, 1964; Nirembirski, 1946; Shuval, 1957/1958, and studies renewed by her). Thus, despite the unusual level of stress to which the inmates were subjected, the occurrence of bizarre behavior was rare. The general pattern of psychiatric dysfunction in camp survivors includes symptoms such as intense fatigue, depression, personality impoverishment, impairment of problem-solving ability, vulnerability to physical illness, and high mortality rate (S. Davidson, 1980; B. P. Dohrenwend & B. S. Dohrenwend, 1969; Dor-Shav, 1978; Eitinger, 1973; Eitinger & Strom, 1981; Nathan et al., 1964; Niederland, 1981). Moreover, according to some other investigators, the stress did not cause any visible long-lasting adjustment difficulties (Leon et al., 1981; Sigal & Weinfeld, 1985; Zlotogorski, 1985). Other data (Shuval, 1957/1958) indicates that the experience actually immunized the survivors to subsequent stresses.

At this point, two objections could perhaps be raised regarding the conclusion that we have drawn from these studies. First, one could argue that psychotic or other types of bizarre symptoms are rare among the camps' survivors since only the strongest survived. This argument implies that in addition to stress, character weakness is a necessary condition for the development of bizarre psychotic symptoms. However, as will be shown in subsequent chapters, while this is apparently true for schizophrenic reactions, it is not true for psychotic depression. Often, depressed psychotic patients have previously been successful, strong-minded persons. Moreover, if indeed the low rate of psychotic breakdown among the survivors was due to their psychological strength, one would expect these disorders to be common, at least among the camp's population during the period of confinement. However, no such indication is in the literature. It is doubtful whether this can be attributed to a lack of observation, as reports about other types of behavioral dysfunction such as depression, apathy, and suicides exist (Bettelheim, 1943; Frankl, 1968). Second, it may further be argued that after the survivors were released, the pressure on them was not such as to arouse bizarre symptoms. However, on their release, the survivors faced homelessness, unemployment, memories of the camps, and the irreversible stress of loss of their families. If the objective level of stress in itself could establish psychosis, without reference to the source of the stress (i.e., universal versus personal), then the camp survivors ought to have displayed bizarre behavior. The fact that they did not convincingly illustrates the significance of the universal–personal stress distinction.

It could still be argued that the data on concentration camp survivors are not sufficient to draw a conclusion that unavoidable universal stress is not likely to cause psychosis. However, we can increase the credibility of our hypothesis by referring to the rarity of these symptoms also among subjects with incurable disease, despite the intensive stress they face. Similarly, there is no indication that the fighters for human rights who spent many years in Soviet labor camps developed bizarre symptoms. For example, Anatoly Sharansky (personal communication) spent 9 years in the Soviet prisons, including 135 days and nights continuously in solitary confinement, yet he did not show any signs of psychotic breakdown. Thus, severe stress is not in itself sufficient to cause psychosis. This fact must be taken into account by any theory that claims stress as one of its basic concepts.

Let us suppose that our conclusion is indeed valid that bizarre psychotic symptoms are associated exclusively with personal but not universal stress. What can be the theoretical basis of this phenomenon? The answer appears to be associated with a cost–benefit expectation. As stated previously, the sources of universal stress are located in the external reality rather than in the self. The best coping strategy in dealing with unavoidable universal stress is to keep in contact with reality while at the same time developing some kind of self-deceptive belief that deflects the noxious effects of the stress. This provides the subject with a degree of relief until his or her objective life conditions are improved and enables the subject to function in a more efficient manner despite the bitter reality. Such contact with reality may prevent further intensification of the stress: it may sometimes provide an unexpected solution to the stressful condition, or it may help to build a new reality. For example, even though many camp survivors had to live with the tragic truth of the annihilation of their entire families, many of them succeeded in alleviating their stress by building happy, new family relationships. Similarly, cancer patients can always hope that new cures for their disease will be discovered or compensate themselves in other spheres of life for the gravity of illness.

We have shown that a coping strategy that incorporates contact with reality and a selective or wise denial policy is the most successful one. Moreover, effecting a total detachment from reality by adopting psychotic symptoms would not only mean giving up any rational endeavor to change the quality of one's life, but these reactions in themselves would be likely to cause serious intensification of stress, given the subject's life conditions. For example, a display of bizarre behaviors in the concentration camps would certainly spell death for the inmate. In a similar manner, such behaviors in a cancer patient would cause social embarrassment and damage his or her social status. Thus, it appears that subjects in unavoidable universal stress situations refrain from adopting psychotic symptoms because the overall expected benefit is much lower than the cost involved.

However, the cost–benefit balance is different in unavoidable personal stress. Here, the prime source of the stress is not the external reality but rather the inadequacy of the self. This is the case at least from the subjects' cognitive appraisal of the situation. Apart from the self, they can see nothing to which they can justifiably attribute their basic incompetence (trait stress) or the irreversible damage for which they consider themselves responsible (state stress). Psychologically, unavoidable personal stress should have a far greater disruptive effect on the emotional well-being and functioning of the individual than unavoidable universal stress. This is mainly because in unavoidable personal stress, the consciousness may become flooded with negative self-reference, self-blame, and self-devaluation, and partly because the individual can see no escape from his or her self-inadequacy or direct responsibility for the stress. The subject has no hope that the situation will ever change. Feelings of despair, depression, and anxiety may accumulate and reach an intolerable level. In such cases, bizarre psychotic symptoms can provide an efficient coping mechanism, mainly because they help to "clear" the attentional system from the tyranny of intense negative self-reference and pessimistic thoughts. Thus, while unavoidable universal stress leaves the ego intact (due to the attribution of the causes of the stress to external sources), unavoidable personal stress damages the ego, sometimes so severely that it essentially stops functioning. One can always flee from a stressful event by directing attention to nonstressful aspects of reality. However, the escape is not so easy when the attentional system is strongly controlled by stressful thoughts related to failure in the functioning of the self. The subject can either remain deeply depressed, commit suicide, or adopt psychotic symptoms. Choosing the psychotic option would improve the quality of the subject's emotional experiences and thereby sustain the ability of the ego to function at some minimal level. In addition to the primary gains of distraction and illusory control, psychotic coping mechanisms also provide secondary gains in the form of attentional services form various social agencies, such as the family and hospital.

The cost of adopting psychotic symptoms may be social embarrassment, loss of status, and loss of friendship. However, for subjects who come from the lower ranks of society and/or whose social relationships are extremely weak, as is often the case with schizophrenic patients (Lukoff et al., 1984), the cost is not so great. These considerations may restrain others from adopting psychotic symptoms or at least lead them to select a more moderate form of these symptoms, as is evidenced by the lower overall rates of psychotic disorders, particularly schizophrenia, among the higher socioeconomic groups (Cockerham, 1978). Nevertheless, some may be willing to pay the price and adopt extreme psychotic symptoms when the stress becomes highly intolerable. The adoption of psychotic symptoms, however, does not altogether relieve the subject of feelings of stress; the subject's disconnection from reality is not complete. For example, as was stated earlier, schizophrenic patients can manipulate at will the emission of pathological responses according to their coping needs (see studies mentioned on p. 103). Thus, a minimal awareness of their miserable life conditions and the price they pay for adopting the psychotic symptoms always remains. This might be one of the reasons why psychotics commit suicide more often than do neurotics or subjects with organic brain disease (Lester, 1983).

The idea that in the vast majority of cases, personal stress is a prerequisite for the onset of psychosis is consistent with psychoanalytic theory. Psychoanalysis places great emphasis on the crucial role of internal stresses, stemming from the impulses of the id or from guilt feelings associated with the superego, in the development of psychotic disorders (Davison & Neale, 1982; Fenichel, 1946; Lewis, 1981; R. W. White & Watt, 1981).

COMMENTS

Some additional comments need to be made with regard to the two basic principles of the psychobizarreness theory:

1. One may point to some cases where psychotic symptoms develop in situations of avoidable stress (in contradiction to our principles) that could have been reduced by

some reality-oriented behaviors or by the adoption of bizarre neurotic symptoms. These cases, though, are the exception rather than the rule. For instance, the most dominant psychiatric disorder during wartime is neurotic or depressive reaction (B. P. Dohrenwend & B. S. Dohrenwend, 1969, p. 130; Kolb, 1977). Hospital admissions for psychosis did not increase in England during the blitz (Hemphill, 1941; Hopkins, 1943; A. Lewis, 1942), and only 3% of the neuropsychiatric casualties following the Normandy offensive were diagnosed as psychotic at the time of discharge (Wagner, 1946). Psychotic symptoms generally appear in the form of what has been called "three-day psychoses" (Kolb, 1977), and the other psychiatric symptoms during wartime are also usually of a transient nature, disappearing spontaneously (B. P. Dohrenwend & B. S. Dohrenwend, 1969). Thus, although war may be considered "a laboratory which manufactures psychological dysfunction" (Grinker & Spiegel, 1963, p. vii), it does not manufacture psychoses. Arieti (1974) suggested that catastrophes such as war may even inoculate against schizophrenia as they breed a sense of solidarity within the community.

We do not feel that an occasional occurrence of temporary schizophrenia in combat situations invalidates our first principle. Psychosis is not normally short-lived, and usually this drastic coping device is not adopted as a tool for achieving some specific goal in the individual's immediate environment. The psychotic symptoms emerge after the subject loses faith in reality or in his or her ability to cope. While in transient psychosis the symptoms are discarded once the specific goal of removing the subject from the threatening environment is achieved, in normal psychosis such short-term specific goals do not exist. Symptoms of schizophrenia or affective disorder are aimed at providing distraction and illusory control and not at effecting some single desirable change in the environment. Our principle of controllability or B. P. Dohrenwend and B. S. Dohrenwend's (1969) principle of compensation, which they suggested for explaining neurotic breakdown during wartime, can fairly be applied to explain the "three-day psychoses." It is only in some very rare cases that psychotic reactions that began during wartime continued beyond. However, most probably these cases relate to the individual's lack of ability to cope with the normal demands of life (Lukoff et al., 1984), and the psychosis would have surfaced sooner or later in a peacetime environment as well.

This argument may also serve to explain research findings by Steinberg and Durell (1968). In reviewing the service records of soldiers in the U.S. Army (during peacetime) who were hospitalized for schizophrenia during the period 1956–1960, the investigators found that the rate of hospitalization was markedly higher in the early months of military service than in the second year. It could be argued that the schizophrenia developed as a means of escaping military demands, heavier in the first year than in the second. Such an interpretation of the results challenges the unavoidability principle. However, this is not the only possible interpretation of the data. The schizophrenic symptoms were not necessarily intended to achieve some concrete goal, such as discharge. It may well be that the symptoms were adopted because of a soldier's deep frustration at his inability to cope and that the stressful military environment only facilitated the psychotic breakdown. Indeed, Steinberg and Durell (1968) noted that the subjects "might well have broken down in civilian life" (p. 1104).

2. Schizophrenic reaction may develop in response to very moderately stressful events or to stresses beyond the individual's control (i.e., universal stresses), such as changes of residence or death of parents (Lukoff et al., 1984; Spring & Coons, 1982), which again appears to be inconsistent with our hypothesis. However, the effect of

these stresses should be judged, not in a vacuum, but rather in the context of the severe deficit in the coping abilities of the schizophrenic and his or her chronic history of stress (see Lukoff et al., 1984; Zubin & Spring, 1977; and chapter 16 in this book). For a person who has great difficulties in making friends (Parnas, Schulsinger, Schulzinger, Mednick, & Teasdale, 1982) and very little social support (Beels et al., 1984; Lukoff et al., 1984), a geographic change or loss of a close relative may cause a serious intensification of social alienation, as evidence reviewed by Lukoff et al. indicates. In many cases, the first schizophrenic attack is preceded by the individual's leaving the family environment in a small town or rural area and moving to a single-person household in the "transitional zone" of a city (Spring & Coons, 1982). Moderate universal stress is not always perceived by an individual as such. For certain individuals, these stresses may have very personal meaning as they may exaggerate their disappointment in themselves. Sometimes, seemingly universal stress factors may encourage ongoing negative self-reference and depression. Attention may thus become so heavily dominated by stress-provoking thoughts that the conscious can be relieved from this "tyranny" only by the adoption of psychotic coping mechanisms.

In subsequent chapters, we will deal with the various types of schizophrenic reactions and affective disorders. We have decided to discuss schizophrenic reactions first because we believe that schizophrenia is a group of coping strategies employed by various subjects, including those who experience severe depression. An explanation of schizophrenia may thus facilitate the understanding of psychotic depression. We now discuss the nature of schizophrenia and then ask what leads people to adopt these types of behaviors.

15

Essence and Characteristics of Schizophrenia

WHAT IS SCHIZOPHRENIA?

It is somewhat disappointing that after so many years of research, there is as yet no wide agreement as to the essence of schizophrenia, and the question "What is schizophrenia?" continues to be asked (Carpenter, 1984; Rifkin, 1984; Skrabanek, 1984; Strauss & Carpenter, 1983; Zigler & Glick, 1984). Strauss and Carpenter (1983) comment that "such a question may seem obvious, naïve, impossible, or any combination of these. And certainly it is a bit demanding to expect that anyone could say what schizophrenia is in 1,000 words" (p. 7). Zigler and Glick (1984) state that "the many symptoms used as the defining features of schizophrenia result in a group of patients extremely heterogeneous in regard to symptoms displayed" (p. 48). Resigned, Rifkin (1984) observes that the "plain fact is that we don't know what schizophrenia is." However, at the same time he argues that "this shouldn't keep us from searching for etiologies and modifying factors and using whatever treatments are shown to work" (pp. 367–368). A more radical approach has been advanced by Sarbin and Mancuso (1980), who claim that there is, in fact, no such thing as schizophrenia, that the disorder is a mythical construction. They consider schizophrenia essentially a "moral verdict" of certain forms of unacceptable behavior rather than a legitimate medical diagnosis.

Why have investigations failed to produce an accurate description of the nature of schizophrenia? In the absence of the psychobizarreness theory, it seems that researchers saw only the similarities of bizarre behavior among schizophrenics and did not pay attention to different etiologies. Nor did they conceptualize schizophrenia as a coping style. Rather, all schizophrenic patients were traditionally regarded as having the same kind of mental illness. It was assumed that they share similar etiological backgrounds and similar behavioral dysfunctions. The fallacy in this traditional approach is its overgeneralization. *Schizophrenia,* which itself is a subcategory of psychosis that includes only the most extreme forms of psychotic disorders, should be no more than an umbrella term covering several distinct disorders that have different etiologies and use totally different coping mechanisms for purposes of distraction.

Psychobizarreness theory identifies the essence of the various forms of schizophrenia as extreme bizarre behavior caused by the malfunctioning of the attentional and thought processes. Coleman, Butcher, and Carson (1984) note that schizophrenic reaction "represents in many ways the ultimate in psychological breakdown. The symptoms of these disorders include the most extreme to be found in human behavior. . . . In short, the schizophrenic disorders may truly be said to be the arena in which all the major problems of the mental health disciplines come together" (pp. 343–344).

Similarly, Bellak (1979) views schizophrenia as "the final common pathway" of severe adaptive breakdown, whatever the source of that breakdown. The fundamental of behavior common to all types of schizophrenia is what R. W. White and Watt (1981) termed *a breakdown of integrated thinking and integrated adaptive behavior*. This element makes "the strongest case for the unity of the several forms of schizophrenia" (p. 481).

The psychobizarreness theory views schizophrenia as a response for coping with stress, in which the subject commits, as it were, a "spiritual suicide." The price of this decision is high. Schizophrenics renounce their rationalism—the essence of their human existence. Depending on the nature of their disorder, they will manipulate their attention to an abnormal state either of inattention (nonparanoid schizophrenia), selective concentration (paranoid schizophrenia), or overconcentration (catatonia). They will also invent bizarre cognitions with which to occupy their residual attention, so that the normal functioning of the cognitive system is in fact destroyed. Their physical existence continues, divorced from their spiritual existence. (This, incidentally, is comparable to the Freudian idea that in schizophrenia the ego almost totally collapses.) The purpose of this spiritual suicide is to liberate the attentional system from stress-producing cognitions and to gain some illusory control over their sources of stress. We will elaborate on the idea of spiritual suicide in the last section of this chapter.

Schizophrenia, according to psychobizarreness theory, can be defined as a group of coping strategies characterized by three basic qualities: (1) the symptoms constitute the most extreme level of bizarre behaviors of the human being; (2) they provide a very powerful distractive tool by which the patient can "fight"[1] stress-provoking thoughts; (3) the subject sacrifices much of the normal functioning of his or her consciousness in order to adjust very marginally to life and thereby continue biological existence.

Despite the similarities in the bizarreness of behavior and the gross malfunction of the cognitive system, schizophrenia can be divided into three groups distinguishable by their stress etiologies and by their coping styles: nonparanoid (disorganized and certain undifferentiated, i.e., with an attentional deficit) schizophrenias, paranoid schizophrenia, and catatonia. The first two are the most common, and the vast majority of research deals with them.

In recent years, though, doubts have been raised with regard to the diagnostic validity of paranoid and catatonic schizophrenia, and it has been suggested that these reactions be viewed as affective disorders (R. W. White & Watt, 1981; Zigler & Glick, 1984). We agree with this suggestion in part. Paranoia ought to be divided into two separate etiological groups: The first—*paranoid affective disorders*—is so termed because of the similarity of its etiology with that of affective disorders; the second—*paranoia, or paranoid nonaffective disorders*—displays a distinct etiology of its own, closer to nonparanoid schizophrenia than to other forms of psychosis, and hence, contradicting the recent suggestion, it is unrelated to affective disorders (see chapter 17). Along with mania, catatonia should be viewed as an extreme strategy of coping with depression. Often the overt symptomatology of both the nonaffective form of paranoia and the catatonic closely matches the symptomatology of the nonparanoid schizophrenic, despite their different etiological background and coping styles. Therefore, as we stated

---

[1]This metaphorical description of the schizophrenic's coping strategy is sometimes used by patients themselves. For example, in a response to the therapist's general question "How are you doing today?" one patient gave the following answer: "I am fighting, Doctor—fighting sin and evil . . . you know what sin and evil are, and you should be down here praying with me for your salvation. . . . I am fighting, Doctor. The devil tries to confuse you, but I am fighting . . ." (Coleman et al., 1980, p. 411).

previously, we believe that the umbrella term schizophrenia should be retained and should apply to cases of extremely disorganized behavior, without reference to etiology and modes of coping.

The present chapter deals with the individual coping styles and self-deception of nonparanoid, paranoid, and catatonic schizophrenics. In chapter 16, we analyze the causes of nonparanoid schizophrenia, and in chapter 17, we discuss paranoia and affective disorders.

COPING STYLES AND SELF-DECEPTION IN SCHIZOPHRENIA

Nonparanoid Schizophrenia

Of all patients with schizophrenic disorders, the nonparanoid (disorganized and certain undifferentiated) schizophrenics display the most extreme bizarre response. Though other schizophrenic patients use sophisticated cognitive strategies to distract their attention, the nonparanoid schizophrenics employ a primitive and very disruptive means of achieving the same end. They effectively put their attention system out of order so that normal functioning of the cognitive system becomes impossible. Inattention and various forms of thought dysfunction, such as thought fragmentation, extreme deviance in thought content, neologism, and speech disorder (Chaika & Lambe, 1985; Davison & Neale, 1982; Lanin-Kettering & Harrow, 1985)—symptoms that were traditionally used to define the essence of schizophrenia (Bleuler, 1964)—are regarded by psychobizarreness theory as behavioral patterns stimulated by a fundamentally deliberate act of the consciousness.

The notion is not new that the prime goal of nonparanoid schizophrenia is distraction obtained by poor attention. For example, Mednick (1958; see also Mednick & Schulsinger, 1968) postulated that the schizophrenic's tangential thinking comprises a set of conditioning avoidance responses having the objective of helping the patient overcome the extreme tendency of schizophrenics to be aroused by relatively minor anxiety-provoking stimuli. The coping mechanism is learned on those occasions when the schizophrenics escape arousal by switching to irrelevant thoughts that successfully interrupt the arousal process. Even though Mednick's learning model has not gone unchallenged (see findings and studies by Kugelmass, Marcus, & Schmueli, 1985), a large body of research does support the idea that nonparanoid schizophrenic patients suffer from gross attentional impairment or increased distractibility (Coleman et al., 1984; Davison & Neale, 1982; Levin, 1984a, 1984b; Nuechterlein & Dawson, 1984). They are easily diverted by stimuli they produce themselves or find in their surroundings. It is the severe attentional deficit that distinguishes nonparanoid schizophrenia from other forms of schizophrenia (Bourne, Dominowski, & Loftus, 1979; Cornblatt & Erlenmeyer-Kimling, 1985; Finkelstein, 1983; Harvey, Winters, Weintraub, & Neale, 1981; R. G. Knight, Youard, & Wooles, 1985; McGhie, 1977; Neale & Cromwell, 1977; Neale, McIntyre, Fox, & Cromwell, 1969; Nuechterlein & Dawson, 1984; Oltmanns, O'Hayon, & Neale, 1978; Rappaport, 1967; Rund, 1983; Shean, 1982; Venables, 1977).

We emphasize that we do not claim that the nonparanoid schizophrenic's inattention is entirely deliberate. Attentional disability is known to be already present among children who are at high risk for developing schizophrenia (Cornblatt & Erlenmeyer-Kimling, 1985). Evidence strongly suggests that attentional impairment is genetically determined (Levin, 1984a; Spring & Coons, 1982) and apparently is further exacerbated by adverse neurochemical changes resulting from stress (Anisman & Lapierre, 1982; Coleman et al., 1984). A high-risk schizophrenic subject who has a constitutional attention deficit and is unable to cope with the extraordinary stress with which he or she is confronted will further aggravate the attentional deficit by turning to daydreams for distraction. Thus, even before adopting bizarre symptoms, the nonparanoid schizophrenic will have an undoubted tendency toward inattention. However, in line with the psychobizarreness principle of saliency–availability, it is argued that this natural attentional-deficit handicap is used and even purposefully intensified by the nonparanoid schizophrenic for coping purposes. Psychobizarreness theory also claims that schizophrenic thought disorders are a pure invention of the consciousness. They form part of the schizophrenic's intended effort to destroy the normal functioning of the cognitive system. The fact that schizophrenic thought disorders have been shown not to be genetically determined (Berenbaum, Oltmanns, & Gottesman, 1985) strengthens the view that they are invented by the subject.

Self-Deception in Nonparanoid Schizophrenics

The claim that schizophrenics' symptoms are largely the result of a deliberate act of the consciousness raises the question of self-deception: How does the consciousness succeed in misleading itself with regard to its own direct responsibility in bringing about extremely bizarre behaviors? As stated previously, neurotic patients need special self-deceptive mechanisms for disguising their direct involvement in the production of their neurotic symptoms. It appears, however, that this is not the case with schizophrenic patients. No special mechanisms are needed. Their pathological coping style alone is sufficient to ensure the success of self-deception as well. As with neuroses, the need for self-deception arises because the subject must cope with the anxiety-arousing questions (e.g., "Why do you behave in such a bizarre way?") that may be posed by the self or by others. In order for these questions to cause uneasiness, two basic requirements must be fulfilled: (1) the anxiety-arousing stimuli must reach the consciousness and (2) the subject must need to relate to himself or herself and to the external world in a rational way. However, in the case of the nonparanoid schizophrenic, these two requirements are not fulfilled. Various extreme distractive measures are employed so that neither of these questions nor any other internal or external threatening stimuli have any chance of gaining access to the patient's attentional domain. Such subjects also renounce the basic human need to be rational though they never actually lose their rationalism (unless drug treatment or electroconvulsive therapy causes irreversible brain damage). According to Coleman et al. (1984), "Most schizophrenic people 'fade in and out of reality' as a function of their own inner state and the environmental situation. They might be in 'good contact' one day and evidence delusions and hallucinations the next" (p. 354). Having no better means at their disposal, schizophrenics consciously resolve to deal with life in an irrational manner.

Distractive Tools Used by Nonparanoid Schizophrenics

Nonparanoid schizophrenics use at least five distractive tools for sealing off access to the attentional domain and for creating a state of unawareness.

Deflection. The subjects deflect threatening stimuli. In order to disguise their ignoring of the stress-arousing questions, subjects may not refrain from responding, but their replies are vague and virtually unrelated to the questions asked. This strategy is demonstrated in the following example (R. W. White & Watt, 1981):

> *"How old are you?"*
> *"Why I am centuries old, Sir."*
> *"How long have you been here?"*
> *"I've been now on this property on and off for a long time. I cannot say the exact time because we are absorbed by the air at night, and they bring back people . . ."*
> *"Who is this?"*
> *"Why, the air."*
> *"What is the name of this place?"*
> *"This is called a star."*
> *"Who is the doctor in charge of your ward?"*
> *"A body just like yours, sir . . ." (pp. 473–474)*

Incoherent Communication. This distractive tactic is similar to deflection, differing in the total unintelligibility of communication.

> *Basically, there is a failure to conform to the semantic and syntactic rules governing verbal communication in the individual's known language—not attributable to low intelligence, poor education, or cultural deprivation . . . Meehal cited as an example the statement "I'm growing my father's hair." (Coleman et al., 1984, p. 350)*

Subjects may create new words (neologisms) that are meaningless to others. They may also fully engage their attention with wandering thoughts that prevent them from maintaining coherent communication. The following excerpt describes the confused state of mind of a schizophrenic:

> *It seems like nothing ever stops. Thoughts just keep coming in and racing round in my head . . . and getting broken up . . . sort of into pieces of thoughts and images . . . like tearing up a picture. And everything is out of control . . . I can't seem to stop it. (Coleman et al., 1984, p. 351)*

Attention Shifting. Attention is rapidly changed from one stimulus to another, barring threatening inputs from occupying the consciousness for the minimum period of time necessary to arouse uncomfortable feelings. The attentional system is not a dichotomous variable but rather a cognitive continuum throughout which different selection processes might be operative before information is consciously identified (Erdelyi, 1974; Nuechterlein & Dawson, 1984). Thus, even if the anxiety-arousing stimuli succeed in penetrating the subject's attentional field, rapid changes of attention (as in the perceptual defense phenomenon described on p. 24) will prevent the "invader" from reaching the focus of attention. Shifting is a relatively easy task for a subject with a chronic attentional deficit.

Schizophrenics are likely to be unaware of their active manipulation of their attention for three reasons. First, attention becomes so rapidly engaged with new nonstressful stimuli that individuals forget their involvement in causing the shift. Second, since attentional shifting in the form of lack of concentration also occurs spontaneously, subjects may not be aware that they are actively causing or intensifying the attentional disturbances. Third, for nonparanoid schizophrenics, attentional shifting becomes highly automatized, requiring, like any overlearned motor skill, only minimal attention (i.e., awareness). Probably, such subjects have been using their attentional deficit for coping purposes for many years, long before schizophrenic symptoms become evident. This is particularly true of cases where the symptoms develop gradually. Our hypothesis is consistent with several models of attention that propose to distinguish automatic from attention-demanding processing (Nuechterlein & Dawson, 1984). Automatic, as opposed to attention-demanding processes have little or no direct access to long-term memory, and as a result the level of awareness necessarily remains low.

Schizophrenic shifting of attention is well illustrated in the following extracts from conversations with three patients (Davison & Neale, 1982):

> My thoughts get all jumped up. I start thinking or talking about something but I never get there. Instead, I wander off in the wrong direction. . . . People listening to me get more lost than I do. . . .

> My trouble is that I've got too many thoughts. You might think about something . . . but I would think of it and then I would think of a dozen different things connected with it at the same time. (pp. 398–399)

> I can't concentrate on television because I can't watch the screen and listen to what is being said at the same time. I can't seem to take in two things like this at the same time especially when one of them means watching and the other means listening. On the other hand I seem to be always taking in too much at one time, and then I can't handle it and can't make sense of it. . . .

> When people are talking, I just get scraps of it. If it is just one person who is speaking, that's not so bad, but if others join in then I can't pick it up at all. I just can't get in tune with the conversation. (pp. 401–402)

Delusions and Hallucinations. Nonparanoid schizophrenics often have hallucinations, particularly auditory ones, and delusions of a sexual, hypochondriacal, religious, or persecutory nature, though they are less profuse and less organized than those of paranoid subjects (Coleman et al. 1984; Davison & Neale, 1982). These cognitive maneuvers no doubt provide individuals with some illusory control over their uncontrollable lives and with an avenue for discharge of sexual tensions and hostile impulses. They also constitute a very powerful tool for distraction. Even though nonparanoid schizophrenic subjects have a severe attentional deficit, threatening perceptions may nevertheless invade their attentional domain. However, by absorbing their residual attentional energy in highly attention-demanding stimuli, they can easily repel the "invader" from their cognitive system.

How are the hallucinations generated, and how do schizophrenics remain unaware of their active responsibility for the creation of hallucinations? Mintz and Alpert (1972) compared the reality perception and vividness of imagination of hallucinating schizophrenics, nonhallucinating schizophrenics, and nonschizophrenic patients. Their results showed that the hallucinating schizophrenics had both a vivid imagination and a defective capacity for perceiving reality, making it hard for them to discriminate daydreaming from real-world events. McGuigan (1966) reported that patients experiencing auditory hallucinations were found merely to be talking to themselves and were not conscious that the internal voices they heard were not coming from the external world.

Thus, based on these findings and the theoretical discussion so far, it seems that nonparanoid schizophrenics remain unaware of their active involvement in producing their hallucinations because (1) they have a strong tendency to daydream, a behavior they have most likely practiced since childhood; (2) they have severe attentional deficits, which they deliberately reinforce; and (3) they renounce rationalism—the basic aspect of human existence.

External Distraction. External agencies, particularly the medical system, that convey a clear message to subjects that they are ill and therefore not responsible for their odd behavior provide them an excuse for not confronting their problems.

Conclusion

In conclusion, "idiotic behavior" seems to be the most suitable coping style for nonparanoid schizophrenics both because of their attentional deficit and because of their typically low intelligence (Albee, Lane, & Reuter, 1964; Lane & Albee, 1965; Sohlberg, 1985). Paranoid or catatonic coping mechanisms, which will soon be described, would be less appropriate in nonparanoid schizophrenics, as they demand superior concentration and greater sophistication.

Paranoid Schizophrenia[2]

An increasing number of investigations (Finkelstein, 1983; McGhie, 1977; McGhie, Chapman, & Lawson, 1965; Rund, 1983; Shean, 1982) have found that, unlike nonparanoid schizophrenic patients, paranoid subjects do not seem to suffer from any cognitive impairments, certainly not attentional ones. Paranoid subjects have been described as alert and vigilant. Their intellectual capacity is preserved. The unique characteristic of paranoid schizophrenics is their ability to narrow their attention and to filter the environmental input according to their needs (Rund, 1983; Zigler & Glick, 1984).

Prior to their psychotic breakdown, paranoid subjects experience wide social rejection and repeated, frustrating failure, particularly in interpersonal relationships (see Coleman et al., 1984; and pp. 246–247 in this book). Paranoid subjects have also cultivated such an intense inferiority complex and negative self-reference that without resorting to paranoid coping tactics, they would have inevitably fallen into deep depression. So close is the connection between depression and paranoid coping strategies that Zigler and Glick (1984) suggest, though in our opinion on insufficient ground, considering all paranoid reactions as affective disorders (see pp. 244–246 in this book).

Coping Styles of Paranoid Schizophrenics

Thus, by inventing the bizarre delusion of persecution and by using their superior attentional capacity to narrow their attention to those environmental inputs that reinforce this delusion, paranoid patients occupy their attention so intensively with thoughts and activities related to their bizarre belief that their attention is no longer available for their real problems.

Paranoid coping strategies may seem odd as the subject merely replaces one type of stress with another. In fact, though, he or she makes a good bargain by replacing an unbearable personal stress with a bearable universal stress. Stress attributed to external or universal sources is much more easily tolerated than is stress related to the self. Moreover, while the original personal stress causes intense feelings of inferiority, self-blame, and depression (Coleman et al., 1984; Zigler & Glick, 1984), the new stress may even lead to an enhancement of the self-concept as the subject fights and sometimes overcomes a powerful "enemy" (e.g., see case study by R. W. White, 1964, pp. 76–84). The paranoid distractive coping mechanism is the most appropriate for paranoid subjects for the following three reasons:

1. The paranoid subject's superior intellectual and attentional capacity appears to be a prerequisite for the efficient use of the paranoid coping style. Just as nonparanoid schizophrenics employ their available "resources" (attentional deficit) for coping purposes (e.g., shifting attention), paranoid subjects make use of their available cognitive abilities (superior attention and high level of intelligence) to achieve the same goal.

[2]In this section, no distinction is drawn between paranoia and paranoid schizophrenia.

2. The coping strategy suits the paranoids' personality. They come from homes in which hostile relationships exist; they are aggressive, have always been suspicious of others, and are particularly sensitive to personal slights (Coleman et al., 1984; Meissner, 1978, 1981). Interestingly, paranoids' family histories frequently reveal that some family members have practiced "mind reading" (Coleman et al., 1984), a technique that the paranoid later employs to "read the mind" of his or her "enemies." Thus, the adoption of a paranoid coping style, rather than other pathological coping strategies, requires a less abrupt change in his or her ordinary pattern of behavior. Consistent with the saliency–availability principle, paranoid subjects meet their coping needs by aggravating their own basic personality maladjustment, aggression, and suspicion to an extreme level of bizarreness.

3. As they are full of anger and resentment and need a target on which to discharge their sometimes violent impulses (Coleman et al., 1984), such subjects prefer the paranoid coping style to any other form of behavior, since it provides them with a "legitimate" excuse for releasing aggressive impulses. Contrary to psychoanalytic theory, it is doubtful whether the need to discharge hostile impulses is anything more than a contributory factor in causing paranoia.

Self-Deception in Paranoid Schizophrenics

Paranoid subjects seem to attain the goal of self-deception by enlisting their intellectual and attentional capacities to collect information that is congruent with their bizarre beliefs. First, their social incompetence increases the likelihood of social rejection and thereby supplies them with a wealth of real information that can "validate" their bizarre persecution belief. For example, Coleman et al. (1984) noted that a rigid, self-important, humorless, and suspicious individual such as the paranoid person inevitably becomes an aversive social stimulus. Consequently, he or she is likely to be "a target of actual discrimination and mistreatment. Ever alert to injustices, both imagined and real, such an individual easily finds 'proof' of persecution" (p. 393). Paranoid bizarre beliefs, then, are not a pure invention of the consciousness, but rather an unusual intensification of a select perception of reality. Second, ambiguous environmental inputs are filtered and interpreted as further reinforcing the paranoid's false belief and self-deception. Third, the patient often produces self-deceptive information by actively attacking innocent people. By these three means, paranoids obtain "evidence" of a conspiracy against them and convince themselves of its verity.

Catatonic Schizophrenia

The measures the catatonic patient uses to achieve distraction differ from those used by the other two schizophrenic types. While distraction in the former two groups is attained by general disruption of the cognitive system or by attuning it to function in a pathologically selective way, catatonics seek distraction through absolute exploitation of their attentional energy, which becomes totally occupied with bizarre thoughts and activities. The catatonic states of both stupor and wild excitement necessitate exhaustive attentional investment as, even in the stuporous state, the subject is highly alert. Indeed, R. W. White and Watt (1981) suggest designating the stupor as a "state of active immobility." As stated previously, hypnosis in recent years has come to be viewed as a kind of superconcentration, and it seems that both types of the catatonic's bizarre motor behavior cause the consciousness to enter a state similar to that in hypnosis.

It appears, then, that the objective of both of the catatonic's modes of response is to maximally utilize all "attentional energy" either by "freezing" the consciousness (stupor) or by occupying it so entirely (wild excitement) that the attentional field is not accessible to stress-producing inputs. Wild excitement fulfills a dual role. Not only does it provide distraction as do all bizarre symptoms, but in addition, it also serves an elating, or antidepressant, function. Thereby, the ego is able to escape deep depression and live a marginally normal life within an institution while not in a catatonic state, until a threatening new input sparks off the catatonic reaction.

The catatonic coping style is more similar to affective disorders than to nonparanoid schizophrenia, because of both the alternation between a state of stupor and wild excitement and the ability of catatonics to concentrate. Abrams and Taylor (1976) found that only 7% of catatonic subjects satisfied research criteria for schizophrenia, whereas 69% had diagnosable affective disorders, mostly mania (62%). At follow-up 1 year later, two thirds of the patients showed either marked improvement or full remission, as is usually the case with mania. Abrams and Taylor reviewed other research (Morrison, 1974) and concluded that their findings were consistent with those of other investigators over the preceding 100 years. These results led R. W. White and Watt (1981) to suggest that catatonia should be classified as an affective disorder rather than as schizophrenia. They also noted that Lewine, Watt, and Fryer (1978) combined catatonics with other affectively colored schizophrenic disorders in a single "schizoaffective" subgroup of schizophrenics that were expected to have had good premorbid adjustment and good prognosis.

The categorization of catatonia as a schizoaffective disorder is preferable, in our opinion, to viewing it simply as an affective disorder. Catatonia should refer to extreme cases of mania, in which thought, speech, and behavior become as disorganized as in nonparanoid schizophrenia (see Andreasen, 1982; case studies mentioned by Coleman et al., 1984, pp. 357–358; Tyrer & Shopsin, 1982; R. W. White & Watt, 1981, p. 477). Although in catatonia, manic coping styles predominate (stupor and wild excitement), attention is further disrupted, as in nonparanoid schizophrenia, by the deliberate production of incoherent speech and thought. It seems, therefore, that two coping styles—mania and nonparanoid schizophrenia—are being combined. Thus the diagnostic term *schizoaffective* may most faithfully represent the catatonic's psychological condition. It may be the extreme cases of mania that breed the confusion that exists in the field of psychopathology in the diagnosis of mania and schizophrenia (Krauthammer & Klerman, 1979; Marengo & Harrow, 1985; Pope & Lipinski, 1978; Sengel, Lovallo, Pishkin, Leber, & Shaffer, 1984).

Few data exist on the catatonic disorder in general and on the self-deceptive mechanisms catatonics employ in particular. It appears that self-deception is achieved simply by blocking. Anxiety-provoking questions are not allowed to penetrate the attentional domain. Under more extreme behavioral deviation, catatonics may employ measures similar to those used by nonparanoid schizophrenics when they adopt negativistic and "idiotic" responses, that is, ceasing normal communication and renouncing rationalism. The discussion on manic alternation in chapter 17 is applicable to catatonic coping devices as well.

Conclusions

The three different types of schizophrenics use different coping mechanisms. Nonparanoid schizophrenics achieve distraction by intensification of their constitutional attentional deficit and by active production of incoherent thoughts and speech. Paranoid schizophrenics, by using their superior cognitive abilities (Zigler & Glick, 1984), change their stress from personal to universal and narrow their attention to those parts of reality that are congruent with their false beliefs. Catatonic coping styles bear a resemblance both to mania and to nonparanoid schizophrenia. Like manics, they alternate between two extremes and prevent access to depressing thoughts by overengagement of their attention. Like schizophrenics, they further disrupt the normal cognitive system by actively producing incoherent responses. As a result, their overt symptomatology is quite similar to the disorganized behavior of the nonparanoid schizophrenics.

SCHIZOPHRENIA: "SPIRITUAL SUICIDE"

The adoption of bizarre neurotic symptoms was compared earlier to an act of suicide. This comparison was drawn to emphasize that like suicide, neurotic symptoms emerge when the subject is in a highly stressful state, that the act is conscious and deliberate, and that the cost involved in adopting this coping strategy is high (though obviously not as high as that of suicide). The comparison is even more appropriate to schizophrenia, and to nonparanoid schizophrenia in particular, for three main reasons. First, schizophrenics are also under tremendous pressure. Second, the personal cost of schizophrenics' pathological escape, that is, their rejection of rationalism and all normal social contact, forces them to live such a poor quality life as to render it virtually valueless. Many normal people would prefer to commit physical suicide rather than imagine themselves schizophrenic. Third, in some chronic cases the spiritual suicide, similar to the physical, is practically irreversible, particularly at an advanced age after the schizophrenic has become accustomed to his or her new mode of life with its secondary gains in terms of care, ease, and no expectations. Frustration, and the convenience of institutionalization may encourage resignation and abort any new endeavor by the patient to resume the hopeless struggle. Despite the fact that adopting bizarre symptoms is a coping strategy chosen in preference to physical suicide, the latter option is not ruled out. No matter how successful subjects are in deceiving themselves, a certain minimal awareness of the very high price paid for the worthless lives they lead always remains. Schizophrenics may reconsider their decision, and many either attempt suicide or neglect to take care of themselves. Indeed, high suicide and mortality rates have been noted by many researchers (Aisenberg, Weizer, & Munitz, 1985; Day & Semard, 1978; Drake, Gates, Whitaker, & Cotton, 1985; Gottesman & Shields, 1982; Lester, 1983; Wilkinson & Bacon, 1984).

The mechanistic medical theorists who conceptualize schizophrenia as an illness and who concentrate their efforts on curing the subject of adverse neurochemical changes neglect the problem of "existence" with which these subjects struggle; such theorists would no doubt strongly oppose the notion of spiritual suicide. However, the fact is that they have no evidence showing that the schizophrenic's crucial symptom—thought disorder—is automatically determined. On the contrary, the evidence suggests that it is not. Various statistical analyses by Berenbaum et al. (1985) reveal that pairs of identical twins, in which one was schizophrenic, were no more similar to each other with respect to the presence or severity of formal thought disorder than a control group of fraternal twins. Similar results were obtained in an earlier study by Slater (1953), who also concluded that thought disorder is not genetically determined. Neurochemical changes in the schizophrenic's physiological system do not necessarily imply that his or her thought responses are biologically controlled. Since neurochemical correlates can be found for all actions, this line of thought would have led to the conclusion that humans are not free to choose their behavior. (This criticism has also been suggested by Skrabanek, 1984.) Moreover, exceptional neurochemical changes are correlated not only with psychotic symptoms but with physical suicide as well. Research shows that attempted suicide among schizophrenics and manics is associated with greater neurochemical activity (A. B. Levy, Kurtz, & Kling, 1984; Nasrallah, McCalley-Whitters, & Chapman, 1984). However, abnormal neurochemical activity has also been found in other subjects, irrespective of their diagnostic category (Banki, Vojnik, Papp, Balla, & Arato, 1985). If the medical theorists wish to claim that neurochemical changes deny schizophrenics the freedom of choice to select their bizarre symptoms, they must also claim that the increased neurochemical activity in the brain of a suicide denied him the freedom of choice to remain alive. Surely it is clear that neurochemistry can do no more than aggravate feelings. It is the individual who always makes the final decision, no matter how impaired his or her judgment may be.

16

Causes of Nonparanoid Schizophrenia

INTRODUCTION

As was shown previously, none of the traditional theories can adequately explain the causes of schizophrenia. We believe that schizophrenia is a coping strategy and that progress can be made in research on the etiology of schizophrenia only by recognizing the centrality of stress. Some awareness in this direction can already be noticed among various investigators who have reviewed studies concerned with the relationship between stress and schizophrenia. While Rabkin (1980) concluded that "the research evidence indicates a weaker relationship between life events and schizophrenia onset than the clinical literature suggests" (p. 408), Spring and Coons (1982) and particularly Lukoff, Snyder, Ventura, & Neuchterlein (1984) seem to be much more convinced that stress is indeed the key factor in understanding this phenomenon. At this stage of scientific inquiry, then, the evidence does not unquestionably support our thesis. It is therefore necessary for us to show that preschizophrenic individuals are indeed subjected to an unusual level of stress and that the schizophrenic option is the best one available to them. As Rabkin demonstrates that in a substantial number of cases no stressful event preceding onset of the disorder can be identified, and that in others the stress was not sufficient to justify a bizarre reaction, our theory must be able to account for the absence of a precipitating stress. As research has shown that a genetic predisposition is essential for development of the disorder, the theory must also describe the interaction of genetics with stress.

Spring and Coons (1982) use the vulnerability model (see Zubin & Spring, 1977) to answer the question of how stress plays a role in bringing about schizophrenia. According to this model, people vary in their vulnerability to schizophrenia, in a manner determined by a genetic predisposition and by the effect of traumatic life events. Vulnerability remains latent until elicited either by "endogenous events" (i.e., neurochemical changes) or by "exogenous" stressful life events. The precipitating events do not create vulnerability, but rather expose it. In order to strengthen the vulnerability concept, Spring and Coons review impressive data showing that remote stresses in the form of trauma during pregnancy, obstetrical complications, early loss of parents, and adverse family relationships were present to a larger degree in the life histories of schizophrenic subjects. Many studies, in addition to those reviewed by Spring and Coons, further strengthen the claim that excessive remote stress is extant in the schizophrenic's early life history (Behring, Cudek, Mednick, Walker, & Schulsinger, 1982; Coleman, Butcher, & Carson, 1984; Silverton, Finello, & Mednick, 1983; Silverton, Finello, & Schulsinger, 1985). However, such traumas can be found among nonschizophrenic people as well. Why, then, does the presence of these variables increase the vulnerability of some people to schizophrenia but not others? What is special about these individuals? In what sense do these people become damaged by their exposure to stress in early life? How crucial can the early environmental stresses be if, for example, high-risk children removed from their pathogenic home environment can still be afflicted with schizophrenia (Davison & Neale, 1982; Kessler, 1980)?

To some extent, Spring and Coons's model makes a fundamental claim similar to that of psychoanalytic theory in that both place great emphasis on the effects of past experiences. However, while psychoanalysis proposed the concept of the unconscious as a mediating mechanism, Spring and Coons do not clearly specify how early stressful experiences are stored in the fetus in the absence of the unconscious until they manifest themselves later in life. The challenging problem of understanding the mediating factors that bring on schizophrenia has occupied many investigators in the field. For example, Lukoff et al. (1984) indicated that "in schizophrenic disorders, the need to understand the mediating variable is especially important because the relationship between life events and psychotic symptoms, although measurable and usually statistically significant, is not very powerful" (p. 285).

The vulnerability model seems to be a revised form of the traditional medical theory. Its emphasis on the role of endogenous events and the constant reference to schizophrenia as an "illness" leave little doubt that according to this model, the mediating mechanisms that directly cause the schizophrenic symptoms are seen as neurochemical. As such, this theory is exposed to all the criticisms raised against the traditional medical model (see pp. 200–203). Nevertheless, the vulnerability theory does have an important advantage over the pure medical one since it takes stress and coping skills into account in the etiology of psychoses.

Research data (Lukoff et al., 1984; Rabkin, 1980) suggest the existence of two major types of schizophrenic patients. One consists of subjects whose bizarre symptoms develop gradually, usually without the presence of a precipitating stress (poor premorbid or chronic schizophrenics). Subjects of the second type (good premorbid or acute schizophrenics) display more or less normal functioning until the occurrence of an excessively stressful, but generally not very unusual event (Rabkin, 1980). It is our opinion that a stress-based theory must distinguish between these two groups of subjects. However, Spring and Coons drew no such distinction in their vulnerability model. They only assumed that a minimal, recent stress is always necessary to provoke the schizophrenic symptoms and that failure to locate it is the fault of the measuring instruments.

To appreciate that stress is the only factor that motivates the subject to adopt schizophrenic symptoms, we need to focus our attention on the abnormal personal deficits of the preschizophrenic individual. Lukoff et al. (1984) strongly emphasize these deficits in their discussion of schizophrenic coping abilities, and it is surprising that they do not come to a more definite conclusion that schizophrenics simply are exposed to extreme pressure. Personality deficits prevent these people from fulfilling their basic psychological needs and increase the likelihood of their suffering from environmental stress. As compared with other people, they are liable to get involved in trouble more easily and may be less able to get out of it.

We contend that nonparanoid schizophrenia stems primarily from the handicapped personality type of the preschizophrenic. In a substantial number of cases, the personality deficits of the high-risk individuals would in themselves be sufficient to cause the adoption of bizarre symptoms simply as a result of failing to deal with chores of daily life. A special stress-arousing event would not even be required. Serban (1975), in comparing the amount of stress experienced by chronic schizophrenics and normal subjects in coping with ordinary life demands, found that the chronic patients suffered the highest levels of stress and normals suffered the lowest. For chronic schizophrenics,

"The surrounding world is a source of turmoil; almost everything creates anxiety and discomfort. . . . Everything appears to represent either an insurmountable demand which society places on them, or worry induced by frustrated expectations" (p. 405). Serban noted that these findings are in contrast to the opinion generally held in psychiatry that chronic schizophrenics endure only a low level of stress. Other high-risk individuals may have less handicapped personalities and be able to maintain a marginal adjustment until the occurrence of a moderately stressful event presents a challenge beyond their coping ability (Lukoff et al., 1984).

The stress faced by chronic and acute schizophrenics is personal, and as they cannot overcome their handicap, it is perceived as unavoidable. Inevitably, their self-concept will be severely damaged. Attention is so heavily loaded with ego-damaging cognitions (i.e., personal stress) that the ego can no longer continue functioning without some pathological coping devices.

THE HANDICAPPED PERSONALITY OF SCHIZOPHRENICS

Overview

Research data suggest that nonparanoid preschizophrenic individuals suffer from three serious deficits (one major and two secondary) that interact to produce a handicapped personality unable to adjust to everyday life demands. The meager coping resources of such individuals prevent them from maintaining productive interchange with the external world. Metaphorically, we might say that their personality "radiates" a highly negative stimulation toward others. Such subjects are characterized by very low cognitive abilities, severe social incompetence, aggression, angry and depressive moods, unrestrained emotions, an extremely negative self-concept, a heightened sensitivity to stress, and very poor coping skills. At a younger age, no pathological coping mechanism is yet needed because the handicapped personality structure has not yet been consolidated and because it is socially legitimate for the subject to be dependent. However, during adolescence or early adulthood, when the subject has to make plans for the future and begin to function independently, the burden on his or her weak personality may become too heavy, leading to the onset of schizophrenia.

Cognitive and Coping Deficits of Schizophrenics

Of the three basic deficits from which these subjects suffer, the first and major one is attentional impairment. The other two are low IQ and a lack of adequate coping skills. We consider a low IQ secondary because it seems to be partly the result of attentional impairment and because we think that on its own, it would not be so damaging. The lack of coping skills is also secondary because it is largely the product of the other two deficits and is only in part due to environmental and/or biological factors related to malfunctioning of the autonomous nervous system.

It is the unique interaction of the severe, constitutional attentional impairment, low IQ, and deficits in coping skills that leads to development of the handicapped personality.

As was stated previously, a great number of studies have found that attentional impairment is one of the most noticeable characteristics of the nonparanoid schizophrenic subject. Furthermore, the evidence strongly suggests that this impairment is genetically determined (Coleman et al., 1984, p. 368; Levin, 1984a; Nuechterlein & Dawson, 1984; Spring & Coons, 1982), that it is one of the most reliable predictors of schizophrenia among high-risk children (Cornblatt & Erlenmeyer-Kimling, 1985; Davison & Neale, 1982, p. 436; Nuechterlein & Dawson, 1984; Sohlberg, 1985; Spring & Coons, 1982, pp. 21–22), and that the impairment is already evident from early infancy (Nuechterlein & Dawson, 1984; Parnas, Schulsinger, Schulzinger, Mednick, & Teasdale, 1982; Silverton et al., 1983). Obstetric complications, more common among subjects who later develop schizophrenia (Behring et al., 1982; Silverton et al., 1983, 1985; Spring & Coons, 1982), are liable to cause minor brain injuries that may be partially responsible for attentional impairment or for other cognitive deficits of the preschizophrenic.

Other research data show that high-risk children also have lower IQs than their siblings, neighborhood peers, and classmates (Albee, Lane, & Reuter, 1964; Lane & Albee, 1965; Sohlberg, 1985; Watt & Lubensky, 1976). In addition, the overall coping ability of these individuals is unusually poor (Coleman et al., 1984; Lukoff et al., 1984; Spring & Coons, 1982; Zubin & Spring, 1977).

No doubt, the adverse family environment of the preschizophrenic plays an important role in causing the reduced IQ and deficiency in coping skills. Abundant evidence in the research literature demonstrates the pathogenic effect of the schizophrenic's home environment (Coleman et al., 1984; Lukoff et al., 1984; Nagler & Mirsky, 1985; Spring & Coons, 1982). We have no intention of detracting from the devastating effects of environmental factors. As will be demonstrated later, the environment alone may be sufficient to bring on another type of psychosis, namely, paranoid schizophrenia. However, in the case of nonparanoid schizophrenics, it is the subject's attentional impairment, in interaction with a low IQ, that seems to be more responsible for impaired coping skills. As Lukoff et al. (1984) noted,

> patients were found to be deficient in most of the cognitive skills necessary for problem solving in comparison with normals. . . . The combination of specific problem-solving skill deficits with more basic impairments in cognitive functioning has the potential to create a severe decrement in the problem-solving ability of schizophrenic patients. (p. 280)

However, there is some evidence that the preschizophrenic deficit in coping skills may also be caused by oversensitivity of the autonomous nervous system. We derive this hypothesis from the fact that like schizophrenic patients (Horvarth & Meares, 1979; Ohman, Nordby, & D'Elia, 1986; Spring & Coons, 1982), high-risk individuals also display intense physiological arousal and a lack of habituation in response to stressful stimuli (Davison & Neale, 1982; Kugelmass, Marcus, & Schmueli, 1985; Ohman et al., 1986; Spring & Coons, 1982).

Consequences of Attentional Deficits

We now discuss the seriously damaging consequences of the schizophrenic's attentional deficit in more detail because, in our opinion, this issue has not received sufficient treatment in the literature.

Attentional impairment first becomes noticeable during the school years. The psychological condition of children who have an attentional deficit during this critical period, particularly if they are of low intelligence, may be compared to the stressful experience of animal subjects in experimental neuroses (Masserman, 1943) and learned helplessness (Telner & Singhal, 1984) studies, which were exposed to environmental demands beyond their coping resources. Handicapped children such as these have no hope of success in academic studies or in social functioning, all the more so when they come from adverse home environments. Their cognitive and social deficits are likely to be reinforced by a total lack of security in family relationships, a severely disturbed home life, parental rejection or maltreatment, "communication deviances" (i.e., conflicting and unclear messages) from parents, a negative parental model for imitation, and other environmental stresses (Behring et al., 1982; Coleman et al., 1984; Davison & Neale, 1982; Lukoff et al., 1984; Silverton et al., 1983, 1985; Spring & Coons, 1982).

As can be expected, the result of all these factors is a failure to cope with academic and social demands at school. Normal attentional functioning is a prerequisite both for academic success and for being able to interact with classmates on the playground. These failures would be expected to cumulatively increase self-resentment, strong feelings of inferiority, insecurity, depression, and anger. This expectation is borne out by recent observations of Blechman and colleagues (Blechman, McEnroe, Carella, & Audette, 1986; Blechman, Tinsely, Carella, & McEnroe, 1985), which demonstrate that children who are academically or socially incompetent tend to be depressed, to experience a greater number of, and more serious, problems, and to have very low self-esteem.

Preschizophrenic children have poor social relationships not only with their peers but with their teachers as well. Because of their inevitable lack of concentration, poor academic achievement, and serious discipline problems, these preschizophrenic children are likely to be rejected by their teachers, particularly when the teachers are unaware of the children's cognitive deficits. The teacher's attitude may serve to further diminish the child's status in the class. Studies of group interaction (Aiken, 1965; Bavelas, Hastorf, Gross, & Kite, 1965; Cieutat, 1959) witness that an individual's social rank and participation in group activities is greatly affected by reinforcements given by the group leader.

The child's failure to cope with school demands may further intensify the parents' rejection of him or her. Parental hostility, in the form of harsh physical punishment, humiliation, and/or excessive criticism (Coleman et al., 1984; Lukoff et al., 1984; Spring & Coons, 1982; Valone, Norton, Goldstein, & Doane, 1983), may reflect in part an understandable dissatisfaction with the child's functioning (which is expressed far too severely) rather than the parents' emotional disturbances per se. As these children are not easy to deal with, a certain remoteness in the parents' relations with them is understandable (Steinglass, 1987).

Thus, it is easy to imagine how difficult the life of high-risk children must be. Too often, there is not one person in their environment with whom they can feel secure and loved. Their severe cognitive deficits, particularly the attentional one, and the extremely stressful environment that constantly conveys negative feedback to their self-image provides them very little chance to develop a properly adjusted personality.

Indeed, all the many studies that have examined the psychological profile of high-risk children are highly consistent with our theoretical expectations (Ayalon & Merom, 1985; Beckfield, 1985; Beisser, Glasser, & Grant, 1967; Grubb & Watt, 1979; Lewine, Watt, & Fryer, 1978; Nagler & Glueck, 1985; Nagler & Mirsky, 1985; Parnas et al., 1982; Rolf, 1972; Rolf & Garmezy, 1974; Schulsinger, 1976; Sohlberg & Yaniv, 1985; Spring & Coons, 1982; Watt, 1978; Watt & Lubensky, 1976; Weintraub, Liebert, & Neale, 1975). Generally speaking, these studies show that high-risk children exhibit a very maladjusted personality profile in school. In class, they have poor concentration as well as low comprehension and creative abilities, and their academic achievement is unsatisfactory. The findings also show that they face discipline problems in school and that teachers tend to relate to them in a remote manner. Their emotional and social behavior tends to elicit the rejection of others. They are emotionally unstable, exhibit difficulties in affective control and are prone to moods of anger and depression. Socially, they tend to be violent, and at the same time, passive, withdrawn, and introverted. No wonder they feel isolated and are disliked by others. Some other data on schizophrenic patients (Davison & Neale, 1974) show that they display oversensitivity to punishment, particularly when administered after unavoidable failure. We would not be surprised if this type of reaction were found among high-risk children as well.

Thus, there seems to be impressive evidence in favor of the idea that the preschizophrenic subject has a very severe personality handicap. We claim that the high-risk child experiences stress above and beyond that encountered by an individual with any other type of disability.

Psychosocial Condition of Preschizophrenics as Compared with Subjects Having Other Disabilities

There are several reasons why the schizophrenic individual is likely to experience more stress than subjects with other disabilities. First, one of the main conditions for coping successfully with the stresses of being disabled is to accept one's limitations and make the appropriate adjustments to them (Russell, 1981). However, the high-risk child faces greater difficulty in this respect than do other disabled people. While other disabled people can observe the difference between themselves and the nondisabled or obtain this information from others, such as in the case of mental retardation (Gibbons, 1985), preschizophrenic children cannot accept their limitations because they cannot identify them. They cannot know in what sense they differ from others, why they constantly fail at school, and why nobody wants their company. Even investigators are still not sure what exactly is wrong with these children, despite the enormous research effort invested. Preschizophrenic children cannot learn to accept their limitations and therefore their stress is inescapably increased.

Second, subjects with observable disorders can attribute their limitations to universal causes and can even gain some limited benefit from being "special" (Gibbons, 1985; Lindemann, 1981, p. 6). For example, being labeled *mentally retarded* produces certain "privileges," foremost among which is a kind of special dispensation for misbehaving or performing poorly in school (Guskin, 1963; Guskin, Bartel, & MacMillan, 1975). Similar "advantages" have been associated with observable physical disabilities. Research findings by Carver and colleagues (Carver, Gibbons, Stephan, Glass, & Katz, 1979; Carver, Glass, & Katz, 1978) show, for example, that successful disabled subjects (e.g., students doing well in college) are likely to receive more favorable evaluations than comparable nondisabled people. Moreover, subjects with observable disabilities can exploit their handicap to avoid blame for failure.

These benefits are totally denied to the preschizophrenic person. In fact, preschizophrenics are likely to be blamed even for their disability. Parents (Lukoff et al., 1984) and teachers are likely to criticize the child for inattentiveness, poor academic performance, and misconduct in the repelling and frustrating environment of school. Thus, while subjects with other disabilities are not likely to develop a negative self-concept (Gibbons, 1985), the high-risk child can be expected to nurture intensive self-resentment. The repeated failure of such children to cope, along with constant harsh parental criticism (Valone et al., 1983), which is not "disproved" by information from other channels, gradually leads to the complete destruction of their self-concept, and with it the total collapse of the ego.

Third, social support, which is of great help in buffering the noxious effects of stress (Eaton, 1978; Gore, 1978; Gottlieb, 1981; Haggerty, 1980; Husaini, Neff, Newbrough, & Moore, 1982; Larocco, House, & French, 1980), though satisfactory among the physically or mentally retarded, is highly restricted among preschizophrenic subjects and becomes even more restricted during the actual breakdown (Beels, Gutwirth, Berkeley, & Struening, 1984; Lukoff et al., 1984). The social networks of schizophrenic patients usually contain a significantly higher proportion of relatives than friends, which Lukoff et al. (1984) note diminishes

> the overall effectiveness of their social support systems in coping with stressful events. In addition, the constricted range of social outlets does not help a schizophrenic patient to cope with any ongoing familial tension because the patient may lack outside alternatives for social contact. (p. 283)

These subjects have great difficulty in making friends (Parnas et al., 1982), and their ability to recruit social support is yet further reduced by their high geographic mobility (Lukoff et al., 1984; Spring & Coons, 1982). Moreover, as we have already noted, schizophrenic patients often lack even the emotional support of their parents. Coleman et al. (1984) indicate that typically the mothers of individuals who have developed schizophrenia have been characterized as rejecting, domineering, cold, overprotective, and impervious to the feelings and needs of others. While verbally the mother may seem accepting, basically she rejects the child. A similar pattern of behavior is displayed by the father.

Fourth, some disabled people can compensate for their disability by succeeding in other areas of life. However, success, which could alleviate stress, is beyond the schizophrenics' abilities. They seem to have no special talent by which they can enhance their self-image. Attentional functioning is necessary for success in any area. The lack of compensatory abilities should, in line with Adler's personality theory, deepen the preschizophrenic's inferiority complex.

Fifth, individuals with other disabilities can prevent or alleviate probable damage to their self-image by comparing themselves with others less fortunate than themselves (Cottrell & Epley, 1977; Gibbons, 1985; Wills, 1981). According to Wills's downward comparison theory, enhancement of subjective well-being can be achieved through comparison with a less or an equally unfortunate other. Gibbons reviewed research data demonstrating that disabled persons use social comparison to maintain or to boost their self-esteem by comparing themselves with equally or less fortunate individuals. However, such self-enhancement mechanisms are unavailable to preschizophrenics both because of the rarity of people in their environment who are less fortunate than themselves and also because, in any case, they probably do not have the cognitive ability to make such a comparison.

Conclusions

Thus, the overall findings clearly demonstrate that high-risk children experience very intense stress throughout their lives. They are severely disabled but because of the invisibility of their disorder, they are denied the social privileges of being "disabled." Perhaps the most frustrating aspect of their condition is their almost absolute social alienation. What can a child with a severely handicapped personality, extreme sensitivity to stress, and poor coping skills do to relieve tension and frustration except to lose himself or herself in a world of fantasy? Isolated children of superior intelligence can distract their attention from their unfortunate condition by reading or by other creative activities; such children may find some consolation in warm family relationships and be redeemed from solitude by parent–child activities. But for high-risk children, daydreaming and nonconstructive behavior seem to be the only coping options available. Repeated flights into daydreaming should ease the escape thereby, further intensifying the subject's attentional deficit and building the foundations of the schizophrenic symptoms that will appear at a later age when the stress becomes intolerable.

RISK YEARS FOR SCHIZOPHRENIC BREAKDOWN

Why should the frequency of onset of schizophrenia reach its peak between adolescence and the first years of adulthood (age 15–25 years, peaking at about age 20; see Bleuler, 1964; Gottesman & Shields, 1982; Richter, 1976)? None of the existing theoretical approaches provides a satisfactory answer to this question. In our view, it is because during this period for the first time stress exceeds the tolerance capacity of the preschizophrenic's handicapped personality. Adolescent stress is a well-recognized phenomenon. References to the "storm and stress" of this period of life have been common among novelists and poets as well as behavioral scientists (Mussen, Conger, & Kagan, 1974). The marked physiological changes of puberty are a contributing factor.

However, the main sources of stress are associated with socialization demands and considerations of the future. The adolescent must gradually achieve independence from parents, establish cooperative workable relationships with peers, and develop self-, gender, and vocational identities (Mussen, Conger, Kagan, & Huston, 1984). While most adolescents eventually make appropriate adjustments to these demands, preschizophrenic subjects cannot cope with any of them. Despite the difficulties of the preadolescent years, the frameworks of family and school at least provided the preschizophrenic subject with psychological support and some sense of belonging. However, in the adolescent years when the young person completes school and starts preparing to leave home, this minimal security is completely shattered. Though most young people are reasonably optimistic and feel that they can exercise some control over their future (Mussen et al., 1984), in the preschizophrenic population, the prospect of "the future" is more likely to arouse feelings of despair, anxiety, and depression. Such young people cannot stay at home, cannot go out to work, and cannot return to school. They are trapped in a den of stress.

Perhaps the most frustrating aspect for the preschizophrenic adolescent is an inevitable intensification of social alienation at an age when peer-group support is especially needed. Throughout the years, the gap between preschizophrenic subjects and their peer group in many psychosocial aspects widens. Mussen et al. (1984) note, for example, that unpopular adolescents may face a "vicious cycle." Being emotionally unstable or lacking the requisite social skills, they

are likely to meet with rejection or indifference from peers. In turn, an awareness of not being accepted by peers and a lack of opportunity to participate in and learn from peer group activities further undermines self-confidence and increases a sense of social isolation. (p. 498)

Preschizophrenic subjects are more vulnerable to adolescent stress if they have experienced loss of a parent (Spring & Coons, 1982). Even when parental loss occurs in early childhood, serious behavioral disturbances usually do not surface before adolescence. Despite their shortcomings, the preschizophrenic's parents can alleviate the stress of this period by providing social support and security and can retard or prevent the adoption of bizarre symptoms, at least where the personality handicap is only moderate.

These considerations explain why the behavioral deviations of the preschizophrenic individual are less prominent during the primary school years, but worsen at the junior and senior high school levels (Nagler & Glueck, 1985; Watt, 1978).

At a somewhat later age, marital status may become another factor in bringing about the schizophrenic breakdown. The rate of marriage among schizophrenics is quite low (Gottesman & Shields, 1982). Unmarried people are exposed to greater stress than married people, and they also lack the socioemotional support that could buffer the harmful effects of pressure (Berkman & Syme, 1979; Bloom, Asher, & White, 1978; Kraus & Lilienfeld, 1959; G. A. Lee, 1974; Pearlin & Johnson, 1977; Udry, 1974). This may explain why single schizophrenics are more severely disturbed than married ones (Gove & Howell, 1974; Turner, Dopkeen, & Labreche, 1970). On the other hand, even if the subject does marry, the chances that the marriage will be unsatisfactory or end in divorce are quite high (Gottesman & Shields, 1982). Divorce or marital disruption constitute profoundly stressful events for most people, and even more so for the emotionally disturbed (Bloom et al., 1978).

Thus, sooner or later the accumulative stress of the high-risk individuals will reach a point where the ego concedes the hopeless struggle with life. This is in accord with the learned helplessness studies, which show that after repeated unsuccessful efforts at control, subjects give up responding (Abramson, Seligman, & Teasdale, 1978; Seligman, 1975). The attention system becomes so despondent that the ego "refuses" to continue doing its job. A very drastic means is needed to clear the attentional system from these pathogenic cognitions, feed the consciousness with unrealistic hopes, in the form of grandiose delusions, and thereby revive the "nearly dead" ego.

EXCESSIVE STRESS

As explained, we have delineated two major categories of schizophrenia—chronic and acute. In chronic cases, the disorder develops gradually, whereas in acute cases, it develops far quicker. The chronic disorder is the more severe as no single stressful event is required to bring on the breakdown. For a breakdown to occur, it is sufficient that a high-risk person with a chronically handicapped personality be placed in a normal demanding environment. This has already been fully discussed. In this section, we turn our attention to acute schizophrenics, whose personalities are also handicapped. However, as they are less vulnerable than the chronics they require at least a moderately stressful event to provoke a breakdown.

Two types of excessive stress that can facilitate the outbreak of schizophrenia are (1) a highly demanding environment (e.g., a kibbutz) and (2) a stressful life event (e.g., the loss of an intimate person).

Demanding Environment: Kibbutz Versus City

It is to be expected that the more demanding the environment, the greater the burden on the already-strained coping resources of the high-risk individual. Support for this assumption can be found in a recent Israeli follow-up study in which high-risk children who had been raised in the kibbutz and in the city were observed over a period of 15 years. The investigators (Mirsky, Silberman, Latz, & Nagler, 1985) found, among other things, that surprisingly (Breznitz, 1985), the occurrence of psychiatric deviations including schizophrenia and affective reactions, at the average age of 25, was significantly greater among the kibbutz subjects than among their city-dwelling counterparts. Attempting to explain this finding, Mirsky et al. (1985) comment that this

> *may be related to the fact that the kibbutz is a relatively small, closed community, with few opportunities for privacy, few opportunities for individual differences that do not contribute to the common goals, and little chance for the pathological history of one's parent to be unknown or forgotten. (p. 153)*

Breznitz (1985), however, suggests that this effect might be attributed to differences in "expressive" (or affectional) child–parent interaction, which he assumes is more intense in the kibbutz. As much of the instrumental (or care-taking) parental role is taken over by the kibbutz supportive organizations, a disproportionate amount of parent–child interaction time is devoted to expressional interaction. Breznitz claims that affectional interaction between a high-risk child and a schizophrenic parent may have a "stronger deleterious impact" on the child's development than instrumental interaction mainly because it is more likely to drift into a "disturbed pattern." However, we doubt the validity of this hypothesis. First, as high-risk children have disciplinary problems and below-normal school and social performance, instrumental interaction may well be more damaging than affectional interaction. Not only are such children unlikely to comply with parents' demands, but parents may also see themselves responsible for their children's inadequacy. As a result, the disturbed parent may harshly criticize the child and employ detrimental disciplinary methods to "teach the child a lesson." In contrast, affectional interaction is less likely to lead to anger and to distancing the child from the parent because, unlike instrumental interaction, it is undemanding. Second, even if expressive interaction does exert a more deleterious impact, this will be balanced by the fact that in the kibbutz, the high-risk child spends less time with the disturbed parent and more time with trained professional caretakers.

Even if the accounts of Mirsky et al. and/or Breznitz are valid, they do not preclude another explanation based on Wills's (1981) downward social comparison theory. It seems that the main reason why the kibbutz is such a pathogenic environment for high-risk children is that kibbutz children are constantly exposed to the adverse effects of downward comparison, which may be very damaging to their self-concept. In the city, high-risk children are obliged to meet their "fortunate peers" only during schooltime, while at other times they can enjoy relief from the emotionally debilitating comparison. Being alone outside of school need not necessarily be perceived as deviance either by the child or by the social environment. In contrast, in kibbutz society, which highly values interpersonal relationships, particularly during the adolescent period (Sohlberg, 1986), interaction within the peer group is exceptionally intensive, and there is great social pressure to "fit in." The socially demanding environment of the kibbutz, populated as it is by socially competent individuals, is the least psychologically healthy for a subject with a handicapped personality. High-risk children are afflicted not only with strong alienation, but also by continuous blows to their self-esteem through constant painful social comparison. Moreover, the unfavorable psychological conditions (isolation, downward comparison by all family members, etc.) may naturally apply to an entire household in which one of the parents is schizophrenic, perpetuating the tension and pressure within the family. By way of contrast, in a big city, not only are the social pressures less noticeable, but the child and/or the family also have a better chance of meeting someone in the same predicament and thereby alleviating their solitude.

Stressful Life Events

As we have stated, schizophrenia is sometimes precipitated by stressful life events (Coleman et al., 1984; Lukoff et al., 1984; Rabkin, 1980; Spring & Coons, 1982). Typically, the stressors are associated with difficulties in intimate relationships, but they may also include events such as changes of residence, arrest, loss of job. However, the stress in itself cannot justify the outbreak of schizophrenia, as many people are subjected to much higher levels of stress and yet do not develop deviant behavior (Taylor, 1983). Thus, it seems that the subject's impoverished personality type, even if it be only moderately impoverished, plays a crucial role. Failures, particularly in intimate social relationships, can be devastating (Coleman et al, 1984; Lukoff et al., 1984). The following factors illustrate how stress can be magnified in preschizophrenics:

1. For those to whom success came only after prolonged deprivation, subsequent failure will have an inordinately detrimental impact.
2. Not only do these subjects lack adequate social support, but the people with whom they interact (e.g., parents, spouses) are also problematic types, emotionally unstable, and themselves in need of support. Thus, when the preschizophrenic fails, the whole family feels the failure; instead of offering comfort and encouragement, family members are far more likely to give vent to their own stresses by reacting with anger and hostility. This serves to build an ever-rising spiral of stress, and it can make a moderately traumatic event extremely traumatic for a high-risk schizophrenic.
3. As schizophrenics have low frustration tolerance and a heightened sensitivity to stress (Coleman et al., 1984; Lukoff et al., 1984; Rabkin, 1980; Spring & Coons, 1982), the same objective level of stress may provoke a more intensive emotional reaction in them than in normals.
4. Research evidence shows that the individual's cognitive appraisal is important in determining the magnitude of stress, and "a few studies in the literature on schizophrenic disorder . . . suggest that the cognitive appraisal process in schizophrenic patients may tend to magnify the stressful events and situations" (Lukoff et al., 1984, p. 278). Thus schizophrenics will have a tendency to "make mountains out of molehills."
5. However, the magnification of stress may be only partly attributable to inadequate cognitive appraisal abilities. The schizophrenic might well be making a realistic assessment of his or her coping potential. For example, loss of one's job or marital separation, though at all times stressful, are tragic for schizophrenics because they encounter far greater difficulty in readjusting—in finding new jobs or friends and in setting up new goals to aim for. Neither can they "compensate" for failure in one field by success in another, as can normals, since usually there is no sphere in which they are successful.
6. Schizophrenics may have poor ability to remove noxious stimuli from their attention by normal distractive means (i.e., denial). Their extreme attention impairment may perhaps assist them in ignoring moderate external stimuli. However, once a stimulus penetrates the conscious, the schizophrenic may be helpless in expelling it. As a result, the subject is continuously exposed to arousal of worry and anxiety until more drastic measures (e.g., daydreaming or bizarre behavior) are taken to ward it off. Some evidence that may support the assertion of the schizophrenic's poor denial ability

is provided by studies on habituation to stressful stimuli. Horvarth and Meares (1979) report that nonparanoid schizophrenics, unlike paranoid schizophrenics and normals, are totally unable to screen out meaningless sound from their attentional system. Similar findings were reported by Ohman et al. (1986). This failure to habituate may testify to their poor cognitive ability to neutralize the noxious element of the stimulus and to remove it from their system.

7. Stress can generate adverse neurochemical changes (Anisman & Lapierre, 1982; Coleman et al., 1984) that disturb the body's normal functioning and thereby aggravate subjects' negative feelings. Preschizophrenic subjects may generate more adverse neurochemical activity either because of an overreaction to stress or because they are genetically programmed to react to stress in this way. The physiological system may further deteriorate due to sleeplessness, loss of appetite, and other somatic problems. For example, see Gottesman and Shields (1982, p. 193) and Aisenberg, Weizer, & Munitz (1985) concerning large weight loss and high mortality rate among schizophrenic patients. Subjects may fail to recognize that their worse emotional state is in part due to physiological deterioration and instead may attribute their overall bad feeling to their own failures. (Drug treatment, therefore, may sometimes be effective in schizophrenia, as it can restore the normal working of the body's neurochemistry.)

Stress cannot be considered in isolation from the person suffering the stress. Acute schizophrenics, though more able than chronics to live an adjusted life, also have handicapped personalities and will also adopt bizarre behavior when stress exceeds their coping resources. Thus, "excessive stress" cannot be given objective parameters. Excessive stress is what triggers schizophrenia, but what that may involve, in practice, will vary from individual to individual.

DISCUSSION

All the evidence reviewed in this chapter demonstrates the sufferings of preschizophrenics. Life starts with a significant incidence of difficult pregnancy and obstetrical complications at the birth of high-risk children. In early childhood, stress is not relaxed. Parents often are emotionally unstable, rejecting, and violent. In school, the child is alienated from peers, fails in the classroom, and begins to display deviant behavior. Social alienation reaches its peak during the "extended adolescence period," which also sees failures in independence, work, and sexual relations. Marriage is rare and invariably unsuccessful. Preschizophrenics hardly receive any social support. From the moment of their conception, they seem virtually fated to fail.

D. A. Lewis and Hugi (1981) examined the personal background of 18 chronically ill psychotic patients who had been hospitalized several times. They found that all these subjects except 2 were unemployed and consequently faced financial hardship. Most were supported by some form of government agency and lacked family or social ties. All the 7 subjects who had been married were divorced. Many lived alone, and several changed their address frequently.

D. A. Lewis and Hugi's findings describe the typical wretched life conditions and horrendous stress to which preschizophrenics are likely to be exposed and which serve as the background for the schizophrenics' collapse of self as a result of their feeling culpable for their failures. In this adverse psychological state, bizarre schizophrenic symptoms become the only method of escaping from deep depression and pressure.

This conclusion is consistent with a point of view expressed by Laing (1964), a Scottish existential psychiatrist who stated that

> *the experience and behavior that gets labelled schizophrenic is a special sort of strategy that a person invents in order to live in an unliveable situation . . . the person has come to be placed in an untenable position. He cannot make a move . . . without being beset by contradictory pressures both internally, from himself, and externally, from those around him. He is, as it were, in a position of checkmate. (p. 186)*

In the light of the preschizophrenics' life conditions, D. A. Lewis and Hugi (1981) suggest regarding the deviant psychotic responses as a rational choice selected to improve their standard of life; the authors indicated that "the continued use of inpatient facilities reflects . . . purposeful behavior of resource-poor citizens who can avail themselves of these stations when they feel it is necessary . . . 'a weekend retreat' for those who have few other places to go" (p. 218). Although the schizophrenic way of life may cause some degree

> *of self-stigmatization and renunciation of personal liberties, these might be mild penalties to pay for escape from constant failure, contempt, rejection, and often brutality. For many, life in a modern mental hospital is distinctly more pleasant in many dimensions than would be life "outside"—in, let us say, an urban ghetto. (Coleman et al., 1984, p. 381)*

However, it would be a misconception to see schizophrenia mainly as a tool for achieving some secondary gains rather than as a coping strategy that frees the conscious from the tyranny of negative self-cognitions and that attains some illusory control on life. Evidence shows that when artificial methods are applied to nullify the schizophrenic coping strategy and resume contact with reality without giving satisfactory answers to the subject's source of stress, depression is likely to replace bizarre symptoms. For example, Van Putten, Crumpton, and Yale (1976) compared two schizophrenic groups. In one group were habitual drug refusers, who invariably discontinued antipsychotic medication and were repeatedly hospitalized. In the second were drug-complier patients. Results showed that the former group experienced resurgence of grandiose psychotic symptoms and a relative absence of dysphoric effects, such as anxiety or depression. By contrast, the drug compliers developed decompensation characterized by depression, anxiety, absence of grandiosity, and some awareness of illness. The authors demonstrated, by referring to the experiences of one of the drug-refuser subjects while on medication, that drug treatment diminishes grandiosity and increases reality contact. The subject became aware of his loneliness and his lack of accomplishments. He resented the increase in reality contact and demanded to leave the hospital. The investigators postulated that "some patients stop medication precisely because they prefer a schizophrenic existence" (p. 1444). Hogarty, Goldberg, and the Collaborative Study Group, Boston (1973) came to the same conclusion in their attempt to explain why 40% of patients in their study stopped medication within the first year after discharge. Another study relevant to this discussion is that of Siris et al. (1984). They reported that among 20 patients diagnosed as having schizophrenia, 4 developed a depression syndrome after their psychotic symptoms were resolved and 4 others developed major depressive syndromes after the first week of hospitalization while they were still psychotic. The authors indicated that the rate of depression might have been higher had they observed the patients after their discharge from the hospital. We do not yet know why drugs sometimes increase reality contact, but it seems obvious that hallucinatory stimuli provide the subject with a valuable distractive tool against depression. It is possible that the spontaneous neurochemical changes that schizophrenics undergo depress attentional arousal and clarity of judgment and thus ease the schizophrenic escape. Medication probably increases alertness and thereby counters the relief of schizophrenic coping maneuvers.

It appears from the research literature reviewed in this chapter that there is little room for doubt that schizophrenia is a coping strategy. In view of the miserable life conditions of preschizophrenic individuals, one may wonder why so many investigators in the field have failed to arrive at the same inevitable conclusion we have, that stress is the major cause of schizophrenia.

The answer is in part related to methodological factors. Lukoff et al. (1984) note that

> one possibility is that major life events occurring before onset were overlooked. The life events schedules used in most studies are oriented toward married, working people, not the typical isolated, single, unemployed schizophrenic patient. Thus, stressful life events which occur commonly to schizophrenic patients . . . are not adequately covered by these schedules. (p. 268)

In our opinion, a second factor that led to the underestimation of the effect of stress in the etiology of schizophrenia is the bias, or what is termed *genetic ideology* (J. R. Marshall & Pettitt, 1985), that unfortunately exists in psychopathology in favor of the medical model. Psychiatrists in general still refuse to believe that extreme bizarre behaviors such as those of schizophrenics can be purposeful, though we are not alone in holding this opinion. However, we shall continue to regard this position as a bias as long as the seven arguments raised against the medical model (pp. 200–203) are not satisfactorily answered.

A third factor retarding recognition of stress as the major factor in psychosis is that not all people exposed to excessive stress become psychotic. We proposed explaining this phenomenon by differentiating between universal unavoidable stress (e.g., concentration camps) and personal unavoidable stress (e.g., handicapped personality). Universal unavoidable stress is not likely to cause any damage to the self, as individuals subject to it cannot hold themselves responsible for their condition. However in personal unavoidable stress, the self is broken and the individual is plagued by helplessness.

It is necessary to explain why stress may lead sometimes to one type of psychosis and sometimes to another. We claim that trait stress (stemming from a genuine pervading incompetence) is associated with unsuccessful people of poor premorbid adjustment and often results in schizophrenia. (In this context, "poor premorbid" adjustment includes both chronic and acute schizophrenics, as the "good premorbid" adjustment of the acute schizophrenic is only relative and is in fact also only marginal adjustment). Affective disorders tend to be found among successful, ambitious, normally adjusted people who encounter a one-time excessive irreversible stress (see chapter 18).

The parsimonious psychobizarreness theory can synthesize within its framework far more data than any other psychopathological theory. It is the only current theory that can account for the etiology and symptomatology of neurosis and psychosis as well as the state of unawareness in psychiatric subjects. This chapter has shown how psychobizarreness theory can explain the causes of nonparanoid schizophrenia. We will now show how the same theory applies to affective disorders and paranoia.

17

Affective Disorders and Paranoia

OVERVIEW

This chapter consists of two main sections. The first discusses the principal determinants of severe depression. The second deals with the major psychotic coping styles employed by severely depressed subjects, namely, paranoia and mania. In recent years, it has been suggested that paranoia, like mania, is a mechanism for coping with depression and that it may be classified as a subcategory of affective disorders. This would oppose the traditional conception of paranoia that considered it either a type of schizophrenia or a distinctive disorder (Zigler & Glick, 1984). Although this new conceptualization of paranoia can advance our understanding of affective disorders, since a significant proportion of severe depressives do indeed employ paranoid coping mechanisms, we believe that paranoia should continue to be viewed partly in the traditional terms. The paranoid coping style is used not only by patients with affective disorders, but also by others with a background similar to that of nonparanoid schizophrenics. Thus, we consider suggestions such as Zigler and Glick's to be overgeneralized, and too radical a departure from the traditional conceptualization of paranoia.

There seem to be two different types of paranoid disorders. Subjects in the first category, which we propose calling *paranoid affective disorders,* have good premorbid adjustment. In the second category, which we call *paranoid nonaffective disorders* or *paranoia,* are subjects with mild paranoia or paranoid schizophrenia, who show severe coping skills deficits and, in their extreme manifestations, display behavior similar to subjects with nonparanoid schizophrenia. According to psychobizarreness theory, the same coping style can be used by subjects with totally dissimilar etiological backgrounds. The reasons why subjects with severe depression tend sometimes to prefer the paranoid coping style will be elaborated later in this chapter.

MAIN DETERMINANTS OF DEPRESSION

Introduction

The traditional mechanistic theories in psychopathology, particularly the medical model, draw no fundamental distinction between depression and bizarre psychiatric symptoms. Such a distinction, however, is basic to our approach. In our view, while bizarre symptoms are unique to humans and are consciously adopted, depression, like anxiety, seems to be a natural, spontaneous reaction to a failure to cope with stress.

The bulk of research findings show that animals may display depressive reactions (unlike bizarre behavior) when exposed to unavoidable stress such as separation from the mother (Costello, 1982; H. F. Harlow & M. K. Harlow, 1965; H. F. Harlow & Zimmermann, 1959; Jesberger & Richardson, 1985; Kaufman & Rosenblum, 1967a, 1967b; McKinney, Suomi, & H. F. Harlow, 1971; Seay, Hansen, & H. F. Harlow,

1963) or to experimentally induced unavoidable stressful situations (Maier & Seligman, 1976; Seligman, 1974; Seligman & Maier, 1967; Telner & Singhal, 1984).

Usually one type of bizarre symptom does not appear in combination with another (e.g., it would be unusual to find agoraphobia and hysteria in the same individual). In contrast, depression is present in virtually all psychiatric disorders. For example, evidence reviewed by Zigler and Glick (1984) shows that "the symptom of depression was manifested by 74% of schizophrenic, 75% of personality disorders, 86% of neurotic, and 86% of affective disorder patients" (p. 56). This fact raises the question of whether classifying depression as a distinctive psychiatric disorder is justified. We think, however, that this diagnosis should continue to be used for cases in which depression is evident in the absence of bizarre symptoms and in which depression remains the predominant psychiatric symptom.

Depression is often triggered by unavoidable stress, particularly loss and failure, or by subjects' helplessness in removing themselves from stress (see Anisman & Lapierre, 1982; Arieti & Bemporad, 1978; Barnes & Prosen, 1985; Billings, Cronkite, & Moos, 1983; Billings & Moos, 1985; Coleman, Butcher, & Carson, 1984; Costello, 1982; I. W. Miller & Norman, 1979; S. M. Miller & Seligman, 1982; Oatley & Bolton, 1985; Paykel, 1982; Roy, 1981; Shaw, 1982; Spring & Coons, 1982; Telner & Singhal, 1984; Warheit, 1979; see also the studies on concentration camp survivors). Depression may, of course, be caused by avoidable stress as well, but only when the stress exceeds one's normal coping resources and the subject is not willing to adopt neurotic bizarre responses. For example, a soldier petrified in battle can escape from this avoidable stress by developing hysteria, forcing his withdrawal from the front line. However the high cost involved (e.g., embarrassment, shame, guilt) may prevent him from choosing this escaping strategy. Similarly, the prolonging of an unhappy marriage, which could be avoided by divorce, may cause depression. If the option of divorce is rejected and subjects fail to cope with the stress by other conventional means, they can still remove themselves from the stressful stimuli by developing neurotic bizarre symptoms such as fugue (see case study, pp. 122–124).

As mentioned earlier, personal stress can cause more serious damage than universal stress. In agreement with psychoanalysis (Bibring, 1953; Paykel, 1982), we emphasize the importance of loss, failure, and blows to self-esteem (Bibring, 1953; Paykel, 1982) as causes of depression, but differ in refuting the relevance of repressed anger, particularly oral aggression (Bibring, 1953; Mendelson, 1982). While research has illustrated that loss, failure, and self-deflation contribute to depression, no such connection has been established for repressed anger (Davison & Neale, 1982; R. W. White & Watt, 1981). For example, loss and failure were found to be themes of depressives' dreams, but anger and hostility were not. If, as psychoanalysis claims, depression results from anger directed at oneself, then depressed people would not be expected to betray hostility toward others. However, contrary to this expectation, they do often express intense anger and hostility to people close to them (Weissman, Klerman, & Paykel, 1971).

Our theory is consistent also with the revised formulation of Seligman's helplessness theory, which claims that depression and self-esteem tend to be lower in cases of universal than personal helplessness (Abramson, Seligman, & Teasdale, 1978; Garber & Hollon, 1980; I. W. Miller & Norman, 1979; S. M. Miller & Seligman, 1982; Seligman, Abramson, Semmel, & Von Baeyer, 1979). Personal helplessness occurs when people believe that they cannot control the outcomes of their actions, while others can. Universal helplessness refers to stressful situations where the subjects believe that neither they themselves nor others can control outcomes.

Factors Precipitating Severe Depression

At least four main factors facilitate the development of severe depression. These are the severity of the stress, certain personality traits, the extent of biological changes, and the lack of social support.

Severity of Stress

The vital role of recent stressful life events in the onset of depression has been unanimously indicated in the research findings (Anisman & Lapierre, 1982; Arieti & Bemporad, 1978; Barnes & Prosen, 1985; Billings & Moos, 1985; Coleman et al., 1984; Costello, 1982; J. W. Miller & Norman, 1979; S. M. Miller & Seligman, 1982; Oatley & Bolton, 1985; Paykel, 1982; Roy, 1981; Shaw, 1982; Spring & Coons, 1982; Telner & Signhal, 1984; Warheit, 1979). The more the subject's dominant life goals are jeopardized and the more the self is perceived as being responsible for the actual occurrence of the stress, the more intense the depression is likely to be.

One of the most frustrating aspects of stress is its irreversibility. The following interview with a 47-year-old patient is, according to Coleman et al. (1980), typical of patients suffering from acute depression:

Therapist: What seems to be your trouble?
Patient: There's just no way out of it . . . nothing but blind alleys . . . it's hopeless . . . everything is hopeless . . . I shouldn't have done it . . . if I had any willpower I would kill myself . . . I don't deserve to live . . . I have ruined everything . . . and it's all my fault . . . there's no use going on . . . I have ruined everything . . . my family . . . and now myself . . . I bring misfortune to everyone . . . I am a moral leper . . . No one can help me . . . it's hopeless. (p. 374)

Even though depressive patients tend to appraise stressful events negatively (Folkman & Lazarus, 1986; Shaw, 1982), they do not necessarily distort reality. As was stated previously, research findings in recent years (Beidel & Turner, 1986; Golin, Terrell, Johnson, 1977; Golin, Terrell, Weitz, & Drost, 1979; Lewinsohn, Mischel, Chaplin, & Barton, 1980; Roth & Ingram, 1985; Taylor, 1983) show depressives to be more reality oriented than nondepressives. The severity of their depression closely reflects the bitter facts of life. This position contradicts Beck's (1967, 1976; Kovacs & Beck, 1978) cognitive theory of depression, which conceives of depressives as people who respond to stress in a distorted way. They tend, for example, to commit logical errors and thereby magnify their troubles. Our position, though, accords with the social cognitive theory of depression recently suggested by Oatley and Bolton (1985), which asserts that depression occurs when life events disrupt the social roles by which people define their worth, and no alternative sources of self-definition are available. Oatley and Bolton (1985) indicate that their theory differs from other cognitive approaches, which claim that

cognitive distortion or bias is essential to the onset of depression. Subjects' assessments of the threatfulness of events correspond closely with those of independent raters. . . . People often become depressed for understandable reasons rather than reasons of irrationality, although distortion may well contribute to chronicity. (p. 384)

Similarly, Beidel and Turner (1986) criticizing the cognitive behavioral theories argued that the cumulative research literature does not support the claim that depressive patients perceive reality less accurately or that they possess distorted cognitive processes, as compared with nondepressives. Beidel and Turner (1986) concluded that *the bulk of the research is contrary to that suggested by cognitive theory. Although the cognitions of depressives may seem more negative, there is little evidence that these cognitions are irrational or patently false, or that they precede the onset of the depressive state. (p. 184)*

Other supportive evidence shows that severity of depression was significantly related both to the incidence of stressful problems experienced prior to the onset of depression and to the subject's problem-solving ability (Billings et al., 1983; Billings & Moos, 1985; Nezu & Ronan, 1985).

That the actual severity of a stressful event constitutes one important factor in the etiology of psychotic depression is axiomatic to psychobizarreness theory. A theory that claims that psychotic disorders are basically the result of stress must specify why stress causes the development of sometimes one type of symptom and sometimes another. As was already explained, the development of nonparanoid schizophrenia is not so much the result of the objective severity of the stressful event itself (state stress) as of the individual's incompetence (trait stress). However, with psychotic depressive patients, the story is completely different. Evidence (Arieti & Bemporad, 1978; Coleman et al., 1984; R. W. White & Watt, 1981) indicates that psychotic depressives had either normal or even very successful premorbid adjustment, particularly during childhood. Some studies (Paykel, 1982) do indicate an adverse childhood environment for neurotic depressives, but not for bipolar or unipolar psychotic depressives. Lewine, Watt, & Fryer (1978) studied school and hospital records to assess the social premorbid competence and psychiatric outcomes in adult schizoaffectives, paranoid schizophrenics, and undifferentiated schizophrenics. Significant differences were found both in childhood interpersonal competence and in adult social competence (especially marital status). The schizoaffectives had the highest levels of competence, the paranoids, intermediate, and the undifferentiated, the lowest levels of competence. The groups did not differ in outcome as measured by total days of hospitalization and a global rating. These results imply that the personality disintegration in affective disorders is a direct consequence not of a handicapped personality, as in nonaffective disorders, but of severe state stress. Therefore it would be expected that affective disorders should have better prognosis, and indeed, research (Coryell & Winokur, 1982) has shown that the recovery rate of schizoaffectives is higher than that of typical schizophrenics, though lower than that of subjects with pure affective disorder. In fact, findings by various investigators (Paykel, 1978, 1982; Rabkin, 1980; Spring & Coons, 1982) show that the stressful events preceding the onset of depression are significantly more severe than those occurring prior to the appearance of schizophrenic symptoms.

A moderate to high level of personal unavoidable stress seems to be a necessary but not a sufficient condition for depression. As they are well-adjusted, were it not for the presence of stress, depressives could live normal satisfying lives. When stress rears its ugly head, however, three additional factors are required to induce psychotic depression.

Personality Traits

In general, subjects with psychotic depression display a firmness of purpose and an obstinate pursuit of their goals. They make great demands on themselves and are highly motivated and energetic (Arieti & Bemporad, 1978; Coleman et al., 1984; Paykel, 1982; Zigler & Glick, 1984). These personality traits, which to a large extent appear to result from the education of very ambitious and demanding parents, are generally positive in normal life, but may have a devastating effect at times of stress. Not only are they likely to intensify the feelings of guilt, self-criticism, and self-deprecation that personal stress tends to cause, but they may also restrict the subject's ability to consider alternative compensation for the lost goal. Exposure of these subjects to severe unavoidable personal stress totally occupies and almost "paralyzes" the attention: the subject cannot divert his or her attention to other more pleasant spheres of life. This is consistent with Bibring's (1953) psychoanalytic approach to depression that "in depression the ego is shocked into passivity not because there is a conflict regarding the goals, but because of its own incapacity to live up to the undisputed narcissistic aspirations" (p. 30). Bibring argued that the depressed person gives up, not the goals, but the pursuit of them.

An inevitable result of such a response style is "cognitive emptiness." As the attention is entirely tuned to the lost goals, rival stimuli cannot penetrate the consciousness. Worrying and negative self-references (Shaw, 1982) expand their "cognitive territory," and depression deepens. Psychoanalysis attributed depression to unconscious childhood experiences of loss. Learning theories explained it in terms of a reduction in reinforcement. Medical models sought disturbances in neurochemical processes to match the change in mood (Davison & Neale, 1982). While these factors should not be discarded wholesale, we believe that depression is caused, first and foremost, by malfunctioning of the conscious. As the body may uncontrollably produce toxic substances in response to disease, so the depressed person may uncontrollably produce a continuous stream of "poisonous" thoughts, in response to stress. This emphasis on the central role of the cognitive components is consistent with several other models of development of depression, anxiety, and fear (Bandura, 1977b; Beck, 1967; Melges & Bowlby, 1969; S. M. Miller, 1981; Persons & Rao, 1985; Shaw, 1982).

Severity of Neurochemical Changes

Although it is accepted that genetic or biological factors are important in the maintenance of depression (Anisman & Lapierre, 1982; Coleman et al., 1984; Davison & Neale, 1982), it seems that in themselves, they are insufficient to set the process in motion. Arieti and Bemporad (1978) state that even with respect to manic–depressive psychosis, where the effect of genetic factors seems to have been convincingly demonstrated, these variables are not in themselves sufficient to cause the reaction; furthermore,

> if studies on heredity are far from conclusive, biochemical studies are even more so . . . I have never seen a patient about whom I could say that his depression was unrelated to a prior anguish, or . . . that . . . its origin had to be sought exclusively in a metabolic disorder. (pp. 4–5)

Thus, stress seems to be the precondition for the development of depression. Neurochemical changes can only perpetuate it.

Stress may cause extensive neurochemical changes similar to those observed in depression (Anisman & Lapierre, 1982; Coleman et al., 1984). These data also suggest that when a subject with a genetic predisposition to depression is exposed to stress, neurochemical changes tend to be more readily and more intensively produced. Furthermore, some authors (Coleman et al., 1984) have raised the possibility that "once the reaction is underway, it becomes relatively 'autonomous' until it runs its course or is interrupted by drugs or other intervention" (p. 314). The very adverse neurochemical changes that characterize subjects with affective disorders (Sachar, 1982; Zis & Goodwin, 1982) should not only have a harmful effect on the subject's general mood but also cause serious disruption of the normal functioning of physiological processes such as sleeplessness and loss of appetite (Hamilton, 1982). This deprivation of the body's needs is likely to further intensify production of the negative neurochemical changes and deterioration of the body. Rimm and Somervill (1977) indicated, for example, that some depressed patients have been hospitalized because of self-starvation more than for depression per se.

Thus, we agree with the medical view, at least in part, that low spirits can result from neurochemical changes and a biological sensitivity to stress. However, we claim that neurochemical changes exert not only a direct influence on depression, as the medical theory would argue, but also an indirect influence through the intensification of adverse psychological processes. Subjects with clear symptoms of physical illness would not necessarily feel depressed, but would, in all probability, attribute the pain and weakness to their physical condition. Depressives, however, are unaware that their emotional affliction is to a certain degree due to the deterioration of their body. They are convinced that all their troubles follow the loss of their goals. Had they the insight to understand that their troubles stem from two separable sources, their depression could be lightened. As it is, they attribute both their emotional and their physical discomfort to the same cause. Thus, in our theory, the conscious is involved even in the effects of neurochemistry on depression. Antidepressants apparently alleviate depression because they reinstate the normal functioning of the body (Jesberger & Richardson, 1985). Cognitive therapeutic strategies may also achieve results (Beck, Rush, Shaw, & Emery, 1979; Rush, Beck, Kovacs, & Hollan, 1977). We have provided a theoretical explanation of why the combination of medical treatment and a cognitive therapy that aims to increase subjects' awareness of their psychological and physiological state may prove much more beneficial than either treatment on its own.

Social Support

Social support and friendship help buffer the potential damage of stress to one's mental and physical well-being (Crinic, Greenberg, Ragozin, Robinson, & Basham, 1983; Eaton, 1978; Gore, 1978; Gottlieb, 1981; Haggerty, 1980; Husaini, Neff, Newbrough, & Moore, 1982; Larocco, House, & French, 1980; Lin, Simeone, Ensel, & Kuo, 1970; Linn & McGranahan, 1980; Mueller, 1980; Sandler & Brian, 1982; A. W. Williams, Ware, & Donald, 1981). Dean and Ensel (1983) found that lack of social support was the single most important factor accounting for depression in young men and women. Similar results were reported by several others (Billings & Moos, 1985; Oatley & Bolton, 1985; Paykel, 1982; Warheit, 1979). The evidence further shows that depressive people seek more social support than do nondepressives (Coyne, Aldwin, & Lazarus, 1981; Folkman & Lazarus, 1986).

Social support seems to be important not only because of the practical help, advice, and encouragement it offers (Coyne et al., 1981; Folkman & Lazarus, 1986; Rofé, 1984), but also because it can provide the individual with distraction. Depressives have a special need for encouragement and distraction because, as stated, they usually have strong reality orientation and lack the ability to delude themselves with false hopes (Abramson & Alloy, 1981; Alloy & Abramson, 1979, 1982; Alloy, Abramson, & Viscusi, 1981; DeMonbreun & Craighead, 1977; Golin et al., 1977, 1979; Lewinsohn et al., 1980; Martin, Abramson, & Alloy, 1984; Roth & Ingram, 1985).

Conclusions

In conclusion, we have seen that four main factors play a dominant role in the development of depression. Distractive coping strategies may prevent the onset of depression, particularly when the stress is unavoidable (see pp. 83–84). If the stress exceeds the individual's coping resources, his or her only alternative to remaining depressed is to adopt more desperate coping strategies, such as bizarre behavior, to which we now turn our attention.

COPING MECHANISMS OF AFFECTIVE DISORDERS

Paranoid Reactions

Paranoid Affective Disorders

As depressives have difficulty in deluding themselves, they strongly object to using psychotic coping mechanisms. It is logical, therefore, that many would attempt to commit suicide (according to Hamilton, 1982, about 15% ultimately kill themselves), become alcoholics, or resort to narcotics as a means of escape (Coleman et al., 1984; Weissman & Klerman, 1977; R. W. White & Watt, 1981; Zigler & Glick, 1984). However, for many patients, these escapes are unacceptable. Suicide might be incompatible with their system of values, and they may be unfamiliar with or morally opposed to the abuse of alcohol and drugs. Such patients, in the face of deep depression, would reluctantly find it necessary to resort to pathological coping mechanisms.

From the perspective of cost–benefit considerations, it seems that of all psychotic coping maneuvers (paranoia, mania, and nonparanoid schizophrenia), the paranoid reaction is the most preferable for depressives. The benefits inherent in this reaction can meet the patient's psychological needs quite well. First, in paranoia, personal stress is converted to universal stress, as an external target is selected to shoulder blame. This saves the self from constant cognitive attack. Second, self-deception is a relatively simple task for many depressives, as their innate intelligence enables them to justify their delusions with "proofs" from reality. Third, it provides them with a legitimized avenue for the discharge of anger and frustration. Fourth, bizarreness in paranoia may be manifested to a greater or lesser extent (Zigler & Glick, 1984). In milder cases, subjects may blame their failure on an external target (e.g., God), which in itself is hardly evidence of bizarre behavior. They may not necessarily develop the full range of symptoms of a persecution complex and so will not incur much social rejection and embarrassment. We believe that extremely bizarre paranoid behavior is more prevalent among individuals with paranoid nonaffective disorders than among those with paranoid affective disorders.

The cost of paranoia is comparatively low. First, the deviance from reality is less than in other psychotic reactions.

> Except for the delusional system, these people are perfectly oriented and are quite normal in their conduct. The personality does not become disorganized, and interest in the environment is substantially preserved. One might say that paranoia is a restricted psychosis . . . it does not invade and disintegrate the personality as a whole. (R. W. White & Watt 1981, p. 479)

Second, the social price is not so great. Depressive subjects are usually of higher social rank than are nonparanoid schizophrenics (Bagley, 1973; Boyd & Weissman, 1982; Cockerham, 1978; Davison & Neale, 1982; Jaco, 1960; Krauthammer & Klerman, 1979; Monnelly, Woodruff, & Robins, 1974). Acting "crazier" may be more effective in the war against depression, but the higher social classes, for whom avoiding social embarrassment is most important, would refrain from greater behavioral deviation.

Paranoid symptoms are frequently preferred by depressives, and the notion that paranoia is a coping style for countering depression is becoming more accepted. Zigler and Glick (1984), following other investigators (Meissner, 1978, pp. 99, 125), describe paranoia as "a mechanism employed by individuals to ward off a breakthrough into consciousness of depressive thought and its accompanying painful affective concomitants" (p. 57). Paranoia, they say, most resembles mania because "in both instances, the disordered individual turns the depression upside-down and asserts his or her worth and well-being" (p. 61).

Paranoia, or Paranoid Nonaffective Disorders

Zigler and Glick (1984) propose classifying all paranoia as affective disorders and abrogating the traditional association of paranoia with schizophrenia. They suggest differentiating between two basic psychiatric disorders, or what they term *genotype* disorders—depression and schizophrenia. Each of these genotypes gives rise to a number of *phenotype* behavioral disorders. The genotype of depression consists of the phenotypes unipolar depression, alcoholism, paranoia, and mania. The schizophrenic genotype includes the phenotypes disorganized hebephrenia, catatonia, and undifferentiated schizophrenia. Thus, for Zigler and Glick, paranoia is merely a kind of affective disorder.

We do not accept this new classification. In our opinion, it is inadequate since it overemphasizes the similarities between paranoia and affective disorders while disregarding the similarities between paranoia and nonparanoid schizophrenia. We argue later in this chapter for preservation of the traditional independent classification of paranoia, to be called in its extreme form *paranoid schizophrenia*. But before forwarding our theory, we first present and comment on Zigler and Glick's new ideas.

Zigler and Glick's Theory. Zigler and Glick (1984) correctly note the similarities that identify paranoia with affective disorders and the differences that distinguish it from nonparanoid schizophrenia. First, they illustrate how paranoid reactions, like depression, are found among many psychiatric subjects. Of all patients admitted to a hospital psychiatric unit, 40% displayed symptoms associated with paranoia. While fewer than one third were actually diagnosed as paranoid schizophrenics, paranoid symptoms were found among 70% of patients with psychotic depression, 50% with affective disorders, and 63% with psychotic organic brain syndrome. Zigler and Glick suggest theoretical justification for this similarity by postulating that both paranoia and depression preoccupy the self and that paranoid symptoms are aimed at assuaging the individual's sense of inadequacy.

Second, they argue that paranoid symptoms, like depression, are common, and can be ordered along a continuum of severity extending from florid delusions of persecution or grandiosity to mild and more reality-based interpersonal sensitivities. Essentially the same ideas were expressed by Meissner (1981).

As part of their argument, Zigler and Glick refer to many stark differences between paranoia and nonparanoid schizophrenia, to which we can add from our own theory. Paranoid and nonparanoid coping mechanisms employ opposite methods of distraction in that the former exploits inattention, and the latter exploits attention. In addition, a substantial number of studies show that paranoids are typically more intelligent, socially more competent, older on their first psychiatric admission, and less disturbed than nonparanoid schizophrenics. Paranoids generally suffer less thought disorder and are more in touch with reality. They are hospitalized for briefer periods, experience fewer readmissions, and react more favorably to psychiatric intervention. Whereas genetic loading has been shown to be a decisive factor in nonparanoid schizophrenia, for paranoia this has as yet to be proven. Most investigators are convinced that psychosocial factors alone are sufficient to account for the development of paranoia (Coleman et al., 1984; M. J. Goldstein, Held, & Cromwell, 1968; Meissner, 1981; Neale, Kopfstein, & Levine, 1972).

Critical Discussion. Zigler and Glick's theoretical conceptualization of paranoia as a strategy for coping with depression constitutes a radical departure from the traditional psychoanalytic notion of paranoia as an unconscious defense mechanism against the id's unacceptable impulses of hostility and/or homosexuality (Fenichel, 1946; H. B. Lewis, 1981; Meissner, 1978; Zamansky, 1958).

However, we have three reservations concerning their theory: (1) they ignore differences between paranoia and affective disorders; (2) we dispute their concept of the severity continuum; (3) we reject the classification of catatonia as nonparanoid schizophrenia.

1. Zigler and Glick overlook six blatant points distinguishing paranoia from unipolar and bipolar depression: family background, personality characteristics, stress background, homosexual tendencies, genetic susceptibility, and the age of onset. In all these aspects, except the last two, paranoids resemble nonparanoid schizophrenics.

Paranoid patients come from disturbed family backgrounds characterized by hostile relationships (Coleman et al., 1984; Meissner, 1978). In contrast, the parents of depressives are typically described as ambitious and the home atmosphere is described as encouraging and achievement oriented (Arieti & Bemporad, 1978; Coleman et al., 1984).

Paranoid and affective disorders differ sharply in personality profile. Paranoid subjects are socially incompetent. As children, they were described as aloof, suspicious, stubborn, and resentful of punishment. Rarely did these subjects have a history of good socialization and normal play with other children. Often, they failed to get along with others, but at the same time, they greatly needed attention (Coleman et al., 1984; Meissner, 1978). Psychotic depressives in childhood, however, were outstandingly competent socially and excelled in independence, scholastic maturity, and leadership qualities (Lewine et al., 1978). Pre-bipolar subjects are described as socially competent, energetic, lively, and full of interest. Warmth radiates from them. With intimates, they are faithful and loving, and they live highly satisfying lives (R. W. White & Watt, 1981, p. 538).

The paranoid subject's stress background is filled with social rejection and with marital and occupational failure. Interestingly, depressives have good premorbid adjustment and normally do not have a history of failure or stress. They are either average or even quite successful individuals prior to their breakdown (Arieti & Bemporad, 1978; Coleman et al., 1984; Paykel, 1982).

Most paranoid subjects encounter sexual difficulties, and frequently they have homosexual conflicts (Coleman et al., 1984; Fenichel, 1946; Hesselbach, 1962; H. B. Lewis, 1981; Meissner, 1978). Psychotic depressives do not. It should be mentioned, though, that schizophrenics sometimes also experience sexual problems. (Coleman et al., 1984; Meissner, 1978).

Paranoia and bipolar depression differ also in terms of genetic loading and age of onset. In paranoia, the genetic component is low and the age of onset is relatively advanced (Zigler & Glick, 1984), whereas in manic depression, as in nonparanoid schizophrenia, the genetic component is high (Mendlewicz, 1979; Nurnberger & Gershon, 1982) and the disorder emerges during young adulthood (Perris, 1982; Shopsin, 1979a).

2. Zigler and Glick see both depression and paranoia as existing on a continuum of severity. While we respect the concept of a continuum for emotions such as depression and anxiety, we strongly oppose the suggestion that bizarre behavior is the end of a behavioral axis on which normal behavior also lies. This is one of the central points on which psychobizarreness theory takes issue with the traditional theories of psychoanalysis, behaviorism, and medical models.

As was stated previously, Freud developed his psychoanalytic ideas (particularly the concepts of the autonomous unconscious, the permanency of childhood traumatic experiences, and defense mechanisms) to account for the inability of his psychiatric patients to provide rational explanations for their bizarre responses. He then generalized these ideas and applied them to normal functioning individuals, arguing that both normal and abnormal behaviors are controlled by the same mechanisms and that they differ only in degree. The behaviorists and the medical model theorists adopted a more radical version of the continuum notion, assuming that our understanding of human bizarre symptoms can be advanced by observing the behavior and neurology of animals. For example, according to McKinney and Moran (1981), exploring the neurochemical factors that govern the cautious behavior of rats can help us understand the physiological mechanisms controlling paranoid humans. Zigler and Glick's notion of a continuum represents the same stream of thought as Freud and Watson. However, the later advocates of these theories have not produced empirical support that is any more convincing than that of their theoretical forefathers for their approach to psychopathology or for the notion that a continuum can advance our understanding of bizarre symptoms.

We therefore suggest abandoning the concept of a continuum and approving instead the idea that bizarre symptoms are unique to abnormal individuals. Any superficial similarity that may be found between the cautious behavior of a normal, reality-oriented human (or rat!) and the persecution complex of a paranoid patient is not attributable to the same psychological mechanisms. No clear-cut evidence can be said to favor either the discontinuity or the continuity theory. However, we have demonstrated the greater explanatory powers of a theory that conceives of bizarre behavior as an abnormal coping strategy, to provide a comprehensive account of the complete range of psychopathological phenomena.

3. Zigler and Glick categorize catatonia—along with disorganized hebephrenia and undifferentiated schizophrenia (which we termed nonparanoid schizophrenia)—under one genotype, namely, schizophrenia. However, as we have shown previously (see p. 219), most researchers now believe that catatonia should be regarded as a schizoaffective disorder instead. Etiologically, there are striking differences between nonparanoid schizophrenia and catatonia in terms of constitutional attentional impairment, premorbid adjustment, and prognosis. The attention of catatonics is over-, rather than underemployed; their premorbid adjustment is good; and their prognosis is hopeful. In all these respects, catatonia resembles affective disorders. Furthermore, the alternation sequence of the catatonic, from wild excitement to stupor, mirrors the bipolar manic cycle. The inclusion of catatonia under the umbrella term schizophrenia is justified only by its extremely bizarre, disorganized behavior.

Psychobizarreness Explanation of Nonaffective Paranoia. The history of nonaffective paranoia starts in the home. Nonaffective paranoids have been raised in pathogenic family environments. Like nonparanoid schizophrenics, they lack social competence and are socially alienated. They have repeatedly failed to meet the critical challenges of life, and they are unable to comprehend their failures and their rejection by others (Coleman et al., 1984). Naturally, they develop a strong inferiority complex, self-rejection, and hostility toward others (Coleman et al., 1984; Meissner, 1978). Hostility is exacerbated by frustration (Feshbach & Weiner, 1982). Nonaffective paranoids, often very talented people, realize at a relatively advanced age (by which time the paranoia is beginning to develop) their failure to accomplish anything significant in life, and they perceive this failure as irreversible. This only serves to intensify frustration and feelings of inferiority (Coleman et al., 1984) and self-resentment and to increase rage toward others. The consciousness reaches a state of readiness for explosion. At this stage of life, moderately or very stressful events, such as marital breakdown or job loss, may make their frustration and depression unbearable. In view of their severe social incompetence, paranoid subjects are likely to have as little social support as nonparanoid schizophrenics. Family relationships will probably be distant and unsupportive, and in such circumstances, the adoption of a paranoid coping style becomes an attractive means of escaping depression and preserving self-integrity. Other psychotic coping mechanisms could also have been effective. However, as we explained previously (pp. 217–218), due to their cognitive competence, family background, personality characteristics, ease of self-deception, and some further considerations to which we will refer later in this chapter, paranoid coping style is the most suitable for them.

We do not preclude the possibility that the course of the disorder is affected by neurochemical changes. These changes may deepen depression or perhaps increase anger and hostility, which, sustained over a prolonged period may cause adverse physiological activity. However, we deny the claim that the body's neurochemistry can directly effect the conscious decision to adopt paranoid bizarre behavior.

Finally, we turn our attention to the question of why sexual maladjustments, particularly homosexual thoughts, are found among both paranoid and nonparanoid schizophrenics (Coleman et al., 1984; Meissner, 1978). Research findings in this area are scant, and therefore we can only speculate on two possible interpretations of this phenomenon.

The first possibility, which seems to be the more probable, is that sexual inadequacy is just one element of the subject's general social inadequacy. Data regarding the etiology of homosexuality, reviewed by R. W. White and Watt (1981), show that as children, male homosexuals are often frail, clumsy, unathletic, feminine, and often isolated. The findings also suggest disturbed social relationships between the family members of homosexuals, characterized by hostility and rejection. Similarly, experiments with monkeys (H. F. Harlow, 1971; Sackett, 1974) show that social deprivation during childhood is likely to lead to social incompetence, characterized by withdrawal, antisocial behavior, and sexual deviation.

Social alienation and a pathogenic home environment are two of the dominant aspects of both paranoid and nonparanoid subjects' childhoods. It appears reasonable, therefore, that subjects in both categories have a high incidence of sexual maladjustment. It should be noted, though, that paranoids only very rarely practice homosexuality. Their sexual deviance is restricted largely to thoughts (Coleman et al., 1984). Most contemporary investigators believe that it is interpersonal stress, and not homosexuality, as Freud had thought, that is the prime cause of paranoia. Paranoid subjects will develop bizarre symptoms even without homosexual tendencies. At most, such tendencies may constitute one additional reason for self-rejection. The bizarre symptoms are aimed at cleansing the attentional system from all antiself cognitions, including homosexual ones.

An interesting case study, illustrating how paranoid schizophrenics can construct coherent, though highly bizarre systems for protecting their self-esteem and for satisfying their sexual needs through fantasy, is reported by R. W. White (1964, pp. 76–84).

The second possible explanation of paranoid homosexuality assumes that a moderate, unaccepted homosexual tendency existed in the preparanoid subject. This tendency was intensified and exploited either to rationalize rejection by others (Coleman et al., 1984, p. 394) or to neutralize aggressive drives, as is suggested by another version of psychoanalysis (Fenichel, 1946; Hesselbach, 1962; R. P. Knight, 1940).

We feel that the former explanation more closely reflects the truth. If indeed homosexuality is used as a coping mechanism to neutralize aggression or to justify the contempt of others, then one would expect that homosexual thoughts would totally occupy the consciousness and that homosexual behavior would be commonplace. The fact that paranoids do not normally engage in homosexual practice argues against this second possibility.

In conclusion, we have seen that paranoia may stem from two completely different etiological backgrounds—affective or nonaffective. The two disorders differ also in severity in that the former condition seems to have a better prognosis than the latter. Affective disorder patients do not typically display severe social incompetence. Because of this and other differences between paranoia and unipolar and bipolar depression mentioned in this chapter, we reject Zigler and Glick's proposal that all paranoid reactions be classified as affective disorders.

Not all severely depressed subjects will necessarily choose the affective paranoid coping style, and some may prefer mania because paranoia may not provide them with sufficient distraction. The strong reality orientation and middle-class respectability that characterize depressives will preclude adoption of the more "idiotic" distractive coping strategies of catatonia or hebephrenia, which indeed are very rare. Mania offers an attractive solution since it provides a high level of distraction and only periodic detachment from reality. The natural excitability, impulsiveness, and hot temper of the younger generation make them more suited to a manic coping style than their more sedate elders.

Mania

Differences Between Mania and Unipolar Depression

Manic subjects have been found to differ from unipolar depressives in several important respects (Boyd & Weissman, 1982; Coleman et al., 1984; Coryell & Winokur, 1982; Mendlewicz, 1979; Nurnberger & Gershon, 1982; Perris, 1982). For example, the genetic component in mania is more significant than in unipolar depression, a lower proportion of women suffer from the disorder, and the age of onset is earlier. As in unipolar depression, excessively stressful events have been found to precede the onset of mania (Dunner, Patrick, & Fieve, 1979; S. Kennedy, Thompson, Stancer, Roy, & Persad, 1983; Lieberman & Strauss, 1984). The data indicate that the stressors are equal in both groups (Bidzinska, 1984; Perris, 1982). It is likely, however, that manics suffer more deeply from stress because of their stronger genetic predisposition.

Mania constitutes about one quarter of all affective disorders (Krauthammer & Klerman, 1979). Rarely, it may occur with no alternation between periods of mania and depression (Krauthammer & Klerman, 1979; Mendlewicz, 1979; Nurnberger, Roose, Dunner, & Fieve, 1979), but even then it is still regarded, theoretically, as a bipolar disorder (Coleman et al., 1984; Krauthammer & Klerman, 1979).

Psychological Function of Mania

In psychoanalysis, all manic reactions are considered denials of depression. Manic symptoms are said to be determined by the unconscious forces established in childhood (particularly during the oral stage), and their appearance in later life reflects the failure of the mechanism of repression (Ginsberg, 1979). The research literature generally accepts the essence of the psychoanalytic theory that mania is mechanism for coping with depression. Coleman et al. (1984) describe the objective of the manic reaction as follows:

> In the case of mania, individuals try to escape their difficulties by a flight into reality. In a less severe form, this type of reaction to stress is shown by the person who goes on a round of parties to try to forget a broken love affair, or tries to escape from a threatening life situation by restless activity, occupying every moment with work, athletics, sexual affairs, and countless other crowded activities—all performed with professional gusto but with little true enjoyment.
>
> In mania this pattern is exaggerated. With a tremendous expenditure of energy, the manic individual tries to deny feelings of helplessness and hopelessness and to play a role of competence. Once this mode of coping with difficulties is adopted, it is maintained until it has spent itself in emotional exhaustion, for the only other alternative is an admission of defeat and inevitable depression. (p. 320)

Psychobizarreness theory agrees with the basic thesis of psychoanalysis, though it rejects the suggestions relating mania with the oral stage and unconscious forces. We also dispute the claim that mania results from a failure of repression. It is unnecessary to say that as in other areas, psychoanalysis has little or no evidence to support its claims. Although the subject's personality profile, shaped in part during childhood, may effect the development of depression, and hence mania, it is recent stresses that precipitate the outbreak of the disorder among patients, not the supposedly unconscious stored traumatic experiences of the "oral stage."

Contrary to psychoanalytic theory, we see mania not as a failure of repression, but as the means of achieving repression. It serves to ward off stress-related thoughts from the domain of the consciousness by inundating the attentional system with erdless activities and antidepressive cognitions of happiness and control. The rival depressive thoughts have no chance of infiltrating. Mania can be compared to fugue, as in both cases the subjects remove themselves from stressful environments. The fugue flees physically, while the manic escapes into a world of imagination.

Like nonparanoid schizophrenics and catatonics, manics exploit the extreme distraction provided by their bizarre coping strategy to preclude the need for a special self-deceptive mechanism. Their coping strategy combines intense concentration with a deliberate disturbance of the conscious functioning. (The strategy is similar to but less extreme than that of catatonics.) So totally are they involved with their highly distractive bizarre responses and thoughts that anxiety-arousing questions regarding their departure from reality have no opportunity to penetrate through to the focus of attention. Even if the "invaders" were to manage to reach the heavily blockaded attentional system, they would have little chance of remaining there for more than a fleeting moment, since the attention is rapidly diverted to unstressful stimuli. This is consistent with observations that distractibility and rapid shifts from topic to topic are among the prominent characteristics of manic subjects (Davison & Neale, 1982; Tyrer & Shopsin, 1982).

Apparently, these manipulations of the attention are not always sufficient to ward off depressive thoughts and ensure self-deception, so that the manic requires another disruptive mechanism, namely, thought disorder. Manics may, therefore, disturb the normal functioning of their consciousness: "Though processes are speeded up to a point where the individual can no longer process incoming information with any degree of efficiency. In a manner of speaking, 'the programmer loses control of the computer' " (Coleman et al., 1984, p. 321). Indeed, various investigators have realized that manic subjects display thought disorders similar to those of nonparanoid schizophrenics (Andreasen, 1979a, 1979b; Andreasen & Powers, 1974; Harrow & Quinlan, 1977; Marengo & Harrow, 1985; Sengel, Lovallo, Pishkin, Leber, & Shaffer, 1984; Tyrer & Shopsin, 1982). Andreasen (1979b) states that tangentiality, derailment, incoherence, and illogicality occur with nearly equal frequency in both mania and schizophrenia. The author, however, indicates that in mania, thought disorder is reversible and appears to be secondary to depression. Sengel et al. (1984) found that paranoid schizophrenics, nonparanoid schizophrenics, and manics did not differ on a measure of severity of psychopathology. Rather, the three manifested equivalent levels of cognitive impairment. Similarly, Marengo and Harrow (1985) reported that thought disorder was significantly more frequent in schizophrenia and mania than in other psychotic disorders.

Thus, there seems to be considerable similarity between the coping strategies of manic and nonparanoid schizophrenic patients. According to evidence reviewed by Tyrer and Shopsin (1982), schizophrenic symptoms were reported in 20%–50% of manic patients. Diagnostic confusion exists between the two disorders (Krauthammer & Klerman, 1979; Pope & Lipinski, 1978). The confusion is also reflected in the classification shift between the second and the third editions of the Diagnostic and Statistical Manual (*DSM II* and *DSM III*) of the American Psychiatric Association. Winters, Weintraub, and Neale (1981) found in a survey that 51% of patients considered schizophrenics under *DSM II* were excluded from this category by *DSM III* and reallocated to affective disorders. Such drastic diagnostic inconsistency shows that accurate diagnosis cannot be made on the basis of symptomatology alone (Tyrer & Shopsin, 1982). Premorbid personality, attentional skills, and the type of stress encountered (state or personal) must be taken into account as well. Consideration should be given to the question of whether all mania should be categorized as an affective disorder or whether extreme cases should be included under the umbrella term schizophrenia.

Causes of the Bipolar Shift

The combination of intense concentration and active disruption of the thought processes seems to mould quite an efficient coping mechanism. However, only a small portion of manic patients (15.7–28%; see Nurnberger et al., 1979) display manic behavior continuously. The majority alternate between mania and depression. Why, then, do these patients use the manic coping style only intermittently? Four factors seem to be involved.

First, the manic expends a tremendous amount of physical and mental energy in sustaining moods of exhilaration and happiness. No special effort is required for nonparanoid schizophrenics to maintain their pathological coping mechanism, which is simply an expansion of a genetically based cognitive impairment and premorbid deviant behavior. Inattention burns up no resources. In contrast, the intensive concentration required for the manic coping style is very taxing. During the manic stage, the individual is thus both mentally and physically exhausted.

Second, any change in stimulus arouses the attention. Continuous utilization of manic (or catatonic) coping styles may gradually diminish their distractive efficiency, while an alternation cycle may enhance it.

Third, the adoption of manic behavior is anathema to reality-oriented individuals. It is more difficult for them than for nonparanoid schizophrenics or paranoid subjects to accept self-deception. Nonparanoid schizophrenics slip into bizarre behavior with relatively little discomfort. Their initial reality testing is low. They are willing to renounce rationalism for prolonged periods, or even permanently, as they know from experience of their inability to adjust rationally to life. Moreover, no sharp contrast exists between their premorbid and schizophrenic way of life. Paranoid patients can sustain their coping style with ease since they have succeeded in developing a powerful bizarre belief in persecution. Whenever the attention is penetrated by stressful input, this readily available "cognitive tool" can at once be called upon to push out the weaker rival cognitions, at the cost of little attentional effort. Furthermore, as paranoid subjects display no gross departure from reality, they have no urgent need to discard the bizarre coping style.

In contrast, manics have neither the comforts of nonparanoid schizophrenics nor the cognitive tool of paranoid subjects. Manics are reluctant to live with self-deception. They are strongly reality oriented and strongly object to a long-term renunciation of their rationalism. However, under the compelling circumstances in which they are trapped, they are willing to endure periodic or temporary irrationalism instead of committing suicide or facing their stress.

They are also accustomed to a better style of life and are shy of the disgrace that accompanies manic behavior. Manics tend to come from the higher social strata and have good premorbid social bonds, at least in comparison with nonparanoid schizophrenics. So they may be embarrassed to continue "crazy" behavior beyond their immediate, urgent needs.

Unlike paranoids, they must be continually on guard (concentration) against infiltrators into the domain of attention. This effort, when prolonged, tires the concentration. When the attention is too fatigued to maintain its guard, it can be swamped with unwanted thoughts, which may trigger the depressive stage. In turn, the depression gradually also becomes intolerable, compelling the subject again to reenter the manic mode. The higher tendency to suicide found among manics than among unipolar depressives (Coleman et al., 1984; Goldring & Fieve, 1984) may be explained by their swinging miserably from one unhappy behavioral option to another.

Fourth, the shifting process may be influenced by neurochemical changes as well. Research findings by Bunney and his colleagues (Bunney, Goodwin, & Murphy, 1972; Bunney, Murphy, Goodwin, & Borge, 1972) indicate that the shift from depression to mania is associated with a marked increase in biogenic amines on the day of the switch. They also showed that the L-dopa drug, which causes a rise in the level of dopamine in the brain, may induce mania in manic–depressive patients (Prange, Wilson, Lynn, Alltop, & Strikeleather, 1974; Zis & Goodwin, 1982). To the best of our knowledge, there is no evidence showing that chemical substances alone can induce the bizarre symptoms of mania in normal individuals. We believe that the physiological changes at the shifting stage produce appropriate conditions for the conscious to adopt manic behavior.

A depressed person undergoes adverse neurochemical changes that are induced by stress (Anisman & Lapierre, 1982) and that may be more intense among subjects with a genetic predisposition to depression. Biological defense mechanisms are then activated to alleviate either the biological imbalance or emotional distress, by secreting substances that improve the mood. Subjects in prolonged deep depression may be particularly sensitive to any positive changes in their psychological system. Some may take advantage of an improvement in mood and deliberately exaggerate it into a bizarre false happiness in a desperate attempt to shake off the depressing cognitions that dominate their mind. However, the activity of the biochemical defense mechanism may be weak and short-lived, and the state of mania will not be sustained. Gradually the substances aggravating depression reaccumulate, and once more depression sets in. The subject must wait for the next round of mood-improving biological substances before readopting mania. Deprived of these substances, he or she is too dejected to put on a show of happiness (mania). Thus, while psychobizarreness theory acknowledges a facilitating role for neurochemical changes, it denies that they alone, with no active intervention of the consciousness, are sufficient to cause the manic bizarre symptoms. Such evidence does not exist, and we believe it will never be found.

It should be noted that the biochemical research of affective disorders is characterized by many inconsistencies (Perris, 1982; Zis & Goodwin, 1982). A proper understanding of the relationship between neurochemical changes and the coping style of depressive individuals requires additional research that must clarify the precise roles of the severity of stress, personality makeup, and genetic predisposition in the onset of the disease.

SEX DIFFERENCES IN DEPRESSION

Women are significantly more susceptible to depression than are men. Evidence shows that the incidence of unipolar depression is two to three times higher among women (Goldring & Fieve, 1984; Krauthammer & Klerman, 1982). The existence of sex differences in bipolar depression is less clear-cut. While some authors (Goldring & Fieve, 1984; Krauthammer & Klerman, 1979; Pope & Lipinski, 1978) report that the ratio of women to men in bipolar depression is still high, though not as high as in unipolar depression, others (Perris, 1982) argue that the ratio is almost equal.

The exact reasons for sex differences in depression are still elusive (Coleman et al., 1984). The possibility that women are under more stress or perceive events as more stressful has been considered and rejected (Weissman & Klerman, 1977). A genetic or some other biological predisposition might be important; while this possibility cannot be ruled out, there is insufficient evidence to justify its acceptance (Weissman & Klerman, 1977). Neither could the sex differences be attributed to the psychosocial variables of marital status, the roles of women as housewives or in other occupations, or their level of education (Amenson & Lewinsohn, 1981; Radloff, 1975; Radloff & Rae, 1979).

The psychological explanations that are most often used to account for these differences are social status and learned helplessness (Radloff, 1975; Radloff & Rae, 1979; Weissman & Klerman, 1977). According to the social status explanation, social regulations place women in an inferior position, preventing them from obtaining the same rewards as men and making it harder for them to achieve control over rewards and punishments. The learned helplessness hypothesis claims that the socialization process encourages women to develop dependency or cognitive set against self-assertiveness and to limit their opportunities to acquire a large repertoire of coping strategies for getting on in the world.

Not only do these explanations lack solid empirical data, but it is also difficult to see how they could account for the other psychiatric sex differences, such as the greater frequency of hysteria and bizarre fears among women and the greater frequency of coronary heart disease, suicide, drug abuse (Goldring & Fieve, 1984; Waldron, 1976,

1978; Weissman & Klerman, 1977), and paranoia among men. We are skeptical as to whether the simple notion of learned helplessness, particularly when it is combined with the traditional mechanistic-automatic theories, can explain why a woman sometimes becomes depressed and sometimes hysterical or agoraphobic. Of course, one can preserve this notion for depression and look for other explanations for the remaining sex differences. However, in the absence of scientific data proving the applicability of learned helplessness or other valid theories to this area, a parsimonious explanation, which can encompass all the abovementioned differences, is surely preferable to a ragbag of disconnected reasons.

Another point of view is expressed in a recent theoretical article entitled "Depression vs. Paranoia: Why Are There Sex Differences in Mental Illness?" by H. B. Lewis (1985). Assuming that mental illness arises out of failure in sociability, and based on some data suggesting that women are more sociable and field dependent, H. B. Lewis claimed that the two sexes develop different superego styles, which cause them to react differently to loss of love. Women have a predisposition to respond with shame and depression and men with aggression and guilt, and "the way is thus paved for the development of paranoia and schizophrenia" (p. 174).

However, it is doubtful whether H. B. Lewis's suggestions can provide an adequate answer to her question. First, like previous approaches, H. B. Lewis fails to refer to the remaining sex differences mentioned previously, and it is hard to see how her ideas can be applied to these differences. Second, the sex differences in schizophrenia exist only with regard to paranoid responses but not with respect to nonparanoid types (Strauss & Carpenter, 1981). Thus, H. B. Lewis must explain why inferiority in sociability causes greater prevalence of paranoid than of nonparanoid reactions among men. Third, as mentioned in this chapter, in view of the strong association between paranoia and depression, there is an increasing awareness among various investigators, such as Zigler and Glick (1984), that these two behavioral disorders have the same etiological background. This theoretical point of view can hardly be accommodated in H. B. Lewis's theoretical framework, which makes a sharp distinction between depression and paranoia. Fourth, it is questionable whether there is enough justification for H. B. Lewis's basic assumptions that women are genetically more sociable and particularly for the idea that mental illnesses stem from failure in sociability.

Usually, psychosocial explanations of sex differences in depression are based on the idea that women are socially discriminated against and disadvantaged. However, although there is no doubt a kernel of truth in this claim, namely, that women have a less favorable position in society than do men, for our case it is far more important to acknowledge that women also enjoy some privileges regarding the manner in which they are allowed to respond to stress. The social training and social expectations of men demand that they face up to and attempt to cope with stress. More allowances are made for women in stressful situations, and escape responses by them are more acceptable. Generally speaking, weaknesses are tolerated more among women than men. For example, although life-endangering illness is more prevalent among men, women use the medical system more frequently and working women are more often absent from work for medical reasons than are working men (Weissman & Klerman, 1977). Work is highly important for the psychological health of an individual (Coleman et al., 1984, pp. 157–159), and this seems to be much more vital for men. Thus, for men, cowardice, displays of weakness, or the adoption of pathological measures aimed at removing themselves from stressful situations may involve a higher cost in terms both of damage to self-esteem and of the social embarrassment of unemployment. In our opinion, this accounts for the relative scarcity of hysteria and agoraphobia among men, as they would entail public weakness, cowardice, and reduced work ability.

Since the cost of adopting bizarre neurotic symptoms for coping purposes seem to be much higher for men, it is to be expected that rather than choosing an escape option, they will remain in the stress situation and attempt to cope. While this gives men better chances of overcoming the stress, it also exposes them to stress for longer periods. Further, some may fail in their coping struggle and remain trapped in the stressful situation. As a result, the risk that the biological system would be damaged is increased to a significant extent. Individuals can certainly refrain from adopting operant responses such as bizarre symptoms, but they would have little control over the arousal of their autonomic nervous system. They can hardly avoid an elevation in heartbeat or blood pressure when their attention is occupied by stress. Therefore, the risk of hypertension and coronary heart disease, in which the component of stress plays a vital role (see studies reviewed by Rofé & Goldberg, 1983; Woolfolk & Lehrer, 1984), and consequently, the mortality rate as well, are expected to be higher for men, as some evidence indeed indicates (Waldron, 1976, 1978; Weissman & Klerman, 1977). Furthermore, because of their difficulties in using pathological coping mechanisms, men may be forced to choose the option of suicide, which is three times higher among them than among women (Coleman et al., 1984) or to adopt more "masculine" coping strategies, such as alcoholism and drug abuse, which are far more common among men than among women (e.g., Goldring & Fieve, 1984; Weissman & Klerman, 1977).

These considerations may of course account for the higher frequency of depression among women as well. Social pressure on men to cope will increase the likelihood of their success, and hence, a smaller percentage of men will develop depression. Moreover, as indicated previously (Weissman & Klerman, 1977), men develop a better repertoire of coping strategies, due mainly to their superior social training, so that even without this pressure, they would in any case have a better chance of overcoming the stress. Furthermore, in cases of depression, they are likely to conceal or deny the existence of these feelings. This conjecture is consistent with research findings reported by Hammen and Peters (1977, 1978), that depressed males elicited greater social rejection than depressed females. The authors inferred from these findings that males tend to judge their own depressive responses more negatively than do females and that social rejection of depressed males follows from the incompatibility of masculinity with helplessness, hopelessness, self-deprecation, and passivity. Hammen and Peters (1978) also found that significantly more feminine traits were attributed to depressed than nondepressed people. They noted that

> depressive behaviors on the part of men may frequently result in rejection and negative evaluation by others, and that men, therefore, learn to express their psychological distress in alternative ways. The consequences of expression of depression may be more benign for women. If this hypothesis is correct, it may partially account for the findings of epidemiological studies, which consistently report higher rates of depression among women than among men. (Hammen & Peters, 1978, p. 332)

The sex differences in affective disorder decrease with the severity of the depression. For example, while in "neurotic" depressions the women : men ratio can rise to as much as 4 : 1 or 5 : 1, in major depression it is generally around 2 : 1, and in bipolar depression it can fall even lower (see studies reviewed by Krauthammer & Klerman, 1979). Some investigators (Perris, 1982) even claim that the women : men ratio reaches parity. It seems that in psychotic depression, the dichotomy is smaller mainly because in severe stress, both men and women encounter insuperable difficulty in coping.

Deep depression thus becomes inevitable, and the gravity of the depression renders concealment impracticable. Both the sexes will have a dire need for bizarre symptoms. A high proportion of men, though, will prefer to commit suicide or become drug addicts, which explains the 2 : 1 ratio in bipolar affective disorders.

CONCLUSIONS

As we have shown, the research evidence suggests that stressful life events are a prerequisite for the outbreak of depression. We have also argued that depression, unlike bizarre symptoms, is a spontaneous reaction to stress, experienced by animals as well as humans, rather than being consciously chosen symptoms, as is the case with bizarre behavior. However, in the vast majority of cases, stress does not automatically cause depression (Taylor, 1983). Depression will follow only when stress exceeds the subject's coping ability and the subject is willing neither to delude himself or herself with false hopes nor to adopt bizarre symptoms. In this respect, the subject's personality, genetic predispositions, and social support are highly important in determining whether depression will ensue and how serious it will be.

Recent evidence, showing that depressives are reality oriented and that the depth of depression corresponds with the level of stress, calls into question the accepted conceptualization of depression as stemming from an illogical and inaccurate distortion of reality.

Throughout this book we have consistently resisted using the term illness when referring to neurotic or psychotic behavioral deviation. If this term does have any value whatsoever in psychopathology, then it is best used, albeit with certain reservations, to describe depression. Illness may be a useful description of depression because massive neurochemical changes and biological deterioration, caused by stress and by refraining from eating and sleeping, play an important role in the development of depression and give the disorder some semblance of an illness. Yet, even here it is the cognitive factors that are decisive. In fact, according to psychobizarreness theory, depression is relieved after depressive thoughts have been eliminated from the attentional domain by the adoption of bizarre symptoms.

Once again, psychobizarreness theory has proven its greater explanatory powers over rival theories. As in other areas of abnormal psychology, psychoanalysis cannot explain the choice of symptoms in affective disorders, that is, the distribution of paranoia and mania. Though the medical model's conception of depression may have some validity, the same cannot be said with regard to its conception of the bizarre symptoms of paranoia and mania. For example, neither psychoanalysis nor the medical models have an explanation for the sex differences or for the disproportionate number of higher class subjects among affective disorder patients. These psychiatric variations can very well be explained by the psychobizarreness theory's cost–benefit principle.

In conclusion, psychopathology today faces a serious theoretical crisis not only with respect to understanding the processes by which pathological behaviors are produced, but also with respect to the ways in which these responses are eliminated. With regard to the first issue, we believe that our theoretical proposals provide a valid solution to this problem. However, the second issue is no less complicated than the first. What psychopathology urgently needs is not the amelioration of the techniques that would facilitate the therapy, although this is no doubt an important goal in itself, but rather a unified theory that can explain why different methods of intervention, which stem from such different theoretical backgrounds, may be effective. Why can behavior therapy, psychoanalysis, family therapy, a witch doctor, friends, and sometimes no intervention at all bring about successful therapeutic outcomes? We believe that psychobizarreness theory adequately synthesizes all these seemingly incompatible variations into one theoretical framework. Originally, we decided to disregard this issue since the massive amount of material it covers warrants a book in its own right. Nevertheless, we present the application of psychobizarreness theory to therapy in brief and general terms in the following chapter with the hope that it will facilitate our better understanding of psychotherapy processes.

VI

TOWARD A UNIFIED THEORY IN PSYCHOTHERAPY

18

Therapeutic Principles of Psychobizarreness Theory

INTRODUCTION

In view of the failure of research efforts to find empirical support for traditional theories in psychopathology, it is little wonder that theoretical confusion characterizes the area of psychotherapy as well. Garfield (1981), in appraising selected issues and developments in the field of psychotherapy over the preceding 40 years, noted that "the issue of effectiveness of psychotherapy has been questioned, debated, reformulated, defended, and still not conclusively settled. In spite of research studies and reviews supposedly showing that psychotherapy is more effective than no therapy, questions and criticisms remain" (p. 181).

So great is the confusion in this field that despite the bitter theoretical disagreements between the various approaches, many investigators (Giles, 1983a, 1983b) seem to remain convinced that "all roads lead to Rome" (Garfield, 1976; see also Garfield, 1987). In other words, all the major psychological therapies are seen as yielding equivalent results. This conviction led investigators such as Strupp (1978) to argue that all psychotherapies are theoretically misguided, that is, there are common mechanisms by which all therapies work, but their exact nature still remains unclear.

As far as psychoanalytic therapy is concerned, serious doubts regarding the validity of the premises of this approach have been raised even by its own advocates. For example, Grusky (1987) indicated that "one cannot help but wonder how much in this field is theory and technique, how much is personal charisma, art, religious conviction, or science" (p. 2). Moreover, behaviorist-oriented investigators (Erwin, 1980; Rachman & Wilson, 1980) tend to devalue the efficiency of psychoanalytic therapy. Giles (1983b) asserts that the data indicating the superiority of nonbehavioral approaches over placebo effect are scanty for the great majority of disorders. Referring to data supporting behaviorist techniques, Giles (1983b) stated: "I am unaware of any evidence that equally beneficial results are obtained solely by providing clients with a warm, accepting and empathetic therapeutic relationship; by encouraging them to scream away unconscious hostilities; by uncovering their erotic repressed impulses . . ." (p. 191).

However, despite this enthusiasm for behavioral techniques (see also Giles, 1983a, 1984), theoretically the behaviorists are in no less trouble than their psychoanalytic rivals. Leaving aside the limited efficiency of behavior therapy (Hafner, 1976, 1983; Hand & Lamontagne, 1976) and its sometimes total lack of success (Rachman & Seligman, 1976), it is doubtful whether their therapeutic success can be attributed to behaviorist learning principles. For example, if they cannot convincingly demonstrate that agoraphobia (see pp. 145–146) or obsessive–compulsive symptoms (Emmelkamp, 1982, 1987) are the result of conditioning processes, it would be implausible to attribute any therapeutic gains achieved by their techniques to those processes. How would they explain the fact that in agoraphobia, unlike normal fears (W. L. Marshall, 1985), not only prolonged but also brief exposure to the fear-arousing conditions (de Silva & Rachman, 1984; Emmelkamp, 1974) may cause significant improvement?

Our critique is directed not only against the traditional behavioral models but also toward cognitive behavioral approaches inasmuch as both paradigms share the same fundamental concepts and therapeutic procedures (Beidel & Turner, 1986; Latimer & Sweet, 1984). Cognitive theorists claim that patients with emotional disorders possess, prior to their breakdown, deviant cognitive processes, the etiology of which is not defined, which are intensified at time of stress and thereby automatically cause the maladaptive behavior. They also believe that their therapeutic procedures are superior to those of the traditional behavioral approaches. However, Beidel and Turner (1986) show, in their critical review article, that the cumulative research data do not support either of these claims. The authors note that cognitive behavior therapists have argued that the validity of their approach has to be

> *evaluated not at the level of procedure, but on the basis of theory and conceptualization of psychopathology. It is on this very basis, however, that the evidence against their case is most damaging. At this time, we must conclude that this new approach to therapy is without a theoretical base. (p. 194)*

Thus, what we most need in the field of psychopathology is a new theoretical base that would explain the behavioral improvements that occur inside and outside the clinical room. Such a new theoretical base would facilitate our understanding of the psychotherapy processes and would perhaps contribute to improvement of therapeutic intervention as well. We believe that our theoretical approach in psychopathology can be of great help in this matter. In this part of the book we will delineate, in very general terms, the theoretical implications of the psychobizarreness theory for therapy.

The first important implication is that we ought to distinguish between normal and bizarre symptoms. We think that symptoms that have clear environmental boundaries— that is, those that are strictly associated with specific environmental stimuli and that therefore do not impose any special burden on the subject's attentional resources (such as fear of heights [acrophobia], fear of confinement [claustrophobia], and fear of animals [zoophobia]), what are called *simple phobias* (McGlynn & Cornell, 1985)— were acquired through behaviorist learning principles. Accordingly, we suggest that behavioral techniques should be employed for undoing the faulty acquired stimulus– response (S–R) bonding. Moreover, we argue further that therapeutic gains in these cases that have been obtained by the employment of other therapeutic methods should be attributed to informal, implicit use of behavioral strategies. For example, in our discussion of the psychoanalytic treatment of fear of dogs by Moss (1960; see pp. 138– 140 in this book), we have demonstrated that in fact it would make more sense if extinguishment of the patient's fear were attributed to an informal application of desensitization procedures rather than to psychoanalytic therapeutic tools. We do not intend to go into detail in discussing the way normal behavioral symptoms should be treated. The conventional behavioral techniques seem perfectly suitable. As was elaborated previously (pp. 172–174), the best strategic intervention in treating normal fears seems to be a combination of prolonged exposure, as the main tool, together with some efforts directed at changing the subject's belief system. A more detailed discussion of various behavioristic techniques available for treating simple fears is found in McGlynn and Cornell (1985).

The second implication of our theoretical approach, to which we now direct our interest, concerns the treatment of bizarre symptoms, that is, behavioral deviations that are not tied to specific environmental stimuli, that seriously disturb the subject's ongoing behavior, and that impose a heavy burden on his or her attentional system (see the four criteria discussed earlier, pp. 89–91). The problem with these symptoms is not so much the lack of adequate techniques for inducing desirable therapeutic outcomes, but rather the inadequacy of the theoretical bases for explaining these changes. Behavioral techniques and to some extent psychoanalytic intervention as well, are sometimes efficient in causing significant improvement in the behavioral functioning of neurotic and psychotic patients. However, this by no means confirms the validity of these theories. These changes can be viewed as specific cases of the psychobizarreness therapeutic program, to which we now turn attention. We divide our discussion into neuroses and psychoses.

NEUROSES

Overview

As was specified earlier, bizarre symptoms have two main functions: controllability and distractibility. In line with this, we maintain that the treatment of neurotic symptoms can be approached by one of two alternative therapeutic methods and sometimes by a combination of the two. One approach, which is characteristic of the behavior therapy paradigm, concentrates its efforts on counteracting the controllability value of the symptoms. The other, which is typical of psychodynamic approaches, sees as its main therapeutic task the counteracting of the symptoms' distractive component. The former approach uses three therapeutic strategies, either separate or in combination, to obtain therapeutic success:

1. Punishment or extinguishing procedures, by which patients are forced to abandon their faulty coping responses. They may then realize that they can endure the stress or overcome it after more careful examination of their repertoire of coping skills. If, however, such capacities are missing, patients may have no alternative but to adopt similar symptoms or even more deviant behavior.
2. Skill training techniques aimed at improving the patients' ability to handle the stress.
3. Direct actions to eliminate the noxious environmental elements and thereby eliminate the factors maintaining the symptoms.

Notice that in all these behavioristic procedures the insight issue is completely ignored.

In contrast, the second therapeutic strategy confronts patients with the underlying stress-bearing causes of their behavior. By creating a comfortable, supporting, and encouraging psychological atmosphere, an attempt is made to motivate patients to select more adaptive coping responses. Thus, the bitter controversy between behaviorist and psychodynamic therapeutic doctrines may be due largely to the exclusive focus of each on one aspect of neurotic symptoms. At this juncture, we discuss in greater detail these two therapeutic methods as well as their combination from the psychobizarreness perspective.

Counteracting the Controllability Function of a Symptom

Decreasing the Benefit or Increasing the Cost of the Symptoms

We have already mentioned that treatment of combat stress disorder is much more effective when performed in close proximity to the combat zone than when the soldier is evacuated and treated behind the lines (Z. Solomon & Benbenishty, 1986). Other data show that extinction procedures by which the reinforcement dimension (i.e., controllability value) of the symptom is removed (i.e., extinguished) or that techniques by which the display of the symptom is accompanied by punishment, such as when aversive training is employed, can sometimes facilitate the treatment of neuroses, such as hysteria (Blanchard & Hersen, 1976) and obsessive–compulsive disorders (Brooker, 1982; Emmelkamp, 1987).

The behaviorists used these successful therapeutic findings to strengthen their automatic and mechanistic conceptualization. However, it may be argued that these procedures are sometimes effective simply because they force patients to abandon their disruptive coping mechanisms and reevaluate whether they can manage without them. Sometimes they may realize that the stress no longer exists or that they have the ability to endure or cope with it in a more adaptive way. For example, a soldier may find it less costly to escape from the combat zone by exhibiting maladaptive behavior such as hysteria than by remaining emotionally aroused. It is also possible that a particularly dreadful combat stress spontaneously arouses a strong emotional reaction that can be eliminated only with a minimal intervention. A quick evacuation of the soldier to a position behind the lines may give him the idea that he ought not easily give up his posed or spontaneous behavioral deviation. However, if the escaping attempts are blocked and the soldier is compelled to reconfront the stressful situation, with or without minimal therapeutic assistance (i.e., encouragement, a little rest, short desensitization training), most subjects will find that they can endure or cope with the stress effectively.

The behavioristic procedures to counteract the controllability value of the symptoms (e.g., by extinction and aversive training) might not be helpful if the patient really had no better coping devices available. In this case, the patient may either desert the therapy, continue maintaining the symptoms (Rachman & Seligman, 1976), show evidence of relapse, or replace the symptom (which meanwhile has become aversive due to its association with the repellent manipulation) by new symptoms, that is, the patient displays symptom substitution (Cahoon, 1968; Kazdin, 1982). Blanchard and Hersen (1976), for example, presented a number of clinical cases of hysteria showing that extinction procedures were not sufficient for producing successful outcomes and that symptom substitution did, in fact, occur.

Sometimes the current pathological response is the best coping device a subject has, and punishment techniques that compel him or her to desert the response may only aggravate the patient's condition. For example, Thorpe and his associates (Thorpe, Schmidt, Brown, & Castell, 1964) employed the electric shock technique (in their terms, "aversive-relief therapy") in their research. Although this technique was useful in treating several cases of sexual deviation, this was not so with two cases of obsessive–compulsive disorder. The "therapy" succeeded in reducing the obsessive–compulsive symptoms, but the patients became anxious and depressed, and they refused to continue therapy. Moreover, they were later diagnosed as hysterical. Thorpe et al. (1964) attributed their failure to the patients' inability to continue the therapy. In our opinion, however, this occurred because the patients lacked healthier devices for coping with their problems. Another study demonstrating our claim that punishment techniques may sometimes aggravate the subject's condition was reported by Kenny, L. Solyom, and C. Solyom (1973). Of five obsessive–compulsive patients who were subjected to aversive therapy, three greatly improved, one moderately improved (although she subsequently developed nightmares about catastrophic situations), and one developed psychotic delusions after her obsessions were removed. Kenny et at. (1973) noted: "it seems that, as therapy progresses, the faradic disruption technique increases anxiety and may even 'push' some susceptible patients into psychosis" (p. 455). Thus, in adopting behavioristic punishment techniques, one must carefully assess whether patients have the resources to cope with their problems if their present deviant coping devices are denied them.

Removal of the Stress

Another way to counteract the controllability value of neurotic symptoms is to eliminate the underlying causes of these symptoms (i.e., remove the stress). This may occur naturally or with direct therapeutic intervention. As was stated previously, two thirds of neurotic patients display spontaneous remission within two years of the time the symptoms were originally developed. Rachman (1985b) noted that in view of these data, "it is essential that the claims made on behalf of any form of treatment should be evaluated against the naturally occurring remission rate" (p. 30). In their explanation of these data, Rachman and Wilson (1980) indicated that discussing one's problems with a relative, friend, priest, etc., or positive events such as promotions, financial windfalls, or successful love affairs may not be regarded as forms of psychological treatment. However, "there is little doubt that such acts and events are potentially therapeutic and may contribute largely to the process of spontaneous remission" (p. 27). A case study relevant to our discussion, reported by Wolpe (1982), is that of a woman who chronically suffered from agoraphobia due to poor marital relations. Her symptoms spontaneously disappeared when she went to live with a man with whom she had fallen in love. However, the symptoms reappeared in full force after she returned to her husband.

Sometimes active intervention may be needed to eliminate the stress or facilitate its reduction. For example, Wolpe (1982) directed his therapeutic efforts at enabling the patient to make a break from her husband, after realizing there was no chance to make her marital relationship more satisfactory. This strategy, combined with self-assertion training and attempts to desensitize her in other areas of unadaptive anxiety, proved effective as the patient became completely free of her symptoms. Often the family is the prime source of the patient's stressful condition such that therapeutic investment in improving the family interaction may eliminate the forces motivating the patient to maintain the symptoms. It is beyond the scope of this book to review the evidence demonstrating the efficiency of family therapy approaches. However, it may be worthwhile mentioning that increasing data indicate that in many cases, it is not enough to focus the entire therapeutic effort on the patient himself or herself, as psychoanalysis and behavioral approaches had traditionally recommended, and that the involvement of family members may sometimes be essential (Bland & Hallam, 1981; Hand & Lamontagne, 1976; Milton & Hafner, 1979).

Coping Skill Enhancement

The need to maintain the symptoms can also be removed by sufficiently enhancing the subject's coping skills. Indeed, Mahoney (1977) views the therapist "as a technical consultant or coach whose assistance will primarily take the form of instruction and training in the development of relevant coping skills" (p. 353). This approach was also taken by Lazarus (1966) and Meichenbaum and Cameron (1982). In the same way, Blanchard and Hersen (1976) noted, in reference to the number of hysterical cases they treated behaviorally, using extinction procedures, that symptom substitution was likely when subjects encountered stressful new situations:

> It would appear that because of a faulty learning history this type of patient has not developed the requisite social skills needed to cope with both the usual and more unusual stresses encountered in life. Therefore, training or retraining in social skills becomes a needed ingredient in a comprehensive therapeutic regime. (p. 127)

The importance of elaborating the subject's coping skills is demonstrated also in cases of obsessive neurosis. Obsessive–compulsive patients usually suffer from an inability to handle their aggressive drives (D. G. Miller, 1983). Accordingly, Emmel-kamp and Van der Heyden (1980) reported that assertiveness training was quite an effective procedure with patients whose major problems were obsessional ruminations concerning harming others or themselves. In four of six cases, a considerable decrease in the frequency of obsessions was obtained. In contrast, in only two control cases who were given thought-stopping training was such a decrease found. With other patients, thought stopping even led to an increase in the number of obsessions.

Improvement of skills to cope with the sources of the stress responsible for a subjects's bizarre symptoms can be induced indirectly through desensitization or relaxation procedures. These were employed with limited success in treating nonspecific phobias such as agoraphobia (Chambless, 1985a) and generalized anxiety (Woolfolk & Lehrer, 1985). Although the effectiveness of these techniques cannot be denied, increasing numbers of researchers have shifted away from the traditional Hullian explanation emphasizing the role of classical conditioning in both acquisition and extinction of maladaptive responses (Sweet, Giles, & Young, 1987). Freudian-oriented investigations (Gordon & Zax, 1981; H. B. Lewis, 1981; Wachtel, 1977; Weitzman, 1967) now attempt to integrate the effectiveness of desensitization procedures within their psychodynamic paradigm. Yet another possible interpretation, and in our view a more valid one, is that desensitization and relaxation training enhance the subject's general ability to cope with the stressful stimuli that initiate and maintain the symptoms. As noted earlier, if Leonard's agoraphobic symptoms had been treated via desensitization or relaxation training, not only would these procedures have helped him deal with the environmental stimuli, which according to the behaviorists aroused his fear, but they might also have allowed him to tolerate the feelings of self-blame that resulted from his wife's suicide as well as the stress caused by his being rejected by the community—two factors that were, in our opinion, the direct causes of the patient's symptoms.

A clinical case that, to some extent, demonstrates that behavioral treatment of anxiety enhances the patient's coping ability in general (rather than reconditioning him) is reported by Woolfolk and Lehrer (1985). The client, a 27-year-old woman, was treated behaviorally for generalized anxiety "tied to no identifiable circumstances or antecedents." First, intensive training in progressive muscle relaxation and desensitization was aimed at reducing her feelings of anxiety in public places; while not very effective in meeting this goal, the training enabled the patient to consciously tolerate some of the underlying causes of her anxiety. The client "began to open up," revealing that she suffered from severe social anxiety and that she was frustrated in many aspects of her marital relationship. The therapy was then refocused on "communication skills training," in which the husband began to be involved, in an attempt to enhance the patient's skills to deal with these problems. Second, the therapy helped the patient to also deal more effectively with stresses not directly addressed. For example, the patient was able to return to work as a teacher, which had been "very stressful" to her. In addition, "she found the students much easier to cope with as a result of her new found ability to assert herself" (p. 105). It should be noted, however, that although the therapy significantly improved the patient's ability to cope with her problems, she was not completely cured. Apparently, the behavioral training did not sufficiently handle the direct causes of the subject's symptoms.

Thus, it seems to be necessary to accept the behavioristic therapeutic framework to explain the limited utility of its techniques. Stress-based concepts, such as those affiliated with psychobizarreness, in contrast to concepts derived from S–R terminology, such as conditioning, appear to be more appropriate. In this light, we may need to consider replacing the term *behavior therapy* with the concept *stress-management techniques,* which is currently used by some investigators (Woolfolk & Lehrer, 1984, 1985).

True and False Insight

Counteracting the Distractibility Function of a Symptom (i.e., Lifting of Repression)

A basic psychoanalytic approach to therapy makes quite a bit of sense. On the one hand, we strongly object to the Freudian archaeological concept (Jacobsen & Steele, 1979) that the therapist's job is to brush away the dirt and debris surrounding the area of unconsciousness and to revive lost childhood memories. However, by the same token, we agree completely that it can be therapeutically useful to make subjects aware of the faulty coping mechanisms they employ and to encourage them to select more appropriate responses. Yet, we believe that only rarely is this a necessary condition for successful therapeutic outcomes.

We share the psychoanalytic assumption that insight therapy is a painful process. Patients must "lift" the deception, becoming aware that they themselves purposely adopted the bizarre symptoms, which means shedding their coping mechanisms and sharing with a stranger this information that they had hidden even from themselves. Therefore, it should be expected, as is argued in psychoanalysis, that patients will not rush to cooperate and that they will tend to desert the therapy unless the penetration into their private world is tactfully conducted and they become convinced that the "stranger" is trustworthy and capable of helping them. In some cases, patients may be so comfortable with the adopted symptom that they feel it to be useless to go through the painful process the therapist has prepared for them. This is why subjects' motivation to recover is so heavily emphasized in psychoanalysis as a precondition for effective therapeutic outcomes (R. W. White, 1964, pp. 61–68). Moreover, the deception may sometimes be so strong and successful that subjects have real difficulties in cooperating with the therapist, particularly when the symptom has been adopted for such a long time that the original circumstances have been forgotten.

All these considerations mean that the process of counteracting the distractibility function of the symptom must be performed skillfully and under special conditions, as advised by orthodox psychoanalysis. First and foremost, it is not advisable to begin the process until good rapport (i.e., emotional attachment and a confident relationship) has been established. Psychodynamic approaches have long argued that a good therapeutic relationship between client and therapist is a prerequisite for successful therapeutic outcomes, and indeed the cumulative research findings (Sweet, 1984) strongly support this claim. Even the behaviorists, who view therapy as a cold, mechanistic application of techniques tested previously on subhuman species, are now becoming increasingly aware of the crucial importance of this factor for therapeutic success. Evidence reviewed by Sweet shows that behaviorists deliver supportive communication that tends to reduce the distance between therapist and client. However, this literature also indicates that the patient–therapist relationship is less crucial in behavioral than in psychoanalytic therapy. It appears, then, that establishing friendly, relaxing relationships and a belief by the client that the therapist is a capable and trustworthy person are essential for easing the client's resistance to the lifting of his or her repression.

Second, all psychodynamic approaches share the belief that insight should be induced in a gradual manner, though they differ with regard to "optimal interpretive procedures" (Bandura, 1971b, p. 92). Thus, it is suggested this idea be followed and a psychodynamic interpretive procedure be adopted in order to lead clients to become aware of the deviant coping mechanisms they employ. The speed by which this goal is achieved should be left to the therapist's assessment, taking into consideration factors such as the quality of rapport and the strength of the patient's resistance and his or her overall coping ability.

Third, successful therapeutic outcomes also require that the patient be given encouragement during and (particularly) immediately after the lifting of repression. Moreover, the therapist must also be ready to push the patient toward certain preferable solutions or prepare him or her to make such a move. For example, if the patient was led to be aware that his or her bizarre symptoms were adopted in response to stressful marital interaction and if there is no hope for a satisfactory relationship, the therapist should help the patient to choose divorce and prepare him or her to make this successful. This was what Wolpe (1982), in the abovementioned case study, and Blanchard and Hersen (1976) did.

As stated, insight-oriented therapy is psychologically painful. Inasmuch as behavioral techniques can in most cases be sufficiently effective, it is suggested that the therapist refrain, as far as possible, from using insight therapy, restricting its use to more complicated cases. Even then, however, a multidimensional approach, which uses the advantages of the two therapeutic methods, should be preferred. This issue will be elaborated following a discussion of false insight in the next section.

False Insight or Positive Self-Deception

Despite the theoretical difficulties and therapeutic inferiority of the traditional psychodynamic approaches (Erwin, 1980; Giles, 1983b, 1984; Rachman & Wilson, 1980), the fact remains that some patients nevertheless do improve when these techniques are applied. Marmor (1962), in his critical discussion of the insight-oriented therapies, noted that patients not only display favorable change but they also strongly accept the

> insights which they have been given. Even admittedly "inexact" interpretations have been noted to be of therapeutic value! Moreover . . . patients of each school seem to bring up precisely the kind of phenomenological data which confirm the theories and interpretations of their analysis! (p. 289; see also Heine, 1953)

In reference to these data, Bandura (1971b) suggested that "interpretive activities might be more accurately represented as a direct social influence rather than as a process involving delicate levitation of repressed forces from the region of the client's unconscious mind" (p. 94). Bandura specified several factors as a result of which the patient might adopt the therapist's belief system. First, the kind of people who seek out and stick with psychotherapy are highly amenable to social influence. Second, the therapist is usually accorded high prestige and credibility. Third, the psychotherapeutic situation is quite ambiguous, and "clients have little objective basis for evaluating whether they possess Oedipus complexes, repressed hostilities . . . and other esoteric motivational forces" (p. 95). Studies of social compliance show that people can be more easily persuaded to accept someone else's opinion on subjective and unfamiliar topics than on objective and familiar matters. Fourth, distress generally facilitates persuasion, especially if solutions that are allegedly effective at stress reduction are also made available. Fifth, the same interpretations, directed toward clients' resistances against the prompted insight, are made over and over during a prolonged period of persuasive attempts.

Although we sympathize with Bandura's claims, it seems that he did not adequately clarify the problem of why traditional insight-oriented therapy is sometimes therapeutically effective. Bandura (1971b) explains these changes behaviorally in terms of reward, punishment, and observational learning, claiming they are unwittingly applied during insight therapy (p. 60). However, in view of the difficulties encountered by the behaviorists themselves, it is doubtful that these principles are sufficient to account for the therapeutic success of the insight therapist. Bandura raises the possibility that friendship experiences may play a role in this process. However, he tends to dismiss the importance of this factor, arguing that "few chronic stutterers, for example, have been cured through amity, introspective conversation, and wise counsel" (p. 59). However, Bandura, as other behaviorists, avoids seeing that the symptoms that usually bring a patient to the psychoanalyst's couch are totally different from symptoms such as stuttering. For example, very rarely, if at all, does stuttering make its first appearance in a sudden and dramatic form, as is usually the case with bizarre symptoms. Moreover, research data do indicate that friendship and social support have a vital therapeutic value and increase the individual's coping ability (Davidson & Packard, 1981; Eaton, 1978; Linn & McGranahan, 1980). Thus, in view of these findings, and the fact that psychoanalytic therapy is usually extended over a relatively prolonged period, it is quite possible that friendship experience did play some important role in producing successful outcomes, and this may also be applied to behaviorism, as Sweet's (1984) review article indicates.

However, friendship, in our opinion, is not the major factor, and certainly not the only one that can account for the positive effects of traditional insight approaches. Positive self-deception or false insight play a vital role in this process. We can demonstrate this claim by referring to two cases: one is the case of Leonard discussed earlier (pp. 108–110), and the other is the psychoanalytic treatment of a homosexual by Messer (1986).

As indicated previously, Leonard was suffering from agoraphobia. He attributed his symptoms to two frightening incidents that he claimed had taken place during his childhood. He reached this "insight," which facilitated his recovery, while he was under "autohypnosis." The insight therapeutic effect here can be attributed neither to friendship experience nor to reward punishment contingencies, which Bandura uses to account for the therapeutic effect of traditional psychodynamic therapy. One possible explanation is that Leonard could no longer bear the burden of his self-imposed restrictions, and he looked for an excuse to give up his symptoms. As indicated previously, Leonard must have been familiar with Freudian conceptualization and was also probably strongly convinced by it; if this were true, then for him this would be the best available formula for positive self-deception.

Thus, it can be imagined that during the formal psychoanalytic therapy, which typically extends over a prolonged period, some patients sometimes would feel uncomfortable in continuing to display their symptoms. Combined with other factors, such as the therapist's convincing efforts, demanding characteristics of the situation, money and time expended, and perhaps pressures from family members as well, subjects become psychologically prepared to abandon their symptoms. Although patients are capable of abandoning their symptoms spontaneously, many may feel cognitively uncomfortable (dissonance) doing so, particularly in cases where the family resists change (see p. 181).

Thus, psychoanalysis can be described as a pseudotherapy whose main benefits are to provide self-deception services, either negative, to assist the patient in maintaining his or her symptoms (see pp. 92–93 and 101), or positive, to enable him or her to get rid of them more easily. A positive self-deception service to relieve subjects' feelings of dissonance, when they feel prepared to desert their symptoms, may also of course be given by other therapeutic interventions, such as behavior therapy (see pp. 180–181). Moreover, sometimes the mere participation in therapy may be sufficient to secure positive outcomes. For example, in one of his early attempts to demonstrate the efficiency of hypnosis, Jung (1961/1965, pp. 118–120) informed a middle-aged woman patient suffering from paralysis of the left leg that he was going to hypnotize her. Without any hypnotic manipulation, the patient immediately fell into a deep trance and talked at length for a half hour, resisting Jung's attempts to awaken her. Soon afterward, she cried out that she was recovered, threw away her crutches, and was able to walk. To cover his embarrassment, before a group of 20 students to whom he planned to show the efficiency of hypnosis, Jung announced, "Now you've seen what can be done with hypnosis." In fact, he had not the slightest idea of what had happened. Similarly, the abrupt disappearance of symptoms has been described in the context of group therapy (Lewis, 1988).

Psychoanalysis apparently provides the best formulation for self-deception because of its claims that the symptom must be eradicated at its roots and that the "sign of all the evils" is to be found in childhood experiences. Such deceptive formulations must be a very convenient way of "purifying" the self, not only because of the abundance of pseudoscientific evidence that psychoanalysis provides, in the form of case studies, but also because of the false generalization one can make from physical illnesses, where a treatment becomes effective only when the illness is treated from its roots. However, a deception-oriented therapy is likely to be effective only if the stress no longer exists or if an appropriate adjustment has already been made to it.

Yet, sometimes a therapy of this kind can facilitate adjustment if it succeeds in deceiving patients to believe that they were not responsible for causing the stress. This possibility is demonstrated in a case study by Messer (1986), which he used to support the claim that, although behavioral therapy may be effective, in some cases a psychoanalytic approach is to be preferred. The case is that of a 20-year-old college student who was concerned "about homosexual feelings, which he was afraid to reveal, particularly because his parents would not accept them" (Messer, 1986, p. 1262). The patient was seen by a therapist experienced in behavior therapy, and initially she inclined to use this approach to help the patient achieve greater comfort with his closeness to men. However, Messer, as the supervisor of the case, advised her to choose the psychoanalytic method, essentially arguing that a patient cannot make a true decision before being aware of the roots of his homosexual drives. Indeed, after one year of treatment the patient eventually "lifted" his repression and talked about his dreadful childhood experiences:

> When he was in the house recently with his girlfriend . . . he was worried that because he was wearing short shorts, his mother may have thought something sexual went on and would disapprove. Suddenly, he remembered an event from the time he was five: "I was in the garage with two girls. I exposed myself to them and my mother found me. It's all black after that. I feel sick to my stomach and weak in my knees as I tell you this. I was also terrified at the time."

In the following session the patient, who was involved in college theater,

> reported that he was in the back-stage dressing room and there was a girl in her pantyhose and bra. He felt disgusted and immediately had an image of himself feeling that same way about his mother. He remembered that when he was a little boy, he had opened the door to her bedroom; she was naked and became upset with him. There was also a skunklike odor that he attached to the scene and that he assumed was the smell of female genitalia. He also remembered quite vividly her big breasts and pubic hair. . . . In the same session . . . he recalled that as a child he would get a bad dream in which his father would get into bed with him and sleep with him. "In the dream my father would be nice, but my mother would get mad. . . . I had a dream this week I didn't want to tell you. I dreamed I was sleeping with my father and that, in the morning, my mother was upset and asked me what my father did to me. She meant I had anal intercourse." (pp. 1265–1266)

Messer, like other psychoanalysts, places full trust in the patient's reports. Furthermore, maintaining that the therapy should try to help the patient expose "the roots" of his problems by brushing away the dirt and debris surrounding fragments of associative memory, Messer interprets these reports in full agreement with orthodox psychoanalytic doctrine. However, there is no proof that these reports reflect actual events and/or that they stimulated the development of the patient's homosexual drives. Based on data reviewed earlier that subjects sometimes make up events (pp. 42–43 and 45), we claim that the patient most likely fantasized the report. Messer provides no data concerning the therapeutic outcomes. However, given the conclusion in the research literature that psychoanalysis is a noneffective therapy (see p. 61), it is unlikely that such a therapy "cured" the patient of his homosexual drives.

We propose that, at most, the "confabulations" helped him to resolve the basic conflict for which he originally came to the therapy, namely, his concern about his parents' response to his homosexual drives. The therapy simply enabled the patient to release the self from blame by attributing the causes for his distorted sexual drives to his parents' failing to be more careful in their behavior or to unfortunate, uncontrollable childhood circumstances. Apparently, the patient had difficulties with complying with the therapist's demand characteristics, and she needed one full year of psychoanalysis to get him to begin thinking in psychoanalytic terms. This may explain why the patient "referred to the therapist as a 'bitch' who pushed him to examine what he preferred not to think about" (p. 1268). Thus, what psychoanalysis would consider as transference, that is, an "intense love . . . or bitter hatred, because the analyst forces him to undergo unpleasant experiences" (Fenichel, 1946, p. 29), may simply reflect the patient's protest at being forced to accept the psychoanalyst's system of belief.

It should be mentioned that concentrated psychoanalytic "brainwashing," particularly when it lasts over an extended period of time, may sometimes lead a patient to accept any absurd idea, no matter what its value. For example, Viktor Frankl (1968) described the case of a high-ranking American diplomat who came to his office in Vienna in order to continue psychoanalytic treatment he had begun in New York 5 years earlier. When the patient was asked why his analysis had been initiated in the first place, he told Frankl that he was discontented with his career and found it most difficult to comply with American foreign policy:

> His analyst, however, had told him again and again that he should try to reconcile himself with his father; because the government of the U.S. as well as his superiors were "nothing but" father images and, consequently, his dissatisfaction with his job was due to the hatred he unconsciously harbored toward his father. Through analysis lasting five years, the patient had been prompted more and more to accept his analyst's interpretations. (pp. 103–104)

In closing this discussion on false insight, it may be worthwhile to note that the placebo effect of therapy is not limited to psychodynamic approaches, but is noticeable in behavior therapy as well (Rachman & Wilson, 1980; Sweet, 1984).

Multidimensional Therapy

The multidimensional strategy that we propose attempts to take advantage of the various available therapeutic models. This strategy consists of three dimensions or stages: rapport and impression making; placebo and enhancement of the patient's general coping skills; insight and stress removal. The first stage seems to be necessary for any therapy to be effective. The second is a diffuse intervention that can be integrated within the first. It can either make the third stage unnecessary or generate appropriate conditions for insight intervention (e.g., strengthening of rapport, better recognition of the patient's problems and coping resources, thereby facilitating the recovery process). Thus, it is proposed that therapy be conceived as a research strategy, that is, a procedure that involves deeper intervention only after simpler and cheaper procedures have proved inadequate. In order to ensure that the therapy is economical, it is suggested that the first two stages be limited to no more than 8–10 therapeutic sessions. These stages are discussed in the following sections, along with a case study of an obsessive–compulsive neurosis treated in line with the multidimensional strategy.

Stage 1: Rapport, Impression Making, and Assessment

As mentioned previously, the research evidence reviewed by Sweet (1984) indicates that establishing good rapport, including a friendly, warm, and permissive relationship, as well as making a good impression (in order to convey competence and credibility) are essential for successful outcomes in any therapeutic intervention, including behavior therapy. This is also consistent with data showing that communication in a therapy like situation is more effective when delivered by a prestigious and knowledgeable communicator (Bergin, 1962).

Assessment procedures should be considered an integral part of the first therapeutic stage, rapport and impression making. We propose, however, abandoning the medical model, which makes a sharp distinction between evaluation and therapy. It is suggested that assessment be extended throughout almost the entire therapeutic relationship. By the same token, while most of the first few sessions should be devoted to this purpose, a significant portion of each session, perhaps excluding the first, should be devoted to therapeutic intervention. This goal should be increased from session to session. Our proposal is recommended for two principal reasons. First, unlike those in medicine, the evaluation methods in psychotherapy are not sensitive enough to detect the patient's problems and assess his or her overall personality immediately. Without denying the importance of these tools, face-to-face contact across the therapeutic sessions can provide much useful information for selecting and modifying the appropriate therapeutic intervention. For example, in Woolfolk and Lehrer's (1985) case study of a woman suffering from general anxiety, it took the patient about 12 sessions to develop a trusting relationship with the therapist and begin to " 'open up' somewhat, revealing that she suffered from severe social anxiety and was rather frustrated with many aspects of her marital relationship" (p. 104). Second, since placebo effect sometimes plays an important role in therapy, there is no reason not to activate this process as early as possible.

Stage 2: Placebo and Enhancement of Coping Skills

Despite their pathological coping strategies, patients with bizarre symptoms, including hysterical ones, suffer from some level of anxiety. Thus, beyond their placebo effect, relaxation procedures, particularly progressive muscle relaxation (Lehrer, 1982; Lehrer, Woolfolk, Rooney, McCann, & Carrington, 1983), significantly help patients reduce their level of anxiety (see p. 264). It is, therefore, suggested that beginning as early as the second session, about 15–20 minutes of the therapy period be devoted to training the patient in progressive muscle relaxation. This practice should be continued in a similar manner for six to seven sessions, and the efficiency of the technique and its importance to everybody should be emphasized. At the end of the second session, the patient can be given Jacobson's (1964) "Self-Operations Control" manual or a tape-recorded training program and asked to practice the relaxation technique for at least a half hour each day. In addition, in the third or fourth session, the patient can be given three to four positive sentences such as "Day by day, in every way, I'm getting better and better" (Coué, 1922; Meichenbaum, 1977) for repetition during the last part of the relaxation state. To strengthen the patient's belief in the efficiency of the method, he or she can be encouraged to read from Meichenbaum's or Coué's book on autosuggestion therapy, where the importance of the technique is explained in simpler terms.

The diffuse therapeutic strategy presented here has these four main objectives:

1. To enhance the placebo effect of the therapy.
2. To strengthen the patient's general coping skills to deal with anxiety-arousing stimuli.
3. To create appropriate conditions for praising the patient for progress at an early stage in the therapy. This is consistent with observations showing that praise for progress in treatment is critical for therapeutic success (Sweet, 1984).
4. To provide the patient with an appropriate distractive tool that can substitute for his or her bizarre symptoms.

This manipulation would in most cases not be sufficient to produce the desired therapeutic effect. Sometimes this may be due to inappropriateness of the specific intervention to produce the placebo effect. For example, a placebo effect can be more easily produced in a subject who has strong religious convictions by also sending him or her to a religious figure to ask for a blessing. This can be applied especially to patients from Eastern countries in which religion more strongly dominates many people's lives. At any rate, there is no need to wait many sessions to see whether or not the placebo-diffuse therapeutic intervention has been effective. Such an evaluation should be made at an early stage. If, after 8–10 sessions, or at some earlier stage, the therapist sees that this manipulation is inadequate, he or she should implement more intensive therapy.

Stage 3: Removal of the Stress and Insight

At this stage of therapy three main therapeutic options seems to be available to the therapist.

First, he or she can actively help the patient remove the causes underlying and maintaining his or her symptoms by one or a combination of these three methods: (1) Continue the coping enhancement training, this time focusing it on the areas that have more relevance to the patient's needs. For example, after realizing the inadequacy of relaxation and desensitization procedures in extinguishing the patient's general anxiety symptoms, Woolfolk and Lehrer (1985) directed therapy efforts toward developing behavioral skills for dealing with problems that became evident in the course of treatment (e.g., sex and intimacy relationships with the husband). (2) Reducing the noxious elements of the environment to make them more tolerable to the patient. Usually, quality of the relationships among family members constitutes one prime source of the patient's stress. For example, this factor was found to be highly important in agoraphobia; behavioral therapy alone, which neglects this factor, failed to produce enduring therapeutic changes for a significant number of cases (Bland & Hallam, 1981; A. J. Goldstein & Chambless, 1978; Goodstein & Swift, 1977; Hand & Lamontagne, 1976; Milton & Hafner, 1979). Thus, involving family members in the therapy and attempting to make the interaction between them and the patient more tolerable should be an important therapeutic goal. (3) Stress can also be reduced by helping the patient remove himself or herself from the noxious environment; Wolpe's (1982) encouragement of his patient's choosing divorce, discussed earlier, is an example.

Second, the therapeutic strategy just discussed is not always the best option available, mainly because of the therapist's limited influence on stress-causing variables (e.g., the family members may refuse to comply to his or her demands) but also because it may be essential for the patient to understand that he or she has had an important role in adopting and maintaining the maladaptive behaviors. Such an understanding would not only retard relapse in the future, but may also facilitate recovery. Thus, another option available to the therapist is to lead the subject to understand his or her active contribution to the process and encourage him or her to adopt a more appropriate coping style. However, this therapeutic option also has prominent disadvantages. Lacking appropriate coping skills, or at least perceiving the situation as such, is likely to strengthen the patient's resistance to complying with the therapist's insight attempts.

The third, and in our opinion, the best option available is a strategy that combines the benefits of the two approaches. A simultaneous effort is invested in both easing the stressful condition and removing the repression. Behavioral and family techniques can be employed for the first purpose, along with inducing insight via psychoanalytic techniques. In particular, we are referring to the gradual manner in which insight is achieved and the sympathy the patient is shown during the process. It may also be worth exploring the possibility of whether an attempt to reduce guilt feelings for selecting the symptoms (e.g., by deceiving the patient into believing that clinical evidence suggests that some unfortunate childhood experiences encourage people to use faulty coping devices) can facilitate the insight process. In the following section, a case study that to some extent demonstrates the clinical use of the latter therapeutic procedure is presented.

The Obsessive–Compulsive Case of Yoni

The client was a 14½-year-old boy who displayed obsessive–compulsive symptoms over a period of 6 months. These included obsessive cleaning and ordering, praying rituals, and excessively bossy and parentlike behavior toward his two younger brothers (8½ and 11 years old).

In the course of therapy the following areas of stress were detected in the patient's current life situation, primarily by interviewing the mother, who had referred the boy to therapy:

1. There was a hostile, tense relationship between the patient, who had his own room, and his two younger brothers, who shared a room and maintained a friendly relationship with each other.

2. A hostile, tense relationship also existed between the parents. The father was a truck driver, with much less education (up to the eighth grade) than the mother, who was a nurse and university student. He was aggressive toward her and the children, and he firmly objected to his wife's studying at the university. (This, however, was based only on the wife's report.) The husband refused to come to the therapist's office, located on the university campus, and several telephone conversations with him did not change his mind. Several months later, he left home, went to live with another woman, and began legal steps toward a divorce.

3. According to the mother's report, the middle child was more talented than the patient, and the parents, particularly the father, displayed more affection toward him than toward the patient. Often the patient was an object of criticism and punishment.

4. The patient had begun attending a new school and was showing deterioration in school performance.

In a search for the motivating bases for the patient's symptoms, we focused our inquiry around sexual problems, both heterosexual and homosexual, as well as hostility. Information derived from the mother and from the patient's responses, including administration of a Rorschach test, tended to reject the hypothesis of sexual bases for the patient's odd behavior. The evidence favored the hostility hypothesis and a desire for attention. For example, when questioned about the patient's hostile behavior, the mother revealed that shortly before the onset of the symptoms, the patient had struck a child in their neighborhood so hard that he had had to be taken to the hospital.

Before discussing the therapy, we should mention that during the entire course of therapy the patient was quite defensive and denied that anything was wrong with him. Therapeutically, the first seven sessions were diffuse and symptom oriented. The mother, who was quite concerned, was given calm messages and encouraged to ignore the symptomatic behavior of the patient and praise him for the positive things he did. She was also instructed to create a relaxing atmosphere at home, to be more friendly with her husband, and to encourage her husband to be less critical of and show more affection toward the patient.

Except for the first session, which was devoted to intake, the patient was given training in progressive muscle relaxation for at least a half hour each session. The general importance of this technique for all people was emphasized, and toward the end of the session he was given Jacobson's (1964) "Self-Operations Control" manual and asked to practice in a quiet place at home for at least 45 minutes each day. When asked his opinion of the training, he responded that he liked it and that he would try to do the homework assignments. In this session, as throughout the entire course of therapy, the patient was often warmly praised for his performance and any sign of progress.

In the third session, the subject continued with relaxation training, this time accompanied by relaxing, hypnoticlike suggestions for 10 minutes. While in a relaxed state, he was asked to repeat several times the following sentences, "From now on I will be relaxed and think only positive thoughts about myself. I must also gradually stop all strange behaviors. These responses do not help to solve my problems and only make my mother sad." At the end of the session, the therapist again encouraged the patient to stop bizarre behavior, emphasizing the sorrow of his mother and explaining to him that this behavior might cause her to fail in her studies. The patient was then given a sheet of paper on which was written these sentences, and he was asked to continue the relaxation training on a daily basis, to be followed by repetition of these sentences. It may be worthwhile noting that a similar therapeutic strategy was used by Spiegel (1970) for treatment of cigarette smoking except that he employed one session of hypnosis accompanied by self-hypnotic practice.

At the beginning of the fourth session, the patient's mother reported that he had showed temporary improvement for a few days, but that he had then resumed his old behavior pattern. In the fourth and fifth sessions, the patient continued in training in the same manner as just described. He again showed great improvement after these two sessions, but later he resumed some of his original behavior as well as adopting new patterns.

The next eight sessions (6–14) were devoted to more intensive intervention. The following actions were taken at this stage: (1) The mother was made aware of the stressful situation confronting her son, particularly the fact that his status as the eldest child was denied him by his more successful brother, that he was constantly criticized, and that his two brothers collaborated against him. The normal stress of adolescence as well as the stress connected with his transfer to a new school were also emphasized. Accordingly, she was encouraged to be less critical and demanding and to display more affection; the importance of making this shift gradually and not overdoing it were explained to her. In an attempt to weaken the coalition between the two brothers, she was advised, after learning that she had a spare room, to move them to separate rooms, and within two weeks this was implemented. (2) Four sessions were devoted to family therapy, in which the two younger brothers, the mother, and the patient took part. In these sessions, the distress that the children were causing to each other, and particularly to the mother, was emphasized in order to motivate them to change their behavior. An agreement was made that the patient would stop displaying bossy behavior toward the two younger brothers, who in turn promised to be more friendly toward the patient. (3) With the mother's permission, a telephone contact was set up with the schoolteacher in which she was asked to be more considerate toward the patient, explaining that he was going through somewhat difficult times. (4) In order to decrease the patient–mother conflicts over homework, a weekly timetable was set up for all of the patient's after-school activities. (5) Since he had some difficulties in mathematics, the mother arranged private tutoring for him. (6) The patient was encouraged to continue with the relaxation training, and this was practiced at the sessions when possible.

At the eleventh session, an attempt was made to "forcefully" lift the patient's repression. On several previous occasions, it had been suggested to him that he had a strong aggressive drive and that his symptoms were aimed at increasing control over his behavior and attracting attention. Nevertheless, the patient denied these possibilities, and the therapist made no attempt to penetrate the patient's defenses. At this session, however, fear of aggression became the central issue. He was told that his fear of aggression was perfectly normal, but that the way he chose to deal with it was not effective. It was recommended that he discuss his problems with his mother and express his anger verbally. At the same time, he was told that some of his difficulties were a result of his own behaviors (e.g., the bossy conduct toward his brothers). The patient was advised to abandon these behaviors, explaining that he was not their father. However, he continued to deny that he had any fear of aggression. He was then asked to recall events in the previous year in which he had behaved aggressively, but he could not recall any such incident.

At this stage, the mother was called in and was asked to remind the patient about the incident that had occurred shortly before the onset of the symptoms, when he had hit the neighborhood child. The story had a dramatic effect on the boy; he burst out crying, indicating that nobody loved him and he did not want to return home. The therapist put his arms around the patient's shoulders, trying to calm him and showing understanding and sympathy for his responses. At the same time, however, he continued to impress upon the patient that he was handling his problems in a self-damaging way. He was warmly praised for the progress he had made and was assured that he had the strength to cope with his difficulties in an efficient and productive manner. He was again reminded that he should discuss his problems with his mother. At the end of the session he was again praised for his progress and was asked to continue the relaxation training at home.

In a telephone conversation the next day, the mother related that on the way home the patient was very sad and solemn. She bought him a favorite goody and tried to cheer him up. At home he behaved quite normally without any symptoms. The therapist asked the patient to come to the telephone and praised him for the improvement in his behavior. The therapy lasted two more sessions. In one, the patient was, as before, encouraged to express his anger and use the relaxation skills to control his anger when necessary. The last session was held 3 weeks later. The main issues discussed were the patient's feelings toward his father, who had in the meantime left home, and his criticism over his mother's relationships with other men. The therapist, while expressing sympathy with the patient's difficulties, led him to understand that the mother had her own private life and that as the eldest son, he should help her rather than criticize her. A follow-up one year later showed no relapse of the patient's symptoms. He behaved quite normally and successfully coped with the school's demands. However, the parents were still in the process of divorce, and the relationship between the patient and his father had become very hostile.

Conclusion

We have attempted to show theoretical inadequacies of the main therapeutic interventions and to demonstrate that the benefits achieved by these techniques could be explained in simpler terms such as those suggested by psychobizarreness theory. Thus, the main contribution of our theoretical model in this respect is that it helps to settle the bitter controversies among the various therapeutic approaches, suggesting that each model deals with only one aspect of a patient's neurotic symptoms—controllability or distractability. The case just presented, while by no means sufficient to demonstrate the validity of our therapeutic approach, does illustrate our psychodynamic integration model, selecting techniques from the traditional approaches, namely, behaviorism, family therapy, and psychoanalysis.

PSYCHOSES: GUIDING PRINCIPLES FOR TREATMENT

The discussion on psychosis will be brief and limited to several basic principles. A more thorough theoretical work, which the field no doubt needs, requires intensive review and careful examination of the literature, which is beyond the scope of this book. We suggest three basic principles.

Principle 1: Treatment of Psychosis Is Most Difficult, and Though Some Neurochemical Reason for This Difficulty Obviously Exists, the Prime Reason Is Psychological

Unlike neurotic symptoms, psychotic symptoms have little controllability function. As indicated earlier, psychotic patients do not try to exert reality control on sources of stress, but the main function of their symptoms is distraction and fantasized control. Patients pay a very heavy price when they decide to detach themselves from reality. Therefore, aversive behavioral techniques aimed at further increasing the "cost" of the symptoms, thereby compelling patients to abandon their faulty coping mechanisms, are unlikely to be successful unless very drastic and unusual punishment, such as electroconvulsive therapy (ECT), is involved. Thus, in the absence of evidence to support an alternative explanation, we tend to attribute the limited efficiency of ECT in the treatment of psychosis (Coleman, Butcher, & Carson, 1984; Kalinowsky, 1980; Weiner, 1984) to the very cruel punishment effect of this method (Frank, 1985). Apart from unusual fear, this therapeutic intervention is likely to cause permanent loss of memory and irreversible brain damage (Breggin, 1979; Frank, 1985). Therefore, we call into question the moral legitimacy of this method.

The treatment of psychosis is also problematic because of the difficulty in undoing the distractibility value of the symptoms. Insight therapy requires that the patient be able to communicate in a rational manner. However, psychotic coping mechanisms preclude this or make it very difficult. Thus, the more severe the patient's cognitive disturbances, the stronger his or her resistance to insight. Furthermore, penetration of the patient's defenses is not recommended unless this constitutes part of a more comprehensive strategy, since it is likely to aggravate his or her difficulties. This is consistent with studies mentioned earlier (see p. 235) showing that drug treatment aimed at reestablishing contact with reality, without providing satisfactory answers to the patient's problems, is likely to replace a schizophrenic coping strategy with deep depression. This is also consistent with some other observations that insight therapy alone may have either no effect or even adverse psychological effects for some schizophrenics (May & Simpson, 1980a, p. 1203 and 1980b, p. 1252; R. W. White & Watt, 1981, p. 513). Thus, it seems that morally, the therapist has no right to dismiss a patient's attempt to find comfort in an illusionary world unless he or she has good reason to believe that the subject has either the strength to cope with the stressful problems or that the therapeutic strategy can produce such an ability.

Principle 2: Of All Psychoses, Nonparanoid Schizophrenia Is the Most Difficult to Treat

The bleak therapeutic prognosis for nonparanoid schizophrenics comes from three basic problems: severe lack of coping skills, severe pathogenic family relationships, and severe lack of self-validation opportunities.

Since nonparanoid schizophrenics lack coping skills to handle life's basic problems, abandoning pathological coping responses could have catastrophic psychological results for them. Apart from losing out on some secondary benefits, abandoning their coping responses is likely to increase their depression to a dangerous and intolerable level. Therefore, it appears that a prerequisite for therapy to be successful is to confront this basic problem. Indeed, research evidence shows that both aversive therapy (ECT) (Kalinowsky, 1980; May & Simpson, 1980b) and psychotherapy aimed at inducing insight (May & Simpson, 1980b) have little or no therapeutic benefit for some psychotics, particularly for chronic and hospitalized patients. With regard to ECT, if there is any validity to our claim that this therapeutic method is no more than severe punishment aimed at forcing a helpless patient to abandon his or her remaining resources for coping, then even if one ignores the probably irreversible damages, this is no less than torture and dehumanization (Breggin, 1979; Frank, 1985) when used with people who lack the capacity to adjust themselves to life. This is like punishing a crippled person for being incapable of running.

With regard to psychotherapy, May and Simpson (1980b) noted that

> positive results seem to be obtained, particularly when treatment focuses on social and occupational rehabilitation, on problem solving, and on cooperation with pharmachotherapy—that is, psychotherapy with outpatients is more likely to be helpful if it is oriented more toward support and rehabilitation than toward formal attempts to promote insight and deep psychological understanding. (p. 1252)

The same approach has recently been taken by behavioral-oriented therapists (Curran, Sutton, Faraone, & Guenette, 1985; J. A. Kelly & Lamparski, 1985), who emphasized the importance of skill training in various areas, particularly social and problem solving.

However, as elaborated earlier, schizophrenics also suffer from a pathogenic family environment. It appears, then, that improving the quality of this environment (e.g., making it less critical and more supportive), particularly in view of the total lack of social support they suffer from, is essential for therapeutic success and prevention of relapse (Lukoff, Snyder, Ventura, & Nuechterlein, 1984; Rabkin, 1980; Steinglass, 1987). Indeed, the importance of this point is highly emphasized in the behavioristic therapeutic approach of Curran et al. (1985). For example, in their therapy

> family members are told that high levels of criticism and too much emotional involvement are toxic to the patient. In order to make this point very clear, a number of examples of what is meant by criticism and emotional involvement are described. (pp. 469–470)

Curran et al. (1985) also attempted to make the communicative interaction among the family members of schizophrenics more effective, to improve the family's ability to solve problems, and to resolve the guilt of family members by explaining to them that schizophrenia is a handicap caused largely by genetic and neurochemical problems. Thus, in recent years, behavioristic approaches to schizophrenia have become quite

TOWARD A UNIFIED THEORY IN PSYCHOTHERAPY

similar to family therapy, particularly the "new psychoeducation family therapy approaches" (see Steinglass, 1987) to schizophrenia.

However, for many patients, skill training and family therapy is not sufficient to bring about a successful outcome. First, the patient's coping skills may be so severely impaired that no therapeutic effort would succeed in raising them to a minimal level necessary for normal functioning. Second, even if the patient reaches the critical therapeutic level, it is doubtful he or she would be able to long endure the social alienation and painful social comparison (see p. 229) that are inevitable for most schizophrenics. Thus, it seems that, at least for more severe cases of schizophrenia, we need to build a small world in which they can meet each other on a regular basis. This may not only allow them to have some minimal social interaction, which appears to be an essential need of every human being, but will also prevent noxious social comparison. Indeed, recent research (Coleman et al., 1984, pp. 681–682) has shown that an after-care program, which helps patients adjust to their communities (e.g., halfway houses that serve as a home base for former patients as they make a transition back to normal functioning in their communities), largely decreases the likelihood of relapse. In our opinion, halfway houses or schizophrenic villages should even be considered a permanent solution for some patients.

It should be noted, however, that while much energy and money is invested in the therapeutic system, very little attention is directed to the prevention of schizophrenia. We believe that many high-risk children would not have become schizophrenics if they had been given proper care. On the basis of the theoretical discussion of the cause of schizophrenia (see chapter 16), we propose the following steps:

1. A national assessment must be conducted on a routine basis (as with the health system) in order to identify from an early age, particularly during the school years, those suffering from gross attentional deficits and social alienation.

2. A modified form of Curran et al.'s (1985) skill-training approach must be developed to specifically handle the constitutional attentional deficit from which high-risk children suffer.

3. The family training suggested for schizophrenics by Curran et al. (1985) should also be given at a very early age.

4. The personality handicap of the high-risk children (see chapter 16) should be brought to the teachers' attention, and they should be advised to avoid criticizing, to display warmth and affection, and to encourage other children to react in a friendly manner to the high-risk children. If the teacher is unsuccessful in preventing social alienation, he or she should bring this fact to the school psychologist's attention.

5. The gap in social skills between the high-risk child and the other children in the school or community may be so high that there may be no better solution than to the transfer of the child to a less demanding environment. This may be an effective solution for high-risk kibbutz children (see pp. 231–233).

6. The children need to be aware that they have an innate handicap or at least they should experience that there are other children like themselves. It is therefore suggested that groups be organized to meet at least once a month; these meetings should also be used for skill training.

7. The mass media should be enlisted to make the public aware of the miserable condition of high-risk children and schizophrenic adults, particularly the painful social alienation to which they are subjected. The goal of this effort would be to motivate the public to respond to these people in a more humane way.

We believe that an intensive effort invested in prevention would not only be beneficial to people at risk for schizophrenia, but, in the long run, it would also significantly decrease the economic burden that they now put on society.

Principle 3: The Main Therapeutic Goal in Treating Depression Is to Turn the Patient's Attention to Positive Aspects of Reality

Unlike schizophrenia, in depression, particularly in psychotic cases, the main therapeutic goal is not improvement of the individual's coping skills. Rather, the therapy can be more effective if it is focused on turning the patient's attention to positive aspects of reality, on convincing him or her to adopt a more optimistic attitude (even if this has no basis in reality), and to a certain extent on restoring the normal functioning of the physiological system. We propose three main arguments in support of this principle.

First, as mentioned earlier, individuals who have psychotic depressions have been, prior to their breakdown, normal and even well adjusted. Thus, their miserable state is not due to deficits in coping skills, but is primarily the result of severely stressful life events or the combination of these and genetic and/or personality variables. Though skill training may help, this does not seem to be what they need most. This claim may be less applicable to neurotic depression, as some evidence suggests that this group of patients has deficits in social skills (e.g., less frequent attempts to initiate conversation, failing to reinforce other sufficiently). Thus, behavioral training intended to overcome these deficits may be helpful in reducing the individual's feelings of depression (Becker & Heimberg, 1985). Nevertheless, this therapeutic approach may not be necessary even with neurotic depression. For example, Shaw (1977) reported that a cognitive strategy (Beck, 1970; Beck, Rush, Shaw, & Emery, 1979) resulted in a better therapeutic outcome than did training in social skills and that the latter intervention left the patient no better off than attention-placebo manipulation, which Shaw referred to as nondirective communication. Although more recent investigations (Bellack, Hersen, & Himmelhoch, 1983; Hersen, Bellack, Himmelhoch, & Thase, 1984) found skill training to be helpful, they too reported that behavioral training was no more effective in decreasing the subject's state of depression than was supportive therapy (which focused on the individual's immediate concerns).

Second, we have argued that the central causes of depression are stressful life events and the subject's inability either to remove the stress by normal means or to release his or her attention from the tyranny of negative cognitions. Consistent with this claim is evidence that cognitive therapy may be more effective than pharmacotherapeutic intervention for treatment of neurotic depression (Kovacs, Rush, Beck, & Hollon, 1981; Rush, Beck, Kovacs, & Hollon, 1977; Shaw, 1977) and may even be sufficient for treatment of psychotics (Bishop, Miller, Normam, Buda, & Foulke, 1986).

The question may be raised as to why cognitive intervention is at all effective. According to Beckian cognitive therapy (Beck, 1970; Hollon & Jacobson, 1985), depressives are characterized by acquired dysfunctional thinking that is largely automatic and that causes them to perceive reality in a distorted way. "Depressive clients extensively distort the past, the present, and the future" (Hollon & Jacobson, 1985, p. 176). Therefore, the therapy should be directed toward correcting the malformed pattern of thinking and, thereby, restoring an accurate picture of reality.

However, as suggested earlier, we object to this theoretical approach because the cumulative research data are clearly contradictory. In fact, not only do depressives not distort reality, but they are more reality oriented than are nondepressives, and they

280   TOWARD A UNIFIED THEORY IN PSYCHOTHERAPY

have difficulty in deluding themselves with nonrealistic optimistic beliefs (Taylor, 1983). Their depression seems to result from an inability to remove the noxious cognitions from their focus of attention. Thus, we propose abandoning the behaviorist–mechanistic explanation of cognitive therapy, adopting instead the view that this approach leads patients to perceive reality from a more convenient angle or, alternatively, convincing them to take a more optimistic attitude. For example, Frankl (1968) using "Logotherapy," his own cognitive approach to depression, convinced a depressive man, who could not overcome the loss of his wife, to adopt a less depressive attitude. Frankl asked the patient "What would have happened . . . if you had died first, and your wife would have to survive you?" The patient replied that this would have been terrible for his wife. Then Frankl commented,

> you see . . . such a suffering has been spared her, and it was you who have spared her this suffering; but now, you have to pay for it by surviving and mourning her. He said no word but shook my hand and calmly left my office. (p. 114)

As part of their efforts to extinguish the faulty automatic thought and restore accurate perception of reality, Beckian cognitive therapists confront clients with discrepant facts. For example, Hollon and Jacobson (1985), in applying this method to treatment of a depressive widow who believed that she could not continue life without her husband, asked the patient to think back and examine if there had been "a time in her life when she had been happy without her husband or whether there had been times in her life when he was still living that she had found solace or pleasure in activities that did not include him" (p. 188). This therapeutic intervention led her to realize that "life was not totally bleak without her husband." Thus, instead of describing this therapy in Beckian terms (i.e., the patient began thinking in a less distorted way), we can argue that the therapy succeeded in shifting the patient's attention to more positive aspects of life.

It is important to emphasize that our dispute with the Beckian approach is not merely semantic, but a fundamental one. The framework of Beck's theory can hardly accommodate cases in which strengthening the patient's unrealistic but optimistic belief or motivating him or her to adopt such a belief can alleviate depression. Using this method, Frankl (1968), for instance, helped a rabbi who had lost his first wife and their six children in Auschwitz and who had recently learned that his second wife was sterile. The rabbi was in despair, particularly because he had to live with the prospect that he would never have a son to say Kaddish (a prayer said by a son following the father's death) for him. Frankl attempted to convince him that he might see his children again in the world to come. At the outset, the rabbi tended to reject the therapist's suggestion, indicating with tears that his children were "worthy of the highest place in Heaven, but as for himself he could not expect, as an old sinful man, to be assigned the same place" (p. 121). However, Frankl (1968) did not give up, stating,

> is it not conceivable, Rabbi, that precisely this was the meaning of your surviving your children; that you may be purified through these years of suffering, so that finally you, too, though not innocent like your children, may become worthy of joining them in Heaven? Is it not written in the Psalms that God preserves all your tears? So, perhaps none of your sufferings were in vain. (p. 121)

Thus, using the patient's belief system, the therapist succeeded in relieving his depression by getting him to accept a more optimistic attitude, one that would most probably be considered as totally unrealistic by Beckian theorists.

Other evidence with which Beck's supporters would have difficulty dealing involves anthropological reports of mysterious circumstances surrounding death, which have been termed *voodoo death* (Richter, 1957):

> A Brazilian Indian condemned and sentenced by a so-called medicine man, is helpless against his own emotional response to this pronouncement—and dies within hours. In Africa a young Negro unknowingly eats the inviolably banned wild hen. On discovery of his "crime" he trembles, is overcome by fear and dies in 24 hours. In New Zealand a Maori woman eats fruit that she only later learns has come from a tabooed place. Her chief has been profaned. By noon of the next day she is dead. In Australian a witch doctor points a bone at a man. Believing that nothing can save him, the man rapidly sinks in spirits and prepares to die. (p. 191)

We are skeptical whether these subjects could have benefited from any Western therapeutic approach, such as Beckian therapy. The most efficient intervention in these cases seems to be to convince the witch doctor to nullify the cognitions or "apply to another therapist" with the same skills. Indeed, Richter reported that the life of the Australian man mentioned was "saved only at the last moment when the witch doctor [was] forced to remove the charm" (p. 191). In the introductory chapter of this book, we mentioned another case of the same sort: a witch doctor cured a woman who suffered from a serious illness and whom several American physicians could not help (N. R. Hll & Goldstein, 1986). This case was originally published by the American Medical Association (Kirkpatrick, 1981), which attests to its validity. These data suggest that Beckian therapy would have little or no effect on Asian–African depressive subjects whose belief system is at variance with the scientific-oriented approach of the Western world.

Furthermore, it seems that even the Beckian therapists use, at least sometimes, what can be termed *deceptive cognitive strategy* in their attempt to convince the patient to abandon his or her "unrealistic" cognitions. In this strategy, the therapist, having difficulty proving to the patient that his or her stress-related thoughts are unrealistic, chooses to challenge cognitions that occupy much lower positions in the hierarchy of the stress-related cognitions, but that can be more easily refuted. As a result, a spreading effect can be developed: The patient either concludes that he or she has a general tendency to perceive life more pessimistically than it really is, or he or she can be more easily convinced that this is so. This strategy is reflected to some extent in a case treated by Hollon and Jacobson (1985).

The case involves a 57-year-old woman who has experienced depression. The woman has six children, but all have grown up and left home and now she was living alone. She divorced her husband 15 years earlier, some years after he had become paralyzed as the result of an illness. The husband is in a nursing home, and she goes to visit him on a somewhat regular basis. The woman expresses much guilt over the divorce, and she wonders whether she should "go back" to her husband. Upon reading the transcript of the conversation between the patient and her therapist, one can see that her marital failure is the prime cause of her depression. Apparently, the woman begins thinking again about her marriage because of the loneliness she experiences after her children left home. However, toward the end of the description of her unfortunate marriage and the difficulties she encountered after the divorce, she sums up in one sentence: "I know that that's when the kids began to resent me so much" (p. 193). Even though it is obvious that this cognition played, at the most, a secondary role in causing the patient's state of depression, the therapist chose to challenge this belief, and he devoted the entire session to it. The conversation between the therapist and the client following the statement just quoted follows:

T: How do you know that?
C: My husband always told me that all the kids were very resentful of me.
T: Did the kids ever tell you that they were resentful?
C: No, but they showed it.
T: . . .
C: . . .
T: Is there any possibility that your children did not resent you?
C: I guess there's a possibility.
T: How could you find out?
C: . . .
T: . . .
C: I think maybe I could write each of them a letter . . ." (pp. 193–194)

Thus, it is difficult to see any other reason for the therapist's choice of challenging this cognition, except the ease by which it could be refuted. The therapist could know in advance that it is unlikely that the children would be so nasty as to tell their mother that they resent her even if they really do. Yet, the children's responses imply that the patient's cognition of resentfulness did have a basis in reality. Although they indicated that they had many pleasant memories of her and never doubted her love, "she had been a tough taskmaster and that as the children grew up they had, indeed, resented her discipline" (p. 194). In line with our expectations, elimination of this cognition caused a significant reduction in the patient's depression, and not only did it change her perception as a mother, but also her perception as a wife. It appears, then, that a broad definition of cognitive therapy as a strategy aimed at directing a patient's attention to the positive elements of the environment and/or encouraging him or her to adopt a more optimistic outlook is more consistent with research and clinical data than is Beck's narrow definition of this therapy.

Third, as suggested previously, one of the stressful causes of depression is the deterioration of the normal functioning of the biological system resulting from the massive production of toxic neurochemical changes set up by environmental stress and the patient's neglect of biological needs such as eating and sleeping. One interesting question that is not yet settled is whether these neurochemical changes are sufficient to cause depression. We believe that they are not. Cancer patients undergo very drastic biological changes, and although they usually feel very bad, they do not necessarily become depressed. The direct causes of depression seem to be cognitive—the subject's psychological response to a stressful life event (Taylor, 1983). It appears that when subjects are helpless in eliminating the stressful cognitions from the focus of their attention, any disruption in the normal functioning of the body is likely to intensify the dominant feelings of depression. The adverse neurochemical changes and neglect of the body's needs, which seem to be the by-product of the adverse psychological condition, cause inconvenient feelings and thereby an intensification of the individual's feelings of depression. Thus, although psychological treatment may be sufficient for eliminating these feelings, as the abovementioned data indicate, antidepressant drugs may also be effective (Coleman et al., 1984) because they eliminate the factors that facilitate depression.

The last issue we would like to address concerns electroconvulsive therapy (ECT), which has proved to be effective in the treatment of severe depression (Weiner, 1984). In the absence of evidence to support an alternative explanation, we regard this method as a cognitive intervention. Thus, we tend to accept the psychodynamic explanation attributing the therapeutic effect of ECT to its severe punishment effect, which assists the individual in releasing himself or herself from guilt-ridden cognitions. If this claim is indeed valid, then morally it is questionable whether a therapist has the right to use such brutal means even if it were to the subject's benefit and would not cause any irreversible damage to his or her neurological system. This claim may be applicable not only to the conventional bilateral form of ECT, but also to its unilateral use, in which the shock is delivered to the nondominant hemisphere as well (Fontaine & Young, 1985). Although the latter form seems to have a lower incidence of adverse cognitive effects, some likelihood of damage, and above all the basic moral question, still remain.

CONCLUSIONS

We have reached the destination of our journey, though many important questions remain to be clarified. While we cannot at this stage say whether or not the journey has been successful—a task that would require the concerted effort of the scientific community in this field—we can conclude this adventure with several well-founded statements:

1. We have demonstrated that none of the mechanistic conceptualizations of the human being, namely, psychoanalysis, behaviorism, and medical models, have succeeded in enlisting much plausible support for their theses in psychopathology despite the tremendous efforts invested in them. In view of this, it seems dubious to continue the search for scientific support.

2. Beyond scientific weaknesses, the conventional theories are also problematic because they cannot provide plausible explanations for many fundamental problems in psychopathology, the most prominent of which are the choice of symptoms, the lack of awareness, and the sheer definition of abnormality.

3. The understanding of human deviation requires differentiation between normal and bizarre symptoms. While normal behavioral dysfunction can be approached in cognitive–behavioral terms, bizarre symptoms should be regarded merely as pathological coping devices.

4. The cognitive–automatic conditioning of fear, which claims that the conditioning process is composed of two distinctive stages, seems to be the most plausible theory that can explain the development of simple fears.

5. Psychobizarreness theory integrates ideas from a variety of schools, not only in the explanation of psychopathological phenomena, but also in the treatment of pathological disorders. For example, it suggests that psychoanalysis, behaviorism, and family therapy deal with limited aspects of the psychotherapy spectrum. The first attempts to induce insight and thus motivate the patient to cope with his or her problems in a normal way. Even though we reject the psychoanalytic "archeological" approach, we believe that a therapy aimed at removal of the patient's deception (in psychoanalysis, the "lifting of repression") may sometimes be the only intervention that can motivate the subject to choose a more adaptive coping mechanism. The second attacks the problem by attempting to enhance the subject's coping skills or by counteracting the controllability value of the symptom, thus forcing him or her to give up the symptom. The third attempts to remove the stressful causes of the symptom. The proposed therapeutic strategy shows that these different approaches can be synthesized into one multidimensional model. Thus, psychobizarreness theory fosters a resolution to the bitter controversies among different schools of thought that have dominated psychopathology in the past century.

6. Psychobizarreness theory emphasizes the uniqueness and complexity of human consciousness without postulating mysterious unconscious phenomena or a "black box" as components of the human cognitive system. Instead, psychobizarreness suggests that the unconscious is better conceptualized as the blocking of free access to one's focus of attention, a blocking which primarily is achieved by using highly demanding attentional stimuli—bizarre symptoms. Verification of the theory thus far has been achieved by demonstrating that it is able to explain and integrate a vast and diverse body of research and clinical observation. The next step is to design research and to refocus clinical observation in order to test basic assumptions and logical ramifications of the theory. It is hoped that the present volume will stimulate and direct such efforts with the goal of integrating and redefining the enormous field of psychopathology.

References

Abbott, R. S. (1972). On confounding of the Repression–Sensitization and Manifest Anxiety Scales. *Psychological Reports, 30,* 392–394.

Abraham, K. (1927). *Selected papers.* London: Hogarth Press.

Abrams, R., & Taylor, M. A. (1976). Catatonia: A prospective clinical study. *Archives of General Psychiatry, 33,* 579–581.

Abramson, L. Y., & Alloy, L. B. (1981). Depression, nondepression, and cognitive illusions: A reply to Schwartz. *Journal of Experimental Psychology: General, 110,* 436–447.

Abramson, L. Y., & Seligman, M. E. P., & Teasdale, J. D. (1978). Learned helplessness in humans: Critique and reformulation. *Journal of Abnormal Psychology, 87,* 49–74.

Abse, D. W. (1959). Hysteria. In S. Arieti (Ed.), *American handbook of psychiatry* (Vol. 1, pp. 272–292). New York: Basic.

Adams, J. A. (1964). Motor skills. *Annual Review of Psychology, 15,* 181–202.

Adler, A. (1964). *Social interest: A challenge to mankind.* New York: Capricorn. (Original work published 1933)

Agras, W. S., Chapin, H. N., & Oliveau, D. C. (1972). The natural history of phobia: Course and prognosis. *Archives of General Psychiatry, 26,* 315–317.

Agras, W. S., Sylvester, D., & Oliveau, D. C. (1969). The epidemiology of common fears and phobias. *Comprehensive Psychiatry, 10,* 151–156.

Aiken, E. G. (1965). Changes in interpersonal descriptions accompanying the operant conditioning of verbal frequency in groups. *Journal of Verbal Learning and Verbal Behavior, 4,* 243–247.

Aisenberg, D., Weizer, N., & Munitz, H. (1985). Morbidity and mortality among schizophrenic patients. *Harefuah, 108,* 67–68. (In Hebrew)

Aitken, R. C. B., Lister, J. A., & Main, C. J. (1981). Identification of features associated with flying phobia in aircrew. *British Journal of Psychiatry, 139,* 38–42.

Albee, G. W., Lane, E. A., & Reuter, J. M. (1964). Childhood intelligence of future schizophrenics and neighborhood peers. *Journal of Psychology, 58,* 141–144.

Alexander, F. (1932). *The medical value of psychoanalysis.* New York: Norton.

Alexander, F. (1939). Emotional factors in arterial hypertension. *Psychosomatic Medicine, 1,* 173–179.

Alexander, F. (1950). *Psychosomatic medicine.* New York: Norton.

Alloy, L. B., & Abramson, L. Y. (1979). Judgment of contingency in depressed and nondepressed students: Sadder but wiser? *Journal of Experimental Psychology: General, 108,* 441–485.

Alloy, L. B., & Abramson, L. Y. (1982). Learned helplessness, depression, and illusion of control. *Journal of Personality and Social Psychology, 42,* 1114–1126.

Alloy, L. B., Abramson, L. Y., & Viscusi, D. (1981). Induced mood and the illusion of control. *Journal of Personality and Social Psychology, 41,* 1129–1140.

Altrocchi, J., & Perlitsh, H. D. (1963). Ego control patterns and attributions of hostility. *Psychological Reports, 12,* 811–818.

Altrocchi, J., Shrauger, S., & McLeod, M. A. (1964). Attribution of hostility to self and others by expressors, sensitizers and repressors. *Journal of Clinical Psychology, 20,* 233.

Amenson, C. S., & Lewinsohn, P. M. (1981). An investigation into the observed sex difference in prevalence of unipolar depression. *Journal of Abnormal Psychology, 90,* 1–13.

Andreasen, N. C. (1979a). Thought, language, and communication disorders: I. Clinical assessment, definition of terms, and evaluation of their reliability. *Archives of General Psychiatry, 36,* 1315–1321.

Andreasen, N. C. (1979b). Thought, language and communication disorders: II. Diagnostic significance. *Archives of General Psychiatry, 36,* 1325–1330.

Andreasen, N. C. (1982). Concepts, diagnosis and classification. In E. S. Paykel (Ed.), *Handbook of affective disorders.* New York: Guilford Press.

Andreasen, N. C., & Powers, P. S. (1974). Overinclusive thinking in mania and schizophrenia. *British Journal of Psychiatry, 125,* 452–456.

Anisman, H., & Lapierre, Y. D. (1982). Neurochemical aspects of stress and depression: Formulations and caveats. In R. W. J. Neufeld (Ed.), *Psychological stress and psychopathology.* New York: McGraw-Hill.

Appley, M. H., & Trumbull, R. (1967). On the concept of psychological stress. In M. H. Appley & R. Trumbull (Eds.), *Psychology of stress* (pp. 1–13). New York: Appleton.

Arconac, O., & Guze, S. B. (1963). A family study of hysteria. *New England Journal of Medicine, 268,* 239–242.

Arieti, S. (1974). *Interpretation of schizophrenia* (2nd ed.). New York: Basic.

Arieti, S. (1979). New views of the psychodynamics of phobias. *American Journal of Psychotherapy, 33,* 82–95.

Arieti, S., & Bemporad, J. (1978). *Severe and mild depression: The psychotherapeutic approach.* New York: Basic Books.

Armstrong, J. S. (1982a). Barriers to scientific contributions: The author's formula. *Behavioral and Brain Sciences, 5,* 197–199.

Armstrong, J. S. (1982b). Research on scientific journals: Implications for editors and authors. *Journal of Forecasting, 1,* 83–104.

Ascher, L. M., Schotte, D. E., & Grayson, J. B. (1986). Enhancing effectiveness of paradoxical intention in treating travel restriction in agoraphobia. *Behavior Therapy, 17,* 124–130.

Atkinson, R. L., Atkinson, R. C., & Hilgard, E. R. (1983). *Introduction to Psychology* (8th ed.). New York: Harcourt Brace Jovanovich.

Averill, J. (1973). Personal control over aversive stimuli and its relationship to stress. *Psychological Bulletin, 80,* 286–303.

Ayalon, M., & Merom, H. (1985). The teacher interview. *Schizophrenia Bulletin, 11,* 117–120.

Baer, P. E., Collins, F. H., Bourianoff, G. G., & Ketchel, M. F. (1979). Assessing personality factors in essential hypertension with a brief self-report instrument. *Psychosomatic Medicine, 41,* 321–330.

Bagby, E. (1922). The etiology of phobias. *Journal of Abnormal Psychology, 17,* 16–18.

Bagley, C. (1973). Occupational class and symptoms of depression. *Social Science and Medicine, 7,* 327–340.

Bahnson, C. D., & Bahnson, M. B. (1966). Role of the ego defenses: Denial and repression in the etiology of malignant neoplasm. *Annals of the New York Academy of Sciences, 125,* 827–845.

Bahrick, H. P. (1979). Maintenance of knowledge: Questions about memory we forgot to ask. *Journal of Experimental Psychology: General, 108,* 296–308.

Bahrick, H. P. (1983). The cognitive map of a city: 50 years of learning and memory. In G. Bower (Ed.), *The psychology of learning and motivation: Advances in research and theory* (Vol. 17, pp. 125–163). New York: Academic Press.

Bahrick, H. P. (1984a). Associations and organization in cognitive psychology: A reply to Neisser. *Journal of Experimental Psychology: General, 113,* 36–37.

Bahrick, H. P. (1984b). Memory and people. In J. E. Harris & P. E. Morris (Eds.), *Everyday memory, actions, and absentmindedness.* New York: Academic Press.

Bahrick, H. P. (1984c). Semantic memory content in permastore: Fifty years of memory for Spanish learned in school. *Journal of Experimental Psychology: General, 113,* 1–29.

Bahrick, H. P., Bahrick, P. O., & Wittlinger, R. P. (1975). Fifty years of memories for names and faces: A cross sectional approach. *Journal of Experimental Psychology: General, 104,* 54–75.

Bahrick, H. P., & Karis, D. (1982). Long-term ecological memory. In C. Puff (Ed.), *Handbook of research methods in human memory and cognition* (pp. 427–465). New York: Academic Press.

Baker, J. W., & Schaie, K. W. (1969). Effects of aggressing "alone" or "with another" on physiological and psychological arousal. *Journal of Personality and Social Psychology, 12,* 80–86.

Baldwin, W. A. (1972). Autonomic stress resolution in repressors and sensitizers following microcounseling. *Psychological Reports, 31,* 743–749.

Bandura, A. (1969). *The principles of behavior modification.* New York: Holt.

Bandura, A. (1971a). *Psychological modeling.* Chicago: Atherton Press.

Bandura, A. (1971b). *Social learning theory.* Morristown, NJ: General Learning Press.

Bandura, A. (1973). *Aggression: A social learning analysis.* Englewood Cliffs, NJ: Prentice-Hall.

Bandura, A. (1977a). Self-efficacy: Toward a unifying theory of behavioral change. *Psychological Review, 84,* 191–215.

Bandura, A. (1977b). *Social learning theory.* Englewood Cliffs, NJ: Prentice-Hall.

Bandura, A. (1978). Reflections on self-efficacy. *Advances in Behaviour Research and Therapy, 1,* 237–269.

Bandura, A. (1982). Self-efficacy mechanism in human agency. *American Psychologist, 37,* 122–147.

Bandura, A., & Rosenthal, T. L. (1966). Vicarious classical conditioning as a function of arousal level. *Journal of Personality and Social Psychology, 3,* 54–62.

Banki, C., M., Vojnik, M., Papp, Z., Balla, K. Z., & Arato, M. (1985). Cerebrospinal fluid magnesium and calcium related to amin metabolites, diagnosis, and suicide attempts. *Biological Psychiatry, 20,* 163–171.

Barber, T. K. (1965). The effect of "hypnosis" on learning and recall: A methodological critique. *Journal of Clinical Psychology, 21,* 19–25.

Barlow, D. H., & Wolfe, B. E. (1981). Behavioral approaches to anxiety disorders: A report on the NIMH–SUNY, Albany, Research Conference. *Journal of Consulting and Clinical Psychology, 49,* 448–454.

Barnes, G. E., & Prosen, H. (1985). Parental death and depression. *Journal of Abnormal Psychology, 94,* 64–69.

Barry, W. (1970). Marriage Research and Conflict: An integrative review. *Psychological Bulletin, 73,* 41–54.

Barton, M., & Buckhout, R. (1969). Effects of objective threat and ego threat on repressors and sensitizers in the estimation of shock intensity. *Journal of Experimental Research in Personality, 3,* 197–205.

Bavelas, A., Hastorf, A. F., Gross, A. E., & Kite, W. R. (1965). Experiments on the alteration of group structure. *Journal of Experimental Social Psychology, 1,* 55–70.

Beck, A. T. (1967). *Depression: Clinical, experimental and theoretical aspects.* New York: Harper & Row.

Beck, A. T. (1970). Cognitive therapy: Nature and relation in behavior therapy. *Behavior Therapy, 1,* 184–200.

Beck, A. T. (1976). *Cognitive therapy and the emotional disorders.* New York: International Universities Press.

Beck, A. T., Rush, A. J., Shaw, B. F., & Emery, G. (1979). *Cognitive therapy of depression: A treatment manual.* New York: Guilford Press.

Becker, R. E., & Heimberg, R. G. (1985). Social skills training approaches. In M. Hersen & A. S. Bellack (Eds.), *Handbook of clinical behavior therapy with adults.* New York: Plenum.

Beckfield, D. F. (1985). Interpersonal competence among college men hypothesized to be at risk for schizophrenia. *Journal of Abnormal Psychology, 94,* 397–404.

Beels, C. C., Gutwirth, L., Berkeley, J., & Struening, E. (1984). Measurements of social support in schizophrenia. *Schizophrenia Bulletin, 10,* 399–411.

Behring, T., Cudek, R., Mednick, S. A., Walker, E. F., & Schulsinger, F. (1982). Vulnerability to environmental stress: High-risk research on the development of schizophrenia. In R. W. J. Neufeld (Ed.), *Psychological stress and psychopathology.* New York: McGraw-Hill.

Beidel, D. C. & Turner, S. M. (1986). A critique of the theoretical bases of cognitive-behavioral theories and therapy. *Clinical Psychology Review, 6,* 177–197.

Beisser, H. R., Glasser, N., & Grant, M. (1967). Psychosocial adjustment of children of schizophrenic mothers. *Journal of Nervous and Mental Diseases, 145,* 429–440.

Bell, P. A., & Byrne, D. (1978). Repression–sensitization. In H. London & J. E. Exner (Eds.), *Dimensions of personality.* New York: Wiley.

Bellack, A. S., Hersen, M., & Himmelhoch, J. M. (1983). A comparison of social-skills training, pharmacotherapy and psychotherapy for depression. *Behaviour Research and Therapy, 21,* 101–107.

Bellak, L. (1979). Introduction: An idiosyncratic overview. In L. Bellak (Ed.), *Disorders of the schizophrenia syndrome.* New York: Basic.

Berenbaum, H., Oltmanns, T. F., Gottesman, I. I. (1985). Formal thought disorder in schizophrenics and their twins. *Journal of Abnormal Psychology, 94,* 3–16.

Berger, S. E. (1971). *The self-deceptive personality.* Unpublished doctoral dissertation, University of Miami, Coral Gables, FL.

Berger, S. M. (1962). Conditioning through vicarious instigation. *Psychological Review, 69,* 450–466.

Bergin, A. (1962). The effect of dissonant persuasive communications upon changes in a self-referring attitude. *Journal of Personality 30,* 423–438.

Bergquist, W. H., Lewinsohn, P. M., Sue, D. W., & Flippo, J. R. (1968). Short and long term memory for various types of stimuli as a function of repression–sensitization. *Journal of Experimental Research in Personality, 3,* 28–38.

Berkman, L. F., & Syme, S. L. (1979). Social networks, host resistance, and mortality: A nine-year follow-up of Alameda Country residents. *American Journal of Epidemiology, 109,* 186–204.

Berkowitz, L. (1962). *Agression: A social psychological analysis.* New York: McGraw-Hill.

Berkowitz, L. (1970). Experimental investigations of hostility catharsis. *Journal of Consulting and Clinical Psychology, 35,* 1–7.

Berkowitz, L., & Geen, R. G. (1967). Stimulus qualities of the target of agression: A further study. *Journal of Personality and Social Psychology, 5*, 364–368.

Berkowitz, L., Geen, J. A., & Macaulay, J. R. (1962). Hostility catharsis as the reduction of emotional tension. *Psychiatry, 25*, 23–31.

Bernstein, M. (1956). *The search for Bridey Murphy.* New York: Lancer.

Bettelheim, B. (1943). Individual and mass behavior in extreme situations. *Journal of Abnormal and Social Psychology, 38*, 417–452.

Bettelheim, B. (1960). *The informed heart.* New York: Free Press.

Bibring, E. (1953). The mechanics of depression. In P. Greenacre (Ed.), *Affective disorders.* New York: International Universities Press.

Bidzinska, E. J. (1984). Stress factors in affective diseases. *British Journal of Psychiatry, 144*, 161–166.

Billings, A. G., Cronkite, R. C., & Moos, R. H. (1983). Social-environmental factors in unipolar depression: Comparisons of depressed patients and nondepressed controls. *Journal of Abnormal Psychology, 92*, 119–133.

Billings, A. G., & Moos, R. H. (1985). Life stressors and social resources affect posttreatment outcomes among depressed patients. *Journal of Abnormal Psychology, 94*, 140–153.

Bilodeau, E. A., & Bilodeau, I. M. (1961). Motor-skills learning. *Annual Review of Psychology, 12*, 243–280.

Bishop, S., Miller, I. W., Norman, W., Buda, M., & Foulke, M. (1986). Cognitive therapy of psychotic depression: A case report. *Psychotherapy, 23*, 167–173.

Bjork, R. A. (1972). Theoretical implications of directed forgetting. In A. W. Melton & E. Martin (Eds.), *Coding processes in human memory.* Washington, DC: Winston.

Blanchard, E. B., & Hersen, M. (1976). Behavioral treatment of hysterical neurosis: Symptom substitution and symptom return reconsidered. *Psychiatry, 39*, 118–129.

Bland, K., & Hallam, R. S. (1981). Relationship between response to graded exposure and marital satisfaction in agorophobics. *Behaviour Research and Therapy, 19*, 335–338.

Blechman, E. A., McEnroe, M. J., Carella, E. T., & Audette, D. P. (1986). Childhood competence and depression. *Journal of Abnormal Psychology, 95*, 223–227.

Blechman, E. A., Tinsely, B., Carella, E. T., & McEnroe, M. J. (1985). Childhood competence and behavior problems. *Journal of Abnormal Psychology, 94*, 70–77.

Bleuler, E. (1964). *Dementia praecox or the group of schizophrenias* (J. Zinkin, Trans.). New York: International Universities Press. (Original work published 1911)

Bloom, B. L., Asher, S. J., & White, S. W. (1978). Marital disruption as a stressor: A review and analysis. *Psychological Bulletin, 85*, 867–894.

Bolles, R. C. (1972). The avoidance learning problem. In G. H. Bower (Ed.), *The psychology of learning and motivation* (Vol. 6). New York: Academic Press.

Bolles, R. C. (1975). *Theory of motivation* (2nd ed.). New York: Harper & Row.

Bolles, R. C. (1978). The role of stimulus learning in defensive behavior. In S. H. Hulse, H. Fowler, & W. K. Honig (Eds.), *Cognitive processes in animal behavior.* Hillsdale, NJ: Erlbaum.

Bootzin, R. R. (1975). *Behavior modification and therapy.* Cambridge, MA: Winthrop.

Bourne, L. E., Dominowski, R. L., & Loftus, E. F. (1979). *Cognitive processes.* Englewood Cliffs, NJ: Prentice-Hall.

Bower, G. H. (1981). Mood and Memory. *American Psychologist, 36*, 129–148.

Bower, G. H., & Hilgard, E. R. (1981). *Theories of learning* (5th ed.). Englewood Cliffs, NJ: Prentice-Hall.

Bowers, K. S. (1975). The psychology of subtle control: An attributional analysis of behavioral persistence. *Canadian Journal of Behavioral Science, 7*, 78–95.

Bowers, K. S. (1984). On being unconsciously influenced and informed. In K. S. Bowers & D. Meichenbaum (Eds.), *The unconscious reconsidered.* New York: Wiley.

Bowers, K. S., & Meichenbaum, D. (Eds.). (1984). *The unconscious reconsidered.* New York: Wiley.

Bowlby, J. (1973). *Attachment and loss: Separation* (Vol. 2). New York: Basic Books.

Boyd, J. H., & Weissman, M. M. (1982). Epidemiology. In E. S. Paykel (Ed.), *Handbook of affective disorders.* New York: Guilford Press.

Bradley, B., & Mathews, A. (1983). Negative self-schemata in clinical depression. *British Journal of Clinical Psychology, 22*, 173–181.

Brady, J. P. (1966). Hysteria versus malingering: A response to Grosz and Zimmerman. *Behaviour Research and Therapy, 4*, 321–322.

Brady, J. P., & Lind, D. L. (1961). Experimental analysis of hysterical blindness. *Archives of General Psychiatry, 4*, 331–339.

Braginsky, B. M., & Braginsky, D. D. (1971). Schizophrenic patients in the psychiatric interview: An experimental study of their effectiveness at manipulation. *Journal of Consulting Psychology, 31,* 543–547.

Braginsky, B. M., Braginsky, D. D., & Ring, K. (1969). *Methods of madness.* New York: Holt, Rinehart and Winston.

Braginsky, B. M., Grosse, M., & Ring, K. (1966). Controlling outcomes through impression-management: An experimental study of the manipulative tactics of mental patients. *Journal of Consulting Pyschology, 30,* 295–300.

Brandon, S. (1960). *An epidemiological study of maladjustment in childhood.* Unpublished M.D. thesis, University of Durham, England.

Breger, L., & McGaugh, J. L. (1965). Critique and reformulation of "learning-theory" approaches to psychotherapy and neurosis. *Psychological Bulletin, 63,* 338-358.

Breggin, P. R. (1979). *Electroshock: Its brain-disabling effects.* New York: Springer.

Bregman, E. (1934). An attempt to modify the emotional attitudes of infants by the conditioning response technique. *Journal of Genetic Psychology, 45,* 169–196.

Breier, A., Charney, D. S., & Heninger, G. R. (1984). Major depression in patients with agoraphobia and panic disorder. *Archives of General Psychiatry, 41,* 1129–1135.

Brewer, W. F. (1974). There is no convincing evidence for operant or classical conditioning in adult humans. In W. B. Weimer & D. S. Palermo (Eds.), *Cognition and the symbolic processes.* New York: Wiley.

Breznitz, S. (1985). Chores as a buffer against risk interaction. *Schizophrenia Bulletin, 11,* 357–360.

Bridger, W. H., & Mandel, I. J. (1964). A comparison of GSR fear responses produced by threat and electric shock. *Journal of Psychiatric Research, 2,* 31–40.

Brooker, A. E. (1982). Behavioral treatment of obsessive–compulsive disorders: Current status. *Psychological Reports, 50,* 1035–1044.

Brown, R., & Kulik, J. (1977). Flashbulb memories. *Cognition, 5,* 73–99.

Brown, S. F. (1970). Defense mechanisms and the behavioral control of stress. *Dissertation Abstracts, 30B,* 5684.

Bruner, J. S. (1973). *Beyond the information given.* New York: Norton.

Bruner, J. S., & Postman, L. (1947). Emotional selectivity in perception and reaction. *Journal of Personality, 16,* 69–77.

Bryant-Tuckett, R., & Silverman, L. H. (1984). Effects of the subliminal stimulation of symbiotic fantasies on the academic performance of emotionally handicapped students. *Journal of Counseling Psychology, 31,* 295–305.

Buckhout, R. (1974). Eyewitness testimony. *Scientific American, 231,* 23–31.

Buglass, D., Clarke, J., Henderson, A. S., Kreitman, N., & Presley, A. S. (1977). A study of agoraphobic housewives. *Psychological Medicine, 7,* 73–86.

Bunney, W. E., Jr., Goodwin, F. K., & Murphy, D. L. (1972). The "switch process" in manic–depressive illness: III. Theoretical implications. *Archives of General Psychiatry, 27,* 312–317.

Bunney, W. E., Jr., Murphy, D. L., Goodwin, F. K., & Borge, G. F. (1972). The "switch process" in manic–depressive illness: A systematic study of sequential behavioral changes. *Archives of General Psychiatry, 27,* 295–302.

Burns, W. J., & Tyler, J. D. (1976). Appreciation of risque cartoon humor in male and female repressors and sensitizers. *Journal of Clinical Psychology, 32,* 315–321.

Button, J. H., & Reivich, R. S. (1972). Obsession of infanticide. A review of 42 cases. *Archives of General Psychiatry, 27,* 235–240.

Byrne, D. (1961). The repression–sensitization scale: Rational, reliability and validity. *Journal of Personality, 29,* 344–349.

Byrne, D. (1964). Repression–sensitization as a dimension of personality. In B. A. Maher (Ed.), *Progress in experimental personality research.* New York: Academic Press.

Byrne, D., Golightly, C., & Sheffield, J. (1965). The repression–sensitization scale as a measure of adjustment: Relationship with CPI. *Journal of Consulting Psychology, 29,* 586–589.

Byrne, D., & Lamberth, J. (1971). The effect of erotic stimuli on sex arousal, evaluative responses, and subsequent behavior. In *Technical report of the Commission on Obscenity and Pornography* (Vol. 8). Washington, DC: U.S. Government Printing Office.

Byrne, D., & Sheffield, J. (1965). Response to sexually arousing stimuli as a function of repressing and sensitizing defenses. *Journal of Abnormal Psychology, 71,* 114–118.

Byrne, D., Steinberg, M. A., & Schwartz, M. S. (1968). Relationship between repression–sensitization and physical illness. *Journal of Abnormal Psychology, 73,* 154–155.

Cahoon, D. D. (1968). Symptom substitution and the behavior therapies: A reappraisal. *Psychological Bulletin, 69,* 149–156.

Campbell, D., Sanderson, R. E., & Laverty, S. G. (1964). Characteristics of a conditioned response in human subjects during extinction trials following a single traumatic conditioning trial. *Journal of Abnormal and Social Psychology, 68,* 627–639.

Campos, J., Emde, R., Gaensbauer, R., & Henderson, C. (1975). Cardiac and behavioral interrelationships in the reactions of infants to a stranger. *Developmental Psychology, 11,* 589–601.

Carpenter, W. T. (1984). A comment on Strauss' and Carpenter's definitions of 'What is schizophrenia': The authors reply. *Schizophrenia Bulletin, 10,* 369–370.

Carroll, D. (1972). Repression–sensitization and the verbal elaboration of experience. *Journal of Consulting and Clinical Psychology, 38,* 147.

Carver, C. S., Gibbons, F. X., Stephan, W. G., Glass, D. C., & Katz, I. (1979). Ambivalence and evaluations of stigmatized others. *Bulletin of the Psychonomic Society, 13,* 50–52.

Carver, C. S., Glass, D. C., & Katz, I. (1978). Favorable evaluations of blacks and the handicapped: Positive prejudice, unconscious denial or social desirability? *Journal of Applied Social Psychology, 8,* 97–106.

Chabot, J. A. (1973). Repression–sensitization: A critique of some neglected variables in the literature. *Psychological Bulletin, 80,* 122–129.

Chaika, E., & Lambe, R. (1985). The locus of dysfunction in schizophrenic speech. *Schizophrenia Bulletin, 11,* 8–15.

Chambless, D. L. (1985a). Agorophobia. In M. Hersen & A. S. Bellack (Eds.), *Handbook of clinical behavior therapy with adults.* New York: Plenum.

Chambless, D. L. (1985b). The relationship of severity of agoraphobia to associated psychopathology. *Behaviour Research and Therapy, 23,* 305–310.

Cheek, D. B., & LeCron, L. M. (1968). *Clinical hypnotherapy.* New York: Grune & Stratton.

Chesney, M. A., Black, G. W., Chadwick, J. H., & Rosenman, R. H. (1981). Psychological correlates of the Type A behavior pattern. *Journal of Behavioral Medicine, 4,* 217–224.

Chodoff, P. (1974). The diagnosis of hysteria: An overview. *American Journal of Psychiatry, 131,* 1073–1078.

Cieutat, V. J. (1959). Surreptitious modification of verbal behavior during class discussion. *Psychological Reports, 5,* 648.

Clark, L. F., & Neuringer, C. (1971). Repressor–sensitizer personality styles and associated levels of verbal ability, social intelligence, sex knowledge, and quantitative ability. *Journal of Consulting and Clinical Psychology, 36,* 183–188.

Cleghorn, R. A. (1967). Hysterical personality and conversion: Theoretical aspects. *Canadian Psychiatric Association Journal, 14,* 553–567.

Clemes, S. (1964). Repression and hypnotic amnesia. *Journal of Abnormal and Social Psychology, 69,* 62–69.

Cobb, S. (1976). Social support as a moderator of life stress. *Psychosomatic Medicine, 38,* 300–314.

Cochrane, R. (1971). High blood pressure as a psychosomatic disorder: A selective review. *British Journal of Social and Clinical Psychology, 10,* 61–72.

Cochrane, R. (1973). Hostility and neuroticism among unselected essential hypertensions. *Journal of Psychosomatic Research, 17,* 215–218.

Cockerham, W. C. (1978). *Medical sociology.* Englewood Cliffs, NJ: Prentice-Hall.

Cofer, C. (1984). Comments on "Semantic memory content in permastore: Fifty years of memory for Spanish learned in school" by Bahrick. *Journal of Experimental Psychology: General, 113,* 30–31.

Cohen, F., & Lazarus, R. S. (1973). Active coping processes, coping dispositions, and recovery from surgery. *Psychosomatic Medicine, 35,* 375–389.

Coleman, J. C. (1964) *Abnormal psychology and modern life* (3rd ed.). Chicago: Scott, Foresman.

Coleman, J. C., Butcher, J. N., & Carson, R. C. (1980). *Abnormal psychology and modern life* (6th ed.). Glenview, IL: Scott, Foresman.

Coleman, J. C., Butcher, J. N., & Carson, R. C. (1984). *Abnormal psychology and modern life* (7th ed.). Glenview, IL: Scott, Foresman.

Collard, R. R. (1967). Fear of strangers and play behavior in kittens with varied social experience. *Child Development, 38,* 877–891.

Condon, T. J., & Allen, G. J. (1980). Role of psychoanalytic merging fantasies in systematic desensitization: A rigorous methodological examination. *Journal of Abnormal Psychology, 89,* 437–443.

Cook, M., Mineka, S., Wolkenstein, B., & Laitsch, K. (1985). Observational conditioning of snake fear in unrelated rhesus monkeys. *Journal of Abnormal Psychology, 94,* 591–610.

Cooper, L. M. (1972). Hypnotic amnesia. In E. Fromm & R. E. Shor (Eds.), *Hypnosis: Research developments and perspectives.* New York: Aldine.

REFERENCES

291

Corballis, M. C. (1980). Laterality and myth. *American Psychologist, 35,* 284–295.
Cornblatt, B. A., & Erlenmeyer-Kimling, L. (1985). Global attentional deviance as a marker of risk for schizophrenia: Specificity and predictive validity. *Journal of Abnormal Psychology, 94,* 470–486.
Coryell, W., & Winokur, G. (1982). Course and outcome. In E. S. Paykel (Ed.), *Handbook of affective disorders.* New York: Guilford Press.
Costello, C. G. (1982). Loss as a source of stress in psychopathology. In R. W. J. Neufeld (Ed.), *Psychological stress and psychopathology.* New York: McGraw-Hill.
Cottrell, N. B., & Epley, S. W. (1977). Affiliation, social comparison, and socially mediated stress reduction. In J. M. Suls & R. L. Miller (Eds.), *Social comparison processes: Theoretical and empirical perspectives.* Washington, DC: Hemisphere.
Coué, E. (1922). *The practice of autosuggestion.* New York: Doubleday.
Coyne, J. C. (1976). Depression and the response of others. *Journal of Abnormal Psychology, 85,* 186–193.
Coyne, J.C., Aldwin, C., & Lazarus, R. S. (1981). Depression and coping in stressful episodes. *Journal of Abnormal Psychology, 90,* 439–447.
Crandall, V. J., & Rabson, A. (1960). Children's repetition choices in an intellectual achievement situation following success and failure. *Journal of Genetic Psychology, 97,* 161–168.
Crinic, K. A., Greenberg, M. T., Ragozin, A. S., Robinson, N. M., & Basham, R. B. (1983). Effects of stress and social support on mothers and premature and full-term infants. *Child Development, 54,* 209–217.
Crowder, R. F. (1976). *Principles of learning and memory.* Hillsdale, NJ: Erlbaum.
Curran, J. P., Sutton, R. G., Faraone, S. V., & Guenette, S. (1985). Inpatient approaches. In M. Hersen & A. S. Bellack (Eds.), *Handbook of clinical behavior therapy with adults.* New York: Plenum.
Dauber, R. B. (1984). Subliminal psychodynamic activation in depression: On the role of autonomy issues in depressed college women. *Journal of Abnormal Psychology, 93,* 9–18.
Davidson, P. O., & Watkins, R. E. (1971). Repressor–sensitizer differences in psychiatric patients on repeated exposures to film induced stress. *Psychological Reports, 28,* 159–162.
Davidson, R. J. (1980). Consciousness and information processing: A biocognitive perspective. In J. M. Davidson & R. J. Davidson (Eds.), *The psychobiology of consciousness.* New York: Plenum.
Davidson, S. (1980). The clinical effects of massive psychic trauma in families of holocaust survivors. *Journal of Marital and Family Therapy, 6,* 11–21.
Davidson, S., & Packard, T. (1981). The therapeutic value of friendship between women. *Psychology of Women Quarterly, 5,* 495–510.
Davison, G. C., & Neale, J. M. (1974). *Abnormal Psychology: An experimental clinical approach.* New York: Wiley.
Davison, G. C., & Neale, J. M. (1982). *Abnormal psychology: An experimental clinical approach* (2nd ed.). New York: Wiley.
Day, M., & Semard, E. V. (1978). Schizophrenic reactions. In A. M. Nicholi, Jr. (Ed.), *The Harvard guide to modern psychiatry.* Cambridge, MA: Harvard University Press.
Dean, A., & Ensel, W. M. (1983). The epidemiology of depression in young adults: The centrality of social support. *Journal of Psychiatric Treatment and Evaluation, 5,* 195–207.
DeCharms, R., & Wilkins, E. J. (1963). Some effects of verbal expression of hostility. *Journal of Abnormal and Social Psychology, 66,* 462–470.
Deese, J., & Hulse, S. H. (1967). *The psychology of learning.* New York: McGraw-Hill.
Delprato, D. J. (1980). Heredity determinants of fears and phobias: A critical review. *Behavior Therapy, 11,* 79–103.
Dember, W. N. (1960). *Psychology of perception.* New York: Holt, Rinehart and Winston.
DeMonbreun, B. G., & Craighead, W. E. (1977). Distortion of perception and recall of positive and neutral feedback in depression. *Cognitive Therapy and Research, 1,* 311–329.
Denike, L. D. (1964). The temporal relationship between awareness and performance in verbal conditioning. *Journal of Experimental Psychology, 68,* 521–529.
Denney, D. R., Sullivan, B. J., & Thiry, M. R. (1977). Participant modeling and self-verbalization training in the reduction of spider fears. *Journal of Behavior Therapy and Experimental Psychiatry, 8,* 247–253.
Derry, P. A., & Kuiper, N. A. (1981). Schematic processing and self-reference in clinical depression. *Journal of Abnormal Psychology, 90,* 286–297.
Diamond, E. L. (1982). The role of anger and hostility in essential hypertension and coronary heart disease. *Psychological Bulletin, 92,* 410–433.
Dixon, N. F. (1958). The effect of subliminal stimulation upon autonomic and verbal behavior. *Journal of Abnormal and Social Psychology, 57,* 29.
Dixon, N. F. (1971). *Subliminal perception: The nature of controversy.* London: McGraw-Hill.

Dixon, N. F. (1981). *Preconscious processing*. New York: Wiley.

Dixon, P. W., Oakes, W. F. (1965). Effect of intertrial activity on the relationship between awareness and verbal operant conditioning. *Journal of Experimental Psychology, 69*, 152–157.

Dohrenwend, B. P., & Dohrenwend, B. S. (1969). *Social status and psychological disorder*. New York: Wiley.

Dollard, J., & Miller, N. E. (1950). *Personality and psychotherapy: An analysis in terms of learning, thinking and culture*. New York: McGraw-Hill.

Donelson, E. (1973). *Personality*. New York: Appleton.

Dor-Shav, N. K. (1978). On the long-range effects of concentration camp internment on Naxi victims: 25 years later. *Journal of Consulting and Clinical Psychology, 46*, 1–11.

Downey, J. (1973). *An interference theory of the catharsis of aggression*. Unpublished doctoral dissertation, University of Missouri, Columbia.

Drake, R. W., Gates, C., Whitaker, A., & Cotton, P. G. (1985). Suicide among schizophrenics: A review. *Comprehensive Psychiatry, 26*, 90–100.

Duke, M., & Nowicki, S. (1979). *Abnormal psychology*. Monterey, CA: Brooks/Cole.

Dulany, D. E. (1961). Hypotheses and habits in verbal "operant conditioning." *Journal of Abnormal and Social Psychology, 63*, 251–263.

Dulany, D. E. (1962). The place of hypotheses and intentions: An analysis of verbal control in verbal conditioning. *Journal of Personality, 30*, 102–129.

Dunner, D. L., Patrick, V., & Fieve, R. R. (1979). Life events at the onset of bipolar affective illness. *American Journal of Psychiatry, 136*, 508–511.

Dykman, R. A., Reese, W. G., Galbrecht, C. R., & Thomasson, P. A. (1959). Psychophysiological reactions to novel stimuli: Measurement, adaptation and relationship of psychological and physiological variables in the normal humans. *Annals of the New York Academy of Sciences, 79*, 43–107.

D'Zurilla, T. (1965). Recall efficiency and mediating cognitive events in "experimental repression." *Journal of Personality and Social Psychology, 3*, 253–256.

Early, C. E., & Kleinknecht, R. A. (1978). The Palmar Sweat Index as a function of repression–sensitization and fear of dentistry. *Journal of Consulting and Clinical Psychology, 46*, 184–185.

Eaton, W. W. (1978). Life events, social supports, and psychiatric symptoms: A reanalysis of the New Haven data. *Journal of Health and Social Behavior, 19*, 230–234.

Eggesen, E. G., Duncan, B., & Konecni, V. J. (1975). Effects of content of verbal aggression on future verbal aggression: A field experiment. *Journal of Experimental Social Psychology, 11*, 192–204.

Eberhage, M. G., Polek, D., & Hynan, M. T. (1985). Similar effects of different threats on perceptual processes. *Bulletin of the Psychonomic Society, 23*, 470–472.

Eitinger, L. (1973). A follow-up of the Norwegian concentration camp survivors' mortality and morbidity. *Israel Annals of Psychiatry, 11*, 199–209.

Eitinger, L., & Strom, A. (1981). New investigations on the mortality and morbidity of Norwegian ex-concentration camp prisoners. *Israel Journal of Psychiatry and Related Sciences, 18*, 173–195.

Ekstrand, B. R. (1967). Effect of sleep on memory. *Journal of Experimental Psychology, 75*, 64–72.

Ekstrand, B. R. (1972). To sleep, perchance to dream. In C. P. Duncan, L. Sechrest, & A. W. Melton (Eds.), *Human memory: Festchrift for Benton J. Underwood* (pp. 59–82). Englewood Cliffs, NJ: Prentice-Hall.

Ekstrand, B. R., Sullivan, M. J., Parker, D. F., & West, J. N. (1971). Spontaneous recovery and sleep. *Journal of Experimental Psychology, 88*, 142–144.

Ellis, A. (1962). *Reason and emotion in psychotherapy*. New York: Lyle Stuart.

Emmelkamp, P. M. G. (1974). Self-observation versus flooding in the treatment of agoraphobia. *Behaviour Research and Therapy, 12*, 229–237.

Emmelkamp, P. M. G. (1982). *Phobic and obsessive–compulsive disorders: Theory, research and practice*. New York: Plenum.

Emmelkamp, P. M. G. (1987). Obsessive–compulsive disorders. In L. Michelson & L. M. Ascher (Eds.), *Anxiety and stress disorders: Cognitive-behavioral assessment and treatment*. New York: Guilford Press.

Emmelkamp, P. M. G., Mersch, P. P., & Vissia, E. (1985). The external validity of analogue outcome research: Evaluation of cognitive and behavioral interventions. *Behaviour Research and Therapy, 23*, 83–86.

Emmelkamp, P. M. G., & Van der Heyden, H. (1980). The treatment of harming obsessions. *Behavioral Analysis and Modifications, 4*, 28–35.

Emmerich, W. (1966). Continuity and stability in early social development: II. Teacher ratings. *Child Development, 37*, 17–27.

Empson, J. A. C., & Clarke, P. R. F. (1970). Rapid eye movements and remembering. *Nature, 227*, 287–288.

Epstein, S., & Fenz, W. D. (1967). The detection of areas of emotional stress through variations in perceptual threshold and physiological arousal. *Journal of Experimental Research in Personality, 2,* 191–199.

Epstein, W., & Shontz, F. (1971). *Psychology in progress.* New York: Holt, Rinehart & Winston.

Erdelyi, M. H. (1970). Recovery of unavailable perceptual input. *Cognitive Psychology, 1,* 99–113.

Erdelyi, M. H. (1974). A new look at the new look: Perceptual defense and vigilance. *Psychological Review, 81,* 1–25.

Erdelyi, M., & Goldberg, B. (1979). Let's not sweep repression under the rug: Toward a cognitive psychology of repression. In J. F. Kihlstrom & F. J. Evans (Eds.), *Functional disorder of memory.* Hillsdale, NJ: Erlbaum.

Ericsson, K. A., & Simon, H. A. (1980). Verbal reports as data. *Psychological Review, 87,* 215–251.

Eriksen, C. W., & Davids, A. (1955). The meaning and clinical validity of the Taylor Anxiety Scale and the hysteria-psychasthenia scales from the MMPI. *Journal of Abnormal and Social Psychology, 50,* 135–137.

Eriksen, C., & Pierce, J. (1968). Defense mechanisms. In E. F. Borgatta & W. Lambert (Eds.), *Handbook of personality theory and research.* Chicago: Rand McNally.

Erwin, E. (1980). Psychoanalytic therapy: The Eysenck argument. *American Psychologist, 35,* 435–443.

Ewart, C. K., Taylor, C. B., Kraemer, H. C., & Agras, W. S. (1984). Reducing blood pressure reactivity during interpersonal conflict: Effects of marital communication training. *Behavior Therapy, 15,* 473–484.

Ewen, R. B. (1980). An introduction to theories of personality. New York: Academic Press.

Eysenck, H. J. (1952). The effects of psychotherapy: An evaluation. *Journal of Consulting Psychology, 16,* 319–324.

Eysenck, H. J. (1960). Learning theory and behavior therapy. In H. J. Eysenck (Ed.), *Behavior therapy and the neuroses: Reading in modern methods of treatment derived from learning theory.* Oxford, England: Pergamon Press.

Eysenck, H. J. (1966). *The effects of psychotherapy.* New York: Interscience Press.

Faraone, S. V., & Tsuang, M. T. (1985). Quantitative models of the genetic transmission of schizophrenia. *Psychological Bulletin, 98,* 41–66.

Feder, C. Z. (1967). Relationship of repression–sensitization to adjustment status, social desirability, an acquiescence response set. *Journal of Consulting Psychology, 31,* 401–406.

Feder, C. Z. (1968). Relationship between self-acceptance and adjustment, repression–sensitization and social competence. *Journal of Abnormal Psychology, 73,* 317–322.

Fenichel, O. (1946). *Psychoanalytic theory of neurosis.* London: Routledge & Kegan Paul.

Fernando, S., & Storm, V. (1984). Suicide among psychiatric patients of a district general hospital. *Psychological Medicine, 14,* 661–672.

Feshbach, S., & Weiner, B. (1982). *Personality.* Lexington, MA: Heath.

Festinger, L., Riecken, H. W., Jr., & Schachter, S. (1956). *When prophecy fails.* Minneapolis: University of Minnesota Press.

Finkelstein, R. J. (1983). Distractibility among paranoid and non-paranoid schizophrenics using subtests matched for discriminating power. *British Journal of Clinical Psychology, 22,* 237–244.

Fischer, K. W., & Pipp, S. L. (1984). Development of the structures of unconscious thought. In K. S. Bowers & D. Meichenbaum (Eds.), *The unconscious reconsidered.* New York: Wiley.

Fisher, L. M., & Wilson, G. T. (1985). A study of the psychology of agoraphobia. *Behaviour Research and Therapy, 23,* 97–107.

Flanagan, J. (1948). *The Aviation Psychology Program in the Army Air Forces* (USAAF Aviation Psychology Research Report No. 1). Washington, DC: U.S. Government Printing Office.

Fleishman, E. A., & Parker, R. F., Jr. (1962). Factors in the retention and relearning of perceptual motor skill. *Journal of Experimental Psychology, 64,* 215–226.

Folkman, S., & Lazarus, R. S. (1986). Stress processes and depressive symptomatology. *Journal of Abnormal Psychology, 95,* 107–113.

Folks, D. G., Ford, C. V., & Regan, W. M. (1984). Conversion symptoms in a general hospital. *Psychosomatics, 25,* 285–295.

Fontaine, R., & Young, T. (1985). Unilateral ECS: Advantages and efficacy of the treatment of depression. *Canadian Journal of Psychiatry, 30,* 142–147.

Fontana, A. F., & Klein, E. B. (1968). Self-presentation and the schizophrenic "deficit." *Journal of Consulting and Clinical Psychology, 32,* 250–256.

Fontana, A. F., Klein, E. B., Lewis, E., & Levine, L. (1968). Presentation of self in mental illness. *Journal of Consulting and Clinical Psychology, 32,* 110–119.

Foulds, M. L. & Warehime, R. G. (1971). Relationship between repression–sensitization and a measure of self-actualization. *Journal of Consulting and Clinical Psychology, 36,* 257–259.

Frank, L. R. (1985). Electroshock: A paradigm of psychiatric tyranny. *Issues in Radical Therapy, 11,* 24–27, 57–59.

Frankl, V. E. (1968). *Man's search for meaning.* Boston: Beacon Press.

Freud, S. (1925). Repression. In J. Strachey (Ed.), *Collected Papers* (Vol. 4, pp. 84–97). London: Hogarth Press. (Original work published 1915)

Freud, S. (1959). On the history of the psychoanalytic movement. In E. Jones (Ed.), *Collected Papers* (Vol. 1, pp. 287–359). New York: Basic Books. (Original work published in 1914)

Galbraith, G. G. & Lieberman, H. (1972). Associative responses to double entendre words as a function of repression–sensitization and sexual stimulation. *Journal of Consulting and Clinical Psychology, 39,* 322–327.

Galin, D. (1974). Implications for psychiatry of left and right central specialization: A neurophysiological context for unconscious processes. *Archives of General Psychiatry, 31,* 572–582.

Galin, D., Diamond, R., & Braff, D. (1977). Lateralization of conversion syndromes: More frequent on the left. *Archives of General Psychiatry, 134,* 578–580.

Gamaro, S., & Rabin, A. I. (1969). Diastolic blood pressure responses following direct and displaced aggression after anger arousal in high-and-low guilt subjects. *Journal of Personality and Social Psychology, 12,* 87–94.

Garber, J., & Hollon, S. D. (1980). Universal versus personal helplessness in depression: Belief in uncontrollability or incompetence. *Journal of Abnormal Psychology, 89,* 56–66.

Garcia, J., Ervin, F. R., & Koelling, R. A. (1966). Learning with prolonged delay of reinforcement. *Psychonomic Science, 5,* 121–122.

Garcia, J., & Koelling, R. A. (1966). Relation of cue to consequence in avoidance learning. *Psychonomic Science, 4,* 123–124.

Garfield, S. L. (1976). All roads lead to Rome. *Contemporary Psychology, 21,* 328–329.

Garfield, S. L. (1981). Psychotherapy: A 40-year appraisal. *American Psychologist, 36,* 174–182.

Garfield, S. L. (1987). Towards a scientifically oriented eclecticism. *Scandinavian Journal of Behaviour Therapy, 16,* 95–109.

Garssen, B., van Veenedaal, W., & Bloemink, R. (1983). Agoraphobia and hyperventilation syndrome. *Behaviour Research and Therapy, 21,* 643–649.

Gauthier, J., & Marshall, W. L. (1977). The determination of optimal exposure to phobic stimuli in flooding therapy. *Behaviour Research and Therapy, 15,* 403–410.

Gedo, J. E. (1979). *Beyond interpretation: Toward a revised theory for psychoanalysis.* New York: International Universities Press.

Geen, R. G., & Quanty, M. B. (1977). The catharsis of aggression: An evaluation of a hypothesis. In L. Berkowitz (Ed.), *Advances in Experimental Social Psychology* (Vol. 10). New York: Academic Press.

Geen, R. G., Stonner, D., & Shope, G. L. (1975). The facilitation of aggression by aggression: Evidence against the catharsis hypothesis. *Journal of Personality and Social Psychology, 31,* 721–726.

Geer, J. H., Davison, G. C., & Gatchel, R. I. (1970). Reduction of stress in humans through nonveridical perceived control of aversive stimulation. *Journal of Personality and Social Psychology, 16,* 731–738.

Geiselman, R. E., Bjork, R. A., & Fishman, D. L. (1983). Disrupted retrieval in directed forgetting: A link with posthypnotic amnesia. *Journal of Experimental Psychology: General, 112,* 58–72.

Geiselman, R. E., Fisher, R. P., MacKinnon, D. P., & Holland, H. L. (1985). Eyewitness memory enhancement in the police interview: Cognitive retrieval mnemonics versus hypnosis. *Journal of Applied Psychology, 70,* 401–412.

Gentry, W. D., Chesney, A. P., Gray, H. E., Hall, R. P., Harburg, E., & Kennedy, C. D. (1983). Behavioral medicine and the risk for essential hypertension. *International Review of Applied Psychology, 32,* 85–94.

Gentry, W. D., Chesney, A. P., Hall, R. P., & Harburg, E. (1981). Effect of habitual anger: Coping pattern on blood pressure in black/white, high/low stress area respondents. *Psychosomatic Medicine, 43,* 83.

Gerard, H. B., & Rabbie, J. M. (1961). Fear and social comparison. *Journal of Abnormal and Social Psychology, 62,* 586–592.

Ghinsberg, Y. (1985). *Back from Tuichi.* Tel-Aviv: Zmora-Bitan. (In Hebrew)

Gibbons, F. X. (1985). A social-psychological perspective on developmental disabilities. *Journal of Social and Clinical Psychology, 3,* 391–404.

Giles, T. R. (1983a). Probable superiority of behavioral interventions: I. Traditional comparative outcome. *Journal of Behavior Therapy and Experimental Psychiatry, 14,* 29–32.

Giles, T. R. (1983b). Probable superiority of behavioral interventions: II. Empirical status of the equivalence of therapies hypothesis. *Journal of Behavior Therapy and Experimental Psychiatry, 14,* 189–196.

Giles, T. R. (1984). Probable superiority of behavioral interventions: III. Some obstacles to acceptance of findings. *Journal of Behavior Therapy and Experimental Psychiatry, 15,* 23–26.

Ginsberg, G. L. (1979). Psychoanalytic aspects of mania. In B. Shopsin (Ed.), *Manic illness.* New York: Raven Press.

Gleason, P. J. (1969). The effects of three types of interaction with another person upon the anxiety levels of repressors and sensitizers. *Dissertation Abstracts, 30B,* 1376–1377.

Gleitman, H. (1971). Forgetting of long-term memories in animals. In W. K. Honig & P. H. R. James (Eds.), *Animal memory.* New York: Academic Press.

Goisman, R. M. (1983). Theraputic approaches to phobia: A comparison. *American Journal of Psychotherapy, 37,* 227–234.

Goldberg, E. L., Comstock, G. W., & Graves, C. G. (1980). Psychosocial factors and blood pressure. *Psychological Medicine, 10,* 243–255.

Goldman, M., Keck, J. W., & O'Leary, C. J. (1969). Hostility reduction and performance. *Psychological Reports, 25,* 503–512.

Goldring, N., & Fieve, R. R. (1984). Attempted suicide in manic-depressive disorder. *American Journal of Psychotherapy, 38,* 373–383.

Goldstein, A. J., & Chambless, D. L. (1978). An analysis of agorophobia. *Behavior Therapy, 9,* 47–59.

Goldstein, M. J., Held, J. M., & Cromwell, R. L. (1968). Premorbid adjustment and paranoid–nonparanoid status in schizophrenia. *Psychological Bulletin, 70,* 382–386.

Goldstein, Y. N. (1977). Electrical skin conductance and cardiac responses of repressors, midlines, and sensitizers to affective stimulus films. *Dissertation Abstracts, 37B,* 4742–4743.

Golin, S., Herron, E. W., Lakota, R., & Reineck, L. (1967). Factor analytic study of the Manifest Anxiety, Extraversion, and Repression–Sensitization Scales. *Journal of Consulting Psychology, 31,* 564–569.

Golin, S., Terrell, F., & Johnson, B. (1977). Depression and the illusion of control. *Journal of Abnormal Psychology, 86,* 440–442.

Golin, S., Terrell, F., Weitz, J., & Drost, P. L. (1979). The illusion of control among depressed patients. *Journal of American Psychology, 88,* 454–457.

Good, L. R., & Levin, R. H. (1970). Pupillary responses of repressors and sensitizers to sexual and aversive stimuli. *Perceptual and Motor Skills, 30,* 631–634.

Goodstein, R. K., & Swift, K. (1977). Psychotherapy with phobic patients: The marriage relationship as the source of symptoms and focus of treatment. *American Journal of Psychotherapy, 31,* 284–293.

Goorney, A. B., & O'Connor, P. J. (1971). Anxiety associated with flying. *British Journal of Psychiatry, 119,* 159–166.

Gordon, K. S., & Zax, M. (1981). Once more unto the breach dear friends. . . . A reconsideration of the literature on symptom substitution. *Clinical Psychology Review, 1,* 33–47.

Gore, S. (1978). The effect of social support in moderating the health consequences of unemployment. *Journal of Health and Social Behavior, 19,* 157–165.

Gossett, J. T. (1964). An experimental demonstration of Freudian repression proper. *Dissertation Abstracts, 25,* 2047–2048.

Gottesman, I. (1962). Differential inheritance of psychoneuroses. *Eugenics Quarterly, 9,* 223–227.

Gottesman, I. I., & Shields, J. (1976). A critical review of recent adoption, twin, and family studies of schizophrenia: Behavioral genetics perspectives. *Schizophrenia Bulletin, 2,* 360–398.

Gottesman, I. I. & Shields, J. (1982). *Schizophrenia: The epigenetic puzzle.* New York: Cambridge University Press.

Gottlieb, B. H. (Ed.). (1981). *Social networks and social support.* Beverly Hills, CA: Sage.

Gove, W. R., & Howell, P. (1974). Individual resources and mental hospitalization: A comparison and evaluation of the societal reaction and psychiatric perspectives. *American Sociological Review, 39,* 86–100.

Gray, J. A. (1971). *The psychology of fear and stress.* New York: McGraw-Hill.

Green, M., Green, R., & Carr, W. J. (1966). The hawk-goose phenomenon: A replication and an extension. *Psychonomic Science, 4,* 185–186.

Greenspoon, J. (1951). *The effect of verbal and non-verbal stimuli on the frequency of members of two verbal response classes.* Unpublished doctoral dissertation, Indiana University, Bloomington.

Greenspoon, J. (1955). The reinforcing effect of two spoken sounds on the frequency of two responses. *American Journal of Psychology, 68,* 409–416.

Grieger, R., & Boyd, J. (1980). *Rational–emotive therapy: A skills-based approach.* New York: Van Nostrand Reinhold.

Grinker, R. R., & Spiegel, J. P. (1945). *Men under stress.* Philadelphia: Blakiston.

Grinker, R. R., & Spiegel, J. P. (1963). *Men under stress.* New York: McGraw-Hill.

Gross, M. L. (1979). *The psychological society.* New York: Simon & Schuster.

Grosz, H. J., & Zimmerman, J. (1965). Experimental analysis of hysterical blindness: A follow-up report and new experimental data. *Archives of General Psychiatry, 13,* 255–260.

Grosz, H. J., & Zimmerman, J. (1970). A second detailed case study of functional blindness: Further demonstration of the contribution of objective psychological laboratory data. *Behavior Therapy, 1,* 115–123.

Grubb, T., & Watt, N. F. (1979, March). *Longitudinal approaches to promoting social adjustment through public school programs.* Paper presented at the meeting of the Society for Research in Child Development, San Francisco.

Grusky, Z. (1987). The practice of psychotherapy: A search for principles in an ambiguous art. *Psychotherapy, 24,* 1–6.

Gunnar, M. R. (1980). Control, warning signals, and distress in infancy. *Developmental Psychology, 16,* 281–289.

Gunnar-von Gnechten, M. (1978). Changing a frightening toy into a pleasant toy by allowing infant to control its actions. *Developmental Psychology, 14,* 157–162.

Gur, R. C., & Sackeim, H. A. (1979). Self-deception: A concept in search of a phenomenon. *Personality and Social Psychology, 37,* 147–169.

Guskin, S. (1963). Social psychologies of mental deficiencies. In N. R. Ellis (Ed.), *Handbook of mental deficiency.* New York: McGraw-Hill.

Guskin, S. L., Bartel, N. R., & MacMillan, D. L. (1975). The perspective of the labeled child. In N. Hobbs (Ed.). *Issues in the classification of exceptional children* (Vol. 2, pp. 189–212). San Francisco: Jossey-Bass.

Haber, R. N., & Hershenson, M. (1973). *The psychology of visual perception.* New York: Holt.

Hafner, R. J. (1976). Fresh symptoms emergence after intensive behavior therapy. *British Journal of Psychiatry. 129,* 378–383.

Hafner, R. J. (1983). Behaviour therapy for agoraphobic men. *Behaviour Research and Therapy, 21,* 51–56.

Hafner, R. J. (1984). Predicting the effects on husbands of behaviour therapy for wives' agoraphobia. *Behaviour Research and Therapy, 22,* 217–226.

Hafner, R. J., & Ross, M. W. (1984). Agoraphobia in women: Factor analysis of symptoms and personality correlates of factor scores in a clinical population. *Behaviour Research and Therapy, 22,* 441–444.

Haggerty, R. J. (1980). Life stress and social supports. *Developmental Medical and Child Neurology, 22,* 391–400.

Haley, G. A. (1974). Eye movement responses of repressors and sensitizers to a stressful film. *Journal of Research in Personality, 8,* 88–94.

Hall, C. S., & Lindzey, G. (1967). *Theories of personality.* New York: Wiley.

Hall, N. R., & Goldstein, A. L. (1986). Thinking well: The chemical links between emotions and health. *The Sciences, 26,* 34–40.

Hallam, R. S. (1978). Agoraphobia: A critical review of the concept. *British Journal of Psychiatry, 133,* 314–319.

Hallam, R. S., & Rachman, S. (1976). Current status of aversion therapy. In M. Hersen, R. Eisler, & P. Miller (Eds.), *Progress in behavior modification* (Vol. 2). New York: Academic Press.

Halpern, H. J. (1944). Hysterical amblyopia. *Bulletin of the United States Army Medical Department, 72,* 84–87.

Hamilton, M. (1982). Symptoms and assessment of depression. In E. S. Paykel (Ed.), *Handbook of affective disorders.* New York: Guilford Press.

Hammen, C. L., & Peters, S. D. (1977). Differential responses to male and female depressive reactions. *Journal of Consulting and Clinical Psychology, 45,* 994–1001.

Hammen, C. L., & Peters, S. D. (1978). Interpersonal consequences of depression: Responses to men and women enacting a depressed role. *Journal of Abnormal Psychology, 87,* 322–332.

Hand, I., & Lamontagne, Y. (1976). The exacerbation of interpersonal problems after rapid phobia-removal. *Psychotherapy: Theory, Research and Practice, 13,* 405–411.

Haney, J. N. (1974). Continuous associative responding to threatening and non threatening stimuli by repressors and sensitizers. *Journal of Consulting and Clinical Psychology, 42,* 152.

Hapsel, K. C., & Harris, R. S. (1982). Effect of tachistoscopic stimulation of subconscious oedipal wishes on competitive performance: A failure to replicate. *Journal of Abnormal Psychology, 91,* 437–443.

Harburg, E., Blakelock, E. H., & Roeper, R. J. (1979). Resentful and reflective coping with arbitrary authority and blood pressure: Detroit. *Psychosomatic Medicine, 41,* 189–202.

Harburg, E., Erfurt, J. C., Hauenstein, L. S., Chape, C., Schull, W. J., & Schork, M. A. (1973). Socio-ecological stress, suppressed hostility, skin color, and black–white male blood pressure: Detroit. *Psychomatic Medicine, 35,* 276–296.

Harder, D. W., Strauss, J. S., Kokes, R. F., Ritzler, B. A., & Gift, T. E. (1980). Life events and psychopathology severity among first psychiatric admissions. *Journal of Abnormal Psychology, 89,* 165–180.

Hare, R. D. (1966). Denial of threat and emotional response to impending painful stimulation. *Journal of Consulting Psychology, 30,* 359–361.

Hariman, J. (1980). What is hypnotism? A proposal. *Australian Journal of Clinical Hypnotherapy, 1,* 2–11.

Hariman, J. (1982). The bearing of the "concentration" theory of hypnosis on the Freudian conception of the unconscious. *Australian Journal of Clinical Hypnotherapy and Hypnosis, 3,* 85–90.

Harlow, H. F. (1971). *Learning to love.* San Francisco: Albion.

Harlow, H. F., & Harlow, M. K. (1965). The affectional systems. In A. M. Schrier (Ed.), *Behavior of nonhuman primates* (Vol. 2, pp. 287–334). New York: Academic Press.

Harlow, H. F., & Zimmermann, R. R. (1959). Affectional responses in the infant monkey. *Science, 130,* 421–432.

Harrell, J. P. (1980). Psychological factors and hypertension: A status report. *Psychological Bulletin, 87,* 482–501.

Harris, B. (1979). Whatever happened to little Albert? *American Psychologist, 34,* 151–160.

Harrow, M., & Quinlan, D. (1977). Is disordered thinking unique to schizophrenia? *Archives of General Psychiatry, 34,* 15–21.

Harvey, P., Winters, K. C., Weintraub, S., & Neale, J. M. (1981). Distractibility in children vulnerable to psychotherapy. *Journal of Abnormal Psychology, 90,* 298–304.

Heath, R. G. (1960). A biochemical hypothesis on the etiology of schizophrenia. In D. D. Jackson (Ed.), *The etiology of schizophrenia.* New York: Basic.

Heath, R. G., & Krupp, I. M. (1967). Schizophrenia as an immunologic disorder. *Archives of General Psychiatry, 16,* 1–33.

Heath, R. G., Martens, S., Leach, B. E., Cohen, M., & Angel, C. (1957). Effect on behavior in humans with the administration of taraxin. *American Journal of Psychiatry, 114,* 14–24.

Heilbrun, K. S. (1980). Silverman's subliminal psychodynamic activation: A failure to replicate. *Journal of Abnormal Psychology, 89,* 560–566.

Heilbrun, K. S. (1982). Reply to Silverman. *Journal of Abnormal Psychology, 91,* 134–135.

Heimberg, R. G. (1985). What makes traumatic stress traumatic? *Behavior Therapy, 16,* 417–419.

Heine, R. W. (1953). A comparison of parents' reports on psychotherapeutic experience with psychoanalytic, nondirective, and Adlerian therapists. *American Journal of Psychotherapy, 7,* 16–23.

Helweg-Larsen, P., Hoffmeyer, H., Kieler, J., Thaysen, E. H., Thaysen, J. H., Thygesen, P., & Wulff, M. H. (1952). Famine disease in German concentration camps: Complications and sequels. *Acta Psychiatrica Scandinavica, Supplementum, 83,* 11–460.

Hemphill, R. E. (1941). The importance of the first year of war in mental disease. *Bristol Medico-Chirurgical Journal, 58,* 11–18.

Herrnstein, R. J. (1969). Method and theory in the study of avoidance. *Psychological Review, 76,* 49–69.

Hersen, M., Bellack, A. S., Himmelhoch, J. M., & Thase, M. E. (1984). Effects of social skill training, amitriptyline, and psychotherapy in unipolar depressed women. *Behavior Therapy, 15,* 21–40.

Hesselbach, C. F. (1962). Superego regression in paranoia. *Psychoanalytic Quarterly, 31,* 341–350.

Highland, A. C. (1980). Confounding of the repression–sensitization scale, controlled for social desirability, with the IPAT anxiety scale. *Psychological Reports, 47,* 1003–1006.

Hilgard, E. R., Atkinson, R. C., & Atkinson, R. L. (1975). *Introduction to psychology* (6th ed). New York: Harcourt Brace Jovanovich.

Hill, K. A. (1984). Verbal reports of stimulus effects on learning: Introspection revisited. *Journal of Research in Personality, 18,* 480–490.

Himadi, W. G., Boice, R., & Barlow, D. H. (1986). Assessment of agoraphobia: II. Measurement of clinical change. *Behaviour Research and Therapy, 24,* 321–332.

Himadi, W. G., Cerny, J. A., Barlow, D. H., & Cohen, S. (1986). The relationship of marital adjustment to agoraphobia treatment outcome. *Behaviour Research and Therapy, 24,* 107–115.

Hinde, R. A. (1970). *Animal behavior: A synthesis of ethology and comparative psychology* (2nd ed.). New York: McGraw-Hill.

Hintzman, D. L. (1978). *The psychology of learning and memory.* San Francisco: Freeman.

Hockey, G. R. J., Davies, S., & Gray, M. M. (1972). Forgetting as a function of sleep at different times of day. *Quarterly Journal of Experimental Psychology, 24,* 386–393.

Hodges, W. F., & Spielberger, C. D. (1966). The effects of threat of shock on heart rate for subjects who differ in manifest anxiety and fear of shock. *Psychophysiology, 2,* 287–294.

Hogarty, G. E., Goldberg, S. C., & the Collaborative Study Group, Baltimore. (1973). Drug and sociotherapy in the aftercare of schizophrenic patients. *Archives of General Psychiatry, 28,* 54–63.

Hokanson, J. E. (1961). The effects of frustration and anxiety on overt aggression. *Journal of Abnormal Psychology, 62,* 346–351.

Hokanson, J. E., & Burgess, M. M. (1962a). The effects of status, type of frustration and aggression on vascular processes. *Journal of Abnormal and Social Psychology, 65,* 232–237.

Hokanson, J. E., & Burgess, H. (1962b). The effects of three types of agression on vascular process. *Journal of Abnormal and Social Psychology, 64,* 446–449.

Hokanson, J. E., & Shelter, S. (1961). The effect of overt aggression on physiological arousal level. *Journal of Abnormal and Social Psychology, 63,* 446–448.

Hokanson, J. E., Willers, K. R., & Koropsak, E. (1968). The modification of autonomic responses during aggressive interchanges. *Journal of Personality, 36,* 386–404.

Hollon, S. D., & Jacobson, V. (1985). Cognitive approaches. In M. Hersen & A. S. Bellack (Eds.), *Handbook of clinical behavior therapy with adults.* New York: Plenum.

Holmes, D. (1972). Repression or interference: A further investigation. *Journal of Personality and Social Psychology, 22,* 163–170.

Holmes, D. S. (1974). Investigations of repression: Differential recall of material experimentally or naturally associated with ego threat. *Psychological Bulletin, 81,* 632–653.

Holmes, D. S., & Schallow, J. R. (1969). Reduced recall after ego threat: Repression or response competition? *Journal of Personality and Social Psychology, 13,* 145–152.

Holt, R. R. (1970). On the interpersonal and intrapersonal consequences of expressing or not expressing anger. *Journal of Consulting and Clinical Psychology, 35,* 8–12.

Hopkins, F. (1943). Decrease in admission to mental observation wards during war. *British Medical Journal, 1,* 358.

Horowitz, M. J. (1977). The core characteristics of hysterical personality. In M. J. Horowitz (Ed.), *Hysterical personality.* New York: Jason Aronson.

Horvath, T., Friedman, J., & Meares, R. (1980). Attention in hysteria: A study of Janet's hypothesis by means of habituation and arousal measures. *American Journal of Psychiatry, 137,* 217–220.

Horvath, T., & Meares, R. (1979). The sensory filter in schizophrenia: A study of habituation, arousal, and the dopamine hypothesis. *British Journal of Psychiatry, 134,* 39–45.

Hudson, B. (1974). The families of agoraphobics treated by behaviour therapy. *British Journal of Social Work, 4,* 51–59.

Hugdahl, K., Fredrikson, M., & Ohman, A. (1977). "Preparedness" and "arousability" as determinants of electrodermal conditioning. *Behaviour Research and Therapy, 15,* 345–353.

Hulse, S. H., Egeth, H., & Deese, J. (1980). *The psychology of learning* (6th ed.). New York: McGraw-Hill.

Husaini, B. A., Neff, J. A., Newbrough, J. R., & Moore, M. (1982). The stress-buffering role of social support and personal competence among the rural married. *Journal of Community Psychology, 10,* 409–426.

Hutt, L. D., & Anderson, J. P. (1967). Perceptual defense and vigilance: Prediction from the Byrne Scale of Repression–Sensitization. *Psychonomic Science, 9,* 473–474.

Ingram, I. M. (1961). Obsessional illness in mental hospital patients. *Journal of Mental Science, 107,* 382–402.

Ironside, R., & Batchelor, I. R. C. (1945). The ocular manifestations of hysteria in relation to flying. *British Journal of Ophthalmology, 29,* 88–98.

Jaco, E. G. (1960). *The social epidemiology of mental disorders.* New York: Russell Sage Foundation.

Jacobs, W. J., & Nadel, L. (1985). Stress induced recovery of fears and phobias. *Psychological Review, 92,* 512–531.

Jacobsen, P. B., & Steele, R. S. (1979). From present to past: Freudian archaeology. *International Review of Psychoanalysis, 6,* 349–362.

Jacobson, E. (1964). *Self-operations control.* Chicago: National Foundation for Progressive Relaxation.

Janet, P. (1929). *The major symptoms of hysteria.* New York: Macmillan.

Janis, I. L. (1951). *Air war and emotional stress.* New York: McGraw-Hill.

Janis, I. L. (1982). *Stress, attitudes, and decisions.* New York: Praeger.

Janis, I. L. (1983). Foreword. In E. J. Langer (Ed.), *The psychology of control.* Beverly Hills, CA: Sage.

Janis, I. L., & Mann, L. (1977). *Decision making.* New York: Free Press.

Jenkins, J. G., & Dallenbach, K. M. (1924). Oblivescence during sleep and waking. *American Journal of Psychology, 35,* 605–612.

Jesberger, J. A., & Richardson, J. S. (1985). Animal models of depression: Parallels and correlates to severe depression in humans. *Biological Psychiatry, 20,* 764–784.

Jones, M. M. (1980). Conversion reaction: Anachronism or evolutionary form? A review of neurologic, behavioral and psychoanalytic literature. *Psychological Bulletin, 87*, 427–441.

Joy, V. L. (1963). *Repression–sensitization and interpersonal behavior*. Paper presented at the meeting of the American Psychological Association, Philadelphia.

Jung, C. G. (1961). *Memories, dreams, reflections* (A. Jaffé, Ed., and R. Wilson and C. Wilson, Trans.) New York: Random House. Paperback reprint: New York: Vintage Books, 1965.

Kahn, M. (1966). The physiology of catharsis. *Journal of Personality and Social Psychology, 3*, 278–286.

Kalinowski, L. B. (1980). Convulsive therapies. In H. I. Kaplan, A. M. Freedman, & B. J. Sadock (Eds.), *Comprehensive textbook of psychiatry* (Vol. 3). Baltimore: Williams & Wilkins.

Kallmann, F. J. (1953). *Heredity in health and mental disorder*. New York: Norton.

Kallmann, F. J. (1958). The use of genetics in psychiatry. *Journal of Mental Sciences, 104*, 542–549.

Kasl, V., & Cobb, S. (1970). Blood pressure changes undergoing job loss: A preliminary report. *Psychosomatic Medicine, 32*, 19–38.

Katkin, E. S. (1965). Relationship between manifest anxiety and two indices of autonomic response to stress. *Journal of Personality and Social Psychology, 2*, 324–333.

Katz, J. L., Weiner, H., Gallagher, T. F., & Hellman, L. (1970). Stress, distress, and ego defenses. *Archives of General Psychiatry, 23*, 131–142.

Kaufman, I. C., & Rosenblum, L. A. (1967a). Depression in infant monkeys separated from their mothers. *Science, 155*, 1030–1031.

Kaufman, I. C., & Rosenblum, L. A. (1967b). The reaction to separation in infant monkeys: Anaclitic depression and conservation withdrawal. *Psychosomatic Medicine, 29*, 648–675.

Kazdin, A. E. (1978). *History of behavior modification: Experimental foundations of contemporary research*. Baltimore: University Park Press.

Kazdin, A. E. (1979). Fictions, factors, and factions of behavior therapy. *Behavior Therapy, 10*, 629–654.

Kazdin, A. E. (1982). Symptom substitution, generalization and response covariation: Implication for psychotherapy outcome. *Psychological Bulletin, 91*, 349–365.

Keane, T. M. (1985). Defining traumatic stress: Some comments on the current terminological confusion. *Behavior Therapy, 16*, 419–423.

Kellogg, R. T. (1980). Is conscious attention necessary for long-term storage? *Journal of Experimental Psychology: Human Learning and Memory, 6*, 379–390.

Kellogg, R. T. (1982). When can we introspect accurately about mental processes? *Memory and Cognition, 10*, 141–144.

Kelly, F. S., Farina, A., & Mosher, D. L. (1971). Ability of schizophrenic women to create a favorable or unfavorable impression on an interviewer. *Journal of Consulting and Clinical Psychology, 36*, 404–409.

Kelly, J. A., & Lamparski, D. M. (1985). Outpatient treatment of schizophrenics: Social skills and problem-solving training. In M. Hersen & A. S. Bellack (Eds.), *Handbook of clinical behavior therapy with adults*. New York: Plenum.

Kendler, H. H. (1968). *Basic psychology*. (2nd ed.). New York: Meredith.

Kennedy, S., Thompson, R., Stancer, H. C., Roy, A., & Persad, E. (1983). Life events precipitating mania. *British Journal of Psychiatry, 142*, 398–403.

Kennedy, T. D. (1970). Verbal conditioning without awareness: The use of programmed reinforcement and recurring assessment of awareness. *Journal of Experimental Psychology, 84*, 487–494.

Kennedy, T. D. (1971). Reinforcement frequency, task characteristics, and interval of awareness assessment as factors in verbal conditioning without awareness. *Journal of Experimental Psychology, 88*, 103–112.

Kenny, F. T., Solyom, L., & Solyom, C. (1973). Faradic disruption of obsessive ideation in the treatment of obsessive neurosis. *Behavior Therapy, 4*, 448–457.

Keppel, G. (1968). Retroactive and proactive intereference. In T. R. Dixon & D. L. Horton (Eds.), *Verbal behavior theory and general behavior theory* (pp. 172–213). Englewood Cliffs, NJ: Prentice-Hall.

Keppel, G. (1972). Forgetting. In C. P. Duncan, L. Sechrest, & A. W. Melton (Eds.), *Human memory: Festschrift for Benton J. Underwood* (pp. 83–109). Englewood Cliffs, NJ: Prentice-Hall.

Kessler, S. (1980). The genetics of schizophrenia: A review. *Schizophrenia Bulletin, 6*, 404–416.

Kihlstrom, J. F. (1979). Hypnosis and psychopathology: Retrospect and prospect. *Journal of Abnormal Psychology, 88*, 459–473.

Kihlstrom, J. F. (1983). Instructed forgetting: Hypnotic and nonhypnotic. *Journal of Experimental Psychology: General, 112*, 73–79.

Kihlstrom, J. F. (1984). Conscious, subconscious, unconscious: A cognitive perspective. In K. S. Bowers & D. Meichenbaum (Eds.), *The unconscious reconsidered* (pp. 149–211). New York: Wiley.

Kipper, D. A. (1977). Behavior therapy for fears brought on by war experiences. *Journal of Consulting and Clinical Psychology, 45*, 216–221.

Kirkpatrick, R. A. (1981). Witchcraft and lupus erythematosus. *Journal of the American Medical Association, 245*, 1937.

Kirsch, I., Tennen, H., Wickless, C., Saccone, A. J., & Cody, S. (1983). The role of expectancy in fear reduction. *Behavior Therapy, 14,* 520–533.

Kline, M. V. (1958). The dynamics of hypnotically induced anti-social behavior. *Journal of Psychology, 45,* 239–245.

Klinger, B. I. (1970). Effect of peer model responsiveness and length of induction procedure on hypnotic responsiveness. *Journal of Abnormal Psychology, 75,* 15–18.

Knight, R. G., Youard, P. J., & Wooles, I. M. (1985). Visual information-processing deficits in chronic schizophrenic subjects using tasks matched for discriminating power. *Journal of Abnormal Psychology, 94,* 454–459.

Knight, R. P. (1940). The relationship of latent homosexuality to the mechanism of paranoid delusions. *Bulletin of the Menninger Clinic, 4,* 149–159.

Kolb, L. C. (1977). *Modern clinical psychiatry.* Philadelphia: Saunders.

Konorski, J. (1967). *Integrative activity of the brain: An interdisciplinary approach.* Chicago: University of Chicago Press.

Kovacs, M., & Beck, A. (1978). Maladaptive cognitive structures in depression. *American Journal of Psychiatry, 135,* 525–533.

Kovacs, M., Rush, A. J., Beck, A. T., & Hollon, S. D. (1981). Depressed outpatients treated with cognitive therapy or pharmacotherapy: A one-year follow-up. *Archives of General Psychiatry, 38,* 33–39.

Kraus, A., & Lilienfeld, A. (1959). Some epidemiologic aspects of the high mortality rate in the young widowed group. *Journal of Chronic Diseases, 10,* 207–217.

Krauthammer, C., & Klerman, G. L. (1979). The epidemiology of mania. In B. Shopsin (Ed.), *Manic illness.* New York: Raven Press.

Kroll, P., Chamberlain, P., & Halpern, D. (1979). The diagnosis of Briquet's syndrome in a male population. *Journal of Nervous and Mental Disease, 169,* 171–174.

Kugelmass, S., Marcus, J., & Schmueli, J. (1985). Psychophysiological reactivity in high-risk children. *Schizophrenia Bulletin, 11,* 66–73.

Kuhn, T. (1962). *The structure of scientific revolutions.* Chicago: University of Chicago Press.

Kundu, R., & Chandidas, B. (1981). Social desirability and sociometric choice status. *Psychologia: An International Journal of Psychology in The Orient, 24,* 185–189.

Lader, M. H., & Mathews, A. M. (1968). A physiological model of phobic anxiety and desensitization. *Behaviour Research and Therapy, 6,* 411–421.

Lader, M. H., & Sartorius, N. (1968). Anxiety in patients with hysterical conversion symptoms. *Journal of Neurology, Neurosurgery and Psychiatry, 31,* 490–495.

Ladouceur, R. (1983). Participant modeling with or without cognitive treatment for phobias. *Journal of Consulting and Clinical Psychology, 51,* 942–944.

Laing, R. D. (1964). Is schizophrenia a disease? *International Journal of Social Psychiatry, 10,* 184–193.

Lane, E. A., & Albee, G. W. (1965). Childhood intellectual differences between schizophrenic adults and their siblings. *American Journal of Orthopsychiatry, 35,* 747–753.

Langer, E. J., Janis, I. L., Wolfer, J. A. (1975). Reduction of psychological stress in surgical patients. *Journal of Experimental Social Psychology, 11,* 155–165.

Lanin-Kettering, I., & Harrow, M. (1985). The thought behind the words: A view of schizophrenic speech and thinking disorders. *Schizophrenia Bulletin, 11,* 1–7.

Laplanche, J., & Pontalis, J. B. (1968). *Vocabulaire de la psychanalyse.* Paris: Universitaires de France. (In French)

Larocco, J. M., House, J. S., & French, R. P. (1980). Social support, occupational stress, and health. *Journal of Health and Social Behavior, 21,* 202–218.

Last, C. G., Barlow, D. H., & O'Brien, G. T. (1984). Precipitants of agoraphobia: Role of stressful life events. *Psychological Reports, 54,* 567–570.

Latané, B., & Wheeler, L. (1966). Emotionality and reactions to disaster. *Journal of Experimental Social Psychology, Supplement, 2,* 95–102.

Latimer, P. R., & Sweet, A. A. (1984). Cognitive versus behavioral procedures in cognitive behavior therapy: A critical review of the evidence. *Journal of Behavior Therapy and Experimental Psychiatry, 15,* 9–22.

Lazarus, R. S. (1966). *Psychological stress and the coping process.* New York: McGraw-Hill.

Lazarus, R. S. (1979). Positive denial: The case of not facing reality. *Psychology Today, 13,* 44–60.

Lazarus, R. S. (1983). The costs of benefits and denial. In S. Breznitz (Ed.), *Denial of stress.* New York: International Universities Press.

Lee, C. (1984). Efficacy expectations and outcome expectations as predictors of performance in a snake-handling task. *Cognitive Therapy and Research, 8,* 509–516.

Lee, G. A. (1974). Marriage and anomia: A causal adjustment. *Journal of Marriage and the Family, 36*, 523–532.

Lehmkuhl, U. (1983). Psychogenic astasia—abasia and transcultural conflict. *Acta Paedopsychiatrica, 49*, 211–219. (From *Psychological Abstracts*, 1984, *71*(10), Abstract No. 26065).

Lehrer, P. M. (1982). How to relax and how not to relax: A reevaluation of the work of Edmund Jacobson: I. *Behaviour Research and Therapy, 20*, 417–428.

Lehrer, P. M., Woolfolk, R. L., Rooney, A. J., McCann, B., & Carrington, P. (1983). Progressive relaxation and meditation. *Behaviour Research and Therapy, 21*, 651–662.

Leon, G. R., Butcher, J. N., Kleinman, M., Goldberg, A., & Almagor, M. (1981). Survivors of the holocaust and their children: current status and adjustment. *Journal of Personality and Social Psychology, 41*, 503–516.

Lester, D. (1983). *Why people kill themselves* (2nd ed.). Springfield, IL: Thomas.

Leuba, C. (1960). Theories of hypnosis: A critique and a proposal. *American Journal of Clinical Hypnosis, 3*. 43–48.

Levin, S. (1984a). Frontal lobe dysfunctions in schizophrenia: I. Eye movement impairments. *Journal of Psychiatric Research, 18*, 27–55.

Levin, S. (1984b). Frontal lobe dysfunctions in schizophrenia: II. Impairments of psychological and brain functions. *Journal of Psychiatric Research, 18*, 57–72.

Levy, A. B., Kurtz, N., & Kling, A. S. (1984). Association between cerebral ventricular enlargement and suicide attempts in chronic schizophrenia. *American Journal of Psychiatry, 141*, 438–439.

Levy, R. S., & Jankovic, J. J. (1983). Placebo-induced conversion reaction: A neurobehavioral and EEG study of hysterical aphasia, seizure and coma. *Journal of Abnormal Psychology, 92*, 243–249.

Lewin, I. (1982). Driver training: A perceptual-motor skill approach. *Ergonomics, 25*, 917–924.

Lewine, R. J., Watt, N. F., & Fryer, J. H. (1978). A study of childhood social competence, adult premorbid competence, and psychiatric outcome in three schizophrenic subtypes. *Journal of Abnormal Psychology, 87*, 294–302.

Lewinsohn, P. M. (1956). Some individual differences in physiological reactivity to stress. *Journal of Comparative and Physiological Psychology, 49*, 271–277.

Lewinsohn, P. M., Mischel, W., Chaplin, W., & Barton, R. (1980). Social competence and depression: The role of illusory self-perceptions. *Journal of Abnormal Psychology, 89*, 203–212.

Lewis, A. (1942). Incidence of neurosis in England under war conditions. *Lancet, ii*, 175–183.

Lewis, D. A., & Hugi, R. (1981). Therapeutic stations and chronically treated mentally ill. *Social Service Review, 55*, 206–220.

Lewis, H. B. (1981). *Freud and modern psychology* (Vol. 1). New York: Plenum.

Lewis, H. B. (1985). Depression vs. paranoia: Why are there sex differences in mental illness? *Journal of Personality, 53*, 150–178.

Lewis, T. H. (1988). The presenting psychiatric problem and its evanescence: The integrative function of group psychotherpy. *Dynamic Psychotherapy, 6*, 55–59.

Ley, R. (1985). Agoraphobia, the panic attack and the hyperventilation syndrome. *Behaviour Research and Therapy, 23*, 79–81.

Lick, J. (1975). Expectancy, false galvanic skin response feedback, and systematic desensitization in the modification of phobic behavior. *Journal of Consulting and Clinical Psychology, 43*, 557–567.

Lick, J., & Bootzin, R. (1975). Expectancy factors in the treatment of fear: Methodological and theoretical issues. *Psychological Bulletin, 82*, 917–931.

Lieberman, P. B., & Strauss, J. S. (1984). The recurrence of mania: Environmental factors and medical treatment. *American Journal of Psychiatry, 141*, 77–80.

Liebson, I. (1969). Conversion reaction: A learning theory approach. *Behaviour Research and Therapy, 7*, 217–218.

Lin, N., Simeone, R. S., Ensel, W. M., & Kuo, W. (1979). Social support, stressful life events, and illness: A model and an empirical test. *Journal of Health and Social Behavior, 20*, 108–119.

Lindemann, J. E. (1981). *Psychological and behavioral aspects of physical disability: A manual for health practitioners*. New York: Plenum.

Linehan, M. M., & Nielsen, S. L. (1981). Assessment of suicide ideation and parasuicide: Hopelessness and social desirability. *Journal of Consulting and Clinical Psychology, 49*, 773–775.

Linehan, M. M., & Nielsen, S. L. (1983). Social desirability: Its relevance to the measurement of hopelessness and suicidal behavior. *Journal of Consulting and Clinical Psychology, 51*, 141–143.

Linn, G. J., & McGranahan, D. A. (1980). Personal disruptions, social integration, subject well-being and predisposition toward the use of counselling services. *American Journal of Community Psychology, 8*, 87–100.

Linton, M. (1975). Memory for real-world events. In D. A. Norman & D. E. Rumelhart (Eds.), *Explorations in cognition*. San Francisco: Freeman.

Loew, C. A. (1967). Acquisition of a hostile attitude and its relationship to aggressive behavior. *Journal of Personality and Social Psychology, 5*, 335–341.

Loftus, E. F., & Loftus, G. R. (1980). On the permanence of stored information in the human brain. *American Psychologist, 35*, 409–420.

Lomont, J. F. (1965). The repression–sensitization dimension in relationship to anxiety responses. *Journal of Consulting Psychology, 29*, 84–86.

Lovatt, D. J., & Warr, P. B. (1968). Recall after sleep. *American Journal of Psychology, 81*, 253–257.

Luborsky, L., Blinder, B., & Schimek, J. (1965). Looking, recalling and GSR as a function of defense. *Journal of Abnormal Psychology, 70*, 270–280.

Lukoff, D., Snyder, K., Ventura, J., & Nuechterlein, K. H. (1984). Life events, familial stress, and coping in the developmental course of schizophrenia. *Schizophrenia Bulletin, 10*, 258–292.

Lynch, S., Watts, W. A., Galloway, C., & Tryphonopoulos, S. (1973). Appropriateness of anxiety and drive for affiliation. *Journal of Research in Personality, 7*, 71–77.

MacKinnon, D., & Dukes, W. (1964). Repression. In L. Postman (Ed.), *Psychology in the making* (pp. 662–744). New York: Knopf.

Mackintosh, N. J. (1983). *Conditioning and associative learning.* New York: Oxford University Press.

MacLeod, C., Mathews, A., & Tata, P. (1986). Attentional bias in emotional disorders. *Journal of Abnormal Psychology, 95*, 15–20.

Maddi, S. R. (1980). *Personality theories: A comparative analysis.* Chicago: Dorsey Press.

Mahl, G. F., Rothenberg, A., Delgado, J. M. R., & Hamlin, H. (1964). Psychological responses in the human to intracerebral electrical stimulation. *Psychosomatic Medicine, 26*, 337–368.

Mahoney, M. J. (1977). Personal science: A cognitive learning therapy. In A. Ellis & R. Grieger (Eds.), *Handbook of rational-emotive therapy* (pp. 352–366). New York: Springer.

Mahoney, M. J. (1985). Open exchange and epistemic progress. *American Psychologist, 40*, 29–39.

Maier, S. F., & Seligman, M. E. P. (1976). Learned helplessness: Theory and evidence. *Journal of Experimental Psychology, 105*, 3–46.

Malmo, R. B. (1970). Emotions and muscle tension: The story of Anne. *Psychology Today, 3*(10), 64–67.

Maltzman, I. (1977). Orienting in classical conditioning and generalization of the galvanic skin response to words: An overview. *Journal of Experimental Psychology: General, 106*, 1977, 111–119.

Mann, A. H. (1977). Psychiatric morbidity and hostility in hypertension. *Psychological Medicine, 7*, 653–659.

Mann, A. (1984). Hypertension: Psychological aspects and diagnostic impact in a clinical trial. *Psychosomatic Medicine: Monograph Supplement 5.* Cambridge, England: Cambridge University Press.

Marcia, J. E., Rubin, B. M., & Efran, J. S. (1969). Systematic desensitization: Expectancy change or counterconditioning? *Journal of Abnormal Psychology, 74*, 382–387.

Marengo, J., & Harrow, M. (1985). Thought disorder: A function of schizophrenia, mania or psychosis? *Journal of Nervous and Mental Disease, 173*, 35–41.

Markowitz, A. (1969). Influence of the repression–sensitization dimension, affect value, and ego threat on incidental learning. *Journal of Personality and Social Psychology, 11*, 374–380.

Marks, I. M. (1969). *Fears and phobias.* New York: Academic Press.

Marks, I. M. (1973). Research in neurosis: A selective review: I. Causes and courses. *Psychological Medicine, 3*, 436–454.

Marks, I. M. (1978). *Living with fear.* New York: McGraw-Hill.

Marks, I. M. & Herst, E. R. (1970). A survey of 1200 agoraphobics in Britain. *Social Psychiatry, 5*, 16–24.

Marmor, J. (1962). Psychoanalytic therapy as an educational process: Common denominators in the therapeutic approaches of different psychoanalytic schools. In J. H. Masserman (Ed.), *Science and psychoanalysis: Vol. 5. Psychoanalytic education* (pp. 286–299). New York: Grune & Stratton.

Marshall, J. R. (1984). The genetics of schizophrenia revisited. *Bulletin of the British Psychological Society, 37*, 177–181.

Marshall, J. R., & Pettitt, A. N. (1985). Discordant concordant rates. *Bulletin of the British Psychological Society, 38*, 6–9.

Marshall, W. L. (1985). The effects of variable exposure in flooding therapy. *Behavior Therapy, 16*, 117–135.

Martin, D., J., Abramson, L. Y., & Alloy, L. B. (1984). Illusion of control for self and others in depressed and nondepressed college students. *Journal of Personality and Social Psychology, 46*, 125–136.

Masserman, J. H. (1943). *Behavior and neurosis.* Chicago: University of Chicago Press.

Masserman, J. H. (1946). *Principles of dynamic psychiatry.* Philadelphia: Saunders.

Mathews, A. M., Gelder, M. G., & Johnston, D. W. (1981). *Agoraphobia: Nature and treatment*. New York: Guilford Press.

Mathews, A., & MacLeod, C. (1985). Selective processing of threat cues in anxiety states. *Behaviour Research and Therapy, 23*, 563–569.

Mathews, A., & MacLeod, C. (1986). Discrimination of threat cues without awareness in anxiety states. *Journal of Abnormal Psychology, 95*, 131–138.

Matthews, K. A., Glass, D. C., Rosenman, R. H., & Bortner, R. W. (1977). Competitive drive, pattern A, and coronary heart disease: A further analysis of some data from the Western collaborative group study. *Journal of Chronic Diseases, 30*, 489–498.

May, P. R. A., & Simpson, G. M. (1980a). Schizophrenia: Overview of treatment methods. In H. I. Kaplan, A. M. Freedman, & B. J. Sadock (Eds.), *Comprehensive textbook of psychiatry* (3rd ed., Vol. 2, pp. 1192–1216). Baltimore: Williams & Wilkins.

May, P. R. A., & Simpson, G. M. (1980b). Schizophrenia: Evaluation of treatment methods. In H. I. Kaplan, A. M. Freedman, & B. J. Sadock (Eds.), *Comprehensive textbook of psychiatry* (3rd ed., Vol. 2, pp. 1240–1274). Baltimore: Williams & Wilkins.

McCandless, B. R., Bilous, C. B., & Bennett, H. L. (1961). Peer popularity and dependence on adults in preschool age socialization. *Child Development, 32*, 511–518.

McCaul, K. D., & Malott, J. M. (1984). Distraction and coping with pain. *Psychological Bulletin, 95*, 516–533.

McCrae, R. R., & Costa, P. T. (1983). Social desirability scales: More substance than style. *Journal of Consulting and Clinical Psychology, 51*, 882–888.

McDonald, R. L. (1965). Ego-control patterns and attribution of hostility to self and others. *Journal of Personality and Social Psychology, 2*, 273–277.

McDonald, R. L. (1967). The effects of stress on self-attribution of hostility among ego control patterns. *Journal of Personality, 35*, 234–245.

McGeoch, J. A. (1932). Forgetting the law of disuse. *Psychological Review, 39*, 352–370.

McGhie, A. (1977). Attention and perception in schizophrenia. In B. A. Maher (Ed.), *Contributions to the psychopathology of schizophrenia*. New York: Academic Press.

McGhie, A., Chapman, J., & Lawson, J. S. (1965). The effect of distraction on schizophrenic performance: I. Perception and immediate memory. *British Journal of Psychiatry, 111*, 383–390.

McGinn, N. F., Harburg, E., Julius, S., & McLeod, J. M. (1964). Psychological correlates of blood pressure. *Psychological Bulletin, 61*, 209–219.

McGinnies, E. (1949). Emotionality and perceptual defense. *Psychological Review, 56*, 244–251.

McGlynn, F. D., & Cornell, C. E. (1985). Simple phobia. In M. Herson & A. S. Bellack (Eds.), *Handbook of clinical behavior therapy with adults*. New York: Plenum.

McGuigan, F. J. (1966). Covert oral behavior and auditory hallucinations. *Psychophysiology, 3*, 73–80.

Mckinney, W. T., & Moran, E. C. (1981). Animal models of schizophrenia. *American Journal of Psychiatry, 138*, 478–483.

Mckinney, W. T., Jr., Suomi, S. J., & Harlow, H. F. (1971). Depression in primates. *American Journal of Psychiatry, 127*, 1313–1320.

McNally, R. J. (1986). Pavlovian conditioning and preparedness: Effects of initial fear level. *Behaviour Research and Therapy, 24*, 27–33.

McNally, R. J., & Reiss, S. (1982). The preparedness theory of phobias and human safety-signal conditioning. *Behaviour Research and Therapy, 20*, 153–159.

McNally, R. J., & Steketee, G. S. (1985). The etiology and maintenance of severe animal phobias. *Behaviour Research and Therapy, 23*, 431–435.

Mechanic, D. (1967). Invited commentary on self, social environment and stress. In M. H. Appley & R. Trumbull (Eds.), *Psychological stress*. New York: Appleton-Century-Crofts.

Mednick, S. A. (1958). A learning theory approach to research in schizophrenia. *Psychological Bulletin, 55*, 316–327.

Mednick, S. A., & Schulsinger, F. (1968). Some premorbid characteristics related to breakdown in children with schizophrenic mothers. In D. Rosenthal & S. S. Kety (Eds.), *The transmission of schizophrenia*. Elmsford, NY: Pergamon Press.

Meichenbaum, D. (1971). Examination of model characteristics in reducing avoidance behavior. *Journal of Personality and Social Psychology, 17*, 298–307.

Meichenbaum, D. (1975). Self-instructional methods. In F. Kanfer & A. Goldstein (Eds.), *Helping people change*. Elmsford, NY: Pergamon Press.

Meichenbaum, D. (1977). *Cognitive-behavior modification*. New York: Plenum.

Meichenbaum, D., & Cameron, R. (1982). Cognitive behavior therapy. In G. T. Wilson & C. M. Franks (Eds.), *Contemporary behavior therapy: Conceptual and empirical foundations* (pp. 310–338). New York: Guilford Press.

Meissner, W. W. (1978). *The paranoid process*. New York: Jason Aronson.

Meissner, W. W. (1981). The schizophrenic and the paranoid process. *Schizophrenia Bulletin, 7*, 611–631.

Melges, F., & Bowlby, J. (1969). Types of hopelessness in psychopathological process. *Archives of General Psychiatry, 20*, 690–699.

Melzack, R. (1952). Irrational fears in the dog. *Canadian Journal of Psychology, 6*, 141–147.

Mendel, J. G. C., & Klein, D. F. (1969). Anxiety attacks with subsequent agoraphobia. *Comprehensive Psychiatry, 10*, 190–195.

Mendelson, M. (1982). Psychodynamics of depression. In E. S. Paykel (Ed.), *Handbook of affective disorders*. New York: Guilford Press.

Mendelwicz, J. (1979). Genetic forms of manic illness and the question of atypical mania. In B. Shopsin (Ed.), *Manic illness*. New York: Raven Press.

Merbaum, M., & Badia, P. (1967). Tolerance of repressors and sensitizers to noxious stimulation. *Journal of Abnormal Psychology, 72*, 349–353.

Merbaum, M., & Kazaoka, K. (1967). Reports of emotional experience by sensitizers and repressors during an interview transaction. *Journal of Abnormal Psychology, 72*, 101–105.

Merskey, H. (1979). *The analysis of hysteria*. London: Bailliere Tindall.

Messer, S. B. (1986). Behavioral and psychoanalytic perspectives at therapeutic choice points. *American Psychologist, 41*, 1261–1272.

Michelson, L., Mavissakalian, M., & Marchione, K. (1985). Cognitive and behavioral treatments of agoraphobia: Clinical, behavioral, and psychophysiological outcomes. *Journal of Consulting and Clinical Psychology, 53*, 913–925.

Michelson, L., Mavissakalian, M., Marchione, K., Dancu, C., & Greenwald, M. (1986). The role of self-directed in vivo-exposure in cognitive, behavioral, and psychophysiological treatments of agoraphobia. *Behavior Therapy, 17*, 91–108.

Miller, B. V., & Levis, D. J. (1971). The effects of varying short visual exposure times to a phobic test stimulus on subsequent avoidance behavior. *Behaviour Research and Therapy, 9*, 17–21.

Miller, D. G. (1983). Hostile emotion and obsessional neurosis. *Psychological Medicine, 13*, 813–819.

Miller, D. G., & Loftus, E. F. (1976). Influencing memory for people and their actions. *Bulletin of the Psychonomic Society, 7*, 9–11.

Miller, E. (1968). A note on the visual performance of a subject with unilateral functional blindness. *Behaviour Research and Therapy, 6*, 115–116.

Miller, I. W., & Norman, W. H. (1979). Learned helplessness in humans: A review and attribution theory. *Psychological Bulletin, 86*, 93–118.

Miller, J. (1981). Discussion of "The stress of deprivation in human relationships." *American Journal of Psychoanalysis, 41*, 235–238.

Miller, N. E. (1944). Experimental studies of conflict. In McV. Hunt (Ed.), *Personality and behavior disorders* (Vol. 1, pp. 431–465). New York: Ronald Press.

Miller, N. E. (1951). Comments on theoretical models illustrated by the development of a theory of conflict behavior. *Journal of Personality, 20*, 82–100.

Miller, R. E., Murphy, J. V., & Mirsky, I. A. (1959). Non-verbal communication of affect. *Journal of Clinical Psychology, 15*, 155–158.

Miller, S. M. (1979). Coping with impending stress: Psychophysiological and cognitive correlates of choice. *Psychophysiology, 16*, 572–581.

Miller, S. M. (1980). When is a little information a dangerous thing? Coping with stressful life-events by monitoring vs. blunting. In S. Levine & H. Ursim (Eds.), *Coping and health*. New York: Plenum.

Miller, S. M. (1981). Predictability and human stress: Toward a clarification of evidence and theory. In L. Berkowitz (Ed.), *Advances in Experimental Psychology* (Vol. 14). New York: Academic Press.

Miller, S. M., & Mangan, C. E. (1983). Interacting effects of information and coping style in adapting to gynecologic stress: Should the doctor tell all? *Journal of Personality and Social Psychology, 45*, 223–236.

Miller, S. M., & Seligman, M. E. P. (1982). The reformulated model of helplessness and depression: Evidence and theory. In R. W. J. Neufeld (Ed.), *Psychological stress and psychopathology*. New York: McGraw-Hill.

Millham, J., & Jacobson, L. I. (1978). Social desirability and the need for approval. In H. London & J. E. Exner (Eds.), *Dimensions of personality*. New York: Wiley.

Millham, J., & Kellogg, R. W. (1980). Need for social approval: Impression management or self-deception. *Journal of Research in Personality, 14*, 445–457.

Milton, F., & Hafner, J. (1979). The outcome of behavior therapy for agoraphobia in relation to marital adjustment. *Archives of General Psychiatry, 36*, 807–811.

Mineka, S., & Cook, M. (1986). Immunization against the observational conditioning of snake fear in rhesus monkeys. *Journal of Abnormal Psychology, 95,* 307–318.

Mineka, S., Cook, M., & Miller, S. (1984). Fear conditioned with escapable and inescapable shock: Effects of a feedback stimulus. *Journal of Experimental Psychology: Animal Behavior Processes, 10,* 307–322.

Mineka, S., Davidson, M., Cook, M., & Keir, R. (1984). Observational conditioning of snake fear in rhesus monkeys. *Journal of Abnormal Psychology, 93,* 355–372.

Mintz, S., & Alpert, M. (1972). Imagery vividness, reality testing, and schizophrenic hallucinations. *Journal of Abnormal Psychology, 79,* 310–316.

Minuchin, S. (1974). *Families and family therapy.* Cambridge, MA: Harvard University Press.

Minuchin, S., Baker, L., Rosman, B. L., Liebman, R., Milman, L., & Todd, T. C. (1975). A conceptual model of psychosomatic illness in children: Family organization and family therapy. *Archives of General Psychiatry, 32,* 1031–1038.

Mirsky, A. F., Silberman, E. K., Latz, A., & Nagler, S. (1985). Adult outcomes of high-risk children: Differential effects of town and kibbutz rearing. *Schizophrenia Bulletin, 11,* 150–154.

Mischel, W. (1971). *Introduction to personality.* New York: Holt, Rinehart & Winston.

Monat, A., & Lazarus, R. S. (1977). *Stress and coping.* New York: Columbia University Press.

Monnelly, E. P., Woodruff, R. A., & Robins, L. N. (1974). Manic–depressive illness and social achievement in a public hospital sample. *Acta Psychiatrica Scandinavica, 50,* 318–325.

Morris, P. (1981). The cognitive psychology of self reports. In C. Antaki (Ed.), *The psychology of ordinary explanations of social behavior* (pp. 183–203). London: Academic Press.

Morrison, J. R. (1974). Catatonia: Prediction of outcome. *Comprehensive Psychiatry, 15,* 317–324.

Moss, C. S. (1960). Brief successful psychotherapy of a chronic phobic reaction. *Journal of Abnormal and Social Psychology, 60,* 266–270.

Mowrer, O. H. (1947). On the dual nature of learning: A reinterpretation of "conditioning" and "problem-solving." *Harvard Educational Review, 17,* 102–148.

Mowrer, O. H. (1960). *Learning theory and behavior.* New York: Wiley.

Mucha, T. F., & Reinhardt, R. F. (1970). Conversion reactions in student aviators. *American Journal of Psychiatry, 127,* 493–497.

Mueller, D. P. (1980). Social networks: A promising direction for research on the relationship of the social environment to psychiatric disorder. *Social Science and Medicine, 14A,* 147–161.

Murphy, G. (1970). Experiments in overcoming self-deception. *Psychophysiology, 6,* 790–799.

Murphy, G. (1975). *Outgrowing self-deception.* New York: Basic Books.

Murray, E. J., & Foote, F. (1979). The origins of fear of snakes. *Behaviour Research and Therapy, 17,* 489–493.

Mussen, P. H., Conger, J. J., & Kagan, J. (1974). *Child development and personality* (4th ed.). New York: Harper & Row.

Mussen, P. H., Conger, J. J., Kagan, J., & Huston, A. C. (1984). *Child development and personality* (6th ed.). New York: Harper & Row.

Nagler, S., & Glueck, Z. (1985). The clinical interview. *Schizophrenia Bulletin, 11,* 38–47.

Nagler, S., & Mirsky, A. F. (1985). Introduction: The Israeli high-risk study. *Schizophrenia Bulletin, 11,* 19–29.

Nasrallah, H. A., McCalley-Whitters, M., & Chapman, S. (1984). Cerebral ventricular enlargement and suicide in schizophrenia and mania. *American Journal of Psychiatry, 141,* 919.

Nathan, T. S., Eitinger, L., & Winnik, H. Z. (1964). A psychiatric study of survivors of the Nazi holocaust: A study in hospitalized patients. *Israel Annals of Psychiatry and Related Disciplines, 2,* 47–76.

Neale, J. M., & Cromwell, R. L. (1977). Attention and schizophrenia. In B. A. Maher (Ed.), *Contributions to the psychopathology of schizophrenia.* New York: Academic Press.

Neale, J. M., Kopfstein, J. H., & Levine, A. (1972). *Premorbid adjustment and paranoid status in schizophrenia: Varying assessment techniques and the influence of chronicity.* Paper presented at the meeting of the American Psychological Association, Honolulu.

Neale, J. M., McIntyre, C. W., Fox, R., & Cromwell, R. L. (1969). Span of apprehension in acute schizophrenics. *Journal of Abnormal Psychology, 74,* 593–596.

Neisser, U. (1967). *Cognitive psychology.* New York: Appleton.

Neisser, U. (1976). *Cognition and reality: Principles and implications of cognitive psychology.* San Francisco: Freeman.

Neisser, U. (1982). Snapshots or benchmarks? In U. Neisser (Ed.), *Memory observed.* San Francisco: Freeman.

Neisser, U. (1984). Interpreting Harry Bahrick's discovery: What confers immunity against forgetting. *Journal of Experimental Psychology: General, 113,* 32–35.

Nelsen, E. A. (1969). Social reinforcement for expression vs. suppression of aggression. *Merill-Palmer Quarterly of Behavior and Development, 15,* 259–278.

Nelson, R. E., & Craighead, W. E. (1977). Selective recall of positive and negative feedback, self-control behaviors and depression. *Journal of Abnormal Psychology, 86*, 379–388.

Nemiah, J. C. (1984). The unconscious and psychopathology. In K. S. Bowers & D. Meichenbaum (Eds.), *The unconscious reconsidered.* New York: Wiley.

Neuringer, C. (1976). Current developments in the study of suicidal thinking. In S. Shneidman (Ed.), *Suicidology: Contemporary developments.* New York: Grune & Stratton.

Nevid, J. S. (1983). Hopelessness, social desirability and construct validity. *Journal of Consulting and Clinical Psychology, 51*, 139–140.

Newman, L. E., & Stoller, R. J. (1969). Spider symbolism and bisexuality. *Journal of the American Psychoanalytic Association, 17*, 862–872.

Nezu, A. M., & Ronan, G. F. (1985). Life stress, current problems, problem solving, and depressive symptoms: An integrative model. *Journal of Consulting and Clinical Psychology, 53*, 693–697.

Niederland, W. G. (1981). The survivor syndrome: Further observations and dimensions. *Journal of the American Psychoanalytic Association, 29*, 413–425.

Nirembirski, M. (1946). Psychological investigation of a group of internees at Belsen Camp. *Journal of Mental Science, 92*, 60–74.

Nisbett, R. E., & Wilson, T. D. (1977). Telling more than we can know: Verbal reports on mental processes. *Psychological Review, 84*, 231–259.

Nuechterlein, K. H., & Dawson, M. E. (1984). Information processing and attentional functioning in the developmental course of schizophrenic disorders. *Schizophrenia Bulletin, 10*, 160–203.

Nurnberger, J. I., & Gershon, E. S. (1982). Genetics. In E. S. Paykel (Ed.), *Handbook of affective disorders.* New York: Guilford Press.

Nurnberger, J., Roose, S., P., Dunner, D. L., & Fieve, R. R. (1979). Unipolar mania: A distinct clinical entity? *American Journal of Psychiatry, 136*, 1420–1423.

Oatley, K., & Bolton, W. (1985). A social-cognitive theory of depression in reaction to life events. *Psychological Review, 92*, 372–388.

Obrist, P. A. (1981). *Cardiovascular psychophysiology.* New York: Plenum.

Ohman, A., Nordby, H., & D'Elia, G. (1986). Orienting schizophrenia: Stimulus significance, attention, and distraction in a signaled reaction time task. *Journal of Abnormal Psychology, 95*, 326–334.

Oliver, J. M., & Burkham, R. (1982). Subliminal psychodynamic activation in depression: A failure to replicate. *Journal of Abnormal Psychology, 91*, 337–342.

Oltmanns, T. F., O'Hayon, J., & Neale, J. M. (1978). The effects of anti-psychotic medication and diagnostic criteria on distractibility in schizophrenia. *Journal of Psychiatric Research, 14*, 81–92.

Orne, M. T. (1959). The nature of hypnosis: Artifact and essence. *Journal of Abnormal and Social Psychology, 58*, 277–299.

Ost, L. G. (1985). Ways of acquiring phobias and outcome of behavioral treatments. *Behaviour Research and Therapy, 23*, 683–689.

Ost, L. G., & Hugdahl, K. (1981). Acquisition of phobias and anxiety response patterns in clinical patients. *Behaviour Research and Therapy, 19*, 439–447.

Ost, L. G., & Hugdahl, K. (1983). Acquisition of agoraphobia, mode of onset, and anxiety response patterns. *Behaviour Research and Therapy, 21*, 623–631.

Ost, L. G., & Hugdahl, K. (1985). Acquisition of blood and dental phobia and anxiety response patterns in clinical patients. *Behaviour Research and Therapy, 23*, 27–34.

Palmer, J., & Altrocchi, J. (1967). Attribution of hostile intent as unconscious. *Journal of Personality, 35*, 164–176.

Parnas, J., Schulsinger, F., Schulzinger, H., Mednick, S., & Teasdale, T. (1982). Behavioral precursors of schizophrenia spectrum: A prospective study. *Archives of General Psychiatry, 39*, 658–664.

Parry-Jones, W. L., Santer-Weststrate, H. C., & Crawley, R. C. (1970). Behaviour therapy in a case of hysterical blindness. *Behaviour Research and Therapy, 8*, 79–85.

Parsons, O. A., Fulgenzi, L. B., Edelberg, R. (1969). Aggressiveness and psychophysiological responsitivity in groups of repressors and sensitizers. *Journal of Personality and Social Psychology, 12*, 235–244.

Paykel, E. S. (1976). Life stress, depression and attempted suicide. *Journal of Human Stress, 2*, 3–12.

Paykel, E. S. (1978). Contribution of life events to causation of psychiatric illness. *Psychological Medicine, 8*, 245–253.

Paykel, E. S. (1982). Life events and early environment. In E. S. Paykel (Ed.), *Handbook of affective disorders.* New York: Guilford Press.

Pearlin, L. I., & Johnson, J. S. (1977). Marital status, life-strains and depression. *American Sociological Review, 42,* 704–715.

Penfield, W. (1969). Consciousness, memory, and man's conditioned reflexes. In K. Pribram (Ed.), *On the biology of learning.* New York: Harcourt, Brace & World.

Penfield, W., & Perot, P. (1963). The brain's record of auditory and visual experience. *Brain, 86,* 595–696.

Penfield, W., & Roberts L. (1959). *Speech and brain mechanisms.* Princeton, NJ: Princeton University Press.

Perris, C. (1982). The distinction between bipolar and unipolar affective disorders. In E. S. Paykel (Ed.), *Handbook of affective disorders.* New York: Guilford Press.

Perry, C., & Laurence, J. R. (1984). Mental processing outside of awareness: The contributions of Freud and Janet. In K. S. Bowers & D. Meichenbaum (Eds.), *The unconscious reconsidered.* New York: Wiley.

Persons, J. B., & Rao, P. A. (1985). Longitudinal study of cognitions, life events, and depression in psychiatric inpatients. *Journal of Abnormal Psychology, 94,* 51–63.

Pervin, L. A. (1985). Personality: Current controversies, issues and directions. *Annual Review of Psychology, 36,* 83–114.

Peters, R. S. (1958). *The concept of motivation.* New York: Humanities Press.

Pinkerton, S. S., Hughes, H., & Wenrich, W. W. (1982). *Behavioral medicine: Clinical applications.* New York: Wiley.

Ploeg, H. M., van der, Buuren, E. T. van, & Brummelen, P. van (1985). *Psychotherapy and Psychosomatics, 43,* 186–193.

Pollak, J. M. (1979). Obsessive–compulsive personality: A review. *Psychological Bulletin, 86,* 225–241.

Pope, H. G., & Lipinski, J. F. (1978). Diagnosis in schizophrenia and manic–depressive illness. *Archives of General Psychiatry, 35,* 811–828.

Porterfield, A. L., & Golding, S. L. (1985). Failure to find an effect of subliminal psychodynamic activation upon cognitive measures of pathology in schizophrenia. *Journal of Abnormal Psychology, 94,* 630–639.

Prange, A. J., Wilson, I. C., Lynn, C. W., Alltop, L. B., & Strikeleather, R. A. (1974). L-*Tryptophan in mania. Archives of General Psychiatry, 30,* 56–62.

Price, R. H. (1972). Psychological deficit versus impression management schizophrenic word association performance. *Journal of Abnormal Psychology, 79,* 132–137.

Putnam, B. (1979). Hypnosis and distortion in eyewitness memory. *International Journal of Clinical and Experimental Hypnosis, 27,* 437–448.

Rabkin, J. G. (1980). Stressful life events and schizophrenia: A review of the research literature. *Psychological Bulletin, 87,* 408–425.

Rachman, S. (1971). *The effects of psychotherapy.* Elmsford, NY: Pergamon Press.

Rachman, S. (1976). The passing of the two-stage theory of fear and avoidance: Fresh possibilities. *Behaviour Research and Therapy, 14,* 125–131.

Rachman, S. (1977). The conditioning theory of fear acquisition: A critical examination. *Behaviour Research and Therapy, 15,* 375–387.

Rachman, S. (1978). *Fear and courage.* San Francisco: Freeman.

Rachman, S. (1984a) Agoraphobia: A safety-signal perspective. *Behaviour Research and Therapy, 22,* 59–70.

Rachman, S. (1984b). The experimental analysis of agoraphobia. *Behaviour Research and Therapy, 22,* 631–640.

Rachman, S. (1984c). Fear and courage. *Behavior Therapy, 15,* 109–120.

Rachman, S. (1985a). A note on the conditioning theory of fear acquisition. *Behavior Therapy, 16,* 426–428.

Rachman, S. J. (1985b). An overview of clinical and research issues in obsessional–compulsive disorders. In M. Mavissakalian, S. M. Turner, & L. Michelson (Eds.), *Obsessive–compulsive disorder: Psychological and pharmacological treatment.* New York: Plenum.

Rachman, S., Craske, M., Tallman, K., & Solyom, C. (1986). Does escape behavior strengthen agorophobic avoidance? *Behavior Therapy, 17,* 366–384.

Rachman, S., & Hodgson, R. J. (1980). *Obsessions and compulsions.* Englewood Cliffs, NJ: Prentice-Hall.

Rachman, S., & Seligman, M. E. P. (1976). Unprepared phobias: "Be prepared." *Behaviour Research and Therapy, 14,* 333–338.

Rachman, S., & Wilson, G. T. (1980). *The effects of psychological therapy* (2nd ed.). Elmsford, NY: Pergamon Press.

Radloff, L. S. (1975). Sex differences in depression: The effects of occupation and marital status. *Sex Roles, 1,* 249–265.

Radloff, L. S., & Rae, D. S. (1979). Susceptibility and precipitating factors in depression: Sex differences and similarities. *Journal of Abnormal Psychology, 88,* 174–181.

Rangaswamy, K., & Kamakshi, G. (1983). Life events in hysteric adolescents. *Child Psychiatry Quarterly, 16,* 26–33.

Ranschburg, J. (1983). Hungary: Aggression research at the Institute for Psychology of the Hungarian Academy of Science. In A. P. Goldstein & M. H. Segall (Eds.), *Aggression in global perspective* (pp. 221–236). Elmsford, NY: Pergamon Press.

Rappaport, M. (1967). Competing voice messages: Effects of message load and drugs on the ability of acute schizophrenics to attent. *Archives of General Psychiatry, 17,* 97–103.

Rappoport, A., & Williams, S. L. (1981, October). *An investigation into the nature and modification of phobic thinking.* Paper presented at the meeting of the Phobia Society of America, San Francisco.

Reason, J. (1983). Absent-mindedness and cognitive control. In J. Harris & P. Morris (Eds.), *Everyday memory, actions and absent-mindedness.* New York: Academic Press.

Reason, J. (1984a). Lapses of attention in everyday life. In R. Parasuraman, R. Davies, & J. Beatty (Eds.), *Varieties of attention.* New York: Academic Press.

Reason, J. (1984b). Little slips and big disasters. *Interdisciplinary Science Review, 9,* 179–189.

Reason, J., & Lucas, D. (1984). Absent-mindedness in shops: Its incidence, correlates and consequences. *British Journal of Clinical Psychology, 23,* 121–131.

Reason, J., &Mycielska, K. (1982). *Absent-minded? The psychology of mental lapses and everyday errors.* Englewood Cliffs, NJ: Prentice-Hall.

Reich, W. (1982). Psychiatry's second coming. *Psychiatry, 45,* 189–196.

Ribot, T. A. (1982). *Diseases of memory: An essay in the positive psychology.* New York: Appleton-Century-Crofts.

Richter, D. (1957). On the phenomenon of sudden death in animals and man. *Psychosomatic Medicine, 19,* 191–198.

Richter, D. (1976). The impact of biochemistry on the problem of schizophrenia. In D. Kemali, G. Bartholini, & D. Richter (Eds.), *Schizophrenia today.* Elmsford, NY: Pergamon Press.

Rifkin, A. (1984). A comment on Strauss' and Carpenter's defintions of "What is schizophrenia." *Schizophrenia Bulletin, 10,* 367–368.

Rimm, D. C., Janda, L. H., Lancaster, D. W., Nahl, M., & Dittmar, K. (1977). An exploratory investigation of the origin and maintenance of phobias. *Behaviour Reserach and Therapy, 15,* 231–238.

Rimm, D. C., & Lefebvre, R. C. (1981). Phobic disorders. In S. M. Turner, K. S. Calhoun, & H. E. Adams (Eds.), *Handbook of clinical behavior therapy.* New York: Wiley.

Rimm, D. C., & Masters, J. C. (1979). *Behavior therapy.* New York: Academic Press.

Rimm, D. C., & Somervill, J. W. (1977). *Abnormal psychology.* New York: Academic Press.

Robbins, L. C. (1963). The accuracy of parental recall of aspects of child development and child rearing practices. *Journal of Abnormal and Social Psychology, 66,* 261–270.

Rofé, Y. (1973). *Acquisition, transfer and retention of verbal conditioning as a function of repression-sensitization, pleasant versus hostile words and induced versus non-induced anxiety.* Unpublished doctoral dissertation, University of Hull, England.

Rofé, Y. (1984). Affiliation and stress: A utility theory. *Psychological Review, 91,* 235–250.

Rofé, Y. (1985). The assessment of marital happiness. In J. N. Butcher & C. D. Spielberger (Eds.), *Advances in personality assessment* (Vol. 4, pp. 55–82). Hillsdale, NJ: Erlbaum.

Rofé, Y., & Goldberg, J. (1983). Prolonged exposure to a war environment and its effects on blood pressure of pregnant women. *British Journal of Medical Psychology, 56,* 305–311.

Rofé, Y., Hoffman, H., & Lewin, I. (1985). Patient affiliation in major illness. *Psychological Medicine, 15,* 895–896.

Rofé, Y., & Lewin, I. (1979). Who adjust better: Repressors or sensitizers? *Journal of Clinical Psychology, 35,* 875–879.

Rofé, Y., & Lewin, I. (1980). Daydreaming in a war environment. *Journal of Mental Imagery, 4,* 59–75.

Rofé, Y. & Lewin, I. (1982a). The effect of war environment on dreams and sleep habits. In C. D. Spielberger, I. G. Sarason, & N. A. Milgram (Eds.), *Stress and anxiety* (Vol. 8, pp. 67–79). Washington, DC: Hemisphere.

Rofé, Y. & Lewin, I. (1982b). Psycho-social factors and blood pressure during pregnancy and delivery. *Psychophysiology, 19,* 7–12.

Rofé, Y. & Lewin, I. (1986). Affiliation in an unavoidable stress situation: An examination of utility theory. *British Journal of Social Psychology, 25,* 119–127.

Rofé, Y., Lewin, I., & Hoffman, M. (1987). Affiliation patterns among cancer patients. *Psychological Medicine, 17,* 419–424.

Rofé, Y., Lewin, I., & Padeh, B. (1977). Affiliation before and after child delivery as a function of repression–sensitization. *British Journal of Social and Clinical Psychology, 16,* 311–315.

Rohrbaugh, M., & Riccio, D. C. (1970). Paradoxical enhancement of learned fear. *Journal of Abnormal Psychology, 75,* 210–216.

Rohrbaugh, M., Riccio, D. C., & Arthur A. (1972). Paradoxical enhancement of conditioned suppression. *Behaviour Research and Therapy, 10,* 125–130.

Rolf, J. E. (1972). The social and academic competence of children vulnerable to schizophrenia and other behavior disorders. *Journal of Abnormal Psychology, 80,* 225–243.

Rolf, J. E., & Garmezy, N. (1974). The school performance of children vulnerable to behavior pathology. In D. F. Ricks, A. Thomas, & M. Roff (Eds.), *Life history research in psychopathology* (Vol. 3). Minneapolis: University of Minnesota Press.

Rose, S. P. (1984). Disordered molecules and diseased minds. *Journal of Psychiatric Research, 18,* 351–360.

Rosenheim, E., & Reicher, R. (1986). Children in anticipatory grief: The lonely predicament. *Journal of Clinical Child Psychology, 15,* 115–119.

Rosenzweig, S., & Mason, G. (1934). An experimental study of memory in relation to the theory of repression. *British Journal of Psychology, 24,* 247–265.

Roth, D. L., & Ingram, R. E. (1985). Factors in the self-deception questionnaire: Associations with depression. *Journal of Personality and Social Psychology, 48,* 243–251.

Roy, A. (1981). Vulnerability factors and depression in men. *British Journal of Psychiatry, 138,* 75–77.

Rozensky, R. H., Rehm, L. P., Pry, G., & Roth, D. (1977). Depression and self-reinforcement behavior in hospitalized patients. *Journal of Behavior Therapy and Experimental Psychiatry, 8,* 35–38.

Rubenstein, R., & Newman, R. (1954). The living out of "future" experiences under hypnosis. *Science, 119,* 472–473.

Rund, B. R. (1983). The effect of distraction on focal attention in paranoid and non-paranoid schizophrenic patients compared to normals and non-psychotic psychiatric patients. *Journal of Psychiatric Research, 17,* 241–250.

Rush, A. J., Beck, A. T., Kovacs, M., & Hollon, S. (1977). Comparative efficacy of cognitive therapy and pharmacotherapy in the treatment of depressed outpatients. *Cognitive Therapy and Research, 1,* 17–37.

Russell, R. A. (1981). Concepts of adjustment to disability: An overview. *Rehabilitation Literature, 42,* 330–338.

Ryan, D. V., & Neale, J. M. (1973). Test-taking sets and the performance of schizophrenics on laboratory tests. *Journal of Abnormal Psychology, 82,* 207–211.

Sachar, E. J. (1982). Endocrine abnormalities in depression. In E. S. Paykel (Ed.), *Handbook of affective disorders.* New York: Guilford Press.

Sackeim, H. A., & Gur, C. R. (1978). Self-deception, self-confrontation and consciousness. In G. E. Schwartz & D. Shapiro (Eds.), *Consciousness and self-regulation* (Vol. 2, pp. 139–197). Chichester, England: Wiley.

Sackeim, H. A., & Gur, C. R. (1979). Self-deception other-deception, and self-reported psychopathology. *Journal of Consulting and Clinical Psychology, 47,* 213–215.

Sackeim, H. A., Nordlie, J. W., & Gur, C. R. (1979). A model of hysterical and hypnotic blindness: Cognition, motivation and awareness. *Journal of Abnormal Psychology, 88,* 474–489.

Sackeim, H. A., Packer, I. K., & Gur, C. R. (1977). Hemisphericity, cognitive set, and susceptibility to subliminal perception. *Journal of Abnormal Psychology, 86,* 624–630.

Sackett, G. P. (1974). Sex differences in rhesus monkeys following varied rearing experiences. In R. C. Friedman, R. M. Richart, & R. L. Van de Wiele (Eds.), *Sex differences in behavior.* New York: Wiley.

Saigh, P. A. (1984a). Pre- and postinvasion anxiety in Lebanon. *Behavior Therapy, 15,* 185–190.

Saigh, P. A. (1984b). An experimental analysis of delayed posttraumatic stress. *Behaviour Research and Therapy, 22,* 679–682.

Saigh, P. A. (1985). On the nature and etiology of traumatic stress. *Behavior Therapy, 16,* 423–426.

Salzman, L. (1968). Obsessions and phobias. *International Journal of Psychiatry, 6,* 451–476.

Sandler, I. N., & Brian, L. (1982). Locus of control as a stress moderator: The role of control perceptions and social support. *American Journal of Community Psychology, 10,* 65–80.

Sarbin, T. R., & Mancuso, J. C. (1980). *Schizophrenia: Medical diagnosis or moral verdict.* Elmsford, NY: Pergamon Press.

Sartory, G., & Eysenck, H. J. (1976). Strain differences in acquisition and extinction of fear responses in rats. *Psychological Reports, 38,* 163–187.

Scarpetti, W. L. (1973). The repression–sensitization dimension in relation in impending painful stimulation. *Journal of Consulting and Clinical Psychology, 40,* 377–382.

Scarpetti, W. L. (1974). Autonomic concomitant of aggressive behavior in repressors and sensitizers: A social learning approach. *Journal of Personality and Social Psychology, 30,* 772–781.

Schill, T. (1969). Repressor–sensitizer differences in free-associative sex responses to double-entendre words. *Journal of Clinical Psychology, 25,* 368–369.

Schill, T. (1972). Agression and blood pressure responses of high- and low-guilt subjects following frustration. *Journal of Consulting and Clinical Psychology, 38,* 461.

Schill, T., Adams, A. E., & Bekker, D. (1982). Repression–sensitization and coping with stressful life events. *Psychological Reports, 50,* 602.

Schill, T., & Althoff, M. (1968). Auditory perceptual thresholds for sensitizers defensive and nondefensive repressors. *Perceptual and Motor Skills, 27,* 935–938.

Schneider, R. H., Egan, B. M., Johnson, E. H., Drobny, H., & Julius, S. J. (1986). Anger and anxiety in borderline hypertension. *Psychosomatic Medicine, 48,* 242–248.

Schneirla, T. C. (1965). Aspects of stimulation and organization in approach/withdrawal processes underlying vertebrate behavioral development. In D. S. Lehrman, R. A. Hinde, & E. Shaw (Eds.), *Advances in the study of behavior* (Vol. 1). New York: Academic Press.

Schulsinger, H. (1976). A ten-year follow-up of children of schizophrenic mothers: Clinical assessment. *Acta Psychiatrica Scandinavica, 53,* 371–386.

Schwartz, B. (1978). *Psychology of learning and behavior.* New York: Norton.

Schwartz, G. E., Weinberger, D. A., & Singer, J. A. (1981). Cardiovascular differentiation of happiness, sadness, anger and fear following imagery and exercise. *Psychosomatic Medicine, 43,* 343–364.

Schwartz, M. S. (1972). The repression–sensitization scale: Normative age and sex data on 30,000 medical patients. *Journal of Clinical Psychology, 28,* 72–73.

Schwartz, M. S., Krupp, N. E., & Byrne, D. (1971). Repression–sensitization and medical diagnosis. *Journal of Abnormal Psychology, 78,* 286–291.

Seay, B. E., Hansen, E., & Harlow, H. F. (1963). Mother–infant separation in monkeys. *Journal of Child Psychology and Psychiatry, 3,* 123–132.

Seligman, M. E. P. (1970). On the generality of the laws of learning. *Psychological Review, 77,* 406–418.

Seligman, M. E. P. (1971). Phobias and preparedness. *Behavior Therapy, 2,* 307–320.

Seligman, M. E. P. (1974). Depression and learned helplessness. In R. J. Friedman & M. M. Katz (Eds.), *The psychology of depression: Contemporary theory and research.* Washington, DC: Winston.

Seligman, M. E. P. (1975). *Helplessness: On depression, development, and death.* San Francisco: Freeman.

Seligman, M. E. P., Abramson, L. V., Semmel, A., & Von Baeyer, C. (1979). Depressive attributional style. *Journal of Abnormal Psychology, 88,* 242–247.

Seligman, M. E. P., & Hager, J. L. (1972). *Biological boundaries of learning.* New York: Appleton-Century-Crofts.

Seligman, M., & Maier, S. (1967). Failure to escape traumatic shock. *Journal of Experimental Psychology, 74,* 1–9.

Sengel, R. A., Lovallo, W. R., Pishkin, V., Leber, W. R., & Shaffer, B. (1984). Associative response bias and severity of thought disorder in schizophrenia and mania. *Journal of Clinical Psychology, 40,* 889–892.

Serban, G. (1975). Stress in schizophrenics and normals. *British Journal of Psychiatry, 126,* 397–407.

Shapiro, D. (1965). *Neurotic styles.* New York: Basic Books.

Shapiro, D. L., & Rosenwald, G. C. (1975). Free association and repression–sensitization. *Journal of Personality Assessment, 39,* 25–27.

Shaw, B. F. (1977). Comparison of cognitive therapy and behavior therapy in the treatment of depression. *Journal of Consulting and Clinical Psychology, 45,* 543–551.

Shaw, B. F. (1982). Stress and depression: A cognitive perspective. In R. W. J. Neufeld (Ed.), *Psychological stress and psychopathology.* New York: McGraw-Hill.

Shean, G. (1982). Cognition, emotion, and schizophrenia. In R. W. J. Neufeld (Ed.), *Psychological stress and psychopathology.* New York: McGraw-Hill.

Sheatsley, P. B., & Feldman, J. J. (1964). The assassination of President Kennedy: A preliminary report on public reactions and behavior. *Public Opinion Quarterly, 28,* 189–215.

Sheehan, P. W., & Bowman, L. (1973). Peer model and experimenter expectancies about appropriate response as determinants of behavior in the hypnotic setting. *Journal of Abnormal Psychology, 82,* 112–123.

Sheehan, P. W., & McConkey, K. M. (1982). *Hypnosis and experience: The exploration of phenomena and process.* Hillsdale, NJ: Erlbaum.

Sheehan, P. W., & Tilden, J. (1983). Effects of suggestibility and hypnosis on accurate and distorted retrieval from memory. *Journal of Experimental Psychology: Learning, Memory, and Cognition, 9,* 283–293.

Sheehan, P. W., & Tilden, J. (1984). Real and simulated occurrences of memory distortion in hypnosis. *Journal of Abnormal Psychology, 93,* 47–57.

Sheingold, K., & Tenney, Y. J. (1982). Memory for a salient childhood event. In U. Neisser (Ed.), *Memory observed.* San Francisco: Freeman.

Shevrin, H., & Dickman, S. (1980). The psychology of unconscious: A necessary assumption for all psychological theory? *American Psychologist, 35,* 421–434.

Shiffrin, R. M., & Atkinson, R. C. (1969). Storage and retrieval processes in long-term memory. *Psychological Review, 76,* 179–193.

Shopsin, B. (1979). Genetic forms of manic illness and the question of atypical mania. In B. Shopsin (Ed.), *Manic illness.* New York: Raven Press.

Shotter, J. (1981). Telling and reporting: Prospective and retrospective uses of self-ascriptions. In C. Antaki (Ed.), *The psychology of ordinary explanations of social behavior* (pp. 157–181). London: Academic Press.

Shuval, J. T. (1957/1958). Some persistent effects of trauma: Five years after the Nazi concentration camps. *Social Problems, 5,* 230–243.

Siegel, M., Niswander, G. D., Sachs, E., & Stavros, D. (1959). Taraxein: Fact or artifact? *American Journal of Psychiatry, 115,* 819–820.

Sigal, J. J., & Weinfeld, M. (1985). Control of aggression in adult children of survivors in the Nazi persecution. *Journal of Abnormal Psychology, 94,* 556–564.

Silber, L. D., & Grebstein, L. C. (1964). Repression–sensitization and social desirability responding. *Journal of Consulting Psychology, 28,* 559.

de Silva, P., & Rachman, S. (1984). Does escape behaviour strengthen agoraphobic avoidance? A preliminary study. *Behaviour Research and Therapy, 22,* 87–91.

de Silva, P., Rachman, S., & Seligman, M. E. P. (1977). Prepared phobias and obsessions: Therapeutic outcome. *Behaviour Research and Therapy, 15,* 65–77.

Silverman, L. H. (1976). Psychoanalytic theory: "The reports of my death are greatly exaggerated." *American Psychologist, 31,* 621–637.

Silverman, L. H. (1978). Unconscious symbolic fantasy: A ubiquitous therapeutic agent. *International Journal of Psychoanalytic Psychotherapy, 7,* 562–585.

Silverman, L. H. (1983). The subliminal psychodynamic activation method: Overview and comprehensive listing of studies. In J. Masling (Ed.), *Empirical studies in psychoanalytic theory* (Vol. 1, pp. 69–97). Hillsdale, NJ: Erlbaum.

Silverman, L. H., Ross, D. L., Adler, J. M. & Lustig, D. A. (1978). Simple research paradigm for demonstrating subliminal psychodynamic activation: Effects of oedipal stimuli on dart-throwing accuracy in college males. *Journal of Abnormal Psychology, 87,* 341–357.

Silverton, L., Finello, K., & Mednick, S. (1983). Children of schizophrenic women: Early factors predictive of schizophrenia. *Infant Mental Health Journal, 4,* 202–216.

Silverton, L., Finello, K. M., & Schulsinger, F. (1985). Low birth weight and ventricular enlargement in a high-risk sample. *Journal of Abnormal Psychology, 94,* 405–409.

Silvestri, R., Rohrbaugh, M., & Riccio, D. C. (1970). Conditions influencing the retention of learned fear in young rats. *Developmental Psychology, 2,* 389–395.

Simal, F. J., & Herr, V. V. (1970). Autonomic responses to threatening stimuli in relation to the repression–sensitization dimension. *Journal of Abnormal Psychology, 76,* 106–109.

Singer, E. (1970). *Key concepts in psychotherapy* (2nd ed.). New York: Basic.

Siris, S. G., Rifkin, A., Reardon, G. T., Endicott, J., Pereira, D. H., Hayes, R., & Casey, E. (1984). Course-related depressive syndromes in schizophrenia. *American Journal of Psychiatry, 141,* 1254–1257.

Skrabanek, P. (1984). Biochemistry of schizophrenia: A pseudoscientific model. *Integrative Psychiatry, 2,* 224–228.

Slade, P. (1974). Psychometric studies of obsessional illness and obsessional personality. In H. Beech (Ed.), *Obsessional states.* London: Methuen.

Slater, E. (1953). *Psychotic and neurotic illnesses in twins.* London: Her Majesty's Stationery Office.

Slater, E. (1961). The thirty-fifth Maudsley lecture: Hysteria 311. *Journal of Mental Science, 107,* 358–381.

Smith, E. R., & Miller, F. D. (1978). Limits on perception of cognitive processes: A reply to Nisbett and Wilson. *Psychological Review, 85,* 355–362.

Smith, M. C. (1983). Hypnotic memory enhancement of witnesses: Does it work? *Psychological Bulletin, 94,* 387–407.

Smith, T. W. (1984). Type A behavior, anger and neuroticism: The discriminant validity of self-reports in a patient sample. *British Journal of Clinical Psychology, 23,* 147–148.

Snortum, J. R., & Wilding, F. W. (1971). Temporal estimation and heart rate as a function of repression–sensitization score and probability of shock. *Journal of Consulting and Clinical Psychology, 37,* 417–422.

Sohlberg, S. (1985). Personality and neuropsychological performance of high-risk children. *Schizophrenia Bulletin, 11,* 48–60.

Sohlberg, S. (1986). Similarity and dissimilarity in value patterns of Israeli kibbutz and city adolescents. *International Journal of Psychology, 21,* 189–202.

Sohlberg, S. C., & Yaniv, S. (1985). Social adjustment and cognitive performance of high-risk children. *Schizophrenia Bulletin, 11,* 61–65.

Solomon, P., Leiderman, P. H., Mendelson, J., & Wexler, D. (1957). Sensory deprivation. *American Journal of Psychiatry, 114,* 357–363.

Solomon, R. L., & Wynne, L. C. (1954). Traumatic avoidance learning: The principles of anxiety, conservation and partial irreversibility. *Psychological Review, 61,* 353–385.

Solomon, Z., & Benbenishty, R. (1986). The role of proximity, immediacy, and expectancy in frontline treatment of combat stress reaction among Israelis in the Lebanon war. *American Journal of Psychiatry, 143,* 613–617.

Solomon, Z., Noy, S., & Bar-On, R. (1986). Risk factors in combat stress reaction: A study of Israeli soldiers in the 1982 Lebanon war. *Israel Journal of Psychiatry and Related Sciences, 23,* 3–8.

Solyom, L., Beck, P., & Solyom, C., & Hugel, R. (1974). Some etiological factors in phobic neurosis. *Canadian Psychiatric Association Journal, 19,* 69–78.

Sosa, J. N. (1968). *Vascular effects of aggression and passivity in prison population.* Unpublished master's thesis, Florida State University, Tallahassee.

Spanos, N. P. (1981). Hypnotic responding: Automatic dissociation or situation–relevant cognizing? In E. Klinger (Ed.), *Imagery: Concepts, results and applications.* New York: Plenum.

Spence, D. P. (1967). Subliminal perception and perceptual defense: Two sides of a single problem. *Behavioral Science, 12,* 183–193.

Sperling, M. (1971). Spider phobias and spider fantasies. *Journal of American Psychoanalytic Association, 19,* 472–498.

Spiegel, H. (1970). A single-treatment method to stop smoking using ancillary self-hypnosis. *International Journal of Clinical and Experimental Hypnosis, 18,* 235–250.

Spielberger, C. D. (1962). The role of awareness in verbal conditioning. In C. W. Eriksen (Ed.), *Behavior and awareness.* Durham, NC: Duke University Press.

Spielberger, C. D., Bernstein, I. H., & Ratliff, R. G. (1966). Information and incentive value of the reinforcing stimulus in verbal conditioning. *Journal of Experimental Psychology, 71,* 26–31.

Spielberger, C. D., & Denike, L. D. (1966). Descriptive behaviorism versus cognitive theory in verbal operant conditioning. *Psychological Review, 73,* 306–326.

Spring, B., & Coons, H. (1982). Stress as a precursor of schizophrenia. In R. W. J. Neufeld (Ed.), *Psychological stress and psychopathology.* New York: McGraw-Hill.

Stafford-Clark, D. (1966). *What Freud really said.* New York: Schocken.

Stam, H. J., Radtke-Bodorik, L., & Spanos, N. P. (1980). Repression and hypnotic amnesia: A failure to replicate and an alternative formulation. *Journal of Abnormal Psychology, 89,* 551–559.

Steinberg, H. R., & Durell, J. (1968). A stressful social situation as a precipitant of schizophrenic symptoms: An epidemiological study. *British Journal of Psychiatry, 114,* 1097–1105.

Steinglass, P. (1987). Psychoeducational family therapy for schizophrenia: A review essay. *Psychiatry, 50,* 14–23.

Stephansson, J. G., Messina, J. A., & Meyerowitz, S. (1976). Hysterical neurosis, conversion type: Clinical and epidemiological considerations. *Acta Psychiatrica Scandinavica, 53,* 119–138.

Steptoe, A. (1981). *Psychological factors in cardiovascular disorders.* London: Academic Press.

Steptoe, A., Melville, D., & Ross, A. (1982). Essential hypertension and psychological functioning: A study of factory workers. *British Journal of Clinical Psychology, 21,* 303–311.

Stone, L. J., & Hokanson, J. E. (1969). Arousal reduction via self-punitive behavior. *Journal of Personality and Social Psychology, 12,* 72–79.

Stone, N. M., & Borkovec, T. D. (1975). The paradoxical effect of brief CS exposure on analogue phobic subjects. *Behaviour Research and Therapy, 13,* 51–54.

Strassman, H. D., Thaler, M. B., & Schein, E. H. (1956). A prisoner of war syndrome: Apathy as a reaction to severe stress. *American Journal of Psychiatry, 112,* 998–1003.

Strauss, J. S., & Carpenter, W. T. (1981). *Schizophrenia.* New York: Plenum.

Strauss, J. S., & Carpenter, W. T. (1983). What is schizophrenia? *Schizophrenia Bulletin, 9,* 7–10.

Strupp, H. (1978). Psychotherapy research and practice: An overview. In S. Garfield & M. Lambert (Eds.), *Handbook of psychotherapy and behavior change*. New York: Wiley.

Sullivan, H. S. (1968). *The interpersonal theory of psychiatry*. Paperback reprint: New York: Norton. (Original work published 1953)

Sullivan, L. G. (1979). *Selective association and long-delay learning*. Unpublished doctoral dissertation, Macquarie University, North Ryde, Australia.

Sullivan, P. F., & Roberts, L. K. (1969). Relationship of manifest anxiety to repression–sensitization on the MMPI. *Journal of Consulting and Clinical Psychology, 33*, 763–764.

Swan, G. E., & MacDonald, M. L. (1978). Behavior therapy in practice: A national survey of behavior therapists. *Behavior Therapy, 9*, 799–807.

Sweet, A. A. (1984). The therapeutic relationship in behavior therapy. *Clinical Psychology Review, 4*, 253–272.

Sweet, A. A., Giles, T. R., & Young, R. R. (1987). Three theoretical perspectives on anxiety: A comparison of theory and outcome. In L. Michelson & L. M. Asher, *Anxiety and stress disorders: Cognitive-behavioral assessment and treatment*. New York: Guilford Press.

Szasz, T. S. (1975). *Pain and pleasure: A study of bodily feelings*. NY: Basic Books.

Taylor, S. E. (1983). Adjustment to threatening events. *American Psychologist, 38*, 1161–1173.

Telch, M. J., Agras, W. S., Taylor, C. B., Roth, W. T., & Gallen, C. C. (1985). Combined pharmacological and behavioral treatment for agoraphobia. *Behaviour Research and Therapy, 23*, 325–335.

Telner, J. I., & Singhal, R. L. (1984). Psychiatric progress: The learned helplessness model of depression. *Journal of Psychiatric Research, 18*, 207–215.

Tempone, V. J. (1964a). Extension of the repression–sensitization hypothesis to success and failure experience. *Psychological Reports, 15*, 39–45.

Tempone, V. J. (1964b). Some clinical correlates of repression–sensitization. *Journal of Clinical Psychology, 20*, 440–442.

Tempone, V. J., & Lamb, W. (1967). Repression–sensitization and its relation to measures of adjustment and conflict. *Journal of Consulting Psychology, 31*, 131–136.

Thelen, M. H. (1969). Repression–sensitization: Its relation to adjustment and seeking psychotherapy among college students. *Journal of Consulting and Clinical Psychology, 33*, 161–165.

Theodor, L. H., & Mandelcorn, M. S. (1973). Hysterical blindness: A case report and study using a modern psychophysical technique. *Journal of Abnormal Psychology, 82*, 552–553.

Thorpe, G. L., & Burns, L. E. (1983). *The agoraphobic syndrome: Behavioral approaches to evaluation and treatment*. New York: Wiley.

Thorpe, J. G., Schmidt, E., Brown, P. T., & Castell, D. (1964). Aversion-relief therapy: A new method for general application. *Behaviour Research and Therapy, 2*, 71–82.

Thyer, B. A., Nesse, R. M., Cameron, O. G., & Curtis, G. C. (1985). Agoraphobia: A test of the separation anxiety hypothesis. *Behaviour Research and Therapy, 23*, 75–78.

Thyer, B. A., Nesse, R. M., Curtis, G. C., & Cameron, O. G. (1986). Panic disorder: A test of the separation anxiety hypothesis. *Behaviour Research and Therapy, 24*, 209–211.

Tinbergen, N. (1951). *The study of instinct*. Oxford, England: Oxford University Press.

Touhey, J. C. (1977). "Penis envy" and attitudes toward castration-like punishment of sexual aggression. *Journal of Research in Personality, 11*, 1–9.

Travers, R. M. W. (1972). *Essentials of learning* (3rd ed.). New York: Macmillan.

Tulving, E. (1974). Cue-dependent forgetting. *American Scientist, 62*, 74–82.

Tulving, E., & Thomson, D. M. (1971). Retrieval processes in recognition memory: Effect of associative context. *Journal of Experimental Psychology, 87*, 116–124.

Tulving, E., & Thomson, D. M. (1973). Encoding specificity and retrieval processes in episodic memory. *Psychological Review, 80*, 353–373.

Turner, R. J., Dopkeen, L. S., & Labreche, G. P. (1970). Marital status and schizophrenia: A study of incidence and outcome. *Journal of Abnormal Psychology, 76*, 110–116.

Turner, R., Giles, T. R., & Marafiote, R. (1983). Agorophobia: A test of the repression hypothesis. *British Journal of Clinical Psychology, 22*, 75–76.

Tyrer, S., & Shopsin, B. (1982). Symptoms and assessment of mania. In E. S. Paykel (Ed.), *Handbook of affective disorders*. New York: Guilford Press.

Udry, J. R. (1974). *The social context of marriage*. Philadelphia: Lippincott.

Ullmann, L. P., & Krasner, L. A. (1975). *Psychological approach to abnormal behavior* (2nd ed.). Englewood Cliffs, NJ: Prentice-Hall.

Underwood, B. J., & Freund, J. S. (1968). The effect of temporal separation of two tasks on proactive inhibition. *Journal of Experimental Psychology, 78*, 50–54.

Valentine, C. W. (1930). The innate basis of fear. *Journal of Genetic Psychology, 37*, 394–420.

Valone, K., Norton, J., Goldstein, M. J., & Doane, J. A. (1983). Parental expressed emotion and affective style in an adolescent sample at risk for schizophrenia spectrum disorders. *Journal of Abnormal Psychology, 92,* 399–407.

Van Egeren, L. (1968). Repression and sensitization: Sensitivity and recognition criteria. *Journal of Experimental Research in Personality, 3,* 1–8.

Van Egeren, L. F., Abelson, J. L., & Thornton, D. W. (1978). Cardiovascular consequences of expressing anger in a mutually-dependent relationship. *Journal of Psychosomatic Research, 22,* 537–548.

Van Ormer, E. B. (1932). Retention after intervals of sleep and waking. *Archives of Psychology, 21,* 1–49.

Van Putten, T., Crumpton, E., & Yale, C. (1976). Drug refusal in schizophrenia and the wish to be crazy. *Archives of General Psychiatry, 33,* 1443–1446.

Venables, P. H. (1977). Input dysfunction in schizophrenia. In B. A. Maher (Ed.), *Contributions to the psychopathology of schizophrenia.* New York: Academic Press.

Vernon, G. M. (1970). *Sociology of death: An analysis of death-related behavior.* New York: Ronald Press.

Volkmar, F. R., Poll, J., & Lewis, M. (1984). Conversion reactions in childhood and adolescence. *American Academy of Child Psychiatry, 23,* 424–430.

Von Baeyer, C. (1982). Repression–sensitization, stress, and perception of pain in others. *Perception and Motor Skills, 55,* 315–320.

Wachtel, P. (1977). *Psychoanalysis and behavior therapy.* New York: Basic.

Wachtel, P. (1984). Foreword. In K. S. Bowers & D. Meichenbaum (Eds.), *The unconscious reconsidered.* New York: Wiley.

Wagner, P. S. (1946). Psychiatric activities during the Normandy offensive, June 20–August, 1944: An experience with 5,203 neuropsychiatric casualties. *Psychiatry, 9,* 341–364.

Waldron, I. (1976). Why do women live longer than men? *Journal of Human Stress, 2,* 2–11.

Waldron, I. (1978). Type A behavior pattern and coronary heart disease in men and women. *Social Science and Medicine, 12B,* 167–170.

Warheit, G. J. (1979). Life events, coping, stress, and depressive symptomatology. *American Journal of Psychiatry, 136,* 502–507.

Watson, J. B., & Rayner, R. (1920). Conditioning emotional reactions. *Journal of Experimental Psychology, 3,* 1–14.

Watt, N. F. (1978). Patterns of childhood social development in adult schizophrenics. *Archives of General Psychiatry, 35,* 160–165.

Watt, N. F., & Lubensky, A. W. (1976). Childhood roots of schizophrenia. *Journal of Consulting and Clinical Psychology, 44,* 363–375.

Weatley, D., Balter, M., Levine, J., Lipman, R., Bauer, M. L., & Bonato, R. (1975). Psychiatric aspects of hypertension. *British Journal of Psychiatry, 127,* 327–336.

Weiner, R. D. (1984). Convulsive therapy: 50 years later. *American Journal of Psychiatry, 141,* 1078–1079.

Weinstein, E. A., Eck, R. A., & Lyerly, O. G. (1969). Conversion hysteria in Appalachia. *Psychiatry, 32,* 334–341.

Weinstein, J., Averill, J. R., Opton, E. M., & Lazarus, R. S. (1968). Defensive style and discrepancy between self-report and physiological indexes of stress. *Journal of Personality and Social Psychology, 10,* 406–413.

Weintraub, S., Liebert, D., & Neale, J. M. (1975). Teacher ratings of children vulnerable to psychopathology. *American Journal of Orthopsychiatry, 45,* 838–845.

Weiskrantz, L., Warrington, E. K., Sanders, M. D., & Marshall, J. (1974). Visual capacity in the hemianopic field following a restricted occipitial ablation. *Brain, 97,* 709–728.

Weissman, M. M., & Klerman, G. L. (1977). Sex differences and epidemiology of depression. *Archives of General Psychiatry, 34,* 98–111.

Weissman, M. M., Klerman, G. L., & Paykel, E. S. (1971). Clinical evaluation of hostility in depression. *American Journal of Psychiatry, 128,* 261–266.

Weitzman, B. (1967). Behavior therapy and psychotherapy. *Psychological Review, 74,* 300–317.

Wheeler, L., & Caggiula, A. R. (1966). The contagion of aggression. *Journal of Experimental Social Psychology, 2,* 1–10.

White, M. D., & Wilkins, W. (1973). Bogus physiological feedback and response thresholds of repressors and sensitizers. *Journal of Research in Personality, 7,* 78–87.

White, P. (1980). Limitations on verbal reports of internal events: A refutation of Nisbett and Wilson and of Bem. *Psychological Review, 87,* 105–112.

White, R. W. (1964). *The abnormal personality* (3rd ed.). New York: Ronald Press.

White, R. W., & Watt, N. F. (1981). *The abnormal personality* (5th ed.). New York: Wiley.

Whitehead, W. E., Blackwell, B., De Silva, H., & Robinson, A. (1977). Anxiety and anger in hypertension. *Journal of Psychosomatic Research, 21,* 283–289.

Wickelgren, W. A. (1977). *Learning and memory.* Englewood Cliffs, NJ: Prentice-Hall.

Wilkinson, G., & Bacon, N. A. (1984). A clinical and epidemiological survey of parasuicide and suicide in Edinburgh schizophrenics. *Psychological Medicine, 14,* 899–912.

Williams, A. W., Ware, J. E., & Donald, C. A. (1981). A model of mental health, life events, and social supports applicable to general populations. *Journal of Health and Social Behavior, 22,* 324–336.

Williams, R. B., Haney, T. L., Lee, K. L., Y.-H. Kong, Blumenthal, J. A., & Whalen, R. E. (1980). Type A behavior, hostility and coronary atherosclerosis. *Psychosomatic Medicine, 42,* 539–549.

Williams, S. L., Turner, S. M., & Peer, D. (1985). Guided mastery and performance desensitization treatments for severe acrophobia. *Journal of Consulting and Clinical Psychology, xx,* 237.

Williams, S. L., & Watson, N. (1985). Perceived danger and perceived self-efficacy as cognitive determinants of acrophobic behavior. *Behavior Therapy, 16,* 136–146.

Wills, T. A. (1981). Downward comparison principles in social psychology. *Psychological Bulletin, 90,* 245–271.

Wilson, H. (1942). Mental reactions to air raids. *Lancet, 1,* 284–287.

Winograd, E., & Killinger, W. A. (1983). Relating age at encoding in early childhood to adult recall: Development of flashbulb memories. *Journal of Experimental Psychology: General, 112,* 413–422.

Winters, K. C., Weintraub, S., & Neale, J. M. (1981). Validity of MMPI code types in identifying DSM-III schizophrenics, unipolars, and bipolars. *Journal of Consulting and Clinical Psychology, 49,* 486–487.

Wolff, D. R. (1966). *The effects of stress on speech characteristics and perceived emotions of repressors and sensitizers.* Unpublished doctoral dissertation, Washington University, St. Louis.

Wolpe, J. (1962). The experimental foundations of some new psychotherapeutic methods. In A. J. Bachrach (Ed.), *Experimental foundations of clinical psychology* (pp. 554–575). New York: Basic.

Wolpe, J. (1982). *The practice of behavior therapy* (3rd ed.). Elmsford, NY: Pergamon Press.

Wolpe, J., & Rachman, S. (1960). Psychoanalytic "evidence": A critique based on Freud's case of little Hans. *Journal of Nervous and Mental Disease, 131,* 135–148.

Woolfolk, R. L., & Lehrer, P. M. (1984). Clinical applications. In R. L. Woolfolk & P. M. Lehrer (Eds.), *Principles and practice of stress management.* New York: Guilford Press.

Woolfolk, R. L., & Lehrer, P. M. (1985). Stress and generalized anxiety. In M. Hersen & A. S. Bellack (Eds.), *Handbook of clinical behavior therapy with adults.* New York: Plenum.

Yarmey, A. D., & Bull, M. P., III (1978). Where were you when President Kennedy was assassinated? *Bulletin of the Psychonomic Society, 11,* 133–135.

Yaroush, R., Sullivan, M. J., & Ekstrand, B. R. (1971). Effect of sleep on memory: II. Differential effect of the first and second half of the night. *Journal of Experimental Psychology, 88,* 361–366.

Yerkes, R. M., & Yerkes, A. W. (1936). Nature and conditions of avoidance (fear) response in chimpanzees. *Journal of Comparative Psychology, 21,* 53–66.

Yuille, J. C., & McEwan, N. H. (1985). Use of hypnosis as an aid to eyewitness memory. *Journal of Applied Psychology, 70,* 389–400.

Zafiropoulou, M., & McPherson, F. M. (1986). Preparedness and the severity and outcome of clinical phobias. *Behaviour Research and Therapy, 24,* 221–222.

Zamansky, H. S. (1958). An investigation of the psychoanalytic theory of paranoid delusions. *Journal of Personality, 26,* 410–425.

Zeller, A. (1950a). An experimental analogue of repression: I. Historical summary. *Psychological Bulletin, 47,* 39–51.

Zeller, A. (1950b). An experimental analogue of repression: II. The effect of individual failure and success on memory by relearning. *Journal of Experimental Psychology, 40,* 411–422.

Zeller, A. (1951). An experimental analogue of repression: III. The effect of induced failure and success on memory measured by recall. *Journal of Experimental Psychology, 42,* 32–38.

Ziegler, F. J., & Imboden, J. B. (1962). Contemporary conversion reactions. *Archives of General Psychiatry, 6,* 279–287.

Ziegler, F. J., Imboden, J. B., & Meyer, E. (1960). Contemporary conversion reactions: A clinical study. *American Journal of Psychiatry, 116,* 901–909.

Zigler, E., & Glick, M. (1984). Paranoid schizophrenia: An unorthodox view. *American Journal of Orthopsychiatry, 54,* 43–70.

Zimmerman, J., & Grosz, H. J. (1966). Visual performance of a functionally blind person. *Behaviour Research and Therapy, 4,* 119–134.

Zis, A. P., & Goodwin, F. K. (1982). The amine hypothesis. In E. S. Paykel (Ed.), *Handbook of affective disorders.* New York: Guilford Press.

Zlotogorski, Z. (1985). Offspring of concentration camp survivors: A study of levels of ego functioning. *Israel Journal of Psychiatry and Related Sciences, 22,* 201–209.

Zubin, J., & Spring, B. (1977). Vulnerability: A new view of schizophrenia. *Journal of Abnormal Psychology, 86,* 103–126.

Index